INTRODUCTION TO INDUSTRIAL/ ORGANIZATIONAL PSYCHOLOGY

Introduction to Industrial/Organizational Psychology provides a complete overview of the psychological study of the world of work. Written with the student in mind, the book presents classic theory and research in the field alongside examples from real-world work situations to provide deeper insight.

This edition has been thoroughly updated to include the latest research on each key topic, and now features:

- A spotlight on diversity, equity, and inclusion throughout, including coverage of LGBTQIA+ inclusion and racial justice
- Expanded coverage of ethics in I/O psychology practice
- Increased emphasis on cross-cultural and international issues
- Coverage of the changing nature of work, post-pandemic, including remote working, worker stress, and burnout
- A new focus on technologies related to I/O such as virtual reality and computer adaptive testing
- New figures, illustrations, and charts to grab the reader's attention and facilitate learning

Accompanied by extensive student and instructor resources, it is a must read for all students on I/O psychology courses and courses in work psychology and organizational behavior, and for practicing managers who want a comprehensive overview of the psychology of work.

Ronald E. Riggio, Ph.D., is the Henry R. Kravis Professor of Leadership and Organizational Psychology at Claremont McKenna College. He has published more than two dozen authored or edited books, more than 200 articles and book chapters, and is a charter member of the Society for Industrial and Organizational Psychology (SIOP).

Stefanie K. Johnson, Ph.D., is a SIOP fellow and Associate Professor of Management at CU Boulder's Leeds School of Business where she studies the intersection of leadership and diversity.

INTRODUCTION TO INDUSTRIAL/ ORGANIZATIONAL PSYCHOLOGY

EIGHT EDITION

Ronald E. Riggio

Stefanie K. Johnson

Routledge
Taylor & Francis Group

NEW YORK AND LONDON

Cover image: Getty

Eighth edition published 2022
by Routledge
605 Third Avenue, New York, NY 10158

and by Routledge
4 Park Square, Milton Park, Abingdon, Oxon, OX14 4RN

Routledge is an imprint of the Taylor & Francis Group, an informa business

First edition published by Pearson Education, Inc. 2003
Seventh edition published by Routledge 2018

Library of Congress Cataloging-in-Publication Data
A catalog record has been requested for this book

ISBN: 9780367699468 (hbk)
ISBN: 9781003143987 (ebk)

DOI: 10.4324/9781003143987

Typeset in Adobe Garamond and Parisine
by ApexCovantage, LLC

Printed and bound in Great Britain by
TJ Books Limited, Padstow, Cornwall

Contents

PREFACE

Ronald E. Riggio and Stefanie K. Johnson

Introduction to Industrial/Organizational Psychology provides an inviting and comprehensive introduction to the field of industrial/organizational (I/O) psychology. Two important themes guided the writing of this textbook. First, because I/O psychology is a field with both a strong scientific base and an applied orientation, the book demonstrates the connection between psychological theory and application: theoretical concepts are shown to lead to useful interventions. Second, this book was designed and written with the student in mind. Whenever possible, the text draws on examples and illustrations from the world of work that students understand. For instance, many work-setting examples include service industries, such as retail chains and fast-food restaurants, and Internet companies and startups rather than concentrating solely on traditional office or factory work settings.

Introduction to Industrial/Organizational Psychology is an introductory textbook that appeals to a wide range of students with varying academic backgrounds. It is designed for use in undergraduate survey courses in I/O psychology or in psychology of work behavior courses and is suited for courses that contain a mix of psychology majors and nonmajors. The text is appropriate for courses at four-year colleges and universities, as well as at two-year community colleges. Although the book is written at a level that makes the material accessible to students who are relatively new to the field of psychology, the coverage of topics is comprehensive. The text includes "classic" theories and research along with the latest developments and innovations to make this a thorough and challenging overview of the field. Instructors will find this the most thoroughly referenced I/O psychology text on the market!

What's New: The Eighth Edition

The world of work and work technology continues to change and evolve. It has been several years since the last edition, so there has been a thorough updating, but the basic structure of the text has remained the same from the last edition. The main changes involve updates related to remote work and diversity and inclusion given the global pandemic and increased focus on diversity, equity and inclusion. We have added research on diversity and inclusion throughout the book along with the marker "D&I insights" to call attention to this important topic whenever diversity and inclusion implications are discussed.

We also updated the research cited through an equity lens to ensure that we are citing male and female scholars equally and ensuring that we are recognizing the research of scholars of color. As part of the publication process we are surveying the cited authors to ask them to report on their race, gender, sexual orientation and disability status and other characteristics. We did this in response to Aguinis and colleagues' 2017 article showing the lack of fender quality in the citations within IO textbooks.

Aguinis, H., Ramani, R. S., Campbell, P. K., Bernal-Turnes, P., Drewry, J. M., & Edgerton, B. T. "This Is Our House!" Why Are IO Psychologists Losing at the Gender Disparity Game?.

Aguinis, H., Ramani, R. S., Campbell, P. K., Bernal-Turnes, P., Drewry, J. M., & Edgerton, B. T. (2017). Most frequently cited sources and authors in industrial-organizational psychology textbooks: Implications for the science-practice divide, scholarly impact, and the future of the field. Industrial and Organizational Psychology: Perspectives on Science and Practice, 10(4), 507–557

We emailed the first authors of the 1127 articles cited in our textbook to request demographic information. Approximately 34% of the authors responded. Based on those who filled out the surveys, 32% of authors who responded were male and 67% were female and 1% were non binary. We assume that this was not a random sample because our own estimate of author gender (based on first author name) was 57% female and 43% male, suggesting that women may have been more likely to respond to our survey than men. Our own estimate of author gender mirror's data collected for a SIOP membership survey which showed that 57% of SIOP members are women (43% men). Regarding race, 77% of our respondents identified as White, 7% as Black, 12% as Asian, and 5% as Hispanic/Latino. These numbers are similar to the SIOP membership data which shows that 75% of members are white, 7% are black, 5% are Asian, and 5% were Hispanic. We did not make our own race assumptions in the way we did gender based on name. In addition, 10% of our surveyed authors identified as members of the LGBTQ community and 10% reported having a disability. Regarding career, 63% were business professors, 30% were Psychology professors, and 7% were practitioners.

There are some new topics added, including:

- A greater focus on issues related to diversity including sexual harassment, racial justice, LGBTQIA+ inclusion, persons with disabilities, among others.
- More student-oriented features to help readers relate to the content in the text.
- New and expanded coverage of international issues.
- Cutting-edge topics related to the global pandemic including remote work, hiring remotely, collaboration in dispersed teams, and worker stress and burnout.
- A focus on new technologies related to IO including virtual reality, computer adaptive testing, gamification, and others.

▌ Thoroughly updated. The latest research on each key topic has been included. There are more than 250 new references in this edition, most published within the last five years. Again, students will find this an excellent resource for term papers and in their future coursework. We worked to include a more equitable coverage of female scholars and scholars of color.

▌ Expanded instructor's manual and ancillaries. The instructor's manual and test bank have been expanded, thoroughly revised, and updated and includes exercises, PowerPoint presentations, and additional material.

Text Structure

Introduction to Industrial/Organizational Psychology is divided into four parts. Part I provides an introduction to the field and an overview of research methods used by I/O psychologists. Part II covers employee and personnel issues, including separate chapters on pre-employment selection issues like job analysis, employee selection and placement, evaluating employee performance, and employee training. Part III is called "Worker Issues" and deals with processes that are worker centered: worker motivation, positive work attitudes and behaviors, and worker stress and burnout. Part IV covers organizational topics that are group oriented: including communication, working in teams, decision making in teams, leadership, organizational power and politics, organizational structure, and culture and development.

Special features included in each chapter of *Introduction to Industrial/ Organizational Psychology* complement the text narrative and provide further illustrations and examples of I/O psychology in the "real world." One of these features, Applying I/O Psychology, takes some of the theoretical and research material presented in the chapter and shows how I/O psychologists apply this knowledge to make positive changes in actual work settings. A second feature, Up Close (which is particularly student oriented), provides students with practical information concerning how I/O psychology can increase understanding of everyday work situations. A third feature, On the Cutting Edge, highlights more current areas of research or practice in I/O psychology. Inside Tips, found at the beginning of each chapter, is designed to connect chapters and help students see the "big picture" of the field of I/O psychology, as well as to provide specific study tips.

The chapters are designed to facilitate learning. Each chapter begins with an outline of the topics and ends with a chapter summary and a series of study questions/ exercises that help students review and think about the chapter material. Stop & Review questions are strategically placed in the margins. These questions are designed to allow the student to "self-test" whether she or he has retained important material just read or studied. A glossary of key terms also appears throughout the chapters, with a more complete alphabetical glossary at the end of the book.

The text is complemented by instructor's resource materials prepared and updated by our team of faculty who have experience with the course and text. We have worked hard to make this ancillary package the best available. It includes detailed outlines, suggestions for lectures, discussion questions, in-class exercises, audiovisual resources, and other special features.

Acknowledgments

We would like to thank the many adopters of the previous editions of the text. Many of you have provided important feedback that has helped in revisions. I would also like to thank the many reviewers whose valuable input helped shape the seven editions of the text. They have become too numerous to list, but special thanks to John F. Binning, Illinois State University, and Chris Cozby, California State University, Fullerton.

Special thanks go to our research assistants throughout the years. We welcome all comments, criticisms, and suggestions. Please contact us at:

Ronald E. Riggio, PhD
Kravis Leadership Institute
Claremont McKenna College
850 Columbia Avenue
Claremont, CA 91711
e-mail: ron.riggio@cmc.edu
Follow me on Twitter: http://twitter.com/#!/ronriggio

Stefanie K. Johnson, PhD
Leeds School of Business
University of Colorado Boulder
995 Regent Drive
Boulder CO 80305
e-mail: Stefanie.Johnson@Colorado.edu
Follow me on Twitter, Instagram, LinkedIn @DrStefJohnson

To the Student (Please Don't Skip This. It Will Help.)

This book was written for you. When the first edition of this text was written in 1987, the textbooks at the time were too technical and not "student friendly." So we have tried to keep our students in mind every step of the way – keeping the book current, readable, and relevant to students' current and future working lives. There are special features, such as the Stop & Review questions, that were created to help you determine if you are retaining the material you are reading and studying.

This text is set up to cover the broad-ranging field of I/O psychology, and we've tried to keep it interesting and lively. In addition, the text is designed not only to maximize learning, but also to be a resource book for continued explorations of the field of I/O psychology. For instance, there is career and educational information about the field, and the book is thoroughly referenced. Although some students may find it distracting to have points referenced with "(Author, year)" throughout, these references will be extremely useful in finding starting points for term papers or future exploration. We hope that you will find this text an important, permanent addition to your personal library. It is a book that can be used in future scholarly work, and you will find it a useful reference in your later career.

We would like to thank the student readers of previous editions for their valuable input, suggestions, and comments about the text. Please let us hear from you as well.

How to Read and Study This Book

This book is set up to maximize your learning about industrial/organizational psychology. Key terms are set in boldface type when they are first discussed, and brief definitions of these terms appear in the adjacent margins (longer definitions are at the end in a glossary). You should look over the key terms before you begin reading a chapter and then alert yourself to them as you read. As you move along, you can test yourself by using the margin definitions. Of course, the key terms deal only with major points in each chapter, for there is much more to mastering the material. Not only should you be able to define important terms and concepts, but you should also know how they apply to work behavior. As you learn the important points made throughout the book, stop occasionally and ask yourself such questions as, "How does this apply to the working world that I know?" "Have I seen examples of this concept before?" "How can the material that I am learning be applied in my own working life?" "How can this new information help me to see work and work behavior in a new way?"

Also located in the margins are brief Stop & Review questions. Their purpose is to stop you at certain points in your reading/studying so that you can go back and review the material just covered. Often, students find that they get caught up in the reading, and they forget to retain, or "encode," the material for later recall. The review questions are intended to help you check if you are retaining important pieces of information.

Three other chapter features are also set off from the text. The first, Applying I/O Psychology, deals with specific applications of I/O psychology theories or concepts. The Up Close feature offers helpful research-based information that can further your understanding of your past, present, or future world of work. These usually take a how-to approach to some common issue or problem at work. On the Cutting Edge offers some of the latest developments in the field including the world of remote work. D&I Insights are included throughout the book so that you are aware of the important opportunities and concerns for employees around diversity and inclusion. Please know that we worked to cover the research of top scholars in an equitable way. We know that you all as students are diverse and care deeply about issues related to diversity and inclusion. So do we! We wanted the topics you read about to reflect the diversity of I/O Psychologists and reflect you, the reader.

At the beginning of each chapter is another learning aid called Inside Tips. This aid will help you understand how the various chapters and topic areas fit together. They may also offer suggestions on how to study the information in the chapter.

At the end of each chapter is a brief summary of the central concepts. There are also study questions and exercises designed to make you think a little more about the topics presented and to review and apply what you have learned. Finally, there are suggestions for additional reading. These usually include at least one reference book related to the general theme of the chapter (useful as a starting point for research papers) and a couple of topical readings—books or journal review articles on a specific topic. Welcome to I/O psychology.

Introduction

CHAPTER 1

Introduction to I/O Psychology

Our History and the Important Role We Play in Ensuring Workplace Equity

Inside Tips

UNDERSTANDING INDUSTRIAL/ORGANIZATIONAL PSYCHOLOGY

This first chapter is intended to define I/O psychology and to give you a feel for what the field is all about and what I/O psychologists do. Because industrial/organizational psychology is so broad in its scope, it is not easy to gain a good understanding of the entire field by simply learning definitions or studying some of its historical roots; to fully comprehend the scope of I/O psychology, you need to get through this entire textbook. Chapters 1 and 2 provide an introduction and an overview of methods used by I/O psychologists to conduct research. In this first chapter, we will do a "deep dive" into issues of measurement because it is so fundamental to what I/O psychologists do. We will also explore employment laws that are critically important for both employers and for I/O psychologists who are called upon to help employers prevent unfair discrimination in the workplace.

Moving beyond the first two chapters, each chapter, from Chapter 3 to Chapter 15, presents a general topic and several specialties that I/O psychologists study. As you go through the book, step back and try to see how the various topics fit together. You will then begin to find the threads that hold the field of I/O psychology together.

Like it or not, we will all spend a big part of our lives working. Not only does work take up a large chunk of the day, it also often governs where we live, how we live, and the kinds of people with whom we associate. It makes sense, then, that we should want to learn more about the world of work and our own work behavior.

Have you ever wondered what motivates people to work, what makes someone a good manager or leader, or why some people are competent, loyal workers, whereas

DOI: 10.4324/9781003143987-2

others are untrustworthy and unreliable? Have you ever considered the ways a particular job might be redesigned to make it more efficient, or the processes by which large organizations make decisions? Have you noticed that work can sometimes be very engaging and a great source of satisfaction, but it can also be terribly stressful at times? Industrial/organizational psychologists have studied all these and other questions and issues.

In this chapter, we will define the field of industrial/organizational psychology, look at some of the specialty areas within the discipline, and learn a bit about what industrial/organizational psychologists do. We will also look briefly at the history of industrial/organizational psychology, focusing on some of the important early developments in the field. Finally, we will explore how industrial/organizational psychology's focus on measurement and compliance with equal employment opportunity laws make diversity and inclusion a central feature of the field.

In fact, we have worked to make diversity and inclusion a core theme of this textbook. Despite federal laws forbidding discrimination based on demographic characteristics, we will show (in this chapter and throughout the textbook) that bias continues to impact employment decisions, and we will provide solutions to create a more equitable workplace. As shared in a 2019 Society for Industrial/Organizational Psychology (SIOP) report (Johnson, 2019), 57% of SIOP members identify as women (43% as men), and 75% identify as White. For the 25% of people of color, the largest proportion was Black (7%), followed by Hispanic/Latino (6%). Chinese, multiracial, and other each comprised 3%, whereas Asian Indian represented 2%.

Despite the prevalence of women as members of SIOP, there is bias against women in terms of access to prestigious roles and in publications. Aguinis and colleagues analyzed the diversity of the most cited authors in I/O textbooks finding that only 17% of the most cited authors were women, and only one textbook author was a woman (Aguinis et al., 2017). The Aguinis study did not examine the race, sexual orientation, or other marginalized identities of textbook authors. Indeed, there is evidence of publication bias in academic journals that actually makes it more difficult to publish studies on diversity (Avery et al., 2021; Cislak et al., 2018; King et al., 2018), so it is not terribly surprising that these studies are not elevated to textbooks.

Thus, not only do we include diversity and inclusion as a central theme throughout the textbook, but we also were intentional about the diversity of the scholars whose research we feature and highlight, so that this edition of the book provides a more accurate representation of the type of work that industrial/organizational psychologists do. We collected data on the race and gender of the authors to ensure that our cited authors are diverse. You will see a feature throughout the book that highlights issues of diversity and inclusion in the workplace.

What Is Industrial/Organizational Psychology?

Psychology
the study of behavior and
mental processes

Psychology is the scientific study of behavior and mental processes. Psychologists use systematic scientific methods in an effort to understand more about the hows and whys of behavior and human thought processes. Within the broad field of psychology are many specialty areas, each of which focuses on a different aspect of behavior. For instance, developmental psychology focuses on developmental behavior over the life span, cognitive psychology studies human thinking (cognition) and how the mind works, and social psychology studies human social behavior. There are also specialties in psychology that are more applied. For example, legal (or forensic) psychology focuses on the law, and school psychology looks at behavior in an educational setting. **Industrial/organizational psychology** is one of the more applied areas of psychology.

As you might imagine, the study of human behavior in work settings is a large undertaking. Most jobs are quite complicated, requiring the use of a wide range of mental and motor skills. Work organizations are often large and complex entities made up of hundreds or even thousands of workers who must interact and coordinate activities to produce some product, service, or information. More and more often, workers are physically distant from one another, working in different parts of the country or the world, coordinating their work activities through online networks and other communication technologies. The COVID-19 global pandemic caused a great increase in the percentage of workers who work partly, or mostly, remotely—a trend that will likely continue into the future.

Some I/O psychologists study the basic personnel functions within organizations, such as the way workers are recruited and selected, how employees are trained and developed, and the measurement of employee job performance. Other I/O psychologists study the psychological processes underlying work behavior, such as the motivation to work and worker feelings of job satisfaction and stress. Still other I/O psychologists focus on group processes in the workplace, including the relationships between workplace supervisors and subordinates and how groups of workers coordinate to get the job done. Finally, some psychologists and other social scientists study the broader picture, including the structure of work organizations and how the physical, social, and psychological environments affect worker behavior. The structure of this textbook will parallel these various areas of subspecialization in I/O psychology and related areas. (It is important to note that "industrial/organizational psychology" is the U.S. term; in Europe and in other parts of the world, this same area of specialization is referred to as "work and organizational psychology".)

Industrial/Organizational (I/O) Psychology
the branch of psychology that is concerned with the study of behavior in work settings and the application of psychology principles to change work behavior

The Science and Practice of Industrial/ Organizational Psychology

I/O psychology has two objectives: first, to conduct research in an effort to increase our knowledge and understanding of human work behavior; and second, to apply that knowledge to improve the work behavior, the work environment, and the psychological conditions of workers. Thus, I/O psychologists are trained to be both scientists and practitioners, in what is referred to as the scientist–practitioner model. Although some I/O psychologists may identify primarily as either scientists or practitioners, most I/O psychologists believe that the best practitioners are strongly based in the science of I/O psychology. There have been many calls for I/O scholars and practitioners to work more closely together so that research informs the practice of I/O psychology, improving workplaces.

The scientific objective of I/O psychology involves the study and understanding of all aspects of behavior at work. As scientists, I/O psychologists conduct research and publish the results of these efforts in professional journals such as those listed in Table 1.1. The information published in these journals helps inform the practice of I/O psychology (Latham, 2001). We will discuss the scientific objective in great depth in Chapter 2.

It is important to realize, however, that the study of work behavior is a multidisciplinary, cooperative venture. Industrial/organizational psychologists are not the only professionals who study work behavior. Researchers in the fields of management, sociology, political science, organizational communication, economics, and several other social sciences contribute to what we know and understand about the worker and work organizations. Because this research takes place on many fronts,

Table 1.1 Journals Publishing Research in Industrial/Organizational Psychology and Related Areas

Academy of Management Journal	*Ergonomics*
International Journal of Selection and Assessment	*The Leadership Quarterly*
Academy of Management Learning and Education	*Group Dynamics*
International Review of I/O Psychology	*Organization Science*
Academy of Management Perspectives	*Group and Organization Management*
Journal of Applied Psychology	*Organizational Behavior and Human Decision Processes*
Academy of Management Review	*Industrial and Organizational Psychology: Perspectives on Science and Practice*
Journal of Applied Social Psychology	*Human Factors*
Administrative Science Quarterly	*Organizational Dynamics*
Journal of Business and Psychology	*Human Performance*
American Psychologist	*Journal of Leadership and Organizational Studies*
Journal of Business Research	*Psychology*
Consulting Psychology Journal	*Personnel*
Annual Review of Psychology	*Human Relations*
Journal of Management	*Leadership*
European Journal of Work and Organizational Psychology	*Personnel Psychology*
Journal of Occupational and Organizational Psychology	*The Industrial/Organizational Psychologist (TIP: the newsletter of the Society for Industrial and Organizational Psychology)*
Applied Psychological Measurement	*Training and Development Journal*
Journal of Organizational Behavior	*Work & Stress*

I/O psychologists need to be aware of recent developments in other fields. A quick look at the titles of journals that publish research of interest to I/O psychologists illustrates the multidisciplinary nature of the study of work behavior, including such terms as *management, business, personnel,* and the related area of *ergonomics* (see Table 1.1).

The multidisciplinary nature of the study of work behavior may be illustrated by current research on virtual work teams. Greater numbers of workers are physically distant from one another, especially after the COVID-19 pandemic shifted the vast majority of employees to working remotely. Yet these workers must collaborate and work together in teams. In studying virtual work teams, an information scientist might be concerned with the issue of improving the information technology so that the team members can coordinate activities efficiently. An organizational communication specialist might be concerned with understanding how the loss of the nonverbal cues present in face-to-face work teams might adversely affect the development of good working relationships among team members. A cognitive scientist might want to study the processes by which virtual teams generate ideas and make decisions. A management expert could be primarily concerned with how to lead and manage virtual work teams, whereas an economist might concentrate on the costs and benefits of virtual organizations. Many work issues are similarly complex and need to be examined from a variety of perspectives. Most importantly, we need to keep an open mind and stay in touch with what other disciplines are doing if we are going to truly understand the working world and human work behavior.

The applied objective of I/O psychology involves the application of psychological principles and of knowledge gleaned from psychological research to work behavior. As practitioners, I/O psychologists may be called on to deal with specific work-related problems or issues. For example, an I/O psychologist might evaluate an employee testing program or conduct an employee attitude survey or some type of employee training program.

The Roots and Early History of Industrial/ Organizational Psychology

To understand the impact that I/O psychology has had on the world of work, it is important to know a little bit about the history of the field. We will examine historical periods in I/O psychology's past and focus on a significant event or important phenomenon in each time period. We will later look at the present and future of I/O psychology.

The Beginnings

Around the turn of the 20th century, when the field of psychology was still in its infancy, a few early psychologists dabbled in the study of work behavior. For example,

Figure 1.1 Frederick W. Taylor was the founder of the scientific management movement.

Source: Photograph by Bettmann/Getty Images.

Hugo Munsterberg was an experimental psychologist who became interested in the design of work and personnel selection for jobs such as streetcar operator (Munsterberg, 1913). Another experimental psychologist who pioneered the field of industrial psychology (the broader label, "industrial/organizational psychology," was not used extensively until the 1970s) was Walter Dill Scott, who was interested in studying salespersons and the psychology of advertising (Scott, 1908). Scott went on to become the first professor in this new field and started a consulting company to practice what was being learned from research.

Another early spark that helped ignite the field of I/O psychology was provided not by a psychologist, but by an engineer named Frederick W. Taylor (Figure 1.1). Taylor believed that scientific principles could be applied to the study of work behavior to help increase worker efficiency and productivity. He felt that there was "one best method" for performing a particular job. By breaking the job down scientifically into measurable component movements and recording the time needed to perform each movement, Taylor believed that he could develop the fastest, most efficient way of performing any task. He was quite successful in applying his methods, which became known as **time-and-motion studies**. These time-and-motion procedures often doubled, tripled, and even quadrupled laborer output! Taylor's system for applying scientific principles to increase work efficiency and productivity eventually became known as scientific management. In addition to applying time-and-motion procedures, Taylor incorporated into his system of **scientific management** other considerations, such as selection of workers based on abilities and the use of proper tools (Taylor, 1911).

Taylor and his followers, including the husband-and-wife team of Frank and Lillian Gilbreth (Lillian Gilbreth was one of the earliest women I/O psychologists; see Figure 1.2), implemented the principles of scientific management and revolutionized several physical labor jobs by making the accepted work procedures more efficient and productive (Gilbreth, 1916). For example, scientific management principles and procedures such as time-and-motion studies greatly improved the efficiency of a wide variety of typical types of jobs, including cabinetmaking, clerical filing, lumber sawing, and the making of reinforced concrete slabs (increased from 80 to 425 slabs per day!; Lowry et al., 1940).

Unfortunately, Taylor's philosophy was quite narrow and limited. In his day, many jobs involved manual labor and were thus easily broken down and made more efficient through the application of principles of scientific management. Today, jobs are much more complex and often require sophisticated problem-solving skills or the use of creative thinking. Fewer and fewer people engage in physical labor. Many of these "higher-level" tasks are not amenable to time-and-motion studies. In other words, there is probably not one best method for creating computer software, developing an advertising campaign, or managing people.

Time-and-Motion Studies
procedures in which work tasks are broken down into simple component movements and the movements are timed to develop a more efficient method for performing the tasks

Scientific Management
begun by Frederick Taylor, a method of using scientific principles to improve the efficiency and productivity of jobs

Figure 1.2 Lillian Gilbreth was an influential early I/O psychologist.

Source: Harris & Ewing, Smithsonian Institution Archives, Accession 90–105, Image #SIA2008–1924, Wikimedia Commons.

UP **CLOSE** **What Does an I/O Psychologist Really Do?**

One of the most common questions asked by students in I/O psychology courses is, "What does an I/O psychologist do, really?" The answer to this question is not simple, for a couple of reasons. First, many undergraduate students and laypersons have not had much exposure to I/O psychologists, either face-to-face or in the media. Unlike clinical psychologists, who are frequently depicted in films, interviewed on news shows, and stereotyped in cartoons and on TV, most people have never seen an I/O psychologist. A second and more important reason why it is difficult to understand what I/O psychologists do is because I/O psychologists do so many different kinds of things. I/O psychology is a broad field encompassing a large number of specialty areas, many of which are quite unrelated to one another. Consequently, it is next to impossible to talk about a "typical" I/O psychologist.

I/O psychologists are prevalent in both academic and applied careers. According to the 2020 SIOP salary survey, 55% of I/O psychologists with a Ph.D. degree and 96% of I/O psychologists with a master's degree work in an applied role (Davison et al., 2020). Applied I/O psychologists tend to work in human resource roles and as consultants. The majority of individuals with master's degrees in I/O psychology are working in the private sector or in government positions. What's more, I/O psychology is a "hot" and growing field. The U.S. Department of Labor predicts that employment for I/O psychologists will grow by 3% from 2019 to 2029.

Applied I/O psychologists with Ph.Ds. are highly paid. The median income for senior consultants with a Ph.D. was $121,000 and with an MA was $108,000. Among

HR directors, the median income for those with a Ph.D. was $153,000 and those with a master's was $108,000. For those Ph.Ds. who stay in academia, full professors in Industrial/Organizational Psychology have a median salary of $122,000.

I/O psychologists work for a variety of major U.S. and international corporations, including Amazon, Dow Chemical, Ford Motor Company, Verizon, Toyota, Disney, Standard Oil, Google, Unisys, United Airlines, and Pepsi. They can hold job titles such as Director of Human Resources, Personnel Research Psychologist, Vice President of Employee Development, Manager of Employee Relations, Senior Employment Specialist, Testing Specialist, Quality Performance Manager, Consultant, and Staff Organizational Psychologist.

To help you better understand what I/O psychologists do, as well as help you understand the diverse areas of specialization within I/O psychology, let's look at some brief profiles of actual I/O psychologists.

Dr. M is an I/O psychologist working for a large aerospace firm. Her main area of expertise is sophisticated robot systems, and she has helped design and test several sophisticated robotlike systems for use in outer space. Dr. M maintains that her training in research methods, which allows her to approach work problems systematically, was the most valuable part of her academic education.

Dr. C received his Ph.D. in I/O psychology in the 1970s. His first job was conducting research for the General Telephone and Electronics Laboratories on the organizational processes in some of the company's

UP CLOSE *(continued)*

operational units, including assessing job satisfaction, facilitating communication, and helping to resolve conflicts. Some years later, Dr. C joined a large consulting firm and was employed by an international consulting company where he conducted survey feedback and other organizational development programs for a variety of businesses and organizations.

Dr. H was originally an I/O psychologist in the U.S. Navy. His responsibilities there included developing and researching placement systems for certain Navy personnel. He currently works for the U.S. government as a grant officer helping to determine funding decisions for psychological research projects.

Dr. R is an I/O psychologist who owns a private consulting practice in a small Midwestern city. Before becoming an independent consultant, Dr. R worked for a large consulting firm in a metropolitan area, where he conducted job analyses and ran training seminars for businesses. His decision to move to a less urban area was primarily responsible for his decision to start an independent practice. Dr. R specializes in personnel selection, job analysis, and the design of training and development programs, although he occasionally engages in other activities such as conducting attitude and marketing surveys and serving as an expert witness in labor-related legal cases. In a sense, he has had to become an industrial/organizational "jack-of-all-trades" because he is one of the few I/O psychologists in his region. Dr. R claims that the most valuable training he received was in statistics, psychology, and the business courses that he took after receiving his Ph.D. so that he could become more knowledgeable about various business operations and learn business terminology.

Ms. O received a master's degree in industrial/organizational psychology just a few years ago. She is an assistant director of marketing research for a national chain of fast-food restaurants. Her duties include researching the sites for new restaurants and designing and organizing customer satisfaction surveys. Ms. O also teaches I/O psychology and marketing courses at a local community college.

Dr. P, an I/O psychologist, is a professor in the School of Management in a large state university. He previously held academic positions in university psychology departments. Dr. P is quite well known and respected for his research in I/O psychology. In addition to his research and teaching, Dr. P has served as a consultant for several large corporations, including many Fortune 500 companies.

Mr. K, who has a master's degree in organizational psychology, is the director of human resources for a biomedical company, which means that he is responsible for the administration of all facets of human resources for his organization. Mr. K oversees payroll, benefits, compensation, and personnel activities such as the development of job descriptions, employee selection, and personnel training. He also has an active internship program that uses undergraduate and graduate students as interns who help set up special human resource programs for his employees.

After a successful career in the finance industry, Dr. A went back to graduate school and received her Ph.D. in industrial/organizational psychology. She has worked in the human resources department at AT&T and has published books and research articles on a variety of topics in I/O psychology. She is currently president of a consulting organization and is quite active in research and professional affairs in the field.

It is important to emphasize that scientific management and I/O psychology are not directly connected, although the principles of scientific management did have an influence on the development of I/O psychology. Today, industrial engineers carry on the tradition of scientific management in efforts to improve the efficiency of jobs. Although work efficiency and increased productivity are certainly important to I/O psychologists, I/O psychology looks beyond efficiency to examine the impact of work procedures and conditions on the working person.

⏱ Stop & Review

Describe in detail the two objectives of I/O psychology.

World War I and the 1920s

At the outbreak of World War I, Robert Yerkes, who was president of the American Psychological Association, and a group of psychologists worked with the U.S. Army to create intelligence tests for the placement of Army recruits. The Army Alpha and Beta tests (the Alpha test was used for those who could read; the Beta test was used for non-literate recruits) represented the first mass testing efforts and set the stage for future testing efforts. Even today, employee testing and selection are important areas of I/O psychology. Following World War I, psychologists began to be involved in the screening and placement of personnel in industry. Throughout the 1920s, while the U.S. was experiencing tremendous industrial growth, industrial psychology began to take hold: the first doctoral degree in industrial psychology was awarded in 1921, and psychologists worked directly with industries as consultants and researchers (Katzell & Austin, 1992).

It was also in the 1920s that the first psychological consulting organizations began. Walter Dill Scott opened a short-lived personnel consulting firm in 1919, and the Psychological Corporation was founded by James McKeen Cattell in 1921 (Vinchur & Koppes, 2011). Today, consulting organizations offer their services to business and industry. In fact, the difficult economic times in the early part of the 21st century led to organizational downsizing, and many larger organizations that employed I/O psychologists eliminated those positions and now outsource their work to consulting firms. As a result, consulting firms are thriving and are a major place of employment for I/O psychologists.

The Great Depression Years and World War II

As the U.S. economy slumped during the 1930s, there was less opportunity for industrial psychologists to work with industries and businesses. Although industrial psychology continued to grow at a slower pace, an important development came out of this period from a group of Harvard psychologists who were conducting a series of experiments at a manufacturing plant of the Western Electric Company in

Hawthorne, Illinois. Researcher Elton Mayo and his colleagues wanted to study the effects of the physical work environment on worker productivity.

In the most famous of the experiments, Mayo explored the effects of lighting on worker productivity. Focusing on a group of women who were assembling electrical relay-switching devices, he systematically varied the level of illumination in the room. He expected to be able to determine the optimal level of lighting for performing the task. However, the results were surprising and dramatically changed psychologists' views of the worker from then on. No matter what level the lighting was set at, productivity increased! When lighting was increased, worker output went up. Further increase to very bright illumination resulted in further improvement. Turning the lights down (even to such low levels that it appeared that the women were working in moonlight) also led to increases in productivity. There was a steady increase in workers' output following any change in lighting. In other studies, Mayo systematically varied the length and timing of work breaks. Longer breaks, shorter breaks, and more or fewer breaks all resulted in a steady increase in worker output (Mayo, 1933).

Mayo knew that every change in the work environment could not possibly be causing the steady rises in worker productivity. Something else had to be affecting output. Upon closer examination, he concluded that the workers were being affected not by the changes in the physical environment, but by the simple fact that they knew they were being observed. According to Mayo, these workers believed that the studies were being conducted in an effort to improve work procedures, and their positive expectations, coupled with their knowledge of the observations, seemed to Mayo to determine their consistent increases in productivity, a phenomenon that has been labeled the **Hawthorne effect**. Although, in the first example discovered by Mayo, the "Hawthorne effect" was positive, resulting in increased productivity, this was not always the case. In another of his studies, work group productivity fell following the introduction of changes in the work environment. Because these workers believed that the results of the studies would lead to more demanding production quotas, they restricted output whenever they were being observed, thus producing a "negative" Hawthorne effect (Roethlisberger & Dickson, 1939).

Although researchers have noted a number of serious flaws in the methods Mayo used to conduct the Hawthorne experiments (see Chapter 2), the general conclusions reached by Mayo and his colleagues resulted in the development of the **human relations movement**, which recognized the importance of social factors and something called "worker morale" in influencing work productivity. In fact, this movement stated that a harmonious work environment, with good interpersonal relationships among coworkers, should be a productive work environment, particularly when the work itself is boring or monotonous. According to Mayo, workers in repetitive or low-level positions—jobs that do not themselves provide satisfaction—will turn to the social environment of the work setting for motivation.

World War II also contributed greatly to the growth of I/O psychology. First, the tremendous need for state-of-the-art machinery, and the increasing complexity of that machinery, was an important impetus for human factors psychology and for training soldiers to operate the equipment. Second, I/O psychologists were called on

Hawthorne Effect
changes in behavior occurring as a function of participants' knowledge that they are being observed and their expectations concerning their role as research participants

Human Relations Movement
a movement based on the studies of Elton Mayo that emphasizes the importance of social factors in influencing work performance

to improve selection and placement of military personnel, continuing the work that psychologists had begun during World War I.

The *Army General Classification Test*, a group-administered, pencil-and-paper test, was developed to separate recruits into categories based on their abilities to learn military duties and responsibilities. Screening tests were also created to select candidates for officer training. In addition, psychologists helped the U.S. Office of Strategic Services (OSS)—the forerunner of today's CIA—develop intensive assessment strategies for selecting candidates for dangerous espionage positions. Some of these techniques included "hands-on" situational tests in which candidates had to perform some tasks under difficult or near-impossible conditions. The aim was to assess their ability to deal with stressful and frustrating circumstances, which is very important for soldiers involved in military espionage.

The Postwar Years

It was after World War II that industrial/organizational psychology truly began to blossom, and specialty areas began to emerge. A distinct focus on personnel issues, such as testing, selection, and the evaluation of employees, was helped in part by the publication of a new journal, *Personnel Psychology*, in 1948. During the Cold War years of the 1950s and 1960s, the growth of the defense industry further spurred the development of a specialty area called engineering psychology (today referred to as human factors psychology, or ergonomics; this has become a separate discipline, but shares roots with I/O psychology). Engineering psychologists were called in to help design control systems that were both sensible and easy to operate. In addition, the contributions of sociologists and social psychologists, who began studying and performing extensive research in work organizations, helped create a subspecialty area of organizational psychology.

The 1960s through the early 1990s was a time when research and practice in I/O psychology flourished. Many of the topics currently associated with I/O psychology were developed and explored in depth during this period, particularly topics such as motivation and goal setting, job attitudes, organizational stress, group processes, organizational power and politics, and organizational development. We will examine a great deal of this work throughout this book.

One historical event during this time period that had a major impact on I/O psychology was civil rights legislation. One portion of the sweeping Civil Rights Act of 1964, Title VII, banned discrimination in employment practices. Designed to protect underrepresented groups such as women and people of color from being unfairly discriminated against in work-related decisions, this legislation forced organizations to take a closer look at the ways people were selected for jobs. Particular attention was given to the fairness of employment selection tests and personnel decisions such as promotions, compensation, and firings. Subsequent civil rights legislation protected other groups from discrimination, including older people (Age Discrimination in Employment Act, 1967 and 1978) and people with disabilities (Americans with Disabilities Act, 1990). As a result, I/O psychologists have played an important part in helping to establish and implement fair employment standards.

Continuing the Timeline—I/O Psychology in the 2020s and Beyond

Today, industrial/organizational psychology is one of the fastest-growing areas of psychology. I/O psychologists are in the forefront of those professionals who are satisfying the huge demand for information leading to greater understanding of the worker, the work environment, and work behavior. They are involved in nearly every aspect of business and industry, and, as we will see, the range of topics they research and the varieties of tasks they perform are extensive.

Perhaps the mission of the Society for Industrial and Organizational Psychology, the professional organization for I/O psychology, most clearly defines this field (and reflects aspirations for the future):

[T]o enhance human well-being and performance in organizational and work settings by promoting the science, practice, and teaching of I-O Psychology.

APPLYING I/O PSYCHOLOGY

Exploring Training and Careers in Industrial/Organizational Psychology

The usual professional degree in industrial/organizational psychology, as in all areas of psychology, is the doctorate (Ph.D.). However, a growing number of programs offer master's degrees in psychology with an emphasis on I/O psychology, and a handful of college programs even offer a bachelor's degree with a major in I/O psychology (Trahan & McAllister, 2002). The master's degree (M.A. or M.S.) can also qualify one as a practitioner of psychology, although licensing requirements may vary from state to state. In recent years, the employment picture for I/O psychologists, particularly those with a Ph.D., has been very good, with salaries among the highest in the field of psychology. To explore graduate training in I/O psychology:

- Talk to your psychology advisor in depth about the process of applying to graduate programs, including the alternatives available, the requirements for admission, the deadlines, letters of recommendations, and the like.
- Find out additional information about graduate programs and the application process by contacting the following professional organizations:
  - The Society for Industrial and Organizational Psychology, Inc. (SIOP) is the U.S.-based professional organization for I/O psychologists. It maintains a website (www.siop.org) and has detailed information available about I/O psychology graduate programs at both the Ph.D. and master's levels.

APPLYING I/O PSYCHOLOGY

(Continued)

- The European Association for Work and Organizational Psychology (EAWOP) is the European counterpart of SIOP (www.eawop.org). (Many countries have national associations for I/O psychology.)
- The American Psychological Association (APA) is the largest professional organization for psychologists. It maintains a website (www.apa.org) with detailed, step-by-step information for exploring and applying to graduate programs (including a "Guide to Getting into Graduate School").
- The Association for Psychological Science has some relevant information about scientific careers in psychology (www.psychologicalscience.org).

To explore a possible career in industrial/organizational psychology:

- Go to your university's career guidance office and to the psychology department advisor to find out what information is available on careers in I/O psychology.
- Both APA and SIOP have career information available at their respective websites.
- Arrange a short "information interview" with a practicing I/O psychologist in your area. Ask for a few minutes of the professional's time to find out first-hand what she or he does for a living. You might talk to several such professionals, because individuals' job duties can vary greatly. Again, the career guidance office may be able to help you locate practicing I/O psychologists.
- Read beyond the textbook. Examine some of the suggested readings at the end of each chapter. Go to the library and scan through some of the journals that publish research in I/O psychology. (There is a list of these journals in Table 1.1.) If you are really serious, you can join SIOP as a student member with a SIOP professional member's sponsorship (your professor may be a SIOP member).

Regardless of whether you choose a career in I/O psychology, the topics studied by I/O psychologists pertain to just about any job in any work setting. A good knowledge of principles of industrial/organizational psychology can help facilitate understanding of human behavior and organizational processes occurring in the workplace.

Note: The professional organizations offer student affiliate memberships that you can join to receive regular correspondence.

SIOP also provides education and training guidelines for students receiving a master's or Ph.D. in industrial/organizational psychology. The most recent guidelines can be found on the SIOP website and are summarized by Gibson and colleagues (Gibson et al., 2018; Society for Industrial and Organizational Psychology, 2016). There are 26 main competencies taught in industrial/organizational psychology that map closely on the topics covered in this text:

Fields of Psychology; History and Systems of Psychology (Chapter 1)

Research Methods; Statistical Methods/Data Analysis (Chapter 2)

Ethical, Legal, Diversity, and International Issues (Chapter 1)

Job Evaluation and Compensation; Job Analysis (Chapter 3)

Personnel Recruitment, Selection, and Placement (Chapters 4 and 5)

APPLYING I/O PSYCHOLOGY

(Continued)

Criterion Theory and Development (Chapter 5)

Human Performance (Chapter 6)

Performance Appraisal/Management (Chapter 6)

Training: Theory, Delivery, Program Design, and Evaluation (Chapter 7)

Work Motivation (Chapter 8)

Attitude Theory, Measurement, and Change (Chapters 9 and 10)

Professional Skills (Communication, Chapter 11)

Groups and Teams (Chapter 12)

Leadership and Management (Chapter 13)

Organization Development (Chapter 15)

Organization Theory (Chapter 15)

Career Development

Individual Assessment

Individual Differences

Judgment and Decision-Making

Occupational Health and Safety

Consumer Behavior

Human Factors

Organizational Downsizing
a strategy of reducing an organization's workforce to improve organizational efficiency and/or competitiveness

A respiratory coronavirus, termed COVID-19, caused significant changes in how many people's work was performed in 2020 and beyond. By March of 2020, the virus had shut down the global economy. In the United States and many other countries, stay at home orders meant that many businesses would have to move to remote work or shut down entirely. By August 2020, a quarter of households were impacted by **organizational downsizing** and layoffs (Parker et al., 2020). Organizational downsizing is a strategy of reducing an organization's workforce to improve organizational efficiency, adapt to supply and demand, and improve productivity and/or competitiveness (Molinsky & Margolis, 2006).

Outsourcing
contracting with an external organization to accomplish work tasks

In addition to using downsizing, many organizations looked to save costs by using **outsourcing** of work—contracting with an external organization to accomplish tasks that were previously done, or could be done, within the organization (Davis-Blake & Broschak, 2009). Outsourcing is used to increase output and can reduce overhead costs associated with the personnel needed to do the tasks in-house. I/O psychologists are involved in helping to understand the effects that the increased use of outsourcing is having on variables such as the way jobs are conducted, group processes, structure and design of organizations, employee commitment, motivation, and other factors.

Employees who kept their jobs transitioned to working from home, with an estimated 85% of people working from home part or full time in September 2020 (Brenan, 2020).

Also in 2020, a social justice movement focused on racial equity began, paralleling the gender movement ignited by #MeToo. The Black Lives Matter (#BLM) movement was largely precipitated by the murder of George Floyd by police officers in Minneapolis and had an immense impact on society, the workplace, and academia (Bell et al., 2021). Many organizations worked to improve their diversity and inclusion practices in the months that followed.

⏱ **Stop & Review**

Name three pre–World War II events that had a significant impact on I/O psychology.

What Makes Industrial/Organizational Psychology Different? Measurement and the Law

The preceding section covering the history of industrial/organizational psychology highlighted the importance of testing and measurement as a central part of what industrial/organizational psychologists do. Because much of the work we do involves creating tests to select and evaluate the performance of employees, there is an incredible focus on how to create tests that accurately measure what they intend to measure without creating bias against certain test-takers. In this section, we will explain central components of measurement (reliability and validity) and then cover how measurement is important from a legal standpoint, given federal legislation related to equal employment opportunity. Finally, we will discuss the broader implications of testing, measurement, and equal employment opportunity laws for diversity and inclusion.

Measurement

One thing that makes I/O psychology unique compared with other areas of psychology is that many I/O psychologists use their skills to help organizations with human resource practices such as selection of employees and performance evaluation. The focus on testing among I/O psychologists and the creation of federal laws to avoid discrimination in the workplace made measurement paramount for I/O psychology. When an I/O psychologist creates a measure to assess talent or knowledge or to measure employees' job satisfaction, there is a heavy focus on the effectiveness of the measures used to ensure that they would hold up to the scrutiny of the law (we will cover the relevant laws next). Any type of measurement instrument used in industrial/organizational psychology, including those used in employee screening and selection, must meet certain measurement standards related to reliability and validity.

Reliability refers to the stability of a measure over time or the consistency of the measure. For example, if we administer a test to a job applicant, we expect to get essentially the same score on the test if it is taken at two different points of time (and if the applicant does not do anything to improve test performance in between). Reliability also refers to the agreement between two or more assessments made of the same event or behavior, such as when two interviewers independently evaluate the appropriateness of a job candidate for a particular position. In other words, a measurement process is said to possess "reliability" if we can "rely" on the scores or measurements to be stable, consistent, and free of random error.

A variety of methods are used for estimating the reliability of a screening instrument. One method is called **test–retest reliability**. Here, a particular test or other measurement instrument is administered to the same individual at two different times, usually involving a 1–2-week interval between testing sessions. Scores on the first test are then correlated with those on the second test. If the correlation is high (a correlation coefficient approaching +1.0), evidence of reliability (at least, stability

Reliability
the consistency of a measurement instrument or its stability over time

Test–Retest Reliability
a method of determining the stability of a measurement instrument by administering the same measure to the same people at two different times and then correlating the scores

Parallel Forms
a method of establishing the reliability of a measurement instrument by correlating scores on two different but equivalent versions of the same instrument

Internal Consistency
a common method of establishing a measurement instrument's reliability by examining how the various items of the instrument are intercorrelated

Validity
a concept referring to the accuracy of a measurement instrument and its ability to make accurate inferences about a criterion

Employee Selection
the process of choosing applicants for employment

Content Validity
the ability of the items in a measurement instrument to measure adequately the various characteristics needed to perform a job

over time) is empirically established. Of course, the assumption is made that nothing has happened during the administration of the two tests that would cause the scores to change drastically.

A second method of estimating the reliability of an employment screening measure is the **parallel forms** method. Here, two equivalent tests are constructed, each of which presumably measures the same construct but using different items or questions. Test-takers are administered both forms of the instrument. Reliability is empirically established if the correlation between the two scores is high. Of course, the major drawbacks to this method are the time and difficulty involved in creating two equivalent tests.

Another way to estimate the reliability of a test instrument is by estimating its **internal consistency**. If a test is reliable, each item should measure the same general construct, and thus performance on one item should be consistent with performance on all other items. Two specific methods are used to determine internal consistency. The first is to divide the test items into two equal parts and correlate the summed score on the first half of the items with that on the second half. This is referred to as split-half reliability. A second method, which involves numerous calculations (and which is more commonly used), is to determine the average intercorrelation among all items of the test. The resulting coefficient, referred to as *Cronbach's alpha*, is an estimate of the test's internal consistency. In summary, reliability refers to whether we can "depend" on a set of measurements to be stable and consistent, and several types of empirical evidence (e.g., test–retest, equivalent forms, and internal consistency) reflect different aspects of this stability.

Validity refers to the accuracy of inferences or projections we draw from measurements. Validity refers to whether a set of measurements allows accurate inferences or projections about "something else." That "something else" can be a job applicant's standing on some characteristic or ability, it can be future job success, or it can be whether an employee is meeting performance standards. In the context of employee screening, the term *validity* most often refers to whether scores on a particular test or screening procedure accurately project future job performance. For example, in employee screening, validity refers to whether a score on an employment test, a judgment made from a hiring interview, or a conclusion drawn from the review of information from a job application does indeed lead to a representative evaluation of an applicant's qualifications for a job, and whether the specific measure (e.g., test, interview judgment) leads to accurate inferences about the applicant's criterion status (which is usually, but not always, job performance). Validity refers to the quality of specific inferences or projections; therefore, validity for a specific measurement process (e.g., a specific employment test) can vary depending on what criterion is being predicted. Therefore, an employment test might be a valid predictor of job performance, but not a valid predictor of another criterion such as rate of absenteeism.

Similar to reliability, discussed above, validity is a unitary concept, but there are three important facets of, or types of evidence for, determining the validity of a predictor used in **employee selection**. A predictor can be said to yield valid inferences about future performance based on a careful scrutiny of its content. This is referred to as **content validity**. Content validity refers to whether a predictor measurement process (e.g., test items or interview questions) adequately sample important job behaviors and elements involved in performing a job. Typically, content validity is established by having experts such as job incumbents (people currently holding the job) or supervisors judge the appropriateness of the test items, taking into account information from the job analysis. Ideally, the experts should determine that the test does indeed sample the job content in a representative way. It is common for organizations constructing their own screening tests for specific jobs to rely heavily on this content-based evidence of validity. As you can guess, content validity is closely linked to job analysis.

A second type of validity evidence is called **construct validity**, which refers to whether a predictor test, such as a pencil-and-paper test of mechanical ability used to screen school bus mechanics, actually measures what it is supposed to measure—(a) the abstract construct of "mechanical ability" and (b) whether these measurements yield accurate predictions of job performance. Think of it this way: many applicants to college take a predictor test of "scholastic aptitude," such as the SAT (Scholastic Aptitude Test). Construct validity of the SAT deals with whether this test does indeed measure a person's aptitude for schoolwork and whether it allows accurate inferences about future academic success. There are two common forms of empirical evidence about construct validity. Well-validated instruments such as the SAT and standardized employment tests have established construct validity by demonstrating that these tests correlate positively with the results of other tests of the same construct. This is referred to as *convergent validity*. In other words, a test of mechanical ability should correlate (converge) with another, different test of mechanical ability. In addition, a pencil-and-paper test of mechanical ability should correlate with a performance-based test of mechanical ability. In establishing a test's construct validity, researchers are also concerned with *divergent*, or *discriminant, validity*—the test should not correlate with tests or measures of constructs that are totally unrelated to mechanical ability. Similarly to content validity, credible judgments about a test's construct validity require sound professional judgments about patterns of convergent and discriminant validity.

Criterion-related validity is a third type of validity evidence and is empirically demonstrated by the relationship between test scores and some measurable criterion of job success, such as a measure of work output or quality. There are two common ways that predictor–criterion correlations can be empirically generated. The first is the *follow-up method* (often referred to as *predictive validity*). Here, the screening test is administered to applicants without the scores being interpreted and without their being used to select among applicants. Once the applicants become employees, criterion measures such as job performance assessments are collected. If the test instrument is valid, the test scores should correlate with the criterion measure. Once there is evidence of the predictive validity of the instrument, test scores are used to select the applicants for jobs. The obvious advantage of the predictive validity method is that it demonstrates how scores on the screening instrument actually relate to future job performance. The major drawback to this approach is the time that it takes to establish validity. During this validation period, applicants are tested, but are not hired based on their test scores.

Construct Validity
refers to whether an employment test measures what it is supposed to measure

Criterion-Related Validity
the accuracy of a measurement instrument in determining the relationship between scores on the instrument and some criterion of job success

Equal Employment Opportunity in Employee Selection and Placement

At least part of the explanation for why measurement is so important to I/O psychology can be explained by federal laws governing discrimination in employment contexts. In theory, employers can hire whomever they choose, as long as their decisions do not discriminate on the basis of categories such as race and gender. If an organization is accused of discrimination, it must show that its hiring decisions were based on one's ability to perform the job. But how can an organization demonstrate that it was hiring on the basis of one's ability to perform the job if it has not established the requisite behaviors and skills required to do the job? In a court of law, the defensibility of that claim rests on the quality of a job analysis. For example, in 2020, Wells Fargo bank settled a lawsuit alleging discriminatory hiring practices against women and people of color and was required to pay nearly $7.8 million to affected applicants. Among other changes, Wells Fargo agreed to change its hiring practices (U.S. Department of Labor Office of Federal Contract Compliance Program, 2020) to reduce subjectivity in hiring by using,

> non-discriminatory qualifications and written criteria to select and/or reject job seekers and applicants at each step of the hiring process, including the qualifications and criteria to be used in any application screen, interview, test, post-offer screening or other selection procedures.

The legal environment in organizations took a dramatic turn in 1964, with the passing of the Civil Rights Act. A section of this major piece of federal legislation, Title VII, was intended to protect against discrimination (i.e., an unfair advantage or disadvantage) in employment on the basis of race, ethnic background, gender, or religious preference. All companies in the U.S. with more than 15 employees are subject to Title VII. Additional laws have since helped protect against age discrimination and discrimination against disabled persons (see Table 1.2). This antidiscrimination legislation led to massive changes in personnel procedures and decision making.

Equal Employment Opportunity Commission (EEOC)
the federal agency created to protect against discrimination in employment

As a result of the Civil Rights Act, a federal agency, the **Equal Employment Opportunity Commission (EEOC)**, was created to ensure that employers' personnel selection and placement procedures complied with the antidiscrimination laws. The EEOC's authority entails the investigation of discrimination claims filed against employers. In an investigation, its role is to conduct a fair and accurate assessment of the allegations. In the 1970s, the EEOC developed the Uniform Guidelines on Employee Selection Procedures (1974, 1978), which serve as the standards for complying with antidiscrimination laws. Three concepts are important for understanding the guidelines and their impact on employee selection procedures.

Protected Class
characteristics of groups for which discrimination is prohibited, including: sex, race, religion, color, national origin, persons over 40, persons with physical or mental disabilities

The first of these concepts is the notion of **protected class**, which includes discrimination on the basis of sex, race, religion, color, national origin, persons over age 40, and persons with physical or mental disabilities. In addition, Title VII of the Civil Rights Act protects individuals based on their nation of origin and religious

Table 1.2 Federal Laws and Key Court Cases Affecting Employment

Civil Rights Act of 1964	Protects against employment discrimination on the basis of "race, color, religion, sex or national origin." Led to the establishment of the Equal Employment Opportunity Commission (EEOC), the federal body that enforces the law
Age Discrimination in Employment Act (passed in 1967, amended in 1978)	Protects against employment discrimination on the basis of age. Specifically targeted toward workers between 40 and 70 years of age
Griggs v. Duke Power Company (1971)	This Supreme Court ruling said that, if hiring procedures led to adverse impact, the employer has the burden of proof to show that the hiring procedures are valid
Albemarle Paper Company v. Moody (1975)	A Supreme Court ruling that required employers to adhere to the Uniform Guidelines, including demonstrating that selection procedures are valid
EEOC Uniform Guidelines (1974, 1978)	Established rules for fair employment practices. Established the notion of adverse impact and the four-fifths rule
Americans with Disabilities Act (1990)	Protects against employment discrimination for qualified individuals with a physical or mental disability. Says that employers must provide "reasonable accommodations" to help the individual perform the job
Civil Rights Act of 1991	Upholds the concepts set forth in *Griggs v. Duke* and allows workers who claim discrimination to have a jury trial and seek both compensatory and punitive damages against employers
Family and Medical Leave Act of 1993	Allows employees in organizations of 50 or more workers to take up to 12 weeks of unpaid leave each year for family or medical reasons
Equal Pay Act 1963	Law that requires employers to pay equal wages for equal work
Pregnancy Discrimination Act 1978	An addition to Title VII of the Civil Rights Act that makes it specifically illegal to discriminate against women on the basis of pregnancy
Sexual Harassment	Considered an illegal form of sex discrimination under Title VII of the Civil Rights Act

affiliation. Later legislation extended protected-class status to older and disabled workers. Employers must keep separate personnel records, including information on all actions such as recruitment, selection, promotions, and firings, for each of these groups and for majority-group workers. If some action is found to discriminate against one or more of these groups, the second concept, adverse impact, comes into play. Discrimination can be either intentional (unequal treatment of employees based on protected status) or unintentional. **Adverse impact** is when members of a protected group are treated unfairly, either intentionally or unintentionally, by an employer's personnel action. For instance, the guidelines state that, if any personnel

Adverse Impact
when members of a protected group are treated unfairly by an employer's personnel action

decision causes a disproportionate percentage of people in a particular group to be hired in comparison with another group, adverse impact exists. Even if it is unintentional, if a test or other selection tool is used that is inherently discriminating against certain protected group members, the use of the test is not legally defensible. The guidelines led to the establishment of the four-fifths rule, which states that a hiring procedure has adverse impact when the selection rate for any protected group is 4/5, or 80%, of the group with the highest hiring rate. In a classic legal decision, *Griggs v. Duke Power Company* (1971), reaffirmed in the Civil Rights Act of 1991, the Supreme Court ruled that, if a selection test has adverse impact, then the employer must demonstrate that the test is a reliable and valid predictor of job performance. The idea behind this law was to stop employers from discriminating against underrepresented groups by using tests that are not job related. If a plaintiff (who may be an individual or a group suing the company or the EEOC) can demonstrate adverse impact, then the burden of proof on whether an employment selection test is fair rests with the employer. This means that the employer must have pre-established data showing that its screening tests and other selection methods are valid indicators of future job performance. This is where measurement comes into the picture. To show that a test predicts future job performance, the test must meet certain standards of reliability and validity. If the test has low reliability (imagine you get a very different score each time you take it), how can it consistently predict job performance?

In addition to Title VII of the Civil Rights Act, the Americans with Disabilities Act (ADA) protects against discrimination for disabled workers and requires employers to make reasonable accommodations for disabled workers to perform jobs. Despite the passage of the law, there is consistent evidence that individuals with disabilities continue to experience discrimination in the workplace. For example, Martinez and colleagues (Martinez et al., 2016) showed that individuals with a history of cancer experience discrimination in selection contexts.

In relation to employee selection, applicants with disabilities may encounter difficulties with certain types of employee screening and selection tests if their disability interferes with test performance. For instance, a vision-impaired applicant may need to be presented with a large-print version of a pencil-and-paper test, or, if vision is severely impaired, an audio test may need to be administered. Any written test might be inappropriate for testing a dyslexic applicant. A difficulty then arises in comparing the test results of the disabled applicant, who received a different version of the test, or who was administered the test in a different format, with applicants completing the regular version of the test. Yet the disability may not hinder the individual's ability to do the job. Therefore, personnel specialists must offer reasonable accommodations so that an applicant's disability does not interfere with test performance.

The passage of the ADA has sparked a great deal of debate about whether or not disabled applicants whose disability interferes with test taking should or should not be tested. It seems the solution lies not in the test scores themselves, but in the judicious interpretation of the scores. An even more fundamental issue is determining if an applicant even has a disability, because it is illegal to ask applicants about disabilities.

The Age Discrimination in Employment Act (1967) protects against discrimination in personnel decisions, including hiring, promotion, and layoffs, for workers aged 40 years and older. The Family Medical Leave Act of 1993 protects employees having children from employment discrimination and allows for up to 12 weeks of unpaid leave for family or medical emergencies. This means that parents caring for a newborn or for an ill family member are protected against being fired or discriminated against because of the need to take extended time from work for family care.

The final important concept from the Uniform Guidelines is **affirmative action**, the voluntary development of organizational policies that attempt to ensure that jobs are made available to qualified persons regardless of sex, age, or ethnic background. In general, affirmative action programs will hire or promote a member of a protected group over an individual from the majority group if the two are determined to be equally qualified. However, if the protected group member is less qualified than a majority group applicant—usually a white male—the organization is under no obligation to hire the less qualified applicant. Affirmative action programs typically deal with all personnel functions, including recruitment, screening, selection, job placements, and promotions.

There are certain exceptions to Title VII coverage, such as in cases where a particular position requires the workers to be of only one class. The term that is used is that the position has **bona fide occupational qualifications (BFOQs)**, or real occupational needs. For example, a fashion designer is allowed to hire only female models for showing her line of women's clothing, or a sports club is allowed to hire only male or female locker-room attendants for their respective locker rooms. Keep in mind, however, that the courts have allowed only very few exceptions to Title VII based on BFOQs. In particular, restaurants that have hired only female waitpersons or airlines with policies of hiring only female flight attendants have not been allowed by the courts to continue this practice.

Affirmative Action
the voluntary development of policies that try to ensure that jobs are made available to qualified individuals regardless of sex, age, or ethnic background

⏱ Stop & Review
Define and discuss the concepts of protected groups, adverse impact, and affirmative action.

Bona Fide Occupational Qualifications (BFOQs)
real and valid occupational needs required for a particular job

Opportunities for I/O Psychologists to Shape the Future

Remote Work

The first major opportunity for I/O psychologists to change the future of work is by focusing on the most effective ways to work in a largely remote environment. The vast majority of workers had to change the ways they did work as a result of the global COVID-19 pandemic. Even when the virus is gone, workers will still expect to work remotely, and I/O psychologists can assist with identifying ways to most effectively attract, select, and hire workers in a remote environment (Phetmisy & King, 2021; Rudolph et al., 2021). I/O psychologists can help companies determine which workers should be remote, how much of one's work time should be spent in the office, and how and when different combinations of employees should be working together in the office. As we go through each of the chapters, consider how basic human resource functions such as recruitment, selection, onboarding, training, performance management, and separation might be different in a fully or partially remote workplace. These are questions that will need to be addressed over the next 5–10 years, and I/O psychologists are well trained to help. Other ideas, such as how to motivate employees in a virtual work environment, how to lead others, and how culture will shift, are all open doors for future inquiry. As we go through the textbook, we will raise this idea of virtual and remote work to ensure that we are capturing the realities of the 21st-century work environment. More employees are doing virtual job interviews, going through employee socialization and onboarding processes in a remote way, and engaging in online training. There is a lot of opportunity to uncover the best practices for how to carry out these tasks in a remote way and the circumstances in which remote options are superior or inferior to face-to-face engagement.

Diversity and Inclusion

The second major opportunity for I/O psychologists to help the organizations of the future relates to diversity and inclusion. From creating "family-friendly" policies such as employer-sponsored childcare and extended family leave (Grandey, 2001; Halpern & Murphy, 2005), to attracting and retaining top talent, to providing training to decrease microaggressions (Williams, 2020), sexual harassment, and racial discrimination (Hayes et al., 2020), industrial/organizational psychologists must be well versed in topics related to diversity and inclusion. Throughout the text, we will discuss the impact of bias in all aspects of the employment cycle. When we touch on an insight related to diversity and inclusion, we will include this symbol:

Despite all of the federal laws aimed at reducing unfair treatment (described earlier in this chapter), the workplace continues to be fraught with bias. Bias is often subtle, but it is pervasive, resulting in severely negative consequences among those who are targeted (Jones et al., 2017). This includes workers with disabilities (Hernandez et al., 2020), workers who are older (Suh, 2021; Zaniboni et al., 2019), people of color (Hernandez et al., 2019; McCord et al., 2018; Rabelo et al., 2020), women (Chang & Milkman, 2020; Hideg & Krstic, 2020), and those who do not fit normative expectations on gender identity and sexual orientation (Christensen, 2020; Christensen et al., 2020; Dray et al., 2020; Melson-Silimon et al., 2019, 2021). When an individual holds more than one marginalized identity, they face different and unique biases based on that intersectionality (Crenshaw, 2017; Voyles & Nadler, 2020).

Even within a broad category such as race, there is evidence of subtle and nuanced bias. For example, those with darker skin tones experience greater discrimination than those with lighter skin (Harrison & Thomas, 2009), particularly in high client-facing roles (Derous, 2017). Black women who wear their hair in a "natural" style experience greater discrimination than those who straighten their hair (Koval & Rosette, 2020). In fact, many states have passed laws to prohibit discrimination against natural hair, including California, Washington, Colorado, New York, New Jersey, Maryland, and Virginia. Although anti-Black racism has received the most attention since events such as the Black Lives Matter protests in 2020, it is important to also examine racism against Hispanic workers and Asian workers (Aguinis et al., 2020; Roth et al., 2017) and, more broadly, confront the problems that colorblind ideologies elicit in the workplace (Offermann, Basford, Graebner et al., 2014).

Many top scholars argue that I/O psychologists must step in to contribute to progress in outreach and education (Roberson et al., 2020; Ruggs & Avery, 2020). Enrica Ruggs and her colleagues have studied several ways that organizations and individuals can work to reduce bias (Ruggs & Hebl, 2012; Ruggs et al., 2011, 2013, 2016).

In education, she suggests ideas such as

- Explaining the benefits of diversity to educators
- Recruiting greater diversity in faculty to act as role models to students
- Ensuring that examples used in class reflect the diversity of the population
- Delivering professional development around diversity to educators.

For individuals working to avoid bias against themselves (see also Singletary & Hebl, 2009)

- Provide personal details about oneself to combat stereotypes
- Acknowledge or disclose stigma
- Enhance positivity during high-stakes situations such as hiring interviews.

Additional research focuses on strategies that individuals can use to improve their cultural competence, such as setting goals for reducing discrimination (Madera et al., 2013), utilizing behavioral scripts for how they can interact with others (Avery et al., 2009), and increasing contact and friendship across differences (Mousa, 2020; Onyeador et al., 2020; Ragins & Ehrhardt, 2021). Across all of these ideas, having high-quality interactions with people who are different from yourself—engaging in perspective-taking and empathy—are the most fruitful steps that any individual can take to reduce their own bias and discomfort when dealing with others across differences.

Each of us can be an ally by learning more about bias and discrimination and stepping in to interrupt it (Brown & Ostrove, 2013). Being an ally involves offering appropriate assistance and advocating for those with marginalized identities, being willing to learn about others' identity, making personal connections, and communicating effectively (Ostrove & Brown, 2018; Ostrove et al., 2019).

As we go through this textbook, we will examine the various ways that organizations can improve their processes to remove bias and more effectively foster diversity and inclusion. Diversity training is among the most popular approaches, although it is clearly not sufficient to eradicate bias (Robinson et al., 2020). There are important steps that can be taken in recruiting diverse candidate pools, designing less biased selection methods, utilizing training to improve inclusion, ensuring performance evaluations are free of bias, employing inclusive leadership, and fostering an inclusive culture, among others.

I/O psychology has had an important impact in how we select, train, develop, and motivate employees; there is huge potential for I/O psychology to play an even bigger part in helping to improve work performance and make the conditions for workers better, more rewarding, and equitable. I/O psychologists can work toward this by researching and taking action on equity. Although increased diversity presents challenges to organizations and managers, this increased workforce diversity also represents a tremendous strength and opportunity. An obvious advantage of increased workforce diversity is the opportunity for different viewpoints and perspectives that will lead to organizational creativity and innovation (Jackson & Joshi, 2011). Increased workforce diversity can also help an organization understand and reach new markets for products or services. An organization's commitment to diversity can also help in recruiting and retaining the best workers. For instance, not only do cutting-edge companies that value workforce diversity attract the most qualified workers, but also the valuing of diversity permeates the entire organizational culture, leading to reduced organizational conflict, greater cooperation among workers, and increased flexibility and innovation (Loden & Rosener, 1991).

Summary

Industrial/organizational psychology is the branch of *psychology* that deals with the study of work behavior. I/O psychologists are concerned with both the science and practice of industrial/organizational psychology. The scientific goal is to increase our knowledge and understanding of work behavior, and the practical goal is to use that knowledge to improve the psychological well-being of workers. The study of work behavior is a multidisciplinary, cooperative venture. Because I/O psychologists are not the only professionals who study work behavior, they combine their research with that of other social sciences.

Important historical contributions that led to the development of the field of I/O psychology include the work of Frederick Taylor, who founded the school of *scientific management*, which held that work behavior could be studied by systematically breaking down a job into its components and recording the time needed to perform each.

The application of such *time-and-motion studies* increased the efficiency of many manual-labor jobs. During both World War I and World War II, psychologists became involved in the psychological testing of military recruits to determine work assignments. This first large-scale testing program was the beginning of formalized personnel testing, which is still an important part of I/O psychology. Elton Mayo and his *human relations movement* emphasized the role that social factors play in determining worker behavior. Through a series of studies, he demonstrated the importance of worker morale or satisfaction in determining performance. Mayo also discovered the *Hawthorne effect*, or the notion that subjects' behavior could be affected by the mere fact that they knew they were being observed and by the expectations they associated with being participants in an experiment. Following World War II, there was tremendous growth and specialization in I/O psychology, including specialties within the field that focus on how work groups and organizations function and on how technology and workers interface. In 2020, the global COVID-19 pandemic and Black Lives Matter movement changed the workplace in important ways.

Next, we focused on what makes I/O psychology different from other fields of psychology, emphasizing the importance of measurement (validity and reliability) because of federal laws that govern workplace discrimination.

Reliability refers to the consistency or stability of a measure. This includes *test–retest* reliability, which measures whether someone gets a similar score when taking a test on separate dates, and *parallel forms* reliability, when different versions of a test are compared and test takers are expected to perform similarly across forms. There is also another form of reliability called *internal consistency*, which examines whether each item on a test correlates with the other items. This can be tested by dividing the test in half to use split-half reliability or determining the average intercorrelation among all items of the test to calculate *Cronbach's alpha*.

Equally important to measurement is the validity of a measure, which refers to whether a test measures what it says it is measuring. This requires *content validity*, which means that a measure captures one's ability to perform the job, and *construct validity*, which refers to whether a measure captures what it is supposed to measure. Finally, there is *criterion-related validity*, which relates to whether scores on a measure predict some future criterion.

One of the reasons measurement is so important to I/O psychology is because measures may cause intentional or unintentional discrimination against members of a protected class (which includes discrimination on the basis of sex, race, religion, color, national origin, persons over 40, and persons with physical or mental disabilities) based on legal guidelines set forth by the federal government. These laws include Title VII of the Civil Rights Act, the Americans with Disabilities Act, the Age Discrimination in Employment Act, and the Family Medical Leave Act. All of these laws are overseen by the Equal Employment Opportunity Commission.

Today, industrial/organizational psychology is a rapidly growing field that has the opportunity to assist companies with two of the most pressing issues facing organizations today—how to redesign the workplace for a more virtual environment, and how to reduce bias and discrimination to create a more equitable workplace.

Study Questions and Exercises

1 Although I/O psychology is a distinct specialty area in the larger field of psychology, consider how the topics studied by I/O psychologists might benefit from other psychology specialty areas. For example, what contributions have social psychology, educational psychology, cognitive psychology, and other areas made to I/O psychology?

2 Consider the historical advancements made by scientific management, human relations, and the army's intelligence testing programs. How has each of these influenced what we know about work and about workers today?

3 Think about tests you have taken, including any tests or interviews that you participated in to obtain a job. Apply the concepts of reliability and validity to those methods. Do you think the methods were reliable? Valid? How could they have been improved?

4 Consider the important trends in I/O psychology today. Are there any ways that these trends have affected or will affect your life as a worker?

5 Imagine that you chose a career path in I/O psychology. What research questions or practice issues interest you? How might these interests affect your choice of training in I/O psychology and the job title you might hold?

Web Links

www.apa.org
American Psychological Association—publisher of journals with information about careers and graduate programs.

www.siop.org
Society for Industrial and Organizational Psychology—excellent information on graduate training in I/O psychology.

www.siop.org/psychatwork.aspx
What do I/O psychologists *really* do? This is a link to the SIOP site that profiles the careers of I/O psychologists.

www.siop.org/gtp/GTPapply.aspx
SIOP website on preparing for and applying to a graduate program.

www.psychologicalscience.org
Association for Psychological Science—includes many links to other psychology websites. Click on "psychology links."

www.siop.org/SIOP-Stands-Against-Racism

Suggested Readings

Gibson, J. L., Payne, S. C., Morgan, W. B., & Allen, J. A. (2018). The Society for Industrial and Organizational Psychology's guidelines for education and training: An executive summary of the 2016/2017 revision. *American Psychologist*, *73*(5), 678.

Kath, L. M., Salter, N. P., Bachiochi, P., Brown, K. G., & Hebl, M. (2020). Teaching IO psychology to undergraduate students: Do we practice what we preach? *Industrial and Organizational Psychology, 13*(4), 443–460.

Powers, K. (2019). History of industrial organizational psychology. In B. Mosher & R. Cox IV (Eds.), *Workplace psychology*. Chemeketa Press. https://workplacepsychology. pressbooks.com/chapter/psy104_ch01/

Salas, E., Kozlowski, S. W., & Chen, G. (2017). A century of progress in industrial and organizational psychology: Discoveries and the next century. *Journal of Applied Psychology, 102*(3), 589.

Society for Industrial and Organizational Psychology, Inc. (SIOP), Division 14 of the American Psychological Association. www.siop.org. *The Industrial/Organizational Psychologist.*

CHAPTER 2

Research Methods in Industrial/ Organizational Psychology

Inside Tips

UNDERSTANDING THE BASICS OF RESEARCH METHODS AND DESIGN

This chapter presents a general overview of selected research method topics and their use, in general and specifically in I/O psychology. Although it is intended to be a basic introduction to research methods, some of the material can be quite complicated, particularly if you have not done a course that has introduced you to these concepts. If this is the case, you might want to devote some extra time to this chapter and consider looking at an introductory research methods textbook, such as the one listed in the Suggested Readings.

Many of the concepts discussed in this chapter will be used throughout the book when presenting and discussing theories, interpreting research results, and studying the effectiveness of various interventions used by I/O practitioners. Because this chapter introduces a number of important terms, you should plan to spend some time studying their definitions and understanding how they are used. In summary, this is an important chapter that serves as a foundation for what is to come.

Imagine that you want to find the answer to a work-related question, such as what qualities make a person an effective manager. How would you go about answering this question? You might ask people you know, but what if you get conflicting answers? Your father might say that a good manager must have a thorough knowledge of the task and of work procedures. A friend might believe that the most

DOI: 10.4324/9781003143987-3

important quality is skill in relating to people. Your boss might answer that the situation determines which type of manager works best. Three people, three answers. Who is correct?

You might then try another strategy: observing some good managers to see for yourself which qualities make someone an effective work group leader. But how do you know who is a "good" manager? Moreover, how will you determine which characteristics make the good manager effective? The only sound procedure for answering the question of what makes a good manager is to use systematic, scientific research methods. Scientific research methods rely not on hunches or beliefs, but on the systematic collection and analysis of data.

How would you approach the problem in a more systematic, scientific fashion? First, to determine the most important characteristics of a successful work group manager, you would need to define "success." Is a successful manager one who leads a productive work group, one who is well liked and respected by subordinates, or one who leads a work group that is both productive and satisfied? Once you have defined your criteria for managerial success, the next step is to figure out how you will measure such success. It is important that the measurement be accurate and precise so that a clear distinction between truly successful and unsuccessful managers can be made. Here, we use the concepts of *reliability* and *validity* that were covered in Chapter 1. Next, you must isolate the specific characteristics that you believe are related to success as a work group manager. From your experience or reading, you may have some informed ideas about the kinds of knowledge, abilities, or personality that make a successful manager, but you must test these ideas in some systematic fashion. This is the purpose of research methods in psychology. Research methodology is a set of procedures that allow us to investigate the hows and whys of human behavior and to predict when certain behavior will and will not occur.

In this chapter, we will study the basic social science research methods used by I/O psychologists to study work behavior. We will learn why the research process is important for industrial/organizational psychology and examine the goals of social science research methods. We will review the step-by-step procedures used in social science research and conclude with a discussion of how research results are interpreted and applied to increase our understanding of actual work behavior.

Social Science Research Methods

One of the prime purposes of the social science research methods used by I/O psychologists is to enable the researcher to step back from any personal feelings or biases to a specific issue objectively. **Objectivity** is the overarching theme of scientific research methods in general and of social science research methods in particular. It is this objectivity, accomplished via the social scientific process, that distinguishes how a social scientist approaches a work-related problem or issue and how a nonscientist practitioner might approach the same problem or issue. Research methodology is simply a system of guidelines and procedures designed to assist the researcher in

Objectivity
the unbiased approach to observation and interpretations of behavior

obtaining a more accurate and unbiased analysis of the problem at hand. Similarly, statistical analysis is nothing more or less than procedures for testing the repeated objective observations that a researcher has collected.

Goals of Social Science Research Methods

Because I/O psychology is a science, it shares the same basic goals of any science: to describe, explain, and predict phenomena (Kaplan, 1964). Because I/O psychology is the science of behavior at work, its goals are to describe, explain, and predict *work* behavior. For example, an I/O psychologist might attempt to satisfy the first goal by describing the production levels of a company, the rates of employee absenteeism and turnover, and the number and types of interactions between supervisors and workers for the purpose of arriving at a more accurate picture of the organization under study. The goal of explaining phenomena is achieved when the I/O psychologist attempts to discover why certain work behaviors occur. Finding out that a company's employee turnover rates are high because of employee dissatisfaction with the levels of pay and benefits would be one example. The goal of prediction would be addressed when a researcher attempts to use the scores from certain psychological tests to predict which employee would be the best candidate for a management position, or when a researcher uses a theory of motivation to predict how employees will respond to different types of incentive programs.

I/O psychology is also an applied science and, therefore, has the additional goal of attempting to control or alter behavior to obtain desired outcomes. Using the results of previous research, an I/O psychologist can attempt to alter some aspect of work behavior. For example, some long-standing evidence indicates a connection between employee participation in organizational decision making and levels of job satisfaction (Argyris, 1964). Knowing this, an I/O psychologist might implement a program of increased employee participation in company policy decision making in an effort to improve levels of employee job satisfaction.

Steps in the Research Process

The process of conducting research typically follows a series of steps (see Figure 2.1). The first step is the formulation of a problem or issue for study. The second step

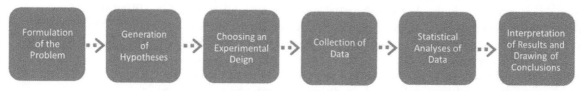

Figure 2.1 Steps in the research process.

is the generation of hypotheses. The third step is designing the research, which includes selecting the appropriate research method or design. The fourth step is the actual collection of data, which is governed by the particular research design used. The fifth step involves analysis of the collected data. This leads to the final step, which involves the interpretation of results and the drawing of conclusions based on the results.

Formulation of the Problem or Issue

The first step in conducting research is to specify the problem or issue to be studied. Sometimes, a researcher develops an issue because of his or her interests in a particular area. For example, an I/O psychologist might be interested in the relationships between worker job satisfaction and employee loyalty to the organization, or between worker productivity and the length of time that employees stay with a particular organization. Often, the selection of a research problem is influenced by previous research. On the other hand, a client company that has a particular problem that needs to be alleviated, such as an extraordinarily high level of employee absenteeism, may provide the practicing I/O psychologist-consultant with an issue. Similarly, large organizations may have I/O psychologists on staff whose job is to study problems using social science methods to better understand the problems or to help solve them.

Generation of Hypotheses

The next step in the research process involves taking those elements that the researcher intends to measure, known as **variables**, and generating statements concerning the supposed relationships between variables. These statements are known as **hypotheses**. In the examples of research issues given earlier, job satisfaction, worker productivity, employee loyalty, employment tenure, and absenteeism are all variables. The hypotheses will later be tested through the analysis of the collected systematic observations of variables, better known as the collection and analysis of research data (see Table 2.1).

By testing hypotheses through the collection of systematic observations of behavior, a researcher may eventually develop a **theory** or **model**, which is an organization of beliefs that enables us to understand behavior more completely. In social science, models are representations of the complexity of factors that affect behavior. In I/O psychology, models are representations of the factors that affect work behavior.

We have all seen architects' cardboard and plaster models of buildings and the plastic models of aircraft that can be purchased in hobby shops. These are concrete models that represent the physical appearance of the actual building or aircraft. The models used

Variables
the elements measured in research investigations

Hypotheses
statements about the supposed relationships between variables

Theory/Model
the organization of beliefs into a representation of the factors that affect behavior

Table 2.1 Examples of Hypotheses in I/O Psychology Research

- Engaging in ethical leadership behavior can cause leaders to become more abusive to their subordinates (Lin et al., 2016)
- Greater gender diversity is related to better company financial performance, particularly in countries with greater gender equality (Zhang, 2020)
- Taking breaks at work earlier in the day is associated with greater recovery than taking later breaks (Hunter & Wu, 2016)
- When customers see employees treated badly by other customers, they leave larger tips and treat the employee better (Hershcovis & Bhatnagar, 2017)
- Responding with anger to negotiation offers can lead to greater concessions (Hillebrandt & Barclay, 2017)
- Employees with high job demands and fewer resources to do their job are more likely to experience job burnout (Nahrgang et al., 2011)
- Asking employees to do illegitimate/non-work-related tasks lowers their self-esteem and well-being (Eatough et al., 2016)
- Confronting someone for prejudice can result in greater workplace belonging as long as you believe people can change (Rattan & Dweck, 2018).

in I/O psychology research are abstract representations of the factors influencing work behavior. Developing a theory and diagramming that theory are convenient ways to organize our thinking and our understanding of complex behavioral processes.

Many people who do not have an understanding of scientific research methodology have misconceptions about theories. Either they believe that theories represent the personal views of scientists, or they believe that theories represent proven facts. Neither is wholly true. Theories are important because they help us represent the complex and often intangible forces that influence human behavior. By using a theory as a guide, I/O psychologists can develop strategies for conducting research to find support for—or against—the theory. A theory is the starting point for understanding and influencing behavior, and theories can be used as guides to improve the work world for all concerned.

Although I/O psychologists use research models to guide their investigations, models of human work behavior are also the products of research. The researcher may use an existing theory or model to develop certain hypotheses about aspects of work behavior and then test those hypotheses through research. These results may then be used to refine the model or create a new, "improved" model. It is through the creation, testing, and refinement of theories that advances are made in the science of I/O psychology.

Selecting the Research Design

Once hypotheses are generated, the researcher chooses a research design that will guide the investigation. The type of design selected depends on such things as the research setting and the degree of control that the researcher has over the research setting. For instance, a researcher may decide that he or she will conduct a study of workers' task performance by observing workers in the actual work setting, during normal working hours, in order to make the setting as "natural" as possible. Alternatively, the researcher may decide instead that it would be less disruptive to bring workers into a laboratory room where the work tasks could be simulated. Different settings may require different research designs.

The researcher may also be constrained in the selection of a research design by the amount of control the researcher has over the work setting and the workers. The company may not allow the researcher to interfere with normal work activities, forcing the researcher to use observational measurement of behavior or to use existing data that the organization has already collected. We shall discuss specific research designs shortly.

Collection of Data

The next step in the research process involves the testing of hypotheses through data collection. The collection of data is governed by the particular research design used. However, an important concern in data collection is **sampling**, or selecting a *representative* group from a larger population for study. The term representative is meant to imply that the sample accurately reflects the characteristics of the larger groups. In many cases, student samples are used to represent workers, which has emerged as a criticism of the sampling methods used in industrial/ organizational psychology (Bergman & Jean, 2016). Alternatively, many studies use employees from online survey sites such as Amazon's Mechanical Turk, where participants receive small monetary benefits for filling in a survey. Although the site is intended to be more representative of workers, because you can choose only to survey full-time employees, there are certainly questions about whether individuals who take surveys for money really are representative of most employees (Cheung et al., 2017).

Even when researchers intend to use a random sample, such as calling or mailing a randomly selected subset of voters, sampling errors can emerge. For example, polling data for the 2016 and 2020 presidential elections overestimated the strength of Democratic presidential candidates Hilary Clinton, in 2016, and Joe Biden, in 2020, against Donald Trump. The Pew Research Center suggests that one possibility for the inaccuracy in polling is that Democratic voters are easier to reach or more willing to respond to surveys (Keeter et al., 2020). If this is the case, then randomly calling voters could result in inaccurate conclusions if more liberal voters are willing to respond. Response rates (who is most likely to respond) should be considered when conducting survey research. Beyond avoiding sampling errors, researchers also need to decide whether they prefer to use random or stratified sampling.

With **random sampling**, research participants are chosen from a specified population in such a way that each individual has an equal probability of being selected.

Sampling
the selection of a representative group from a larger population for study

Random Sampling
the selection of research participants from a population so that each individual has an equal probability of being chosen

For example, to choose a random sample of 20 workers from a company employing 200 workers, we would begin with a list of all workers and, using a table of random numbers or a computer program that generates random numbers, randomly select 20 workers. The concept of sampling also applies to studying behaviors in certain individuals or groups of individuals. For example, if we wanted a random sampling of a particular employee's typical work behavior, we might study different, random 5-minute time periods throughout a typical workday or week.

Stratified Sampling
the selection of research participants based on categories that represent important distinguishing characteristics of a population

Stratified sampling begins with the designation of important variables that divide a population into subgroups, or strata. For example, we might want to consider male and female employees and management and nonmanagement personnel as different strata. We then randomly select a specified number of employees in such a way that our research sample mirrors the actual breakdown of these groups in the total population. For example, assume that 40% of the individuals in our total worker population are female and 60% are male, and 25% are management and 75% are nonmanagement. We would want to choose a sample that represented these percentages. Of the individuals in our selected sample, 40% should be female, and 25% should be management personnel. We may also want to ensure that the percentages of male and female managers and nonmanagers in our sample are representative of the larger population.

Both of these sampling techniques help ensure that the sample is representative of the population from which it is drawn. The random selection procedure also protects against any sorts of biases in the choice of participants for study.

Analyses of Research Data

Once data are gathered, they are subjected to some form of analysis for interpretation. Most often, this involves statistical analysis of quantitative data (i.e., data with numerical values), although data can be analyzed using qualitative data analysis techniques (not based on the numerical values of the data). Statistical analysis of data requires that the research observations be quantified in some way. Statistics are simply tools used by the researcher to help make sense of the observations that have been collected. Some statistical analyses are simple and are used to help describe and classify the data. Other statistical techniques are quite complex and help the researcher make detailed inferences. For example, some statistics allow the researcher to determine the causes of certain observed outcomes. A brief discussion of certain statistical analysis techniques is presented in the appendix at the end of this chapter.

Interpretation of Research Results

The final step in the research process is interpretation of the results. Here, the researcher draws conclusions about the meaning of the findings and their relevance to actual work behavior, as well as their possible limitations. For example, imagine that a researcher decides to study the effects on work group productivity of two managerial styles: a directive style, whereby the manager closely supervises workers, telling them what they should be doing and how they should be doing it; and a nondirective, participative style, whereby the manager allows the workers a great deal of freedom in deciding how they will get the work task done. The researcher conducts the study on groups of directive and nondirective frontline managers who are employed at several factories that manufacture jet aircraft parts. By collecting and analyzing data, the researcher concludes that directive managers lead more productive groups. However, the researcher might want to set some limits for the use of these findings. The researcher might caution that these results may only apply to managers who are supervising factory work groups and might not pertain to managers of service organizations, such as hospitals or restaurants, to more creative jobs, such as developing smartphone apps, or to managers of salespersons (Figure 2.2). The researcher might also mention that, although a directive management style appears to be related to productivity, it is not known whether it is related to other important variables, such as employee satisfaction or work quality.

In the next few sections, we will examine in depth some of the steps in the research process. First, we will examine the various research designs used to govern the collection of research data. Second, we will briefly discuss how research variables

Figure 2.2 A researcher who studied management styles of structural engineers would need to be cautious in interpreting data. Would the same kind of supervision produce the same results in a retail store? In a law firm?

Souce: Photograph found on Unsplash (https://unsplash.com/photos/CUA-_IGpXXo).

are measured. Next, we will discuss some of the problems and limitations of conducting research in I/O psychology and will consider the ways that research results and theories can be applied to the practice of I/O psychology. Finally, we will discuss rules of conduct for researchers who are studying people and their work behavior. Research methods are obviously important to practicing I/O psychologists. See the "Up Close" feature to learn how knowledge of research methods can help you in your working life.

Major Research Designs

When testing theories and collecting data, researchers use specific research designs. Two of the most common designs are the experimental design and the correlational design, although other methodologies can be used. We will begin by looking at each of these two general research designs. Another method of conducting research is called meta-analysis. This is a method that allows researchers to "combine" results from different studies in a systematic way (Schalken & Rietbergen, 2017). Finally, researchers will occasionally conduct an in-depth, descriptive investigation of a particular issue, which is known as a case study. Each of these research designs will be explored.

The Experimental Method

Experimental Method
a research design characterized by a high degree of control over the research setting to allow for the determination of cause-and-effect relationships among variables

The **experimental method** is most commonly associated with research conducted in a laboratory, although it can also be applied in an actual work setting, in which case it is known as a field experiment. The experimental method is designed to give the researcher a very high degree of control over the research setting. In a laboratory experiment, the researcher has a great deal of control, which is a major advantage of conducting research in a laboratory. In a field experiment, the researcher typically has less control than in the laboratory, but the researcher must still maintain control over the situation in a field experiment to draw strong conclusions.

 UP CLOSE **How to Use Research Methods in Your Own Life**

Although a thorough knowledge of social science research methods is critical for an I/O psychologist, how might this knowledge apply to the life of the typical working person?

Perhaps the greatest value of social science research methods is that the general principles of trying to take an objective (unbiased) perspective, using caution concerning cause-and-effect interpretations, and basing

UP CLOSE *(continued)*

interpretations on repeated observations can be extremely useful as guidelines for decision making. Rather than basing important work-related decisions on hunches, previous experience, or personal preferences, approach the problems as a scientist would. Step back from your own biases. Try to collect some objective data to clarify the problems and base your decisions on the data.

For example, a student approached me about her part-time job, which had been a source of grief to her and to others who worked with her at the customer service desk of a large department store. The problem was that the manager never seemed to schedule hours in a way that satisfied all the employees. Some employees seemed to get the "better" hours, whereas others were complaining that they consistently had to work the "bad" shifts. The student believed that she had the perfect solution: the employees would all submit their ideal work schedules and possible alternatives, and the manager would arrange them in a way that was satisfactory to everyone.

I suggested that, rather than assuming she had reached a workable solution, she should go back and approach the problem from a research perspective. First, I recommended that she determine the magnitude and scope of the problem. She developed a brief survey that she gave to all the department employees, asking about their satisfaction with the current work scheduling. The results indicated that the majority of the workers did indeed have difficulties with the scheduling. She next approached the manager to see whether she would be open to suggestions for change, which she was. Rather than relying on just her solution, the student then solicited suggestions for dealing with the difficulties from all the employees. When a new strategy was eventually selected (they did try a variation of her suggestion), it was implemented on a trial basis, with careful assessment of its effects on employee attitudes and on difficulties related to scheduling conflicts. By following this systematic method of relying on data, the workers were thus able to improve their situation.

A sound background in research methods can also assist in the evaluation of new work techniques or management strategies. Whenever you hear of some revolutionary strategy for increasing work performance or efficiency, do what a good social scientist would do: go directly to the primary source. Find out what research evidence (if any) supports the technique and read those reports with a critical eye. See if there are serious flaws in the ways that the technique was tested, flaws that might make you doubt whether it really works.

In the experimental method, the researcher systematically manipulates levels of one variable, called the **independent variable**, and measures its effect on another variable, called the **dependent variable**. The dependent variable is the outcome variable, or the behavior that is of primary interest to the investigator. In the experimental method, other variables in the setting are presumed to be held constant. That is, no elements except the independent variable are allowed to vary. As a result, any change in the dependent variable is presumed to have been caused by the independent variable. The primary advantage of the experimental method is that it allows us to determine cause-and-effect relationships among variables.

Independent Variable
in the experimental method, the variable that is manipulated by the researcher

Dependent Variable
in the experimental method, the variable that is acted on by the independent variable; the outcome variable

Treatment Group
the group in an experimental investigation that is subjected to the change in the independent variable

Control Group
a comparison group in an experimental investigation that receives no treatment

To determine whether the manipulation of an independent variable produces any significant change in a dependent variable, following the experimental method, researchers often compare the results of two groups of participants. One group, called the experimental group, or **treatment group**, is subjected to the change in the independent variable. The second group, called the **control group**, receives no change. In other words, the second group is not subjected to the treatment. This comparison of treatment and control groups allows the researcher to determine the magnitude of the effect produced by the manipulation of the independent variable (the treatment). Measuring the dependent variable of the control group allows the researcher to rule out any normal fluctuations that might have occurred naturally in the absence of the treatment. The comparison of treatment and control groups gives the researcher greater confidence that the treatment was (or was not) effective.

For example, imagine that a researcher wants to test the effectiveness of a new training program for sales skills. A number of salespersons are randomly assigned to the treatment group and attend the training session. Other salespersons are randomly assigned to the control group and do not receive the training content. (In a good experimental design, the control group should also attend "a session," but one that does not have the training content; this allows the researcher to control for any effects that may result from participants' simply attending a program.) A comparison of the subsequent sales records of the two groups allows the researcher to determine the effectiveness of the program. In this case, the independent variable is whether the salespersons did or did not receive the training content; the dependent variable would be the amount of sales. It is also possible to expand the experimental method to include a number of different treatment groups—for example, different types of sales training programs—and to compare the effectiveness of these various treatments with one another and with a control group. Of course, the experimental method is not used only for comparing treatment and control groups. Any variable that can be broken into distinct categories or levels can serve as an independent variable in an experimental design. For instance, we might examine differences between male and female workers or among "high-," "medium-," and "low-" producing workers (as determined by productivity measures).

Aside from the specified independent variables, other variables that may be affecting the dependent variable are termed **extraneous variables**. It is these variables that increase the difficulty of conducting research because they can be any factors other than the independent variables that influence the dependent variable. Consider, for example, the Hawthorne studies discussed in Chapter 1. In these studies of the influence of lighting and other work conditions on assembly line productivity (the independent variables), the attention paid to the workers by the researchers was an extraneous variable that affected productivity (the dependent variable).

The key to the success of the experimental method is to hold all extraneous variables constant. For example, observing all research participants, treatment and control groups, at the same time of day, using the same methods, same equipment, and so forth. This is, of course, much easier to do in a laboratory setting than in an actual work setting. Sometimes, extraneous variables result from systematic differences in

⏱ Stop & Review

Describe the six steps in the research process.

Extraneous Variables
variables other than the independent variable that may influence the dependent variable

the individuals being studied. For example, if participants are given the opportunity to volunteer to participate in a particular treatment group (with the nonvolunteers serving as a control group), there may be some motivational differences in the treatment volunteers that might act as a moderating or confounding variable, thus affecting the results. That is, participants in the treatment group might be more energetic and "helpful" than those in the control group, and it would thus be impossible to tell whether any differences between the two groups resulted from the treatment or from these inherent motivational differences. Many potential extraneous variables can be controlled through the **random assignment** of participants to the experimental and control groups. Random assignment ensures that any motivational differences or other individual characteristics show up in equivalent proportions in both groups. In other words, assigning participants randomly to treatment and control groups serves to control for the effects of extraneous variables.

Random Assignment
a method of assigning subjects to groups by chance to control for the effects of extraneous variables

One of the major drawbacks of the experimental method is its artificiality. A researcher who controls the experimental setting may create a situation that is quite different from the actual work setting. There may, thus, be some concern about whether the results will apply or generalize to real settings. In field experiments, there is less concern about the generalizability of findings because the participants and the setting are usually representative of those that can be affected by the results. However, any time that a researcher creates an experimental situation, he or she runs the risk of generating artificial conditions that would not exist in the usual work setting.

Two Examples of the Experimental Method: A Laboratory and a Field Experiment

One experimental study was designed to determine which of two decision-making styles was most effective when individuals were working under high-stress conditions (Johnston et al., 1997). In this laboratory experiment, 90 U.S. Navy–enlisted personnel volunteered and were required to take part in a simulation where they would be working as a ship's radar screen operator. The participants were randomly assigned to one of two training groups. The first group learned a "vigilant" decision-making style. Vigilant decision making is where the decision maker scans and considers all information in an orderly, sequential fashion, taking into account all information and reviewing all alternatives before making a decision. Participants in the second group were trained in "hypervigilant" decision making. In hypervigilant decision making, the decision maker scans only the information that is needed in a particular circumstance, and scanning of information does not follow a systematic, ordered sequence. The type of training participants received constituted the independent variable. Stress was created by having distracting radio communications played and by an experimenter who told the participants to "hurry up" and "perform better" at regular intervals.

The participants were seated at a computer screen that presented a simulation of a ship's radar screen that systematically presented images representing approaching ships, submarines, and aircraft. Participants had to identify each object, determine if it was a "friendly" or enemy craft, and engage enemy craft. The dependent variable in this study consisted of the number of objects that were correctly identified and dealt with appropriately. The results of the study confirmed the researchers' hypothesis that hypervigilant decision making was best under high-stress conditions, primarily because it is quicker and more efficient and provides less of a cognitive "load" on the radar operator.

Our second example of the experimental method is a field experiment designed to test the effects on safe driving behavior of worker participation in setting safety-related goals (Ludwig & Geller, 1997). The study participants were 324 college-aged pizza deliverers from three pizza stores. Observation of the drivers showed that they often did not stop completely at a stop sign as they headed out on deliveries. Pizza deliverers were randomly assigned to one of two types of safety meetings focusing on the importance of making a full and safe stop. In one condition, driving-related safety goals were set by store managers. In the other condition, the deliverers participated in setting their own driving safety goals. The type of goal setting constituted the independent variable. At certain intervals, the managers observed stopping behaviors as the drivers exited the stores' parking lots and headed down the road on their deliveries. During the posttraining period, managers posted the rates of safe stopping for the drivers to see. Also recorded were other safety behaviors, such as whether or not the drivers wore their seat belts and used their turn signals when turning onto the highway. Each of these safe driving behaviors constituted the study's dependent variables.

The results showed that both groups, those who helped set their own safety goals and those whose goals were set by managers, engaged in safer stopping behavior during the time period when their managers were watching and providing feedback. But only the group who had set their own stopping safety goals showed increased use of turn signals and seat belt use. In other words, the safe stopping behavior "generalized" to other safety behaviors, but only for the group that participated in setting its own goals.

Although both of these studies were fairly well designed and executed and produced some useful knowledge, both have limitations. The laboratory investigation used Navy-enlisted personnel, not actual ship radar operators, which raises the question of whether the results would generalize to actual radar operators or to other similar workers, such as air traffic controllers. As presented, the dependent variables in the studies are fairly limited. (Both studies were presented in simplified format. Additional variables were measured in each.) For example, although the safety study found that drivers increased seat belt usage and the use of their turn signals, we don't know if other driving behaviors (e.g., speeding) were similarly affected. Although the results of studies such as these may answer some questions, additional ones might arise. For example, from the results of these experiments, we still don't know for sure why one particular decision-making style was better or exactly why setting your own safety goals had better effects on safe driving.

This is the research process. Results of one study may stimulate subsequent research in the same area. Scientific research builds on the results of previous studies, adding and refining, to increase our knowledge of the behavior in question.

Quasi-Experiments

In many cases, a researcher does not have the control over the situation needed to run a true experiment. As a result, a **quasi-experiment** is used, which is a design that follows the experimental method but lacks features such as random assignment of participants to groups and manipulation of the independent variable. For example, a researcher might compare one group of workers who have undergone a particular training program with another group of workers who will not receive the training, but, because they were not randomly assigned to the groups, the groups are not equivalent. As a result, cause-and-effect relationships cannot be determined. For example, one study examined the effectiveness of a management coaching program and compared managers in the coaching programs to other managers who did not receive coaching, but who were matched on age, years of experience, and salary (Evers et al., 2006).

Quasi-experiments are quite common in I/O psychology because of the difficulties in controlling extraneous variables, and, often, the unit of analysis is groups or organizations, rather than individuals. Quasi-experiments can be used, for example, to compare departments or organizations on some variables of interest. It is important in making these comparisons, however, that the groups be as equivalent as possible. Moreover, in quasi-experimental designs, researchers often try to measure as many possible extraneous variables as they can in order to statistically control for their effects. This helps strengthen the results obtained in quasi-experiments. As mentioned, many of the studies we will explore in this book are quasi-experimental designs, and they are quite frequent in I/O psychology.

Quasi-Experiment
follows the experimental design but lacks random assignment and/or manipulation of an independent variable

The Correlational Method

The second major method for data collection, the **correlational method** (also referred to as the observational method), looks at the relationships between or among variables as they occur naturally. When the correlational method is used, in contrast to the experimental method, there is no manipulation of variables by the experimenter. A researcher simply measures two or more variables and then examines their statistical relationship to one another. Because the correlational method does not involve the manipulation of independent variables, distinctions between independent and dependent variables are not nearly as important as they are in the experimental method. Because the correlational method does not require the rigid control over

Correlational Method
a research design that examines the relationship between variables as they naturally occur

variables associated with the experimental method, it is easy to use in actual work settings. In addition, correlational research can be conducted with archival data—data that an organization has already collected. For example, an organization might use data on employee absenteeism and look at the relationship between number of sick days and ratings on a job satisfaction survey that was administered to employees. Because of its ease of use, a great deal of the research on work behavior thus uses the correlational method. The major drawback of this method is that we cannot determine cause-and-effect relationships. A common problem is the tendency of people to try to make causal statements from correlations, which leads to many misconceptions and faulty interpretations of data. Many students of statistics quickly learn that correlation does not necessarily imply causality. However, with advancements in "big data" (extremely large data sets, often collected online, that are too large to analyse with traditional data analysis software) (Oswald et al., 2020), and data visualization tools (Tay et al., 2018), there is immense opportunity to utilize correlational research to draw strong conclusions.

Considerable caution must be exercised when interpreting the results of correlational research. For example, suppose that a researcher finds a relationship between workers' attitudes to their employer and the amount of money they invest in a company stock program. Employees with very positive attitudes tend to use a greater portion of their income to purchase stock. It could be that their favorable attitudes cause them to demonstrate their support for (and faith in) the company by buying stock, but the cause-and-effect relationship could also go the other way: employees who purchase stock at bargain prices may develop more positive attitudes about the company because they now have an investment in it. On the other hand, a third variable (an extraneous variable), such as the length of time employees have worked for the company, may actually be the cause of the observed correlation between employee attitudes and stock purchases. Employees with a long tenure may generally have more favorable attitudes about the company than newcomers (over time, those with negative attitudes usually leave the organization). These employees are also older and may be able to invest a larger proportion of their incomes in stock options than younger workers, who may be raising families and purchasing first homes. Length of time on the job may thus influence both of the other two variables. The simple correlation between employee attitudes and stock purchases, therefore, does not lead us to any firm cause-and-effect conclusions.

Two Examples of the Correlational Method

Two researchers studied the ability of certain tests and other assessment methods to predict future managerial success. The participants were more than 1,000 entry-level women managers, all of whom took part in a 2-day testing program at an assessment center. The assessment techniques included an interview, some standardized tests, and several scored exercises. (We will discuss assessment centers and employee assessment techniques in Chapters 4 and 5.) At the end of the assessment, each woman was rated on a 4-point scale of "middle-management potential," with endpoints ranging from *not acceptable* to *more than acceptable*. Seven years later, measures of the women's "management progress" were obtained. Results indicated "a sizable correlation between predictions made by the assessment staff and subsequent progress seven years later" (Ritchie & Moses, 1983).

In a study of secretaries and managers in seven German companies, researchers examined the relationship between the time it took for these office workers to deal with computer errors and the workers' "negative emotional reactions," such as voicing frustration or outbursts of anger (Brodbeck et al., 1993). This study was an observational field study, because the researchers observed the workers as they went through their normal daily routine at work. The observers merely recorded the errors workers made while working at computers, noted the time that it took workers to deal with the computer errors, and noted their emotional reactions. As you might expect, there was a significant positive relationship (a positive correlation) between the length of time workers spent trying to solve computer errors and their reactions of frustration and anger. In other words, the more time the workers spent trying to solve computer errors, the more angry and frustrated they became.

As mentioned, each of the methods, experimental and correlational, has its own strengths and weaknesses. Sometimes, researchers might use both methods in a large-scale investigation. Although the experimental method is most commonly associated with laboratory studies, and correlational research is most often associated with field research, either method can be used in either setting. The key to using the experimental method in a field investigation is gaining control over the environment by manipulating levels of the independent variable and holding extraneous variables constant. Because the correlational method looks at the relationships among variables as they naturally exist, a correlational design may often be easier to implement, particularly in actual work settings, as the study of German office workers demonstrates.

Complex Correlational Designs

Although simple correlational designs do not allow the determination of cause-and-effect relationships, most correlational designs in modern I/O psychology research involve complex statistical analyses that allow for combining predictor variables and statistically controlling for possible extraneous variables, and methods that allow for inferring the likelihood of cause and effect.

A **multiple regression design** allows a researcher to examine the relationship between a particular outcome variable and multiple predictors. This allows the researcher to determine how a number of variables correlate with a certain outcome. For example, a researcher might be interested in how ability in combination with motivation predicts job performance. For example, a study of nurses might use a

Multiple Regression Design examines the relationship between a particular outcome variable and multiple predictors

measure of technical nursing skills and motivation to predict the nurses' on-the-job performance evaluations. The simple correlations between technical skills and performance and between motivation and performance can be examined, but, through multiple regression (we will learn more about this in the appendix at the end of the chapter), the researcher can see how skills and motivation in combination predict performance and understand the relative contribution each of the variables makes in predicting job performance.

The multiple regression design also allows a researcher to control for possible extraneous variables and examine the effect of one variable on another after controlling for (or "holding constant") the effects of extraneous variables. In the study of nurses, for example, the researcher might measure and control for possible extraneous variables, such as the age and years of experience of the nurses, in examining how skills and motivation affect performance.

Certain complex designs can also be used to infer causality. One example that is quite common in the I/O psychology literature is the use of a *mediation model*. In a mediation model, the relationship between two variables is hypothesized to be explained by, or mediated by, a third variable—the *mediator variable* (see Figure 2.3). For example, the relationship between job satisfaction and employee turnover (assuming that less satisfied employees are more likely to quit their jobs) is mediated by a third variable—the intention to quit.

Meta-Analysis

As we have seen, the results of a single research study provide some answers, but often raise other questions. Moreover, different research investigations of the same topic or issue may reach inconsistent, and sometimes totally contradictory, conclusions. For example, one study may find strong support for a given hypothesis, a second study may find only weak support, and a third study may have results that are opposite to

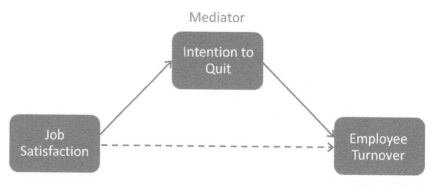

Figure 2.3 A mediation model for the job satisfaction–employee turnover relationship.

those of the first study. Students who are just beginning to explore research in I/O psychology or other social sciences seem to get particularly frustrated by such inconsistencies. How can any conclusions be drawn from the varying and often conflicting results of several independent research investigations?

The answer is found in a methodological technique called **meta-analysis**, which allows the results of a number of studies to be combined and analyzed together to draw a summary conclusion (Rosenthal, 1991; Wolf, 1986). Meta-analyses are usually conducted when there are 20 or more separate studies of a given hypothesis or topic. Meta-analysis may be used for several purposes, including summarizing the relationship between variables examined in each of a set of studies and determining other factors that are associated with increases or decreases in the magnitude of relationships between variables of interest (these "other factors" are often referred to as moderating variables). Although it depends on the research question and the types of studies and their specific research designs, meta-analysis will typically use an indicator of effect size from each examined study. **Effect size** refers to an estimate of the magnitude of the relationship between any variable X and any variable Y (in a correlational design) or the size of the effect of an independent variable on a dependent variable (in an experimental design). One measure of effect size is the correlation coefficient, which is provided in many studies to describe relationships between variables (see the appendix at the end of the chapter for more information on correlation coefficients).

Meta-analysis is used to compare and combine data from all of the examined studies, taking into account the effect sizes and the number of participants in each of the independent studies. Typically, meta-analytic techniques yield a summary statistic that tells us something about the overall relationship between the variables examined in each of the studies and whether the results from the independent studies are significantly different from each other in meaningful ways. For example, different studies examining the relationship between job satisfaction and employee absenteeism have produced different results, with some studies reporting higher levels of job satisfaction associated with lower rates of absenteeism (e.g., Ostroff, 1993, and others reporting no association between the two factors (Ilgen & Höllenback, 1977); see Chapter 9 for more information). Meta-analytic procedures may suggest that different studies yield different results because each uses a different measure of absenteeism or job satisfaction, or because the participants in studies were different. Meta-analyses have been used to summarize the research results from many studies of the absenteeism–job satisfaction relationship and have found that the two factors are indeed related—low satisfaction is related to higher rates of absenteeism—but the relationship is not as strong as most people believe (e.g., Scott & Taylor, 1985).

Meta-analytic studies have become quite popular, particularly in I/O psychology and other fields studying work behavior. These analyses have addressed variables such as the effects of: personality and intelligence on counterproductive academic behaviors such as cheating (Cuadrado et al., 2021); justice perceptions of workplace behaviors (Cohen-Charash & Spector, 2001) empowering leadership on employee performance (Kim et al., 2018); situational factors, interpersonal interactions, and personal factors

Meta-Analysis
a technique that allows results from several different research studies to be combined and summarized

Effect Size
an estimate of the magnitude of a relationship or effect found in a research investigation

on safety climate (He, Wang & Payne, 2019), team training in health-care settings (Hughes et al., 2016); organizational climate on decisions to disclose sexual orientation at work (Wax et al., 2018); thriving at work affecting job outcomes (Kleine et al., 2019); and job insecurity on employee outcomes (Jiang & Lavaysse, 2018).

One meta-analysis confirmed the widely held view that more physically demanding jobs, such as hazardous jobs with high risk for injury, were related to workers becoming stressed and "burned out" (Nahrgang et al., 2011). In another meta-analysis of 55 studies investigating the relationship between workers' personalities, positive job attitudes, and organizational citizenship behaviors—pro-company behaviors exhibited by employees—it was found that positive job attitudes were a better predictor of organizational citizenship behaviors than were workers' personalities (Organ & Ryan, 1995).

The Case Study Method

We have stated that there are difficulties in conducting controlled research in actual work settings. Often, a researcher or scientist-practitioner will have the opportunity to conduct research in a business or industry, but will find it impossible to

Figure 2.4 In one example of the case study method, a psychologist found that company picnics, games, and other social activities increased employees' loyalty to the organization.

Souce: Photograph by You X Ventures, found on Unsplash (https://unsplash.com/photos/NdZ 08c-zu0c).

follow either the experimental or the correlational method. The study may involve a one-time-only assessment of behavior or the application of an intervention to only a single group, department, or organization. Such research is known as a **case study**. The results of a single case study, even if the study involves the application of some highly researched intervention strategy, do not allow us to draw any firm conclusions. A case study is really little more than a descriptive investigation. We are unable to test hypotheses or to determine cause-and-effect relationships from a case study because it is like conducting research with only one participant. What may have seemed to work in this one instance may not work in a second or third case. However, this does not mean that the case study method is not valuable, and, in fact, many exploratory studies follow this method. Case studies can provide rich, descriptive information about certain work behaviors and situations. In some topic areas, where it has been impossible to conduct controlled experimental studies, the results of case studies may be the only evidence that exists. Moreover, such results might inspire the development of hypotheses that will later be tested with experimental or correlational studies.

Case Study
a research investigation involving a one-time assessment of behavior

Measurement of Variables

One of the more difficult aspects of research is the measurement of variables. A variable must be **operationalized**—that is, brought down from the abstract level to a more concrete level and clearly defined so that it can be measured or manipulated. In the first example of the correlational method outlined earlier, the variable "middle-management potential" was operationalized as a rating on a 4-point scale. In the experimental study of pizza delivery drivers, "safe driving behavior" was operationalized as wearing a seat belt, using a turn signal, and coming to a full stop at an intersection. Both variables could be considered operational definitions of the more general variable of "performance."

During the process of operationalizing a variable, a particular technique for measuring the variable is usually selected. We will examine two of the general categories of techniques used to measure variables in I/O psychology: observational techniques and self-report techniques.

Operationalized
clearly defining a research variable so that it can be measured

⏱ Stop & Review

Describe and contrast the experimental and correlational methods.

Observational Techniques

One procedure for measuring research variables is through direct, systematic observation. This involves the researchers themselves recording certain behaviors that they have defined as the operationalized variables. For example, a researcher might consider the number of items manufactured as a measure of productivity or may look for certain defined supervisory behaviors, such as demonstrating work techniques to subordinates, giving direct orders, and setting specific work quotas, to assess whether a manager has a "task-oriented" supervisory style.

The measurement of variables through direct observation can be either obtrusive or unobtrusive. With **obtrusive observation**, the researcher is visible to the persons being observed. The primary disadvantage of this technique is that the participants may behave differently because they know they are a part of a research investigation. This is exactly what happened in the original Hawthorne experiments. Researchers engaging in obtrusive observation must always consider how their presence will affect participants' behavior, and thus the results of the study.

Unobtrusive observation also involves direct observation of behavior, but in this case participants are unaware of the researcher's presence and do not know that their behavior is being studied (or may not know which behaviors are being studied). The primary advantage of unobtrusive observation is that the researcher can be fairly confident that the recorded behavior is typical. The major drawback to unobtrusive observation lies in ethical concerns about protecting the privacy of the participants.

Self-Report Techniques

Direct observational measurement techniques are often costly and difficult to obtain, requiring the assistance of trained observers. More commonly, researchers measure variables through **self-report techniques**, which include a variety of methods for assessing behavior from the responses of the research participants themselves. One of the most popular self-report techniques is the **survey**. Surveys can be used to measure any number of aspects of the work situation, including workers' attitudes about their jobs, their perceptions of the amount and quality of the work that they perform, and the specific problems they encounter on the job. Most typically, surveys take the form of pencil-and-paper or online measures that the participants can complete either in a group session or on their own time. However, surveys can also involve face-to-face, telephone, or video (e.g., Zoom) interviews.

The most obvious problem with surveys is the possibility of distortion or bias of responses (either intentional or unintentional). If the survey is not conducted in a way that protects respondents' anonymity, particularly when it deals with sensitive issues or problems, workers may feel that their answers can be traced back to them and possibly result in retribution by management. In these cases, workers may temper their responses and give "socially desirable" answers to survey questions.

Self-report techniques are also used in I/O psychology research to assess workers' personalities, occupational interests, and management or supervisory style; to obtain evaluations of job candidates; or to elicit supervisors' ratings of worker performance. Compared with observational techniques, self-reports allow the researcher to collect massive amounts of data relatively inexpensively. However, developing sound self-report tools and interpreting the results are not easy tasks and require thorough knowledge of measurement theory, as well as research methods

Obtrusive Observation
research observation in which the presence of the observer is known to the participants

Unobtrusive Observation
research observation in which the presence of the observer is not known to the participants

Self-Report Techniques
measurement methods relying on research participants' reports of their own behavior or attitudes

Survey
a common self-report measure in which participants are asked to report on their attitudes, beliefs, and/or behaviors

and statistics. Many I/O psychologist researchers and practitioners use self-report measures extensively in their work.

Measuring Work Outcomes: The Bottom Line

There are a tremendous number of potential independent variables in I/O psychology research. I/O psychologists have examined how characteristics of workers such as personality, attitudes, and education affect work behavior. As we saw in Chapter 1, factors in the physical and social work environment can be manipulated to see how they affect worker performance and satisfaction and engagement with their work. Other variables, such as the amount and frequency of compensation, styles of supervision, work schedules, and incentive programs, also serve as independent variables in research on work behavior.

Many dependent variables are also studied in I/O research. However, a great deal of research in I/O psychology focuses on dependent variables such as productivity, work quality, employee turnover, employee absenteeism, and employee satisfaction/engagement. These key dependent variables represent work outcomes—what often translates to the "bottom line" in work organizations. Most commonly, changes in these important variables result in financial losses or gains for businesses.

Of these important dependent variables, the first two, work productivity and quality, are usually theoretically linked because a company's goals should be to produce as much as possible while ensuring that the output is of high quality. However, although these variables are linked, they are typically considered separately by many businesses. For example, in many manufacturing plants, the departments responsible for production volume and for quality control are separate.

On the surface, it may seem that the measurement of a variable such as productivity is relatively simple and accurate. This may be true if the task involves production of concrete objects, such as the number of hamburgers sold or the number of books printed. However, for companies that deal with more abstract products, such as services, information, or ideas, the measurement of productivity is not as easy, nor as precise.

The accurate measurement of quality is often more difficult (Hoffman et al., 1991). For example, in a department store, productivity may be assessed by the dollar amount of sales, which is a fairly reasonable and simple assessment. However, the quality of the salespersons' performance might involve factors such as the friendliness, courteousness, and promptness of their service, which are usually more difficult to measure. Similarly, a writer's productivity might be defined as the number of books or articles the author produced (a straightforward assessment), although the quality of the writing might be more difficult to measure. Thus, quality is often quite difficult to define operationally. We will deal with the measurement of worker productivity and worker performance in more detail in upcoming chapters, particularly in Chapter 5.

Although they are distinct variables, employee absenteeism, turnover, and satisfaction/engagement are also theoretically tied to one another (Vroom, 1964). In

Chapter 1, we saw that Mayo believed that there was a strong relationship between employee satisfaction and productivity. However, this is not always the case; the happy worker is not necessarily the productive worker. There may be a relationship between employee satisfaction and a tendency to show up for work and stay with the job. Specifically, it is thought that higher satisfaction leads to lower absenteeism and turnover. Although the reasons for being absent and individual differences can alter the relationship between job satisfaction and absenteeism. For example Schaumberg and Flynn (2017) showed that job satisfaction predicts absenteeism for individuals who are not prone to feeling guilty, but does not for those who are more prone to experience guilt. Individuals who feel guilt may avoid playing "hooky" from work regardless of whether or not they like their jobs. We will discuss this issue in detail in Chapter 8.

In any case, the interrelationships between job satisfaction, absenteeism, and turnover are important. If negative relationships do indeed exist between employee satisfaction and rates of absenteeism and turnover (they are negative relationships, because higher satisfaction would be associated with lower absenteeism and lower turnover), it is important that companies strive to keep workers satisfied. Happy workers may be less likely to be absent from their jobs voluntarily or to look for work elsewhere. Reduced rates of absenteeism and turnover can translate into tremendous savings for the company.

Turnover and absenteeism can be measured fairly easily, but the assessment of worker satisfaction is much less precise, because attitudes about a wide range of elements in the work environment must be considered. Moreover, the worker attitude–behavior relationship needs to be studied in depth. A more complex construct is replacing the simple notion of job satisfaction, and that is the notion of *employee engagement*, which involves not only employees' attitudes about their jobs, but also their broader attitudes about the organization and their commitment to it. We will deal more deeply with these issues in Chapter 8.

Although these key variables are most commonly considered dependent variables, this does not preclude the possibility that any one of them could be used as an independent variable. For example, we might classify workers into those who are "good attenders" with very few absences and "poor attenders" who have regular absences. We could then see whether there are differences in the good and poor attenders' performance levels or in their attitudes about their jobs. However, certain variables, such as productivity, absenteeism, and turnover, represent the bottom-line variables that translate into profits or losses for the company, whereas job satisfaction tends to be the bottom-line variable for the employee. These bottom-line variables are most often considered dependent variables.

Interpreting and Using Research Results

When a researcher conducts a study and obtains research results, it is the researcher's task to make sense of those results. To interpret research data accurately, an I/O psychologist must be very knowledgeable about methods of data collection and statistical analysis and be aware of potential research problems and the strengths and limitations of the methods that have been used. We covered these topics in Chapter 1 in relation to measurement.

When interpreting results, it is important to consider the limitations of the findings. One concern is the extent to which we are successful in eliminating extraneous, or "confounding," variables. This is called **internal validity**. In an experiment, internal validity deals with how confident we are that the change in a dependent variable was actually caused by the independent variable, as opposed to extraneous variables. A second concern is the **external validity** of the research results—that is, whether the results obtained will generalize to other work settings. In other words, how well do the findings apply to other workers, jobs, and/or environments? For example, say that the results of research on patterns of interactions between workers in an insurance claims office indicate a significant positive relationship between the amount of supervisor–supervisee contact and worker productivity: as supervisors and workers interact more, more work is completed. Can these results be generalized to other settings? Maybe, but maybe not. These findings might be particular to these workers and related to their specific characteristics. The participants may be the kind of workers who need a lot of supervision to keep them on task. Other groups of workers might view interactions with supervisors negatively, and the resulting dissatisfaction might lead to a restriction of output. Alternatively, the results might be specific to the type of tasks in which workers are engaged. Because insurance claims often need to be approved by supervisors, a worker must interact with the supervisor to complete the job. As a result, increased supervisor–supervisee contact may be a sign of increased efficiency. For assembly line workers, however, supervisor–supervisee interactions might be a distraction that reduces productivity, or they might have little effect on output. To know whether research results will generalize to a variety of work settings, results must be replicated with different groups of workers in different work settings. Eventually, further research may discover the moderating variables that determine when and where supervisor–subordinate contacts have beneficial effects on work productivity.

External validity is especially important for research conducted under tightly controlled circumstances, such as a laboratory investigation, where the conditions of the research setting may not be very similar to actual work conditions. One solution is to combine the strength of experimental research—well-controlled conditions—with the advantage of real-world conditions by conducting experimental research in actual work settings.

Once these issues have been considered fully, scientists must consider how they report their results for academic publication. Careful reporting of methods and statistics ensures that academic rigor has been taken, allows other scientists to replicate their results, and creates greater transparency in what was done for the research study (Eby et al., 2020). Table 2.2 contains a checklist designed by Eby and colleagues for ensuring the best academic methods are utilized in research.

So far, we have been discussing only one objective of research in I/O psychology: the scientific objective of conducting research to understand work behavior

Internal Validity
the extent to which extraneous or confounding variables are removed

External Validity
whether research results obtained in one setting will apply to another setting

 Stop & Review

List the five common work outcomes that are often measured in I/O psychology.

Table 2.2 This useful checklist helps authors ensure that they are following best practices for research quality and transparency

Checklist Item	Rigor	Replication	Transparency/Openness
Description of Research Sample			
1. Sampling plan and recruitment strategy	X		X
2. Inclusion/exclusion criteria	X	X	X
3. Number of cases excluded/Final sample size for each analysis	X	X	X
4. Basic sociodemographic info on sample		X	X
Description of Measures/Manipulations			
5. Basic information on scales (e.g., # items, anchors, instructional prompts, coding of dichotomous items), and their descriptive statistics (e.g., M, SD, skewness, reliability coefficients)		X	X
6. Scale adaptations (e.g., shortening, changing language)/Translated scales	X	X	X
7. Provide access to all scale items (e.g., in Table, Appendix, cite original source with all items)	X	X	X
8. Manipulation checks reported, along with how failed manipulation checks were handled	X	X	X
Description of Analyses and Interpretation			
9. Correlation matrix including ALL variables (including controls, sociodemographics, multiplicative and transformed variables)	X	X	X
10. Full results from model testing (e.g., if testing moderated mediation, include all steps in analysis, full reporting of regression models, standard errors or 95% CI)	X		X
11. Effect size and variance accounted for estimates included (e.g., R2, odds ratio)	X		X
12. Using relative ("higher/lower") rather than absolute ("high/low") language when depicting and discussing interactions			X

Source: Created by Eby et al., 2020.

more completely. As you recall, in Chapter 1, we mentioned that there are two goals in industrial/organizational psychology: the scientific and the practical, whereby new knowledge is applied toward improving work conditions and outcomes. Although some research in I/O psychology is conducted merely to increase the base of knowledge about work behavior, and some I/O practitioners (and practicing managers) use strategies to affect work behavior that are based on hunches or intuition rather than on sound research evidence, the two facets of I/O psychology should work together. To be effective, the applications used by I/O practitioners to improve work behavior must be built on a strong foundation of research. Through sound research and the testing of hypotheses and theories, better applications develop. Moreover, the effectiveness of applications can be demonstrated conclusively only through additional evaluation and research (see the box "Applying I/O Psychology").

Ethical Issues in Research and Practice in I/O Psychology

It is very important when conducting any type of psychological research involving human beings that the researcher—whether student or professional—adhere to ethical principles and standards. The American Psychological Association (APA) lists several core principles that should guide the ethical conduct of research in psychology, including I/O psychology (American Psychological Association, 2002). These guiding principles include striving to benefit the persons with whom the psychologist is working and taking care to do no harm; being honest and accurate in the science, teaching, and practice of psychology; and respecting the rights of people to privacy and confidentiality.

Although the ethical issues pertaining to I/O psychologists are complex, we will review a few of the key elements for research and practice of I/O psychology.

APPLYING I/O PSYCHOLOGY

The Hawthorne Effect: A Case Study in Flawed Research Methods

The initial Hawthorne studies clearly followed the experimental method, because Mayo and his colleagues manipulated levels of lighting and the duration of work breaks. Furthermore, because the studies were conducted in the actual work setting, they were also field experiments. The result, particularly the discovery of the Hawthorne effect, is a classic in the field of I/O psychology. In fact, this effect is studied in other areas of psychology and social science.

Although the original Hawthorne studies were set up in the experimental method, the discovery of the Hawthorne effect actually resulted from a breakdown in research procedures. The changes observed in the dependent variable (productivity) were caused not by the independent variable (lighting), but by an extraneous variable that was not controlled by the researchers: the attention the workers received from the observers. Although Mayo and his colleagues eventually became aware of this unanticipated variable, which led to the discovery of the Hawthorne effect, the design and implementation of the studies had other methodological problems.

In the 1970s, researchers reexamined the data from the original Hawthorne experiments, combing through the records and diaries kept by Mayo and his colleagues. These investigators found a series of very serious methodological problems that cast doubt on the original conclusions drawn from the Hawthorne studies. These

APPLYING I/O PSYCHOLOGY

(Continued)

reanalyses indicated difficulties with the number of participants (one of the studies used only five participants), the experimenters' "contamination" of the participant population (two of the five participants were replaced because they were not working hard enough), the lack of control or comparison groups, and the absence of appropriate statistical analyses of data (Franke & Kaul, 1978; Parsons, 1974). The I/O psychologist Parsons discovered not only serious flaws in the published reports of the Hawthorne experiments, but also a number of extraneous variables that were not considered, further confounding the conclusions. For example:

> [U]nlike the big open floor of the relay assembly department, the test room was separate, smaller, and quieter . . . and the supervisors were friendly, tolerant observers, not the usual authoritarian foremen . . . Back in their relay-assembly department, the women had been paid a fixed hourly wage plus a collective piecework rate based on the department's total output. In the test room, the collective piecework rate was based on the output of only the five workers, so that individual performance had a much more significant impact on weekly pay. The monetary reward for increased

individual effort thus became much more evident and perhaps more effective than in the department setting.

(Rice, 1982)

All in all, there are significant flaws in the research design and execution of the Hawthorne experiments. Of course, this does not mean that a Hawthorne effect cannot exist, because we do know that the presence of others can affect behavior. What it does mean is that the original Hawthorne studies were too methodologically muddled to enable researchers to draw any firm conclusions from them. On the one hand, we must forgive Mayo and his associates on some of these issues because their studies were conducted before many of the advancements in research methodology and design were made. On the other hand, some of the errors in data collection were obvious. In many ways, the Hawthorne studies illustrate some of the difficulties of conducting research and the dangers of drawing conclusions based on flawed research methods. The moral is that conducting research is a complex but important endeavor. Researchers and users of research must display caution in both the application of methods and the interpretation of results to avoid errors and misinformation.

Informed Consent
a research participant is fully informed of the nature of the experiment and has the right to not participate

The researcher must obtain participants' **informed consent**—a sort of "full disclosure." That is, participants must be told in advance the purposes, duration, and general procedures involved in the research, and they have the right to decline participation at any point. At the end of the research, participants should be fully debriefed, and the researcher should ensure that no harm has been caused. Researchers must also protect the privacy of research participants by either collecting data anonymously or keeping the data confidential—with identities known only to the researchers for purposes of accurate recordkeeping.

The same general principles apply to the practice of I/O psychology. In addition, practicing I/O psychologists should not misrepresent their areas of expertise and should be honest, forthright, and fair in their dealings with clients and client organizations. An excellent case reader deals specifically with ethical issues for the practicing I/O psychologist, entitled *Ethics and Values in Industrial-Organizational Psychology* (Lefkowitz, 2017). Another resource is the book *Decoding the Ethic Code: A Practical Guide for Psychologists* (Fisher, 2016).

Summary

The goals of I/O psychology are to describe, explain, predict, and then alter work behavior. Research methods are important tools for I/O psychologists because they provide a systematic means for investigating and changing work behavior. *Objectivity* is the overriding theme of the social scientific method used to study work behavior.

The first step in conducting research involves the formulation of the problem or issue. The second step is the generation of *hypotheses*, which are simply statements about the supposed relationships among variables. It is through the systematic collection of observations of behavior that a researcher may develop a set of hypotheses into a more general *theory*, or *model*, which is a way of representing the complex relationships among a number of variables related to actual work behavior. The third step in conducting research is choosing a particular design to guide the actual collection of data—the fourth step. The data collection stage includes sampling, the methods by which participants are selected for study. The final steps in the process are the analyses of research data and the interpretation of research results.

I/O psychologists use two basic types of research designs. In the *experimental method*, the researcher manipulates one variable, labelled the *independent variable*, and measures its effect on the *dependent variable*. In an experimental design, any change in the dependent variable is presumed to be caused by the manipulation of the independent variable. Typically, the experimental method involves the use of a *treatment group* and a *control group*. The treatment group is subjected to the manipulation of the independent variable, and the control group serves as a comparison by not receiving the treatment. Variables that are not of principal concern to the researchers but that may affect the results of the research are termed *extraneous variables*. In the experimental method, the researcher attempts to control for extraneous variables through the *random assignment* of participants to the treatment and control groups in order to ensure that any extraneous variables will be distributed evenly between the groups. The strength of the experimental method is the high level of control that the researcher has over the setting, which allows the investigator to determine cause-and-effect relationships. The weakness of the method is that the controlled conditions may be artificial and may not generalize to actual, uncontrolled work settings. *Quasi-experiments* follow the experimental method, but do not involve random assignment or manipulation of the independent variable. The other type of research method, the *correlational method* (sometimes called the observational method), looks at the relationships among measured variables as they naturally occur, without the intervention of the experimenter and without strict experimental controls. The strength of this design is that it may be more easily conducted in actual settings. However, the correlational method does not allow the specification of cause-and-effect relationships.

Meta-analysis is a method that allows the results of a number of studies to be combined and analysed together to draw an overall summary or conclusion. Meta-analysis may also be used to determine if the results of different studies of the same factors are significantly different from each other.

The *case study* is a commonly used descriptive investigation that lacks the controls and repeated observations of the experimental and correlational methodologies. The case study can provide important information, but does not allow the testing of hypotheses.

An important part of the research process involves the measurement of variables. The term *operationalization* refers to the process of defining variables so that they can be measured for research purposes. I/O psychology researchers use a variety of measurement techniques. Researchers may measure variables through the direct obtrusive or unobtrusive observation of behavior. In *obtrusive observation*, the researcher is visible to the research participants, who know that they are being studied. *Unobtrusive observation* involves observing participants' behavior without their knowledge. Another measurement strategy is *self-report techniques*, which yield information about participants' behavior from their own reports. One of the most widely used self-report techniques is the *survey*.

When interpreting research results, attention must be given to *internal validity*—whether extraneous variables have been accounted for in the research—as well as the *external validity* of the findings—that is, whether they will generalize to other settings. A critical concern for I/O psychologists is the interrelation of the science and practice of industrial/organizational psychology and adhering to ethical principles and guidelines that govern research and practice in I/O psychology.

Study Questions and Exercises

1 Consider the steps in the research process. What are some of the major problems that are likely to be encountered at each step in the research process?

2 What are the strengths and weaknesses of the experimental and the correlational methods? Under what circumstances would you use each?

3 Consider the various measurement techniques used by I/O psychologists. Why are many of the variables used in I/O psychology difficult to measure?

4 Choose some aspect of work behavior and develop a research hypothesis. Now try to design a study that would test the hypothesis. Consider what your variables are and how you will operationalize them. Choose a research design for the collection of data. Consider who your participants will be and how they will be selected. How might the hypothesis be tested statistically?

5 Using the study that you designed earlier, what are some of the ethical considerations in conducting the research? What information would you include in an informed consent form for that study's participants?

Web Links

www.simplypsychology.org/research-methods.html
A general psychology website that discusses research methods and has a number of methods-related definitions and explanations.

www.apa.org/ethics/code/index.aspx
APA site for ethics in conducting research.

Suggested Readings

Aron, A., Aron, E. N., Coups, E. (2013). *Statistics for psychology* (6th ed.). Boston: Pearson. *This straightforward text examines basic methods students in the social and behavioral sciences need to analyze data and test hypotheses.*

Brough, P. (Ed.). (2018). *Advanced research methods for applied psychology: Design, analysis and reporting.* Routledge.

Statistical Analyses of Research Data

Although a comprehensive treatment of research methods and statistics is beyond the scope of this text, it is important to emphasize that the science and practice of industrial/organizational psychology require a thorough knowledge of research methods and statistics and some experience using them. More important for our present concerns, it is impossible to gain a true understanding of the methods used by I/O psychologists without some discussion of the statistical analyses of research data.

As mentioned earlier in this chapter, research methods are merely procedures or tools used by I/O psychologists to study work behavior. Statistics, which are arithmetical procedures designed to help summarize and interpret data, are also important research tools. The results of statistical analyses help us to understand relationships between variables. In any research investigation, there are two main questions: (1) is there a statistically significant relationship between the variables of interest, and (2) what is the strength of that relationship? For example, does the independent variable have a strong, moderate, or weak effect on the dependent variable (e.g., What is the effect size?)? Statistics provide the answers to these questions.

There are many types of statistical analyses, and which is most appropriate in a given study depends on such factors as the variables of interest, the way these variables are measured, the design of the study, and the research questions. Concerning the measurement of variables, it is important to point out that variables can be described as being either *quantitative* or *qualitative* in nature. The term **quantitative data** (also known as *measurement* data) refers to a numerical representation of a variable, such as an individual's weight provided by a scale, a score on a cognitive ability test, a student's grade point average, and so on. In all cases, some sort of measurement instrument has been used to measure some quantity. The term **qualitative data** (also referred to as *categorical* or *frequency* data) refers to numbers that are used as labels to categorize people or things; the data provide frequencies for each category. When data collection involves methods such as discussion or focus groups, for example, the

Quantitative (Measurement) Data
data that measure some numerical quantity

Qualitative (Categorical or Frequency) Data
data that measure some category or measurement quality

data are likely to be qualitative and expressed in such statements as, "Twelve people were categorized as 'highly favorable' to changes in work schedules, 20 as 'moderately favorable,' and 9 as 'not favorable.'" Here, we are categorizing participants into groups, and the data represent the frequency of each category. In contrast, if, instead of categorizing participants into high, moderate, and low favorability, we assigned each of them a score based on some continuous scale of favorability (scale from 1 to 10), the data would be measurement data, consisting of scores for each participant on that variable. Independent variables are often qualitative, involving categories, although they may also involve quantitative measurement, whereas dependent variables are generally quantitative. Different types of statistical techniques are used to analyze quantitative and qualitative data. Because they tend to be more frequently used in I/O psychology, our discussion will focus on procedures used to analyze quantitative, or measurement, data.

We will discuss two types of statistics: (1) *descriptive statistics*, used to summarize recorded observations of behavior, and (2) *inferential statistics*, used to test hypotheses about research data.

Descriptive Statistics

The simplest way to represent research data is to use **descriptive statistics**, which describe data in ways that give the researcher a general idea of the results. Suppose we have collected data on the job performance ratings of 60 employees. The rating scale ranges from 1 to 9, with 9 representing outstanding performance. As you can see in Table 2.3, it is difficult to make sense out of the raw data. A **frequency distribution**, which is a descriptive statistical technique that presents data in a useful format, arranges the performance scores by category so that we can see at a glance how many employees received each numerical rating. The frequency distribution in Figure 2.5 is in the form of a bar graph or histogram.

Descriptive Statistics
arithmetical formulas for summarizing and describing research data

Frequency Distribution
a descriptive statistical technique that arranges scores by categories

Table 2.3 Performance Rating Scores of 60 Employees

Employee	Score	Employee	Score	Employee	Score
Adams	5	Alva	6	Ang	6
Bates	4	Bender	1	Berra	7
Brown	6	Cadiz	5	Camus	8
Chow	7	Cisneros	4	Crow	5
Davis	8	Dawes	7	DeRios	4
Driver	4	Dudley	6	Evans	S
Ewing	5	Exner	4	Fang	2
Farris	3	Fernal	5	Ford	9

(continued)

Table 2.3 (Continued)

Employee	Score	Employee	Score	Employee	Score
Frank	5	Gant	3	Ghent	5
Gower	3	Grant	6	Gwynne	2
Hall	6	Hawkes	7	Horner	4
Hull	4	Hu	8	Jacobs	S
Justin	3	Kee	5	Kubiak	9
Lang	5	Lantz	7	Leong	5
Mayes	5	Mertz	3	Mio	4
Murphy	4	Nguyen	5	Page	5
Pierce	2	Rabago	S	Richards	3
Sherrod	7	Simpson	8	Suls	S
Taylor	3	Tucker	2	Tran	4
Woll	5	Young	6	Zapf	5

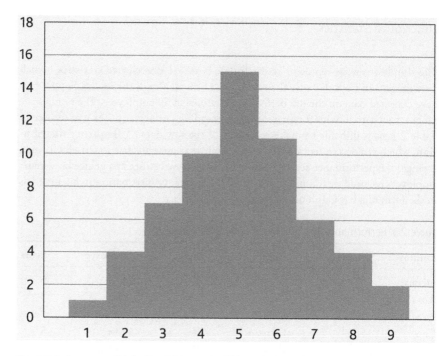

Figure 2.5 Frequency distribution (histogram) of 60 employee performance ratings scores.

Measures of Central Tendency
present the center point in a distribution of scores

Other important descriptive statistics include **measures of central tendency** and **variability**. Measures of central tendency present the center point of a distribution of scores. This is useful in summarizing the distribution in terms of the middle or average score. The most common measure of central tendency is the **mean**, or average, which is calculated by adding all the scores and dividing by the number of scores. In our performance data, the sum of the scores is 303, and the number of scores is 60. As a result, the mean of our frequency distribution is 5.05. Another measure of central tendency is the **median**, or the midpoint of the distribution, such that 50% of the scores (in this example, 50% would be 30 of the 60 scores) fall below the median and 50% fall above the median. In this distribution of scores, the median is in the center rating category of 5.

Measures of **variability** show how scores are dispersed in a frequency distribution. If scores are widely dispersed across a large number of categories, variability will be high. If scores are closely clustered in a few categories, variability will be low. The most commonly used measure of distribution variability is the **standard deviation**. In a frequency distribution, the standard deviation indicates how closely the scores spread out around the mean. The more widely dispersed the scores, the greater the standard deviation. The more closely bunched the scores, the smaller the standard deviation. For example, imagine that two managers each rate 15 subordinates on a 5-point performance scale, and the mean (average) ratings given by each manager are the same: 2.8 on the 5-point scale. However, manager A's ratings have a large standard deviation, whereas manager B's ratings have a very small standard deviation. What does this tell you? It means that manager A gave more varied ratings of subordinate performance than did manager B, because the standard deviation represents the variance of the distribution of scores. In contrast, manager B gave similar ratings for all 15 subordinates, such that all the ratings are close in numerical value to the average and do not vary across a wide numerical range. Both the mean and the standard deviation are important to more sophisticated inferential statistics.

Mean
a measure of central tendency; also known as the average

Median
a measure of central tendency; the midpoint of a distribution of scores

Variability
estimates the distribution of scores around the middle or average score

Standard Deviation
a measure of variability of scores in a frequency distribution

Inferential Statistics

Although descriptive statistics are helpful in representing and organizing data, **inferential statistics** are used to test hypotheses. For example, assume that we wanted to test the hypothesis that a certain safety program effectively reduced rates of industrial accidents. One group of workers is subjected to the safety program, whereas another (the control group) is not. Accident rates before and after the program are then measured. Inferential statistics would tell us whether or not differences in accident rates between the two groups were meaningful. Depending on the research design, different sorts of inferential statistics will typically be used.

When inferential statistics are used to analyze data, we are concerned about whether a result is meaningful, or statistically significant. The concept of **statistical significance** is based on theories of probability. A research result is statistically significant if its probability of occurrence by chance is very low. Typically, a research result is statistically significant if its probability of occurrence by chance is less than 5 out of 100 (in research terminology, the probability, or p, is less than 0.05; $p < 0.05$). For example, say we find that a group of telephone salespersons who have

Inferential Statistics
statistical techniques used for analyzing data to test hypotheses

Statistical Significance
the probability of a particular result occurring by chance, used to determine the meaning of research outcomes

undergone training in sales techniques have average (mean) sales of 250 units per month, whereas salespersons who did not receive the training have mean sales of 242 units. Based on the difference in the two means and the variability (standard deviations) of the two groups, a statistical test will determine whether the difference in the two groups is statistically significant (and thus if the training program actually increases sales).

The concept of the **normal distribution** of variables is also important for the use of inferential statistics. It is assumed that many psychological variables, especially human characteristics such as intelligence, motivation, or personality constructs, are normally distributed. That is, scores on these variables in the general population are presumed to vary along a continuum, with the greatest proportion clustering around the midpoint and proportions dropping off toward the endpoints of the continuum. A normal distribution of scores is symbolized visually by the bell-shaped curve. The bell-shaped curve, or normal distribution, is a representative distribution of known mathematical properties that can be used as a standard for statistical analyses. The mathematical properties of the normal distribution are represented in Figure 2.6. The exact midpoint score, or median, of the normal distribution is the same as its mean. In a normal distribution, 50% of the scores lie above the midpoint and 50% below. The normal distribution is also divided in terms of standard deviations from the midpoint. In a normal distribution, approximately 68% of all scores lie within one standard deviation above or below the midpoint or mean. Approximately 95% of all scores in a normal distribution lie within two standard deviations above or below the midpoint. Now that you know the properties of the bell-shaped, or normal, curve, go back to the frequency distribution in Figure 2.5. You should notice that this distribution closely approximates the bell-shaped, normal distribution.

Normal Distribution
(bell-shaped curve) a distribution of scores along a continuum with known properties

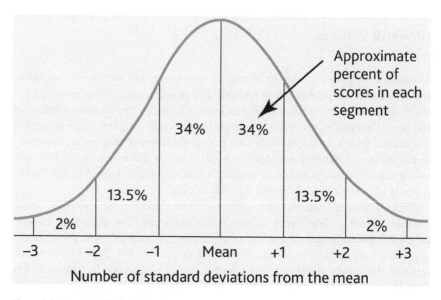

Figure 2.6 A normal distribution.

Statistical Analysis of Experimental Method Data

As mentioned, depending on the research design, different inferential statistics may be used to analyze data. Typically, one set of statistical techniques is used to test hypotheses from data collected in experimental methods, and another set is used to analyze data from correlational research.

The simplest type of experimental design would have a treatment group, a control group, and a single dependent variable. Whether or not a group receives the treatment represents levels of the independent variable. The most common statistical technique for this type of study is the *t*-test, which examines the difference between the means on the dependent variable for the two groups, taking into account the variability of scores in each group. In the example of trained and untrained salespersons used earlier, a *t*-test would determine whether the difference in the two means (250 units vs. 242 units) is statistically significant—that is, not due to chance fluctuations. If the difference is significant, the researcher may conclude that the training program did have a positive effect on sales.

When an experimental design moves beyond two group comparisons, a statistical method called *analysis of variance*, or ANOVA, is often used. Analysis of variance looks at differences among more than two groups on a single dependent variable. For example, if we wanted to examine differences in sales performance between a group of salespersons exposed to 2 weeks of "sales influence tactic training," a group exposed to only 3 days of the training program, and a group with no training, analysis of variance would be the appropriate technique. In this instance, we still have one dependent variable and one independent variable, as in the two-group case; however, the independent variable has three, rather than two, levels. Whenever a research design involves a single independent variable with more than two levels and one dependent variable, the typical statistical technique is referred to as a one-way analysis of variance (it is called "one-way" because there is a single independent variable). The one-way ANOVA would tell us whether our three groups differed in any meaningful way in sales performance.

When a research design involves more than one independent variable, which is very common, the technique that is typically used is the factorial analysis of variance. For example, we may wish to examine the effect of the three levels of our influence training program on sales performance for a group of salespersons who receive a sales commission compared with a group who do not. This design involves a single dependent variable (sales performance) and two independent variables, one with three levels (training) and one with two levels (commission vs. no commission). The number of different groups in a research study is determined by the number of independent variables and their levels. In this case, our design would result in six groups of salespersons ($2 \times 3 = 6$), and the analysis would involve a 2×3 factorial analysis of variance.

There is a major advantage to examining more than one independent variable in a research study, and it involves the types of effects that may be detected. Suppose that, in our study, we find that sales influence tactic training significantly increases

t-Test
a statistical test for examining the difference between the means of two groups

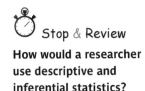

Stop & Review

How would a researcher use descriptive and inferential statistics?

sales performance. This change in the dependent variable due to the independent variable of training is called a *main effect*. Similarly, we may find a main effect of the sales commission variable, such that salespersons who receive a commission have significantly higher sales performance than those who do not. This type of effect could not be detected if we were examining either independent variable alone. However, by examining both independent variables at the same time, we may detect a different type of effect called an *interaction*. Two variables are said to interact when the effect of one independent variable on the dependent variable differs, depending on the level of the second independent variable. In our study, an interaction between sales influence tactic training and sales commission would be indicated if our training program only increased the sales performance of salespersons who received a commission and did not affect the performance of salespersons who did not receive commissions.

An even more sophisticated technique, *multivariate analysis of variance* (MANOVA), examines data from multiple groups with multiple dependent variables. The logic of MANOVA is similar to that of ANOVA, but more than one dependent variable is investigated at a time. For instance, we may want to investigate the effects of training or receiving a sales commission (or both) on sales performance and worker job satisfaction. MANOVA procedures would tell us about differences between our groups on each of these dependent variables. Understanding how these complex statistical techniques work and how they are calculated is not important for our discussion. These terms are presented only to familiarize you with some of the statistics that you might encounter in research reports in I/O psychology or in other types of social science research and to increase your understanding of the purposes of such procedures.

Statistical Analysis of Correlational Method Data

Correlation Coefficient
a statistical technique used to determine the strength of a relationship between two variables

When a research design is correlational, a different set of statistical techniques is usually used to test hypotheses about presumed relationships among variables. As mentioned earlier, the distinction between independent and dependent variables in a correlational design is not as important as in the experimental method. In a correlational design, the independent variable is usually called the predictor, and the dependent variable is often referred to as the criterion (we will discuss predictors and criterion variables more fully in Chapter 4). In a simple correlational design with two variables, the usual statistical analysis technique is the **correlation coefficient**, which measures the strength of the relationship between the predictor and the criterion. The correlation coefficient ranges from +1.00 to –1.00. The closer the coefficient is to either +1.00 or –1.00, the stronger the linear relationship between the two variables. The closer the correlation coefficient is to 0, the weaker the linear relationship. A positive correlation coefficient means that there is a positive linear relationship between the two variables, where an increase in one variable is associated with an increase in the other variable.

Assume that a researcher studying the relationship between the commuting distance of workers and work tardiness obtains a positive correlation coefficient of 0.75. This correlation indicates that the greater the commuting distance of employees, the greater the likelihood that they will be late for work. A negative correlation coefficient indicates a negative relationship: an increase in one variable is associated with a decrease in the other. For example, a researcher studying workers who cut

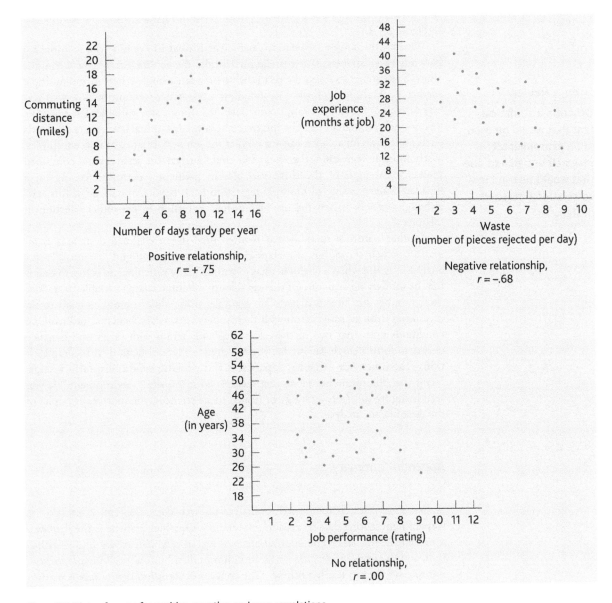

Figure 2.7 Plots of scores for positive, negative, and zero correlations.

out patterns in a clothing factory hypothesizes that there is a relationship between workers' job experience and the amount of waste produced. Statistical analysis indicates a negative correlation coefficient of –0.68: the more experience workers have, the less waste they produce. A correlation coefficient of 0 indicates that there is no relationship between the two variables. For example, a researcher measuring the relationship between the age of factory workers and their job performance finds a correlation coefficient of approximately 0.00, which shows that there is no relationship between age and performance. (These relationships are presented graphically in Figure 2.7.)

Whereas the simple correlation coefficient is used to examine the relationship between two variables in a correlational study, the *multiple regression* technique allows a researcher to assess the relationship between a single criterion and multiple predictors. Multiple regression would allow a researcher to examine how well several variables, in combination, predict levels of an outcome variable. For example, a personnel researcher might be interested in how educational level, years of experience, and scores on an aptitude test predict the job performance of new employees. With multiple regression, the researcher could analyze the separate and combined predictive strength of the three variables in predicting performance. Again, a detailed understanding of multiple regression is far beyond the scope of this text, although we will discuss the use of multiple regression in personnel selection in Chapter 4.

Another statistical method that is often used in correlational designs is *factor analysis*, which shows how variables cluster to form meaningful "factors." Factor analysis is useful when a researcher has measured many variables and wants to examine the underlying structure of the variables or combine related variables to reduce their number for later analysis. For example, using this technique, a researcher measuring workers' satisfaction with their supervisors, salary, benefits, and working conditions finds that two of these variables, satisfaction with salary and benefits, cluster to form a single factor that the researcher calls "satisfaction with compensation." The other two variables, supervisors and working conditions, form a single factor that the researcher labels "satisfaction with the work environment." If you read literature in I/O psychology or related social sciences, you may see examples of the use of factor analysis.

Stop & Review

Describe a statistical test that would be used in an experimental research design and one that would be used in a correlational research design.

Appendix Summary

Statistics are research tools used to analyze research data. *Descriptive statistics* are ways of representing data to assist interpretation. One such statistic is the *frequency distribution*. The *mean* and *median* are *measures of central tendency* in a distribution, and the *standard deviation* is an indicator of distribution variability. *Inferential statistics* are used to test hypotheses. The concept of *statistical significance* is used to determine whether a statistical test of a hypothesis produced a meaningful result. The concept of the *normal distribution* provides a standard for statistical analyses.

Different inferential statistics are typically used to analyze data from different research designs. For example, a *t-test* is used to examine the difference between two groups on some dependent variable. *Analysis of variance* (ANOVA) is used for statistical analyses when there are more than two groups, and a *multivariate analysis of variance* (MANOVA) is used when there is more than one dependent variable. Statistical analyses of correlational method data rely on the *correlation coefficient*, a statistic that measures the strength and direction of a relationship between two variables. *Multiple regression* involves correlational research with more than two variables. *Factor analysis* allows for statistical clustering of variables to form meaningful factors or groupings of variables.

Human Resources Issues

CHAPTER 3

Pre-Employment Planning

Inside Tips
UNDERSTANDING HOW ORGANIZATIONS PLAN FOR AND RECRUIT
FOR HIRING TALENT

In this chapter we will begin to understand the foundation of personnel/human resources processes, beginning with job analyses. Conducting a job analysis is an example of the implementation of the research methods and measurement issues that were covered in the first two chapters. Understand that personnel processes—those related to the creation, development, and maintenance of an organization's human resources—lie on a foundation of understanding what the jobs employees do every day are all about. Here is your first opportunity to begin to apply your knowledge of the research methods that are so important to I/O psychology.

Imagine that you have finished school and chosen an exciting, rewarding career. Armed with your new knowledge, and a highly polished resume, you start searching for the right position in the right organization. From the applicant's perspective, a job search can be an exhausting, stressful, but exciting task. Just as you are looking for potential employers, organizations are out looking for talented new employees through campus recruiters and online job postings. Organizations spend a tremendous amount of time, money, and energy trying to recruit and select a qualified, capable, and productive workforce. Although there are always significant numbers of unemployed workers in the population, the market for truly skilled workers is tight. Organizations continue to compete with one another for the most skilled and productive employees. More and more, companies are realizing the importance of developing comprehensive programs for employee recruitment, screening, testing, and selection. They are also becoming more forward thinking—planning ahead several years to try to predict their future human resources needs. Moreover, they are beginning to understand that the costs of hiring the wrong types of workers greatly

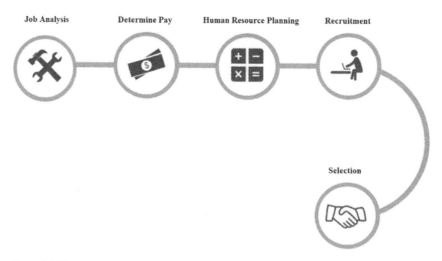

Figure 3.1 There are many stages in the employment cycle that occur before anyone ever applies to a job. It starts with a job analysis, followed by the determination of a pay range for the job. Then, human resource planning might occur to determine how many employees are needed before the recruitment process. In the next chapter we will cover the selection process itself.

outweigh the investment of developing good recruitment and screening programs. Depending on the job level, the costs of recruiting, selecting, training, and then releasing a single employee can range from a few thousand dollars to several hundreds of thousands of dollars, depending on the level of the position—it has been estimated that the hiring costs are approximately three times the person's annual salary (Cascio, 2003).

This chapter will take you through the pre-employment process. First, organizations must conduct a job analysis to determine the tasks and skills required for each job. Second, they must determine the pay for each job. Third, they must engage in human resource planning to determine the number of employees they need. Fourth, they engage in recruitment efforts to attract talent. All of these steps occur before an applicant ever enters the door. We will dive into selection methods in the next chapter (see Figure 3.1).

UP CLOSE **What Do You Want to Do for a Living?—Using O*NET for Your Career Search**

"My Next Move" (www.mynextmove.org/) is a useful online tool for your career search. It is managed by the National Center for O*NET Development, and it lists over 900 different careers from the O*NET database.

UP CLOSE *(continued)*

There are three ways to use this website, depending upon your answer to the question: *What do you want to do for a living?* Think about it for a moment.

1. "I want to be a . . ."

   If you have a clear idea about what you want to do for a living, you can search careers using key words. In this case, the website asks you to describe your dream career in a few words. For instance, you can type "doctor." Then, it directs you to a list of career options (e.g., physician assistants, optometrists, surgeons). Once you click a career option, it directs you to the page that summarizes the required knowledge, skills, abilities, tasks, and responsibilities in your chosen job. It also displays the appropriate educational training and personality for the job, together with a job outlook on the average salary and likelihood of new job opportunities.

2. "I'll know it when I see it."

   If you think you will know when you actually see some career options, you can browse careers by industry. Over 900 career options are organized by different industries (e.g., arts and entertainment, construction, education, government, and health and counseling). You can look for a list of career options based on your choice of industries.

3. "I'm not really sure."

   If you are not quite sure about your career, you can tell the website what you like to do by answering questions regarding the type of work you might enjoy. Based on your answers, it will suggest potential career options that meet your interests and training. The questions constitute a self-assessment tool for career exploration called the O*NET Interest Profiler (www.onetcenter.org/IP.html). The O*NET Interest Profiler gives you scores for six broad occupational interest areas: realistic, investigative, artistic, social, enterprising, and conventional. Once you have scores for each area, follow the instructions on the O*NET Interest Profiler page to discover your career options.

In addition to scores for interest areas, you will be asked to specify one among five job zones. Each of the five job zones corresponds to a level of preparation (from "little or no preparation" to "extensive preparation") required for the job in terms of experience, education, and training. You can also specify your job zone based on your plans for preparation. The website will then present careers that fit your interests and preparation level.

It is worth noting that a recent meta-analysis of 926,462 people revealed some racial/ethnic differences in interests (Jones et al., 2020). According to the study, for example, Black Americans have stronger social, enterprising, and conventional interests than White Americans, and White Americans have stronger realistic and investigative interests compared with Black Americans. The findings have implications for recruiting diverse applicants and for creating greater equality in access to careers.

Job Analysis

Imagine that you are scanning online for available job openings in your chosen field. You see a variety of openings with finely crafted job descriptions, requiring specific skills and offering competitive salaries. Have you ever stopped to wonder how companies come up with those job descriptions or salary ranges? The answer is **job analysis**, or the systematic study of the tasks, duties, and responsibilities of a job and the knowledge, skills, and abilities needed to perform it. Job analysis is the starting point for nearly all personnel functions, from selection, to pay, to training, to performance appraisal (Wheaton & Whetzel, 1997).

Because most jobs consist of a variety of tasks and duties, gaining a full understanding of a job is not always easy. Most jobs are quite complex and require workers to possess certain types of knowledge and skills to perform a variety of different tasks. Workers might need to operate complex machinery or software to perform their jobs, or they might need to possess a great deal of information about a particular product or service, particularly in this ultra-competitive global marketplace. Jobs might also require workers to interact effectively with different types of people, or a single job might require a worker to possess all these important skills and knowledge. As jobs become more and more complex, the need for effective and comprehensive job analyses becomes increasingly important.

To perform a good job analysis, the job analyst must be well trained in the basic research methods we discussed in Chapter 2 and the knowledge of measurement we addressed in Chapter 1. Job analysis typically involves the objective measurement of work behavior performed by actual workers. Therefore, a job analyst must be an expert in objective measurement techniques to perform an accurate job analysis. In fact, a review of research on job analysis suggests that experience and training in job analysis methods are critical for effective job analysis (Voskuijl & van Sliedregt, 2002).

A job analysis leads directly to the development of several other important personnel "products": a job description, a job specification, a job evaluation, and performance criteria. Using the methods described in the next sections, the job analyst will determine the key behaviors done in the job. These behaviors will be used to create a **job description**: a detailed accounting of the tasks, procedures, and responsibilities required of the worker; the machines, tools, and equipment used to perform the job; and the job output (end product or service).

From the job description, a job analyst will determine information about the human characteristics required to perform the job, such as physical and personal traits, work experience, and education needed to do the job, which become a **job specification.** The job specification includes the knowledge, skills, abilities, and other characteristics (KSAOs) needed to do the job. Usually, job specifications give the minimum acceptable qualifications that an employee needs to perform a given

Job Analysis
the systematic study of the tasks, duties, and responsibilities of a job and the qualities needed to perform it

Job Description
a detailed description of job tasks, procedures, and responsibilities; the tools and equipment used; and the end product or service

Job Specification
a statement of the human characteristics required to perform a job

Table 3.1 Examples of a Job Description and a Job Specification

Partial Job Description for Human Resources Assistant

Job summary: Supports human resources processes by administering employment tests, scheduling appointments, conducting employee orientation, maintaining personnel records and information

Job tasks and results: Schedules and coordinates appointments for testing; administers and scores employment tests; conducts new employee orientation programs; maintains personnel databases, involving assembling, preparing, and analyzing employment data; must maintain technical knowledge by attending educational workshops and reviewing publications; must maintain strict confidentiality of HR information

Partial Job Specification for Human Resources Assistant

Minimum of 2 years' experience in human resources operations. Bachelor's degree in business, psychology, social sciences, or related area; master's degree in HR-related discipline desired; proficiency in database management programs and statistical analysis software; good interpersonal skills, with training and presentation experience

Source: Adapted from Plachy, 1998.

job. A sample job description and job specification are presented in Table 3.1. A third personnel "product," **job evaluation**, is the assessment of the relative value or worth of a job to an organization to determine appropriate compensation, or wages. We will come back to the concept of the job evaluation in the determining pay section that follows job analysis.

Job Evaluation
an assessment of the relative value of a job to determine appropriate compensation

Sources of Information for Job Analysis

A variety of methods and procedures are available for conducting a job analysis, including observational techniques, examination of existing data on jobs, interview techniques, and surveys. Each method will yield a different type of information, and each has its own strengths and weaknesses. In certain methods, such as interviewing, the data may be obtained from a variety of sources, such as the job incumbent (the person currently holding the job), supervisory personnel, or outside experts. Moreover, different job analysis methods are often used in combination to produce a detailed and accurate description of a certain job (Brannick et al., 2007).

Figure 3.2 This job analyst uses observational methods to analyze this machinist's job.

Observations

Observational methods of job analysis are those in which trained job analysts gather information about a particular job. To do this, the analyst usually observes the job incumbent at work for a period of time (Figure 3.2). Job analysts may also make use of videos to record work behavior for more detailed analysis. Typically, in observational analysis, the observer takes detailed notes on the exact tasks and duties performed. However, to make accurate observations, the job analyst must know what to look for. For example, a subtle or quick movement, but one that is important to the job, might go unnoticed. Also, if the job is highly technical or complex, the analyst may not be able to observe some of its critical aspects, such as thinking or decision-making processes. Observational techniques usually work best with jobs involving manual operations, repetitive tasks, or other easily seen activities. For example, describing the tasks and duties of a sewing machine operator is much simpler than describing the job of a computer technician, because much of the computer technician's job involves cognitive processes employed in troubleshooting computer problems.

With observational techniques, it is important that the times selected for observation are representative of the worker's routine, especially if the job requires that the worker be engaged in different tasks during different times of the day, week, or year. For example, an accounting clerk may deal with payroll vouchers on

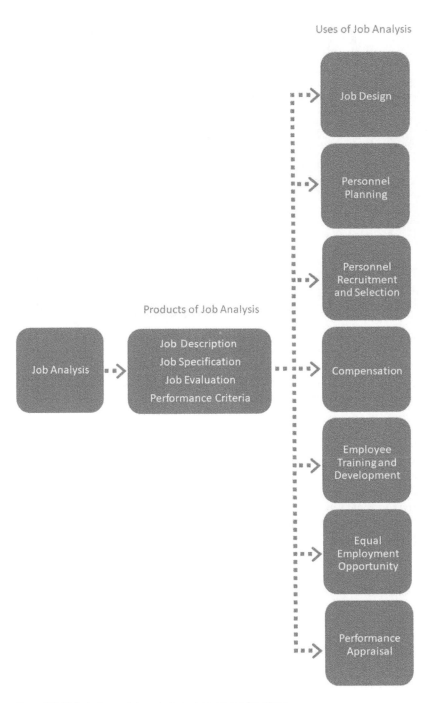

Figure 3.3 Links between job analysis and personnel functions.

Source: Based on Ghorpade, 1988.

Figure 3.4 Job analysis can even be used for complex jobs such as this thermochemical process/
control engineer at NREL's Thermochemical User Facility Pilot Plant in the Field Test
Laboratory Building.

Source: Photograph by Science in HD on Unsplash (https://peacockengineering.com/increasing-
your-first-time-fix-rate/science-in-hd-i4abhj811n0-unsplash/).

Stop & Review

**List and define three
products of a job
analysis.**

Thursdays, may spend most of Fridays updating sales figures, and may be almost
completely occupied with preparing a company's tax records during the month of
January.

One concern regarding observational methods is whether the presence of the
observer in some way influences workers' performance. There is always the chance
that workers will perform their jobs differently simply because they know that they
are being watched (recall the Hawthorne effect discussed in Chapter 1).

Participation

In some instances, a job analyst may want to actually perform a particular job or job
operation to get a firsthand understanding of how the job is performed. For example,
several years ago, one of us was involved in conducting a job analysis of workers
performing delicate microassembly operations. These microassemblers were working
on fitting together extremely tiny electrical components. The only way to gain a true

understanding of (and appreciation for) the fine hand–eye coordination required to perform the job was to actually attempt the assembly task.

Existing Data

Most large, established organizations usually have some information or records that can be used in the job analysis, such as a previous job analysis for the position or an analysis of a related job. Such data might also be borrowed from another organization that has conducted analyses of similar jobs. Human resources professionals often exchange such information with professionals at other organizations. In addition, government sources, such as the U.S. Department of Labor, might provide data that can assist in a specific job analysis (Dierdorff, 2012). Existing data should always be checked to make sure they conform to the job as it is currently being performed and to determine if the existing data account for the inclusion of new technology in the job.

APPLYING I/O PSYCHOLOGY

A Detailed Job Analysis of Real Estate Agents

In one project, the State of California hired an industrial/organizational psychologist to undertake a detailed job analysis of real estate salespersons and brokers (Buckly, 1993). The state wanted to understand the real estate professionals' job better in order to improve the existing state licensing exam for real estate agents/brokers.

The I/O psychologist began by surveying nearly 1,000 real estate salespersons and brokers, asking them about the activities they engaged in and the knowledge they needed to perform their jobs. The results of this job analysis indicated that real estate salespersons typically engaged in the following activities:

1. *Locating and listing property*—Includes inspecting the property, performing a market analysis, and suggesting a price range for the property.
2. *Marketing property*—Includes promoting the property through advertising, finding prospective buyers, and showing and describing features of the property to prospective buyers.
3. *Negotiating sales contracts*—Includes preparing and presenting offers and counteroffers and negotiating deals.
4. *Assisting with transfer of property*—Includes arranging for escrow; assisting the buyer to find financing; coordinating with inspectors, appraisers, and the escrow and title companies; and reviewing closing documents with clients.

APPLYING I/O PSYCHOLOGY

(Continued)

5. *Maintaining professional image*—Includes staying informed about changes in real estate laws, market trends, and the community.

In addition to these activities, real estate salespersons had to demonstrate knowledge of:

- Types of properties and ownerships (e.g., leases, common interest properties)
- Land use controls and regulations (zoning, property taxes, building codes, etc.)

- Market value and market analysis
- Property financing and financing regulations
- Contracts
- Transfer of property rules and laws.

The result of this project was that the I/O psychologist recommended that the state change the licensing examination test items in order to better reflect the job as described by real estate salesperson job incumbents.

Interviews for Job Analysis

Interviews are another method of job analysis. They can be open-ended ("Tell me all about what you do on the job") or they can involve structured or standardized questions. Because any one source of information can be biased, the job analyst may want to get more than one perspective by interviewing the job incumbent, the incumbent's supervisor, and, if the job is a supervisory one, the incumbent's subordinates. The job analyst might also interview several job incumbents within a single organization to get a more reliable representation of the job and to see whether various people holding the same job title in a company actually perform similar tasks.

Surveys

Survey methods of job analysis usually involve the administration of a pencil-and-paper or online questionnaire that the respondent completes and returns to the job analyst. Surveys can consist of open-ended questions ("What abilities or skills are required to perform this job?"); closed-ended questions ("Which of the following classifications best fits your position: (a) supervisory, (b) technical, (c) line, (d) clerical?"); or checklists ("Check all of the following tasks that you perform in your job.").

The survey method has two advantages over the interview method. First, the survey allows the collection of information from a number of workers simultaneously.

This can be helpful and very cost-effective when the analyst needs to study several positions. Second, because the survey can be anonymous, there may be less distortion or withholding of information than in a face-to-face interview. One of the drawbacks of the survey, however, is that the information obtained is limited by the questions asked. Unlike an interview, a survey cannot probe for additional information or for clarification of a response.

Often, in the conducting of job analyses, job incumbents or knowledgeable supervisors of job incumbents are referred to as **subject matter experts (or SMEs)**. Subject matter experts can provide job analysis information via interviews or through survey methods.

Subject Matter Expert (SME)
an individual who has detailed knowledge about a particular job

Job Diaries

Another method for job analysis is to have job incumbents record their daily activities in a diary. An advantage of the job diary is that it provides a detailed, hour-by-hour, day-by-day account of the worker's job. One difficulty of diary methods, however, is that it is quite time-consuming, both for the worker who is keeping the diary and for the job analyst who has the task of analyzing the large amount of information contained in the diary.

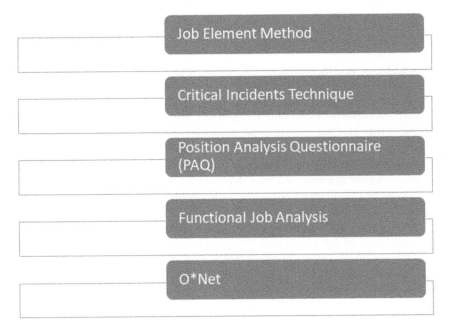

Figure 3.5 Specific job analysis techniques

Specific Job Analysis Techniques

In addition to these various general methods for conducting job analyses, there are a number of specific, standardized analysis techniques. These techniques have not only been widely used but have also generated a considerable amount of research on their effectiveness. We will consider four of these specific techniques: the job element method, the critical incidents technique, the Position Analysis Questionnaire, and functional job analysis.

Job Element Method

Job Element Method
a job analysis method that analyzes jobs in terms of the knowledge, skills, abilities, and other characteristics (KSAOs) required to perform the jobs

The **job element method** of job analysis looks at the basic knowledge, skills, abilities, or other characteristics—KSAOs—that are required to perform a particular job (Primoff, 1975). These KSAOs constitute the basic job elements.

In the job element method, the job analyst relies on "experts" (subject matter experts, or SMEs) who are informed about the job to identify the job elements (KSAOs) required for a given job. The experts then rate or rank the different elements in terms of their importance for performing the job. The job element method is "person oriented" (or personality based) in that it focuses on the characteristics of the individual who is performing the job (Morgeson et al., 2019). This method has been used most often in jobs in the federal government. Because of its limited scope, the job element method is often combined with other job analysis methods outlined next.

Critical Incidents Technique

Critical Incidents Technique (CIT)
a job analysis technique that relies on instances of especially successful or unsuccessful job performance

The **critical incidents technique (CIT)** of job analysis records the specific worker behaviors that have led to particularly successful or unsuccessful job performance (Flanagan, 1954). For example, some critical incidents for the job of clerical assistant might include the following: "Possesses knowledge of word processing programs"; "Notices an item in a letter or report that doesn't appear to be right, checks it, and corrects it"; "Misfiles charts, letters, etc., on a regular basis"; and "Produces a manuscript with good margins, making it look like a professional document." All of these behaviors presumably contribute to the success or failure of the clerical assistant. Research indicates that information is best provided by experts on the job and that careful qualitative analysis methods should be used (Butterfield et al., 2005). Therefore, information on such incidents is obtained by questioning—either through interviews or questionnaires—job incumbents, job supervisors, or other knowledgeable individuals. Through the collection of hundreds of critical incidents, the job analyst can arrive at a very good picture of what a particular job—and its successful performance—is all about. CIT is particularly suited to analyzing complex jobs

The following is an example of an interview question designed to elicit critical incidents for a particular job. This question focuses on an incident where a subordinate was behaving in a "helpful" way. Another question might try to elicit when workers are not being helpful; in other words, when they may be hurting group productivity.

"Think of the last time you saw one of your subordinates do something that was very helpful to your group in meeting their production schedule." (Pause until the respondent has such an incident in mind.) "Did the subordinate's action result in an increase in production of as much as one percent for that day?–or some similar period?"
(If the answer is "no", say) "I wonder if you could think of the last time that someone did something that did have this much of an effect in increasing production." (When respondent indicates he/she has such a situation in mind, say) "What were the general circumstances leading up to this incident?"

"Tell me exactly what this person did that was so helpful at that time."
"Why was this so helpful in getting your group's job done?"
"When did this incident happen?"
"What was this person's job?"
"How long has the person been on this job?"

Another example of a question designed to elicit critical incidents may be as simple and general as, "Think of the best (worst) subordinate you have known. Tell me about a time that shows why this person was the best (worst)."

Figure 3.6. Critical incidents interview form.

Source: Adapted from Flanagan, 1954.

(Anderson & Wilson, 1997). An example of a critical incidents interview form is presented in Figure 3.6.

The real value of the CIT is in helping to determine the particular knowledge, skills, and abilities that a worker needs to perform a job successfully. For example, from the critical incidents given for the clerical assistant position, we know that the successful worker will need to know how to file, use a word processing program, check basic grammar and sentence structure, and set up a typed manuscript page. The CIT technique is also useful in developing appraisal systems for certain jobs by helping to identify the critical components of successful performance. In fact, recently, the results of CIT analyses have been used to teach "best practices" in professions such as medicine, counseling, and customer service (Rademacher et al., 2010).

Position Analysis Questionnaire

One of the most widely researched job analysis instruments is the **Position Analysis Questionnaire (PAQ)** (McCormick et al., 1969), which is a structured questionnaire that analyzes various jobs in terms of 187 job elements that are arranged into six categories, or divisions, as follows:

▎ *Information input*—Where and how the worker obtains the information needed to perform the job. For example, a newspaper reporter may be required to use published, written materials as well as interviews with informants to write a news

Position Analysis Questionnaire (PAQ)
a job analysis technique that uses a structured questionnaire to analyze jobs according to 187 job statements, grouped into six categories

story. A clothing inspector's information input may involve fine visual discriminations of garment seams.

- *Mental processes*—The kinds of thinking, reasoning, and decision making required to perform the job. For example, an air traffic controller must make many decisions about when it is safe for jets to land and take off.
- *Work output*—The tasks the worker must perform and the tools or machines needed. For example, a word processor must enter text using keyboard devices.
- *Relationships with other persons*—The kinds of relationships and contacts with others required to do the job. For example, a teacher instructs others, and a store clerk has contact with customers by providing information and ringing up purchases.
- *Job context*—The physical and/or social contexts in which the work is performed. Examples of job context elements would be working under high temperatures or dealing with many conflict situations.
- *Other job characteristics*—Other relevant activities, conditions, or characteristics necessary to do the job.

Each of these job elements is individually rated using six categories: extent of use, importance to the job, amount of time, applicability, possibility of occurrence, and a special code for miscellaneous job elements. The standard elements are rated on a scale from 1, for minor applicability, to 5, for extreme applicability. There is an additional rating for "does not apply" (McCormick, 1979). A sample page from the PAQ is shown in Figure 3.7.

The PAQ results produce a detailed profile of a particular job that can be used to compare jobs within a company or similar positions in different organizations. Because the PAQ is a standardized instrument (meaning it has been extensively validated), two analysts surveying the same job should come up with similar profiles. This might not be the case with interview techniques, where the line of questioning and interpersonal skills specific to the interviewer could greatly affect the job profile.

As mentioned, the PAQ has historically been one of the most widely used and thoroughly researched methods of job analysis (Hyland & Muchinsky, 1991). In one interesting study, the PAQ was used to analyze the job of a homemaker. It was found that a homemaker's job is most similar to the jobs of police officer, firefighter, and airport maintenance chief (Arvey & Begalla, 1975).

Functional Job Analysis (FJA)
a structured job analysis technique that examines the sequence of tasks in a job and the processes by which they are completed

Dictionary of Occupational Titles (DOT)
a reference guide that classifies and describes over 40,000 jobs

Functional Job Analysis

Functional job analysis (FJA) has been used extensively by organizations in both the public and private sectors (Morgeson et al., 2019). It was developed in part to assist the U.S. Department of Labor in the construction of a comprehensive job classification system and to help create the ***Dictionary of Occupational Titles*** (**DOT**) (U.S. Department of Labor, 1991). The *DOT* was a reference guide that classified and gave general descriptions for over 40,000 different jobs. The *DOT* has been replaced by the online O*NET system that we will discuss shortly.

INFORMATION INPUT

1. INFORMATION INPUT

1.1 Sources of Job Information

Rate each of the following items in terms of the extent to which it is used by the worker as a source of information in performing his job.

Code	Extent of Use (U)
N	Does not apply
1	Nominal/very infrequent
2	Occasional
3	Moderate
4	Considerable
5	Very substantial

1 _____ Written materials (books, reports, office notes, articles, job instructions, signs, etc.).

2 _____ Quantitative materials (materials which deal with quantities or amounts, such as graphs, accounts, specifications, tables of numbers, etc.).

3 _____ Pictorial materials (pictures or picturelike materials used as **sources** of information, for example, drawings, blueprints, diagrams, maps, tracings, photographic films, x-ray films, TV pictures, etc.).

4 _____ Patterns/related devices (templates, stencils, patterns, etc., used as **sources** of information when **observed** during use; do **not** include here materials described in item 3 above).

5 _____ Visual displays (dials, gauges, signal lights, radarscopes, speedometers, clocks, etc.).

6 _____ Measuring devices (rulers, calipers, tire pressure gauges, scales, thickness gauges, pipettes, thermometers, protractors, etc., used to obtain visual information about physical measurements; do **not** include here devices described in item 5 above).

7 _____ Mechanical devices (tools, equipment, machinery, and other mechanical devices which are **sources** of information when observed during use or operation).

8 _____ Materials in process (parts, materials, objects, etc., which are **sources** of information when being modified, worked on, or otherwise processed, such as bread dough being mixed, workpiece being turned in a lathe, fabric being cut, shoe being resoled, etc.).

9 _____ Materials **not** in process (parts, materials, objects, etc., not in the process of being changed or modified, which are sources of information when being inspected, handled, packaged, distributed, or selected, etc., such as items or materials in inventory, storage, or distribution channels, items being inspected, etc.).

10 _____ Features of nature (landscapes, fields, geological samples, vegetation, cloud formations, and other features of nature which are observed or inspected to provide information).

11 _____ Constructed features of environment (structures, buildings, dams, highways, bridges, docks, railroads, and other "man made" or altered aspects of the indoor or outdoor environment which are **observed** or **inspected** to provide job information; do not consider equipment, machines, etc., that an individual uses in work, as covered by item 7).

Figure 3.7 Sample page from the Position Analysis Questionnaire (PAQ).

Source: McCormick et al., 1969.

Table 3.2 Hierarchy of Work Functions Used in Functional Job Analysis

Data	People	Things
0 Synthesizing	0 Mentoring, leading	0 Setting up
1 Coordinating, innovating	1 Negotiating	1 Precision working
2 Analyzing	2 Instructing, consulting	2 Operating-controlling
3 Compiling	3 Supervising	3 Driving-operating
4 Computing	4 Diverting	4 Manipulating
5 Copying	5 Persuading	5 Tending, data processing
6 Comparing	6 Exchanging information	6 Feeding, off bearing
	7 Serving	7 Handling
	8 Taking instructions, helping	

Source: Fine & Cronshaw, 1999; U.S. Department of Labor, 1991.

Functional job analysis uses three broad categories representing the job's typical interaction with data, people, and things. *Data* refers to information, knowledge, and conceptions. Jobs are evaluated with an eye to the amount and type of interaction the person performing the job has with data—numbers, words, symbols, and other abstract elements. *People* refers to the amount of contact with others that a job requires. These people can be coworkers, supervisors, customers, or others. *Things* refers to the worker's interaction with inanimate objects such as tools, machines, equipment, and tangible work products. Within each of these categories there is a hierarchy of work functions that ranges from the most involved and complex functions (given the numerical value of "0") to the least involved and least complex (the highest digit in the category; see Table 3.2).

For example, using FJA, the job of industrial/organizational psychologist requires "coordinating" data (value of "1"), "mentoring/leading" people (the highest value of "0"), and "handling" things (relatively low value of "7"). For the occupation of job analyst, the corresponding numbers are 2, 6, and 7, meaning that this job involves "analyzing" data, "exchanging information" with people, and "handling" things (see Figure 3.5). For instance, in a study of over 200 nursing assistants in nursing homes, functional job analysis discovered that nursing assistants were spending too little time dealing with the people aspects of their jobs (e.g., giving attention to elderly residents) and a disproportionately large amount of time dealing with data (e.g., reports) and things, such as changing bedding (Brannon et al., 1992).

O*Net: A Useful Tool for Understanding Jobs

O*NET
the U.S. Department of Labor's website that provides comprehensive information about jobs and careers

O*NET—the Occupational Information Network (www.onetcenter.org) is the U.S. Department of Labor's website that is intended to be the primary source of information about occupations. O*NET is an extensive database of information about jobs. O*NET has career exploration tools to assist individuals in evaluating their career interests; information on the job-related skills and training needed for particular jobs; consumer guides that explain personnel testing and assessment; and a clearinghouse for information for I/O psychologists, human resources professionals, and career and vocational counselors. The Department of Labor intends to make the ever-evolving O*NET the central source for information about jobs, careers, and the world of work.

Measurement Issues

Reliability
the consistency of a measurement instrument or its stability over time

As the job analysis will lead us to determine how we recruit, screen, and pay employees, it is important to reintroduce the topic of validity and reliability. Any type of measurement instrument used in industrial/organizational psychology, including those used in employee screening and selection, must meet certain measurement

Table 3.3 O*NET Summary Report for Occupation: Industrial/Organizational Psychologists (greatly abbreviated)

Sample of Reported Job Titles: Consultant, I/O Psychologist, Consulting Psychologist Management Consultant, Research Scientist

Tasks
Develop and implement employee selection and placement programs
Analyze job requirements and content . . . for classification, selection, training
Identify training and developmental needs
Assess employee performance

Knowledge
Personnel and human resources
Psychology
Education and training
Administration and management
Customer personal service
Sales and marketing

Skills
Critical thinking
Active listening
Complex problem solving
Service orientation
Speaking

Abilities
Oral and written comprehension and expression
Problem sensitivity
Deductive and inductive reasoning
Originality

Work Activities
Getting information and interpreting its meaning for others
Organizing, planning, prioritizing work
Analyzing data
Making decisions and problem solving
Providing consultation and advice to others
Interacting with computers, etc.
[Other information includes: Interests, Work Styles, Work Values, Related Occupations, and Wages & Employment Trends. (2020 median wages are over $96,000 per year, by the way, with good growth prospects.)]

standards. Two critically important concepts in measurement (as we covered in Chapter 1) are reliability and validity. You can review the material from Chapter 1, but we also provide the definitions here.

We build on those concepts from Chapter 1, here, and dive deeper into how criterion-related validity is assessed. There are two common ways that predictor–criterion correlations can be empirically generated. The first is the *follow-up method*

Test–Retest Reliability
a method of determining the stability of a measurement instrument by administering the same measure to the same people at two different times and then correlating the scores

Parallel Forms

a method of establishing the reliability of a measurement instrument by correlating scores on two different but equivalent versions of the same instrument

Internal Consistency

a common method of establishing a measurement instrument's reliability by examining how the various items of the instrument are intercorrelated

Validity

a concept referring to the accuracy of a measurement instrument and its ability to make accurate inferences about a criterion

Content Validity

the ability of the items in a measurement instrument to measure adequately the various characteristics needed to perform a job

Construct Validity

refers to whether an employment test measures what it is supposed to measure

Criterion-Related Validity

the accuracy of a measurement instrument in determining the relationship between scores on the instrument and some criterion of job performance

Figure 3.8 According to functional job analysis, the job of restaurant cook involves compiling data, speaking to people, and doing precision work with things.

Source: Photograph by Herman Latawa, found on Unsplash (https://unsplash.com/photos/RKdkETvcYn4).

(often referred to as *predictive validity*). Here, the screening instrument (for example, a skill test) is administered to applicants without interpreting the scores and without using them to select among applicants. Once the applicants become employees, criterion measures such as job performance assessments are collected. If the test instrument is valid, the scores should correlate with the criterion measure. Once there is evidence of the predictive validity of the instrument, scores are used to select the applicants for jobs. The obvious advantage of the predictive validity method is that it demonstrates how scores on the screening instrument actually relate to future job performance. The major drawback to this approach is the time that it takes to establish validity. During this validation period, applicants are tested, but are not hired based on their test scores.

In the second approach, known as the *present-employee method* (also termed *concurrent validity*), the screening instrument is given to current employees, and their scores are correlated with some criterion of their current performance. Again, a relationship between test scores and criterion scores supports the measure's validity. Once there is evidence of concurrent validity, a comparison of applicants' test scores with the incumbents' scores is possible. Although the concurrent validity method leads to a quicker estimate of validity, it may not be as accurate an assessment of criterion-related validity as the predictive method because the job incumbents represent a select group, and their test performance is likely to be high, with a restricted range of scores. In other words, there are no test scores for the "poor" job performers, such as workers who were fired or quit their jobs or applicants who were not chosen for jobs. Interestingly, available research suggests that the estimates of validity derived from both methods are generally comparable (Barrett et al., 1981).

Standardized tests and other assessment instruments can be reliable and valid screening devices for many jobs. However, two important issues must be considered: validity generalization and test utility. The **validity generalization** of a screening test refers to its validity in predicting performance in a job or setting different from the one in which the instrument was validated. For example, a standardized test of managerial potential is found to be valid in selecting successful managers in a manufacturing industry. If the test is also helpful in choosing managers in a service organization, its validity has generalized from one organization to another. Similarly, validity generalization would exist if a test of clerical abilities is successful in selecting applicants for both secretarial and receptionist positions. Of course, the more similar the jobs and organizations involved in the validity studies are to the jobs and organizations that subsequently use the screening tests, the more likely it is that validity will generalize from one situation to another.

High validity generalization of a standardized test will greatly increase its usefulness—and reduce the workload of I/O psychologists—because the instrument may not need to be validated for use with each and every position and organization. Some I/O psychologists argue that the validity generalization of most standardized employee screening procedures is quite high, which means that they can be used successfully in a variety of employment settings and job classifications (Ones et al., 2017). At the other extreme is the view that the ability of tests to predict future job success is situation-specific, and validity should be established for each use of a screening instrument. Although few I/O psychologists believe that the validity of test instruments is completely situation-specific, there is some disagreement over how well their validity generalizes.

From an international perspective, some types of tests may generalize better across countries and cultures. For example, tests of cognitive abilities should be important for many jobs throughout the world, and evidence suggests they are less prone to cultural effects (Salgado et al., 2003), whereas personality tests, for example, may be more susceptible to cultural effects (Hough & Connelly, 2013).

Test utility is the value of a screening test in helping to effect important organizational outcomes. In other words, test utility determines the success of a test in terms of dollars gained by the company through the increased performance and productivity of workers selected based on test scores. For example, in one organization, a valid screening test was used to select applicants for 600 jobs as computer programmers (Schmidt et al., 1979). The estimated money gained in 1 year from the increased speed and efficiency of the chosen workers was more than $97 million. The initial cost of the screening tests was only $10 per applicant, a very good return on investment.

Validity Generalization
the ability of a screening instrument to predict performance in a job or setting different from the one in which the test was validated

Test Utility
the value of a screening test in determining important outcomes, such as dollars gained by the company through its use

Determining Pay

Before recruiting for a job, the organization also needs to know the pay range it can offer for each position. Pay is heavily influenced by the KSAOs and behaviors determined to be important for the job during job analysis and described in the job evaluation. The job evaluation is one important part of the pay decision (Conroy, 2019). Detailed job evaluations typically examine jobs on a number of dimensions, called **compensable factors**. Examples of compensable factors might be the physical demands of a job; the amount of education, training, or experience required; the working conditions associated with the job; and the amount of responsibility the job carries. Each job may be given a score or weighting on each factor. The summed total of the weighted compensable factors indicates the value of the job, which is then translated into the dollar amount of compensation. Bear in mind that a compensable factors analysis of a job determines rates of compensation based solely on the training, responsibility, and conditions associated with a job. It does not take into account market conditions, such as the supply and demand for workers for a certain job.

Compensable Factors
the job elements that are used to determine appropriate compensation for a job

The compensable factors determined to be important for the job are really only half of the equation. Human resources professionals will consider how this job relates to other jobs in the organization to ensure that the pay rate for different jobs matches market pricing (Conroy, 2019). Imagine that a job evaluation shows that the salary for a new position in digital marketing should have a pay range of $100,000–120,000. The human resources professional would then consider what other marketing positions get paid to ensure there are not large disparities. The salary might also be compared with what engineers or human resources representatives are paid. And, one would consider what the typical pay range is for this type of job outside of the organization. Through consideration of all of these factors, a final pay range would be determined. Of course, these decisions should be made in the context of the organization's overall strategic goals (Conroy, 2019).

A common question that arises about pay is whether or not to openly share pay information with employees. Pay transparency can be useful in determining pay equity but can also have unintended consequences. If there are pay inequities, pay transparency can have negative effects for those who learn they are underpaid (SimanTov-Nachlieli & Bamberger, 2021) or if it reveals inequities where some employees are receiving idiosyncratic deals related to pay (Abdulsalam et al., 2020). On the other hand, transparency around how pay is determined, especially if pay is determined in a consistent fashion, has generally positive outcomes (SimanTov-Nachlieli & Bamberger, 2021), and pay transparency can contribute to greater pay equity between men and women.

For decades, the issue of how jobs are compensated has been a source of controversy because of pay inequality between men and women, often referred to as the gender pay gap. Although the most recent research shows that pay for women is catching up to the wages paid men, these gains are slow in coming. According to the United States Census Bureau (Leisenring, 2020), the pay gap was at its largest in 1973, when full-time working women earned 57 cents for each dollar that their male counterparts earned. That difference has decreased over time to 82 cents in 2019. At this rate, it will take until 2059 for women to achieve equal pay. This disparity amounts to a difference of between $700,000 and $2,000,000 per woman over her lifetime. The pay gap is even greater for women of color and for better-educated women compared with White women and less well-educated women.

According to the World Economic Forum (2019), the gender wage gap persists in all countries, although Western Europe has the smallest gap, followed by North America, and the Middle East and North Africa have the largest pay gap. Three issues bear directly on the "gender gap" in wages (Klein et al., 2021). The first concerns access to higher-paying jobs (Wittig & Berman, 1992). Traditionally, many such jobs were primarily held by men, but, throughout the 1960s and 1970s, the women's rights movement helped increase the access of women to these positions. However, although women are now found in nearly every type of job, there is still considerable sex stereotyping of jobs, which means that many relatively high-paying jobs and professions are still filled mainly by men. For example, men are found in large numbers in skilled craft jobs that receive higher wages than clerical and service jobs, which are filled mainly by women. In corporations, men fill more finance positions, and women are overrepresented in lower-paying human resources posts.

Second, female-dominated jobs may pay less than male-dominated jobs, even when they involve similar tasks. In the 1980s, this gender-based pay disparity gave birth to the concept of **comparable worth**, or equal pay for equal work. For example, the job of human resources clerk, a traditionally "female" job, and the position of records manager in the production department, a job usually filled by men, both require workers to perform similar tasks, such as keeping records and managing data files. Because of the similarity in duties, both positions should be paid equal wages. However, the job of records manager typically pays higher wages than the position of HR clerk.

Because of its focus on evaluating the worth of work tasks, the issue of comparable worth is tied to the ability of organizations to conduct valid and fair job evaluations, which should reveal instances of equal jobs receiving unequal compensation. However, opponents of the comparable worth movement argue that job evaluation methods may be inaccurate because they do not account for factors such as the oversupply of female applicants for certain jobs, such as teachers and airline attendants, the lower levels of education and work experience of women relative to men, and women's preferences for certain types of "safe" jobs with "pleasant working conditions." Advocates of the comparable worth movement argue that even these factors do not account for the considerable disparity in pay for men and women (Aisenbrey & Brückner, 2014; Pinzler & Ellis, 1989; Thacker & Wayne, 1995). For a number of reasons, women are simply not paid the same wages for the same level of work. One argument is that society does not value the type of work required by many jobs that are filled primarily by women, such as secretarial, clerical, teaching, and

Comparable Worth
the notion that jobs that require equivalent KSAOs should be compensated equally

nursing positions. Alternatively, certain jobs that are filled primarily by men may be compensated at higher levels because more value is ascribed to them (Aisenbrey & Brückner, 2014).

Exceptioning
the practice of ignoring pay discrepancies between particular jobs possessing equivalent duties and responsibilities

Another reason for gender-based pay disparity is the practice of **exceptioning**, whereby a job evaluation reveals that two jobs, with equivalent duties and responsibilities, receive very different rates of pay, and yet no steps are taken to rectify the inequality. In other words, an "exception" is made because it is too costly or too difficult to raise the wages of the lower-paid job. An example of exceptioning is the pay rates for physicians and nurses. The average salary of a physician is three to five times that of a nurse, and yet the two jobs have many comparable duties and responsibilities. Although the imbalance in salaries is known to exist, hospitals are financially unable to pay nurses what they are worth, and so an exception is made.

The issue of comparable worth has been hotly debated by both business and government officials. Certain cases of sex discrimination in employee compensation have reached the courts, highlighting the issue of comparable worth. For example, in *AFSCME v. State of Washington* (1983), a job evaluation of state employee positions found that women's job classes were paid approximately 20% less than comparable men's classes. It was recommended that women state employees be paid an additional $38 million annually. Because the State of Washington did not act on the recommendation, the women employees' union sued. The court ruled that the state was discriminating against its women employees and awarded them nearly $1 billion. In a highly controversial decision, the U.S. Supreme Court would not allow the largest gender discrimination case, involving 1.5 million women employees of Walmart to go forward, even though there was evidence that the women were paid less than men in comparable positions.

Stop & Review
What two issues are involved in the wage gender gap?

If the comparable worth movement goes forward, and the government decides to take steps to correct pay inequalities, the impact on workers and work organizations will be tremendous. First, job evaluations will have to be conducted for nearly all jobs in the country—a staggering and expensive task. Second, because it is unlikely that workers and unions will allow the wages of higher-paid workers to be cut, the salaries of the lower-paid workers will have to be raised—also an enormous expense. Regardless of what takes place in the next several years, the issue of comparable worth has focused greater attention on job evaluations and job evaluation procedures. It is, thus, likely that greater attention will be given to improving such procedures in the near future.

The final interpretation of the gender wage gap is that women receive lower pay for the same job within the same firm, known as within-job pay inequality (Klein et al., 2021). And the differences in equity-based awards (such as stock options) add additional gaps to pay differences (Klein et al., 2021). At least some of the pay differential may relate to inferences that women are less likely to stay with the organization (Klein et al., 2021), although questions about past pay history have also been shown to contribute to within-job pay inequality (Gottsacker, 2020). As a result, many states have banned inquiries about pay history, although the U.S. Supreme Court has not made it illegal at the federal level. The idea behind the ban is that if there has been a history of pay inequity, which we know there has been, then anchoring women's salary against their previous salary perpetuates pay inequality (Gottsacker, 2020). Initial analyses of the impact of such laws show that states that have enacted pay bans have narrowed the gender pay gap by as much as 1% in a short period of time (Hansen & McNichols, 2020).

In today's global environment, many organizations are multinational, with offices around the world. As a result, attention is being paid to employees selected for international assignments. Researchers have suggested that cultural sensitivity and ability to adapt to different situations and surroundings are important for employees working in other countries and cultures (Caligiuri et al., 2009). Importantly, it has been suggested that selecting and placing the right employees for global assignments are not enough. Attention must be paid to the ongoing development and training for workers going abroad (Mesmer-Magnus & Viswesvaran, 2007). We will discuss this further in Chapter 6, which focuses on employee training and development.

Human Resource Planning

With job analysis in hand and pay determined, the human resources professional determines how many and what types of employees need to be hired. We often think of selection as refilling a single position that has been vacated. But refilling vacancies is a reactive response to hiring. The best organizations continually evaluate their human resources needs and plan their hiring and staffing in order to meet their companies' business goals. This means forecasting what types of positions organizations think they will need in the subsequent year, including new positions that they may create and refilling positions that may become vacant.

Effective human resource planning (HR planning) begins with the strategic goals of the organization. For example, imagine an internet-based marketing company that provides marketing services for small businesses. This company has recently branched out and now provides clients with websites that the clients can control themselves. The marketing company will need web experts to build and maintain the infrastructure for the sites and will need to provide customer support services to help clients maintain their own websites. This will mean that the company needs to hire a certain number of web design experts and customer service agents with web knowledge to staff the customer help lines.

Human resources professionals need to consider a number of factors in HR planning: What are the organization's goals and strategic objectives? What are the staffing needs required for the organization to accomplish its goals? What are the current human resource capacities and existing employee skills in the organization? Which additional positions are needed to meet the staffing needs (sometimes referred to as a "gap analysis"—i.e., what is the gap between the HR capacities the company has and what it needs)?

Staffing today's organizations requires that companies take into account a number of critical issues, such as the changing nature of work and the workforce (e.g., greater need for experienced, "knowledge" workers), increased competition for the best workers, ensuring that there is good "fit" between workers and organizations, and increasing workforce diversity.

Human resource planning also considers the short- and long-term time frames and begins to ask the broader HR questions: What are the training needs of employees going to be in the future? How can we competitively recruit the highest potential employees? How competitive are we in our compensation and benefit programs? How can we find employees who are a "good fit" for our company and its culture?

One model of human resource planning suggests that companies need to focus on four interrelated processes (Cascio, 2003). These are:

- **Talent inventory**: an assessment of the current KSAOs (knowledge, skills, abilities, and other characteristics) of current employees and how they are used.
- **Workforce forecast**: a plan for future HR requirements (i.e., the number of positions forecasted, the skills those positions will require, and some sense of what the market is for those workers).
- **Action plans**: development of a plan to guide the recruitment, selection, training, and compensation of the future hires.
- **Control and evaluation**: having a system of feedback to assess how well the HR system is working and how well the company met its HR plan (you will find that evaluation is critical for all HR functions—we need to constantly evaluate I/O programs and interventions to determine their effectiveness).

Employee Recruitment

Employee Recruitment
the process by which companies attract qualified applicants

⏱ Stop & Review

What are the four processes in a model of human resource planning? How are they connected or related?

Once an organization knows how many employees it needs and what skills those employees should have, it can move into the recruitment phase of employee selection. **Employee recruitment** is the process by which organizations attract potential workers to apply for jobs. If you have ever applied for a job, then you know that the job description, job specification, and pay range are determined before the recruitment process ever begins.

One of the primary objectives of a successful program is to attract a large pool of qualified applicants. A wide variety of recruitment techniques and tactics can be used, including job advertisements on internet sites (e.g., Monster.com, CareerBuilder.com), employment agencies (including executive search firms—i.e., "headhunters"—for high-level positions), and referrals by current employees. College students are most familiar with on-campus recruitment programs and web-based career sites that post openings as well as allowing applicants and employers to "connect" online through professional social networking sites (e.g., LinkedIn.com, Indeed.com). The larger internet job sites, such as Monster.com, have millions of registered job seekers and employers, allowing a potential applicant to search hundreds of jobs in minutes, post a resume, and get career advice. The downside of internet recruitment, however, is the large number of potential applicants who need to be sifted through. Recently, there have been attempts to provide detailed information about what sort of applicants might best fit the positions and the organization and jobs on companies' websites.

Recruitment from the Perspective of the Recruit

Recruitment is a two-way process: while the recruiting organization is attempting to attract and later evaluate prospective employees, job applicants are evaluating various potential employers. Job search is a shared experience for almost all college students who seek employment (or a better job) after graduating college. This can be a very exciting process, but can also be stressful and exhausting. A study examining college students' motivation during the job search process showed that internal motivation tends to decrease over time during the job search, whereas external motivation remains stable (da Motta Veiga & Gabriel, 2016). Both types of motivation are important in determining one's level of effort in searching for a job as long as students utilize goal strategies such as setting goals, developing a plan, and using feedback related to the job search. Importantly, receiving feedback on one's job search can be a double-edged sword such that college students who receive useful, high-quality feedback tend to invest more time in job search, whereas those who receive low-quality feedback may withdraw effort (Chawla et al., 2019)

Research shows that a majority of young job applicants have preferred larger, multinational firms, with a smaller subset preferring working for small organizations (Barber et al., 1999). In addition, job seekers are influenced by the type of industry, the profitability of the company, the company's reputation, the opportunities for employee development and advancement, and the company's organizational culture. Applicants also form judgments of organizations based on their thorough recruitment materials (Rynes, 1993). Potential applicants examine online reviews of the organization from past employees on sites such as Glassdoor and Indeed (Evertz et al., 2019). Organizations that convey a clear and consistent positive image of the organization, often referred to as organizational branding, are more attractive to potential applicants (Ghielen et al., 2021; Lawong et al., 2019).

ON THE *CUTTING* EDGE

On the *Cutting* Edge: Job Search in a Pandemic

In December of 2019, a new respiratory coronavirus, COVID-19, was identified in Wuhan, China. By early 2020, the pandemic had spread across the globe, including the United States. As of the end of 2021, there were hundreds of millions of cases of the virus, causing many millions of deaths across the globe. In March of

ON THE *CUTTING* EDGE (*continued*)

2020, the spread of the virus had virtually shut down the global economy. In the United States, and in many other countries, stay at home orders were issued, schools were closed, and most in-person businesses were shut down, with the exception of essential services such as grocery stores and medical care. Massive layoffs swept the nation, and those who did not lose their jobs started to work remotely. Researcher Lynn McFarland and her colleagues examined the impact of COVID-19 on job search behavior (McFarland et al., 2020). They found that job search greatly increased in the weeks following the onset of the pandemic. In addition, the types of jobs people searched for also changed such that there was an increase in applications to work-from-home jobs, although there was no increase in face-to-face jobs. The question remains, at this point in time, how the pandemic will change the nature of work in the long term, although we expect that employees will continue to work from home to some extent long after the pandemic is gone.

In their efforts to attract applicants, however, many companies will "oversell" a particular job or their organization. Advertisements may say that "this is a great place to work" or that the position is "challenging" and offers "tremendous potential for advancement." This is not a problem if such statements are true, but, if the job and the organization are presented in a misleading, overly positive manner, the strategy will eventually backfire. Although the recruitment process may attract applicants, the new employees will quickly discover that they were fooled and may look for work elsewhere or become dissatisfied and unmotivated.

Realistic Job Preview (RJP)
an accurate presentation of the prospective job and organization made to applicants

Therefore, organizations should consider using a **realistic job preview (RJP)**, which is an accurate description of the duties and responsibilities of a particular job, in order to mitigate overly positive and unrealistic expectations from employees. For example, many people are drawn to careers in consulting or to certain health-care professions because the jobs seem important, interesting, and exciting. But, there are also downsides to those jobs, and knowing those as well can allows applicants to determine their own suitability (and capabilities) for performing a job (Callinan & Robertson, 2000). Indeed, applicants who receive a realistic job preview have higher job commitment and satisfaction and lower turnover (Shibly, 2019). Realistic job previews can take the form of an oral presentation from a recruiter, supervisor, or job incumbent; a visit to the job site; or a discussion in a brochure, manual, video, or company website.

Another important goal for any recruitment program is to avoid intentional or unintentional discrimination against underrepresented groups such as women, people of color, workers who are older, and persons with disabilities (Breaugh, 2017). One recent suggestion that serves to offer a realistic job preview while also reducing bias in the selection process is offering practice employment tests during the recruitment process. Although not a common practice, one study showed that offering job applicants the opportunity to take an exam related to occupational knowledge and writing ability offered several important benefits (Campion et al., 2019). Taking the practice test allowed for a realistic job preview for potential applicants and allowed many potential applicants to opt out of applying for a position. In addition, for those who did apply for the job, taking the practice test resulted in score gains on the actual employment task for Black and Hispanic applicants.

In addition to offering practice tests, organizations can take other steps to increase the diversity in their recruitment pool. Employers should take steps to attract applicants from underrepresented groups in proportion to their numbers in the population from which the company's workforce is drawn, at a minimum. In other words, if a company is in an area where the population within a 10–20-mile radius is 40% White, 30% African American, 10% Asian American, and 10% Hispanic, the recruitment program should draw applicants in roughly those proportions to avoid unintentionally discriminating against any group. Many organizations make efforts to over-recruit from underrepresented groups to improve their chances of capturing the most diverse talent. This type of targeted recruitment can increase diversity among new hires (Newman & Lyon, 2009).

Not only is it important to be able to attract underrepresented applicants, it is also important to be able to get them to accept job offers. If an organization is perceived as not welcoming to members of underrepresented groups, it will be difficult to get candidates to accept jobs. For example, research has shown that qualified members of minority groups lost enthusiasm for jobs in organizations that had few minority group members and few minorities in higher-level positions (Avery & McKay, 2006; McKay & Avery, 2006).

For applicants with disabilities, the application process itself can create barriers to employment (Bonaccio et al., 2020). For example, persons with visual impairment may be unable to see small text used in online applications. Organizations that are mindful of these challenges can increase their success at recruiting this underutilized segment of the workforce. Owing to the competitive nature of recruiting the very best employees, companies need to give greater consideration to recruitment methods and processes. Some researchers have specifically looked at recruitment efforts that target specific groups of potential employees, such as college students. For example, many innovative organizations, particularly those creating web-based innovations (e.g., Google/Alphabet, Facebook, Zynga) are competing hard to recruit high-potential college graduates. Retail giants, such as Walmart, have actively targeted seniors through associations such as the American Association for Retired Persons (AARP).

Summary

There are many stages in the preselection process, beginning with job analysis, followed by determining pay, engaging in human resource planning, and finally recruiting a broad pool of applicants. *Job analysis* is the systematic study of a job's tasks, duties, and responsibilities and the knowledge, skills, and abilities needed to perform the job. The job analysis, which is the important starting point for many personnel functions, yields several products: a *job description*, which is a detailed accounting of job tasks, procedures, responsibilities, and output; a *job specification*, which consists of information about the physical, educational, and experiential qualities required to perform the job; a *job evaluation*, which is an assessment of the relative value of jobs for determining compensation; and performance criteria, which serve as a basis for appraising successful job performance.

Job analysis methods include observation, use of existing data, interviews, and surveys. One structured job analysis technique is the *job element approach*, a broad approach to job analysis that focuses on the knowledge, skills, abilities, and other characteristics (KSAOs) required to perform a particular job. The *critical incidents technique* of job analysis involves the collection of particularly successful or unsuccessful instances of job performance. Through the collection of hundreds of these incidents, a detailed profile of a job emerges. Another structured job analysis technique, the *Position Analysis Questionnaire (PAQ)*, uses a questionnaire that analyzes jobs in terms of 187 job elements arranged into six categories. *Functional job analysis (FJA)* is a method that has been used to classify jobs in terms of the worker's interaction with data, people, and things. FJA relies on the U.S. Labor Department's *O*NET* database. FJA examines the sequence of tasks required to complete the job, as well as the process by which the job is completed. Research has determined that all these specific, standardized methods are effective.

In preparing for screening and selection of employees, it is important to consider the measurement properties of any screening instruments, such as employment tests. This includes issues of the reliability and validity of the screening instruments, which should be thoroughly evaluated before they are utilized.

With job analysis in hand, organizations can begin *determining pay* for different positions, depending on the skills required for the job. Then, the organization will determine how many employees it projects needing in the subsequent year using *human resource planning*. *Human resource planning* involves thinking forward to the positions that need to be filled, the talent needed to fill them, and the process of how the organization will fill these positions.

Finally, *employee recruitment* begins. *Employee recruitment* is the process of attracting potential workers to apply for jobs. There are a variety of employee recruitment methods, such as advertisements, college recruitment programs, employment agencies, and employee referrals. An important element of the recruitment process is presenting applicants with an accurate picture of the job through the use of *realistic job previews (RJPs)*, which help increase satisfaction and decrease turnover of new employees.

Study Questions and Exercises

1. Consider each of the products of a job analysis. How do these products affect other organizational outcomes?

2. Compare and contrast the four specific, structured methods of job analysis: the functional job analysis, the job element method, the Position Analysis Questionnaire, and the critical incidents technique. Make a table listing their respective strengths and weaknesses.

3. Consider your current job, or a job that you or a friend had in the past. How would you begin to conduct a job analysis of that position? What methods would you use? What are the important components of the job?

4. Using the preceding job, go to O*NET and find the code for that job title using the "Occupational listings," sorted by title (www.onetcenter.org/occupations. html). Using the code, look up the online job using the occupational title (http:// online.onetcenter.org/find/) and find the information for that job, or you can put in the code for I/O psychologist (19–3032.00).

5. List some of the reasons why women are paid less than men are for comparable work. Think of some stereotypically "female" jobs and comparable jobs that are stereotypically held by men. Are there inequities in compensation between the "male" and "female" jobs? Why or why not?

Web Links

www.onetcenter.org
The U.S. Department of Labor's "one-stop" site for job career information.

www.job-analysis.net
An interesting site, part of a larger human resources site, with detailed information and links on job analysis methods and practice.

www.siop.org/Research-Publications/Items-of-Interest/ArtMID/19366/Article ID/4977/How-Can-Organizations-Help-Close-the-Pay-Gap

Suggested Readings

Morgeson, F. P., Brannick, M. T., & Levine, E. L. (2019). *Job and work analysis: Methods, research, and applications for human resource management.* Sage.

Voskuijl, O. F. (2017). Job analysis: Current and future perspectives. In A. Evers, N. Anderson, & O. Voskuijl (Eds.), *The Blackwell handbook of personnel selection* (pp. 25–46). Blackwell.

CHAPTER 4

Assessing and Selecting Employees

Inside Tips
UNDERSTANDING THE HIRING AND ASSESSMENT PROCESS

In this chapter, we will continue our look at how employees are selected into organizations by focusing directly on assessment techniques used in hiring. As mentioned earlier, we will be applying some of the research and measurement methods discussed in Chapter 2, so make sure to review the concepts if necessary.

A study hint for organizing and understanding the many screening and testing proce-dures presented in this chapter is to consider those processes in the context of some of the methodological issues discussed previously. In other words, much of the strength or weak-ness of any particular employment method or process is determined by its ability to predict important work outcomes, which are usually defined as "job performance." The ability to predict future employee performance accurately from the results of employment tests or from other employee screening procedures is critical. However, other important considerations for screening methods concern their cost and ease of use, or, in other words, their utility. Hiring interviews, for example, are considered to be relatively easy to use, whereas testing programs are thought (rightly or wrongly) to be costly and difficult to implement. Often, our own experiences in applying for jobs give us only a limited picture of the variety of employee screening methods.

You have found what you consider to be the perfect job. You polish up your resume (and hopefully have some friends, and perhaps your career services counselor, read it over and make suggestions) and spend a lot of time crafting a dynamic cover letter. You then begin the online application process. A week later, you receive an e-mail scheduling you for an "employment testing session and interview." You begin to wonder (and worry) about what the testing session and interview will be about.

DOI: 10.4324/9781003143987-6

In this chapter, we will focus on the methods used in assessing and screening applicants for jobs. This is an area where I/O psychologists have been greatly involved—in the development of employment tests, work simulations, hiring interview protocols, and other methods used to predict who, among a large pool of applicants, might be best suited for success in a particular job.

A Model for Employee Selection

The model for recruiting and hiring effective and productive employees is actually quite simple. It consists of two categories of variables: criteria and predictors. **Criteria** (or the singular, criterion) are measures of success. The most common way to think of success on the job is in terms of performance criteria. A performance criterion for a cable TV installer may be the number of units installed. For a salesperson, dollar sales figures may be a performance criterion (we will discuss performance criteria in more depth in Chapter 5). Yet, when it comes to hiring good employees, we may want to go beyond these rather simple and straightforward performance criteria. The general criterion of "success" for an employee may be a constellation of many factors, including performance, loyalty, and commitment to the organization; a good work attendance record; ability to get along with supervisors and coworkers; and ability to learn and grow on the job. Thus, for the purpose of hiring workers, we might want to think of "success on the job" as the ultimate criterion—a criterion we aspire to measure, but something that we may never actually be able to capture with our limited measurement capabilities.

Criteria
measures of job success typically related to performance

Predictors are any pieces of information that we are able to measure about job applicants that are related to (predictive of) the criteria. In employee selection, we measure predictors, such as job-related knowledge and expertise, education, and skills, in an effort to predict who will be successful in a given job. Figure 4.1 illustrates this model for employee selection. Through evaluation of resumes and hiring interview performance and from the results of employment tests, applicants are measured on a number of predictors. These predictor variables are then used to select applicants for jobs. Evaluation of the success of an employee selection program involves demonstrating that the predictors do indeed predict the criterion of success on the job.

Predictors
variables about applicants that are related to (predictive of) the criteria

Early Screening Methods

A wide variety of data sources, such as resumes, job applications, letters of recommendation, employment tests, and hiring interviews, can be used in screening and selecting potential employees (Figure 4.2). If you have ever applied for a job, you

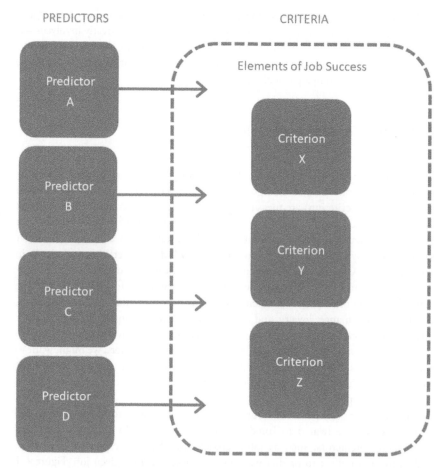

Figure 4.1 Multiple predictors are used in selection decisions to get at the different success criteria.

have had firsthand experience of some of these. We will consider all these screening methods in this first section, except for employment tests and interviews. Because of the variety and complexity of tests used in employee screening and selection, we will consider employment testing and hiring interviews in a later section of this chapter.

Application/ Resumes

The first step in the screening process involves the evaluation of application blanks, cover letters, and resumes. Usually, standard application forms are used for screening lower-level positions in an organization, whereas resumes are used to hire for higher-level jobs. Often, these applications are submitted online. The main purpose of the

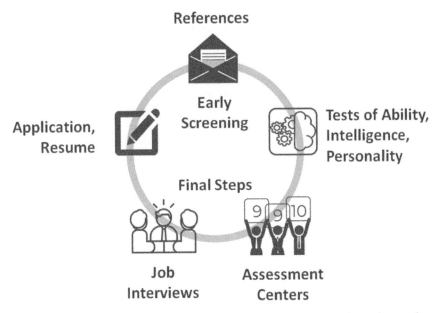

Figure 4.2 Multiple assessment methods are often used during selection. During early screening, most job openings require a resume or application along with references and testing. Once a finalist slate has been determined, most organizations will conduct job interviews and sometimes use assessment centers for higher-level jobs.

application and resume is to collect background information about the applicant such as education, work experience, and outstanding work or school accomplishments to determine if the applicant meets the minimum requirements for the job in terms of education or experience. Work experience can be measured in both quantitative (e.g., time in a position, number of times performing a task) and qualitative (e.g., level of complexity or challenge in a job) terms (Sajjadiani et al., 2019).

As with all employment screening devices, the application form should collect only information that has been determined to be job related. Questions that are not job related, and especially those that may lead to job discrimination, such as inquiries about age, ethnic background, religious affiliation, marital status, or finances, should not be included. In addition, there is evidence from numerous research studies that race and gender inferred from applications and resumes can elicit illegal and unfair bias from evaluators, although training may reduce those effects (Derous et al., 2020).

One difficulty with application forms lies in evaluating and interpreting the information obtained to determine the most qualified applicants. For example, it may be difficult to choose between an applicant with little education but ample work experience and an educated person with no work experience. There have been attempts to quantify data related to experience and education from application forms through the use of weighted application forms. **Weighted application forms** assign different weights to each piece of information on the form. The weights are determined

Weighted Application Forms
forms that assign different weights to the various pieces of information provided on a job application

through detailed research, conducted by the organization, to determine the relationship between different types of education or experience and success on the job (Ryan & Ployhart, 2014).

In addition to demonstrating that an applicant meets the minimum requirements for a job, resumes and cover letters provide the employer with a first impression of the applicant (Soroko, 2012). In fact, research has shown that impressions of qualifications from written applications influenced impressions of applicants in their subsequent interviews (Macan & Dipboye, 1994). Therefore, applicants should ensure that there are no typos or mistakes on their resumes and cover letters.

References and Letters of Recommendation

Two other sources of information used in employee screening and selection are references and letters of recommendation. Typically, reference checks and letters of recommendation can provide four types of information: (1) employment and educational history, (2) evaluations of the applicant's character, (3) evaluations of the applicant's job performance, and (4) the recommender's willingness to rehire the applicant (Cascio, 1987).

There are important reasons why references and letters of recommendation may have limited importance in employee selection. First, because applicants can usually choose their own sources for references and recommendations, it is unlikely that they will supply the names of persons who will give bad recommendations. Therefore, letters of recommendation tend to be distorted in a highly positive direction—so positive that they may be useless in distinguishing among applicants. One interesting study found that both longer reference letters and letters written by persons with more positive dispositions tended to be more favorably evaluated than either short letters or those written by less "positive" authors (Judge & Higgins, 1998). In addition, because of increased litigation against individuals and former employers who provide negative recommendations, many companies are refusing to provide any kind of reference for former employees except for job title and dates of employment. Thus, some organizations are simply forgoing the use of reference checks and letters of recommendation.

Letters of recommendation are still widely used, however, in applications to graduate schools and in certain professional positions. One study examined the use of reference letters by academics and personnel professionals in selection. As expected, letters of reference are used more frequently for selection of graduate students than for selection of employees, although neither group relied heavily on reference letters, primarily because most letters tend to be so positively inflated that they are considered somewhat useless in distinguishing among applicants (Nicklin & Roch, 2009). Beyond their low validity levels, letters of recommendation have also been shown to have an adverse impact on women, who are often described in letters in ways that focus on their ability to get along well with others rather than their ability to execute tasks (Madera et al., 2009). To avoid those risks, letter writers should think twice

D&I
INSIGHT
☼

about describing women in terms of their good social skills and, instead, focus on their competence.

In many graduate programs, steps have been taken to improve the effectiveness of these letters as a screening and selection tool by including forms that ask the recommender to rate the applicant on a variety of dimensions, such as academic ability, motivation/drive, oral and written communication skills, and initiative. These rating forms often use graphic rating scales to help quantify the recommendation for comparison with other applicants. They also attempt to improve the accuracy of the reference by protecting the recommender from possible retaliation by having the applicants waive their rights to see the letter of reference.

The use of background checks for past criminal activity has been on the rise and has fueled an industry for companies providing this service. Although quite common for applicants for positions in law enforcement, jobs working with children and other vulnerable populations, and positions in government agencies, many companies are routinely conducting background checks on most or all candidates for jobs before hire in an attempt to protect employers from litigation and to prevent hiring poor workers (Duane et al., 2017). The Society for Human Resource Management (SHRM, 2012) found that the vast majority of employers are routinely conducting criminal background checks on potential employees. Interestingly, although background checks are becoming commonplace, there has been very little research examining the impact on organizations. This is an important concern, because companies who routinely refuse to hire applicants with criminal or arrest records can come under fire from the EEOC owing to adverse impact concerns, because African Americans and Hispanics are more likely, as a group, to have arrest records (Viswesvaran & Ones, 2018). Likewise, the use of credit checks as a selection tool can have an adverse impact on applicants of color (Volpone et al., 2015).

 CLOSE ## Using Social Network Sites when Prescreening Job Applicants

The use of social network sites (SNS), such as Facebook and LinkedIn, has become so common that many hiring managers are now searching their job applicants' comments, pictures, and profiles on SNS. According to a survey conducted by CareerBuilder.com, 45% of hiring managers reported that they searched applicants on SNS. The same report also revealed that 35% of employers decided not to hire certain applicants because they found unfavorable comments or pictures of the applicants on the internet. However, the survey also found that information on a more professional SNS (e.g., LinkedIn) could help strengthen a candidate's likelihood of getting hired.

Are you a potential job applicant? Activity on SNS has both pros and cons. You can now share your life with many friends. You can also join a community to share similar interests or enhance professional skills. Occasionally, however, you may accidentally share information that you did not intend to share, or you may post

UP CLOSE *(continued)*

comments that would be considered unacceptable in a professional situation.

One study found that the information on SNS can reveal an individual's personality, work ethics, behavior, and tendencies (Back et al., 2010). Therefore, investigating job applicants' daily behaviors on SNS to see if candidates are suitable for positions may seem to make sense to many employers (Brown & Vaughn, 2011). Nevertheless, organizations need to be cautious when using the information found on SNS for their hiring decisions. For their selection processes to be legally defensible, the information they obtain and utilize should be relevant to job requirements (i.e., ensuring the validity of such information). The use of SNS allows employers to unearth a variety of information about job applicants, including age, marital status, or religious affiliation. The discovery of such information is prohibited in traditional job application and interview processes. Moreover, contrary to the common perception that SNS reveals undisclosed information about a person, these sites are places where people may present themselves in a socially desirable manner. As a result, employers may end up with inaccurate assessments of job applicants. In addition, there is no consistency in the type of information employers can find, because SNS users can edit privacy settings and customize their profiles. This leads to inconsistent assessment across different job applicants.

Despite these limitations in using information from SNS, such information does have some impact on hiring decisions. If you are an SNS user, you may want to reconsider how and why you use certain SNS. Ultimately, acting more professionally in the "bare-all" online world is advisable.

Employment Testing

After the evaluation of the biographical information available from resumes, application forms, or other sources, the next step in comprehensive employee screening programs is employment testing. As we saw in Chapter 1, the history of personnel testing in I/O psychology goes back to World War I, when intelligence testing of armed forces recruits was used for employee placement. Today, the use of tests for employment screening and placement has expanded greatly. A considerable percentage of large companies and most government agencies routinely use some form of employment test to measure a wide range of characteristics that are predictive of successful job performance. For example, some tests measure specific skills or abilities required by a job, whereas others assess more general cognitive skills as a means of determining if one has the aptitude needed for the successful performance of a certain job. Still other tests measure personality dimensions that are believed to be important for particular occupations.

One concern with testing is that women and people of color often face stereotype threat when taking exams. According to the theory, stereotype threat refers to the "predicament" in which members of a social group (e.g., African Americans, women) fear being judged in a way that is consistent with negative stereotypes about their group or behaving in a way that could confirm the stereotype (Steele & Aronson, 1998). For instance, when stereotyped group members take standardized ability tests, such as in educational admission or employment selection contexts, their performance may be partially undermined when they encounter cues of a salient negative stereotype in the testing environment (e.g., women are not good at math, or ethnic minorities are inferior in intellectual abilities; Steele et al., 2002). Stereotype threat is a situational stressor that occurs when someone feels performance pressure because they are aware of negative stereotypes related to their race or gender group. Knowing that one's group is stereotyped as performing less well in certain domains can create a self-fulfilling prophecy, causing the individual to perform poorly.

Considering that there is an expectation that tests will not have an adverse impact on different demographic groups, it is important that I/O psychologists effectively mitigate stereotype threat (Roberson & Kim, 2014; Roberson & Kulik, 2007). Importantly, stereotype threat is communicated and reinforced through cultural, societal, and organizational levers, making it difficult to eradicate (Jones & Carpenter, 2014). Nonetheless, there is evidence that stereotype threat can be mitigated in test-taking environments through simple interventions such as telling test-takers that there are no mean differences across race or gender (Nguyen & Ryan, 2008). Alternatively, placing demographic questions such as asking someone's race and gender at the end of a test instead of as the first questions actually can reduce the salience of race and gender (Kirnan et al., 2009). A meta-analysis (a study of studies) on stereotype threat interventions showed that interventions do improve performance, but there are certainly differences in the types of interventions (Liu et al., 2021). For example, promoting social belonging and providing in-group role models had a medium effect on reducing stereotype threat, whereas interventions focused on boosting resilience such as self-affirmation and improving confidence have small, but still significant, effects.

🕐 Stop & Review

What are some diversity and inclusion issues related to selection?

Test Formats

Test formats, or the ways in which tests are administered, can vary greatly. Several distinctions are important when categorizing employment tests:

▎ *Individual versus group tests*—Individual tests are administered to only one person at a time. In individual tests, the test administrator is usually more involved than in a group test. Typically, tests that require some kind of sophisticated apparatus, such as a driving simulator, or tests that require constant supervision are administered individually, as are certain intelligence and personality tests. Group tests are designed to be administered simultaneously to more than one person, with the administrator usually serving only as a test monitor. The obvious advantage to group tests is the reduced cost for administrator time. More and more, tests of all types are being administered online, so the distinction between individual and group testing is becoming blurred, as many applicants can complete screening instruments online simultaneously.

- **Speed versus power tests**—Speed tests have a fixed time limit. An important focus of a speed test is the number of items completed in the time period provided. A typing test and many of the scholastic achievement tests are examples of speed tests. A power test allows the test-taker sufficient time to complete all items. Typically, power tests have difficult items, with a focus on the percentage of items answered correctly.
- **Paper-and-pencil versus performance tests**—"Paper-and-pencil tests" refers to both paper versions of tests and online tests that require some form of written reply, in either a forced choice or an open-ended "essay" format. Many employee screening tests, and nearly all tests in schools, are of this format. Performance tests, such as typing tests and tests of manual dexterity or grip strength, usually involve the manipulation of physical objects.

As mentioned, most written-type tests are now administered via computer (usually web-based), which allows greater flexibility in how a test can be administered. Certain performance-based tests can also be administered via computer simulations (see Figure 4.3)

Figure 4.3 Some employment tests involve sophisticated technology, and may even use virtual reality to test applicants.

Source: Photograph by Laurens Derks, found on Unsplash (https://unsplash.com/photos/bCdlx5LjrYo).

Although the format of an employment test is significant, the most important way of classifying the instruments is in terms of the characteristics or attributes they measure, such as biographical information (biodata instruments), cognitive abilities, mechanical abilities, motor and sensory abilities, job skills and knowledge, or personality traits (see Table 4.1 for examples of these various tests).

Types of Tests

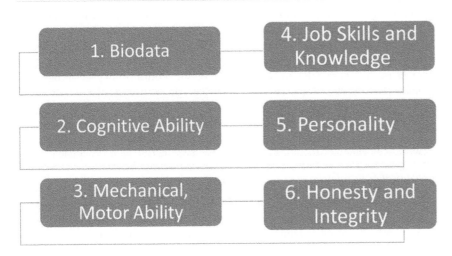

Figure 4.4 Types of tests.

Biodata Instruments

Biodata tests measure background information and personal characteristics that can be used in a systematic fashion to select employees (Ryan & Ployhart, 2014). Developing biodata instruments typically involves taking information that would appear on application forms and other items about background, personal interests, and behavior and using that information to develop a form of forced-choice employment test. Along with items designed to measure basic biographical information, such as education and work history, the biodata instrument might also involve questions of a more personal nature, probing the applicant's attitudes, values, likes, and dislikes. Biodata instruments are unlike the other test instruments we will discuss because there are no standardized biodata instruments. Instead, biodata instruments take a great deal of research to develop and validate. Because biodata instruments are typically designed to screen applicants for one specific job, they are most likely to be used only for higher-level positions.

Biodata
background information and personal characteristics that can be used in employee selection

Table 4.1 Some Standardized and Well-Researched Tests Used in Employee Screening and Selection

---

Cognitive Ability Tests

Comprehensive Ability Battery (Hakstian & Cattell, 1975–82): Features 20 tests, each designed to measure a single primary cognitive ability, many of which are important in industrial settings. Among the tests are those assessing verbal ability, numerical ability, clerical speed and accuracy, and ability to organize and produce ideas, as well as several memory scales.

Wonderlic Cognitive Ability Test (formerly the *Wonderlic Personnel Test*) (Wonderlic, 1983): A 50-item, pencil-and-paper test measuring the level of mental ability for employment, which is advertised as the most widely used test of cognitive abilities by employers.

Raven Progressive Matrices (Raven & Raven, 2003): A nonverbal test of general cognitive ability that consists of sequences of figures that get progressively harder. It measures intelligence without using any verbal content.

Wechsler Adult Intelligence Scale-Revised or WAIS-R (Wechsler, 1981): A comprehensive group of 11 subtests measuring general levels of intellectual functioning. The WAIS-R is administered individually and takes more than an hour to complete.

Mechanical Ability Tests

Bennett Mechanical Comprehension Test (Bennett, 2008): A 68-item, pencil-and-paper test of the ability to understand the physical and mechanical principles in practical situations. Can be group administered; comes in two equivalent forms.

Mechanical Ability Test: A 35-item, multiple-choice instrument that measures natural mechanical aptitude. Used to predict potential in engineering, assembly work, carpentry, and building trades.

Motor and Sensory Ability Tests

Hand-Tool Dexterity Test (Bennett, 1981): Using a wooden frame, wrenches, and screwdrivers, the test-taker takes apart 12 bolts in a prescribed sequence and reassembles them in another position. This speed test measures manipulative skills important in factory jobs and in jobs servicing mechanical equipment and automobiles.

O'Connor Finger Dexterity Test (O'Connor, 1977): A timed performance test measuring fine motor dexterity needed for fine assembly work and other jobs requiring manipulation of small objects. Test-taker is given a board with symmetrical rows of holes and a cup of pins. The task is to place three pins in each hole as quickly as possible.

Job Skills and Knowledge Tests

Minnesota Clerical Assessment Battery or MCAB (Vale & Prestwood, 1987): A self-administered battery of six subtests measuring the skills and knowledge necessary for clerical and secretarial work. Testing is completely computer administered. Included are tests of typing, proofreading, filing, business vocabulary, business math, and clerical knowledge.

Purdue Blueprint Reading Test (Owen & Arnold, 1942): A multiple-choice test assessing the ability to read standard blueprints.

Various Tests of Software Skills. Includes knowledge-based and performance-based tests of basic computer operations, word processing, and spreadsheet use.

Personality Tests

California Psychological Inventory or CPI (Gough, 1987): A 480-item, pencil-and-paper inventory of 20 personality dimensions. Has been used in selecting managers, sales personnel, and leadership positions.

Hogan Personnel Selection Series (Hogan, 1985): These pencil-and-paper tests assess personality dimensions of applicants and compare their profiles to patterns of successful job incumbents in clerical, sales, and managerial positions. Consists of four inventories: the prospective employee potential inventory, the clerical potential inventory, the sales potential inventory, and the managerial potential inventory.

Revised NEO Personality Inventory or NEO-PI-R (Costa & McCrae, 1992): A very popular personality inventory used in employee screening and selection. This inventory measures the five "core" personality constructs of Neuroticism (N), Extraversion (E), Openness (O), Agreeableness (A), and Conscientiousness (C).

Bar-On Emotional Quotient Inventory (EQ-I; Bar-On, 1997) and the Mayer–Salovey–Caruso Emotional Intelligence Test (MSCEIT) (Mayer, 2002): Two measures of emotional intelligence.

Comprehensive biodata instruments can give a highly detailed description and classification of an applicant's behavioral history—a very good predictor of future behavior (sample biodata items are given in Figure 4.5). One potential problem in the use of biodata instruments concerns the personal nature of many of the questions and the possibility of unintentional discrimination against minority groups because of items regarding age, financial circumstances, and the like. Thus, biodata instruments should only be developed and administered by professionals trained in test use and validation. It has been suggested that, given the success of biodata in employee selection, it is surprising that biodata instruments are not more widely used.

Cognitive Ability Tests

Tests of cognitive ability range from tests of general intellectual ability to tests of specific cognitive skills. Group-administered pencil-and-paper tests of general intelligence have been used in employee screening for some time (Georgiou et al., 2019).

The following is an example of an interview question designed to elicit critical incidents for a particular job. This question focuses on an incident where a subordinate was behaving in a "helpful" way. Another question might try to elicit when workers are not being helpful; in other words, when they may be hurting group productivity.

"Think of the last time you saw one of your subordinates do something that was very helpful to your group in meeting their production schedule." (Pause until the respondent has such an incident in mind.) "Did the subordinate's action result in an increase in production of as much as one percent for that day?—or some similar period?" (If the answer is "no", say) "I wonder if you could think of the last time that someone did something that did have this much of an effect in increasing production." (When respondent indicates he/she has such a situation in mind, say) "What were the general circumstances leading up to this incident?"

"Tell me exactly what this person did that was so helpful at that time."
"Why was this so helpful in getting your group's job done?"
"When did this incident happen?"
"What was this person's job?"
"How long has the person been on this job?"

Another example of a question designed to elicit critical incidents may be as simple and general as, "Think of the best (worst) subordinate you have known. Tell me about a time that shows why this person was the best (worst)."

Figure 4.5 Sample biodata items.

Two such widely used older instruments are the Otis Self-Administering Test of Mental Ability (Otis, 1929) and the Wonderlic Personnel Test (now called the Wonderlic Cognitive Ability Test; Wonderlic, 1983). Both are fairly short and assess basic verbal and numerical abilities. Designed to measure the ability to learn simple jobs, to follow instructions, and to solve work-related problems and difficulties, these tests are used to screen applicants for positions as office clerks, assembly workers, machine operators, and certain frontline supervisors.

One criticism of using general intelligence tests for employee selection is that they measure cognitive abilities that are too general to be effective predictors of specific job-related cognitive skills. However, research indicates that such general tests are reasonably good predictors of job performance (Bertua et al., 2005). In fact, it has been argued that general intelligence is the most consistent predictor of performance across all types and categories of jobs. One meta-analysis of workers in the United Kingdom found that tests of cognitive abilities predicted both job performance and the success of employee training efforts (Bertua et al., 2005). However, there is concern that cognitive ability tests can also have an adverse impact on women, people of color (Rupp et al., 2020), and older applicants (Fisher et al., 2017).

Mechanical, Motor, and Sensory Ability Tests

Standardized tests have also been developed to measure abilities in identifying, recognizing, and applying mechanical principles. These tests are particularly effective in screening applicants for positions that require operating or repairing machinery, for construction jobs, and for certain engineering positions. The Bennett Mechanical Comprehension Test (BMCT; Bennett, 2008) is one such commonly used instrument. The BMCT consists of 68 items, each of which requires the application of a physical law or a mechanical operation. One study using the BMCT and several other instruments determined that the BMCT was the best single predictor of job performance for a group of employees manufacturing electromechanical components (Muchinsky, 1993). A UK military study also found that a mechanical comprehension test predicted recruits' abilities to handle weapons (Munnoch & Bridger, 2008).

A number of tests measure specific motor skills or sensory abilities. Tests such as the Crawford Small Parts Dexterity Test (Crawford, 1981) and the Purdue Pegboard (Tiffin, 1968) are timed performance instruments (speed tests) that require the manipulation of small parts to measure the fine motor dexterity in hands and fingers required in jobs such as assembling computer components and soldering electrical equipment. For example, the Crawford test uses boards with small holes into which tiny pins must be placed using a pair of tweezers. The second part of the test requires screwing small screws into threaded holes with a screwdriver. Sensory ability tests include tests of hearing, visual acuity, and perceptual discrimination. The most common test of visual acuity is the Snellen Eye Chart, which consists of rows of letters that become increasingly smaller. Various electronic instruments are used to measure hearing acuity. No doubt you have taken one or more of these in school or in a doctor's office. In employment settings, they are used in basic screening for positions such as inspectors or bus drivers who require fine audio or visual discrimination.

Job Skills and Knowledge Tests

Various standardized tests also assess specific job skills or domains of job knowledge. Examples of job skill tests for clerical workers would be a standardized typing test or tests of other specific clerical skills such as proofreading, alphabetical filing, or correction of spelling or grammatical errors, as well as the use of software. For example, the Judd Tests (Simmons, 1993) are a series of tests designed to assess competency in several areas of computer competence, including word processing, spreadsheet programs, and database management.

A special sort of job skill test involves the use of **work sample tests**, which measure applicants' abilities to perform brief examples of some of the critical tasks that the job requires (Thornton III & Kedharnath, 2013). The sample tasks are constructed as tests, administered under standard testing conditions, and scored on some predetermined scale. Their obvious advantage is that they are clearly job-related. A drawback is that work samples are usually rather expensive to develop and take a great deal of time to administer.

Work Sample Tests
used in job skill tests to measure applicants' abilities to perform brief examples of important job tasks

One example of a work sample test was developed for applicants for the job of concession stand attendant at a city park's snack bar. The test required applicants to use the cash register, make change, fill out a report, page someone over a loudspeaker, and react to an "irate customer" who was arguing about receiving the wrong change. Research suggests that work sample tests can be a very good predictor of job performance (Roth et al., 2005). In addition to being an effective screening device, this work sample served as a realistic job preview, providing applicants with a good idea of what the job was all about.

Job knowledge tests are instruments that assess specific types of knowledge required to perform certain jobs. For example, a job knowledge test for nurses or paramedics might contain questions asking about appropriate emergency medical procedures. A job knowledge test for a financial examiner might include questions about regulations governing financial transactions and securities regulations. Research has demonstrated good predictive validity for job knowledge tests (Ones & Viswesvaran, 2007).

Personality Tests
instruments that measure psychological characteristics of individuals

Personality tests are designed to measure certain psychological characteristics of workers. A wide variety of these tests are used in employee screening and selection in an attempt to match the personality characteristics of job applicants with those of workers who have performed the job successfully in the past. Although personality tests were met with skepticism in the past, they are widely accepted today (Hough & Oswald, 2005), given their predictive validity in selection contexts (Ones, 2005). Like many other types of tests, personality tests are delivered online, and online testing yields quite similar outcomes as in-person testing (Meade et al., 2007), offering an increase in flexibility and options for administering the tests (see the "On the Cutting Edge" box on page 120).

General personality inventories, such as the Minnesota Multiphasic Personality Inventory (MMPI; Hathaway & McKinley, 1970), are used to screen out applicants who possess some psychopathology that might hinder the performance of sensitive jobs, such as police officer, airline pilot, or nuclear power plant operator. However, most of the time, personality tests are used to assess the "normal" characteristics that are deemed to be important for the performance of certain jobs. For example, personality dimensions such as achievement motivation or persistence might be used to screen applicants for positions in sales jobs, and tests for traits of responsibility and service orientation may be administered to applicants for bank teller positions. Other commonly used personality tests include the 16 Personality Factor Questionnaire (Cattell et al., 1970), which measures normal personality, and the California Psychological Inventory (Gough, 1984), which assesses managerial potential.

The most widely used personality tests are the Big Five model and the newer variation of the Big Five called the HEXACO model (see Feher & Vernon, 2021, for a review). The Big Five assesses emotional stability (neuroticism), extraversion, agreeableness, conscientiousness, and openness to experience; HEXACO adds honesty-humility, resulting in: honesty-humility, emotionality, extraversion, agreeableness, conscientiousness, and openness to experience (He et al., 2019). Of these facets, meta-analytic research shows that conscientiousness is the strongest predictor of job performance, followed by emotional stability (neuroticism). According to the meta-analysis (He, Donnellan & Mendoza, 2019), extraversion has a weak relationship to job performance overall, although some facets of extraversion (such as assertiveness and positive emotions) predicted job performance to a greater extent than others (such as gregariousness and excitement-seeking).

Although widely used, there is some concern that personality tests could violate the Americans with Disabilities Act by adversely affecting individuals with psychological or personality disorders (Melson-Silimon et al., 2019). Even the most widely used personality measure, the Big Five, which assesses conscientiousness, extraversion, agreeableness, openness to experience, and emotional stability (neuroticism), has been shown to correlate with personality disorders (Melson-Silimon et al., 2019). This does not mean that personality tests cannot be used in selection contexts, as it is possible to develop job-related personality tests that have no adverse impact (Gonzalez et al., 2019). Another concern relates to the Big Five factor of extraversion, because the assertiveness factor in this personality dimension can be perceived negatively for women because of gender stereotypes, whereas it is perceived positively for men (Kim et al., 2020).

A relatively new construct that has begun to capture the attention of I/O psychologists interested in the selection of employees is that of **emotional intelligence**. Emotional intelligence involves knowledge, understanding, and regulation of emotions; ability to communicate emotionally; and using emotions to facilitate thinking (Mayer et al., 2016). As such, emotional intelligence is partly personality, partly an ability, and partly a form of intelligence, and so it does not fit neatly into any of our categories of tests. However, it is easy to see how this interesting construct might be related to performance as a supervisor or workplace leader who needs to inspire followers and be aware of their feelings, and how the ability to regulate emotions in a positive way might be beneficial for any worker, particularly when facing interpersonal problems or conflicts with other employees or when under stress. Emotional intelligence is growing in popularity as a tool for employee selection (Herpertz et al., 2016; Ryan & Ployhart, 2014) because of its benefits to performance, but, importantly, research shows that the skills associated with emotional intelligence can also be trained (Mattingly & Kraiger, 2019).

Emotional Intelligence
ability to understand, regulate, and communicate emotions and use them to inform thinking

Honesty and Integrity Tests

In the past, **polygraphs**, or lie detectors—instruments designed to measure physiological reactions presumably associated with lying such as respiration, blood pressure, or perspiration—were used in employee selection. Most often, polygraphs were used to screen out "dishonest" applicants for positions in which they would have to handle cash or expensive merchandise, although they were also used by a wide number of organizations to screen and select employees for almost any position. Research, much

Polygraphs
instruments that measure physiological reactions presumed to accompany deception; also known as lie detectors

of it conducted by industrial/organizational psychologists, called into question the validity of polygraphs. A major problem concerned the rate of "false-positive" errors, or innocent persons who are incorrectly scored as lying. Because of this questionable validity and the potential harm that invalid results could cause innocent people, the federal government passed legislation in 1988 that severely restricted the use of polygraphs in general employment screening. However, polygraphs are still allowed for the testing of employees about specific incidents, such as thefts, and for screening applicants for public health and safety jobs and for sensitive government or police positions (Linos & Riesch, 2020).

Integrity Tests
measures of honest or dishonest attitudes and/or behaviors

Since the establishment of restrictions on the use of polygraphs, many employers have turned to using paper-and-pencil measures of honesty, referred to as **integrity tests**. Typically, these tests ask about past honest/dishonest behavior or about attitudes condoning dishonest behavior. Typical questions might ask, "What is the total value of cash and merchandise you have taken from your employer in the past year?" or "An employer who pays people poorly has it coming when employees steal. Do you agree or disagree with this statement?" Like polygraphs, these tests also raise the important issue of "false positives," or honest persons who are judged to be dishonest by the instruments. On the other hand, meta-analyses of validity studies of integrity tests indicate that integrity tests (and the personality-based correlate of

Figure 4.6 Much employment testing today is computer administered.

Source: Photograph by Christina Wocintechchat, found on Unsplash (https://unsplash.com/photos/y3YyxZA7bjs).

honesty-humility) predict employee "counterproductive behaviors," such as chronic tardiness, taking extended work breaks, and "goldbricking" (ignoring or passing off assigned work tasks), organizational citizenship (or helping) behaviors, and task performance (Lee, Berry & Gonzalez-Mule, 2019).

Other Employee Screening Tests

In addition to the categories of employee tests we have discussed, there are other types of tests that do not fit neatly into any of the categories. For example, in the U.S., many employers concerned about both safety issues and poor work performance screen applicants for drug use, usually through analysis of urine, hair, or saliva samples. Unfortunately, current laboratory tests are not 100% accurate, raising additional concerns about fairness. Unlike the polygraph, however, today there are few restrictions on drug testing in work settings. The most controversial issue surrounding drug testing relates to marijuana, which has been made legal in many states for medical and recreational use (Hazle et al., 2020). Some states have limited pre-employment screening of cannabis use, others only allow the use of prescribed medical marijuana to avoid violating the Americans with Disabilities Act, and others continue to allow employers to deny work to those who test positive for cannabis use (Hazle et al., 2020). The issue is particularly complex because use of cannabis before work is related to declines in workplace performance, whereas use of cannabis after work hours was found to be unrelated to job performance (Bernerth & Walker, 2020).

The Effectiveness of Employee Screening Tests

The effectiveness of using standardized tests for screening potential employees remains a controversial issue. Critics of testing cite the low validity coefficients (approximately 0.20) of certain employment tests. (As the model at the beginning of Chapter 4 illustrates, the validity coefficient is the correlation coefficient between the predictor, or the test score, and the criterion, usually a measure of subsequent job performance.) However, supporters believe that a comparison of all screening methods—tests, biographical information, and hiring interviews—across the full spectrum of jobs reveals that employment tests are the best predictors of job performance (Ployhart et al., 2017). Obviously, the ability of a test to predict performance in a specific job depends on how well it can capture and measure the particular skills, knowledge, or abilities required. For example, tests of word processing and other clerical skills are good predictors of success in clerical positions because they do a good job of assessing the skills and knowledge needed to be a successful clerical assistant.

ON THE *CUTTING* EDGE

The Future of Employment Testing: "Smart" Tests, Performance-Based Simulations, and Video Interviews

Most companies today use computer-based testing (CBT) or web-based programs to administer pencil-and-paper employment tests (Kantrowitz et al., 2011; Ryan & Derous, 2019; Tippins, 2015). In CBT, applicants complete the test instruments on a PC or online. Computers can then immediately score the tests, record the results in databanks, and provide the test-taker with feedback if appropriate. A more sophisticated development is the use of computer-adaptive testing (CAT). Despite its prevalent usage in educational and governmental institutions, organizations have only recently started to adopt CAT for pre-employment testing purposes (Tippins, 2015). In computer-adaptive tests (often referred to as "smart" tests), the computer program "adjusts" the difficulty of test items to the level of the person being tested. For example, if a test-taker misses several questions, the computer will adjust the level of test difficulty by asking easier questions. If the test-taker is getting several answers correct, the computer will present more difficult questions. Although CAT is typically only used with knowledge-based tests where there are right and wrong answers, it has also been applied to personality tests. Computer-adaptive testing is usually quicker and more efficient than traditional testing because, by adjusting the test's difficulty to fit the test-taker, the computer can get an accurate assessment using fewer questions. You may soon encounter a CAT program because many of the standardized graduate school entrance exams are now available in CAT form.

Traditional employment tests, whether they be on paper or computer-administered, are limited by the fact that they present only written information. A novel approach to testing makes use of either computer-based or interactive video-computer technology (Ryan & Derous, 2019). In interactive video testing, an applicant views a videotaped example of a simulated work setting. The video scene usually presents a realistic, work-related problem situation. The applicant is then asked to respond with an appropriate solution. In effect, through video-computer technology, the applicant is "transported" into the work situation and required to "perform" work-related tasks and make work-related decisions. In addition to testing an applicant's work-related knowledge and decision making, such interactive testing provides applicants with a realistic preview of the job. The major drawback to interactive computer-video testing is the cost of development of such testing programs. Computerized testing programs can also use gamification to make the experience more engaging for test-takers (Georgiou et al., 2019).

Amidst the COVID-19 pandemic in 2020–2021, most hiring interviews were also done virtually, creating a great deal of interest in the design and impact of video-based interviews, including asynchronous video interviews (Lukacik et al., 2020). Although video interviewing became a necessary evil because of the virus, using video-based interviewing also allows for improvements to selection practices such as ensuring that the same questions are asked of all candidates and the potential for all decision makers to see the exact same information when making their hiring decisions. There is a great deal of potential for video- and technology-based selection practices, although more research is needed

ON THE *CUTTING* EDGE *(continued)*

on applicant reactions and adverse impact of such tests (McCarthy et al., 2017). To meet this need, one study designed an automated video interview to score personality through artificial intelligence (Hickman et al., 2021). The computer program was able to identify some aspects of personality (such as emotional stability) better than others and was more effective when trained on interviewer judgments of personality than when trained on interviewee's self-reported personality, raising some question as to the reliability and validity of these instruments that are increasingly common in use.

Another benefit of computer-based testing is that it can be converted into a more enjoyable experience for the test-taker through gamification. Employment tests can be intimidating, with images of school-based testing and pressures to perform well. A new advancement

in the area of employment testing involves using game-based technology to turn tests of certain skills and abilities into games. This is particularly effective with younger applicants who grew up with online games. One example of a "gamified" test assesses an applicant's interpersonal skills (Georgiou et al., 2019). The applicant's avatar moves through a series of situations with other avatars (the applicant's "crew"). In the game, the applicant has to interact with the others, make decisions, and deal with conflict. The "correct" actions/responses have been predetermined and lead to an assessment of the applicant's ability to interact with others—their "soft skills." Gamification is also being used as a technology for training employees because it leads to greater motivation and involvement in the material.

The most effective use of screening tests occurs when a number of instruments are used in combination to predict effective job performance. Because most jobs are complex, involving a wide range of tasks, it is unlikely that successful performance is due to just one particular type of knowledge or skill. Therefore, any single test will only be able to predict one aspect of a total job. Employment screening tests are usually grouped together into a **test battery**. Scores on the various tests in the battery are used in combination to help select the best possible candidates for the job. Importantly, using a combination of tests, such as a personality test and an ability test, are a better predictor of job performance than either test used alone (Nesnidol & Highhouse, 2020).

All in all, utility analyses of standardized employee testing programs indicate that such tests are usually cost-effective. Many years ago, Hunter and Schmidt (1982) went so far as to estimate that the U.S. gross national product would be increased by tens of billions of dollars per year if improved employee screening and selection procedures, including screening tests, were routinely implemented. Utility analyses allow the employer to determine the financial gains of a testing program and then compare them with the costs of developing and implementing the program.

Test Battery
a combination of employment tests used to increase the ability to predict future job performance

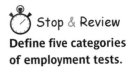 Stop & Review
Define five categories of employment tests.

Another important issue in testing is the importance of ethics in the administration and use of employment testing, including the protection of the privacy of persons being tested (Bauer, Truxillo et al., 2020). I/O psychologists are very concerned about ethical issues in testing. In fact, the Society for Industrial and Organizational Psychology (SIOP) published a fifth edition of its *Principles for the Validation and Use of Personnel Selection Procedures* (2018). This publication outlines important ethical concerns for employment testing.

Faking
purposely distorting one's responses to a test to try to "beat" the test

A final issue concerning testing is the issue of **faking**. Faking is trying to "beat" the test by distorting responses to the test in an effort to present oneself in a positive, socially desirable way. Faking is a particular concern for personality and integrity tests (Geiger et al., 2018; Lopez et al., 2019). Laypersons tend to believe that employment tests are easily faked, but this is not the case. First, some tests have subscales designed to determine if a test-taker is trying to fake the test. Second, it is often difficult for the test-taker to determine exactly which responses are the correct (desired) responses. Finally, there is evidence that personality and integrity tests are quite robust, still validly measuring their intended constructs even when test-takers are trying to fake (Ones & Viswesvaran, 1998).

Final Steps in the Selection Decision

Once the large pool of applicants has been trimmed to the most qualified few, employers usually meet with job finalists for some type of in-person assessment. This can take the form of a very intensive assessment center. More common is the traditional job interview.

Assessment Centers

Assessment Center
a detailed, structured evaluation of job applicants using a variety of instruments and techniques

One of the most detailed forms of employment screening takes place in an **assessment center**, which offers a detailed, structured evaluation of applicants on a wide range of job-related knowledge, skills, and abilities (Ingold et al., 2018). Specific managerial skills and characteristics an assessment center attempts to measure include oral and written communication skills; behavioral flexibility; creativity; tolerance of uncertainty; and skills in organization, planning, and decision making. Because a variety of instruments are used to assess participants, the assessment center often makes use of large test batteries. As we saw in Chapter 1, the assessment center approach was developed during World War II by the U.S. Office of Strategic Services (the forerunner of the CIA) for the selection of spies. Today, it is used primarily to select managers, but it is also being used extensively for managerial development purposes—to provide feedback to managers concerning their job performance-related strengths and weaknesses (Parr et al., 2016).

We will discuss this use of assessment centers again in the chapter on employee training (Chapter 6). In assessment centers, applicants are evaluated on a number of job-related variables using a variety of techniques, such as personality and ability tests, that are considered to be valid predictors of managerial success. Applicants also take part in a number of **situational exercises**, which are attempts to approximate certain aspects of the managerial job. These exercises are related to work samples, except that they are approximations rather than actual examples of work tasks (Buckett et al., 2020; Keeler et al., 2019).

Sometimes, these situational exercises are used independently in employment screening as a situational test. Situational tests can be written, live tests or be presented via video (Bardach et al., 2020). One popular situational exercise is the in-basket (or "inbox") test (Frederiksen, 1962), which requires the applicant to deal with a stack of memos, letters, and other materials that have supposedly collected in the "in-basket" of a manager (see Figure 4.7). The applicant is given some background information

Situational Exercise
assessment tools that require the performance of tasks that approximate actual work tasks

---

Instructions:

You are now Mr. C. D. Evans, Plant Superintendent of the East District in Division A of the Green Area of the Eastern Telephone Company. You have just arrived in your new job. Mr. I. W. Prior, your predecessor, died suddenly of a heart attack last Wednesday, March 28. You were notified Friday at 4 p.m. of your new appointment, but you could not get here until today, Sunday, April 1.

Today is your first day on your new job, and here is what your secretary has left for you. Since it is Sunday, no one else is around and you cannot reach anyone on the telephone. You must leave in exactly three hours to catch a plane for an important meeting connected with your previous assignment . . . In the large envelope in front of you, you will find three packets. One contains an organization chart, a map of the district and the division, a copy of the management guide, and a copy of the union contract. The second packet contains the materials your secretary has left on your desk for your attention. These materials include letters, reports, memoranda, etc. Your secretary has attached materials from the files to some of the documents. The third packet contains . . . office forms, memo pads, pencils, and paper. You can use these materials to write letters, memos, notes to yourself, etc. (Bray, Campbell, & Grant, 1974, pp. 24–25).

The second packet on the hypothetical desk contained 24 problems that the participants had to address.

Figure 4.7 Example of an Assessment Center In-basket Exercise.

about the job and then must actually take care of the work in the in-basket by answering correspondence, preparing agendas for meetings, making decisions, and the like. A group of observers considers how each applicant deals with the various tasks and assigns a performance score.

Another situational exercise is the leaderless group discussion (Bass, 1954). Here, applicants are put together in a small group to discuss some work-related topic. The goal is to see how each applicant handles the situation and who emerges as a discussion leader. Other assessment center exercises might require the assessee to make a presentation, role-play an encounter with a supervisee, or engage in a team exercise with other assessees (Oostrom et al., 2019). Trained observers rate each applicant's performance on each exercise. Because evaluation of assessment center exercises is made by human observers/assessors, to avoid systematic biases and to ensure that assessors are in agreement on ratings of assessees (in other words, that there is reliability in the ratings), training of assessors is critical (Schleicher et al., 2002), but most data suggest that assessment center ratings demonstrate high levels of reliability across raters (Putka & Hoffman, 2013).

The result of testing at the assessment center is a detailed profile of each applicant, as well as some index of how a particular applicant rated in comparison with others. Research has indicated that assessment centers are relatively good predictors of managerial success (Parr et al., 2016). Of course, the major drawback is the huge investment of time and resources they require, which is the major reason that assessment centers are usually only used by larger organizations and for the selection of candidates for higher-level management positions. However, recent innovations using videotape and computerized assessment of participants has led to a recent renewal of interest in assessment centers, both in managerial selection and in other forms of evaluation (see box on "Applying I/O Psychology").

APPLYING I/O PSYCHOLOGY

The Use of Assessment Center Methodology for Assessing Employability of College Graduates

Since the early 1990s, the use of assessment centers and assessment center methods has grown. There has been an increase in the use of assessment centers in managerial selection, and assessment centers are also being used as a means of training and "brushing up" managers' skills. In addition, assessment center methods are being expanded to facilitate screening and orientation of entry-level employees. In colleges and universities, assessment center methodologies are being used to evaluate new students or in outcome evaluation—measuring the managerial skills and potential "employability" of students as they graduate.

For instance, in one university's master's-level program in industrial/organizational psychology, first-year

APPLYING I/O PSYCHOLOGY

(Continued)

master's students are put through an assessment center evaluation, with second-year master's students serving as evaluators (Kottke & Shultz, 1997). This not only allows for an assessment of student skills, but also provides students with direct, hands-on experience with assessment. In another project, all graduates of a state university's business school underwent a "mini" assessment center, including completing a computerized in-basket test that assessed both managerial skills and skills in operating computer software, participation in a leaderless group discussion, mock hiring interview, and formal presentation (Riggio et al., 2003). The goal was to evaluate the "managerial potential" of business school graduates and to track them during their early careers as a way of determining if the knowledge and skills measured in the assessment center were indeed predictive of future career success. A follow-up study did indeed demonstrate that college assessment center ratings of leadership potential correlated with later ratings of leadership made by the former college students' work supervisors (Schleicher et al., 2002). In another student assessment center, assessment center ratings were related to early career progress of the alumni (Waldman & Korbar, 2004).

Why the surge of interest in assessment centers? There are several reasons. First, the assessment center methodology makes sense. It offers a detailed, multimodal assessment of a wide range of knowledge, skills, abilities, and psychological characteristics. This is the test battery approach we discussed earlier. Second, much of the measurement in assessment centers is "performance-based," and there is a trend in assessment away from pencil-and-paper assessment and toward more behavior- or performance-based assessment. Third, assessment centers are easier to conduct today. With computer and video technology, it is easy to conduct an assessment center and store the participants' performance data for later, more convenient evaluation (Jackson et al., 2016). Finally, evidence indicates that assessment centers serve a dual purpose by assessing participants and helping them to develop managerial skills by undergoing the assessment center exercises (Herd et al., 2018).

Hiring Interviews

To obtain almost any job in the U.S., an applicant must go through at least one hiring interview, which is the most widely used employee screening and selection device. Despite its widespread use, if not conducted properly, the hiring interview can be a poor predictor of future job performance. I/O psychologists have contributed greatly to our understanding of the effectiveness of interviews as a hiring tool. Care must be taken to ensure the reliability and validity of judgments of applicants made in hiring interviews (see "Up Close" box). Part of the problem with the validity of interviews is that many interviews are conducted haphazardly, with little structure to them (Kausel et al., 2016).

You may have experienced one of these poor interviews that seemed to be nothing more than a casual conversation, or you may have been involved in a job interview in which the interviewer did nearly all of the talking. Although you might have learned a lot about the company, the interviewer learned little about your experience and qualifications. In these cases, it is obvious that little concern has been given to the fact that, just like a psychological test, the hiring interview is actually a measurement tool, and employment decisions derived from interviews should be held to the same standards of reliability, validity, and predictability as tests.

A number of variations on the traditional interview format have been developed to try to improve the effectiveness of interviews as a selection tool, including situation and behavior descriptive interviews (Culbertson et al., 2017). In situational interviews, applicants are asked to imagine how they would deal with specific job-related, hypothetical situations. In contrast, job descriptive interviews (also called structured behavioral interviews) ask interviewees to draw on past job incidents and behaviors to deal with hypothetical future work situations. It is interesting to note that, in a review of court cases involving allegations of discrimination in hiring, judges also valued good measurement properties in hiring interviews—ruling more favorably for the organization if the interviews were objective, job-related, structured, and based on multiple interviewers' evaluations (Williamson et al., 1997).

There has been increased use of videoconference technology to conduct hiring interviews. This can be done either via a live videoconference or via a computer–video interface. I/O psychologists have only begun studying videoconference interviews. One interesting finding is that interviewers tend to make more favorable evaluations of videoconference applicants than in face-to-face interviews, likely because there are some nonverbal cues, particularly cues that reveal anxiety and discomfort, absent in videoconference interviews (Blacksmith et al., 2016; Lukacik et al., 2020). During the COVID-19 pandemic, most businesses were working remotely and needed to utilize technology-based interviews in order to hire new employees, including both synchronous and asynchronous video interviews (Lukacik et al., 2020).

When used correctly as part of an employee screening and selection program, the hiring interview should have three major objectives. First, the interview should be used to help fill in gaps in the information obtained from the applicant's resume and application form and from employment tests and to measure the kinds of factors that are only available in a face-to-face encounter, such as poise and oral communication skills. Second, the hiring interview should provide applicants with realistic job previews, which help them decide whether they really want the job and offer an initial orientation to the organization (Rynes, 1988).

Finally, because the hiring interview is one way that an organization interacts directly with a portion of the general public, it can serve an important recruitment tool for the company (Wilhelmy et al., 2016).

There are serious concerns about the accuracy of judgments made from hiring interviews, however, because, unlike screening tests or application forms, which ask for specific, quantifiable information, hiring interviews are typically more free-wheeling affairs (Levashina et al., 2014). Interviewers may ask completely different questions of different applicants, which makes it very difficult to compare responses.

⏱ Stop & Review

Define and describe an assessment center.

Figure 4.8 The hiring interview should maintain high standards of measurement, the same as other screening methods.

Source: Photograph by Tim Gouw, found on Unsplash (https://unsplash.com/photos/bwki71ap-y8).

Interviews that lack structure yield very little information about the applicant and probably no valid assessment of the person's qualifications.

The reliability of interviewer judgments is also problematic. Different interviewers may arrive at completely different evaluations of the same applicant, even when evaluating the same interview. Also, because of nervousness, fatigue, or some other reason, the same applicant might not perform as well in one interview as in another, which further contributes to low reliability.

Perhaps the greatest source of problems affecting hiring interview validity is interviewer biases. Interviewers may allow factors such as an applicant's gender (Koch et al., 2015), race (Pogrebtsova et al., 2020), physical disability (Brecher et al., 2006), physical attractiveness (Johnson et al., 2014), appearance (Madera & Hebl, 2012), weight (Pingitore et al., 1994), pregnancy (Bragger et al., 2002), class (Chua & Mazmanian, 2020), or age (Gioaba & Krings, 2017) to influence them.

There may also be a tendency for an interviewer to make a **snap judgment**, arriving at an overall evaluation of the applicant in the first few moments of the interview (Luan et al., 2019). The interviewer may then spend the remainder of the time trying to confirm that first impression, selectively attending to only the information that is consistent with the initial evaluation. Structured interviews, where a series of questions are asked of all applicants, may help lessen snap judgments (Frieder et al., 2016). Another potential source of bias is the *contrast effect*, which can occur after the interview of a particularly good or bad applicant. All subsequent applicants may then be evaluated either very negatively or very positively in contrast to this person.

Snap Judgment
arriving at a premature, early overall evaluation of an applicant in a hiring interview

In general, the hiring interview may fail to predict job success accurately because of a mismatch between the selection instrument and the information it obtains and the requirements of most jobs (Hamdani et al., 2014). Receiving a positive evaluation in an interview is related to applicants' abilities to present themselves in a positive manner and to carry on a one-on-one conversation. In other words, evaluations of interviewees may be strongly affected by their level of communication or social skills. Therefore, for some jobs, such as those that involve primarily technical skills, performance in the interview is in no way related to performance on the job, because the types of skills required to do well in the interview are not the same as those required in the job. Researchers have also found a relationship between general cognitive ability and interview performance, suggesting that more intellectually gifted persons receive more positive interview evaluations (Huffcutt et al., 1996). Despite this relationship, research suggests that interview performance from a well-conducted, structured interview can predict job performance above and beyond the effects of cognitive ability (Cortina et al., 2000).

Stop & Review

Name and define four potential biases in hiring interviews.

UP **CLOSE** **How to Conduct More Effective Hiring Interviews**

A great deal of research indicates that typical hiring interviews, although widely used, are not always effective predictors of job performance. There are, however, ways to improve their reliability and validity, some of which are outlined here.

Use Structured Interviews, Job-Related Interview Questions

Structured interviewing, in which the same basic questions are asked of all applicants, is nearly always more effective than unstructured interviewing because it allows for comparisons among applicants (Dipboye, 1994). The use of structured questions also helps prevent the interview from wandering off course and assists in keeping interview lengths consistent. Just like any

other selection method, interview questions should be developed from a detailed job analysis to ensure that they are job-related. At least one study has shown that gender bias, often prevalent in job interviews, did not occur when the interview was structured (Pogrebtsova et al., 2020).

Provide for Some Rating or Scoring of Applicant Responses

To interpret the applicant responses objectively, it is important to develop some scoring system (Graves & Karren, 1996). Experts could determine beforehand what would characterize good and poor answers. Another approach is to develop a scale for rating the quality of the responses. It may also be beneficial to make some

UP CLOSE *(continued)*

record of responses to review later and to substantiate employment decisions, rather than relying on memory.

Use Trained Interviewers

Interviewer training improves the quality of hiring interview decisions (Campion et al., 1998) and can be used to reduce bias (Derous et al., 2016). Interviewers can be instructed in proper procedures and techniques and trained to try to avoid systematic biases (Howard & Dailey, 1979). Training is also important because of the public relations function of hiring interviews (e.g., the interviewer is representing the organization to a segment of the public; Stevens, 1998).

Consider Using Panel or Multiple Interviews

Because of personal idiosyncrasies, any one interviewer's judgment of an applicant may be inaccurate. One way to increase interview reliability is to have a group of evaluators assembled in a panel (Roth & Campion, 1992). Although panel interviews may improve reliability, they may still have validity problems if all interviewers are incorrect in their interpretations or share some biases or stereotypes. Also, the use of panel interviews is costly. Using multiple (separate) interviews is another way to increase the reliability of judgments made in hiring interviews (Conway et al., 1995).

Making Employee Selection Decisions

You have data from all of your finalists: their scores on the application blank, personality, intelligence, physical ability test, and an integrity test. You just completed your job review and you think you have the job in the bag because you nailed the interview. But whether you are to be hired or not might depend on how the organization scores job applicants. There are two types of decision errors in employee selection. When we erroneously accept applicants who would have been unsuccessful on the job, we are making **false-positive errors** (see Figure 4.9). On the other hand, when we erroneously reject applicants who would have been successful in the job, we are making **false-negative errors**. Although both errors are problematic to the organization, it is more difficult to identify false-negative errors than false-positive errors. We cannot eliminate these errors entirely, but we can minimize them by using more objective decision strategies.

All too often, employee selection decisions are made subjectively, using what is often referred to as the clinical approach. In this approach, a decision maker simply combines the sources of information in whatever fashion seems appropriate to obtain some general impression about applicants. Based on experience and beliefs about which types of information are more or less important, a decision is made. Although some good selection decisions may be made by experienced decision makers, subjective, clinical decisions are error prone and often inaccurate (Meehl, 1954).

False-Positive Errors erroneously accepting applicants who would have been unsuccessful

False-Negative Errors erroneously rejecting applicants who would have been successful

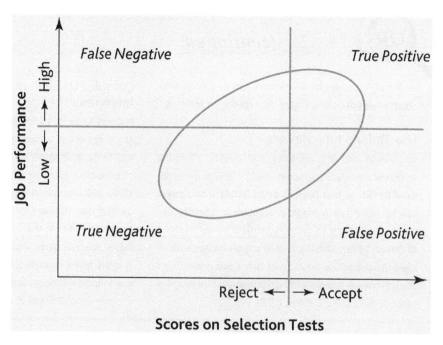

Figure 4.9 Accuracy of prediction in employee screening.

Source: Figure in Millsap and Kwok (2004)

The alternative is to use a statistical decision-making model, which combines information for the selection of applicants in an objective, predetermined fashion. Each piece of information about job applicants is given some optimal weight that indicates its strength in predicting future job performance. It makes sense that an objective decision-making model will be superior to clinical decisions because human beings, in most cases, are incapable of accurately processing all the information gathered from a number of job applicants. Statistical models are able to process all of this information without human limitations.

Multiple Regression Model
an employee selection method that combines separate predictors of job success in a statistical procedure

One statistical approach to personnel decision making is the **multiple regression model**, an extension of the correlation coefficient (see the Appendix in Chapter 2). As you recall, the correlation coefficient examines the strength of a relationship between a single predictor, such as a test score, and a criterion, such as a measure of job performance. However, rather than having only one predictor of job performance, as in the correlation coefficient or bivariate regression model, multiple regression analysis uses several predictors. Typically, this approach combines the various predictors in an additive, linear fashion. In employee selection, this means that the ability of all the predictors to predict job performance can be added together, and that there is a linear relationship between the predictors and the criterion: higher scores on the predictors will lead to higher scores on the criterion. Although the statistical assumptions and calculations on which the multiple regression model is based are beyond the scope of this text, the result is an equation that uses the various types of screening information in combination.

The multiple regression model is a compensatory type of model, which means that high scores on one predictor can compensate for low scores on another. This is both a strength and a weakness of the regression approach. For example, an applicant's lack of previous job-related experience can be compensated for by test scores that show great potential for mastering the job. However, in other situations, this may be problematic. Take, for example, the screening of applicants for a job as an inspector of microcircuitry, a position that requires the visual inspection of very tiny computer circuits under a microscope. From her scores on a test of cognitive ability (i.e., general intelligence), an applicant might show great potential for performing the job. However, the applicant might have an uncorrectable visual problem that leads her to score poorly on a test of visual acuity. Here, the compensatory regression model would not lead to a good prediction, for the visual problem would mean that the applicant would fail, regardless of her potential for handling the cognitive aspects of the job.

A second type of selection strategy, one that is not compensatory, is the **multiple cutoff model**, which uses a minimum cutoff score on each of the predictors. An applicant must obtain a score above the cutoff on each of the predictors to be hired. Scoring below the cutoff on any one predictor automatically disqualifies the applicant, regardless of the scores on the other screening variables. For example, a school district may decide to hire only those probationary high school teachers who have completed a specified number of graduate units and who have scored above the cutoff on a national teacher's examination. The main advantage of the multiple cutoff strategy is that it ensures all eligible applicants have some minimal amount of ability on all dimensions that are believed to be predictive of job success. The difference between the multiple cutoff model and the multiple hurdle model (see below) is that the multiple cutoff method is non-compensatory, meaning that someone cannot make up for a low score on one predictor by receiving a particularly high score on another predictor.

Cutoff scores are most commonly used in public-sector organizations that give employment tests to large numbers of applicants (Truxillo et al., 1996). The setting of cutoff scores is an important and often controversial decision because of the legal issues involved. Particular care needs to be taken by I/O psychologists to set cutoff scores that distinguish the best candidates for jobs, but do not unfairly discriminate against people of color, women, or older workers (see Cascio et al., 1988).

The multiple regression and multiple cutoff methods can be used in combination. If this is done, applicants will be eligible for hire only if their regression scores are high and if they are above the cutoff score on each of the predictor dimensions. Of course, using both strategies at the same time greatly restricts the number of eligible applicants, and so they are used together only when the pool of applicants is very large.

Another type of selection decision-making method is the **multiple hurdle model**. This strategy uses an ordered sequence of screening devices. At each stage in the sequence, a decision is made either to reject an applicant or to allow the applicant to proceed to the next stage. An example of the multiple hurdle model would be

Stop & Review
Define and discuss the concepts of predictors and criteria.

Multiple Cutoff Model
an employee selection method using a minimum cutoff score on each of the various predictors of job performance

D&I INSIGHT

Multiple Hurdle Model
an employee selection strategy that requires that an acceptance or rejection decision be made at each of several stages in a screening process

one used for hiring police officers (Figure 4.10). The first stage, or *hurdle*, might be receiving a passing score on a civil service exam. If a passing score is obtained, the applicant's application blank is evaluated. An applicant who does not pass the exam is no longer considered for the job. A third hurdle is a physical exam and fitness test. Those who pass that test then move on to an interview. The final hurdle is attendance at a 6-month-long police academy training. Typically, all applicants who pass all the hurdles are then selected for jobs.

One advantage of the multiple hurdle strategy is that unqualified persons do not have to go through the entire evaluation program before they are rejected. Also, because evaluation takes place at many times on many levels, the employer can be quite confident that the applicants who are selected do indeed have the potential to be successful on the job. Because multiple hurdle selection programs are expensive and time-consuming, they are usually only used for jobs that are central to the operation of the organization.

Employee Placement

Employee Placement
the process of assigning
workers to appropriate jobs

Whereas employee selection deals with how people are hired for jobs, **employee placement** is the process of deciding to which job hired workers should be assigned. Employee placement typically only takes place when there are two or more openings that a newly hired worker could fill. Placement also becomes important when large organizations close departments or offices and do not want to lay off the workers from the closed sites, but instead want to reassign these workers to other positions within the organization. Although placement is a different personnel function, many of the methods used in placement are the same as those used in employee selection. The main difference is that, in placement, the worker has already been hired. Therefore, the personnel specialist's job is to find the best possible "fit" between the worker's attributes (KSAOs) and the requirements of the job openings.

Personnel specialists are looking more broadly at the issue of employee selection and placement. Rather than just focusing on fitting potential employees into the right job, researchers and practitioners are concerned with how particular individuals might fit with a particular work group or team and with a specific organization (Kristof-Brown et al., 2005). Assuring that there is good fit between individuals and their work organizations and work environments not only allows organizations to predict who will be the better performers, but also helps to increase well-being among the selected employees.

Summary

Criteria are measures of job success, most often related to performance. *Predictors* are variables about applicants that should be predictive of criteria. Generally,

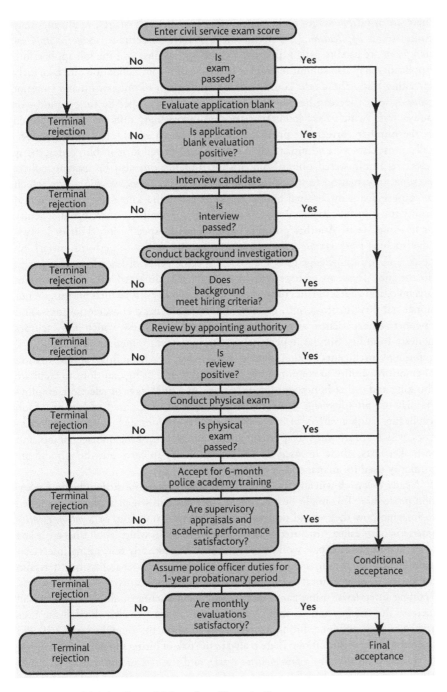

Figure 4.10 Multiple hurdle model for police officer selection.

Source: Found in Cascio, 1987, p. 282.

there are multiple stages of employee selection. In early stages, applicants may complete an *application form* or submit a *resume*. Sometimes, *weighted application forms* are used to assign different weights to responses on the job application. Applicants may also submit references or letters of recommendation and take early screening tests. These tests could be *individual* (given to one person at a time) or *group*-based. They can be *speed* tests—tests that have a specific time period—or power tests, which have items that become increasingly difficult and are scored as the number correct but provide sufficient time to get the test done. Historically, most tests were administered in a paper-and-pencil format, but, today, many tests are administered online. Biodata instruments can also be used to collect personal information from applicants. There are also *cognitive ability tests*, which measure general intellectual ability or domain-specific knowledge, and physical ability tests, such as mechanical, motor, and sensory ability—such as visual acuity or hearing—tests. Another group of tests relates to specific job skills or knowledge such as *work sample tests*, which measure the ability to perform critical job tasks, and job knowledge tests that assess specific types of knowledge needed to do the job. There are also *personality tests* that are designed to measure certain psychological characteristics of workers, such as the *Big Five*, which measures emotional stability (neuroticism), extraversion, agreeableness, conscientiousness, and openness to experience, and the more recent *HEXACO* test, which also includes honesty-humility. Similar to personality, employers will sometimes test applicants' emotional intelligence, which involves knowledge, understanding, and regulation of emotions; ability to communicate emotionally; and using emotions to facilitate thinking and utilize honesty or integrity tests. As a final stage of selection, employers may use an *assessment center*, which is a detailed, structured evaluation of job applicants using a variety of instruments and techniques such as situational exercises, which are attempts to approximate certain aspects of the managerial job, and in-basket tests. These are used to assess one's ability to carry out the job and are primarily used for managerial-level jobs.

Nearly every job will also use some type of *hiring interview* during the final selection procedure. This might be a *situational interview*, in which applicants are asked to imagine how they would deal with a hypothetical situation, or a *job descriptive interview* (also called structured behavioral interview), in which applicants are asked to recall and describe past workplace behaviour. Just like any test, hiring interviews should consider measurement issues such as validity and reliability, but it is also important to reduce interviewer biases by asking all applicants the same questions. Training interviews, using panel interviews, or conducting multiple interviews all increase the validity and reliability of interview ratings. Finally, when all the tests and interviews are done, hiring managers get to select the candidate who will add the most to the organization. There is always the risk of hiring someone who will not be successful in the job (a *false-positive error*), and the risk of eliminating an applicant who would have been successful (a *false-negative error*). All too often, subjective decision-making processes are used. Statistical models of decision making include the *multiple regression model*, an approach that allows predictors to be combined statistically; the *multiple cutoff* strategy, a method of setting minimum cutoff scores for each predictor; and the *multiple hurdle* approach, a stringent method that uses an ordered sequence of screening devices. *Employee placement* involves assigning selected employees to jobs to which they are best suited.

Study Questions and Exercises

1 Imagine that you were in charge of hiring new employees for a particular job that you are familiar with. Which screening methods would you choose and why?
2 Search for a detailed job advertisement or a job description. What are the KSAOs that the job seems to require? Suggest which sorts of tests or other screening procedures might best measure the KSAOs associated with the job.
3 Consider the last job you applied for. What kinds of screening procedures did you encounter? What were their strengths and weaknesses? How could they have been improved?
4 It is clear that, in much of the hiring that takes place, subjective evaluations of applicants are often the basis for the decisions. Why is this the case? What are some reasons that more objective—and more valid—hiring procedures are often ignored by employers?

Web Links

www.siop.org/Research-Publications/Items-of-Interest/ArtMID/19366/ ArticleID/4979/Using-Personality-to-Improve-Diversity-Equity-and-Inclusion-Practical-Evidence-Based-Recommendations

www.siop.org/Research-Publications/Items-of-Interest/ArtMID/19366/ ArticleID/4976/Diversity-Equity-Inclusion-in-the-Prehire-Process

www.ipacweb.org
Site for the International Personnel Assessment Council, an organization devoted to personnel testing and assessment.

www.cpp.com

www.wonderlic.com
Two test publisher sites (Consulting Psychologists Press and the Wonderlic site) where you can look at some of the employment tests available.

www.siop.org/workplace/employment%20testing/testtypes.aspx
SIOP provides a list of categories of employment screening tests, listing advantages and disadvantages of each type.

Suggested Readings

Colella, A., Hebl, M., & King, E. (2017). One hundred years of discrimination research in the *Journal of Applied Psychology*: A sobering synopsis. *Journal of Applied Psychology, 102*(3), 500–513.

Ployhart, R. E., Schmitt, N., & Tippins, N. T. (2017). Solving the supreme problem: 100 years of selection and recruitment at the *Journal of Applied Psychology. Journal of Applied Psychology, 102*(3), 291–304.

Society for Industrial and Organizational Psychology SIOP (2018). Principles for the validation and use of personnel selection procedures. *Industrial and Organizational Psychology: Perspectives on Science and Practice, 11(Supl 1),* 2–97. https://doi.org/10.1017/iop.2018.195. College Park, MD: Society for Industrial and Organizational Psychology. *This handbook is a statement of the principles, adopted by the Society for Industrial and Organizational Psychology, of "good practice in the choice, development, evaluation and use of personnel selection procedures."*

Zhang, L., Van Iddekinge, C. H., Arnold, J. D., Roth, P. L., Lievens, F., Lanivich, S. E., & Jordan, S. L. (2020). What's on job seekers' social media sites? A content analysis and effects of structure on recruiter judgments and predictive validity. *Journal of Applied Psychology, 105*(12), 1530–1546.

CHAPTER 5

Evaluating Employee Performance

Inside Tips

EMPLOYEE PERFORMANCE: A CRITERION FOR SUCCESS

This chapter looks at how employees' job performance is measured and appraised in organizations. Often, measures of performance are the criteria used to determine the effectiveness of an employee testing or screening program, as discussed in the previous chapter. Because job performance is such an important outcome variable in I/O psychology, it is important to understand the measurement issues concerning this factor. For example, when reviewing studies that discuss influences on job performance, you should investigate how performance was operationally defined and measured. Were objective or subjective criteria used? How accurate or inaccurate might the assessments of performance be? How can performance assessments and appraisals be improved?

Job Performance and Performance Appraisals

From the first few days on the job, you have wondered, "How am I doing?" Are you performing at an acceptable (or better) level? How are you performing in comparison with others in a similar position or compared with what your supervisor expects? You wait for some assessment of your job performance with a mixture of eager anticipation and trepidation.

The evaluation of employees' job performance is a vital personnel function and of critical importance to the organization. In this chapter, we will consider the very important variable of job performance in the context of assessments and evaluations. We will discuss the importance of performance appraisals, procedures for appraising performance, and the difficulties encountered in attempting to appraise performance.

DOI: 10.4324/9781003143987-7

We will also look at research on performance appraisals and assessment and discuss the legal concerns in performance appraisals.

In work organizations, measurement of performance typically takes place in the context of formalized **performance appraisals**, which measure worker performance in comparison with certain predetermined standards. Performance appraisals serve many purposes for the individual worker, for the worker's supervisor, and for the organization as a whole (Cleveland et al., 1989).

For the worker, performance appraisals are linked to development and career advancement. Performance appraisals function as the foundation for pay increases and promotions, provide feedback to help improve performance and recognize weaknesses, and offer information about the attainment of work goals. Work supervisors use performance appraisals to make personnel decisions such as promotions, demotions, pay raises, and firings and to give workers constructive feedback to improve work performance. Moreover, the formal performance appraisal procedure facilitates organizational communication by helping to encourage interaction between workers and supervisors. Research has shown that employees who receive regular performance appraisals that are characterized as "helpful" to the performance of their job show stronger commitment to their jobs and organizations (see Schleicher et al., 2019, for a review). For the organization, performance appraisals provide a means of assessing the productivity of individuals and work units (see Table 5.1).

Performance Appraisals
the formalized means of assessing worker performance in comparison with certain established organizational standards

Table 5.1 The Many Purposes of Performance Appraisals

For the Worker

Means of reinforcement (praise, pay raises)
Career advancement (promotions, increased responsibility)
Information about work goal attainment
Source of feedback to improve performance
Can lead to greater job engagement

For the Supervisor

Basis for making personnel decisions (promotions, firings, etc.)
Assessment of workers' goal attainment
Opportunity to provide constructive feedback to workers
Opportunity to interact with subordinates

For the Organization

Assessment of productivity of individuals and work units
Validation of personnel selection and placement methods
Means for recognizing and motivating workers
Source of information for personnel training needs
Evaluation of the effectiveness of organizational interventions (e.g., training programs, system changes, etc.)

The Measurement of Job Performance

As we have seen, job performance is one of the most important work outcomes. It is the variable in organizations that is most often measured and that is given the most attention. This makes sense, because the success or failure of an organization depends on the performance of its employees.

There are many ways to measure job performance. Yet, as we saw in our discussion of personnel selection in Chapter 4, I/O psychologists typically refer to measures of job performance as performance criteria. **Performance criteria** are the means of determining successful or unsuccessful performance. As we saw in Chapter 3, performance criteria are one of the products that arise from a detailed job analysis, for, once the specific elements of a job are known, it is easier to develop the means to assess levels of successful or unsuccessful performance.

Performance Criteria
measures used to determine successful and unsuccessful job performance

Objective versus Subjective Performance Criteria

One important categorization of job performance assessments is to distinguish between objective and subjective measures. Objective and subjective performance criteria are also sometimes referred to as "hard" and "soft" performance criteria, respectively (see Ramawickrama et al., 2017, for a review). **Objective performance criteria** involve the measurement of some easily quantifiable aspects of job performance, such as the number of units produced, the dollar amount of sales, or the time needed to process some information. For example, an objective criterion for an assembly-line worker might be the number of products assembled. For an insurance claims adjuster, the average amount of time it takes to process a claim might be an objective measure of performance (see Table 5.2). Such criteria are often referred to as measures of productivity.

Objective Performance Criteria
measures of job performance that are easily quantified

Subjective performance criteria consist of judgments or ratings made by some knowledgeable individual, such as a worker's supervisor or coworker. These criteria are often used when objective criteria are unavailable, difficult to assess, or inappropriate. For example, it is usually inappropriate to use objective performance criteria to assess a manager's job because it is difficult to specify the exact behaviors that indicate successful managerial performance. Instead, subjective criteria, such as subordinate or superior ratings, are used.

Subjective Performance Criteria
measures of job performance that typically consist of ratings or judgments of performance

Objective performance criteria offer two main advantages. First, because objective criteria typically involve counts of output or the timing of tasks, they are less prone to bias and distortion than subjective performance ratings. Second, objective criteria are usually more directly tied to "bottom-line" assessments of an organization's success, such as the number of products assembled or dollar sales figures. It is often more difficult to determine the links between subjective criteria and bottom-line outcomes.

As mentioned, it is often difficult, if not impossible, to obtain objective performance criteria for certain jobs, such as graphic artist, software developer, and executive vice president (see Figure 5.1). Jobs such as these may best be assessed through ratings

⏱ **Stop & Review**
Describe nine purposes of performance appraisals.

Table 5.2 Examples of Objective Job Performance Criteria

Job Title	Measure
Social worker	Number of clients helped, number of people diagnosed
Real estate agent	Number of houses sold
Customer service (telephone)	Number of people helped, number of complaints received
Cashier	Number of products purchased, people helped
Hotel maid	Number of rooms cleaned, towels replaced
Truck driver	Miles driven, weight of cargo carried, amount of time taken per trip
Aircraft maintenance worker	Number of planes serviced
Receptionist	Number of people checked in, appointments scheduled
Cabinet worker	Number of cabinets made
Fast-food cook	Number of burgers cooked, amount of time to cook burger
Bartender	Number of drinks served, amount of tips given
Bill collector	Amount of debt collected, number of people contacted
Hair stylist	Number of haircuts given
Pharmacy technician	Number of prescriptions filled
Telemarketer	Number of people called, number of rejections received

Source: Adapted from Landy et al., 1983.

or judgments. Another drawback of objective assessments is that they may focus too much on specific, quantifiable outcomes. Because many jobs are complex, looking at only one or two objective measures of performance may not capture the total picture of performance. Some aspects of job performance, such as work quality, worker initiative, and work effort, are difficult to assess objectively. For example, a salesperson might have high dollar sales figures, but may be so pushy and manipulative that customers are unlikely to return to the store. Likewise, a research analyst may have relatively low output rates because he spends a great deal of time teaching new workers valuable work techniques and helping coworkers solve problems. It is important to emphasize that comprehensive evaluation of employee performance might include both very positive, outside-of-the-job-description activities, such as helping other workers, and counterproductive behaviors, such as "goofing off," substance abuse on the job, or disrupting the work team (Ramawickrama et al., 2017).

In many cases, collecting objective performance data is time-consuming and costly (although see "On the Cutting Edge"). By contrast, subjective performance criteria are usually easy and relatively inexpensive to obtain and, thus, may be the preferred method of assessment for many organizations. Moreover, subjective performance criteria can be used to assess variables that could not be measured objectively, such as employee motivation or "team spirit."

Figure 5.1 How would the performance of this tattoo artist best be assessed?

Source: Photograph by Janko Ferlič, found on Unsplash (https://unsplash.com/photos/Visezp_DeTU).

Regardless of the criteria used to evaluate performance of a job, a number of important criterion concerns or issues have implications for conducting accurate performance appraisals. A primary issue is whether the criteria identified in the job analysis relate to the true nature of the job. A particular concern here is **criterion relevance**: the notion that the means of appraising performance is, indeed, pertinent to job success, as identified in the job analysis. A performance appraisal should cover only the specific KSAOs needed to perform a job successfully. For example, the performance criteria for a bookkeeper should deal with knowledge of accounting procedures, mathematical skills, and producing work that is neat and error-free, not with personal appearance or oral communication skills—factors that are clearly not relevant to the effective performance of a bookkeeper's job. However, for a public relations representative, personal appearance and communication skills may be relevant performance criteria.

Criterion Relevance
the extent to which the means of appraising performance is pertinent to job success

ON THE *CUTTING* EDGE

The Boss Is Watching: Electronic Monitoring of Employee Performance

"Your call may be monitored in an effort to improve our customer service." How many times have you heard that when calling a helpline? Probably most of the time. Workers in call centers, as well as many employees who work online or on company computer networks, can have their performance monitored electronically. For example, employees in the collections department of a credit card company must maintain computerized records of phone calls, correspondence, and other activity for all accounts. The computerized monitoring system allows supervisors to note the number and length of calls to each account, as well as the amount of money collected. Supervisors receive a detailed weekly report of employee computer activities that gives a good indication of how the workers spent their time. A hard measure of employee performance is obtained from the amount of money collected from each account. Twenty years ago, 80% of employers were using some sort of electronic surveillance of employee performance (Alge, 2001), and that number has vastly increased over the last two decades. According to research by the American Management Association (2019), organizations monitor computer keystrokes, computer files, and internet histories in addition to phone calls and video camera surveillance.

When the COVID-19 pandemic began in March of 2020, many employees switched to remote work. A survey by Stanford University (Bloom, 2020) reported a 12,000% increase in working from home, with 42%

of employees working from home full-time in June of 2020. This shift in employment practices ignited a corresponding increase in employee monitoring amounting to a 50% increase (Migliano, 2020) in the demand for employee monitoring systems. The most popular surveillance tools according to the study were Hubstaff, Time Doctor, and FlexiSPY. Microsoft also announced new software for monitoring employee performance, "Productivity Score," that documents how many minutes per day an individual employee spends on Word, Excel, Outlook, etc. However, the article also says that, following backlash and criticism, Microsoft changed the program to remove individual employee names from the reports. Even in-person workers experienced an increase in electronic monitoring during the pandemic. For example, retail giant Amazon installed cameras to detect whether employees were engaging in social distancing (staying at least 6 feet apart from each other), according to CNBC (Palmer, 2020).

Although electronic monitoring can be a highly effective and inexpensive way to increase and monitor employee performance (Claypoole & Szalma, 2019), it can also negatively impact employee well-being. One study showed that employees believe electronic monitoring invades their privacy, eliciting anger, decreased helping behaviors, and increased counterproductive workplace behavior (Yost et al., 2019).

Criterion Contamination
the extent to which performance appraisals contain elements that detract from the accurate assessment of job effectiveness

A related concern is **criterion contamination**: the extent to which performance appraisals contain elements that detract from the accurate assessment of job effectiveness—elements that should not be included in the performance assessment. A common source of criterion contamination stems from appraiser biases. For example, a supervisor may give an employee an overly positive performance appraisal because the employee has a reputation of past work success or because the employee was a graduate of a prestigious university. Criterion contamination can also result from extraneous factors that contribute to a worker's apparent success or failure in a job. For instance, a sales manager may receive a poor performance appraisal because of low sales levels, even though the poor sales actually result from the fact that the manager supervises a young, inexperienced sales force.

It is unlikely that any criterion will capture job performance perfectly; every criterion of job performance may fall short of measuring performance to some extent. **Criterion deficiency** describes the degree to which a criterion falls short of measuring job performance perfectly. Criterion deficiency occurs when the measurement of the performance criteria is incomplete. An important goal of performance appraisals is to choose criteria that optimize the assessment of job success, thereby keeping criterion deficiency to a minimum.

A final concern is **criterion usefulness**, or the extent to which a performance criterion is usable in appraising a particular job in an organization. To be useful, a criterion should be relatively easy and cost-effective to measure and should be seen as relevant by the appraiser, the employee whose performance is being appraised, and the management of the organization.

Criterion Deficiency
the degree to which a criterion falls short of measuring job performance

Criterion Usefulness
the extent to which a performance criterion is usable in appraising a particular job

Sources of Performance Ratings

Because performance ratings play such an important role in performance assessment in organizations, a great deal of personnel research has focused on the process and methods of rating performance. Most supervisors provide annual performance reviews, although an industry report released by SHRM (Society for Human Resource Management; O'Connell, 2020) suggests that this number is dropping, with 82% of employees reporting the use of annual reviews in 2016, 65% in 2017, 58% in 2018, and 54% in 2019. In addition to performance reviews by one's supervisor, reviews can also contain data from a worker's peers, subordinates, the worker himself or herself, or even customers evaluating the performance of a service worker. The obvious advantage of getting these different perspectives on performance assessment is that each type of appraiser—supervisor, self, peer, subordinate, and customer—may see a different aspect of the worker's performance, and thus, may offer unique perspectives (Thomason et al., 2011). Moreover, multiple-perspective performance appraisals are perceived as fairer and, therefore, are more likely to be accepted by those evaluated (Karkoulian et al., 2016).

⏱ Stop & Review
Compare and contrast objective and subjective performance criteria and give examples of each.

Supervisor Appraisals

Conducting regular appraisals of employee performance is considered one of the most important supervisory functions. Supervisor performance appraisals are so common because supervisors are usually quite knowledgeable about the job requirements and are often in a position to provide rewards for effective performance and suggestions for improvement for substandard performance. Supervisors play a large role in how a performance appraisal is perceived by employees. Managers who have supervisors who are perceived as fair and those who are trusted by their employees tend to elicit more positive reactions from their direct reports when delivering performance feedback (Schleicher et al., 2019).

Yet supervisors do not witness all employee behavior, and so collecting data from additional sources can be beneficial.

Self-Appraisals

Self-appraisals of performance have been used by many companies, usually in conjunction with supervisor appraisals. Although there is evidence that self-appraisals correlate slightly with supervisor performance appraisals, self-appraisals tend to be more lenient and focus more on effort exerted rather than on performance accomplishments (DeNisi & Murphy, 2017). Quite often, there are large discrepancies between how supervisors rate performance and the worker's self-rating. It has been suggested that part of the discrepancy between self- and supervisor appraisals can be overcome if both the worker and the supervisor are thoroughly trained to understand how the performance rating system works and when workers receive more frequent, regular performance feedback from supervisors. One advantage of appraisal discrepancies, however, may be that they highlight differences in supervisor and worker perceptions and can lead to an open dialogue between supervisor and supervisee (Campbell & Lee, 1988). Self-appraisals of performance are also useful in encouraging workers to be more committed to performance-related goals (Riggio & Cole, 1992). One advantage of appraisal discrepancies, however, may be that they highlight differences in supervisor and worker perceptions and can lead to an open dialogue between supervisor and supervisee (Campbell & Lee, 1988).

Although studies of U.S. workers have found that self-appraisals tend to be more lenient than supervisor performance ratings, individuals from more collectivistic cultures, including individuals from countries such as China, Korea, and Japan, generally rate themselves lower than individuals from individualistic cultures such as the United States (Cho & Payne, 2016). Considering that different cultures may have different levels of modesty, the accuracy of self-appraisals and their discrepancy from supervisor ratings may need to be evaluated with culture taken into account.

Peer Appraisals

Peers are another source of ratings. Particularly among individuals who work on teams, peers are keenly aware of what constitutes good performance and have the most information about one's workplace contributions. One obvious problem with peer ratings of performance is the potential for conflict among employees who are evaluating each other, a particular problem when peers are competing for scarce job rewards. Further, not all peer ratings are equally valid. Research shows that ratings from peers who are more central to one's workplace network provide more valid ratings of performance (Zhao et al., 2020).

⏱ Stop & Review

Define four important criterion concerns in performance appraisals.

Subordinate Appraisals

Subordinate ratings are most commonly used to assess the effectiveness of persons in supervisory or leadership positions. Research on subordinate appraisals indicates considerable agreement with supervisor ratings (Riggio & Cole, 1992). Subordinate ratings may be particularly important because they provide a different, meaningful perspective on a supervisor's performance—the perspective of the persons being supervised.

For example, one study (Hoffman & Woehr, 2009) examined the validity of subordinate ratings by having participants obtain ratings from peers, supervisors, and subordinates and then participate in an assessment center. The assessment center provided data on leadership skills such as decision making, influencing others, and coaching. Subordinate ratings were more strongly related to leadership effectiveness than peer ratings or manager ratings. Simply put, if you are trying to measure leadership, then subordinates may be the best source of information.

Customer Appraisals

Another form of performance rating for employees working in customer service positions is ratings made by customers. Although customer ratings are not commonly considered a method of performance appraisal, they can be because they offer an interesting perspective on whether certain types of workers (salespersons, waitpersons, telephone operators) are doing a good job. Customer evaluations of an individual employee's performance are most appropriate when the employee and customer have a significant, ongoing relationship, such as customers evaluating a supplier, a sales representative, a real estate agent, a stockbroker, or the like. One might say that customer appraisals are inherently valid (if the customer is satisfied, then the employee has done his or her job). In addition, research shows that customer appraisals also correlate with observer ratings (Demerouti et al., 2019).

360-Degree Feedback

A comprehensive form of performance appraisal gathers ratings from all levels that were mentioned above in what is commonly called **360-degree feedback** (Waldman et al., 1998). In 360-degree feedback programs (sometimes referred to as multirater

360-Degree Feedback
a method of gathering performance appraisals from a worker's supervisors, subordinates, peers, customers, and other relevant parties

feedback), performance ratings are gathered from supervisors, subordinates, peers, customers, and suppliers (if applicable). The obvious advantages of 360-degree feedback include improved reliability of measurement because of the multiple evaluations, the inclusion of more diverse perspectives on the employee's performance, the involvement of more organizational members in the evaluation and feedback process, and improved organizational communication (Campion et al., 2015). Although 360-degree feedback programs may have distinct advantages, including enhanced development and improved performance of employees, they are also time-intensive and costly. Despite being costly, however, the data largely suggest that 360-degree feedback improves employees' engagement in knowledge sharing and the overall level of employees' ability to do their job, especially when the feedback is used for both developmental and assessment purposes (Kim et al., 2016). Because 360-degree feedback programs are often used as a management development tool, rather than being used only as a performance appraisal system, we will discuss 360-degree feedback more fully in the next chapter, on employee training.

Methods of Rating Performance

When it comes to subjectively evaluating employee performance, a variety of rating methods can be used. We will review some of the more common methods. These methods can be classified into two general categories: those that can be termed "comparative methods" and those that can be labeled "individual methods."

Comparative Methods

Comparative Methods
performance appraisal methods involving comparisons of one worker's performance against that of other workers

Comparative methods of performance appraisal involve some form of comparison of one worker's performance with the performance of others. These procedures are relatively easy to implement in work organizations and include *rankings*, *paired comparisons*, and *forced distributions*.

Rankings

Rankings
performance appraisal methods involving the ranking of supervisees from best to worst

The comparative method of **rankings** requires supervisors to rank their direct reports from best to worst on specific performance dimensions or to give an overall comparative ranking on job performance (see Dominick, 2009). Although this is a simple and easy technique that supervisors are not likely to find difficult or time-consuming, it has several limitations. Although ranking separates the best workers from the worst, there are no absolute standards of performance. This is a problem if few or none of the entire group of workers are performing at "acceptable" levels. In this case, being ranked second or third in a group of 15 is misleading, because even the highest-ranking workers are performing at substandard levels. Conversely, in a group of exceptional workers, those ranked low may actually be outstanding performers in comparison with other employees in the organization or workers in other companies.

Paired Comparisons

Another comparative method of performance appraisal uses **paired comparisons**, in which the rater compares each worker with every other worker in the group and then simply has to decide who is the better performer. Of course, this technique becomes unwieldy when the number of group members being evaluated becomes large (for instance, there are 6 possible paired comparisons for a group of 4 workers, but 28 paired comparisons for a 7-member group). Each person's final rank consists of the number of times that individual was chosen as the better of a pair. The drawbacks of this technique are similar to those of the ranking method. However, both these comparative techniques have the advantage of being simple to use and of being applicable to a variety of jobs. One possible use for this technique might be to decide which team member(s) to eliminate when downsizing.

Paired Comparison
performance appraisal method in which the rater compares each worker with each other worker in the group

Forced Distributions

In the comparative method known as **forced distributions**, the rater assigns workers to established categories, ranging from poor to outstanding, on the basis of comparison with all other workers in the group. Usually, the percentage of employees who can be assigned to any particular category is controlled to obtain a fixed distribution of workers along the performance dimension. Most often, the distribution is set up to represent a normal distribution (see Figure 5.2). This forced distribution evaluation technique is similar to the procedure used by an instructor who grades on a so-called "normal curve," with preassigned percentages of A, B, C, D, and F grades. One large U.S. company established a policy of placing all employees in a performance distribution, with the bottom 10% of performers fired each year in an effort to continually upgrade the performance level of the entire workforce.

One possible problem with the forced distribution occurs when there is an abundance of either very good or very poor workers in a supervisor's work group. This can create a situation where a supervisor might artificially raise or lower some employees' evaluations to fit them into the predetermined distribution. In some situations, forced distribution may lead to employee dissatisfaction if it is perceived as unfair (Schleicher et al., 2009) and, if used in a layoff situation, may raise concerns about adverse impact (Giumetti et al., 2015).

Information comparing the performance of one employee with that of others can be used in conjunction with other performance appraisal methods. For example, a

Forced Distributions
assigning workers to established categories of poor to good performance, with fixed limitations on how many employees can be assigned to each category

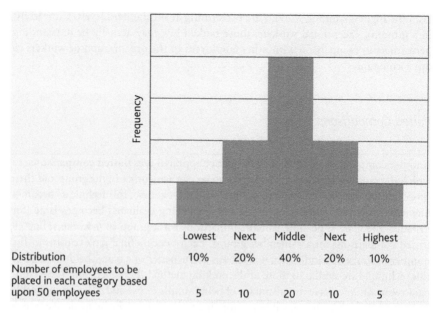

Distribution	Lowest	Next	Middle	Next	Highest
	10%	20%	40%	20%	10%
Number of employees to be placed in each category based upon 50 employees	5	10	20	10	5

Figure 5.2 **A forced distribution performance rating using five categories with a sample of 50 employees.**

study by Farh and Dobbins (1989) found that, when subordinates were presented with information comparing their job performance with that of their peers, their self-ratings of performance were more accurate and there was greater agreement between self-appraisals and appraisals made by supervisors. Thus, although comparative methods may sometimes yield misleading results, the use of comparative information may increase the accuracy and quality of self-appraisals of performance.

Individual Methods

Individual Methods
performance appraisal methods that evaluate an employee by himself or herself, without explicit reference to other workers

It is more common for employees to be evaluated using what could be termed "individual methods." **Individual methods** involve evaluating an employee by himself or herself. However, even though ratings are made individually, appraisals using individual methods may still make comparisons of one individual employee's rating with individual ratings of other employees. We will begin our discussion of individual methods with the most widely used method of performance rating: graphic rating scales.

Graphic Rating Scales

Graphic Rating Scales
performance appraisal methods using a predetermined scale to rate the worker on important job dimensions

The vast majority of performance appraisals use **graphic rating scales**, which offer predetermined scales to rate the worker on a number of important aspects of the job, such as quality of work, dependability, and ability to get along with coworkers. A graphic rating scale typically has a number of points with either numerical or verbal labels, or both. The verbal labels can be simple, one-word descriptors, or they can be quite lengthy and specific (see Figure 5.3). Some graphic rating scales use only verbal endpoints, or anchors, with numbered rating points between the two anchors.

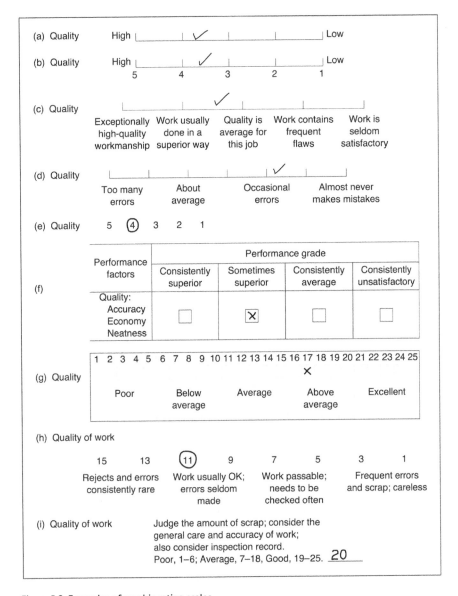

Figure 5.3 Examples of graphic rating scales.

Source: Found in Guion, 1965.

When graphic rating scales are used in performance assessment, appraisals are usually made on anywhere from 7 to 12 key job dimensions, which are derived from the job analysis. Better graphic rating scales define the dimensions and the particular rating categories quite clearly and precisely. In other words, it is important that the rater know exactly what aspect of the job is being rated and what the verbal labels mean. For instance, in Figure 5.3, examples (f) and (i) define the job dimension, whereas example (h) defines the rating categories.

Although good graphic rating scales take some time to develop, often the same basic scales can be used for a number of different jobs by simply switching the relevant job dimensions. However, a common mistake made by many organizations is attempting to develop a "generic" set of performance rating scales for use with all persons and all jobs within the company. Because the relevant job dimensions change drastically from job to job, it is critical that the dimensions being rated are those that actually assess performance of the particular job. The major weakness of graphic rating scales is that they may be prone to certain biased response patterns, such as the tendency to give everyone "good" or "average" ratings. Also, limiting ratings to only a few job dimensions may constrain the appraiser and may not produce a total picture of the worker's job performance.

Behaviorally Anchored Rating Scales

Behaviorally Anchored Rating Scales (BARS) performance appraisal technique using rating scales, with labels reflecting examples of poor, average, and good behavioral incidents

An outgrowth of the critical incidents method of job analysis is the development of **behaviorally anchored rating scales (BARS)**, which attempt to clearly define the scale labels and anchors used in performance ratings. Rather than having scale labels such as poor, average, or good, BARS have examples of behavioral incidents that reflect poor, average, and good performance in relation to a specific dimension.

Figure 5.4 presents a behaviorally anchored rating scale for appraising the job of Navy recruiter on the dimension of salesmanship skills. Note first the very detailed definition of the job dimension at the top of the scale. On the left are the rating points, ranging from 8 to 1. The verbal descriptors to the right of each category give examples of behavioral incidents that would differentiate a recruiter's sales skills, from highest levels to lowest.

As you might imagine, the development of BARS is a lengthy and tedious process. The result, however, is a rating instrument that focuses clearly on performance behaviors relevant to a particular job. An appraiser is forced to spend a great deal of time just thinking about what adequate or inadequate performance of a certain job dimension entails, particularly if the rater had a hand in developing the scale. This increased attention to job behaviors helps to overcome some of the general biases and stereotyping that may occur in other performance ratings, for a worker cannot be summarily judged without consideration of how the person's past behavior supports the rating.

Job: Navy Recruiter

Job dimension: Salesmanship skills

Skillfully persuading prospects to join the Navy, using Navy benefits and opportunities effectively to sell the Navy; closing skills; adapting selling techniques appropriately to different prospects; effectively overcoming objections to joining the Navy.

8 A prospect stated he wanted the nuclear power program or he would not sign up. When he did not qualify, the recruiter did not give up; instead, he talked the young man into electronics by emphasizing the technical training he would receive.

7 The recruiter treats objections to join the Navy seriously; he works hard to counter the objections with relevant, positive arguments for a Navy career.

6 When talking to a high school senior, the recruiter mentions names of other seniors from that school who have already enlisted.

5 When an applicant qualifies for only one program, the recruiter tries to convey to the applicant that it is a desirable program.

4 When a prospect is deciding on which service to enlist in, the recruiter tries to sell the Navy by describing Navy life at sea and adventures in port.

3 During an interview, the recruiter said to the applicant, "I'll try to get you the school you want, but frankly it probably won't be open for another three months, so why don't you take your second choice and leave now."

2 The recruiter insisted on showing more brochures and films even though the applicant told him he wanted to sign up right now.

1 When a prospect states an objection to being in the Navy, the recruiter ends the conversation because he thinks the prospect must not be interested.

Figure 5.4 A behaviorally anchored rating scale (BARS).

Source: Found in Borman, 1986, p. 103.

Behavioral Observation Scales

A performance assessment technique related to the BARS is **behavioral observation scales (BOS)**. With this method, raters indicate how often the worker has been observed performing key work-related behaviors. Whereas BARS focus on expectations that a worker would be able to perform specific behaviors that are typical of certain performance levels, behavioral observation scales concentrate on critical behaviors that were actually performed. Bear in mind that behavioral observation scales do not involve the direct observation and assessment of performance behaviors,

Behavioral Observation Scales (BOS)
performance appraisal methods that require appraisers to recall how often a worker has been observed performing key work behaviors

but rather the recollections of observers, who may be biased or selective in what they remember. Studies have compared behavioral observation scale and graphic rating scale assessments of performance and showed that employees preferred the BOS method (see Schleicher et al., 2019, for a review).

Checklists

Checklists
performance appraisal methods using a series of statements about job performance

Another individual method of performance rating is the use of **checklists**, which consist of a series of statements about performance in a particular job. The statements are derived from a job analysis and can reflect either positive or negative aspects of performance (see Figure 5.5). The rater's task is to check off the statements that apply to the worker being evaluated. Each of the statements is given a numerical value reflecting the degree of effective performance associated with it. The numerical values assigned to the checked items are then summed to give an overall appraisal of the worker's performance. There is some evidence that rating inflation may be reduced when using checklists rather than graphic rating scales (Yun et al., 2005).

A variation of checklist rating is the forced-choice scale, developed in an attempt to overcome the rater's tendency to give generally positive or negative performance

Instructions: Below you will find a list of behavioral items. Read each item and decide whether it describes the person being evaluated. If you feel the item does describe the person, place a checkmark in the space provided. If the item does not describe the person, leave the space next to the item blank.

- ☐ 1 Regularly sets vague and unrealistic program goals
- ☐ 2 Is concerned only with the immediate problems of the day and sees very little beyond the day-to-day
- ☐ 3 Develops work schedules that allow for completion of projects provided no major problems are encountered
- ☐ 4 Is aware of needs and trends in area of responsibility and plans accordingly
- ☐ 5 Follows up on projects to ensure that intermediate goals are achieved
- ☐ 6 Looks for new markets and studies potential declines in current markets
- ☐ 7 Anticipates and plans for replacement of key personnel in the event of corporate relocation

Figure 5.5 A checklist rating scale for a project manager.

Note: This is only a portion of the checklist. Scores are derived based on the number of items checked and the scale values of those items.

Source: Found in Jacobs, 1986.

appraisals. While using the forced-choice technique, the rater is unaware of how positive an appraisal is being made. This format presents groups of descriptive statements from which the rater must select the one that is either most or least descriptive of the worker. The statements carry different values that are later added to form the overall performance appraisal.

Although checklists are easy to use and provide detailed appraisals of performance that are focused on job-related behaviors, they do have some drawbacks. The development of such techniques is expensive and time-consuming, requiring the generation of applicable work-related statements and the assignment of accurate performance values. Also, checklists may limit the focus of a performance appraisal, because the rater must choose among a finite set of statements that might not capture all aspects of an individual's performance of a particular job.

⏱ **Stop & Review**

List and define three comparative methods of performance appraisal.

Narratives

A relatively simple form of individual performance evaluation is the use of **narratives**, which are open-ended, written accounts of the worker's performance or listings of specific examples of performance strengths and weaknesses. The advantage of narratives is that appraisers have the freedom to describe performance in their own words and to emphasize elements that they feel are important. Their major drawback is that they offer no quantification of performance, which makes it very difficult to compare workers' performance. An additional problem with narratives is that the worker may misinterpret the meaning of the report. For example, an appraiser may write that the worker is doing a "fair job," meaning that some improvement is needed, but the worker may interpret the word "fair" to mean "adequate" or "good" and may, thus, believe that no improvement is necessary. Another concern is that subtle bias may easily enter into the performance narrative that a supervisor writes (Wilson, 2010).

Narratives
open-ended written accounts of a worker's performance used in performance appraisals

We have seen that there are quite a number of methods for rating employee job performance, but what works best? All forms of ratings suffer from the same limitation: they are subjective and, thus, prone to the unique perspective and biases of the person doing the rating. No one method of rating performance has emerged as superior to the others. However, a key issue is the focus of the rater's attention on actual job performance. Therefore, methods that focus raters on performance-related job behaviors—the BARS and BOS methods—should theoretically improve rater accuracy.

Problems and Pitfalls in Performance Appraisals

Despite the various performance appraisal tools designed to help obtain more objective assessments, the appraisal evaluation process remains highly subjective. Because appraisers selectively observe on-the-job performance and rate what they believe to be an individual's performance level, their judgments are prone to a number of systematic biases and distortions. A great deal of research has helped uncover some of these problems. Understanding these potential errors in the performance appraisal process can make it easier to develop the means to combat them and to produce better appraisals of work performance. We will consider several types of such systematic problems, including leniency/severity errors, halo effects, recency effects, causal attribution errors, and personal biases.

Leniency/Severity Errors

Leniency Error
the tendency to give all workers very positive performance appraisals

Severity Error
the tendency to give all workers very negative performance appraisals

Central Tendency Error
the tendency to give all workers the midpoint rating in performance appraisals

A **leniency error** in performance ratings occurs when an appraiser tends to judge all workers leniently, routinely giving them very positive appraisals. A **severity error** is the exact opposite and arises when an appraiser tends to rate employees on the low end of performance scales, giving generally negative appraisals. For the rater making a severity error, no performance ever seems good enough. There is also a **central tendency error**, whereby the appraiser tends always to use the midpoint of the rating scale. All three of these errors lead to the same problem: a short-circuiting of the appraisal process because the rater's tendency to use only one area of the performance scale does not actually discriminate between poor, fair, and outstanding workers. In statistical terms, the ratings show little variance. As shown, some techniques, such as the various comparative methods, help combat such response tendency errors.

Halo Effects

Halo Effect
an overall positive evaluation of a worker based on one known positive characteristic or action

A **halo effect** in performance appraisal occurs when appraisers make overall positive appraisals of workers on the basis of one known positive characteristic or action. If a particular worker did an outstanding job on a particular task, the supervisor assumes that all of this person's work is also outstanding, regardless of whether it really is. Certain personal characteristics such as physical attractiveness or being labeled a "rising star" may also lead to halo effects. Research indicates that halo effects occur because raters use the one salient characteristic as the basis for forming an overall, generally positive or negative, impression of the worker's performance. There is also a "reverse" halo effect, sometimes called the "rusty halo" or "horns" effect, in which an overall negative performance appraisal is made on the basis of one instance of failure or one negative characteristic.

Because halo effects are such a common source of bias in performance appraisals, a number of rater training programs have been developed to try to control for them. Many of these training programs involve simply making raters more aware of the phenomenon of halo effects and helping them to focus on behavioral dimensions of job performance.

Recency Effects

Another potential error in performance appraisals is the tendency to give greater weight to recent performance and lesser value to earlier performance; this can be referred to as the **recency effect**. Because performance assessments usually rely on the appraiser's memory of a worker's past performance, there are bound to be problems related to accurate recall. In general, the greater the delay between the performance and the appraisal of work behaviors, the less accurate the appraisal will be. The lesser value given to earlier performance because of the recency effect may not always be detrimental to accurate performance appraisals, however. Earlier performance by a relatively new employee may reflect the employee's learning period, where mistakes may be more numerous, whereas later performance may reflect the employee's performance once he or she has more completely learned about the job.

Recency Effect
the tendency to give greater weight to recent performance and lesser weight to earlier performance

Causal Attribution Errors

The process by which people ascribe cause to events or behaviors is known as **causal attribution**. Research has uncovered a number of systematic biases in causal attribution that have important implications for the accuracy of performance appraisals. Two of these attributional biases are particularly relevant to performance appraisals. The first causal attribution bias is the tendency for appraisers to give more extreme appraisals if they believe that the cause of a worker's performance is rooted in effort rather than ability. That is, if an appraiser feels that particularly high levels of performance were the result of great effort on the part of a worker, that worker will receive a more positive performance appraisal than one whose high levels of performance were perceived as resulting from possession of natural ability or talent. Similarly, a performance failure due to a lack of sufficient effort will be judged more harshly than a failure believed to be caused by lack of ability.

The second pertinent bias in causal attribution is called the **actor–observer bias**. This bias is founded in the notion that, in any event, there is an actor—the person performing a behavior—and an observer—the person watching and appraising the event and the actor's behavior. In performance appraisals, the worker is the actor, and the appraiser is the observer. The bias in causal attribution occurs when the actor and observer are each asked to state the cause of the particular event. In the case of performance appraisals, the event could be a particularly successful or unsuccessful work outcome. The actor tends to overemphasize the role that situational factors, such as luck, task difficulty, and the work environment, played in the result.

Causal Attribution
the process by which people assign cause to events or behaviors

Actor–Observer Bias
the tendency for observers to overattribute cause to characteristics of the actor and the tendency for the actor to overattribute cause to situational characteristics

In contrast, the observer has a tendency to attribute cause to dispositional factors, or personal characteristics of the actor such as ability, effort, and personality. This means that the performance appraiser tends to believe that performance is due primarily to qualities in the worker and tends to neglect the role that situational factors played in the performance outcome. Therefore, in certain situations of poor work performance, the supervisor may blame the worker, when the failure was actually due to circumstances beyond the control of the worker. On the other side, the worker is prone to overemphasizing situational factors and, in cases of failure, will try to lay the blame elsewhere—for example, by faulting the working conditions or coworkers. The actor–observer bias not only leads to inaccurate perceptions of work performance, but is also one of the main reasons that supervisors and supervisees do not always see eye to eye when it comes to performance appraisals (see "Applying I/O Psychology"). Interestingly, in one study, it was found that actors, but not observers, were aware of the actor–observer bias in specific rating situations, suggesting that workers may realize that supervisors are being biased, but may not be able to make their supervisors aware of it.

Personal Biases

In addition to the biases and errors that can afflict any appraiser of work performance, the personal biases of any particular appraiser can distort the accuracy of assessments. The most common personal biases are those based on the worker's sex, race, age, and physical characteristics, including disabilities. It even has been found that pregnancy can be a source of negative bias in performance appraisals. It is no secret that women, ethnic minorities, older people, and people with disabilities are sometimes discriminated against in performance appraisals, despite legislation specifically designed to ensure fairness. However, reviews of research on racial and gender bias in performance appraisal concluded that such bias may be less of a problem than commonly believed. On the other hand, having a close personal relationship with a supervisee, or merely a liking for that individual over others, could bias appraisals in a favorable direction.

There is also evidence that certain types of individuals are more prone to bias in performance appraisals. For example, in an interesting review of research, it was found that supervisors who have high levels of power over those they are evaluating tended to make more negative performance evaluations than supervisors who did not have as much power over supervisees (Georgesen & Harris, 1998). One explanation is that powerful individuals attend more to negative stereotypic information about their subordinates, such as being particularly harsh in an evaluation when an inexperienced, young worker makes a mistake (Rodríguez-Bailón et al., 2000).

Certain personal biases may be deeply ingrained in individuals and are, therefore, difficult to overcome. As with other biases, one way to deal with personal biases is to make appraisers more aware of them. Because discrimination in personnel procedures has been outlawed through federal civil rights legislation, most organizations and managers are on the lookout to prevent such biases from leading to discrimination. Ironically, programs designed to protect against personal biases and subsequent discrimination may lead to instances of reverse discrimination, a bias toward favoring a member of a particular underrepresented group over members of the majority group.

Cross-Cultural and International Issues

The individual focus of performance appraisals, where a single worker is the focus of the evaluation, is, in many ways, a Western/U.S. view of evaluating performance (Fletcher & Perry, 2001). In many non-U.S. cultures, the focus is on the work group, or collective, instead of on individual performance. For instance, Japanese and Russian workers may prefer receiving performance feedback at the group, rather than the individual, level (Elenkov, 1998). Research has also suggested that cultures that are less egalitarian are less accepting of 360-degree performance appraisals, presumably because there is resistance to the idea of having lower-level workers and peers evaluate managers' performance (Peretz & Fried, 2012). There may also be cultural norms regarding how direct and "blunt" feedback can be (Fletcher & Perry, 2001). Because of the personal nature of traditional performance appraisals, it is important that cultural norms and expectations be considered in the development and delivery of a performance appraisal system.

Stop & Review

Describe five sources or types of error/bias in performance appraisals.

APPLYING I/O PSYCHOLOGY

Combating the Actor–Observer Bias in Performance Appraisals

The actor–observer bias, or the tendency for actors to make situational attributions and for observers to make dispositional attributions, is a particular problem in performance appraisals that can lead to inaccurate assessments and cause rifts between the evaluating supervisor and subordinates. How can this bias be overcome?

One way to try to combat this problem is to create performance rating forms that require the evaluator to take into account the various situational factors that may have hampered the employee's performance (Bernardin et al., 1998). Although this strategy can avoid

some of the observer bias, there may still be some tendencies toward overattributing cause to dispositional characteristics of the worker. An even better remedy is to change the perspective of the observers/evaluators by providing them with direct experience with the actor's job. Because much of the actor–observer bias is the result of the differing perspectives of the actor and the observer, putting the observer/appraiser "in the shoes" of the actor/worker can help the observer see conditions as the actor sees them (Mitchell & Kalb, 1982).

A large savings and loan organization has done just that. All supervisors who are responsible for

APPLYING I/O PSYCHOLOGY

(Continued)

conducting the performance appraisals of customer service representatives—tellers and loan officers—must spend 1 week during each appraisal period working in customer service. The belief is that, because many of these supervisors are far removed from the customer service situation, they are unable to evaluate objectively the pressures that the workers have to deal with, such as difficult or irate customers. Providing appraisers with this direct experience helps them take into account the situational variables that affect employees' performance, thus leading to more accurate assessments.

A common misconception is that the actor–observer bias will be overcome if both supervisor performance appraisals and workers' self-appraisals are obtained. However, if the actor–observer bias is operating, all this will produce is two very discrepant performance appraisals: one from the supervisor, blaming the worker for poor performance, and one from the worker, blaming the situation. Peer evaluations, likewise, will not be of much help, because coworkers are also subject to the actor–observer bias. Peer evaluations will also over-attribute cause to characteristics of the person being appraised, because the coworker is also an observer.

The Dynamic Nature of Performance Today

In today's modern world of work, many jobs constantly change and evolve. The measures used to evaluate performance at one point in a job may not still be valid a short time later, as the job requirements "morph" into something very different. This is particularly true in start-up organizations, where jobs may become either more specialized over time or become broader, quickly encompassing new duties and responsibilities.

Another concern is that annual, biannual, or even quarterly performance reviews are far too infrequent to adequately assess ongoing performance and provide more immediate performance feedback. Many managers, and even HR professionals, are becoming disenchanted with traditional performance reviews owing to concerns about the accuracy of measurement and the long time intervals between evaluations (Wilkie, 2015). As a result, many organizations are abandoning traditional performance reviews and using briefer, and more frequent, "check-ins"—which are like mini performance assessments. For example, General Electric (GE) has eliminated annual performance reviews and, instead, has managers conduct regular feedback sessions via a smartphone app that was designed in-house (Baldassarre & Finken, 2015).

Other organizations are turning to more frequent assessment of performance goals, believing there are important advantages to using smartphone apps or online check-ins to provide more immediate feedback from managers and from other team members. There are several advantages:

- Problems and issues can be dealt with more quickly.
- The instant electronic technology appeals to younger workers.
- It allows for quicker assessment of performance goal attainment, leading to faster raises and promotions.
- It creates a more engaged workforce.

In addition to the use of apps and other sorts of "immediate" technology to give workers performance feedback, many organizations are outsourcing the performance appraisal process to firms that collect performance evaluations online and aggregate and summarize the data to produce reports to the workers being evaluated and their supervisors. This is particularly true when companies decide to use 360-degree evaluations, which require sophisticated technology to collect and analyze the data. As a result, there is a growing industry that helps organizations with performance reviews, often offering their own evaluation instruments and rating scales that the organization can adopt or customize for their own use. When using these outside services, however, it is important that the organization be engaged in the selection and/or the creation of the performance review measures and should monitor the process to make sure that it is being done correctly and effectively.

Positive Employee Behaviors

Although employers want their employees to be satisfied and committed to the organization, job satisfaction and organizational commitment are attitudes. What employers really care about is how job satisfaction and organizational commitment translate into positive employee behaviors. We have already explored the connections between job satisfaction, organizational commitment, and the important work behaviors of job performance, absenteeism, and turnover. However, there are other forms that positive employee behaviors can take.

Organizational Citizenship Behaviors

Early research on positive employee behaviors focused on altruistic, or prosocial, behaviors. Prosocial behaviors are those that go beyond specific job requirements to promote the welfare of the work group and the organization (Organ, 2018). Protecting an organization from unexpected dangers, suggesting methods of organizational improvement without expecting a payoff, undertaking deliberate self-development, preparing oneself for higher levels of organizational responsibility, and speaking favorably about the organization to outsiders are all forms of prosocial behavior. Subsequent research suggested that workers have deep-seated motives for performing prosocial behaviors (Rioux & Penner, 2001). Not only do prosocial behaviors have positive influences on the ability of individuals and teams to do their jobs, but there is also evidence of a positive relationship with job satisfaction (Smith et al., 1983).

Researchers have looked more broadly at worker behaviors that benefit the organization. This cluster of "pro-organizational" behaviors, which includes organizational prosocial behaviors, has been termed "organizational citizenship behavior" (Organ, 1988). **Organizational citizenship behavior (OCB)** consists of efforts by organizational members to advance or promote the work organization, its image, and its goals (Figure 5.6). Job satisfaction, as well as motivating job characteristics, such as jobs that provide workers with autonomy and meaningful work (we will discuss such motivating "job characteristics" in Chapter 8), combine to help produce organizational citizenship behaviors (Van Dyne et al., 1994). In addition, certain personality types, particularly persons who are "agreeable" and conscientious employees, are more likely to perform OCBs (Chiaburu et al., 2011). Table 5.3 presents a list of categories of OCB.

OCBs are positively correlated with both job satisfaction and organizational commitment (Podsakoff et al., 2000). In addition, employees who engage in more OCBs are less likely to turn over than those who do not engage in OCBs (Chen

Organizational Citizenship Behavior (OCB)
efforts by organizational members to advance or promote the work organization and its goals

Figure 5.6 Demonstrating positive feelings about your organization is an example of organizational citizenship behaviors.

Source: Photograph by Brooke Cagle, found on Unsplash (https://unsplash.com/photos/TxSVq Ngnjq4).

Table 5.3 Types of Organizational Citizenship Behaviors (OCBs)

Helping Behavior—voluntarily helping others with work-related problems; helping prevent others from encountering problems; keeping the peace/managing conflict

Sportsmanship—maintaining a positive attitude in the face of challenges or problems; tolerating inconveniences and impositions; not taking rejection personally; sacrificing personal interests for the sake of the group

Organizational Loyalty—promoting the organization to outsiders; defending the organization from external threats; remaining committed to the organization even under adverse conditions

Organizational Compliance—accepting and adhering to the organization's rules and procedures; being punctual; not wasting time

Individual Initiative—volunteering to take on additional duties; being particularly creative and innovative in one's work; encouraging others to do their best; going above and beyond the call of duty

Civic Virtue—participating in organizational governance; looking out for the organization (e.g., turning out lights to save energy, reporting possible threats, etc.); keeping particularly informed about what the organization is doing

Self-Development—voluntarily working to upgrade one's knowledge and skills; learning new skills that will help the organization

Source: Podsakoff et al., 2000.

et al., 1998) and are less likely to be voluntarily absent (Lee et al., 2004). Moreover, there is evidence that supervisors notice OCBs, tending to give more positive performance appraisals to employees who engage in citizenship behaviors as opposed to those who simply do their jobs. In addition, managers and leaders have been found to play a critical role in the incidence of employees' OCBs if the leaders engage in OCBs themselves (Yaffe & Kark, 2011). An important question, however, is, "Do OCBs affect the bottom line?" Do employees' organizational citizenship behaviors affect organizational performance? Research suggests that employees who "go the extra mile" and exhibit OCBs do indeed have work groups and organizations that are more productive and produce higher-quality work than work groups exhibiting low levels of OCBs (Podsakoff & MacKenzie, 1997). Organizational citizenship behaviors seem to affect work performance in groups as diverse as salespersons (Podsakoff & MacKenzie, 1997), manufacturing workers (Allen & Rush, 1998), machine crews in a paper mill (Podsakoff & MacKenzie, 1997), and restaurant crews (Walz & Niehoff, 1996).

Podsakoff and MacKenzie (1997) suggested a number of reasons why OCBs may be related to organizational effectiveness. They include the following:

- Workers who help new coworkers "learn the ropes" help them to speed up the orientation and socialization process and become more productive employees faster.
- Employees who help each other need less managerial supervision, freeing up the managers' time for other important duties.

- Employees who have positive attitudes toward one another are more cooperative and avoid destructive conflicts with other workers.
- Workers freely and voluntarily meet outside work times and regularly touch base with one another, improving the flow of organizational communication.
- OCBs lead to a positive work environment and help in the recruitment and retention of the best-qualified workers.
- Workers pick up the slack and "cover" for one another during absences or times of heavy individual workloads.
- Employees are more willing to take on new responsibilities or learn new technology or work systems.

As can be seen, organizational citizenship behaviors lead to work groups that engage in the best sorts of organizational and personnel processes and may help explain what separates the top-performing work groups and organizations from those who have substandard levels of performance. On the other hand, some workers might be so involved in work and going above and beyond their job descriptions, engaging in so many OCBs, that it might interfere with their personal lives. Indeed, it is critically important that management recognize employees' OCBs, acknowledging and rewarding employees for engaging in these positive work behaviors, or else workers will experience a sort of "citizenship fatigue" ("I do all of this for the organization, but no one cares")—leading to a negative impact on the employee and the organization (Bolino et al., 2015).

An interesting question concerns whether workers in various countries engage in the same organizational citizenship behaviors and at the same levels. Research suggests that, although OCBs seem to be more or less universal, there are differences in how workers and organizations view these behaviors. For example, workers and supervisors in China and Japan are more likely to view OCBs as an everyday, expected part of one's job than do workers in the U.S. or Australia (Lam et al., 1999). Nevertheless, there is evidence that OCBs are positively correlated with measures of the productivity and service quality of Taiwanese bank employees (Yen & Niehoff, 2004), government and manufacturing employees in China (Liu et al., 2013), and Korean travel agents (Yoon & Suh, 2003).

Counterproductive and Deviant Work Behaviors

Counterproductive Work Behaviors (CWBs)
deviant, negative behaviors that are harmful to an organization and its workers

Beyond the role of negative emotions, what are some negative employee behaviors that are of major concern to organizations? I/O psychologists have investigated **counterproductive work behaviors (CWBs)**, which are deviant behaviors that are harmful to an employee's organization and the organization's members (Bennett & Robinson, 2000). Counterproductive work behaviors include such things as stealing from employers, vandalism, sabotage, harassment of coworkers, deliberately missing work, and using drugs or alcohol on the job (see Table 5.4 and Figure 5.7).

Research has shown that CWBs can result from stress, frustration at work, feelings of inequity, or even from jealousy, which cause attempts to retaliate against the employer and seek revenge (Jensen et al., 2010; Shoss et al., 2016). Meta-analyses suggest that CWBs are more prevalent in younger employees and those with lower job

Table 5.4 Examples of Counterproductive Work Behaviors (CWBs)

Said something hurtful to or made fun of a coworker

Acted rudely or publicly embarrassed a coworker

Took property from work without permission

Falsified a receipt to get reimbursed for more than you spent on a business expense

Took an additional or longer work break than is acceptable

Came in late to work without permission

Neglected to follow your boss's instructions

Used an illegal drug or consumed alcohol on the job

Dragged out work in order to get paid overtime

Discussed confidential company information with an unauthorized person

Made a derogatory ethnic, religious, or racial remark at work

Littered your work environment

Intentionally worked slower than you could have worked

Source: Bennett & Robinson, 2000.

Figure 5.7 Employee theft is one form of counterproductive work behaviour.

Source: Photograph by Tim Gouw, found on Unsplash.

satisfaction (Lau et al., 2003). Just like many of the other work-related attitudes and behaviors, there are personality correlates of CWBs. Bolton and colleagues (2010) showed that the personality dimensions of agreeableness and conscientiousness negatively relate to CWBs. Agreeableness was most highly related to interpersonally directed CWBs, while conscientiousness was most related to organizationally directed CWBs such as workplace sabotage and withdrawal. Extraversion was negatively related to theft, and openness to experience positively predicted employees purposely doing their job wrong.

Researchers suggest that organizations should engage in programs to try to alleviate sources of stress and provide strategies to give workers greater control over their jobs as a way to reduce CWBs. There is evidence that CWBs are not just individually motivated ("bad apples"), but can also be influenced by the norms and values of the group and organization ("bad barrels"; O'Boyle et al., 2011). (We will discuss group level influences on behavior fully in Chapter 12.) Also, making sure that employees are treated fairly, providing reasonable workloads, clearly defining jobs, and having supervisors trained to mediate interpersonal disputes among workers are other strategies to prevent counterproductive behavior and workplace violence (Atwater & Elkins, 2009).

Stop & Review

Give five examples of counterproductive work behaviors.

The Performance Appraisal Process

In the past few decades, research on performance appraisals has increasingly focused on the cognitive processes underlying performance appraisal decisions—how an evaluator arrives at an overall evaluation of a worker's performance (e.g., Kravitz & Balzer, 1992). This research views performance appraisal as a complex, decision-making process, looking at (a) how information about the worker's performance is acquired, (b) how the evaluator organizes and stores information about a worker's performance behaviors, and (c) how the evaluator retrieves and translates the stored information in making the actual performance appraisal (Howell et al., 2015). Evaluators form ongoing, or "online," evaluations of others from observing behavior day to day, rather than just waiting until the time a formal performance rating is required and then forming an opinion based solely on memory (Pulakos et al., 2015). Because evaluation of performance is an ongoing, information-processing task, evaluators should be presented with the performance appraisal rating instruments up front so that they can familiarize themselves with the rating dimensions before they begin to observe and evaluate performance.

In addition to evaluating workers' performance, the performance appraisal must include **performance feedback**, which is the process of providing information to a worker regarding performance level with suggestions for improving future performance (Boswell & Boudreau, 2002). Performance feedback typically occurs in the context of the performance appraisal interview. Here, the supervisor typically sits down face-to-face with the worker and provides a detailed analysis of the worker's

Performance Feedback
the process of giving information to a worker about performance level with suggestions for future improvement

performance, giving positive, constructive criticism and suggestions and guidelines for improvement. Guidelines for effective feedback are given in Table 5.5. Although constructive feedback is critical to a good performance appraisal, more "informal" feedback from supervisor to subordinate should take place regularly, on a day-to-day basis.

Because of the importance of performance appraisals, the appraisal process is likely to have some psychological and emotional effects on the worker. It is crucial that the supervisor be aware of this potential impact of the procedure and be equipped to deal with the worker's possible reactions (O'Malley & Gregory, 2011). Whether the worker perceives the performance appraisal process positively or negatively, and how the worker acts on the information provided in the feedback session, are in large part determined by how the information is presented by the supervisor. Supervisors who have a more positive orientation toward feedback themselves are perceived more positively than those who do not (Steelman & Wolfeld, 2018). O'Malley and Gregory (2011) further suggest that supervisors should use empathy during the feedback session and focus on what success will look like for the employee, taking a learning goal orientation and focusing on how performance can be improved. At the end of the day, performance appraisals are so important that we suggest managers should be appraised on their ability to deliver effective appraisals. Those who do a good job should be rewarded, and those who do not should receive coaching to improve. (See "Up Close" for suggestions on how to improve performance appraisals, and see Table 5.6, which provides suggestions for appraiser training programs.)

Table 5.5 Guidelines for **Effective Performance Feedback**

1 Feedback should be descriptive rather than evaluative
2 Feedback should be specific rather than general
3 Feedback should be appropriate, taking into account the needs of the employer, the worker, and the situation
4 Feedback should be directed toward behavior that the worker can do something about or is able to change
5 Feedback should be well timed. More immediate feedback is usually more effective
6 Feedback should be honest rather than manipulative or self-serving
7 Feedback should be understood by both parties. If necessary, additional input should be sought to enhance and clarify the feedback process
8 Feedback should be proactive and coactive. When change in past behavior is required, specific directions for change should be provided. Both parties should agree on the need for change and the remedy
9 Feedback should not be used as an opportunity to criticize or to find fault with the worker. It should be a natural process in the ongoing superior–subordinate relationship

Source: Harris, 1993.

Table 5.6 Suggestions for a Good Appraiser Training Program

Hauenstein (1998) suggests that a good training program for performance appraisers should have the following:

1 Appraisers should be familiarized with the performance dimensions used in the evaluation system
2 Appraisers should be provided with opportunities for practice and feedback (using written or videotaped examples)
3 Appraisers should be informed about common rating biases and trained to reduce these biases
4 Appraisers should be trained to improve their observational skills and use notes and behavioral diaries
5 Training should improve appraiser's self-confidence in conducting performance appraisals
6 Appraisers should be trained to provide good feedback, to be sensitive to employees' reactions to evaluations, and to involve employees in the process as much as possible

 UP Close   How to Improve Performance Appraisals

Given the importance of performance appraisals and the difficulties associated with conducting appraisals, Wallace et al. (2016) offered these evidence-based suggestions:

1 *Train the appraisers*—Because conducting good performance appraisals is a difficult process, prone to error and potential bias, it is imperative that appraisers be adequately trained. They must be taught how to use the various appraisal instruments and should be instructed to avoid possible errors, such as halo effects and leniency/severity errors. Appraisers should be knowledgeable of the performance appraisal methods and procedures up front, before they begin observing workers' performance, so they know what they should look for in their direct reports' performance.
2 Encourage employee participation. Performance appraisals are not supposed to be unidirectional conversations. Both the appraiser and the appraised should contribute to the conversation, state opinions, and shape the course of the discussion to make the appraisal as fair and effective as possible. Yet, one study showed that appraisers speak three times as long as those being appraised, and this was particularly true during the performance review portion of the meeting compared with the developmental portion of the meeting (Meinecke et al., 2017).
3 Create transparent systems. All employees should understand how performance appraisals are conducted and what is expected of them. Not only will this make the appraisal feel fairer, but it is useful for employees to understand what is being measured so they can allocate their efforts in a way that is consistent with expectations.

Legal Concerns in Performance Appraisals

In theory, employers in the U.S. have had the right to terminate an employee, with or without cause, in what is called "employment-at-will" rights. With increased employment litigation, however, this right to fire at will has been challenged. Most often, discharged employees have argued that there was an "implied employment contract," such as promises made by an employer. For example, before deregulation of provision of utilities (e.g., electricity), many utility employees were led to believe that they had "lifetime employment," because workers were rarely fired or laid off. However, in the more competitive post-deregulation environment, utility companies needed to downsize, causing many of the laid-off workers to seek legal recourse. To prevent problems in this area, employers should be careful to fully inform new employees about employment-at-will and should avoid making any sort of real or implied "contracts" or promises regarding future employment. This is also another reason why performance appraisals need to be accurate, frequent, and backed up with good recordkeeping. For instance, if an employee has a record of mediocre or substandard performance and is one of the first to be let go during a workforce reduction, having accurate records of the employee's performance will reduce the company's exposure should the employee seek legal recourse.

Because performance appraisals are tied to personnel actions such as promotions, demotions, and raises, they are carefully scrutinized in terms of fair employment legislation. Under these legal guidelines, any performance appraisal must be valid. As we covered in Chapter 3, if a performance appraisal intentionally or unintentionally discriminates against employees of a particular race, gender, religion, color, or national origin, then the appraisal design must stand up to legal standards. Supreme Court cases have ruled that appraisals must be based on a job analysis and validated against the job duties that the workers actually perform (*Albemarle Paper v. Moody*, 1975; *United States v. City of Chicago*, 1978). In addition, performance appraisals must also be administered and scored under controlled and standardized conditions (*Brito v. Zia Company*, 1973), and appraisers should receive training, or at least written instructions, on how to conduct performance appraisals (Dorsey & Mueller-Hanson, 2017). Further, additional case law has determined that not having a performance appraisal cannot be used as a defense for alleged discrimination (*Watson v. Fort Worth Bank & Trust*, 1988).

In addition to civil rights legislation, the Americans with Disabilities Act (ADA) requires that employers make reasonable accommodations for disabled workers in performing their jobs, and performance appraisals of these workers need to take into account both the disability and the accommodations to avoid discrimination in the appraisal. Despite these laws, there is consistent evidence that women, people of color, those with disabilities, members of the LGBTQ+ community, and pregnant employees experience discrimination in performance evaluations (Colella et al., 2017). In some instances, bias in performance appraisals can be intentional. But,

⏱ Stop & Review
Outline five techniques for improving performance appraisals.

in many other instances, bias is unintentional and based on unconscious biases and performance expectations that individuals hold for different groups. For example, a creative, innovative idea might actually be more likely to be noticed and encoded when exhibited by a man than a woman (Howell et al., 2015). In addition, the very same behavior can be interpreted differently when exhibited by White men than when exhibited by women or people of color, having differential impacts on performance evaluations (Hekman et al., 2017).

Summary

A thorough job analysis is the starting point for measuring and evaluating actual job performance. *Performance appraisals* involve the assessment of worker performance on the basis of predetermined organizational standards. Performance appraisals serve many important purposes, including being the basis for personnel decisions and a means of assessing performance. One way to categorize performance is in terms of objective and subjective criteria. *Objective performance criteria* are more quantifiable measurements of performance, such as the number of units produced or dollar sales. *Subjective performance criteria* typically involve judgments or ratings of performance. Concerns for a performance criterion include whether it is relevant to job success, called *criterion relevance*; whether the criterion contains elements that detract from the "pure" assessment of performance, termed *criterion contamination*; the degree to which a criterion falls short of perfect assessment of job performance, called *criterion deficiency*; and whether the criterion is usable, called *criterion usefulness*.

Research on ratings of job performance has examined who is making performance ratings. Self-appraisals are ratings or evaluations made by the workers themselves. Peer appraisals involve coworkers rating each other's performance. In some instances, subordinates may rate the performance of their supervisors. Most common, of course, are supervisory ratings of subordinates' performance. The type of feedback called *360-degree feedback* involves getting multiple performance evaluations from supervisors, peers, subordinates, and customers.

There are a variety of methods for rating performance. *Comparative methods* of appraisal, such as the paired comparison and forced distribution techniques, directly compare one worker's performance with that of another worker's. *Individual methods* of appraisal do not make direct comparisons with other workers. Individual methods include *checklists* and forced-choice scales and are easy-to-use methods of appraisal that require the evaluator simply to check off statements characteristic or uncharacteristic of a particular worker's job performance. The most common method of individual performance appraisal involves the use of *graphic rating scales*, whereby an appraiser uses a standardized rating instrument to make a numerical and/or verbal rating of various dimensions of job performance. A specific type of rating technique, the *behaviorally anchored rating scale* (BARS), uses examples of good and poor behavioral incidents as substitutes for the scale anchors found in traditional rating instruments.

A major problem in rating job performance is caused by systematic biases and errors. Response tendency errors, such as *leniency/severity* or *central tendency errors*, lead to consistently good, bad, or average ratings, respectively. *Halo effects* occur when appraisers make overall positive (or negative) performance appraisals because of one known outstanding characteristic or action. There are also errors caused by giving greater weight to more recent performance, known as *recency effects*, and various attribution errors, including *actor–observer bias*. The latter may lead an appraiser to place greater emphasis on dispositional factors and lesser emphasis on situational factors that may have affected performance.

In addition to in-role job performance, employees are also evaluated on their *organizational citizenship behaviors* (going above and beyond) and *counterproductive work behaviors (CWBs)*, which are deviant behaviors that are harmful to an employee's organization such as stealing, vandalism, sabotage, harassment of coworkers, deliberately missing work, and using drugs or alcohol on the job.

A good performance appraisal consists of two parts: the performance assessment and *performance feedback*. The feedback should occur in a face-to-face situation in which the supervisor provides constructive information, encouragement, and guidelines for the improvement of the worker's future performance.

Because performance appraisals are important to the worker's livelihood and career advancement, there are considerable legal overtones to the appraisal process. Performance appraisals must be valid procedures, resulting from job analysis, that do not unfairly discriminate against any group of workers.

Study Questions and Exercises

1 Think of a job you have had in the past, or talk to someone you know about his or her job. Using what you know about the position, try to determine what the relevant performance criteria would be for the job. Develop methods for assessing the performance criteria. Would you measure these criteria objectively or subjectively?

2 Using the job from question 1, design a performance appraisal system for the position. What does it consist of? Who will do the evaluations?

3 What are the advantages and disadvantages of using graphic rating scales versus comparative methods in performance appraisals?

4 In some organizations, performance appraisals are taken too lightly: they receive little attention and are conducted irregularly and infrequently, and there is little motivation for appraisers to do a good job. Why might this occur? Imagine that your task is to convince the management of one of these organizations to improve its performance appraisal system. What would you say to convince the management? What components of a good performance appraisal system would you suggest be implemented?

5 When considering organizational citizenship behaviors (OCBs) and counterproductive work behaviors (CWBs), what would the organization or your supervisor have to do to motivate you to engage in OCBs? Is there anything that would cause you to engage in CWBs?

Web Links

www.performance-appraisal.com
This site, maintained by Archer North Consultants, has some interesting information on performance appraisals.
http://performance-appraisals.org
This site has a wealth of resources to help understand performance appraisals, including many suggested books and a Q&A area.

Suggested Readings

Bayo-Moriones, A., Galdon-Sanchez, J. E., & Martinez-de-Morentin, S. (2020). Performance appraisal: dimensions and determinants. *The International Journal of Human Resource Management, 31*(15), 1984–2015.

DeNisi, A., Murphy, K., Varma, A., & Budhwar, P. (2021). Performance management systems and multinational enterprises: Where we are and where we should go. *Human Resource Management, 60*(5), 707–713.

Maley, J. F., Marina, D., & Moeller, M. (2020). Employee performance management: charting the field from 1998 to 2018. *International Journal of Manpower, 42,* 131–149.

Trost, A. (2017). *The end of performance appraisal: A practitioners' guide to alternatives in agile organisations.* Switzerland: Springer.

CHAPTER 6

Employee Training and Development

Inside Tips
ISSUES OF TRAINING AND TRAINING METHODS

This chapter concludes the focus on personnel processes by looking at how employees are trained and developed over their careers. We will also touch on topics that were introduced in several of the earlier chapters. We return to methodological issues (particularly experimental design issues) when considering the evaluation of training programs. The section on assessing training needs is in some ways related to the discussion of job analysis procedures in Chapter 3, except that now we are assessing what knowledge, skills, abilities, and other characteristics (KSAOs) workers need to perform their jobs, rather than analyzing the jobs themselves. Analyses of employee performance data (Chapter 5) can also assist in training needs analysis. When going through the discussion on employee training, you should see some similarities to the sort of "training" and education you are receiving in college. After all, learning is learning.

You have just graduated from college. You went through the arduous process of applying for jobs, being screened, interviewed, and "courted" to some extent by your employer. You are anxious to get to work—to show them what you can do and to make your mark on the company. However, before you are able to get started, the company sends you to a training center where you will learn the basics of the job, learn company policies and procedures, and learn about the culture of your new organization (we will discuss organizational culture and onboarding in Chapter 11 on Socialization and Working in Groups).

Employee training is a planned effort by an organization to facilitate employees' learning, retention, and transfer of job-related behavior. In most organizations, training is not limited to new employees, as various types of training and development programs are offered at all stages of an employee's career.

Employee Training
planned organizational efforts to help employees learn job-related knowledge, skills, and other characteristics

In this chapter, we will begin by examining areas of employee training. We will also examine the fundamentals of the learning process and how learning applies to employee training and development. We will then look at factors that affect the success of training programs. Next, we will look at how employee training needs are assessed and study general training methods. Finally, we will examine how training programs are evaluated.

Areas of Employee Training

Training, like learning, is a lifelong process. Organizations need to provide for the wide variety of training needs of workers to stay competitive. We will briefly examine some of these specific focuses of employee training and development programs. One of the most common types of training, new employee training, will be covered in Chapter 11, in our discussion of employee socialization, along with diversity training and team training. Leadership training will be discussed in the leadership chapter (Chapter 14). We will focus here on the fundamentals of training design.

Retraining and Continuing Education Programs

Considerable evidence indicates that a certain amount of the knowledge and skills of workers either erodes or becomes obsolete during their work careers, and this reality is only increasing with advancements in artificial intelligence (Ghislieri et al., 2018). To maintain workers' proficiencies, organizations must encourage and support basic "refresher courses," as well as continuing education programs that provide workers with new information. With rapid technological advancements, it is critical that the skills and knowledge of persons employed in jobs that require the use of advanced technology be constantly updated.

Certain professionals, particularly those in licensed health-care professions such as medicine, dentistry, and clinical psychology, require some form of continuing education to continue to work in the field. Other professionals, such as managers, lawyers, engineers, and architects, are also increasingly encouraged to participate in continuing education programs.

Research on employee training/retraining suggests that organizations' investment in employee training pays off. For example, in one study, employees showed more commitment to the organization after training, and there was a short-term decrease in absenteeism, presumably because employees realize that the firm is investing in them (Kampkötter & Marggraf, 2015). Another study found that training reduced employee turnover, but that the effect was mediated by employee job satisfaction (Koster et al., 2011).

Retirement Planning and Preparation

The training departments of many organizations offer employees assistance in planning and preparing for retirement (Figure 6.1). Research suggests that many workers do not prepare well (or at all) for retirement (Kim & Moen, 2001). Seminars are offered on such topics as making the retirement decision, retirement plans and options, investment and money management, and services and opportunities for retirees and seniors. More general programs aimed at helping retirees adjust to a nonworking lifestyle are also offered. An increase in preretirement training programs reflects a general trend toward more employee training and greater concern for employees' pre- and postretirement welfare. One study found that both pre- and postretirement planning were needed for employees to successfully retire (Donaldson et al., 2010). Another study suggested that employees who think about retirement early by contributing to a retirement savings plan tended to be healthier than noncontributors—a positive outcome for both employees and organizations (Gubler & Pierce, 2014).

Employee Career Development

Organizations are becoming more and more aware of the need for greater attention to be given to the development and planning of employees' careers. Helping

Figure 6.1 An employer-sponsored session for retirement planning.

Source: Photograph by Amy Hirschi, found on Unsplash (https://unsplash.com/photos/W7aX Y5F2pBo).

workers plan their careers can help lead to a more productive, more satisfied, and more loyal workforce (Gaffney, 2005). This may be particularly true for younger workers (Akkermans et al., 2014). Many organizations have developed formal career development systems, which benefit all parties involved, including workers, managers, and the organization (Maurer & Chapman, 2013; see Table 6.1).

Career development systems typically offer a variety of programs, including career counseling, courses in career planning, and workshops that provide tools and techniques for helping employees manage their careers. For example, career counseling programs might help individuals set career goals and develop a plan for getting the type of training and education necessary to meet those goals. They may also assist in finding jobs for employees who are about to be laid off. With increased job mobility and organizational downsizing, research has demonstrated that it is very important today for employees to learn to take responsibility for and "self-manage" their careers (Barnett & Bradley, 2007). Moreover, companies that demonstrate they are concerned about employee career advancement are going to be more successful at attracting and retaining employees.

Table 6.1 Benefits of a Career Development System

For Managers/Supervisors	For Employees	For the Organization
Increased skill in managing own careers	Helpful assistance with career decisions and changes	Better use of employee skills. Increased loyalty
Greater retention of valued employees	Enrichment of present job and increased job satisfaction	Dissemination of information at all organizational levels
Better communication between manager and employee	Better communication between employee and manager	Better communication within organization as a whole
More realistic staff and development planning	More realistic goals and expectations. Better feedback on performance	Greater retention of valued employees
Productive performance appraisal discussions	Current information about the organization and future trends	Expanded public image as a people-developing organization
Increased understanding of the organization	Greater sense of personal responsibility for managing career	Increased effectiveness of personnel systems and procedures
Enhanced reputation as a people developer		
Employee motivation for accepting new responsibilities		
Building of talent inventory for special projects		
Clarification of fit between organizational and individual goals		

Source: Leibowitz et al., 1986.

Fundamental Issues in Employee Training

Employee training is rooted in basic theories of learning. Designers of good employee training programs are familiar with learning theories and principles. The most relevant theories for employee training are social learning theory and cognitive theories of learning. **Social learning theory** emphasizes the observational learning of behavior (Bandura, 1997; Bandura & Walters, 1977). A key process in social learning theory is modeling. **Modeling** is imitative learning that occurs through observing and reproducing another person's action, such as when an employee learns to operate a piece of machinery by watching a supervisor work with the equipment and imitating the supervisor's actions. **Cognitive theories of learning** view workers as information processors, focusing on how new information is stored and retrieved and how that information is used to produce work behavior (Cooke et al., 2003). Cognitive theories are particularly useful in understanding complex thought processes, such as how workers can go beyond learned information and come up with novel and creative solutions or ideas.

Social Learning Theory
learning theory that emphasizes the observational learning of behavior

Modeling
learning that occurs through the observation and imitation of the behavior of others

Cognitive Theories of Learning
learning theories that emphasize that humans are information processors

Key Issues in the Success of Training Programs

If employee training programs are to be successful, a number of key issues should be considered. For example, we must take care to see that learning achieved during the training sessions actually transfers to new behaviors at the worksite. We also need to consider the trainees' willingness and readiness to learn. In addition, we need to look at the structure of the training program in terms of when, where, and how training will take place. Let's look more closely at these key training issues.

Transfer of Training

An important concern is the **transfer of training** (Ford et al., 2018). How well does learning transfer from the training situation to the actual work environment? Because training transfer is influenced by the degree of similarity between the training tasks and the actual job tasks, the most useful training programs directly address the actual tasks that are performed on the job. Positive transfer of learned tasks has been found to be maximized when the training mirrors the job and when the job environment allows for and is supportive of practicing newly acquired skills (see Grossman & Salas, 2011, for a review). Given this fact, organizations need to consider the very real

Transfer of Training
concept dealing with whether training is actually applied in the work setting

problem of developing training in one culture and then utilizing the same training design globally or in different cultures (Sarkar-Barney, 2004).

There are numerous other factors that can increase transfer of training. Training transfer is also more likely to occur if the employee voluntarily chooses to enroll in the training program, as opposed to being required to attend the training (Curado et al., 2015). Setting training goals positively affects training transfer (Johnson et al., 2012). Goals are just one piece of creating accountability for transfer of training (Grossman & Burke-Smalley, 2018). Other types of accountability, such as feedback from supervisors and positive reinforcement of utilizing new skills, also help to maintain transfer of training. One study found that, when trainees set goals for implementing the training strategies and feedback was given concerning the achievement of those goals, the trained behaviors tended to stay in place (Wexley & Baldwin, 1986). Without feedback and reinforcement, learned skills or procedures may deteriorate as workers forget some of their important elements, pick up bad habits that interfere with their application, or lapse into using old work strategies (Marx, 1982). Thus, attention should be given to the maintenance of newly learned work behaviors. It is also important that workers see the connection between the learning of new behaviors and how the use of the new learning will enhance their working lives. "Brush-up" or reminder training sessions should follow a few months down the line. In short, training should take place on a regular basis, be thorough, and continue throughout an employee's career. For effective transfer and maintenance of learning, employees must see that learning new work skills helps them to be better, more productive workers, which in turn can lead to promotions and other forms of career advancement.

APPLYING I/O PSYCHOLOGY

Diversity and Sexual Harassment Training

One of the common ways that industrial/organizational psychologists have worked to improve diversity and inclusion in organizations is through diversity training. With internationalization and increased access to jobs, work groups are becoming increasingly diverse, with greater national and cultural diversity and more women in the workforce. This has prompted organizations to allocate resources to diversity training programs and efforts to prevent harassment, including sexual harassment. However, from a training perspective, many of these programs have fallen short in terms of demonstrating changes in behavior. Hayes et al., (2020) argue that diversity and sexual harassment training has utilized relatively poor training design and evaluation. Although meta-analyses show positive effects for diversity training, at least on attitudes, and particularly when combined with other diversity initiatives (Bezrukova et al., 2016), there is still much room for improvement. For example, the benefits of training can be enhanced by doing a needs analysis (Brummel et al., 2019), by ensuring that training is ongoing rather than a one-time event (Robinson et al., 2020), by using training sessions

APPLYING I/O PSYCHOLOGY

(Continued)

that last over 4 hours and involve social interaction (Kalinoski et al., 2013), and by increasing accountability for transfer of training back on the job (Sachdev et al., 2019). Other suggestions include extending diversity training from a focus on perpetrators to also focusing on creating allies (Gardner & Alanis, 2020) and engaging bystanders in training efforts (Lee, Hanson & Cheung, 2019). Yet, others still suggest that training is not the full answer. Hernandez et al. (2020) argue that I/O psychologists should consider as well how recruitment, selection, and performance management systems could also be used to reduce discrimination and harassment.

Trainee Readiness

A second consideration is what could be termed **trainee readiness**. A great deal of research indicates that positive employee attitudes toward training programs are critical for training success (Noe, 1986). Is the trainee prepared to learn? Does the trainee feel the need for training and see the usefulness of the material that will be learned? Trainee ability, or "trainability," is another important factor to consider (Kanfer & Ackerman, 1989). For example, does the employee possess the basic prerequisites to be a good candidate for learning these new behaviors? In other words, does the trainee have the aptitude to learn? Finally, if a training program is going to be successful, we must consider the trainee's motivation (Tharenou, 2001). If a learner has no desire to learn new tasks, it is unlikely that much learning will take place (see Kraiger & Ford, 2021, for a review). Or if a trainee feels unable to master the material—if he or she feels the material is "beyond reach"—learning will be adversely affected (Mathieu, Hofmann et al., 1993; Mathieu, Martineau et al., 1993).

The concept of readiness is particularly important when looking at the training and development of higher-level positions in management and leadership (Day, 2013). Moreover, research has indicated that both giving employees a realistic preview of what the training program is about and providing them with the personal and career-related benefits have positive effects on both trainee reactions to the program and their learning (Smith-Jentsch et al., 1996).

An important issue in some highly skilled, highly specialized jobs, such as surgeon or air traffic controller, is the readiness for a trainee to move from working in a simulated environment to actually performing the job. This sort of trainee readiness has been studied in the medical profession, where simulations are used extensively before the doctor is allowed to practice on an actual patient (Gorman et al., 2020).

Trainee Readiness
the individual's potential for successful training

Training Program Structure

A third issue concerns the structure of the training program. When and how often does training take place? How long are the training sessions? How much opportunity is there for trainees to practice or apply what they have learned? How much guidance and individual attention does each trainee receive?

The bulk of research evidence does indeed support the old adage that "practice makes perfect." In fact, evidence indicates that practice should continue to the point of overlearning, or where practice continues even after the trainee has established that the material has been learned (Driskell et al., 1992). Should the practice be continuous, in what is called massed practice, or should practice sessions be spaced over time? Nearly all evidence supports spaced over massed practice, particularly if the practice involves retrieval-type learning (such as a recall test) rather than recognition learning (Schmidt & Bjork, 1992). Students are probably familiar with this. Studying course material in continuous, spaced sessions over the semester beats intense, last-minute "cramming" nearly every time!

Training research has also looked at whether it is better to segment the material into parts, in what is called part learning, or to present the material as a whole (*whole learning*). The research evidence suggests that whole learning is better than *part learning*, particularly when the trainees have high levels of cognitive abilities (Adams, 1987). For example, teaching a worker to operate a bulldozer would be more successful if presented as a whole task, such as learning to manipulate the controls that both drive the vehicle and operate the shovel, as opposed to learning the two tasks separately, particularly because operating a bulldozer requires driving while simultaneously controlling the shovel.

Another critical element is providing trainees with feedback about learning accomplishments. To be effective, feedback must be immediate rather than delayed. If the feedback is delayed, it will be less effective, because workers tend to distance themselves from past actions. More feedback is generally better, although there is a point where too much feedback may only serve to overload and confuse trainees. Research has also shown that positive feedback—information about what a trainee has done right—is more effective than negative feedback, which focuses on what the trainee has done wrong (Martocchio & Webster, 1992).

Finally, evidence indicates that, to be effective, training programs should be highly structured to increase the meaningfulness of the material to be learned (Fantuzzo et al., 1989). Adding structure to training programs may involve presenting a general overview of the material to trainees before actual training begins and imposing a logical or orderly sequence on the presentation of the training material. Trainees should also be made aware of the importance and goals of practicing newly learned skills (Cannon-Bowers et al., 1998).

A review of various meta-analyses on training program structure identified several key best practices of training design: active learning, training techniques that encourage errors (so that trainees can learn how to deal with them), prompting trainees to continue paying attention, and the use of technology-delivered instruction (Kraiger et al., 2015).

Common Problems in Employee Training Programs

Estimates of the cost of personnel training in the U.S. alone range from the tens of billions to the hundreds of billions of dollars per year. Yet, one problem with many personnel training programs is that, although organizations make a major commitment to training in terms of time, money, and other resources, training programs are not as effective as they could be, partly because they do not adequately follow sound learning principles. Another problem is that employee training programs in some companies are not well organized. Perhaps you have even experienced such "haphazard" training in one of your jobs, where you received little formal training and were expected to learn "on-the-job," with little guidance.

A Model for Successful Training Programs

Theories and principles of learning should be taken into account in the design and implementation of any good employee training program (Bisbey et al., 2020). In addition, to be successful, training programs need to follow a structured, step-by-step model (see Figure 6.2). A successful training program should begin by *assessing training needs*. In other words, the organization must first have some idea of what workers need to know to perform their jobs.

The next step is *establishing training objectives*—goals for what the training is supposed to accomplish. Training objectives need to be specific and related to measurable outcomes because they are used both to set a course for the training program and to help later in determining if the training was indeed successful (Goldstein & Ford, 2002).

The next step in the training program involves the *development and testing of training materials*. A variety of factors must be taken into account in developing training materials, such as the trainees' educational and skill levels, whether the training material focuses on the areas that are directly related to successful job performance, and what training methods will provide the best cost–benefit trade-off. It is also important that training materials be thoroughly tested before they are put into regular use.

The actual *implementation of the training program* is the next step in the training model. Important considerations in implementing the training program include

Figure 6.2. A model for successful employee training programs.

when and how often the training will take place, who will conduct the training, the assignment of trainees to sessions, and where the training will be conducted.

The final step is the *evaluation of the training program* to determine if the training was effective. This step involves a detailed analysis of whether training objectives were met and whether the training translates into trainees using the newly learned behaviors on the job.

Let's look more closely at some of the issues related to successful personnel training programs, starting with a discussion of training needs assessment.

Assessing Training Needs

⏱ **Stop** & **Review**

List and define four key issues that are important in determining the success of training programs.

A successful training program should begin by assessing training needs (Ferreira et al., 2015). In other words, the organization must have some idea of what workers need to know to perform their jobs. Typically, an assessment of training needs should include analyses on many levels: the organizational level (the needs and goals of the organization), the task level (the requirements for performing the task), and the person level (the skills and knowledge required to do the job). An additional analysis can be done at the demographic level (determining training needs for specific demographic groups).

Organizational Analysis

The organizational level of needs analysis considers issues such as the long- and short-term organizational goals and their implications for training, the available training resources, and the general climate for training (that is, the workers' and supervisors' commitment to participation in the training program). In addition, organizational analysis considers training needs that are the result of internal and external factors affecting the organization. For example, the introduction of a new manufacturing system and technology would require the organization to plan the kinds of technical skills, managerial skills, and support that workers will need to use the new machines and processes (Salas & Cannon-Bowers, 2001). An organization might also make a commitment to improving issues around diversity and inclusion and make that a training priority for the organization. Support from peers, supervisors, and the organization all increase transfer of training (Hughes et al., 2020). In an organizational analysis, a strategy for assessing the training climate might involve surveying employees regarding their perceptions of training needs and their attitudes toward participation in training programs. The organizational level of needs analysis would also want to determine whether managers' expectations regarding training needs were consistent with organizational goals.

Task Analysis

The task level of analysis is concerned with the knowledge, skills, abilities, and other characteristics (KSAOs) that a worker requires to perform a specific job effectively. The starting point for obtaining this information is the job description derived from a detailed job analysis. (As you may recall from Chapter 3, a job analysis is the starting point for just about any personnel operation.) The next and most difficult step involves translating the specific task requirements of the job into the basic components of knowledge and skill that can be incorporated into a training program. For example, a job as department store assistant manager might require the worker to handle customer complaints effectively. However, it may be difficult to determine the specific skills required to perform this task to train prospective employees.

Person Analysis

The person analysis of employee training needs examines the current capabilities of the workers themselves to determine who needs what sort of training. Person analysis usually relies on worker deficiencies outlined in performance appraisals for incumbent workers and information derived from employee selection data, such as screening tests, for new workers. Another important source of information is job incumbents' self-assessments of training needs (Ford & Noe, 1987), which may also help build employee commitment to the training program.

The use of the three levels of training needs analysis—organizational, task, and person—can help determine which workers need training in which areas and provide information to guide the development of specific training techniques. It has been argued that effective training programs should be based on an analysis of training needs on many levels, rather than simply focusing on one level of analysis (Ostroff & Ford, 1989). In addition, the organization must consider the impact of a proposed training program in terms of both the potential benefits, such as increased efficiency and productivity, and the potential costs of the program itself.

Demographic Analysis

It has been suggested that training needs analysis may have to be conducted on a fourth level, demographic analysis (Latham, 1988). A demographic analysis involves determining the specific training needs of various demographic groups, such as women and men, certain ethnic minorities, and workers of different age brackets. For example, a study of the perceived training needs of workers 40 years of age and older found that the younger workers (aged 40–49 years) believed that they needed training in management skills, and the middle-aged group (aged 50–59 years) preferred training in technological skills, whereas the oldest group (60 years and older) showed little interest in any type of training, perhaps because they felt that they had little to gain from additional training (Tucker, 1985). We will discuss training for special groups later in the chapter.

Establishing Training Objectives

The second step in a successful training program, after assessing needs, is establishing training objectives. As mentioned earlier, it is important that objectives be specific and that they be associated with measurable outcomes. Training objectives should specify what the trainee should be able to accomplish on completion of the training program (Goldstein & Ford, 2002). For example, objectives for a training program for cashiers might be that the trainee will be able to operate and maintain the cash register and make change on completion of training.

Training objectives are important in guiding the design of the training program and the selection of training techniques and strategies. Moreover, the emphasis on establishing training objectives that are specific and measurable is particularly important in eventually evaluating the effectiveness of the training program (Kraiger et al., 1993).

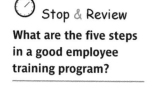

Stop & Review

What are the five steps in a good employee training program?

Developing and Testing of Training Materials: Employee Training Methods

The next step in our employee training model involves developing and testing the training materials. A wide variety of employee training methods are available, ranging from the relatively simple and straightforward to the fairly complex and sophisticated. In actual practice, most comprehensive training programs utilize a combination of several training methods and techniques.

It is important to pilot test the training materials, perhaps by using a group of workers who can provide their reactions to the materials and the program. This process leads to a refinement of the training materials and improvement in the program. Let's look at some of the more common training materials and methods.

Employee training methods can be grouped into two broad categories: the on-site methods—those conducted on the job site—and the off-site methods—those conducted away from the actual workplace.

On-Site Methods

On-site training methods may be further divided into several categories, including on-the-job training, apprenticeship, vestibule training, and job rotation.

On-the-job training—One of the oldest and most widely used training methods, **on-the-job training** consists simply of putting an inexperienced worker in the workplace and having a more experienced worker teach that person about the job. This technique thus relies on principles of modeling, with the experienced worker serving as the role model. Also, because actual hands-on learning is involved, the worker can receive immediate feedback, be reinforced for successful efforts, and have a chance to learn how to correct errors.

Reasons for the popularity of on-the-job training are obvious: it requires little preparation and has few costs to the organization, aside from the time invested by the experienced worker. Moreover, because the trainee is actually working while learning, certain small levels of output offset the costs of the supervising worker's time. However, problems occur when the organization neglects to consider the abilities and motivations of the experienced workers who serve as trainers. If these trainers do not see the personal benefits of serving as trainers (especially when there are no obvious benefits!), they will not be motivated to do a good job. Also, being a good trainer requires certain qualities, such as patience and an ability to communicate. If the trainer lacks these characteristics, this can interfere with trainees' learning. For example, one study found that experienced trainers often presented ideas abstractly or spoke "over the heads" of trainees (Hinds et al., 2001). Problems can also arise if the trainer does not know or follow proper work procedures. In this case, the trainer may teach the new worker wrong or inefficient methods.

On-the-job training is best used when the trainers have been carefully selected because of their ability to teach and when they have received systematic training to help them be more effective. Trainers should also receive some type of reward or recognition for performing their training duties, and the best trainers tend to be committed and take pride in the work they do (Choi et al., 2015). Finally, the organization must accept the fact that, during the on-the-job training period, production rates will suffer. It is impossible to expect the trainer–trainee team to do a good job of training while simultaneously maintaining high output rates. It has been suggested that, to be effective, on-the-job training should be used with other training methods, including off-site methods such as seminars and programmed instruction (Wexley & Latham, 2001).

Apprenticeship—Skilled trade professions, such as carpentry, printing, masonry, and plumbing, use a very old type of training program called apprenticeship. A typical **apprenticeship** can last for several years and usually combines some supervised on-the-job training experience (usually at least 2,000 hours) with classroom instruction. The on-the-job experience allows the apprentice to learn the mechanics of the profession, whereas the classroom training usually teaches specific cognitive skills and rules and regulations associated with the profession

On-the-Job Training
an employee training method of placing a worker in the workplace to learn firsthand about a job

 Stop & Review

Describe the four levels of training needs analysis.

Apprenticeship
a training technique, usually lasting several years, that combines on-the-job experience with classroom instruction

(Harris et al., 2003). For example, an apprentice in the housing construction industry will learn the mechanical skills of building a house while on the job and will learn about building codes and how to read blueprints in the classroom. The obvious advantage of apprenticeship programs is the detailed, long-term nature of the learning process. There is good evidence of the business benefits of apprenticeships in terms of increased productivity and lowered turnover (Kenyon, 2005; Smith & Smith, 2005).

It is important to mention that the term *apprenticeship* has been used to describe a number of training programs that are quite different from traditional, formal apprenticeships. These informal "apprenticeships" might be better labeled "mentorships," because they typically do not have the strict combination of hands-on learning and classroom training required by formal apprenticeships. We will discuss mentoring a bit later when we look at the use of mentoring in managerial training.

Vestibule Training

training that uses a separate area adjacent to the work area to simulate the actual work setting

Vestibule training—**Vestibule training** is another on-site training method. This method uses a separate training area adjacent to the actual work area to simulate that setting, complete with comparable tools and equipment. In vestibule training, professional trainers teach the new workers all aspects of the job, allowing them hands-on experience in the work simulation area. The main advantage of vestibule training is that there is no disruption of actual production, because trainers rather than experienced workers provide instruction, and the novice workers are not in the actual work setting. The major drawback to this method is its costs in terms of the trainers, space, and equipment needed. In recent years, some large supermarkets have set up vestibule training areas at closed check-out stations to teach prospective checkers how to operate laser scanners and cash registers to ring up goods. Vestibule training is used to eliminate the delays to customers that inevitably occur when using on-the-job training.

Job Rotation

a method of rotating workers among a variety of jobs to increase their breadth of knowledge

Job rotation—A final on-site training method is **job rotation**, in which workers are rotated among a variety of jobs, spending a certain length of time (usually several weeks to 2 months) at each. The basic premise behind job rotation is to expose workers to as many areas of the organization as possible so they can gain a good knowledge of its workings and how the various jobs and departments fit together. Job rotation can also be beneficial to the organization because of "cross-training" of workers. Thus, if a worker is absent or quits, another worker has already been trained to perform the job. Most commonly, job rotation is used to help entry-level management personnel find the positions for which they are best suited. It can also be used to groom managers for higher-level positions, presumably making them more effective by enabling them to see the organization from a variety of perspectives. Research has shown that job rotation not only increases learning, but also has positive effects on employees' career progression and development (Ortega, 2001). Job rotation has also been used in various team approaches to work-task design to increase worker flexibility, eliminate boredom, and increase worker job satisfaction and commitment to the organization (Wexley & Latham, 2001). When done within a team, job rotation can also enhance team performance by helping team members understand each other's work (Marks et al., 2002).

It is important to mention, however, that job rotation does not consist of simply moving workers from task to task with little or no preparation. A careful analysis of training needs should be done for each position to which a worker is rotated. It is also important to orient and train the worker adequately on each task. Finally, an evaluation should be done of the worker's performance at each task, assessment of the effectiveness of the overall job rotation training experience should be conducted, and feedback to the worker should be provided.

Off-Site Methods

Training that takes place in a setting other than the actual workplace uses off-site methods. Because of the greater flexibility and control over the situation they afford, off-site methods are more varied and diverse than the on-site techniques. We will consider several off-site methods: seminars/webinars, audiovisual instruction, behavior modeling training, simulation techniques, programmed instruction, and computer-assisted instruction.

Seminars/webinars—A common method of employee training, and one that is likely familiar to students, is the **seminar**, which typically involves some expert providing job-related information orally in a classroom-like setting. An online form of seminar, or **webinar**, allows for greater reach to workers in multiple locations, typically with an opportunity to ask questions live or via online text. Although these methods of training allow a large number of workers to be trained simultaneously at relatively low cost, there are some drawbacks. First, because the seminar/webinar is primarily a one-way form of communication, employees may not become highly involved in the learning process. Also, it is unclear whether workers will be able to translate the information they receive from seminars/webinars into actual performance of work behaviors. Finally, the seminar/webinar method is often only as good as the presenter. A training program presented by a speaker who is unprepared and speaks in a monotone is unlikely to lead to any significant learning. In fact, one early study found that the seminar was one of the least effective of various employee training methods (Carroll et al., 1972). On a more positive note, however, seminar methods of instruction have been shown to be an effective learning strategy, particularly when used with more educated workers, such as when seminars are used in managerial and leadership training (Avolio et al., 2009). Another study found a positive impact of an employee health promotion program on healthful behaviors of employees and reduced absenteeism (Mills et al., 2007). A large study of webinars across 419 trainees in 48 webinars, focusing on four content areas (early childhood education, supply chain management, industrial management, and mathematics), demonstrated that trainees generally had positive reactions toward webinar training, but those reactions were particularly positive in sessions that involved greater trainer interaction (such as questions and answers) and those that were shorter (about 90 minutes) in length (Gegenfurtner et al., 2020).

Seminar
a common training method in which an expert provides job-related information in a classroom-like setting

Webinar
an online training method similar to a lecture or seminar

Audiovisual Instruction
the use of pre-recorded videotapes and other electronic media to convey training material

Audiovisual instruction—**Audiovisual instruction** uses videos to train workers. In effect, audiovisual instruction is a seminar or webinar provided in a pre-recorded format—this would include training podcasts. Although there may be some fairly large initial costs for purchase or development of training materials, the audiovisual method can be even more cost-effective than traditional seminar or webinar techniques if large numbers of employees are going to be trained.

As in seminars or webinars, the quality of audiovisual instruction determines its effectiveness as a training tool. In many instances, a video can be more entertaining than a seminar and may do a better job of attracting the audience's attention. An obvious problem occurs, however, when the informational content is sacrificed for entertainment value.

Audiovisual presentations are especially effective when the information is presented visually rather than verbally. A few minutes of video can visually demonstrate manual operations (with instant replay, stop action, or slow motion) or can expose workers to a number of different locations and settings, both of which would be impossible in a seminar presentation. Moreover, the pre-recorded nature of audiovisual programs can ensure uniformity of training by exposing all workers to the same information. For example, one company has prepared a video presentation giving new employees information about company policies, procedures, and employee rights and benefits in a thorough, graphic, and cost-effective manner.

Behavior Modeling Training
a training method that exposes trainees to role models performing appropriate and inappropriate work behaviors and their outcomes and then allows trainees to practice modeling the appropriate behaviors

Behavior modeling training—Another employee training technique is behavior modeling training (Decker & Nathan, 1985). In **behavior modeling training**, which is based on social learning theory, trainees are exposed to videotaped or live role models displaying both appropriate and inappropriate work behaviors as well as their successful or unsuccessful outcomes. Trainees are then allowed an opportunity to try to replicate and practice the positive work behaviors. Research indicates that behavior modeling training, if used correctly, can effectively improve employee job performance (Mann & Decker, 1984). Behavior modeling training was also shown to be effective in computer software training (Gist et al., 1989) and in training U.S. government employees for work in Japan (Harrison, 1992). In another interesting study, behavior modeling training was found to be more effective than either seminars or programmed instruction (see discussion later in the chapter) in training computer operators (Simon & Werner, 1996). Behavior modeling may be a particularly effective strategy for ethics training, where models can demonstrate complex ethical and moral decision making and actions (Kaptein, 2011a).

Simulation Training
training that replicates job conditions without placing the trainee in the actual work setting

Simulation training—**Simulation training** is a method of replicating job conditions to instruct employees in proper work operations without actually putting them in the job setting (Marlow et al., 2017). Jet pilots, astronauts, and nuclear power plant operators are all subjected to intensive simulation training before they are allowed to control the complex and dangerous machinery that they will operate on the job. Simulation training allows the worker hours of practice under conditions that are quite similar to the actual work setting, without allowing the possibility of damaging the equipment, the product, the environment, or themselves.

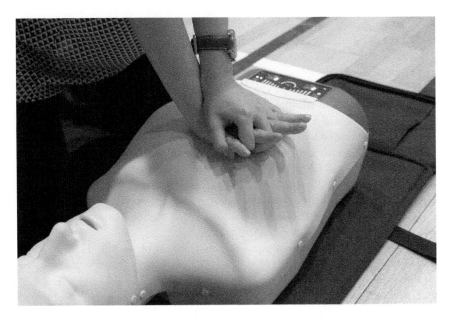

Figure 6.3 CPR (cardio pulmonary resuscitation) training involves hands on training methods using CPR training mannequins.

Source: Image by Manseok Kim, from Pixabay (https://pixabay.com/users/manseok_kim-1005494/).

Most commonly, simulation training uses replications of complex machinery or equipment, such as jet cockpit flight simulators or mock-ups of the control panels used by nuclear power plant operators. Other simulations may be designed to give trainees exposure to what would normally be very hazardous working conditions. For example, a Southern California police department has constructed a mock city (complete with a bank and a convenience store!) for use in training police personnel in simulated emergency conditions. Police trainees attempt to foil simulated robbery attempts and rescue hostages from terrorists using the mock city and blank ammunition. According to the police authorities, the realism of this simulation has led to better preparation of new officers in dealing with actual life-threatening situations. As you can imagine, simulation training is often quite expensive. However, the chance for hands-on experience, immediate feedback, and repeated practice makes it a highly effective technique.

Web-based training—More and more, employee training is being done virtually through web-based, interactive programs, including the previously discussed webinars and podcasts (Gurtner, 2015). Some time ago, Whalen and Wright (2000) argued that much of future training will be web-based owing to the flexibility and scope of the training programs that can be delivered via the web, the convenience of having training "on demand" when employees need it, and the relatively low cost of web-based training in comparison with "live" employee training programs. Little did they know that, essentially, all training would become online training amidst the COVID-19 pandemic in 2020. The World Economic Forum reported that 1.2 billion children in 186 countries around the world experienced school closures as a result of the pandemic (Cathy & Farah, 2020). In many cases, this meant turning to remote learning through online education. Although there is evidence that e-learning can be just as effective as face-to-face instruction (Paul & Jefferson, 2019), it had not been normalized until the pandemic. As a result, many organizations were not ready for online education. One study on ophthalmologist training showed that COVID-19 had greatly impacted doctors' training. In a field where much is learned through clinical hours under supervision, 55% of doctors said that they were doing less than 25% of their normal clinical training hours because of COVID-19 (Ferrara et al., 2020). The ophthalmologists also reported that they would find web-based case presentations, web-based discussion of surgical videos, and simulation-based training effective additions to their training.

Web-based training has incorporated an older form of learning known as *programmed instruction*.

Programmed instruction involves the use of self-paced individualized training. Each trainee is provided with either printed materials or, more commonly, web-based content to learn and then answers a series of questions that test how much learning has taken place. When test answers are substantially correct, the trainee is instructed to move on to the next unit. If the questions are answered incorrectly, some review of the previous unit is required. Most of the student study guides that accompany college textbooks are examples of programmed instruction.

The benefits of programmed instruction are that it is efficient, because individuals proceed at their own pace, and that it provides immediate feedback. In addition, programmed instruction is an "active," involved form of learning. Furthermore, although the development of such programs is time-consuming, the initial cost diminishes greatly over time if large numbers of employees are trained. A problem can arise, however, in keeping the programs up-to-date, especially in fields where there are rapid changes in technology or in the types of products produced or services performed, requiring that new instruction programs be continually created.

Computer-assisted instruction (CAI) is a more sophisticated approach to individualized employee training. Although CAI is actually a form of programmed instruction, CAI systems offer the flexibility to change and update the instructional programs continually. CAI also allows for immediate testing of the trainee's learning, because the computer can ask questions and instantly score the correctness of responses, automatically returning the trainee to an earlier lesson if the answers are incorrect and quickly presenting the next unit when the answers are correct (recall the computer-adaptive and web-based testing discussed in Chapter 4). Typically, training organizations offer web-based courses that can also generate detailed data on each trainee's performance across all the lessons. One problem with individualized instruction such as CAI is that some employees may not have the self-motivation to learn, although interventions that help students plan their

Programmed Instruction
self-paced individualized training in which trainees are provided with training materials and can test how much they have learned

Computer-Assisted Instruction
programmed instruction delivered by computer that adapts to the trainee's learning rate

learning schedule and remind them to pay attention to the material can increase their effectiveness (Sitzmann & Johnson, 2012).

A recent development in CAI is computerized, interactive programs that combine audiovisual techniques, programmed instruction, and simulation techniques. With these programs, a trainee may be presented with a video representation of a work situation, and the computer asks questions about which course of action the trainee would like to take. The response is then used to choose the next video segment, where the trainee can see the results of the choice played out. One such program used for management training exposes the trainee to a variety of difficult interpersonal and decision-making situations. The trainee is brought into a simulated work situation with actors portraying the roles of coworkers. In one setting, the trainee might need to deal with a subordinate who is angry about having been given a negative performance appraisal. In another situation, the trainee may be asked to play the role of leader of a decision-making group and choose one of several possible courses of action. Choosing the correct management strategies leads to a positive outcome. If an incorrect choice is made, the trainee will view the disastrous results played out in the subsequent scene.

There has also been some use of online gaming platforms to develop teams—putting team members through simulated environments in order to build coordination and cooperation among team members. We will discuss team training in Chapter 12. As the Millennial generation becomes more prominent in the workforce, it is likely that we will see a large increase in web-based training, including the use of gaming platforms for training (Grossman et al., 2015). For example, in one study, it was found that gaming-based training led to better employee performance than when employees were trained using non-gamified training (Alcivar & Abad, 2016).

Management/Leadership Training Methods

Because managers and organizational leaders are considered to play such a central role in administrative functions, coordinating organizational activities, and motivating workers, and because managerial skills are abstract and difficult to learn, a large share of training resources goes into the training and development of managers. In fact, a variety of special techniques are used almost exclusively in management training.

One common and popular management training technique is the **problem-solving case study**, which presents trainees with a written description of a real or hypothetical organizational problem. Each trainee is allowed time to study the case individually and come up with a solution. The trainees then meet in small groups to present and critique their solutions and discuss the problem further, helping trainees recognize that there is not always a simple answer—or one correct answer.

Problem-Solving Case Study
a management training technique that presents a real or hypothetical organizational problem that trainees attempt to solve

Analyzing real company decisions helps trainees apply management theories to organizational problems, providing a concrete application to enhance learning (Hack-Polay, 2018).

Role-Playing

a management training exercise that requires trainees to act out problem situations that often occur at work

An extension of this method is to have trainees engage in **role-playing** a certain management situation. For example, in a role-playing exercise to develop managers' abilities to handle difficult interpersonal situations, a trainer may play a subordinate who has chronic performance problems. The trainee plays the manager, and the trainer may later offer feedback concerning how the situation was handled. In role-playing, the basic idea is that trainees will become more involved in a problem situation if they act it out. Sometimes, participants will reverse roles to gain a different perspective on the problem situation. A beneficial side effect of role-playing may be that management trainees simultaneously learn to develop their presentational and communication skills.

Management Games

a management training technique using scaled-down enactments of the operations and managements of organizations

Another management training technique that is becoming increasingly popular is the use of simulations of organizations or **management games**, which are usually scaled-down enactments of the management of organizations (Cruz-Cunha, 2012). They are, in many ways, similar to some of the more complicated board or computer simulation games that people play at home. One example is called "Tinsel Town," where trainees function as the top management team of a fictional movie studio (Devine et al., 2004). Participants may either play in groups, forming management teams to compete against other teams, or play against one another individually. One concern about management games is participants may become so caught up in the game that they do not comprehend the management principles that are being taught. An early review of research on management games, however, indicated that they are an effective management training technique (Keys & Wolfe, 1990).

Action Learning

teams assemble to work on a company-related problem or issue to learn by doing

Action learning, a highly complex, involved type of managerial training/development, consists of teams of employees who are assembled to work on a company-related problem or issue (Volz-Peacock et al., 2016). Rather than being a simulation, action learning has the team working on an actual assignment such as developing a new product or solving an organizational problem (O'Neil & Marsick, 2014). The concept behind action learning is that managers learn by doing, while the organization benefits from the results of the action learning team's project. For example, action learning teams at General Electric have been formed to deal with issues as diverse as investigating markets for leasing locomotive engines, developing new applications for plastic in the design of automobile bodies, and developing marketing plans for foreign markets—with the team members learning as they contribute to expanding GE's businesses (Dotlich & Noel, 1998). Interest in action learning in organizations is on the rise, with an academic journal, *Action Learning: Research & Practice*, devoted to the topic.

Becoming very popular in management development is the use of *360-degree feedback*—the multisource, multi-perspective performance appraisal method that we discussed in Chapter 5. It can be an effective management development tool, but only if the manager is open to and accepting of the potentially critical feedback

(Fletcher, 2015). Atwater et al. (2003) suggest that 360-degree feedback will be most successful when participants are trained in the technique, when feedback is honest and constructive, when the feedback is combined with other training efforts so that the manager can see how to improve performance, and when there is careful follow-up monitoring and feedback. As in all types of training, there are individual differences. Some managers may react favorably to 360-degree feedback, but others may not benefit and may have a negative reaction (Atwater et al., 2000). A longitudinal study of managers who received 360-degree feedback suggested that the technique led to improved managerial competence over time (Bailey & Fletcher, 2002).

An increasingly popular training program for new managers that combines elements of on-the-job training and a sort of informal "apprenticeship" is **mentoring**, a process by which an inexperienced worker develops a relationship with an experienced worker to promote the former's career development (Eby, 2007). Much of the learning that takes place in these relationships involves the protégé attempting to imitate the mentor's work and interpersonal style. Modeling thus appears to be one key learning process in mentoring. Mentoring among managers in large organizations is becoming more and more common as young, inexperienced workers typically look to older, more experienced workers to help them to "learn the ropes" of the job (Ragins et al., 2000). It has even been suggested that women executives will have difficulty moving up the corporate ladder unless they receive some mentoring from higher-ups (Ragins & Cotton, 1999).

Mentoring
a training program in which an inexperienced worker develops a relationship with an experienced worker who serves as an advisor

Since its appearance as a formal training strategy in the late 1970s (Roche, 1979), there has been extensive research, as well as popular interest, in mentoring as a management training and development technique. For the most part, there are many positive results of good mentoring relationships. For instance, protégés generally advance more quickly in their careers, have greater job and career satisfaction, and have lower turnover than workers without mentors (Allen et al., 2009). Of course, a mentoring program is only going to be successful if there are good relationships between mentors and protégés (Young & Perrewé, 2000), and mentoring programs using more "powerful," senior mentors seem to be more effective than peer mentoring programs (Ensher et al., 2001). Research, however, suggests that mentoring relationships that develop on their own, informally, are typically more successful than formal, assigned mentoring relationships (Scandura & Williams, 2001). Research has also indicated that a number of factors may influence workers' willingness to serve as mentors. For instance, managers are more willing to mentor newer workers if those workers show greater promise and if they are more similar to the mentor in terms of factors such as educational background (Olian et al., 1993). Gender may also play a part in willingness to mentor (Ragins & Cotton, 1993), with women less likely than men to volunteer as mentors, particularly if the protégé is a man, than men to volunteer as mentors, particularly if the protégé is a man.

Mentoring as a management development technique is quite popular in organizations today (Figure 6.4). Although the benefits of mentorship to protégés are obvious, there are also some payoffs for the mentor and for the organization (Fagenson, 1989).

Figure 6.4. Formal mentoring programs are common in organizations today.

Source: Found on AllGo, an app for plus-sized people found on Unsplash (https://unsplash.com/photos/rvbOhjX1uGc).

The mentor, who may be at a midlife career standstill, may become energized by the chance to assist in the development of an eager young worker's career. The organization also benefits, because mentoring leads to a better-trained and more satisfied young workforce. On the other hand, mentors may find mentoring time-consuming and burdensome (Ragins & Scandura, 1993). Protégés may also react negatively if they feel forced into participating in mentorship programs (Chao et al., 1992; Ensher & Murphy, 2005).

Ensher and Murphy (2005) looked at various alternatives to formal mentoring programs, including "virtual mentoring" and the use of multiple individuals as mentoring role models.

Coaching
a one-on-one relationship where a consultant helps an executive improve performance

One management development technique that is becoming wildly popular with high-level executive leaders is "executive coaching" (McLaughlin & Cox, 2015). **Coaching** is typically a one-on-one relationship between a consultant and a key executive/manager that is designed to help develop and improve the executive's professional performance (Van Coller-Peter & Burger, 2019). Although coaches use a wide range of techniques, perhaps their most important function is providing frank feedback to managers and executives and helping in setting developmental goals. There is very limited research on the effectiveness of coaching, but its use is on the rise, and a few studies suggest that it is effective (e.g., Williams & Lowman, 2018). A review of the literature suggests that coaching does positively impact the development of leaders and positively impacts organizational outcomes (Athanasopoulou & Dopson, 2018).

Given the "counseling" nature of executive coaching, issues regarding the ethics of psychological practice are extremely important. For example, in a study of over 1,000 sales representatives in a pharmaceuticals company receiving coaching, managers' coaching skill was related to annual sales goal attainment, highlighting the importance of ensuring that coaches are well trained and highly skilled if they are to have a positive impact (Dahling et al., 2016).

 Stop & Review

Give three examples each of off-site and on-site employee training methods.

Implementation of the Training Program

Once the training materials and methods have been selected and pilot tested, the next step in the training model is the implementation of the training program. When implementing the training program, factors such as trainee readiness, trainee expectations, and the climate for training—whether the employees and the organization feel positively about the training and encourage it—need to be considered. It is also important to provide trainees with a "rationale" for training—to let them know how the training will benefit them and the organization (Quiñones, 1997). As training progresses, it is important that trainees be given feedback about their learning and opportunities to practice newly learned techniques or behaviors.

Evaluation of the Training Program

A crucial component of any employee training program is the evaluation of training effectiveness, for there is no use in investing money and resources in training programs unless they do indeed work. As such, researchers suggest that companies engage in much deeper evaluation of training effectiveness, including individual-, group-, and organization-level outcomes and return on investment (Sitzmann & Weinhardt, 2019). Yet, many experts suggest that greater rigor is needed in the evaluation of training programs (Garavan et al., 2019), potentially including both standard surveys and qualitative responses (Harman et al., 2015). Sometimes, training programs are not evaluated because the organization's trainers lack the expertise to conduct the evaluations or the administration does not support evaluation efforts (Marshall & Rossett, 2014).

The evaluation of a training program should first outline the criteria that indicate the program's success and develop the means for measuring these criteria. One very useful framework suggests that there are four types of criteria for evaluating a program's effectiveness (Kirkpatrick, 1959):

1 ***Reaction criteria***—measure the impressions of trainees, including their assessments of the program's value, the amount of learning they received, and their enjoyment of the program. Reaction criteria are usually assessed via training

evaluation rating surveys given to trainees immediately after training sessions or workshops. It is important to note that reaction criteria do not measure whether any learning has taken place. Rather, they assess trainees' opinions about the training and their learning.

2 *Learning criteria*—measure the amount of learning that has taken place. Typically, these take the form of some sorts of tests assessing the amount of information retained from the program.

3 *Behavioral criteria*—measure the amount of newly learned skills displayed once the trainee has returned to the job. Observational methods of measurement are typically used to assess behavioral criteria, with supervisors recording the use of newly learned behaviors.

4 *Results criteria*—measure the outcomes that are important to the organization, such as increased trainee work output as expressed by production rates, dollar sales figures, or quality of work. Using the results criteria, a cost–benefit analysis can be performed by comparing the costs of the program with the dollar value of the results. This is usually the most important evaluation of a program's effectiveness. However, it is sometimes difficult to translate training outcomes into dollars and cents. For example, if one of the goals is to improve employee attitudes, it may be hard to place a dollar value on such results.

The important question in the evaluation of programs is whether any measured changes in criteria are indeed the result of training. The methods used in the proper evaluation of a training program are those used to determine the effectiveness of any other type of program introduced into an organization. For a formal evaluation to demonstrate conclusively that training has caused certain outcomes, it should be based on experimental designs. Unfortunately, many evaluations use what might be called "pre-experimental designs," which do not allow for proper assessments (Campbell & Stanley, 1963; see Figure 6.5). One example, the **posttest-only design**, simply measures criteria following the completion of a training program. However, this does not tell us anything conclusive about its effectiveness because we have no basis for any sort of comparison.

A **pretest–posttest design**—measuring behavior before and after training—is also an inadequate experimental design. Although this approach compares the criterion measures collected before and after the training program, we cannot be sure that the differences from pretest to posttest were due to the program. Consider the example of a training program designed to teach customer service agents to be more friendly and attentive to customer needs. With a simple pretest–posttest evaluation, we can never be sure that later observed increases in the quality of customer service were due to training or to other factors, such as a recent pay raise or change in management. Although these limited designs do not allow us to draw clear conclusions, even such limited evaluations are better than no evaluation at all (Sackett & Mullen, 1993).

To be sure of the effectiveness of a training program, one should apply a more sophisticated, true experimental design that uses at least one treatment group, which

Posttest-Only Design
a program evaluation that simply measures training success criterion following completion of the training program

Pretest–Posttest Design
a design for evaluating a training program that makes comparisons of criterion measures collected before and after the introduction of the program

receives the training, and one control group, which does not undergo any training. The simplest and most common experimental design for evaluation research uses one training group and one control group, both of which are measured before and after the program. To ensure that there are no unexpected differences in members of the training and control groups, employees are randomly assigned to the two groups. The pretest and posttest scores are then compared. This experimental design makes it clear that any positive changes in the criterion measures of the training group, relative to the control group, are most likely due to the training program.

A more sophisticated experimental design is the **Solomon four-group design** (Solomon, 1949). This method of evaluation uses four groups, two that are trained and two that are not. In the Solomon design, two of the groups are identical to those in the basic experimental design mentioned earlier. That is, one training group and one control group are measured both before and after the training program. However, the additional training and control groups are measured only after the program, which is intended to help rule out the fact that administering a pretraining measure might sensitize employees to what the program is designed to do and might thus produce certain changes in the criterion measures that occur without the benefit of training. For example, if our customer service agents are given a pretraining test of their customer service knowledge, they might realize that management is very interested in this issue, which might cause all agents to give greater attention to customers, regardless of whether they later receive customer service training. Although the Solomon four-group design is an effective design for evaluating training programs, it is underused, primarily because of the large number of participants and groups required (Braver & Braver, 1988).

The Solomon four-group design can be used, however, for more than just an evaluation of training programs. One study used the design to evaluate employee reactions to a major organizational restructuring (Probst, 2003). Figure 6.5 summarizes the various evaluation designs.

A comprehensive evaluation of a training program must be well designed and executed to ensure that the training is indeed effective. This means careful consideration must be given to the selection and measurement of criteria, an experimental design with adequate control groups must be used, and the costs versus benefits of the program must be assessed (Arvey et al., 1992).

An obvious problem in evaluating the effectiveness of training programs is the inability to use a true experimental design owing to constraints imposed by the particular work organizations. However, quasi-experimental designs can be used, such as lagged-intervention studies (Schwatka et al., 2019). As discussed in Chapter 2, quasi-experiments are approximations of experimental designs. One example is the nonequivalent control group design. This design is typically used when it is impossible to assign trainees randomly to experimental and control groups. A nonequivalent control group might consist of similar employees from another company location that is not undergoing the new training program. The training and control groups are "nonequivalent" because they may differ systematically on variables such as experience,

Solomon Four-Group Design
a method of program evaluation using two treatment groups and two control groups

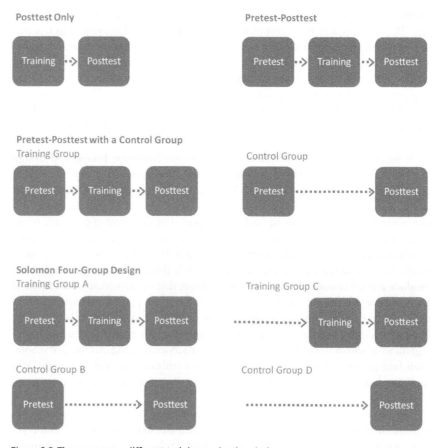

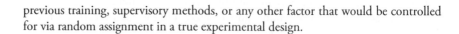

Figure 6.5 There are many different training evaluation designs.

Stop & Review

Illustrate the four types of criteria for evaluating employee training programs.

D&I
INSIGHT
☼

previous training, supervisory methods, or any other factor that would be controlled for via random assignment in a true experimental design.

Equal Employment Opportunity Issues in Employee Training

Because training is linked to job performance and can lead to personnel actions such as pay increases, promotions, and terminations, several equal employment opportunity concerns are related to personnel training (Russell, 1984). One such issue deals with educational or training prerequisites for certain jobs. Because members of underprivileged groups are likely to have less education and formal job training than members of more privileged groups, setting certain levels of education or training as job prerequisites may be considered discriminatory. As mentioned in Chapter 3, equal employment opportunity legislation protects against discrimination against specific groups in providing access to jobs. If access to some jobs requires certain training, employers must take steps to guard against any discrimination in this area by providing remedial education or training for groups of workers who lack the educational prerequisites. For example, some employers are supporting agencies that will train chronically unemployed or underemployed individuals in basic job skills, either by making financial contributions or by hiring persons who have undergone the training.

The methods used in employee training programs may also create instances of potential discrimination. For example, the lectures offered in many seminar programs may lead to different rates of learning in different groups of trainees. If certain groups lack the education needed to process the information and to perform well on any examinations administered, using the results of such training classes to screen or place workers can lead to unintentional discrimination. A similar case occurs in training courses that require certain strenuous activities, such as lifting and carrying heavy materials, in which women may be at some disadvantage. One example was a training course for firefighters that demanded that trainees lift and carry a 150-pound dummy over their shoulders for several yards or down a flight of stairs to simulate carrying an unconscious person from a burning building. A question arose as to whether this part of the course discriminated against women. Critics stated that firefighters rarely carried a person out of a burning building, and that the ability to do this was not a critical requirement for adequate performance of their job. Because of the possibility of discrimination and because the fire department could not prove that this was a necessary skill for the position, the training task was eliminated.

Similarly, organizations that require workers to attend and complete some type of training program to gain a position or a promotion must demonstrate that completion of the program is predictive of success in the jobs that trainees will be holding. If not, there is the possibility that certain disadvantaged groups of trainees may not do as well in the program because of unfamiliarity with the training procedures and format. In other words, because of their lack of experience with the classroom situation, they may not learn as well as members of the majority group, which can lead to discrimination. For example, if being promoted to a frontline supervisory position in a factory requires attending classes in supervisory skills and passing an examination to complete the course, the organization must prove that completion of the training is related to later success as a supervisor, and that the program itself does not discriminate in terms of ability to pass the course. In these cases, the training program is just like any other selection tool. It must be shown to be valid, fair, and job-related.

ON THE *CUTTING* EDGE

Training for the 21st Century: Adaptability, Creativity, and Proactive Thinking

Today's organizations exist in a rapidly changing environment. Likewise, jobs are constantly changing in terms of structure, technology, and tasks. Your job today might be completely different 6 months from now. As a result, I/O psychologists and human resources professionals are giving greater attention to training the skills required in ever-changing jobs and work environments.

One model suggests that the skills needed for adaptive performance include *solving problems creatively*, *dealing with uncertain work situations*, *handling emergencies*, and *being interpersonally* and *culturally adaptable* (Pulakos et al., 2000). Other research suggests that effective, adaptable workers need to develop what is called "proactive thinking," which involves a willingness and ability to take action to change a situation to one's advantage (Kirby et al., 2002). There is evidence that both adaptive performance and proactive thinking can be trained.

Organizations are realizing that the greatest source of information and ingenuity is in the company's own employees. This is particularly true in technology-oriented organizations and companies that rely heavily on innovation (think Silicon Valley). As a result, training employees to use and manage the knowledge already existing in the company—knowledge management— is becoming popular (Nisula & Kianto, 2016). Another approach is to develop workers to be more entrepreneurial and innovative. This approach is labeled "agile management" (Adkins, 2010) and involves developing employees to behave like entrepreneurs—to try new ideas and nurture those that look promising, but quickly abandon those that aren't working and move on to another innovative idea (i.e., to learn to "fail quickly").

Another area that is receiving a great deal of attention is training workers to be more creative. Special attention has been given to developing creative and innovative workers and organizational leaders (Birdi, 2020). A meta-analysis of 70 studies suggests that creativity training is generally effective in getting people to be more creative and innovative in approaching tasks (Scott et al., 2004). In all likelihood, work-related training in the future will focus more on strategies to be creative and adaptive, rather than learning specific tasks and procedures.

Summary

Employee training is a planned effort by an organization to facilitate the learning, retention, and transfer of job-related behavior. Training is not limited to new employees, but often involves various types of training and development programs offered throughout an employee's career. Specific areas of employee training include new employee orientation; employee retraining and continuing education; retirement planning and career development; and worker training for international assignments, for diversity, to reduce sexual harassment, and to increase ethical behavior at work.

An understanding of learning theories is fundamental in the design of employee training programs. For example, the concept of *modeling*, which is imitative of learning, is expressed in *social learning theory*. If training programs are to be successful, a number of key issues will affect their effectiveness. For example, *transfer of training*, or how the learning translates into use of the newly learned behaviors, and the job characteristics of the trainees, such as *trainee readiness*, must be taken into account. Finally, concern must be given to how training programs are structured and how they are conducted.

The first step in a successful employee training program is assessing training needs, which occurs on several levels. Organizational analysis considers the organization's goals, resources, and the climate for training; task analysis evaluates the specific knowledge, skills, and abilities that a job requires; and person analysis examines the capabilities and deficiencies of the workers themselves. Training needs may also have to be conducted through demographic analysis, which is targeted toward assessing the training needs of specific groups, such as males versus females or the old versus the young. The second step involves establishing training objectives, whereas the third step focuses on employee training methods. The various training methods can be broken down into two general categories: on-site methods and off-site methods. Of on-site methods, *on-the-job training* is the most widely used, consisting of putting inexperienced workers into the work site under the direction of an experienced teacher-worker. *Apprenticeship* is a much more long-term on-site method, combining classroom training with supervised on-the-job training. *Vestibule training* sets up a model training area adjacent to the actual work site, using professional trainers and hands-on experience. *Job rotation* is a training technique designed to broaden workers' experience by rotating employees among various jobs.

Off-site methods include the common *seminar* method and *audiovisual instruction* that provides graphic depictions of work activities and web-based training (webinars). A technique that uses aspects of both audiovisual technology and concepts of social learning theory is *behavior modeling training*, a method of exposing trainees to videotapes of models engaged in appropriate work behaviors and then having them practice the observed behaviors. *Simulation techniques* involve classroom replications of actual workstations. *Programmed instruction* is a form of self-paced training in which workers can learn at their own pace. A sophisticated version of programmed instruction is *computer-assisted instruction* (CAI).

Several specific methods and techniques used in management training include *problem-solving case studies*, *role-playing*, and *management games*, which all involve simulations of actual management situations. *Action learning* is a complicated form of training in which teams are formed to perform a special project or assignment that benefits the organization, while the team members learn and develop managerial skills. A 360-degree feedback is also used as a management development tool. *Mentoring* is a management training program in which an inexperienced worker is assigned to an experienced mentor who serves as a role model. *Coaching* is where a consultant advises an executive to improve performance.

Once training programs have been implemented, the evaluation of their effectiveness is very important. The first step in evaluation is to determine criteria of training effectiveness. Four types are typically used: reaction criteria, learning criteria, behavioral criteria, and results criteria. Once the criteria are established, basic research methods and design should be used to evaluate the training programs. The *pretest–posttest* design is a common but inadequate means of assessing a program in which measures of criteria are collected both before and after a training intervention, allowing for a comparison of changes in learning or work behaviors. However, this method is inadequate because of the lack of a good comparison group. Better evaluation designs use both a training group and a comparison, or control, group that is not subjected to the training program. A complex and sophisticated evaluation design is the *Solomon four-group design*, which uses two training groups and two control groups.

Finally, certain legal issues must be considered in the design and implementation of training programs. Training or educational prerequisites and the training programs themselves must not unfairly discriminate on the basis of ethnicity, age, sex, or disability.

Study Questions and Exercises

1 Consider how learning takes place in work organizations. How does employee training relate to learning in college classrooms? What are the similar methods and underlying theories/concepts of learning?

2 Consider a work organization that you have had some contact with, either one in which you were employed or one in which a friend or relative is working. Based on your knowledge, how might a training needs assessment be conducted? Consider all four levels of assessment: organizational, task, person, and demographic analysis.

3 Compare and contrast the advantages and disadvantages of on-site versus off-site training methods.

4 Consider the various designs for evaluating employee training programs. Although the more complex and sophisticated designs usually provide better evaluation, what are some of the difficulties of conducting an assessment in actual work organizations?

5 Review the discussion of equal employment opportunity (EEO) issues in personnel training. What are the various ways that training programs could discriminate against members of **protected groups** (ethnic minorities, women, people with disabilities, or the elderly)?

Protected Groups
groups, including women and certain ethnic and racial minorities, that have been identified as previous targets of employment discrimination

Web Links

www.td.org
Association for Talent Development is a professional organization devoted to employee training.

www.eeoc.gov
Site for the federal agency dealing with employment discrimination issues.

**www.siop.org/Research-Publications/Items-of-Interest/ArtMID/19366/ArticleID/
4978/Achieving-Equity-and-Inclusion-Through-Civility-Training**

Suggested Readings

Kraiger, K., Passmore, J., Rebelo dos Santos, N., & Malvezzi, S. (Eds.). (2015). *The Wiley Blackwell handbook of the psychology of training, development, and performance improvement*. Chichester, UK. This edited collection has scholarly reviews of most every area of employee training in organizations and professional development.

Noe, R. A., & Kodwani, A. D. (2018). *Employee training and development* (7th ed.). McGraw-Hill Education.

Olenick, J., Blume, B. D., & Ford, J. K. (2020). Advancing training and transfer research through the application of nonlinear dynamics. *European Journal of Work and Organizational Psychology, 29*(4), 541–555.

Robinson, A. N., Arena, D. F., Lindsey, A. P., & Ruggs, E. N. (2020). Expanding how we think about diversity training. *Industrial and Organizational Psychology, 13*(2), 236–241.Protected Groups

PART III

Worker Issues

CHAPTER 7

Motivation

Inside Tips

MOTIVATION WITHIN THE CONTEXT OF
INDUSTRIAL/ORGANIZATIONAL PSYCHOLOGY

Two areas of I/O psychology involve a tremendous amount of theorizing: motivation and leadership (the topic of leadership will be discussed in Chapter 14). Because both motivation and leadership are extremely complex and important topics in the work world, they have historically been given a great deal of attention by I/O psychologists. This chapter introduces a variety of theories of motivation. Rather than viewing these as isolated models, consider the ways in which they are similar. Some of these similarities are reflected in the grouping of theories into categories, such as need theories and job design theories, as shown in the chapter outline. Other similarities can also help draw related concepts together. For example, the need theories emphasize the satisfaction of basic human needs as a key to motivation, whereas reinforcement theory argues that motivation is caused by work-related rewards, or reinforcers. However, the satisfaction of human needs can also be seen as the experience of a reward. By understanding similarities such as these, you can begin to synthesize what at first appears to be an overwhelming mass of abstract and unrelated theories.

Besides looking for similarities among motivation theories and noticing topics that were previously discussed, pay close attention to the last section of the chapter, which emphasizes that motivation is only one of the many variables that can affect work outcomes. This is an important point because it reminds us to consider the "total picture"— the interrelationships between many organizational variables—when studying work behavior.

It's still the first month of your new job. You have noticed that some of your colleagues seem to put lots of energy and drive into their work. Others try to get by with minimal effort. Why is this the case? When we begin to infer some underlying processes of effort, energy, or drive, we are trying to capture the elusive construct of motivation. If you surveyed managers and asked them to list the most difficult aspects of their jobs, odds are that the majority would mention difficulties in motivating workers as a particular problem.

Motivation is complex and elusive and has historically been of great interest to the wider field of psychology. As a result, work motivation is one of the more widely researched topics in I/O psychology.

In this chapter, we will begin by defining motivation. Next, we will examine the various theories of work motivation and see how some of them have been applied in attempts to increase worker motivation. Finally, we will look at how work motivation relates to work performance.

Defining Motivation

Motivation
the force that energizes, directs, and sustains behavior

According to one definition (Steers & Porter, 1991), **motivation** is a force that serves three functions: it energizes, or causes people to act; it directs behavior toward the attainment of specific goals; and it sustains the effort expended in reaching those goals.

Because motivation cannot be observed directly, it is difficult to study. We can only infer motives either by observing goal-directed behavior or by using some psychological measurement technique. Throughout its history, I/O psychology has offered many theories of work motivation (Kanfer et al., 2017). We have already touched on the simplistic models put forth by scientific management and the human relations movement (Chapter 1). According to Frederick Taylor, workers are motivated by money and material gains, whereas Elton Mayo stressed the role that interpersonal needs play in motivating workers. Since these early days, more sophisticated theories of motivation have been developed. Some stress the importance of specific needs in determining motivation. Other theories emphasize the connection between work behaviors and outcomes—the influence of attaining rewards and achieving goals. Other theories focus on the role of job design in affecting motivation. Still another category of theories argues that motivation is a cognitive process, and that workers rationally weigh the advantages and disadvantages of expending work energy. We will review examples of each of these categories of work motivation theories.

Need Theories of Motivation

Needs
physiological or psychological deficiencies that an organism is compelled to fulfill

Several motivation theories assert that people have certain needs that are important in determining motivation. **Needs** involve specific physiological or psychological deficiencies that the organism is driven to satisfy. The need for food and the drive of hunger are a physiological need and a drive inherent in all living organisms; the need for human contact is a psychological need. Need theories of motivation propose that motivation is the process of the interaction among various needs and the drives to satisfy those needs. We will first look at some basic need theories and then examine one need theory, McClelland's achievement motivation theory, in more depth.

Basic Need Theories

Two basic need theories are those proposed by Abraham Maslow and Clayton Alderfer. Both of these theories maintain that several different types or categories of needs play a role in human motivation. Maslow's theory, called the **need hierarchy theory**, proposes five categories of needs, which form a hierarchy from the more basic human needs to more complex, higher-order needs (Maslow, 1965, 1970). See Table 7.1 for a description of these needs.

According to Maslow, the lower-order needs (physiological needs, safety needs, and social needs)—what Maslow called "deficiency needs"—must be satisfied in a step-by-step fashion before an individual can move on to higher-order needs (esteem and self-actualization needs)—what Maslow referred to as "growth needs." Because higher-order needs are unlikely to be satisfied in the typical worker, there is also a constant upward striving that explains why, for example, even successful, high-level executives continue to exhibit considerable motivation. In other words, they are no longer motivated by money to provide for subsistence needs, but by a need for esteem, recognition, or self-growth.

Building in part on Maslow's theory is Clayton Alderfer's (1972) **ERG theory**, which collapses Maslow's five categories of needs into three: existence needs, which are similar to Maslow's basic physiological and safety needs; relatedness needs, which

Need Hierarchy Theory
a motivation theory proposed by Maslow that arranges needs in a hierarchy from lower, more basic needs to higher-order needs

ERG Theory
Alderfer's motivation model that categorizes needs into existence, relatedness, and growth needs

Table 7.1 Maslow's Hierarchy of Needs (arranged from lowest- to highest-order needs)

1 *Physiological needs*: the basic survival needs of food, water, air, sleep, and sex
2 *Safety needs*: the needs for physical safety (need for shelter) and needs related to psychological security
3 *Social needs*: the need to be accepted by others and needs for love, affection, and friendship
4 *Esteem needs*: the needs to be recognized for accomplishments and to be admired and respected by peers
5 *Self-actualization needs*: the needs to reach one's highest potential and to attain a sense of fulfillment; the highest level of needs

stem from social interaction and are analogous to the social needs in Maslow's hierarchy; and growth needs, which are the highest-order needs, dealing with needs to develop fully and realize one's potential. Alderfer made predictions, similar to Maslow's, that, as each level of need becomes satisfied, the next higher level becomes a strong motivator.

Although both basic need theories have received a great deal of attention from professionals in psychology, business, and other areas, neither theory has led to any type of useful application or strategy for improving work motivation (Miner, 1983). Both theories do a good job of describing various types of needs and of distinguishing the lower- from the higher-order needs. Although all aspects of the theories have not held up to research (Rasskazova et al., 2016, for example), they do provide insight as to the importance of internal psychological motivation and brought to light the importance of intrinsic needs for growth and development (Van den Broeck et al., 2019).

McClelland's Achievement Motivation Theory

Achievement Motivation Theory
McClelland's model of motivation that emphasizes the importance of three needs—achievement, power, and affiliation—in determining worker motivation

A more comprehensive need theory of motivation, and one that deals specifically with work motivation, is David McClelland's **achievement motivation theory** (McClelland, 1961, 1975). This theory states that three needs are central to work motivation: the needs for achievement, power, and affiliation. According to McClelland, people are motivated by different patterns of needs, or motives, terms that he uses interchangeably. The factors that lead to work motivation may differ from person to person, depending on their particular pattern of needs. Unlike Maslow's hierarchy of needs and Alderfer's ERG theory, the needs in McClelland's theory are not arranged in a hierarchical order. Instead, he suggests that we all hold all of these needs, but that individuals differ on which need within them is strongest. The three key motives, or needs, in his theory are as follows:

1. *Need for achievement*—the compelling drive to succeed and to get the job done. Individuals with a very high need for achievement are those who love the challenge of work. They are motivated by a desire to get ahead in the job, to solve problems, and to be outstanding work performers. Need for achievement is also associated with being task-oriented, preferring situations offering moderate levels of risk or difficulty, and desiring feedback about goal attainment.
2. *Need for power*—the need to direct and control the activities of others and to be influential. Individuals with a high need for power are status-oriented and are more motivated by the chance to gain influence and prestige than that to solve particular problems personally or reach performance goals. McClelland talks

about two sides to the need for power: one is personal power that is used toward personal ends, and the other is institutional power, or power that is oriented toward organizational objectives (McClelland, 1970).

3. *Need for affiliation*—the desire to be liked and accepted by others. Individuals motivated by affiliation needs strive for friendship. They are greatly concerned with interpersonal relationships on the job and prefer working with others on a task. They are motivated by cooperative rather than competitive work situations.

To assess an individual's motivational needs, McClelland used a variation of the **thematic apperception test (TAT)**. Respondents are instructed to study each of a series of fairly ambiguous pictures for a few moments and then "write the story it suggests" (see Figure 7.1). The brief stories are then scored using a standardized procedure that measures the presence of the three basic needs to obtain a "motivational profile" for each respondent. The TAT is known as a projective test—that is, respondents project their inner motivational needs into the content of the story they create. One criticism of McClelland's theory concerns the use of the TAT, for its scoring can sometimes be unreliable, with different scorers possibly interpreting the stories

Thematic Apperception Test (TAT)
a projective test that uses ambiguous pictures to assess psychological motivation

Figure 7.1 Sample item from a variation of the thematic apperception test (TAT) used by McClelland.

Source: Ridofranz/iStock.

differently. Also, there is a tendency for participants who write longer "stories" to be given higher scores on achievement motivation. Despite the criticisms of McClelland's version of the TAT and criticisms of the measurement properties of projective tests in general, meta-analysis shows that the TAT is a reasonably good measurement tool (McCredie & Morey, 2019). It is important to note that there are alternative self-report measures of motives and that these measures also do a good job of assessing basic underlying motivational needs.

The majority of research on McClelland's theory has focused on the need for achievement (Kanfer et al., 2017). Evidence indicates that individuals with a high need for achievement attain personal success in their jobs, but only if the type of work they do fosters personal achievement. That is, there must be a match between the types of outcomes a particular job offers and the specific motivational needs of the person. For example, people who have a great need for achievement might do best in a job in which they are allowed to solve problems, such as a scientist or engineer, or in which there is a direct relation between personal efforts and successful job outcomes, such as a salesperson working on commission. For example, need for achievement tends to be positively correlated with workers' incomes—high achievers made more money than those with a low need for achievement (McClelland & Franz, 1992). High need-achievement individuals are also more attracted to and successful in entrepreneurial careers (Collins et al., 2004). However, persons high in need for achievement might be less effective in team situations, and they have a tendency to try to accomplish goals by themselves rather than delegate to others or work with them as a unit (a reason why, perhaps, many high-achieving college students prefer individual over group projects and assignments).

High need for achievement is also positively related to students' grades in college (Bipp & van Dam, 2014). Alternatively, those high in the need for affiliation should do best in a job in which they work with others as part of a team. Finally, persons with a high need for power should thrive in jobs that satisfy their needs to be in charge. In fact, research shows that many successful managers are high in the need for power, presumably because much of their job involves directing the activities of others (McClelland & Boyatzis, 1982). One study showed that the effects of need for power on leadership outcomes were more positive when leaders also had a high need for affiliation (Steinmann et al., 2016).

The work of McClelland and his associates has led to several applications of the achievement motivation theory toward improving motivation in work settings. One strategy is a program that matches workers' motivational profiles to the requirements of particular jobs to place individuals in positions that will best allow them to fulfill their predominant needs (McClelland, 1980). A second application, effective in positions that require a strong need for achievement, is an achievement training program in which individuals are taught to be more achievement-oriented by role-playing achievement-oriented actions and strategies and developing plans for setting achievement-related goals (Miron & McClelland, 1979).

Behavior-Based Theories of Motivation

The next two motivation theories have been categorized as "behavior-based theo-ries" because each theory focuses on behavioral outcomes as critical to affecting work motivation. These two theories are reinforcement theory and goal-setting theory.

Reinforcement Theory

Reinforcement theory draws on principles of operant conditioning and states sim-ply that behavior is motivated by its consequences. A consequence that follows a behavior and serves to increase the motivation to perform that behavior again is a reinforcer. These reinforcers can be of two types. **Positive reinforcers** are events that are in and of themselves desirable to the person. Receiving praise, money, or a pat on the back are all common positive reinforcers. **Negative reinforcers** are events that lead to the avoidance of an existing negative state or condition. Being allowed to escape the noise and confusion of a busy work area by taking a short break in a quiet employee lounge or working hard at a task to avoid the wrath of a watchful supervisor are negative reinforcement situations. Negative reinforcement increases the motivation to perform the desired behavior again in an effort to keep the aversive negative condition from returning. For example, if a clerical worker feels that being behind schedule is a particularly aversive condition, the individual will be motivated to work hard to avoid the unpleasant state of being behind schedule. It is important to reemphasize that both negative and positive reinforcement can increase the moti-vation to repeat a behavior.

Punishment is the term used to describe any unpleasant consequence that directly follows the performance of a behavior. The effect of punishment is to weaken the tendency to perform the behavior again. Punishment is applied to behaviors that are deemed inappropriate. Receiving a harsh reprimand from your boss for too much socializing on the job and receiving a demotion because of sloppy work are examples of punishment. Reinforcement theory argues that reinforcement is a much better motivational technique than is punishment, because the goal of punishment is to stop unwanted behaviors, whereas reinforcement is designed to strengthen the motivation to perform a particular *desired* behavior. In addition, it is important to emphasize that punishment is generally a poor managerial strategy for several reasons. First, the chronic use of punishment can create feelings of hostility and resentment in workers and reduce morale and job satisfaction. Second, punished workers may try to retaliate and "get back" at punitive supervisors (de Lara, 2006). Third, punishment tends only to suppress behavior; once the threat of punishment is taken away, the worker may continue to use the undesirable behavior. Fourth,

Reinforcement Theory
the theory that behavior is motivated by its consequences

Positive Reinforcers
desirable events that strengthen the tendency to respond

Negative Reinforcers
events that strengthen a behavior through the avoidance of an existing negative state

Punishment
unpleasant consequences that reduce the tendency to respond

Stop & Review

What are the three needs in McClelland's theory? How are they measured?

continual use of punishment leads to inefficient supervisors—ones who must spend too much of their time constantly "on watch" to catch workers committing undesirable behaviors and administer the punishment. Finally, there is some evidence that women supervisors who use punishment are evaluated more harshly than their male counterparts, and the women's use of discipline is perceived to be less effective (Atwater et al., 2001).

UP CLOSE   What Is a Workaholic?

According to McClelland, the need for achievement is a continuum ranging from very low to very high levels of achievement. Typically, we consider a high achievement level to be positive, but can we ever have too much need for achievement? The answer appears to be yes. When an individual's compelling drive to succeed in a job becomes so great that all other areas of life (family, health concerns, and leisure) are given little or no concern, we may label the person a workaholic or "achievement addicted" (Andreassen, 2013). Spence and Robbins (1992) suggested that, although workaholics are highly involved in work, they do not necessarily enjoy working—they experience high levels of stress and may have related psychological and physical health issues (Aziz et al., 2015; Burke, 2000). The concept of the workaholic is related in many ways to the hard-driving "Type A," or "coronary-prone," behavior pattern, a topic we will discuss in Chapter 9, on worker stress.

Based on interviews with workaholics, Machlowitz (1976) derived 15 characteristics common to them. Look over the list and see how you match up to the definition:

1 An ongoing work style
2 A broad view of what a job requires
3 A sense of the scarcity of time
4 The use of lists and time-saving gadgets
5 Long work days

6 Little sleep
7 Quick meals
8 An awareness of what one's own work can accomplish
9 An inability to enjoy idleness
10 Initiative
11 Overlapping of work and leisure
12 A desire to excel
13 A dread of retirement
14 Intense energy
15 An ability to work anywhere (workaholics can always be spotted taking work into the bathroom)

It is interesting to note that many workers and work organizations place a high value on workaholics, and many companies actually encourage workaholism. For example, workaholic bosses may be singled out as role models for younger managers, and workaholic supervisors might encourage and reward similar workaholic behaviors in subordinates. In addition, as more and more companies downsize and eliminate personnel, it may promote workaholism because fewer workers must handle all of the work duties. Research suggests that workaholism does not necessarily lead to stress if the workaholic employee is engaged in and enjoys his or her job (van Beek et al., 2011). Malissa Clark and her colleagues (2020) recently came out with a scale that measures workaholism and can help you tell if you fall into this category.

One way to better understand reinforcement theory is to focus on *schedules of reinforcement*. Reinforcement in the work environment typically takes place on a partial or intermittent reinforcement schedule, which can be of either the interval or ratio type. When interval schedules are used, the reinforcement is based on the passage of time, during which the individual is performing the desired behavior. When ratio schedules are used, reinforcement follows the performance of a number of desired behaviors. Both interval and ratio schedules can be either fixed or variable. Thus, there are four reinforcement schedules: fixed interval, variable interval, fixed ratio, and variable ratio. Most typically, in work settings, we think of these four types of schedules as representing different schedules of pay.

In the **fixed-interval schedule**, the reinforcement occurs after the passage of a specified amount of time. Employees who are paid an hourly or daily wage or a weekly or monthly salary are being reinforced on this schedule, which has two important characteristics. First, the reinforcement is not contingent on the performance of the desired behavior. Of course, it is assumed that during the intervening time period, people are performing their jobs. However, reinforcement follows regardless of whether the rate of performing job-related behaviors is high or low. Second, the fixed-interval schedule is predictable. People always know when a reinforcement is coming.

A **variable-interval schedule** is a somewhat rare means of work compensation. On these schedules, reinforcement is also determined by the passage of time, but the interval varies. For example, a worker for a small business might be paid on the average of once a month, but the exact time depends on when the owner does the payroll. Bonuses that are given on bosses' whims are also on a variable-interval schedule.

In a **fixed-ratio schedule**, reinforcement depends on the performance of a set number of specified behaviors. Examples include workers who are paid for the number of components assembled, baskets of fruit picked, or reports written. This type of fixed-ratio payment is commonly referred to as "piecework." The strength of such a schedule is that reinforcement is contingent on execution of the desired behavior. Individuals on ratio schedules have high rates of responding in comparison with persons on interval schedules, who are merely "putting in time."

A **variable-ratio schedule** also involves reinforcement that is contingent on the performance of behaviors, but the number of responses required for a particular reinforcement varies. An example of a variable-ratio schedule is a salesperson on commission (Figure 7.2.), who is required to give a number of sales presentations (the work behavior) to make a sale and receive a commission (the reinforcement). Variable-ratio schedules usually lead to very high levels of motivation because the reinforcement is contingent on performance and because of the "surprise element": you never know when the next reinforcement is coming. Gambling is reinforced on a variable-ratio schedule, which is why it is such an addicting behavior.

Fixed-Interval Schedule
reinforcement that follows the passage of a specified amount of time

Variable-Interval Schedule
reinforcement that follows the passage of a specified amount of time, with exact time of reinforcement varying

Fixed-Ratio Schedule
reinforcement that is contingent on the performance of a fixed number of behaviors

Variable-Ratio Schedule
reinforcement that depends on the performance of a specified but varying number of behaviors

Figure 7.2 A car salesperson is on a variable-ratio schedule of compensation: their earnings depend on the number of successful sales pitches they make.

Source: Photograph by Ron Porter, found on Pixabay (https://pixabay.com/photos/ultima-gtr-motor-car-hand-built-1498756/).

Research indicates that different types of schedules lead to various patterns of responding and thus have important implications for the use of reinforcement in motivating workers. Generally, evidence suggests that ratio schedules result in higher levels of motivation and subsequent task performance than do fixed-interval schedules (Pritchard et al., 1980). These findings are important, especially because the majority of U.S. workers are paid on fixed-interval reinforcement schedules.

Obviously, reinforcement principles are used informally on a day-to-day basis to motivate workers through compensation systems and other forms of rewards for work outcomes. However, when reinforcement theory is applied formally as a program to increase worker motivation, it most often takes the form of **organizational behavior modification**, in which certain target behaviors are specified, measured, and rewarded. For example, one model of organizational behavior modification takes a four-step approach, involving:

1. Specifying the desired work behaviors;
2. Measuring desired performance of these behaviors using trained observers;

Organizational Behavior Modification
the application of conditioning principles to obtain certain work outcomes

3. Providing frequent positive reinforcement, including graphs demonstrating individual and group performance of desired behaviors; and

4. Evaluation of the program's effectiveness.

(Komaki et al., 1991)

Extrinsic versus Intrinsic Motivation

Intrinsic Motivation
the notion that people are motivated by internal rewards

One limitation to reinforcement theory is that it emphasizes external, or extrinsic, rewards. That is, persons are motivated to perform a behavior because they receive some extrinsic reward from the environment. Yet research shows that people are often motivated by internal or **intrinsic motivation** (Delaney & Royal, 2017). Delaney and Royal's (2017) data from consulting firm Korn Ferry show that 70% of employees report feeling intrinsically motivated, whereas only 59% of employees report feeling extrinsically motivated. Intrinsic rewards are derived from workers' sense of accomplishment and competence at performing and mastering work tasks and from a sense of autonomy or control over one's own work. According to the notion of intrinsic motivation, workers are motivated by challenges at work, with the reward being the satisfaction of meeting the challenge of a job well done. You have probably experienced firsthand intrinsic motivation at school or work when you felt the glow of accomplishment with a particularly challenging assignment. Likewise, people who say they love their work because of its challenge and opportunity to "stretch" their skills and abilities are intrinsically motivated workers.

According to intrinsic motivation theorists, it is not enough to offer tangible, extrinsic rewards to workers. To motivate workers intrinsically, jobs need to be set up so that they are interesting and challenging and so that they call forth workers' creativity and resourcefulness (Gagné & Deci, 2005). Another approach used to promote intrinsic motivation at work is to allow workers some control, or autonomy, in deciding how their work should be planned and conducted (Gagné & Deci, 2014). As we will see as we discuss additional theories of motivation, many models of motivation focus on intrinsic rewards as critical for work motivation. Although intrinsic motivation comes from within, Delaney and Royal (2017) suggest there are still things that organizations can do to support intrinsic motivation (p. 137):

Create opportunities for employees to do challenging and interesting work that fully leverages their skills and abilities

Remove bureaucracy, poorly designed processes, and other institutional barriers that stand in the way

Empower employees to devise new ways of working based on their unique differences and perspectives

Encourage managers to recognize employees who go above and beyond.

Self-Determination Theory

Expanding on the construct of intrinsic motivation, Ryan and Deci (2000) proposed **self-determination theory**, which focuses on the conditions and processes that lead to self-motivation, as well as growth on the job. According to self-determination theory, three factors—feelings of *autonomy*, *competence*, and *relatedness*—are critical for spurring motivation, particularly in the workplace. Autonomy is when workers feel as if they have options and choices in how to accomplish their tasks, as opposed to being directed to perform using particular, specific procedures. Competence deals with the sense of mastery that a worker experiences through becoming more skilled at their job. Relatedness is the feeling of social connections with others in the workplace. When a work situation provides for these important needs, a worker becomes more motivated to both perform and master a job.

Research has found support for self-determination theory. In one study, managers who were supportive of workers and who allowed them to work autonomously, as opposed to controlling subordinates' behavior, produced greater employee motivation (Deci et al., 1989). Likewise, Patall et al. (2008) found that providing individuals with the opportunity to make choices increases autonomy and enhances intrinsic motivation. One meta-analysis of over 30,000 employees, from 70 firms in nine countries, showed that managers who supported autonomy experienced greater need satisfaction and autonomy, resulting in more positive work behavior (Slemp et al., 2018). As a result of its robust effects, self-determination theory has been applied to other domains such as health (Standage & Ryan, 2020), technology use (Peters et al., 2018), and education (Nie et al., 2015).

Goal-Setting Theory

Goal-setting theory emphasizes the role of specific, challenging performance goals and workers' commitment to those goals as key determinants of motivation. Typically, goal-setting theory is associated with Edwin Locke (1968). Goal-setting techniques have also been used in nonwork settings to motivate people to lose weight, to exercise regularly, and to study.

Goal-setting theory states that, for employees to be motivated, goals must be clear, specific, attainable, and, whenever possible, quantified. General goals, such as urging employees to do their best or to work as quickly as possible, are not as effective as defined, measurable goals. In addition, goal-setting programs may emphasize taking a large, challenging goal and breaking it down into a series of smaller, more easily attained goals. For example, as we sat down to revise this textbook, the task seemed overwhelming. It was much easier (and more motivating) to view the book as a series of chapters, tackle each chapter individually, and feel a sense of accomplishment each time the first draft of a chapter was completed. (You may be faced with something similar as you try to study and master the book.) There are various characteristics of more effective goals (see Van den Broeck et al., 2019). Steps to making goals more effective include: ensuring goals are challenging but not impossible, encouraging employees to participate in goal-setting so they accept the goals, making employees accountable for goals by publicly sharing them, and rewarding or supporting goal attainment.

Research on goal setting has also stressed the importance of getting workers committed to goals, for, without such commitment, it is unlikely that goal setting will be motivating (Locke et al., 1988). A number of strategies have been used to influence employees' commitment to performance goals. These include the use of extrinsic rewards (e.g., bonuses), the use of peer pressure via setting both individual and group goals, and the encouragement of intrinsic motivation by providing workers with feedback about goal attainment (Sawyer et al., 1999). In addition, providing feedback about what goals other high-performing individuals or groups are achieving can also encourage motivation toward goal attainment (Vigoda-Gadot & Angert, 2007). Van den Broeck et al.'s (2019) review of meta-analyses of goal setting shows that setting specific difficult goals leads to a 10% increase in performance, whereas adding feedback to goal setting can result in an additional 7% increase in performance.

Although goal-setting theory has stimulated a great deal of research, there has been considerable interest from practitioners in applying goal-setting theory to increase worker motivation. A wide variety of motivational techniques and programs, such as incentive programs and management by objectives, or MBO (which we will discuss in Chapter 15), are consistent with goal-setting theory. Because goal setting is a relatively simple motivational strategy to implement, it has become quite popular.

⏱ Stop & Review

Give examples of the four types of reinforcement schedules. How are punishment and negative reinforcement different?

Job Design Theories of Motivation

The need theories emphasize the role that individual differences in certain types of needs play in determining work motivation. The behavior-based theories focus on behavioral outcomes as the key to motivation. By contrast, two job design theories—Herzberg's two-factor theory and the job characteristics model—stress the structure and design of jobs as key factors in motivating workers. They argue that, if jobs are well designed, containing all the elements that workers require from their jobs to satisfy physical and psychological needs, employees will be motivated.

Herzberg's Two-Factor Theory

Influenced greatly by the human relations school of thought, Frederick Herzberg developed a theory of motivation that highlighted the role of job satisfaction in determining worker motivation (we will discuss job satisfaction in great depth in Chapter 9, but we are here looking at job satisfaction as one element in the motivation "equation"; Herzberg, 1966). He stated that the traditional, single-dimension approach to job satisfaction, with its continuum ends ranging from job dissatisfaction to job satisfaction, is wrong, and that job satisfaction and job dissatisfaction are actually two separate and independent dimensions. Herzberg arrived at these conclusions, called the **two-factor theory**, after analyzing the survey responses of many white-collar, professional workers who were asked to describe what made them feel especially good or bad about their jobs. What he found was that the factors clustered into one of two categories. Certain factors, when present, seemed to cause job satisfaction, and Herzberg labeled them **motivators**. Other factors, when absent, tended to cause job dissatisfaction, and he called them **hygienes**. Motivators are factors related to job content; they are inherent in the work itself. The type of work, the level of responsibility associated with the job, and the chances for recognition, advancement, and personal achievement are all motivators. Hygienes are related to the context in which people perform their jobs. Common hygienes include benefits, working conditions (including both physical and social conditions), type of supervision, base salary, and company policies (see Table 7.2).

To illustrate Herzberg's concepts of hygienes and motivators, consider the jobs of high school teacher and paramedic. Neither job is particularly well paid, and the working conditions of the paramedic, with odd hours, out in the field, working under high pressure to save lives, are not too appealing. In other words, the hygienes in the two jobs are low to moderate. And, as you might expect with reduced hygienes, teachers and paramedics might often voice their dissatisfaction over low pay and poor working conditions. However, the positions of teacher and paramedic have high levels of responsibility, shaping young minds and saving lives, respectively. Moreover, both teachers and paramedics consider themselves to be professionals, doing work that has value to society. These are the motivators that, according to Herzberg, will lead to job satisfaction and keep levels of motivation high for people in these professions. Indeed, one study of social service workers found that motivators such as having a variety of tasks, supportive supervisors, and chances to be creative led to greater satisfaction and motivation—consistent with Herzberg's predictions (Smith & Shields, 2013).

Two-Factor Theory
Herzberg's motivational theory that proposes that two factors—motivators and hygienes—are important in determining worker satisfaction and motivation

Motivators
elements related to job content that, when present, lead to job satisfaction

Hygienes
elements related to job context that, when absent, cause job dissatisfaction

Table 7.2 Profile of Herzberg's Motivators and Hygienes

Motivators	Hygienes
Responsibility	Company policy and administration
Achievement	Supervision
Recognition	Interpersonal
Content of work	Working
Advancement	Salary
Growth on job	

Herzberg's theory indicates that, if managers are to keep workers happy and motivated, two things must be done. First, to eliminate job dissatisfaction, workers must be provided with the basic hygiene factors. That is, they must be compensated appropriately, treated well, and provided with job security. However, furnishing these hygienes will only prevent dissatisfaction; it will not necessarily motivate workers. To get workers to put greater effort and energy into their jobs, motivators must be present. The work must be important, giving the workers a sense of responsibility, and should provide chances for recognition and upward mobility.

Unfortunately, research has not been very supportive of Herzberg's theory. In particular, the two-factor theory has been criticized on methodological grounds, because subsequent research did not replicate the presence of the two distinct factors (Schneider & Locke, 1971). There also have been difficulties in clearly distinguishing hygienes and motivators. For example, salary, which should be a hygiene because it is external to the work itself, may sometimes act as a motivator because pay can be used to recognize outstanding employees and indicate an individual's status in the organization. It has also been suggested that Herzberg's theory applies more to white-collar than to blue-collar workers (Dunnette et al., 1967). As a result, some scholars do not consider it to be a viable theory of motivation, although it continues to be used as a theory to explain worker motivation in a number of jobs (Lundberg et al., 2009).

Despite criticisms and a lack of supportive research, Herzberg's theory helped stimulate the development of an innovative strategy used to increase worker motivation known as *job enrichment*. We will discuss job enrichment shortly, but first we must consider our second job design theory of motivation: the job characteristics model.

Stop & Review

Under what conditions is goal setting most effective?

Job Characteristics Model

The **job characteristics model** emphasizes the role of certain aspects or characteristics of jobs in influencing work motivation (Hackman et al., 1980; Hackman & Oldham, 1976). According to the theory, employees must experience three important psychological states to be motivated: workers must perceive their work as meaningful, associate a sense of responsibility with the job, and have some knowledge of the results of their efforts. Five core job characteristics contribute to a worker's experience of the three psychological states:

1. *Skill variety*—the degree to which a job requires the worker to use a variety of abilities and skills to perform work-related tasks. A job that demands a range of skills is likely to be perceived as challenging and meaningful.

Job Characteristics Model a theory that emphasizes the role that certain aspects of jobs play in influencing work motivation

2. **Task identity**—the degree to which a job requires the completion of an entire job or function. The worker needs to see the observable outcome or product of work efforts.
3. **Task significance**—the degree to which a job has a substantial impact on other people within the organization, such as coworkers, or persons outside of the organization, such as consumers.
4. **Autonomy**—the degree to which the job gives the worker freedom and independence to choose how to schedule and carry out the necessary tasks.
5. **Feedback**—the degree to which the job allows the worker to receive direct and clear information about the effectiveness of performance.

Skill variety, task identity, and task significance all affect the experience of meaningfulness in work; autonomy influences the sense of responsibility associated with the job and with work outcomes; and feedback influences the worker's experience of work results.

These five core job characteristics can be assessed and then combined into a single motivating potential score (MPS) using the following formula:

$$MPS = \frac{Skill\ Variety + Task\ Identity + Task\ Significance}{3} \times Autonomy \times Feedback$$

Hackman and Oldham used this formula to show that motivation is not a simple combination of the five job characteristics. In the formula, skill variety, task identity, and task significance are averaged, which means that jobs can have low levels of one or two of these characteristics that are compensated for by a high score on the third. This average score is then multiplied by the core characteristics of autonomy and feedback. However, if any of the levels of autonomy, feedback, or skill variety plus task identity plus task significance are zero, the MPS will be zero—no motivating potential! For a job to have any motivating potential, it must have both autonomy and feedback and at least one of the other three characteristics.

To summarize the basic job characteristics model, the five core job characteristics influence the three critical psychological states—meaningfulness, responsibility, and knowledge of results—that in turn lead to motivation and certain work outcomes, such as the motivation to work, improve performance, and grow on the job (Figure 7.3). Actually, the job characteristics model is more complex. According to Hackman and Oldham, certain "moderators" can affect the success of the model in predicting worker motivation. One such moderator is **growth need strength**, or an individual's need and desire for personal growth and development on the job. In other words, some workers desire jobs that are challenging, responsible, and demanding, whereas others do not. According to the theory, improving the dimensions of the five core job characteristics should have motivating effects only on those workers who are high in growth need strength. Workers low in this moderator are not likely to be motivated by jobs that offer enriched opportunities for responsibility, autonomy, and accountability.

Growth Need Strength
the need and desire for personal growth on the job

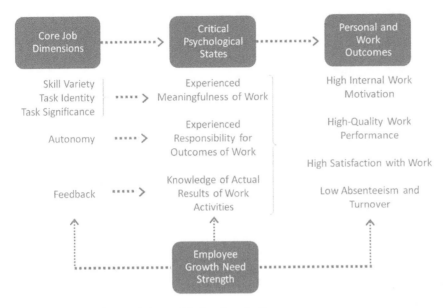

Figure 7.3 The job characteristics model of work motivation.

Source: Found in Hackman & Oldham, 1976.

To validate their theory, Hackman and Oldham (1975) developed a questionnaire to measure the five core characteristics, called the **Job Diagnostic Survey (JDS)**. Other questionnaires have also been created, but the use of self-reported job characteristics has been criticized as a methodological flaw of research in this area (see Kanfer & Chen, 2016). Nonetheless, the job characteristics model has been found to predict motivation to come to work, with workers who have enriched, "motivating" jobs having better attendance records than workers whose jobs lack the critical job characteristics (Rentsch & Steel, 1998).

One important difficulty with the use of the JDS (and other similar self-report measures of job characteristics) to test the job characteristics model relates to the old problem with correlation and causality that we discussed in Chapter 2. Research has found a positive correlation between the presence of core job characteristics and employee satisfaction and self-reported motivation. However, because most of this research is based on self-report measures of both job characteristics and job satisfaction/motivation, we cannot be sure of the direction of causality. Is it the presence of motivating job characteristics that causes job satisfaction and motivation, as the job characteristics model predicts, or is it the case that motivated, satisfied workers see their jobs as being rich in key job characteristics? Some researchers have criticized the use of self-report measures of job characteristics, advocating instead the use of job analysis methods to determine if jobs have "motivating" job characteristics (Spector, 1992).

These two job design theories of motivation—Herzberg's theory and the job characteristics model—have led to the development and refinement of a strategy

Job Diagnostic Survey (JDS)
a questionnaire that measures core job characteristics

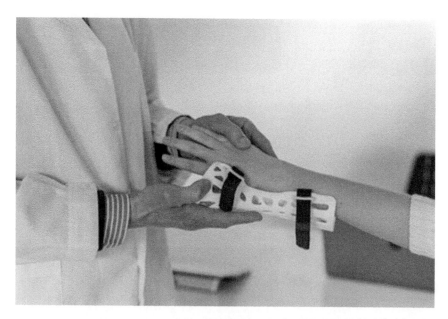

Figure 7.4 This physical therapist experiences at least two of the psychological states identified by the job characteristics model: she knows her work is meaningful and she sees the results.

Source: Photography by Tom Claes, found on Unsplash (https://unsplash.com/photos/HIdUi amYIs0).

Job Enrichment
a motivational program that involves redesigning jobs to give workers a greater role in the planning, execution, and evaluation of their work

used to motivate workers through job redesign. This intervention strategy is called **job enrichment**, and it involves redesigning jobs to give workers greater responsibility in the planning, execution, and evaluation of their work. (Note that job enrichment is not the same as job enlargement, because job enrichment raises the level of responsibility associated with a job, whereas job enlargement does not.) When job enrichment is used as a motivational strategy, workers may actually take on some of the tasks that were previously performed by higher-level supervisors, such as allocating work tasks, appraising their own work performance, setting output quotas, and making their own personnel decisions (including hiring, firing, giving raises, and the like). These programs typically include the following elements:

- Increasing the level of responsibility associated with jobs, as well as the workers' sense of freedom and independence
- Wherever possible, allowing workers to complete an entire task or function
- Providing feedback so that workers can learn to improve their own performance
- Encouraging workers to learn on the job by taking on additional, more challenging tasks and by improving their expertise in the jobs they perform.

As you can see, these elements of job enrichment programs are quite similar to the job characteristics outlined in the Hackman and Oldham model. (For an illustration of job enrichment programs in action, see "Applying I/O Psychology.")

Although job enrichment programs have been implemented in quite a few large companies in the U.S. and Europe, their effectiveness is still in question. Because job enrichment usually takes place at an organizational or departmental level, it is very difficult to conduct a well-controlled evaluation of the effectiveness of the program. Specifically, because the unit of analysis—the participant—is usually the organization or department, it is difficult to compare the success of various job enrichment programs. Most often, support for or against job enrichment is based on the results of a series of case studies. Although many of these case studies find job enrichment programs to be successful, other case studies illustrate failed job enrichment programs. It is clear, however, that some of these failures may be due more to faulty implementation of the program (e.g., management does not support the program; jobs aren't truly enriched), rather than to any weakness in the concept and theory of job enrichment. In addition, the idea from the job characteristics model that workers vary in growth need strength indicates that some workers (those high in growth need) will benefit and be motivated by enriched jobs, and some will not. Thus, levels of growth need strength in the workforce may also play a role in the success or failure of job enrichment. In addition, in monotonous and boring jobs, such as working in a call center or customer service positions, job enrichment may be required in order to improve employee motivation (Parker, 2014).

Cognitive Theories of Motivation

This category, labeled "cognitive theories of motivation," presents two theories that view workers as rational beings who cognitively assess personal costs and benefits before taking action: equity theory and expectancy theory.

APPLYING I/O PSYCHOLOGY

Job Enrichment in a Manufacturing and a Service Organization

In 1971, a decision was made to implement a job enrichment program in a Volvo automobile assembly plant in Kalmar, Sweden, that was suffering from extremely high levels of absenteeism and turnover. First, the traditional assembly-line workers were separated into teams with 15–25 members. In keeping with the general principles of job enrichment, each team was made responsible for an entire auto component or function (for example, upholstery, transmission assembly, or electrical system wiring). Each team was given the freedom to assign members to work tasks, to set their own output rates, to order supplies, and to inspect their own work, all of which had previously been performed by supervisors. To encourage team spirit, each group was given carpeted break rooms, and job rotation (rotating workers periodically from one task to another) was encouraged to alleviate boredom. The results of the program indicated a significant decline in both absenteeism and turnover

APPLYING I/O PSYCHOLOGY

(Continued)

along with improved product quality, although there was a slight decline in productivity, and the costs of implementing the program were great. It was also discovered that some workers did not adapt well to the enriched jobs and preferred the more traditional assembly line (Goldman, 1976). However, management proclaimed the program a success and implemented the strategy in several other plants (Gyllenhammer, 1977).

In another job enrichment program, a large U.S. financial institution decided to introduce job enrichment into its credit and collections department, which serviced the company's credit card account activity, collected on overdue accounts, and dealt with any credit-related difficulties experienced by cardholders, such as changes of address, lost cards, and credit inquiries. In the existing situation, each type of work was handled by a specialist, so that an inquiry on a single account might be handled by several workers. This often led to confusion and to frustration on the part of cardholders, who felt as if they were being passed from worker to worker

for even simple service requests. On the employee side, jobs were repetitive and monotonous, which led to high rates of absenteeism and turnover.

The job enrichment program involved dividing the department into two distinct operating units, each composed of a number of two-member teams. One unit dealt solely with actions on current accounts, and the other unit only with past due accounts. Rather than assigning work based on the type of task that needed to be performed, each team was now given complete responsibility for certain accounts. This restructuring increased the level of responsibility required of each worker and reduced the routine nature of the jobs. Also, workers were able to receive feedback about their work because they dealt with an action on an account from start to finish. Nine months after the implementation of the job enrichment program, productivity had increased without any increase in staff, collection of past due accounts was more efficient, absenteeism was down 33%, and the 9-month turnover rate was zero (Yorks, 1979).

Equity Theory of Motivation

Equity Theory
a theory that workers are motivated to reduce perceived inequities between work inputs and outcomes

Inputs
elements that a worker invests in a job, such as experience and effort

Outcomes
those things that a worker expects to receive from a job, such as pay and recognition

Equity theory states that workers are motivated by a desire to be treated equitably or fairly. If workers perceive that they are receiving fair treatment, their motivation to work will be maintained, and steady performance can be expected. If, on the other hand, they feel that there is inequitable treatment, their motivation will be channeled into some strategy that will try to reduce the inequity.

Equity theory, first proposed by J. Stacey Adams (1965), has become quite popular. According to this theory, the worker brings **inputs** to the job, such as experience, education and qualifications, energy, and effort, and expects to receive certain **outcomes**, such as pay, fringe benefits, recognition, and interesting and challenging work, each in equivalent proportions. To determine whether the situation is equitable, workers make some social comparisons between their own input–outcome ratio and those of **comparison others**, who can be coworkers, people with a similar job or occupation, or the workers' own experiences. It must be stressed that equity theory is based on workers' perceptions of equity/inequity. In certain instances, workers may perceive that an inequity exists when there is not one, but equity theory's predictions are still valid because they operate on worker perceptions.

According to equity theory, lack of motivation is caused by two types of perceived inequity. **Underpayment inequity** results when workers feel they are receiving fewer outcomes from the job in ratio to inputs. Imagine that you have been working at a particular job for over a year. A new employee has just been hired to do the same type of job. This person is about your age and has about the same background and level of education. However, your new coworker has much less work experience than you. Now, imagine that you find out that this new employee is making $2.50 per hour more than you are. Equity theory predicts that you would experience underpayment inequity and would be motivated to try to balance the situation by doing one of the following:

- *Increasing outcomes*—You could confront your boss and ask for a raise or find some other way to get greater outcomes from your job, perhaps even through padding your expense account or taking home office supplies.
- *Decreasing inputs*—You might decide that you need to limit your work production or quality of work commensurate with your "poor" pay.
- *Changing the comparison other*—If you find out that the new employee is actually the boss's daughter, she is clearly not a similar comparison other.
- *Leaving the situation*—You might decide that the situation is so inequitable that you are no longer motivated to work there.

Now, imagine that you are on the receiving end of that extra $2.50 per hour. In other words, compared with your comparison others, you are receiving greater outcomes from your average-level inputs. This is referred to as **overpayment inequity**, which also creates an imbalance. In this case, equity theory predicts that you might try doing one of the following:

- *Increasing inputs*—You might work harder to try to even up the input–outcome ratio.
- *Decreasing outcomes*—You might ask for a cut in pay, although this is extremely unlikely.
- *Changing comparison others*—An overpaid worker might change comparison others to persons of higher work status and ability. For example, "Obviously my boss sees my potential. I am paid more because she is grooming me for a management position."
- *Distorting the situation*—A distortion of the perception of inputs or outcomes might occur. For example, "My work is of higher quality and therefore deserves more pay than the work of others."

Comparison Others
persons used as a basis for comparison in making judgments of equity/inequity

Underpayment Inequity
worker's perception that inputs are greater than outcomes

⏱ Stop & Review
Define Herzberg's concepts of motivators and hygienes and give examples of each.

Overpayment Inequity
worker's perception that outcomes are greater than inputs

It is this last outcome, the possibility of psychological distortions of the situation, that weakens the predictive power of this cognitive theory of motivation. Equity theory has difficulty predicting behavior when people act irrationally, as they sometimes do.

Although most of the research on equity theory has used pay as the primary outcome of a job, other factors may constitute outcomes. For example, one study found that workers would raise their inputs in response to receiving a high-status job title (Greenberg & Ornstein, 1983). In other words, the prestige associated with the title served as compensation, even though there was no raise in pay. There was one catch, however: the workers had to perceive the higher job title as having been earned. An unearned promotion led to feelings of overpayment inequity. Another study looked at Finnish workers who felt inequity because they were putting too much effort and energy into their work compared with the norm. The greater the felt inequity, the more likely these workers reported being emotionally exhausted and stressed (Taris et al., 2002).

Research has also examined the role of individual differences as moderators of equity. In particular, this research has focused on the construct of *equity sensitivity*. It has been suggested that individuals vary in their concern over the equity of input–outcome ratios. In other words, some people are quite sensitive to equity ratios and prefer balance, whereas others may be less concerned with equitable relationships, and still other individuals may prefer to have either an outcome advantage or an input advantage, preferring to be overcompensated or undercompensated for their work (Woodley et al., 2016; see Table 7.3). Obviously, if only certain individuals are motivated by equity, it will limit the theory's ability to predict which employees are influenced by equity.

Expectancy (VIE) Theory of Motivation

One of the most popular motivation theories is **expectancy theory**, which is also known as *VIE theory*, referring to three of the theory's core components: valence, instrumentality, and expectancy. Expectancy theory is most often associated with Vroom (1964), although there were some later refinements and modifications of the theory (see Van den Broeck et al., 2019). Like equity theory, expectancy theory

Stop & Review
According to the MPS, which job characteristics are most important in motivating workers?

Expectancy Theory
a cognitive theory of motivation that states that workers weigh expected costs and benefits of particular courses before they are motivated to take action

Table 7.3 Equity Sensitivity: Three Types of Individuals

Benevolents—These individuals are "givers." They are altruistic and are relatively content with receiving lower outcomes for their inputs

Entitleds—These individuals are "takers." They are concerned with receiving high outcomes, regardless of their levels of inputs

Equity sensitives—These individuals adhere to notions of equity. They become distressed when feeling underpayment inequity and feel guilt when overrewarded

assumes that workers are rational, decision-making persons whose behavior will be guided by an analysis of the potential costs and benefits of a particular course of action. Also, like equity theory, expectancy theory focuses on the particular outcomes associated with a job, which refer not only to pay, but also to any number of factors, positive or negative, that are the potential results of work behavior. For example, positive outcomes include benefits, recognition, and job satisfaction, and negative outcomes include reprimands, demotions, and firings.

As mentioned, the three core components of expectancy theory are **valence**, which refers to the desirability (or undesirability) of a particular outcome to an individual; **instrumentality**, which is the perceived relationship between the performance of a particular behavior and the likelihood that a certain outcome will result—in other words, the link between one outcome (the worker's behavior) and another outcome (obtaining recognition or a pay raise, for example); and **expectancy**, which is the perceived relationship between the individual's effort and performance of the behavior. Both the expectancy and the instrumentality components are represented as probabilities (for example, "If I expend X amount of effort, I will probably complete Y amount of work"—the expectancy component; "If I complete Y amount of work, I will likely get promoted"—the instrumentality component). Expectancy theory states that the motivation to perform a particular behavior depends on a number of factors: whether the outcome of the behavior is desirable (valence); whether the individual has the ability, skills, or energy to get the job done (expectancy); and whether the performance of the behavior will indeed lead to the expected outcome (instrumentality). In research and applications of expectancy theory, each of the components is measured, and a complex predictive formula is derived.

Consider as an example the use of expectancy theory in studying how students might be motivated, or not motivated, to perform exceptionally well in college courses. For these students, the particular outcome will be acceptance into a prestigious graduate (Ph.D.) program in I/O psychology. First, consider the valence of the outcome. Although it may be a very desirable outcome for some (positively valent), it is not for others (negative or neutral valence). Therefore, only those students who view being admitted to a graduate program as desirable are going to be motivated to do well in school to achieve this particular outcome. (Note: This does not mean that there are not other reasons for doing well in school, or that good grades are the only requirements for admission to graduate school.) For those who desire the graduate career, the next component to consider is expectancy. Given what you know about your own abilities, study habits, and effort, what is the probability that you will actually be able to achieve the required grades? Here, you might consider your willingness to sacrifice some of your social life to study more, as well as considering your past academic performance. Should you say, "Yes, I have the 'right stuff' to get the job done," it is likely that you will be highly motivated. For those individuals unwilling to expend the time and energy required, motivation will be much less. Finally, what about instrumentality? It is well known that there are many more qualified applicants to graduate programs than there are openings. Therefore, the probability of actually achieving the desired outcome, even if you perform at the required level, is less than certain. It is here that motivation might also potentially break down. Some people

Valence
the desirability of an outcome to an individual

Instrumentality
the perceived relationship between the performance of a particular behavior and the likelihood of receiving a particular outcome

Expectancy
the perceived relationship between the individual's effort and performance of a behavior

might believe that the odds are so poor that working overtime to get good grades is simply not worth it. Others might figure that the odds are not so bad, and thus the force of their motivation, in expectancy theory terms, will remain strong.

At work, expectancy theory might be applied using promotions, the performance of special work projects, or avoidance of a supervisor's displeasure as potential outcomes. For example, if an employee's goal is to avoid her supervisor's criticism (which is negatively valent), she might consider the expectancy ("Can I perform the job flawlessly to avoid my supervisor's displeasure?") and the instrumentality ("Even if I do an error-free job, will my supervisor still voice some displeasure?") of that goal before being motivated even to try to avoid having the boss become displeased. If the supervisor is someone who never believes that an employee's performance is good enough, it is unlikely that the employee will exhibit much motivation to avoid the boss's displeasure because it is perceived as inevitable.

Expectancy theory illustrates the notion that motivation is a complex phenomenon affected by a number of variables. This theory looks at factors such as individual goals, the links between effort and performance (expectancy), the links between performance and outcomes (instrumentality), and how outcomes serve to satisfy individual goals (valence). It is one of the most complicated yet thorough models of work motivation. The theory has generated a considerable amount of research, with evidence both supporting and criticizing certain aspects of the theory (Van Eerde & Thierry, 1996). For example, Van Eerde and Thierry's (1996) meta-analysis suggests that expectancy theory more accurately predicts which of two tasks an employee might be more motivated to complete, rather than predicting how motivated that employee will be to persist and complete the task.

Expectancy theory continues to be a popular cognitive model for understanding work motivation. Although there is no single agreed-upon strategy for its application, it does lead to many practical suggestions for guiding managers/leaders in their attempts to motivate workers (e.g., Isaac et al., 2001), including the following:

- Managers should try to define work outcomes—potential rewards and costs associated with performance—clearly to all workers.
- The relationships between performance and rewards should also be made clear. Workers need to know that, if they achieve certain goals, rewards are sure to follow.
- Any performance-related goal should be within the reach of the employee involved.

In sum, both expectancy theory and equity theory are based on cognitive models of motivation. They assume that individuals are constantly aware of important elements in their work environment, and that motivation is determined by a conscious processing of the information received. The problem is that some people may simply be more rational than others in their usual approaches to work. The effectiveness of these cognitive models of motivation is also weakened by the fact that, in some situations, individuals, regardless of their usual rational approach, may behave in a nonrational manner (for example, when workers become so upset that they impulsively quit their job without considering the implications).

Comparing, Contrasting, and Combining the Different Motivation Theories

Work motivation is an important topic. The importance of the construct is reflected in the many theories that have been generated to try to "capture" motivational processes and predict when workers will and will not be motivated. In reviewing the various motivational models, it is important to examine the ways in which the theories are similar and how they are different. (See Table 7.4 for a summary of the motivation theories we have discussed.)

The early need theories of motivation, those of Maslow and Alderfer, are primarily descriptive models that explain that people's motivation is rooted in different levels of needs. Reinforcement theory, on the other hand, focuses on the role of the environment in "drawing out" a person's motivation. Need theories can be viewed as the "push" from within, whereas reinforcement represents the "pull" from without. Yet more complex versions of need theories, such as McClelland's, go beyond the simple categorization of needs. In McClelland's model, the needs for achievement, power, and affiliation interact with how a worker views the job and the work environment. For example, someone with a high need for achievement will be concerned with how the job can meet her achievement-related goals. Someone with high power needs will seek out ways to direct others' activities. In other words, there is an interaction between needs from within the individual and what the work environment, external to the person, has to offer. Of course, the fact that workers evaluate how their needs

Table 7.4 Summary of Theories of Motivation

Theory	Elements/Components	Applications
Need Theories: Maslow's need hierarchy	Levels of needs arranged in a hierarchy from lower- to higher-order needs	(No direct intervention programs)
Alderfer's ERG theory	Three levels of needs: existence, relatedness, growth	
Behavior-Based Theories: Reinforcement theory	Consequences of behavior: reinforcers and punishment	Organizational behavior modification
Goal-setting theory	Setting of challenging goals and commitment to goals	Various goal-setting programs (e.g., MBO)
Job Design Theories: Herzberg's two-factor theory	Jobs must provide hygienes and motivators	Job enrichment
Job characteristics model	Jobs must provide five key job characteristics	Job enrichment
Cognitive Theories: Equity Theory	Inputs = outcomes; emphasizes drive to reduce inequities	(Various applications but no agreed-upon intervention programs)
Expectancy (VIE) theory	Valence, instrumentality, expectancy	

can be achieved suggests that rational, cognitive factors also come into play. Thus, there is some overlap between McClelland's need theory and aspects of the cognitive models of motivation.

Similar connections can be made between the behavior-based theories of motivation and the cognitive models. For example, the notion of intrinsic rewards suggests that workers think rationally about their accomplishments, and the setting and achieving of performance goals are important components of both goal-setting theories and the expectancy/VIE model of motivation (Kanfer et al., 2017).

The Relationship Between Motivation and Performance

Motivation is central to any discussion of work behavior because it is believed that it has a direct link to good work performance. In other words, it is assumed that the motivated worker is the productive worker.

Yet this may not always be true, because many other factors can affect productivity, independent of the effects of worker motivation. Furthermore, having highly motivated workers does not automatically lead to high levels of productivity. The work world is much more complex than that. As mentioned at the beginning of the chapter, many managers consider motivation to be the primary problem when they see low levels of productivity. However, a manager must approach a productivity problem as a social scientist would. Before pointing the finger at worker motivation, a detailed assessment of all the other variables that could affect productivity must first be undertaken. These variables can be divided into four categories: systems and technology variables, individual difference variables, group dynamics variables, and organizational variables.

ON THE *CUTTING* EDGE

On the *Cutting* Edge: Motivating through Team-Based Rewards

Traditionally, organizations reward, through pay and bonuses, the performance of individual workers. However, in keeping with the trend toward greater use of work teams, there has been growing interest in team-based strategies for motivating workers. This involves making both pay contingent on team, rather than individual, performance and payment of bonuses and other financial incentives. Although team-based rewards should, in theory, foster greater cooperation and teamwork, how is individual motivation affected when rewards are based on group rather than individual efforts? Research indicates that team-based rewards can be as motivating as individual rewards in many cases, especially if the work team is not too large (Honeywell-Johnson & Dickinson, 1999). Team-based rewards work best when members are committed to the

ON THE *CUTTING* EDGE (*continued*)

team, when their work is highly interdependent so that they must rely on one another to get the job done, when workers are fully informed about the incentive system and how it works, and when the system is perceived as fair (DeMatteo et al., 1998). Furthermore, team rewards are most appropriate when the group performance is easily identified, but when it is difficult to determine specific individual contributions to the team output. Researchers have also begun exploring team-based rewards in virtual work teams (Hertel et al., 2004). Beyond just looking at motivation, a meta-analysis of 30 studies, including more than 7,000 teams, showed that team-based rewards can have positive effects on performance (Garbers & Konradt, 2014).

Systems and Technology Variables

Regardless of the level of motivation, if workers are forced to work with inadequate work systems, procedures, tools, and equipment, productivity will suffer. Poor tools and systems will affect work productivity independent of employee motivation. This is often seen in the low agricultural production of some developing countries.

Figure 7.5 Lack of technology, not motivational problems, often limits agricultural production in developing countries.

Source: Photograph by Abhishek Baru, found on Unsplash (https://unsplash.com/photos/eINs9_ly73c).

Stop & Review

Explain the three components of the expectancy theory of motivation.

A common mistake is to assume that these disadvantaged nations suffer from a lack of worker motivation. A more reasonable (and accurate) explanation is that they lack the appropriate agricultural technology to be as productive as other countries (Figure 7.5).

Individual Difference Variables

A variety of factors within the individual can affect work productivity regardless of motivation. For example, lacking the basic talents or skills to get the job done will hamper productivity, even in the most motivated worker. Perhaps the least productive workers in any work setting are also the most motivated: new employees. At least initially, the novice employee is energized and determined to make a good impression on the boss. Unfortunately, a total lack of knowledge about the job makes this person relatively inefficient and unproductive, despite high motivation. Other workers, because of a lack of basic abilities or education, or perhaps because of being placed in a job that is incompatible with their own interests and talents, may be particularly unproductive. What may appear on the surface to be a motivational problem is actually a problem of individual abilities. We have already touched on some of these individual factors that affect performance when we looked at employee screening, selection, and placement.

Group Dynamics Variables

Rather than working by themselves, most workers are a part of a larger unit. For the group to be efficient and productive, individual efforts must be coordinated. Although most members may be highly motivated, group productivity can be poor if one or two key members are not good team workers. In these situations, the influence of motivation on productivity becomes secondary to certain group dynamics variables. We will discuss the group processes that come into play in affecting work performance in Chapters 11 and 12.

Organizational Variables

The productivity of an organization requires the concerted and coordinated efforts of a number of work units. High levels of motivation and output in one department may be offset by lower levels in another department. Organizational politics and conflict may also affect the coordination among groups, thus lowering productivity despite relatively high levels of motivation in the workforce. We will look at the effects of such variables as organizational politics and conflict in upcoming chapters.

As you can see, the role of motivation in affecting work outcomes is important, but limited. The world of work is extremely complex. Focusing on a single variable, such as motivation, while ignoring others leads to a narrow and limited view of work behavior. Yet motivation is an important topic, one of the most widely researched in I/O psychology. However, it is only one piece of the puzzle that contributes to our greater understanding of the individual in the workplace.

Summary

Motivation is the force that energizes, directs, and sustains behavior. The many theories of work motivation can be classified as need theories, behavior-based theories, job design theories, and cognitive theories. Maslow's and Alderfer's basic need theories propose that needs are arranged in a hierarchy, from the lowest, most basic needs to higher-order needs such as the need for esteem or self-actualization. McClelland's *achievement motivation theory* proposes that the three needs important in work motivation are needs for achievement, power, and affiliation, which can be measured with a projective test known as the *thematic apperception test*. Unlike Maslow's and Alderfer's need theories, McClelland's theory has been used extensively in work settings to encourage worker motivation.

Behavior-based theories include both reinforcement and goal-setting approaches to motivation. *Reinforcement theory* stresses the role that *reinforcers* and *punishments* play in motivation. Reinforcement theory is evident in the various schedules used to reward workers. The theory is applied to increase motivation through *organizational behavior modification* programs. *Goal-setting theory* emphasizes setting challenging goals for workers and getting workers committed to those goals as the keys to motivation.

While reinforcement theory focuses on external, or *extrinsic*, motivation, we are also motivated from within, in what is termed *intrinsic* motivation. Also, *self-determination theory* suggests that other factors, such as autonomy, a sense of competence, and relationships at work, also affect motivation.

Job design theories of motivation stress the structure and design of jobs as key factors in motivating workers. Herzberg's *two-factor theory* focuses on job satisfaction and dissatisfaction as two independent dimensions important in determining motivation. *Motivators* are factors related to job content that, when present, lead to job satisfaction. *Hygienes* are elements related to job context that, when absent, cause job dissatisfaction. According to Herzberg, the presence of hygienes will prevent job dissatisfaction, but motivators are needed for employee job satisfaction and, hence, motivation. Hackman and Oldham have proposed the *job characteristics model*, another job design theory of motivation, which states that five core job characteristics influence three critical psychological states that in turn lead to motivation. This model can be affected by certain moderators, including *growth need strength*, the notion that certain workers feel a need to grow in their jobs. Workers must be high in growth need strength if programs such as job enrichment are indeed going to produce motivation. *Job enrichment*, which involves redesigning jobs to give workers greater responsibility in the planning, execution, and evaluation of their work, is the application that grew out of the job design model of motivation.

Cognitive theories of motivation emphasize the role that cognition plays in determining worker motivation. *Equity theory* states that workers are motivated to keep their work *inputs* in proportion to their *outcomes*. According to equity theory, workers are motivated to reduce perceived inequities. This perception of equity/inequity is determined by comparing the worker's input–outcome ratio to similar *comparison others*. *Expectancy (VIE) theory* (with its three core components of valence, instrumentality, and expectancy) is a complex model that states that motivation is dependent on expectations concerning effort–performance–outcome relationships.

Motivation is indeed a complex construct. Yet, despite the importance given to worker motivation in determining work performance, numerous variables related to systems and technology, individual differences, group dynamics, and organizational factors may all affect work performance directly, without regard to worker motivation. Thus, although motivation is important, it is only one determinant of work behavior.

Study Questions and Exercises

1. Motivation is an abstract concept, one that cannot be directly observed. Using your knowledge of research methods, list some of the methodological issues/problems that motivation researchers must face.
2. Some theories of motivation have led to successful strategies for enhancing work motivation, whereas others have not. What are some of the factors that distinguish the more successful theories from the less successful?
3. Apply each of the various theories to describing/explaining your own level of motivation at school or at work. Which model gives the best explanation for your personal motivation?
4. Basic need theories, goal-setting theory, and reinforcement theory are very general models of work motivation. What are the strengths and weaknesses of such general theories?
5. How would you design a program to improve motivation for a group of low-achieving high school students? What would the elements of the program be? What theories would you use?

Suggested Readings

Latham, G. P. (2012). *Work motivation: History, theory, research, and practice* (2nd ed.). Thousand Oaks, CA: Sage. *A thorough examination of work motivation from one of the leading scholars in the field.*

Van den Broeck, A., Carpini, J. A., & Diefendorff, J. M. (2019). How much effort will I put into my work? It depends on your type of motivation. In R. Ryan, *Oxford Handbook of Human Motivation* (2nd ed., pp. 354–372). John Wiley. DOI:10.1093/oxfordhb/9780190666453.013.27

Kanfer, R., Frese, M., & Johnson, R. E. (2017). Motivation related to work: A century of progress. *Journal of Applied Psychology, 102*(3), 338.10.4324/9781315620589-8

Positive Employee Attitudes

Inside Tips

POSITIVE EMPLOYEE ATTITUDES

This chapter more than any other pulls together a number of issues and topics from I/O psychology. We will look at the positive aspects of jobs—what causes workers to be engaged in their jobs, their organizations, and their careers. We will explore how positive employee attitudes and behaviors are connected to job performance. This is really an issue of motivation, similar to those examined in Chapter 7. This chapter also deals with some measurement issues that were introduced in Chapters 1 and 2. The measurement of employee attitudes, for example, presents a number of measurement problems. The connection between attitudes and their ability to predict important behaviors has a long and important history in both social and industrial/organizational psychology.

You are getting settled into your new job. A great deal of effort went into finding the position, making it through the screening process, and landing the job, and into your initial training and orientation. You've learned the ropes and know what to do. There are a lot of positive aspects to the job, but it's not all rosy. Your attitudes and evaluation of your working situation will determine if you stay in this job, with this company, and even on this career path. We work partly out of necessity, but we stay in a job or an organization because of the positive things that come from the job, the company, and the career.

In the early 20th century, the only compensation that most workers received from their jobs was a paycheck. As time went on, this changed, as workers began to demand and receive more from their jobs. Today's workers receive a variety of forms of compensation, including health care, retirement, and numerous other benefits and programs.

DOI: 10.4324/9781003143987-11

However, one thing that the workers of the past and today's workers have in common is that their jobs constitute a major part of their lives and are one of the greatest sources of personal pleasure and pain. Although jobs can be satisfying in some ways, with positive feelings of accomplishment and purpose, they can also be stressful and the source of negative feelings. Such negative feelings may, in turn, affect worker attitudes and behaviors.

In the next two chapters, we will explore the positive and negative effects of jobs on workers. In this chapter, we will focus on employee engagement, including job satisfaction, organizational commitment, and positive employee attitudes and behaviors. We will examine how these influence work performance, absenteeism, and turnover. We will also focus on some of the programs and techniques designed to increase employees' engagement in their work and their organizations. We will then focus on positive employee behaviors and how we can encourage the best from workers, for the good of the organization and to improve employee well-being.

Employee Engagement

Employee engagement is a psychological state that is characterized by vigor (energy), dedication, and absorption in one's work and organization (Schaufeli et al., 2019). Highly engaged employees are enthusiastic about their jobs, committed to their work and the organization, and it is assumed that this state leads them to be more motivated and productive and more likely to engage in positive work behaviors (Macey & Schneider, 2008). We will use employee engagement as an "umbrella" term to focus on positive employee attitudes, including the related (and much more thoroughly researched) constructs of job satisfaction and organizational commitment; Mackay et al., 2017).

What factors contribute to employee engagement? Saks (2006) suggests that jobs that are high in job characteristics (recall the job characteristics model discussed in Chapter 7) are more meaningful and more likely to engage employees. In addition, if employees feel that they are supported by their supervisors and their organization, they are more likely to experience high levels of engagement. Finally, being recognized and rewarded for one's accomplishments and working in an organization that treats people fairly all contribute to employee engagement.

The construct of employee engagement has received a great deal of attention from consultants and HR professionals, but, until recently, has received less attention from researchers. It does, however, represent a more global way of looking at the positive attitudes and feelings of employees about their work and their work organizations. One self-report measure of employee engagement assesses two separate, but related, components, *job engagement* (sample scale items: "Sometimes I am so into my job that I lose track of time" and "I am highly engaged in this job") and *organization*

Employee Engagement
a psychological state characterized by vigor, dedication, and absorption in one's work/organization

Figure 8.1 Employees who are engaged are more satisfied with their jobs and less likely to quit.

engagement (sample items: "Being a member of this organization is very captivating" and "I am highly engaged in this organization"; Saks, 2006). This research found that employee engagement was positively related to job satisfaction and negatively related to employees' stated intentions to quit their jobs (Figure 8.1).

Inclusion

Inclusion
the feeling that one can be one's unique self and still belong

A second workplace attitude that is conceptually distinct from engagement is **inclusion**. We will discuss inclusive climates (Nishii & Rich, 2014)—organizational climates that facilitate the feeling of inclusion among employees—in Chapter 15, but inclusion can also be conceptualized as an individual attitude. Lynn Shore and her colleagues have conceptualized the feeling of inclusion through Brewer's (1991) optimal distinctiveness framework (Shore et al., 2011). This theory says that, to feel inclusion, employees need to feel that they can be their unique selves while simultaneously being able to experience belonging. These two elements, uniqueness and belonging, are considered basic and essential human needs, and one cannot experience the feeling of inclusion without both. Additional research shows that feelings of inclusion predict employee helping behavior, creativity, and

Figure 8.2 When employees feel that they can be their unique selves and still belong they feel included.

Source: Photograph by Christina @ wocintechchat.com, found on Unsplash (https://unsplash.com/photos/RMweULmCYxM).

job performance (Chung et al., 2020). Diversity climate and inclusive leadership both predicted feelings of inclusion. Although everyone wants to feel included, this construct is particularly important when working in diverse organizations. Women, people of color, and those who hold other marginalized identities are often faced with the choice of either: (1) changing who they are to fit in, causing people to feel incomplete, or (2) choosing to be their authentic selves at the cost of belonging, causing them to feel insular or alone (Johnson, 2020). Of course, the ideal state is that of inclusion, where employees feel that they can fit in while being themselves (Figure 8.2).

Job Satisfaction

Although job engagement is a broad construct that refers to how much employees are psychologically and emotionally committed to their jobs and their organizations, it is a relatively new variable in I/O psychology. A related variable—one that has been extensively studied—is job satisfaction.

Job satisfaction consists of the feelings and attitudes one has about one's job. All aspects of a particular job, good and bad, positive and negative, are likely to contribute to the development of feelings of satisfaction (or dissatisfaction). Job satisfaction, along with productivity, quality, absenteeism, and turnover, is one of the key dependent variables commonly considered (and measured) in research in I/O psychology. There are two approaches to conceptualizing job satisfaction: the global approach and the facet approach (Ironson et al., 1989). The **global approach** considers overall job satisfaction. This way of looking at job satisfaction simply asks if the employee is satisfied overall, using a yes/no response, a single rating scale, or a small group of items that measure global job satisfaction. The **facet approach** considers job satisfaction to be composed of feelings and attitudes about a number of different elements, or facets, of the job. For example, overall satisfaction may be a composite of numerous factors: satisfaction with pay, the type of work itself, working conditions, the type of supervision, company policies and procedures, relations with coworkers, opportunities for promotion and advancement, and even the extent to which one derives meaning from one's work (Rothausen & Henderson, 2019). The facet approach considers each of these aspects individually, assuming that a particular worker might be quite satisfied with some facet, such as the amount of pay, but unsatisfied with others, such as the quality of supervision and the opportunities for promotion.

Proponents of the global approach argue that it is overall satisfaction with a job that is important, and that such complete satisfaction is more than the sum of satisfaction with separate job facets (Scarpello & Campbell, 1983). Moreover, evidence suggests that even single-item measures of job satisfaction work reasonably well for assessing job satisfaction (Wanous et al., 1997). Alternatively, single-item measures for each facet have also been used (Lepold et al., 2018). Advocates of the facet approach maintain that this view provides better and more detailed assessments of job satisfaction, allowing a researcher insight into how a particular individual feels about the various facets of the job and the work situation. One or more facets may be the primary cause of lack of job satisfaction. Moreover, there may be tremendous variation in how highly individual workers value certain facets of job satisfaction (Bowling et al., 2018). For example, satisfaction with pay may be an important element of job satisfaction for one worker but not for another. In addition, some facets may not apply to all types of jobs. For instance, CEOs of companies and self-employed professionals are not affected by opportunities for promotion—a facet that may be an important contributor to job satisfaction of lower-level managers in large organizations.

Proponents of the facet definition argue that it helps to indicate specific areas of dissatisfaction that can be targeted for improvement (Smith et al., 1969). Still others believe there are advantages to using both types of measurement approaches, based on findings that indicate that each approach offers interesting and important information (Ironson et al., 1989).

Job Satisfaction
the positive and negative feelings and attitudes about one's job

Global Approach
views job satisfaction as an overall construct

Facet Approach
views job satisfaction as made up of individual elements, or facets

The Measurement of Job Satisfaction

Regardless of the approach, when considering the measurement of job satisfaction, it is important to bear in mind the difficulties encountered in attempting to define the factors that may influence satisfaction, as well as the difficulties inherent in trying to measure any attitude.

As mentioned earlier, most instruments designed from the facet approach measure satisfaction with such things as pay, working conditions, and relationships with supervisors and coworkers. However, other variables, such as pre-employment expectations, individual personality characteristics, and the fit between the organization or job and the employee, may also affect worker satisfaction (Ostroff, 1993). Satisfaction with career choice and the employee's career progression can also contribute to job satisfaction (Scarpello & Vandenberg, 1992). Research has suggested that elements of job satisfaction may be deeply rooted in the individual workers. These researchers have suggested that there may be genetic "predispositions" to be satisfied or dissatisfied with one's job (see "On the Cutting Edge" box).

One major obstacle in the measurement of job satisfaction is the same obstacle encountered in the measurement of any attitude—the necessary reliance on respondents' self-reports. Recall that problems with self-report measures include the fact that workers may (intentionally or unintentionally) fail to report their true feelings. Strategies for measuring job satisfaction have included interviews, group meetings, and a variety of structured survey methods, such as rating scales or questionnaires. The obvious advantages of using a rating scale or questionnaire instead of a face-to-face meeting are the reduced time invested in the administration of the instrument and the fact that anonymity of responses can often be maintained (particularly if large numbers of employees are being surveyed). Such anonymity may help to ensure that worker responses are more candid than they might be in a face-to-face interview. That is, some workers, fearing retaliation from management, may not give an accurate representation of their levels of job satisfaction in an interview or a meeting and may try to present an overly positive picture of their feelings.

ON THE *CUTTING* EDGE

On the *Cutting* Edge: Personality, Genetics, and Job Satisfaction

Can job satisfaction be a reality for all workers? And how much can the organization do toward increasing or maintaining job satisfaction for its workers? Although the organization can do much to foster job satisfaction,

ON THE *CUTTING* EDGE *(continued)*

the factors that cause job satisfaction are not entirely under the control of the organization. Workers can influence their own levels of job satisfaction through such actions as performing their jobs well and maintaining good attendance at work. Even if we could set up the ideal workplace, would this lead all workers to enjoy high levels of job satisfaction? Research on the influences of personality and genetic factors on job satisfaction suggests that the answer is "no."

For example, workers who score high on personal alienation—indicating deep-set tendencies toward feeling isolated, lonely, and powerless—do not seem to be as affected by interventions designed to increase workers' job satisfaction as are workers scoring low on this personality characteristic (Efraty & Sirgy, 1990). Persons high on trait positive affectivity might be more likely to experience positive moods and emotions at work, which relate to various measures of job satisfaction (Fisher, 2000). Likewise, workers' personality based on the five-factor model (Törnroos et al., 2019) and individuals' core self-evaluation, a construct related to how positively one sees oneself (Bono & Judge, 2003), both relate to job satisfaction. Indications are that workers' personalities may vary in terms of the amount of job satisfaction they are able to achieve and under what conditions they are best able to achieve it. In fact, it has been argued that dispositional factors may be responsible for the fact that surveys of U.S. workers during both good and bad economic times seem to show approximately the same percentages of satisfied and dissatisfied workers (Staw & Ross, 1985). In other

words, although economic conditions fluctuate, the distribution of different personality types in the workforce remains relatively stable.

Perhaps more interesting is the finding that genetic factors present at birth can influence a worker's job satisfaction. Studies examining the genetic and environmental components of job satisfaction using identical twins who were reared apart in different homes found a higher correlation in the twin adults' job satisfaction than would be found between persons in the general population (Keller et al., 1992). In other words, despite the fact that the identical twins were raised in totally different environments and likely were in completely different job environments, the twins' levels of job satisfaction were quite similar. Research has discovered some of the genetic markers associated with job satisfaction (Song et al., 2011), worker reactions to jobs, and their overall well-being (Li et al., 2016).

Of course, such findings do not suggest that organizations have no responsibility in helping workers to achieve job satisfaction. What these findings do suggest is that job satisfaction may not be completely determined by characteristics of the organization or of the job (Dormann & Zapf, 2001). Although organizations must provide an environment where employees can meet their job-related needs, they cannot guarantee that every worker will achieve the same level of satisfaction. Likewise, workers should not place the entire responsibility for their own job satisfaction (and other work attitudes) on the employer.

On the other hand, meetings or interviews can provide richer information because the interviewer can ask follow-up questions or request further elaboration or clarification of an answer. In addition, response biases (e.g., tendencies for all or most employees to give overly positive or negative responses) and ambiguous items that employees may interpret differently may seriously damage the validity of a pencil-and-paper/online job satisfaction measure. In summary, no matter which type of measurement is selected, careful thought and planning must go into the development and administration of job satisfaction measures.

Despite the complexities, many organizations develop their own interviews, scales, or surveys that are used to measure employee job satisfaction. Although such in-house techniques can be designed to assess satisfaction with specific issues relevant to each company's employees, their results may be difficult to interpret. First, these measures may not be reliable or valid. To construct measures that are reliable and valid, one must have a rather extensive background in survey development and measurement techniques. Moreover, it takes quite a bit of research to establish the reliability and validity of a job satisfaction measure. Many organizations do not have employees with the skills needed to construct such measures. Second, it is difficult to know what a particular rating or score means without being able to compare it with some standard. For example, if employees indicate relatively low levels of satisfaction with salary on some scale, does this mean that they are actually dissatisfied with the money they make? They may merely be stating a desire for more money—a desire shared by most employees of most organizations.

Standardized Job Satisfaction Surveys

Because of these problems in creating and interpreting in-house job satisfaction measures, many companies use standardized surveys. Recall that "standardized" instruments means that the measures have established reliability and validity and have been widely used. Besides being cost-effective, a major advantage of using such standardized measures is that they provide normative data that permit the comparison of ratings with those from similar groups of workers in other companies who have completed the survey. This allows the organization to know whether the job satisfaction levels of its employees are low, high, or in the "normal" range, as compared with other workers in other organizations. As demonstrated earlier in the comparison of levels of satisfaction with salary, if a company simply assumes its employees' ratings are low (when, in fact, they are average when compared with the norm), management may spend time and resources on a problem that doesn't exist.

The ability to compare scores from standardized job satisfaction measures that have been obtained from different groups of workers in different companies also allows researchers to investigate the various organizational factors that cause job satisfaction and dissatisfaction. In other words, if different questionnaires were used for all studies, researchers could not be sure that the studies were measuring and comparing the same things.

Two of the most widely used standardized surveys of job satisfaction are the *Minnesota Satisfaction Questionnaire* (*MSQ*) and the *Job Descriptive Index* (*JDI*). The

Stop & Review

Describe the two approaches to conceptualizing job satisfaction.

Minnesota Satisfaction Questionnaire (MSQ)
a self-report measure of job satisfaction that breaks satisfaction down into 20 job facets

Minnesota Satisfaction Questionnaire (Weiss et al., 1967) is a multiple-item rating scale that asks workers to rate their levels of satisfaction/dissatisfaction with 20 job facets, including supervisor's competence, working conditions, compensation, task variety, level of job responsibility, and chances for advancement. Ratings are marked on a scale from "very dissatisfied" to "neutral" to "very satisfied." Sample items from the MSQ are presented in Figure 8.3.

On my present job, this is how I feel about	Very Dissatisfied	Dissatisfied	Neutral	Satisfied	Very Satisfied
1 Being able to keep busy all the time	1	2	3	4	5
2 The chance to work alone on the job	1	2	3	4	5
3 The chance to do different things from time to time	1	2	3	4	5
4 The chance to be somebody in the community	1	2	3	4	5
5 The way my boss handles his or her workers	1	2	3	4	5
6 The competence of my supervisor in making decisions	1	2	3	4	5
7 The way my job provides for steady employment	1	2	3	4	5
8 My pay and the amount of work I do	1	2	3	4	5
9 The chances for advancement on this job	1	2	3	4	5
10 The working conditions	1	2	3	4	5
11 The way my coworkers get along with each other	1	2	3	4	5
12 The feeling of accomplishment I get from the job	1	2	3	4	5

Figure 8.3 Sample items from the Minnesota Satisfaction Questionnaire.

Source: Adapted from Weiss et al., 1967.

The **Job Descriptive Index** (Smith et al., 1969) is briefer than the MSQ and measures satisfaction with five job facets: the job itself, supervision, pay, promotions, and coworkers. Within each of the five facets is a list of words or short phrases. Respondents indicate whether the word or phrase describes their job, using the answers "yes," "no," and "undecided." Each of the words or phrases has a numerical value that reflects how well it describes a typically satisfying job. Items checked within each scale are summed, yielding five satisfaction scores that reflect the five facets of job satisfaction. In the past, it was suggested that the five scales could be summed into a total score of overall job satisfaction. However, one study indicates that such a

Job Descriptive Index (JDI)
a self-report job satisfaction rating scale measuring five job facets

---

Think of your present work. What is it like most of the time? In the blank beside each word given below, write:

Y for "Yes" if it describes your work
N for "No" if it does NOT describe it
? if you cannot decide

Work on present job

  Routine

  Satisfying

  Good

Think of the kind of supervision that you get on your job. How well does each of the following words describe this supervision? In the blank beside each word below put:

Y if it describes the supervision you get on your job
N if it does NOT describe it
? if you cannot decide

Supervision on present job

  Impolite

  Praises good work

  Doesn't supervise enough

Think of the pay you get now. How well does each of the following words describe your present pay? In the blank beside each word, put:

Y if it describes your pay
N if it does NOT describe it
? if you cannot decide

Present pay

  Income adequate for normal expenses

  Insecure

Think of the majority of the people that you work with now or the people you meet in connection with your work. How well does each of the following words describe these people? In the blank beside each word below, put:

Y if it describes the people you work with
N if it does NOT describe them
? if you cannot decide

People on your present job

  Boring

  Responsible

  Intelligent

Think of the opportunities for promotion that you have now. How well does each of the following words describe these? In the blank beside each word, put:

Y for "Yes" if it describes your opportunities
N for "No" if it does NOT describe them
? if you cannot decide

Opportunities for promotion

  Dead-end job

  Unfair promotion policy

  Regular promotions

Think of your job in general. All in all, what is it like most of the time? In the blank beside each word below, write:

Y for "Yes" if it describes your job
N for "No" if it does NOT describe it
? if you cannot decide

Job in general

  Undesirable

  Better than most

  Rotten

Figure 8.4 Sample items from the Job Descriptive Index, Revised (each scale is presented on a separate page).

Note: The Job Descriptive Index is copyrighted by Bowling Green State University.

Source: Smith et al., 1985.

total score is not the best overall measure and suggests the use of a global assessment instrument called the Job in General (JIG) scale as an accompaniment to the five JDI scales (Ironson et al., 1989).

Since its development in the 1960s, the JDI has become the most widely used standardized measure of job satisfaction (Roznowski, 1989). Moreover, the JDI has been revised and improved several times over the years (e.g., Smith et al., 1969). Figure 8.4 presents sample items from the JDI.

Both the MSQ and the JDI have been widely researched and both have established relatively high levels of reliability and validity (Smith et al., 1969, 1987). One obvious difference between the two measures is the number of job satisfaction facets measured: the JDI measures 5 facets; the MSQ assesses 20. An important question is how many or how few facets are needed to measure job satisfaction adequately. Although there has been a century of research on the topic, to date, there is not consensus as to the ideal or best measurement of job satisfaction (Judge et al., 2017). However, most researchers do agree that a valid, reliable, and standardized instrument will provide the most accurate assessment.

In addition to the MSQ and JDI, a number of job satisfaction scales have been developed for research purposes, such as the *Job Satisfaction Survey* (Spector, 1997), a briefer facet measure of job satisfaction that has been used sporadically in research. From the practitioner standpoint, numerous consulting firms specialize in job satisfaction/employee satisfaction surveys, although companies need to use caution because many of these surveys have not, like the MSQ and JDI, been subjected to rigorous research evaluation.

The complete forms, scoring key, instructions, and norms can be obtained from Department of Psychology, Bowling Green State University, Bowling Green, OH 43403.

 CLOSE **Job Satisfaction at the International Level**

As you read this chapter, you will become more aware of some of the aspects of work that are related to job satisfaction for workers. However, the large majority of these studies are done in the U.S. As with research in all areas of psychology, we cannot conclude that the results of studies conducted with workers within the U.S. will generalize to workers in other countries and cultures. For example, you probably find that good relationships with your coworkers and supervisors add to the satisfaction that you find in your job. Are such personal relationships at work as important to workers throughout the world as they appear to be with American workers? And what other aspects of work add to job satisfaction for workers outside the U.S.?

One study conducted in Japan found that supportive supervision, as well as support from coworkers,

UP CLOSE *(continued)*

was positively correlated with workers' job satisfaction (Kumara & Koichi, 1989). According to this study, support from coworkers and supervisors was especially important to employees who did not feel positive about the work they performed (e.g., those who found their jobs unpleasant, very difficult, or stressful). These workers in "unfulfilling" jobs depended on good interpersonal relationships to feel satisfied, similar to findings of studies conducted using U.S. workers.

Along with having good social relationships at work, many U.S. workers prefer to have a variety of tasks to do and to have some autonomy in performing those tasks. Similarly, workers' job satisfaction in Australia (Sawang et al., 2020), Canada (Barken et al., 2018), and the Netherlands (van Dorssen-Boog et al., 2020) is positively related to having autonomy. These facets of the job may also account for the findings in the U.S. that blue-collar and white-collar workers have different levels of job satisfaction along with different factor structures of what constitutes job satisfaction (Hu et al., 2010). Specifically, Hu and colleagues found that white-collar workers distinguish two different aspects of their work: whether it is boring and whether it provides a sense of accomplishment, whereas blue-collar workers rate these various factors as a single measure ranging from negative to positive. Consistent with these findings, one comparison of white-collar workers in the U.S. and India

found remarkable similarity in the factors that contributed to these workers' job satisfaction (Takalkar & Coovert, 1994).

Obviously, the international findings discussed here are mostly based on studies of workers in developed countries, where workers enjoy a certain level of job security, adequate pay, and good working conditions. For example, one study found differences in job satisfaction levels between U.S. workers and workers in the Philippines (Rothausen et al., 2009). Another study found differences in job satisfaction among workers from countries in Central and Eastern Europe (Lange, 2009). Whether or not workers in more underdeveloped nations would look to such things as task variety and autonomy for sources of job satisfaction has not yet been determined (Judge et al., 2001). Perhaps workers in underdeveloped nations have different sources of satisfaction, which are possibly related to more basic survival needs (e.g., pay) than workers in more developed nations. However, one would expect that, as these nations develop and gain economic strength, workers the world over will look to their jobs to fulfill higher-level needs, such as support from coworkers, recognition, and the opportunity to control their own work behaviors and reach their highest potential. Indeed, having control over one's work decisions is positively related to job satisfaction (Keller & Semmer, 2013).

It is important to mention that cultural factors can affect both how workers define and perceive job satisfaction and how members of different countries or cultural groups respond to job satisfaction measures. As a result, there have been many attempts to understand job satisfaction globally (see the "Up Close" box, "Job Satisfaction at the International Level").

Stop & Review

Compare and contrast the MSQ and the JDI.

Job Satisfaction and Job Performance

As you recall from our discussion of the human relations movement, Mayo and his colleagues proposed that there was a relationship between one aspect of job satisfaction—employee satisfaction with social relationships at work—and work productivity. Moreover, the job design theories of motivation discussed in Chapter 7—Herzberg's two-factor theory and the job characteristics model—are as much theories of job satisfaction as they are of motivation. Both theories emphasize that satisfaction with the job is key to determining motivation. Is there any truth to this notion that the "happy worker is the productive worker"?

A meta-analysis suggests that there is indeed a moderate correlation between job satisfaction and job performance (Judge et al., 2001). But what is the causal relationship? Does job satisfaction cause job performance? One early theory of the job satisfaction–performance relationship suggests that it may be the other way around: good job performance leads to (causes) job satisfaction! (But, of course, it is not that simple, as other factors mediate the relationship.)

This early theory, suggested by Porter and Lawler (1968), clarifies how this process might operate. According to them, job satisfaction and performance are not directly linked. Instead, effective job performance leads to job-related rewards, such as pay increases, promotions, or a sense of accomplishment. If the process for offering these rewards is perceived as fair, receiving these rewards leads to job satisfaction and to higher and higher levels of performance. This creates a situation in which job satisfaction and job performance are actually independent of one another but are linked, because both are affected by job-related rewards (see Figure 8.5). Interestingly, the **Porter–Lawler model** builds on the equity theory of motivation discussed in Chapter 7, because notions of equity—fairness in job-related inputs and outcomes—are central to the argument. Specifically, motivation to perform the job and the satisfaction derived from the job are both caused by the relationship between what an individual puts into the job and what is received from the job in terms of rewards. In other words, both motivation and job satisfaction come from the perceived equitable relationship between the employee's inputs to the job and the job outcomes.

Many other factors could potentially affect the job satisfaction–performance relationship—for example, the types of jobs that people perform. In fact, evidence suggests that job satisfaction might be more strongly related to job performance for individuals in complex jobs, such as managers, scientists, and engineers, than in more structured jobs such as accounting and sales (Judge et al., 2001).

Complex jobs, because they require creativity and ingenuity, might offer more opportunity for intrinsic reinforcement, and that may strengthen the connection between satisfaction and performance, in comparison with more routine jobs, where satisfaction may be more affected by the structure or conditions of work, or extrinsic rewards.

Some researchers emphasize that the perception of fairness or justice in pay is the most important part of this link between performance and job satisfaction (Miceli,

Porter–Lawler Model
a theory where the relationship between job satisfaction and performance is mediated by work-related rewards

Instructions: Listed below are a series of statements that represent possible feelings that individuals might have about the company or organization for which they work. With respect to your own feelings about the particular organization for which you are now working (company name), please indicate the degree of your agreement or disagreement with each statement by indicating one of the seven scale points listed in the note below these statements.*

☐ 1 I am willing to put in a great deal of effort beyond that normally expected in order to help this organization be successful.

☐ 2 I talk up this organization to my friends as a great organization to work for.

☐ 3 I feel very little loyalty to this organization. (R)

☐ 4 I would accept almost any type of job assignment in order to keep working for this organization.

☐ 5 I find that my values and the organization's values are very similar.

☐ 6 I am proud to tell others that I am part of this organization.

☐ 7 I could just as well be working for a different organization as long as the type of work was similar. (R)

☐ 8 This organization really inspires the very best in me in the way of job performance.

☐ 9 It would take very little change in my present circumstances to cause me to leave this organization. (R)

☐ 10 I am extremely glad that I chose this organization to work for over others I was considering at the time I joined.

☐ 11 There's not too much to be gained by sticking with this organization indefinitely. (R)

☐ 12 Often, I find it difficult to agree with this organization's policies on important matters relating to its employees. (R)

☐ 13 I really care about the fate of this organization.

☐ 14 For me this is the best of all possible organizations for which to work.

☐ 15 Deciding to work for this organization was a definite mistake on my part. (R)

Figure 8.5 The Porter–Lawler model of the job performance–job satisfaction relationship.

Note: Responses to each item are measured on a 7-point scale with scale point anchors labeled as follows: (1) strongly disagree, (2) moderately disagree, (3) slightly disagree, (4) neither disagree nor agree, (5) slightly agree, (6) moderately agree, (7) strongly agree. An "R" denotes a negatively phrased and reverse-scored item.

Source: Porter & Lawler, 1968, as adapted by Baron, 1986.

1993). That is, "relative deprivation" (a discrepancy between a worker's expectations and rewards) and perceived fairness of pay may mediate the relationship between performance and job satisfaction, regardless of the actual rewards obtained. For example, if highly paid workers do not perceive their pay to be fair or to meet their expectations, their satisfaction is likely to be negatively affected. This may extend beyond pay. A sense of being fairly treated is a very important determinant of job satisfaction (Clay-Warner et al., 2005).

In summary, both job satisfaction and job performance are important but complex work outcomes. There is some evidence that these two variables are linked, but the relationship is not necessarily direct and is likely influenced by a variety of other variables, such as job-related rewards, job complexity, feelings of equity and justice, and other factors.

Organizational Commitment

Just as there are different operational definitions of job satisfaction, so, too, are there different definitions of the construct of organizational commitment. For example, is it an attitude, a behavior, or both? Previously, organizational commitment, also referred to as company loyalty, was associated with an acceptance of the organization's goals and values, a willingness to exert effort on behalf of the organization, and a desire to remain with the organization (Porter et al., 1974). This definition encompasses both attitudes and behaviors. More recently, the concept of organizational commitment has been taken to imply worker attitudes, such as those just mentioned, whereas the concept of organizational citizenship behaviors (OCBs) refers to commitment-related behaviors (Organ, 1990). (Recall that we discussed OCBs in Chapter 5.) For example, there is a negative correlation between the attitude of organizational commitment and the behavior of quitting a job. Organizational commitment is similar to job satisfaction because both involve feelings about the work situation (and both can be seen as components of the "umbrella" construct of employee engagement). However, because organizational commitment deals specifically with workers' attitudes about the organization, it may be more directly linked to employee attendance variables such as absenteeism and turnover than is job satisfaction. A good definition of **organizational commitment** is that it is the worker's attitudes about the entire work organization.

Organizational Commitment
a worker's feelings and attitudes about the entire work organization

The most widely used organizational commitment measure is a 15-item self-report instrument called the Organizational Commitment Questionnaire (OCQ), which is presented in Figure 8.6. Another model of organizational commitment views it as composed of three dimensions: *affective commitment*, which is the employee's emotional attachment to the organization; *continuance commitment*, which refers to commitment to continue with the organization because there are costs associated with leaving; and *normative commitment*, which is like a sense of duty or obligation to stay with the company (Meyer & Allen, 1997). Separate scales are used to measure

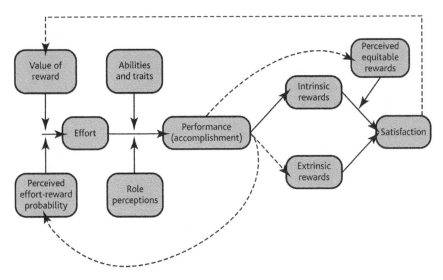

Figure 8.6 Organizational Commitment Questionnaire (OCQ).

Source: Mowday et al., 1979, p. 228.

each of these three commitment dimensions (Meyer et al., 1993). Research has demonstrated that self-report measures of organizational commitment such as these do a good job of measuring the construct (Goffin & Gellatly, 2001).

⏱ Stop & Review

Describe the Porter–Lawler model.

Organizational Commitment and Job Satisfaction

The concepts of job satisfaction and organizational commitment are closely related, although distinct. Research indicates a fairly high positive correlation between the two factors (Tarigan & Ariani, 2015). Part of this high positive correlation may be due to the fact that workers respond positively to both job satisfaction and organizational commitment measures, or due to a positive response bias, or due to workers having a desire to avoid *cognitive dissonance*.

Cognitive dissonance is an unpleasant state of perceived self-inconsistency (see Festinger, 1957). Workers thus avoid cognitive dissonance by convincing themselves that they are satisfied simply because they are loyal to the organization ("I have stayed with this company through thick and thin, therefore I must like my job"). Although it is conceivable that a worker could be quite satisfied with a job but have low feelings of commitment to the organization, or vice versa, the feelings tend to be positively related.

Both organizational commitment and job satisfaction are most likely affected by numerous factors, including the type and variety of work, the autonomy involved in the job, the level of responsibility associated with the job, the quality of the social relationships at work, compensation, and the chances for promotion and advancement in the company. However, there appears to be some consensus that organizational values influence organizational commitment, whereas perceived equity of rewards influences job satisfaction. That is, perceived fairness in rewards influences job satisfaction, whereas perceived congruence between organizational and employee values, and between organizational values and actions, tends to influence organizational commitment (Finegan, 2000). If employees feel that the organization cares about them and supports them, organizational commitment tends to be higher (Kim et al., 2016). Organizational commitment also tends to be weakened by the perceived chances of finding a job with another company (Gilbert & Ivancevich, 2000). For instance, if highly skilled worker, Carol, could easily find a job with another company, but her friend, Kim, had difficulty finding her current job, Carol will likely have a lower level of organizational commitment than Kim.

Beginning in the 1990s and into the financial "meltdowns" of past decades, many organizations found it necessary to reduce the size of their workforces by laying off or terminating workers. This was certainly true in many organizations during the COVID-19 pandemic. Thousands of people at a time can lose their jobs when a major corporation reduces the number of people it employs. Such actions, called *downsizing* (although some companies have tried to soften this term by relabeling it "rightsizing"), can have an impact on the workers who are retained, as well as on those who lose their jobs. For many of the remaining employees, feelings of organizational commitment and job satisfaction can decline following downsizing, especially if the employees are close to those who were laid off or if they feel that their own jobs may be in jeopardy. However, studies show that explanations from management giving the reasons for the layoffs and treating people fairly improve reactions to layoffs (Holten et al., 2019).

As you might imagine, maintaining job satisfaction and organizational commitment is a challenge to both employers and employees—a challenge that becomes even more difficult during trying economic times. Yet organizations must be concerned with both employee job satisfaction and organizational commitment if they are to maintain a high-quality, loyal workforce.

Employee Attitudes and Employee Attendance

As previously mentioned, employee attendance variables such as absenteeism and turnover are associated with employee engagement, job satisfaction, and organizational commitment. Employees who are engaged, or who have positive feelings about their job and work organization, should be less likely to be absent from work and to leave for a job elsewhere than those who are disengaged and hold negative attitudes about their job. However, before considering these relationships, we must consider how employee attendance variables are defined and measured.

Employee Absenteeism

Both absenteeism and turnover can be categorized into voluntary and involuntary forms. Voluntary absenteeism is when employees miss work because they want to do something else. Calling in sick to take a 3-day weekend or taking a day off to run errands or to go shopping are examples of voluntary absenteeism. Involuntary absenteeism occurs when the employee has a legitimate excuse for missing work, typically illness. Involuntary absenteeism also occurs when employees are absent because of factors beyond their control, such as lack of transportation or childcare problems (Goldberg & Waldman, 2000). It is very difficult to distinguish voluntary from involuntary absenteeism because most employees are unlikely to admit that they were voluntarily absent (Hammer & Landau, 1981).

One factor that might affect the use of involuntary sick leave is the presence of paid sick leave. Only 13 states and Washington D.C. require paid sick leave as of 2020— Connecticut, California, Massachusetts, Oregon, Vermont, Arizona, Washington, Rhode Island, Maryland, New Jersey, Michigan, Nevada, and Maine—in order of when each state passed the law (www.ncsl.org/research/labor-and-employment/paid-sick-leave.aspx). Of course, organizations can offer paid sick leave regardless of state law, and, although common sense might suggest that individuals who have paid sick leave would be more likely to take time off from work, research studies consistently show the opposite: providing paid sick leave actually reduces sick leave by keeping ill employees out of the office, reducing the spread of infectious illnesses (Stearns & White, 2018).

While involuntary absenteeism may be the result of actual illness and an organization's paid sick leave policy, voluntary absenteeism is more strongly related to work attitudes, such that job satisfaction has a negative but weak relationship to absenteeism (Ostroff, 1993). However, that relationship may depend on individual differences. One study on customer service agents within a major telecommunications company showed that individuals who were not prone to experience guilt reported a negative relationship between job satisfaction and absenteeism. However, individuals who were not guilt-prone did not allow their job satisfaction to impact their absenteeism (Schaumberg & Flynn, 2017). Of course, it is also important to make the distinction between voluntary and involuntary absenteeism. Job satisfaction and guilt proneness are most likely to impact voluntary, but not involuntary, absenteeism.

Additionally, there is evidence that individual absenteeism may be affected by coworkers' absenteeism rates and by the organization's policy and "climate" toward absenteeism (see Miraglia & Johns, 2021). For example, if coworkers are frequently absent, or if management has a lenient policy that is tolerant of absences, employees might be inclined to miss work regardless of how satisfied or dissatisfied they are with their job (Lieke et al., 2016).

It seems apparent that absenteeism, especially voluntary absenteeism, would be related to turnover (e.g., workers who have a lot of unexcused absences don't last long on the job). A meta-analysis found a small positive relationship ($r = 0.25$) between absenteeism and turnover and a pattern of employee "withdrawal," as tardy workers who tended to be late arriving at work had greater rates of absenteeism, which, in turn, led to higher rates of turnover (Berry et al., 2012).

Employee Turnover

As with absenteeism, there are difficulties in defining and measuring turnover. Involuntary turnover occurs when an employee is fired or laid off. A certain amount of involuntary turnover is likely to be considered inevitable and possibly even beneficial. Firing workers who are not performing at desirable levels can be viewed as a positive, "weeding" process (Manz et al., 2015). Even employee quitting (voluntary turnover) can yield positive results for the organization if those who quit are poor performers (Eberly et al., 2009).

In contrast, turnover of high-performing employees can cost organizations in terms of bottom-line outcomes such as sales and profit (Kacmar et al., 2006). According to one school of thought, voluntary turnover is likely to be influenced by lack of job satisfaction and organizational commitment, whereas involuntary turnover is not. As is the case with absenteeism, research that does not distinguish between voluntary and involuntary turnover may not find the expected relationships between employee attitudes and turnover simply because the two types of turnover are lumped together.

Both job satisfaction and organizational commitment have been investigated as predictors of employee turnover. Meta-analyses indicate that low levels of both job satisfaction and organizational commitment are related to higher rates of turnover (see Eberly et al., 2009, for a review). Interestingly, one of the best predictors of employee turnover is absenteeism, particularly the rate of absences in the years immediately before the employee leaves (Griffeth et al., 2000). There is also some evidence that voluntary turnover can occur in clusters of employees—what can be referred to as *collective turnover* (Heavey et al., 2013). This makes sense because employees develop social networks, and negative attitudes toward the organization may develop and be reinforced by other employees in the network. Whereas a network of strongly committed employees can reduce turnover, growing dissatisfaction within the group may lead to employees leaving in clusters (Porter & Rigby, 2021).

Researchers have turned their attention to measuring employees' self-reported intentions to leave, or turnover intentions, in an effort to prevent the loss of valuable employees. We have already seen that employee engagement leads to reduced

turnover intentions. The obvious problem with measuring turnover intentions is that many workers who report that they intend to quit their jobs may not actually turn over because they lack alternative employment, because they reevaluate the situation, or because they are not risk takers (Allen et al., 2005). Regardless of the strength of the connection between intentions to turn over and actual turnover, measuring employees' intentions to quit their jobs can be a measure of dissatisfaction with the job or organization and used by employers to try to remedy the situation to prevent costly turnover.

Because voluntary turnover can be costly to an organization, it is important to understand some of the reasons why good performers may leave their jobs. Productive, valuable employees who do not receive work-related rewards, such as promotions and pay raises, are likely candidates for leaving their jobs (Trevor et al., 1997). Studies also indicate that perceived lack of influence or power within the organization can cause workers to seek employment elsewhere, especially if they feel positive about the other job opportunities available to them (Lee & Mitchell, 1994). As stated earlier, both job satisfaction and organizational commitment are associated with turnover, and this need for workers to feel that they have some influence within the organization may help explain this association. That is, those workers who have such influence are probably more satisfied with their jobs and, thus, more committed to the organization (Dwyer & Ganster, 1991). This may also help explain the reason that giving workers a sense of power over their jobs or allowing them to participate in decision-making processes is associated with higher levels of job satisfaction, as we shall see later in this chapter.

In summary, when examining the relationships between job satisfaction and other outcome variables such as absenteeism and turnover, it is important to consider the type of absenteeism and turnover being measured. Voluntary absenteeism and turnover are most likely to be affected by employee attitudes. Unfortunately, many studies do not distinguish between voluntary and involuntary absenteeism and turnover, which leads to a possible "watering down" of any observed effects. Moreover, cause-and-effect relationships often cannot be assumed. In fact, some studies indicate that the relationships are reciprocal, with each variable sometimes being the "cause" and at other times being the "effect."

Increasing Employee Engagement, Job Satisfaction, and Organizational Commitment

As we have seen, employee engagement, job satisfaction, and organizational commitment are considered important by organizations because they are linked to costly absenteeism and turnover. Job satisfaction is particularly important to the employee because it reflects a critical work outcome: feelings of fulfillment from the job and the work setting. Because of this, organizations have implemented a number of programs and techniques in an effort to increase employees' engagement, satisfaction, and commitment. These programs take many forms. Some change the

Turnover Intentions
workers' self-reported intentions to leave their jobs

structure of work, others alter the methods of worker compensation, and still others offer innovative fringe-benefit plans and packages. We will examine some of these techniques.

Changes in Job Structure

Three techniques have been used to try to increase employee satisfaction and engagement by changing the structure of jobs. The first technique, job rotation, which was first introduced in Chapter 6, involves moving workers from one specialized job to another. Although job rotation can be used to train workers in a variety of tasks, it can also be used to alleviate the monotony and boredom associated with performing the same work, day in and day out. For example, an employee in a retail store may move from maintenance and cleanup duties to stocking merchandise to bagging merchandise on a weekly basis. A receptionist in a large organization might rotate from greeting visitors and answering telephones to simple clerical duties such as filing and photocopying. Research shows that job rotation can be related to job satisfaction, as well as contributing to increases in salary and opportunities for promotion (Campion et al., 1994).

Job Enlargement
the expansion of a job to include additional, more varied work tasks

Job enlargement is the practice of allowing workers to take on additional, varied tasks in an effort to make them feel that they are more valuable members of the organization. For example, a custodian who is responsible for the cleaning and upkeep of several rooms might progressively have the job enlarged until the job's duties involve the maintenance of an entire floor. Job enlargement is tricky to implement because it means that workers are required to do additional work, which some might perceive as negative. However, if used correctly, job enlargement can positively affect job satisfaction by giving an employee a greater sense of accomplishment and improving valuable work skills. One study of enlarged jobs found that they led to greater employee satisfaction, improved employee initiative, and better customer service than nonenlarged jobs. However, enlarged jobs carried the "costs" of requiring more skilled, more highly trained, and more costly (higher-paid) workers than nonenlarged jobs (Campion & McClelland, 1991).

Job enrichment, which we studied in depth in Chapter 7, can also be used to increase employee engagement and job satisfaction. Recall that job enrichment involves raising the level of responsibility associated with a particular job by allowing workers a greater voice in the planning, execution, and evaluation of their own activities. For example, in one such program, assembly-line workers were divided into teams, each of which was given many of the responsibilities that were previously held by frontline supervisors, including ordering supplies, setting output rates, creating quality control inspection systems, and even appraising their own performance. This independence and increased responsibility can go a long way toward increasing motivation and job satisfaction for many workers, and enriched jobs may be more important today to younger workers (Beltrán-Martín & Roca-Puig, 2013). Although job enrichment and job enlargement seem somewhat similar, because both require more work from employees, job enrichment raises the level of tasks, whereas job enlargement does not raise the level of responsibility associated with the work.

Changes in Pay Structure

According to research, the perception of fairness in pay is associated with greater job satisfaction (Witt & Nye, 1992). Although the relationship between pay and job satisfaction is not always a direct, positive one, pay and opportunities to develop relate to affective commitment (Jayasingam & Yong, 2013). Although most innovative compensation programs are introduced primarily in an effort to improve job performance, many changes also increase levels of job satisfaction.

One innovative compensation program is **skill-based pay** (also known as *knowledge-based pay*), which involves paying employees an hourly rate based on their knowledge and skills rather than on the particular job to which they are assigned (Lawler et al., 1992). In other words, workers are paid for the level of the job that they are able to perform, rather than paid for the title or particular position that they hold. For example, two individuals may both have the job title of auditor, but one, who is more skilled, receives higher pay because she had advanced auditing skills and the other doesn't.

For skill-based pay programs to be cost-effective, it is imperative that employees be assigned to jobs that match the levels of their skills and knowledge. Research indicates that workers are more satisfied in organizations that use this system than in those that use conventional pay plans, and there is also evidence that they are more productive, more concerned with quality, less prone to turnover, and more likely to be motivated to grow and develop on the job (Dierdorff & Surface, 2008). There is also some evidence that skill-based pay works better in manufacturing as opposed to service organizations (Shaw et al., 2005). Particularly satisfied are those who receive skill-based pay and who also have high levels of ability and motivation (Tosi & Tosi, 1987). One explanation for the effectiveness of skill-based pay systems is that employees may perceive these compensation plans as fairer and the organization as more supportive (Mitra et al., 2011). With the current emphasis on the "knowledge worker" and with a dwindling supply of workers possessing the highest levels of technical knowledge and skills, skill-based pay systems may increase in the future.

The Porter–Lawler model suggested that job performance leads to job satisfaction by way of increased rewards, one of the most important of which is pay. If this is the case, then a system of compensation based directly on performance should be an effective strategy for increasing job satisfaction. One such pay-for-performance system is **merit pay**, a plan in which the amount of compensation is directly a function of an employee's performance. In merit pay plans, workers receive a financial bonus based on their individual output. Although sensible in theory, such systems do not work well in practice for a number of reasons (Campbell et al., 1998). First, and perhaps most important, difficulties in the objective assessment of performance mean that it is often impossible to distinguish the truly good performers from the more average performers. This leads to feelings of unfairness in the distribution of merit

Skill-Based Pay
a system of compensation in which workers are paid based on their knowledge and skills rather than on their positions in the organization

Merit Pay
a compensation system in which employees receive a base rate and additional pay based on performance

pay and subsequent employee dissatisfaction (Salimäki & Jämsén, 2010; St-Onge, 2000). Second, most merit pay systems emphasize individual goals, which may hurt the organization's overall performance and disrupt group harmony, especially if jobs require groups to collaborate for the production of a product. Finally, in many such plans, the amount of merit compensation is quite small in proportion to base salaries. In other words, the merit pay is simply not viewed as a strong incentive to work harder (Balkin & Gomez-Mejia, 1987; Pearce et al., 1985). Research has suggested that a merit pay raise needs to be at least 7% to have a significant impact on employee attitudes and motivation (Mitra et al., 1997).

Another strategy for the implementation of pay-for-performance systems is to make pay contingent on effective group performance, a technique termed **gainsharing** (Lawler, 1987). The notion of group- or team-based rewards was introduced in Chapter 7. In gainsharing, if a work group or department reaches a certain performance goal, all members of the unit receive a bonus (Figure 8.7). Because the level of productivity among workers usually varies, the gainsharing program must be viewed as being fair to all involved (Welbourne & Ferrante, 2008). For example, in one program, workers decided that the fairest plan was to set a minimum amount that could be received by any worker and then base additional pay on each worker's level of productivity. Thus, the low producers received some base compensation, but they found that greater pay would result only if they increased production. The high producers, on the other hand, were well rewarded for their efforts (Cooper et al., 1992). One longitudinal study of gainsharing found that it was related to more positive employee attitudes and greater commitment than when employees did not participate in gainsharing (Hanlon et al., 1994). Another study found that gainsharing improved members' teamwork as well as their satisfaction with pay (O'Bannon & Pearce, 1999). Rather than focusing on productivity increases, some gainsharing programs reward workers who cut production costs through suggestions and innovations and then pass a portion of the savings on to the workers (Arthur & Huntley, 2005). Gainsharing may not be appropriate for all organizations or for all groups of workers. Therefore, implementation of a gainsharing program must be based on careful planning and a thorough knowledge of the groups of workers involved. One important consideration is that a failed attempt at a major change in pay structure, such as a gainsharing plan, could lead to massive worker dissatisfaction (Collins, 1995).

A more common plan is **profit sharing**, in which all employees receive a small share of the organization's profits (Rosen et al., 1986). The notion underlying profit sharing is to instill a sense of ownership in employees, to increase both commitment to the organization and to improve motivation and productivity (Chiu & Tsai, 2007). For profit-sharing programs to be effective, it is imperative that employees buy into the program and understand that profit sharing is linked to performance (Han et al., 2015). One drawback is that it is often difficult for employees to see how their individual performances have an impact on the company's total output. This may be one reason why profit sharing seems to work better in small companies than in large ones (Bayo-Moriones & Larraza-Kintana, 2009). In addition, there is typically quite a long delay between reaching performance goals and receiving individual shares of the company's profits (see the box "Applying I/O Psychology").

Gainsharing
a compensation system based on effective group performance

🕐 Stop & Review

Describe three techniques for changing job structure.

Profit Sharing
a plan where all employees receive a small share of an organization's profits

Figure 8.7 As part of a gainsharing system, an auto mechanic competes with others for monthly bonuses.

Source: Image by Ryan Doka, found on Pixabay (https://pixabay.com/photos/auto-repair-oil-change-oil-auto-3691963/).

Employee ownership is a program where employees own all or part of an organization. Employee ownership can take one of two forms: direct ownership or employee stock ownership. In direct ownership, the employees are the sole owners of the organization. In employee stock ownership programs, which are the more common of the two, stock options are considered part of a benefit package whereby employees acquire shares of company stock over time. Each employee eventually becomes a company stockholder and has voting rights in certain company decisions. Proponents of these programs claim that, although they are expensive, the costs are offset by savings created by increased employee organizational commitment, productivity, work quality, and job satisfaction and decreases in rates of absenteeism and turnover (Buchko, 1992).

Of course, tales of the quick success of employee-owned companies in the 1990s, such as Southwest Airlines, United Airlines, and Wheeling Steel, quickly became legendary, but were offset by the ethical scandals of the early 2000s and the financial meltdown, which meant that employees who had their retirement funds in stock in Enron, WorldCom, or a variety of Wall Street firms lost a bundle.

Research on the success of employee ownership programs is somewhat inconsistent, and results show that employee ownership does not necessarily lead to increased job satisfaction or organizational commitment (Oliver, 1990). Other research indicates that, if employee ownership is going to increase organizational commitment, certain criteria must be met, the most obvious being that the program must be

Employee Ownership
a program where employees own all or part of an organization

financially rewarding to employees (French & Rosenstein, 1984). Moreover, higher-level employees may have more positive reactions to employee ownership programs than do lower-level workers (Wichman, 1994). One investigation further qualified the conditions required for the success of employee ownership programs. Examining 37 employee stock ownership companies, the study found that rates of employee organizational commitment and satisfaction were highest when the companies made substantial financial contributions to the employee stock purchases, when management was highly committed to the program, and when there was a great deal of communication about the program (Klein, 1987). In addition, the Oliver (1990) study found that the rewards of employee ownership would only have a positive impact on the workers if they placed a high value on those rewards. For example, if a worker valued the work for its own merits, the worker would likely feel about the same level of satisfaction whether she was working for an employee-owned company or not.

Flexible Work Schedules

Another strategy for improving worker satisfaction and commitment is to provide alternative or flexible work schedules. Flexible work schedules give workers greater control over their workday, which can be important in large urban areas, where workers are able to commute at nonpeak times, or for workers with childcare responsibilities. One study showed that flexible schedules are related to lower sick day use and improved health perceptions, but only for older workers who are most likely to have health concerns (Piszczek & Pimputkar, 2020). In addition, flexible work schedules were related to improved attitudes around balancing work and family, but only for middle-aged workers who are most likely to have children. Flexible work schedules were positively related to affective commitment across age.

APPLYING I/O PSYCHOLOGY

Interventions to Enhance Employee Engagement?

Given the benefits of employee engagement, many scholars and practitioners have asked—is it possible to do an intervention to increase engagement in the workplace? And, if so, what should you do?

According to Knight and colleagues, there are four common "types" of work engagement interventions (Knight et al., 2017):

1. Personal resource-building interventions: interventions focused on increasing employees' individual strengths such as self-efficacy (confidence), resilience, or optimism.

2. Job resource-building interventions: interventions focused on improving the work environment such as increasing autonomy, social support, feedback, or developmental opportunities.

APPLYING I/O PSYCHOLOGY

(Continued)

3. Leadership training interventions: interventions focused on developing managers' leadership skills though offering education, practicing goal-setting, and engaging in problem solving.

4. Health promotion interventions: interventions focused on enhancing the health and well-being of employees by reducing stress, increasing mindfulness, and offering stress management or exercise/relaxation opportunities.

In one study, researchers implemented an engagement intervention that focused on increasing personal resources and job resources and challenging job demands in a health-care organization (Van Wingerden et al., 2016). The intervention involved three training sessions that were delivered in a 5-week period. They completed four activities:

1. The first activity focused on accepting the past, appreciating the present, and viewing the future as a source of opportunities.

2. The second activity involved giving and receiving feedback.

3. The third activity required participants to practice refusing requests.

4. The fourth activity related to job crafting and asked participants to consider their job tasks and personal strengths before designing a plan and goals that might increase their social job resources, structural job resources, and challenging job demands.

The researchers used a quasi-experimental design and showed that employees who received the intervention reported increased work engagement and increased job performance (self-rated).

Another study used mindfulness training to increase engagement among surgical intensive care unit personnel and involved meditation, yoga, and music for an hour-long, weekly session for 8 weeks (Steinberg et al., 2017). Participants who received the training also reported increased work satisfaction and reported being more resilient to stress.

Meta-analyses support the general effectiveness of interventions to increase engagement (Knight et al., 2019), suggesting that it is quite possible for organizations to increase employee engagement through a variety of workplace interventions.

One type of flexible schedule is **compressed workweeks**, in which the number of workdays is decreased while the number of hours worked per day is increased. Most common are four 10-hour days, and certain groups, such as nurses, may work three 12-hour shifts per week. Workers may prefer a compressed schedule because the extra day off allows workers time to take care of tasks that need to be done Monday through Friday, such as going to the doctor, dentist, or tax accountant. Usually, compressed workweeks include a 3-day weekend, which allows workers more free time to take weekend vacations. Both of these benefits should cut down on absenteeism, because workers previously might have called in sick to take an extra day of "vacation" or to run errands. An extended shift might also allow a worker to miss peak traffic

Compressed Workweeks schedules that decrease the number of days in the workweek while increasing the number of hours worked per day

times. However, a drawback is that working parents might have difficulty finding childcare for the extended workday. Also on the negative side, a 10-hour (or 12-hour) workday is more exhausting than the typical 8-hour day (see Bolino et al., 2021, for a review). This fatigue may lead to decreases in work productivity and concern for work quality (although many people say that the extra couple of hours are not necessarily tiring). Meta-analyses suggest that, although employees tend to be satisfied with compressed workweeks and exhibit higher overall job satisfaction, there is no reduction in absenteeism associated with compressed schedules (Baltes et al., 1999). In addition, one study found that workers had more favorable attitudes toward compressed work schedules if they had participated in the decision to implement the schedule change (Latack & Foster, 1985).

Flextime

a schedule that commits an employee to working a specified number of hours per week, but offers flexibility in regard to the beginning and ending times for each day

Flextime is a scheduling system whereby a worker is committed to a specified number of hours per week (usually 40) but has some flexibility concerning the starting and ending times of any particular workday. Often, flextime schedules operate around a certain core of hours during which all workers must be on the job (such as from 10 a.m. to 2:30 p.m.). However, the workers can decide when to begin and end the workday, as long as they are present during the core period and work an 8-hour day. Some flextime schedules even allow workers to borrow and carry hours from one workday to the next or, in some extremely flexible programs, from one week to another. The only stipulation is that an average of 40 hours per week is maintained. Obviously, only certain types of jobs can accommodate flextime.

What are the primary advantages of flextime? For the worker, it creates greater freedom and can improve well-being (Spieler et al., 2017). Workers can sleep in and begin work later in the morning, as long as they make up the time by staying late. Employees who want to leave work early to do some late-afternoon shopping can arrive early to work that day. One study of commuting workers showed that flextime commuters reported less driver stress than workers not on flextime (Lucas & Heady, 2002). A study of flextime programs found that flextime reduced stress levels for workers in three countries (Canada, Israel, Russia; Barney & Elias, 2010). Research indicates that flextime programs increase employee satisfaction and commitment (Chen & Fulmer, 2018). Interestingly, flextime pays off for companies that can implement this type of schedule, resulting in reduced absenteeism and increased productivity (Berkery et al., 2017), as well as lower turnover and higher revenue well above any costs associated with flextime (Berkery et al., 2020).

Benefit Programs

Perhaps the most common way for employers to try to increase employees' job satisfaction and organizational commitment is through various benefit programs. Benefit programs can include flexible working hours, a variety of health-care options, different retirement plans, profit sharing, career development programs, health promotion programs, and employee-sponsored childcare. Interestingly, however, not all programs have their intended effects. For example, although on-site childcare programs increase worker job satisfaction, the expected reductions in absenteeism rates have been small (Kossek & Nichol, 1992).

Growing in popularity are flexible, or "cafeteria-style," benefit plans, where employees choose from a number of options (Barringer & Milkovich, 1998). Lawler (1971) long ago argued that allowing employees to choose their own benefits led to increases in job satisfaction and ensured that the benefits suited each employee's unique needs. One study demonstrated, however, that it is important that employees receive adequate information and guidance regarding the characteristics of the various benefit programs, to help them make an informed choice of benefits that best suit their needs and to avoid dissatisfaction caused by making incorrect choices (Sturman et al., 1996). Research suggests that cafeteria-style benefits are perceived as a fairer system than traditional benefit plans (Cole & Flint, 2004).

It is important to bear in mind that the costs of employee benefits are rising rapidly—with benefits costing U.S. employers 30–40% of total compensation (U.S. Department of Labor, 2016). Benefit costs in some European countries are even higher. As a result, organizations often reduce benefit programs as a cost-saving strategy during times of economic downturn. Yet, organizations must be aware of the potentially damaging effects of such cuts in benefits on employee job satisfaction and morale.

The effectiveness of programs designed to increase job satisfaction and organizational commitment depends on various factors. Although most of the techniques intended to increase job satisfaction do indeed appear to do so, there is less evidence that these programs then lead to changes in other important outcome variables such as productivity, work quality, absenteeism, and, ultimately, turnover. If a company implements a program aimed at increasing employee job satisfaction, and if management is perceived by employees to be taking positive steps toward improvement of the workplace, job satisfaction will likely improve immediately after the introduction of the program. However, it may be unclear whether the program actually caused the increase or if it is really a sort of Hawthorne effect, in which employees' positive expectations about management's good intentions lead to increases in satisfaction merely because something was done. Regardless of the reason for measured improvements following the implementation of some satisfaction-enhancing program, the increases may tend to disappear over time as some of the novelty wears off, which long-term follow-up evaluations would reveal.

Stop & Review

List and define four alternative pay structure techniques.

Positive Affect and Employee Well-Being

Another factor influencing prosocial behaviour is one's mood at work (George, 1991). **Positive affect**, which includes positive moods and emotions, influences a host of employee attitudes and behaviors (Fisher, 2000). Positive mood at work is negatively related to both absenteeism (George, 1989) and turnover (George & Jones, 1996). Not only is a person's emotional state important, but also there are clearly individual differences in dispositions toward positive or negative affect that

Positive Affect
positive emotions that affect mood in the workplace

are genetically determined, as discussed in "On the Cutting Edge." Just like moods and emotions, dispositional affect (affectivity) relates to workplace outcomes such as absenteeism and turnover (Pelled & Xin, 1999).

A major source of moods and emotions at work is one's manager. One study used an experience sampling methodology to examine the impact of leaders on employees' affect at work (Bono et al., 2007). Health-care workers completed a survey four times a day for 2 weeks and reported that they experienced fewer positive emotions when interacting with their supervisors than their coworkers and customers, but certain types of leaders (transformational leaders) elicited more positive emotions than others. Further, laboratory (Johnson, 2009) and field (Johnson, 2008) studies show that managers' affect influences employee affect, which can impact additional outcomes such as organizational citizenship behavior and performance.

So, is a positive disposition or emotional state and resulting job satisfaction the "cure-all"? Not necessarily. There is some evidence that, when workers become dissatisfied with some aspect of the work situation, they become motivated to change it. Job dissatisfaction has been linked to both creativity and voicing of concern (Zhou & George, 2001). Importantly, no matter how strong an individual's positive emotions or disposition, if the person is not fairly treated or is undercompensated, job satisfaction and positive work behaviors will decline.

It is important to also mention that satisfaction with one's job is not enough. Workers may have job satisfaction, but other aspects of their lives (family relationships, physical health, etc.) may not be as positive. I/O psychology has two important objectives in this regard: to improve the physical and social environment at work in an effort to enhance worker well-being, satisfaction, and life quality, and to improve organizational outcomes, such as increased productivity, work quality, and reduced absenteeism and turnover by increasing employee participation in, and commitment to, organizational processes (Danna & Griffin, 1999).

Stop & Review

List and define five categories of organizational citizenship behaviors.

Summary

There are a number of ways to assess positive employee attitudes at work. *Employee engagement* reflects a psychological state in which one feels vigor (energy), dedication, and absorption in one's work and organization. *Inclusion* involves the feeling that one belongs, but can still be one's unique self. The most commonly used construct is *job satisfaction*, which involves the positive feelings and attitudes one has about a job, can be conceptualized in overall, or global, terms or in terms of specific components or facets, and can be measured through interviews or with self-report instruments. The most widely used self-report measures are the *Minnesota Satisfaction Questionnaire (MSQ)* and the *Job Descriptive Index (JDI)*. Research indicates that there is a slight positive relationship between job satisfaction and job performance, although the link may be moderated by another variable, such as the receipt of work rewards. Job satisfaction is positively correlated with *organizational commitment*, or employees' feelings and attitudes about the entire work organization.

Both job satisfaction and organizational commitment tend to be negatively correlated with voluntary employee absenteeism. However, the relationships are complex and difficult to decipher, partly owing to the difficulty involved in distinguishing voluntary absenteeism from involuntary absenteeism. Job satisfaction and organizational commitment are also related to voluntary employee turnover.

Programs designed to increase job satisfaction include changes in job structure through techniques such as *job rotation, job enlargement,* and *job enrichment.* Other satisfaction-enhancing techniques suggest changing the pay structure by using methods such as *skill-based pay, pay-for-performance* programs such as *merit pay, gainsharing,* or *profit sharing,* which are sometimes contingent on effective group performance. Flexible work schedules, such as *compressed workweeks* and *flextime,* improve satisfaction by giving workers greater control over their jobs. Still other methods of improving satisfaction involve increasing job-related benefits.

Most recently, research has focused on the role of *positive affect* in employee behavior, with job satisfaction mediating the relationship between affect and work outcomes. This emphasis on positive employee attitudes, emotions, and behaviors reflects I/O psychology's concern with both organizational functioning and employee well-being.

Study Questions and Exercises

1. What are some of the difficulties in the measurement of employee job satisfaction?
2. How might I/O psychologists try to deal with these problems?
3. How does job satisfaction relate to the important "bottom-line" outcome variables of performance, absenteeism, and turnover?
4. What would a good, comprehensive program to increase job satisfaction contain? What elements would you include?
5. Consider a job or occupation that you are familiar with. What are the "normal" job duties associated with this job, and what might be considered "organizational citizenship behaviors" for this job or occupation? Try to come up with examples of each type of OCB for this job.

Web Links

https://positivepsychology.com/job-satisfaction/

Inclusify.com

www.bgsu.edu/arts-and-sciences/psychology/services/job-descriptive-index. html
Information on the Job Descriptive Index (JDI).

Suggested Readings

Daus, C. S., Cropanzano, R., Martinez-Tu, V., & Yang, L.-Q. (2020). Emotion at work. In L.-Q. Yang, R. Cropanzano, C. S. Daus, & V. Martínez-Tur (Eds.), *The Cambridge handbook of workplace affect*. Cambridge University Press, p. 1.

Knight, C., Patterson, M., & Dawson, J. (2017). Building work engagement: A systematic review and meta-analysis investigating the effectiveness of work engagement interventions. *Journal of Organizational Behavior*, *38*(6), 792–812.

Smith, R. W., Kim, Y. J., & Carter, N. T. (2020). Does it matter where you're helpful? Organizational citizenship behavior from work and home. *Journal of Occupational Health Psychology*, *25*(6), 450.

CHAPTER 9

Worker Stress and Burnout

Inside Tips
WORKER STRESS AND BURNOUT

Life stress is a topic with which most of us will be familiar because it is discussed often in the popular press and media. This chapter deals primarily with worker stress: the stress that occurs at work and affects work behavior. So be careful not to confuse what you have heard from the media about life stress and what you read in this chapter. For instance, a common misconception is that all stress is bad. As you will find out, a little bit of stress can be motivating and challenging. Yet it is the negative type of stress that gets most of the attention. Another misconception is that the strategies used in dealing with stress in everyday life will also work in dealing with worker stress. This is not always the case. For example, some stressors can be alleviated by organizational changes and are, therefore, under the control of management, whereas others must be addressed by the individual worker. In addition, some of the techniques for dealing with stress in the workplace are not so much stress-reduction techniques as they are simply good management and human resource practices. Social scientists have had a great deal of difficulty in precisely defining and measuring stress. Be aware of this. Some of the concepts in this chapter are quite abstract and are initially difficult to understand.

This chapter fits well with Chapter 8, which focused on worker satisfaction and positive worker attitudes. In some ways, satisfaction and stress can be opposite sides of the same coin. Jobs can create a great deal of satisfaction, contributing to a sense of well-being and "worth." At the same time, however, jobs can subject us to uncomfortable (and potentially harmful) stress and can lead to negative attitudes and work behaviors.

The first few weeks of your job were exciting: you were challenged to learn new things and accomplish important objectives. You felt good about the job and about yourself.

But now, work has become routine, and there is a great sense of pressure. It is sometimes hard to drag yourself out of bed in the morning. Some of this is due to the increasing workload, but you are also having trouble getting along with a particularly difficult coworker. Sometimes, the pressure from work makes it hard to concentrate; other times, you feel sick and unhappy.

As we saw in Chapter 8, most workers feel some sense of purpose and accomplishment about their jobs, which can be highly rewarding and self-satisfying. However, work can also be a tremendous burden. Deadlines, work overload, and difficult bosses or coworkers can all place considerable pressure and strain on workers. Thus, jobs and the work environment commonly produce stress, and workers must learn to deal with that stress. Moreover, the negative behaviors of people at work, ranging from bad attitudes to acts of sabotage and workplace violence, make the work world a difficult (and sometimes dangerous) place. In this section, we will define worker stress, see how it affects work behavior, look at how it is measured, examine ways that the individual worker can attempt to cope with it, and consider strategies that organizations can use to try to decrease stress. We will also look at negative attitudes and dysfunctional behaviors at work and what organizations and individuals can do to try to limit or eliminate these.

Defining Worker Stress

The construct of stress is quite complex. So much so, that there are at least eight different definitions (models) for stress (Cooper et al., 2002). According to the early stress researcher Hans Selye (1976), stress is primarily a physiological reaction to certain threatening environmental events. From Selye's perspective, worker stress would simply refer to the stress caused by events in the work environment. Psychologist John French and his colleagues (1982) say that worker stress results from a lack of "fit" between a person's skills and abilities and the demands of the job and the workplace. In other words, a worker who is totally unqualified for a particular job should feel a tremendous amount of stress. For example, imagine a worker with little previous experience with computer systems applying for and being hired as a communication specialist, only to find out that the job requires a thorough knowledge of various computer networking systems. Richard Lazarus (1991), in his "transactional" view of worker stress, saw stress as resulting from the worker's perception that a certain environmental event is a threat or a challenge, factoring in their perception of how capable they will be at managing the threat. From Richard Lazarus's perspective, you and I might interpret the same event very differently—I might find it stressful; you might view it as totally harmless (or perhaps even as pleasantly challenging!).

To arrive at a definition of worker stress for our purposes, we need to look at what these three different approaches to stress have in common. All three definitions view worker stress as an interaction between the person and some environmental event, or **stressor**. In addition, all the definitions emphasize that there are some important reactions to the stressful event. These reactions can be either physiological or

Stressor
an environmental event that is perceived by an individual to be threatening

psychological in nature, or both. Therefore, we will define **worker stress** as physiological and/or psychological reactions to an event that is perceived to be threatening or taxing.

Although we most often think of stress as an unpleasant state, it can have both negative and positive aspects. For example, imagine that you have been working for several years as an assistant manager for a large company and find out that you have just received a promotion to department manager, a position you have been trying to obtain for some time. With your new position come feelings of stress. Some of these are negative, such as the stress that will result from having to work many overtime hours without additional compensation, being required to make formal presentations regularly to your peers and superiors (and having your presentations critically evaluated by them), and taking on the responsibility to take the criticism for any problems occurring in your department. On the other hand, many positive reactions are associated with the promotion, including feelings of accomplishment, anticipation, pride, and challenge. Like the negative aspects, these positive responses also induce physiological and psychological reactions in the body. Some stress researchers distinguish the negative stress, termed *distress*, from the positive kind of stress, called *eustress* (see, e.g., Parker et al., 2015).

We are all likely familiar with the physiological reactions to stress. They include signs of arousal such as increased heart and respiratory rates, elevated blood pressure, and profuse sweating. The psychological reactions to distress include feeling anxiety, fear, frustration, and despair, as well as appraising or evaluating the stressful event and its impact, thinking about the stressful experience, and mentally preparing to take steps to try to deal with the stress. In many ways, stress is a perceptual process. An event that one individual perceives to be stressful may not be labeled as such by someone else. For example, making a formal presentation in front of a large audience may be perceived as extremely stressful for the average college student, but may be perceived as energizing (and perhaps fun) by a person who is accustomed to public speaking. Because stress may cause a variety of reactions and feelings, and because perceptions of stress may vary from person to person, stress has not been particularly easy to define, and it is very difficult to measure. We will deal with methods of measuring stress shortly.

Events that might not be terribly stressful alone can build up over time if exposure to stressful events is sustained over time, creating more deleterious outcomes for individuals and organizations (Fuller et al., 2003). For workers, stress can have long-term health-related effects (Ganster & Rosen, 2013). Stress-related illnesses include ulcers, hypertension and coronary heart disease, migraines, asthma attacks, and colitis. If worker stress leads to stress-related illnesses, rates of absenteeism can increase. At the psychological level, stress can cause mental strain, feelings of fatigue, anxiety, and depression that can reduce worker productivity and quality of work. If a job becomes too stressful, a worker may be compelled to quit and find a less stressful position. Thus, worker stress may influence turnover as well.

Managers and workers may also be concerned about stress at a more personal level. Worker stress can be, in many ways, the flip side of job satisfaction. Whereas job satisfaction represents the "positives" associated with work, stress is a way of

Worker Stress
the physiological and/or psychological reactions to events that are perceived to be threatening or taxing

conceptualizing the "negatives" associated with jobs—the pressures, the strains, the conflicts. No doubt, much of the interest in worker stress results from the fact that managers, business owners, and all other sorts of workers experience stress on a day-to-day basis.

Sources of Worker Stress

Situational Stress

stress arising from certain conditions that exist in the work environment or in the worker's personal life

Generally, stress can arise from either the environment (situational stress) or from an individual's personal characteristics (dispositional stress). **Situational stress** can come from all aspects of our lives. We are subjected to a wide range of stressors at home, at school, and in our interpersonal relationships, as well as the stressors we encounter at work. No doubt, all these various sources of stress accumulate and add to our overall stress levels. That is, stress at home can spill over to work situations and vice versa. Most stress researchers realize this and emphasize that, when studying stress, it is important to look at the broad picture of an individual's total stress, rather than focusing narrowly on stress derived from work (Erickson et al., 2000).

For our purposes, however, we will focus primarily on the stress that comes from workplace sources. We will first examine stressful occupations and then focus on the elements of jobs and of work organizations that can cause worker stress. Finally, we will look at how worker stress can result from characteristics of the workers themselves as we examine individual sources of worker stress, or what we might call dispositional stress.

Stressful Occupations

It is generally believed that certain occupations, such as air traffic controller, physician or other health-care provider, police officer, and firefighter, are particularly stressful. Several years ago, there was increased attention given to postal workers' stress following highly publicized cases of postal workers attacking and killing coworkers. This led to the slang term "going postal." Is it true that certain occupations are particularly stress prone? There is some evidence to support this. For example, studies of air traffic controllers indicate that they do indeed experience high levels of work-related stress, as do medical doctors and nurses (Sparks & Cooper, 1999). Similarly, studies of dentists suggest that dentistry is a high-stress occupation (DiMatteo et al., 1993). High-level managers and business executives are also believed to hold extremely stressful jobs.

Certain jobs, such as being a police officer, can be particularly stressful because of the physical dangers involved (Tehrani & Piper, 2011). Likewise, we saw the dangers associated with other first responders during and after the September 11, 2001, tragedy. The day-to-day dangers facing police officers and firefighters are indeed stressful. However, some studies suggest that, rather than causing stress, the excitement and challenge of dealing with physical danger may actually be motivating and "enriching" to many police officers and firefighters (Riggio & Cole, 1995). Interestingly, studies of police officers suggest that they suffer from the same sources of stress, such as increased responsibilities and workloads and difficulties with coworkers, as persons in other occupations (Brown et al., 1996). In sum, trying to determine levels of worker stress merely by looking at a person's occupation or job title may not be very accurate.

Research on these and other stereotypically stressful occupations has begun to discover exactly why these jobs are characterized as stressful. For instance, air traffic controllers' jobs are stressful because of the heavy workloads, the constant fear of causing accidents, equipment problems, and poor working environments (Shouksmith & Burrough, 1988). The primary sources of dentists' occupational stress are

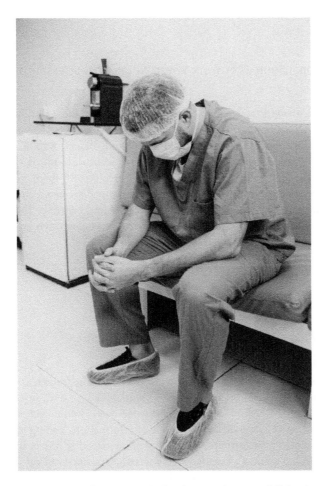

Figure 9.1 Although they are often seen as having fewer work responsibilities than physicians, nurses often experience very high levels of work stress.

Source: Image by Jonathan Borba, found on Unsplash (https://unsplash.com/photos/9Ov8ofh7URg).

difficult patients, heavy workloads, and the dentists' own concern that their patients hold negative views about them and about dentists in general (DiMatteo et al., 1993).

Rather than focusing only on high-stress occupations, it makes sense to examine those sources of worker stress that are common to all kinds of jobs, even those that are not typically considered high-stress jobs. Such sources of stress can be divided into two general categories: organizational and individual. Organizational sources of stress come from the work environment and can be broken down into two subcategories: stress derived from work tasks and stress resulting from work roles. Individual sources of stress include a person's history of exposure to stress, as well as certain stress-related personality characteristics and behavioral patterns. For example, there is evidence that certain personality traits make people more prone to stress (and stress-related illnesses), and some characteristics seem to make people more resistant to stress and its negative outcomes.

⏱ Stop & Review
Discuss why worker stress is difficult to define.

Organizational Sources of Work Stress: Situational Stressors

A great deal of worker stress is caused by stressors in the environment of the work organization. Some of this organizational stress is caused by the work tasks themselves—the physical and psychological demands of performing a job. Organizational stress may also be caused by work roles, because work organizations are complex social systems in which a worker must interact with many people. Therefore, the work relationships of various kinds that must be created and maintained for a worker to perform the job adequately can also lead to stress. These two types of situational stress—work task and work role stressors—can often be alleviated by management actions.

Work Task Stressors

Work Overload

Work Overload
a common source of stress resulting when a job requires excessive speed, output, or concentration

A common work task source of stress is **work overload**, also known as *role overload*, which results when the job requires excessive work speed, output, or concentration (Bowling et al., 2015). More recently, attention has been given to technology-related work overload, such as the increased volume of information, leading to things such as "e-mail overload" (Bellotti et al., 2005). Work overload is widely believed to be one of the greatest sources of work stress. Research on work overload indicates that it is related to physiological indicators of stress, such as elevated serum cholesterol and increased heart rate (Caplan & Jones, 1975); to psychological measures of stress (Spector, 1987); and to lower quality of work and job dissatisfaction (Kirmeyer & Dougherty, 1988). In fact, work overload has been reported as a common source of stress for jobs as diverse as clerical workers, soldiers, air traffic controllers, courtroom attorneys, and health-care workers (Carayon, 1994).

Underutilization

Work overload can cause stress, but having too little to do—**underutilization**—can also be stressful (Ganster et al., 1986). Underutilization may also occur when workers feel that the job does not use their work-related knowledge, skills, or abilities, or when jobs are boring and monotonous (Weinberg, 2016). Some college graduates in low-level clerical or customer service positions may feel some stress owing to under-utilization of their knowledge and skills (French et al., 1982). There is also evidence that some individuals may be more susceptible to stress relating to underutilization than others (Vodanovich, 2003).

Underutilization
a source of stress resulting from workers feeling that their knowledge, skills, or energy are not being fully used

Physical Work Conditions

Physical conditions in the work environment are another organizational source contributing to worker stress (Frese & Zapf, 1988). Jobs that must be performed in extreme temperatures, loud and distracting noise, or poor lighting or ventilation can be quite stressful. Dangerous jobs that place workers at risk of loss of health, life, or limb are an additional source of work stress (Booth, 1986). Cramped, crowded, and excessively noisy work environments can also cause stress (Ashkanasy et al., 2014). For example, one study showed that noise levels in open-space office environments (offices with partitioned cubicles and open ceilings) constituted a significant source of stress (Evans & Johnson, 2000). Similarly, working late-night ("graveyard") shifts can disrupt natural sleep and waking cycles and may lead to problems such as high stress, fatigue, job dissatisfaction, and performance errors (Smith & Folkard, 1993).

Interpersonal Stress

One of the greatest sources of work stress results from difficulties in interpersonal relationships on the job. **Interpersonal stress** stems from difficulties in developing and maintaining relationships with other people in the work setting. Having a harsh, critical boss with a punitive management style would likely be stressful for just about anyone. With the rise of virtual work, some workers feel a lack of social connections and support and experience a stressful sense of social isolation (Wiesenfeld et al., 2001).

Interpersonal stress can also result when coworkers are placed in some sort of conflict situation. Imagine, for example, that two employees are both being considered

Interpersonal Stress
stress arising from difficulties with others in the workplace

Figure 9.2 The physical work environment, including loud noise and hot temperatures, can be a source a stress for many workers.

Source: Photo by Ahsanization ッ on Unsplash (https://unsplash.com/photos/wpvEMgFV4w0).

for an important promotion. A great deal of stress may be generated if the two individuals must work together while both are competing for the same honor.

There is also evidence that organizational politics and struggles over power can be important sources of stress in the workplace (Ferris et al., 1994). We will discuss power and politics in depth in Chapter 13. Whatever its causes, the inability to get along with other workers is one of the most common sources of stress in the workplace (Matteson & Ivancevich, 1987).

Another form of interpersonal stress occurs frequently in service organizations and involves the stress of providing good customer service. When one is dealing with impatient and difficult customers, the pressure to maintain one's cool and offer service with a smile can be quite taxing and stressful. Researchers have examined this **emotional labor**—the demands of regulating and controlling emotions and emotional displays as part of a job requirement (Hochschild, 1983). The very common stress caused by emotional labor can cause workers to become dissatisfied and cynical about their jobs, reduce job satisfaction, affect performance, and lead to frequent absenteeism and turnover (Bono & Vey, 2005; Hülsheger et al., 2010).

Emotional Labor
the demands of regulating and controlling emotions in the workplace

Workplace Mistreatment

Related to interpersonal stress is workplace mistreatment from colleagues and supervisors. All forms of harassment, including sexual harassment, harassment due to group membership (e.g., gender, race, sexual orientation), and being singled out by an abusive supervisor or colleague, are extremely stressful (Raver & Nishii, 2010). Not surprisingly, workplace abuse is negatively related to job satisfaction and organizational commitment and positively related to higher turnover intentions (see Hackney & Perrewé, 2018, for a review). For example, a study of over 6,000 telephone company employees across the U.S. showed that experiencing sexual harassment (see Chapter 6 for a more in-depth discussion of sexual harassment) resulted in increased stress and decreased job satisfaction (Law et al., 2011). This study further showed that the culture of the organization/unit in terms of whether the culture fostered and appeared to tolerate harassment or discouraged it also played a part in levels of employee stress (Law et al., 2011). Sexual harassment and other forms of harassment result in increased odds of work-related illness, injury, or being assaulted (Rospenda et al., 2005).

In addition to overt forms of workplace mistreatment such as sexual harassment and bullying (see the box "On the Cutting Edge"), researchers have become interested in the effects of subtle discrimination or microaggressions at work. For example, being left out or ostracized results in lowered self-esteem and increased negative affect at work (Smart Richman & Leary, 2009). Because subtle forms of workplace mistreatment are likely to occur with greater frequency, they can have equally negative effects as more overt harassment on physical, psychological, and work-related outcomes (Jones et al., 2016). Rather than categorizing mistreatment as overt or subtle, an informative way of thinking about workplace mistreatment was offered by Jones and colleagues (2017). They categorize workplace mistreatment along two axes: interpersonal to formal, and covert to overt. This allows us to see how the various forms of workplace treatment are related and different from one another.

Workplace mistreatment is particularly nefarious because it has the potential to impact those who are not the targets of harassment and has the potential to escalate over time. For example, one study showed that just observing hostile sexism can also reduce performance-based self-esteem and career aspirations among women

(Bradley-Geist et al., 2015). Workplace mistreatment can have a spiraling effect such that even small acts of incivility can become contagious and escalate over time, creating greater acts of aggressive behavior (Andersson & Pearson, 1999). Not surprisingly, discrimination and other forms of harassment tend to co-occur in some organizations, along with generally uncivil behavior (Lim & Cortina, 2005). A more specific type of stress that can result from stereotypes is stereotype threat, which we covered in Chapter 4.

Organizational Change

A common organizational source of stress is change (Rafferty & Griffin, 2006). (We will spend a great deal of time on organizational change in Chapter 15.) People tend to grow accustomed to certain work procedures and certain work structures, and they resist change. Most of us prefer things to remain stable and predictable. Such stability in our working environments seems comforting and reassuring. Therefore, it should not be surprising that major changes in a work organization tend to cause stress (Dahl, 2011). Some common change situations that lead to worker stress include company reorganizations, mergers of one company with another or acquisitions of one organization by another, changes in work systems and work technology, changes in company policy, and managerial or personnel changes (see Table 9.1; Wanberg & Banas, 2000). For example, research has shown that physiological stress responses are stronger in novel or unfamiliar circumstances that involve a threat or challenge (Rose, 1987).

An event such as a company-wide reorganization or a merger or acquisition would certainly be perceived as threatening and stressful by many employees (Marks & Mirvis, 2010). Coping with the loss of a job or potential job loss is another major stressor (Moore et al., 2006).

Table 9.1 Characteristics of Jobs that Cause Worker Stress

Work overload (e.g., time pressures and too much work)	Interpersonal conflict
	Decision making
Underutilization of worker knowledge, skills, ability, or energy	Organizational change
	Lack of support from supervisors or coworkers
Dangerous work conditions	Lack of control over the work situation
Responsibility for the health and well-being of others	Work–family conflict
Difficult or complex work tasks	Personal factors (e.g., Type A behavior or stress-prone personality)
Unpleasant or uncomfortable physical work conditions	

ON THE *CUTTING* EDGE

Workplace Bullying: An "Invisible" Epidemic?

A 2017 survey by the Workplace Bullying Institute found that 19% of employees in the United States have experienced bullying at work, and another 19% have observed bullying at work. Bullying behaviors include threats, aggression, ridiculing, sabotage of employees' work, and giving them the silent treatment. Targets of workplace bullying become emotionally depleted, which affects their motivation and can lead to disengagement at work (Tuckey & Neall, 2014), and experience severe stress reactions, including psychological and physical illness (Hogh et al., 2012). The cost of workplace bullying to organizations in terms of reduced productivity and increased absenteeism and turnover likely runs into the billions of dollars (Paludi, 2015). In Australia, where combating workplace bullying is a priority, it was estimated that bullying led to depression that cost hundreds of millions of dollars annually in increased absenteeism and lost productivity (McTernan et al., 2013).

Some countries have begun to enact legislation to combat workplace bullying, including Australia, Canada, and several European nations. In the U.S., there is currently no federal law to reduce bullying, but many states have passed antibullying legislation that requires employers to offer harassment training and increases accountability over bullying (https://healthywork.org/wp-content/uploads/2019/09/015-HWC-Website-Page-Content-Resources-Healthy-Work-Strategies-Workplace-Bullying-Prevention-Laws-Regs-v1–092019–300res-CYMK.pdf). As of 2020, Connecticut, Missouri, New York, Oregon, Illinois, and Rhode Island have introduced legislation allowing employees who have been victims of workplace bullying to sue their organizations. Further, it is important to note that, because bullying is often aimed at marginalized groups, it can fall under Civil Rights Act legislation (Cortina, 2008).

Individual Sources of Work Stress: Dispositional Stressors

Although a great deal of worker stress is created by factors in the organization or by features of jobs and work tasks, some is caused by characteristics of the workers themselves. We will consider two such individual sources of work stress: the Type A behavior pattern and susceptibility to stress and to stress effects. It is the individual worker—not management—who must work to alleviate these sources of stress.

Type A Behavior Pattern

When many people think of individuals who are extremely stressed in the workplace, they immediately picture the stereotypical hard-driving, competitive executive who seeks a job with a heavy workload and many responsibilities—a person who takes on too much work and never seems to have enough time to do it. Is there any truth

Type A Behavior Pattern
a personality characterized by excessive drive, competitiveness, impatience, and hostility that has been linked to greater incidence of coronary heart disease

to this characterization? Research evidence indicates that there is. Researchers have uncovered the **Type A behavior pattern,** or Type A personality, which is characterized by excessive drive and competitiveness, a sense of urgency and impatience, and underlying hostility (Table 9.2; Rosenman, 1978). This behavior pattern is particularly significant because there is evidence that persons who possess the Type A personality are slightly more prone to develop stress-related coronary heart disease, including fatal heart attacks, than persons who do not have the behavior pattern, termed Type Bs (Booth-Kewley & Friedman, 1987).

An important question is, how does the Type A behavior pattern relate to stress and to stress-related heart disease? Early research on Type A behavior hypothesized that it was the Type A's hardworking, competitive drive that caused stress and subsequent heart problems (Rosenman et al., 1964). Later research, however, suggested that the Type A's underlying hostility, and the lack of appropriate expression of that hostility, is also partly responsible for increased stress reactions in Type As (Friedman et al., 1985). Other studies suggest that the more global construct of "negative affectivity"—the expression of negative emotions, such as anger, hostility, anxiety, impatience, and aggression—is what combines with a Type A personality to increase stress-related health risks (Chen & Spector, 1991). (We will discuss negative affectivity in more depth later.)

Do Type As experience more stress than others? Research into this question has produced mixed results. For example, some studies indicate that Type As are more likely to experience or report high stress than are other personality types under the same workload (Kirmeyer & Dougherty, 1988). Other studies show that Type As do not report or experience greater stress, but simply have stronger physiological stress reactions to stressful situations (Ganster et al., 1986). Perhaps the subjective experience of stress has less negative influence on health than the physiological responses.

Table 9.2 Type A Behavior Pattern

Two popular self-report instruments are designed to assess Type A behavior. They are the Jenkins Activity Survey (JAS; Jenkins et al., 1979) and the Framingham Type A Scale (FTAS; Haynes et al., 1978). Following are examples of questions that determine Type A behavior:

- Are you a hard-driving and competitive person?
- Do you always seem pressed for time to get errands done?
- Are you the type of person who has a strong desire to excel and accomplish things?
- Are you impatient when you have to wait for service?
- Are you the kind of person who gets easily irritated?
- Would other people consider you bossy?
- Is your temper sometimes fiery and hard to control?
- Do you often feel like there is too much to do and not enough time to do it?

Affirmative answers to these questions indicate a Type A behavior pattern.

In other words, Type As may have stronger stress-induced physiological responses that they are not necessarily aware of, and it is these strong physiological responses over time that lead to increased health risks. If this is the case, Type As may simply not realize that their long, intense work style is creating wear and tear on their bodies.

Although there are obvious stress-related costs to the Type A behavior pattern, there are also some gains. Studies consistently show that Type As tend to work harder (Byrne & Reinhart, 1989), work well in high-variety jobs (Lee et al., 1988), and have higher positions and salaries than Type Bs (Chesney & Rosenman, 1980). This aspect of Type A behavior is conceptually related to strong achievement orientation or "workaholism," discussed in the motivation chapter (see the "Up Close" box in Chapter 7).

An important question is whether the Type A behavior pattern is something related to Western or U.S. work culture, or whether Type As occur in other countries and cultures. Although there is some evidence that other cultures have Type A and Type B workers (e.g., Jamal, 1999), there are most certainly differences across cultures and countries in the prevalence and rates of the Type A behavior pattern (Al-Mashaan, 2003).

Susceptibility/Resistance to Stress

Another dispositional source of stress may stem from the fact that some persons are simply more susceptible to stress, whereas others have stress-resistant, hardy personalities. Individuals with mental illness may be more prone to suffer from stress-related outcomes (see Follmer & Jones, 2018). In contrast, hardy individuals may suffer less from stress. The concept of **hardiness** was outlined by psychologist Suzanne Kobasa (1982), who argued that hardy personality types are resistant to the harmful effects of stress because of their style of dealing with stressful events. A meta-analysis shows that hardy individuals experience less stress and are better at coping with stress than nonhardy individuals (Eschleman et al., 2010). Rather than viewing a stressful situation as a threat, hardy types view it as a challenge and derive meaning from these challenging experiences (Britt et al., 2001). Moreover, they also believe that they can control and influence the course of their lives (a sense of lack of control can contribute to stress) and are committed to their jobs. Conversely, a lack of hardiness is associated with higher levels of self-perceived stress, and there is evidence that such "unhardy" or "disease-prone" persons may be more susceptible to stress-related illnesses and depression (Kobasa & Puccetti, 1983). Thus, it appears that certain types of workers are more "stress prone." That is, they are more likely to suffer stress-related physical illness and psychological symptoms (depression, anxiety, etc.) than are more hardy workers.

There have been attempts to increase hardiness through what has been called HardiTraining (Kobasa, 1982). Hardiness training was found to be successful in

Stop & Review

List and define five organizational/ situational sources of worker stress.

Hardiness
the notion that some people may be more resistant to the health-damaging effects of stress

helping college students deal with the stresses of college life (Maddi et al., 2009). We will examine other programs to cope with stress later in this chapter.

Self-Efficacy

Self-Efficacy
an individual's beliefs in his or her abilities to engage in courses of action that will lead to desired outcomes

Research has also identified another characteristic that seems to increase resistance to stress: self-efficacy. **Self-efficacy** is defined as an individual's beliefs in his or her abilities to engage in courses of action that will lead to desired outcomes (Bandura, 1997). In other words, self-efficacy is related to one's sense of competence and effectiveness. Self-efficacy is a very important concept that not only relates to one's ability to cope with stressful situations (i.e., the possession of *coping* self-efficacy), but is also an important factor relating to a worker's ability to perform his or her job (*job-related* self-efficacy), to lead a work team (*leadership* self-efficacy), and to deal effectively with relationships at work (*relationship* self-efficacy). There is evidence that a sense of self-efficacy can have positive effects in reducing stress in the workplace (Rennesund & Saksvik, 2010). In one study, it was found that having a sense of control over a stressful work situation only decreased stress if the employees had a high sense of self-efficacy about their abilities to do their jobs under stress and strain (Jimmieson, 2000).

Measurement of Worker Stress

Because stress is such a complex phenomenon, and because stress researchers cannot agree on a single definition of stress, you might suspect that the measurement of stress is extremely difficult. For the most part, measurement of stress in general, and of worker stress in particular, is problematic. There have been a number of approaches to measuring stress. We will consider several of these.

Physiological Measures

As has been stated, the stress response involves physiological reactions as well as psychological and emotional responses. Therefore, one strategy for measuring stress has focused on measuring signs of physiological arousal and strain that accompany stress. This includes blood pressure monitoring, an electrocardiogram (EKG) for monitoring heart rate, or blood tests for monitoring levels of certain hormones, such as the stress-linked hormone, cortisol, and cholesterol in the bloodstream. One problem with using such physiological indicators of stress is the amount of variation that can occur from hour to hour, day to day, or person to person (Herd, 1988). Another drawback to the use of such stress tests is the requirement for trained medical personnel, as well as the associated costs for equipment and analysis procedures.

Self-Report Assessments

Another approach to measuring stress, one that is favored by psychologists, is to ask people directly to report on their own perceived stress through various rating scales. Most self-report assessments fall into one of two major categories: reports about organizational conditions or reports about psychological and/or physical states.

Reports on organizational conditions typically contain items that ask about facets of the job such as autonomy, feedback, task identity, task significance, skill variety, complexity, dealing with others, ambiguity, and workload (Spector, 1992). For example, questions dealing with workload might include the following (Matteson & Ivancevich, 1987):

- Number of projects/assignments you have
- Amount of time spent in meetings
- Amount of time spent at work
- Number of phone calls and visitors you have during the day.

There are several standardized self-report measures of psychological and physiological stress and strain, such as the *Stress Diagnostic Survey* (SDS; Ivancevich & Matteson, 1980), the *Occupational Stress Indicator* (OSI; Cooper et al., 1988), and the *Job Stress Survey* (JSS; Spielberger & Reheiser, 1994). For example, the SDS measures workers' perceptions of stress in 15 work-related areas, including time pressure, workload, role ambiguity, and supervisory style. The JSS is a 30-item instrument that measures the severity and frequency with which workers experience certain stressful working conditions. These instruments have been used in research or by organizations to quickly gauge employees' stress levels.

⏱ Stop & Review
What is the Type A behavior pattern, and how does it relate to worker stress?

Measurement of Stressful Life Events

As was mentioned earlier, situational stress in one area of an individual's life, such as the home or school, can affect stress levels at work (Levi et al., 1986). Particularly important is the worker's experience of traumatic or **stressful life events**, which include negative events such as the death of a spouse or loved one, divorce or separation, major illness, and financial or legal troubles, as well as positive events such as marriage, the birth of a child, and vacations. This approach to measuring stress assumes that such events can bring on stress-related illness and may impair job performance.

Stressful Life Events
significant events in a person's recent history that can cause stress

One measure is a checklist where individuals total the numerical "stress severity" scores associated with the significant life events that they have experienced in the past year (Holmes & Rahe, 1967; see Table 9.3). This provides a personal life events stress index. Note that half of the ten most stressful life events are directly related to work (Hobson & Delunas, 2001). Research suggests that persons with high personal stress indexes tend to perform more poorly, have higher absenteeism, and change jobs more frequently than persons who experience fewer stressful life events (Bhagat, 1983). Moreover, there is some evidence that stressful life events have a greater stress impact on younger as opposed to older persons, based on the notion that young people do not have as well-developed coping mechanisms (Jackson & Finney, 2002). Yet there has been a great deal of criticism of the stressful life events approach to

Table 9.3 Sample Items from the Social Readjustment Rating Scale

Life Event	Stress Value
Death of spouse	100
Divorce	73
Marital separation	65
Jail term	63
Death of close family member	63
Personal injury or illness	53
Marriage	50
Fired at work	47
Change to different line of work	36
Change in number of arguments with spouse	35
Mortgage over $10,000	31
Foreclosure of mortgage or loan	30
Change in responsibilities at work	29
Outstanding personal achievement	28
Spouse begins or stops work	26
Trouble with boss	23
Change in work hours or conditions	20
Change in residence	20
Change in schools	20
Change in number of family get-togethers	15
Change in eating habits	15
Vacation	13
Christmas	12
Minor violations of the law	11

Source: Holmes & Rahe, 1967.

assessing stress (e.g., Hurrell et al., 1988). Much of the criticism is that this approach is too general. Certain life events may affect people very differently. For example, it has been suggested that a simple additive weighting of the Social Readjustment Rating Scale does not accurately assess the effect of an additional stressful event when an individual is already experiencing other stressful events (Birnbaum & Sotoodeh, 1991). In addition, assessment of stressful life events may not reveal the impact of day-to-day stressors influencing the individual.

Effects of Worker Stress

Much of the growing interest in worker stress (it is one of the most studied areas of I/O psychology) is due to the very powerful impact that it can have on workers and work behavior and, most dramatically, on employee health. It is believed that more than one half of all physical illnesses are stress-related. As mentioned, some common stress-related illnesses are ulcers, colitis, high blood pressure, heart disease, respiratory illnesses, and migraine headaches. Moreover, stress can worsen common colds, flus, and infections, making recovery time longer. It is estimated that these illnesses, attributed in part to work stress, cost billions of dollars annually in health-care costs and in employee absenteeism and turnover (Clark, 2005).

Worker stress can also have an adverse impact on employees' psychological states. High levels of stress are associated with depression, anxiety, and chronic fatigue. Stress may also contribute to alcoholism and drug abuse in workers and may influence accident rates on the job (Frone, 2008; we will discuss these in more depth later in this chapter). Emotional exhaustion, detachment from coworkers, negative self-evaluations, and lowered self-esteem are also associated with worker stress (Cordes & Dougherty, 1993).

As you might imagine, stress can have an effect on important work outcomes. Stress is believed to cause decreased work performance and increased absenteeism and turnover. However, the relationships between work stress and these key bottom-line variables are quite complex. For example, it has been suggested that the relationship between stress and performance may often take the form of an inverted U (see Figure 9.3), rather than being direct and linear, with greater stress leading to poorer performance.

In other words, very low levels of stress (or no stress) and very high levels of stress are associated with poor work performance, whereas low to moderate levels of stress seem to be related to better performance (Muse et al., 2003). This makes sense, because very high levels of stress will interfere with job performance. For instance, there is evidence that severe, acute stress results in poor performance because stress interferes with workers' mental processing (Ellis, 2006). On the other end, having little or no stress likely means that workers are not being challenged or motivated (LePine et al., 2005). In short, a little bit of stress might not be a bad thing. Of course, both stress and job performance are extremely complex variables, and this

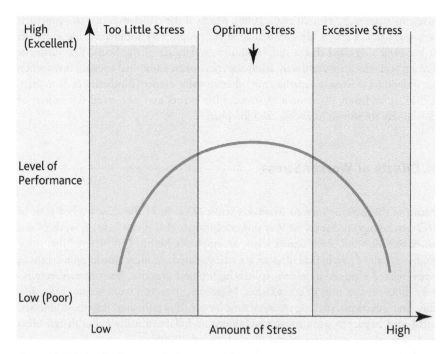

Figure 9.3 Relationship between performance and stress.

Source: Adapted from Cohen, 1980, p. 85.

inverted U relationship may not hold for all types of stressors or for all aspects of job performance (Beehr, 1985).

The effects of work stress on job performance might also be affected by other variables. For example, one study showed that the effect of stress on the job performance of nurses was mediated by feelings of depression. That is, work stress caused the nurses to be depressed, and the depression led to decreased quality of patient care and problems with relationships with coworkers (Motowidlo et al., 1986). If stress is caused by an inability to get along with a certain coworker, an employee may try to cope with this situation by avoiding all interactions with the individual. This avoidance strategy may impair the employee's job performance if the coworker has some valuable information that the employee needs to perform his or her job. In this case, it is not the stress that is causing poor job performance, but the coping strategy!

A great deal of evidence suggests that work stress can lead to increased turnover/ turnover intentions and absenteeism (Boswell & Olson-Buchanan, 2004). Gupta and Beehr (1979) found this to be true for a variety of occupations in five organizations. Another study concluded that it was a combination of high levels of work stress and low levels of organizational commitment that predicted voluntary turnover rates for workers in a food processing company (Parasuraman & Alutto, 1984). Further, if stress levels are to blame for certain illnesses, it is a given that stress must be responsible for some absenteeism and some turnover caused by disabling illness.

Job Burnout

Employees exposed to such things as unresolved interpersonal conflicts, lack of clearly defined work tasks and responsibilities, extreme overwork, lack of appropriate rewards, or presence of inappropriate punishment may become victims of **burnout**, a process by which they become less committed to their job and begin to withdraw from work. The process of withdrawal may include such reactions as increased tardiness and absenteeism and decreased work performance and work quality (Sutherland & Cooper, 1988). Moreover, work-related burnout can spill over to an individual's family life, as we saw with stress earlier (Maslach, 2005).

Burnout usually occurs in three phases. The first phase is *emotional exhaustion* caused by excessive demands placed on the worker. The second phase is *depersonalization*, or the development of a cynical, insensitive attitude toward people (other workers or customers) in the work site. The third phase is marked by feelings of

Burnout
a syndrome resulting from prolonged exposure to work stress that leads to withdrawal from the organization

Table 9.4 Sample Items from the Maslach Burnout Inventory (MBIHSS)

Directions: The purpose of this survey is to discover how various persons in the human services or helping professions view their jobs and the people with whom they work closely. Because persons in a wide variety of occupations will answer this survey, it uses the term "recipients" to refer to the people for whom you provide your service, care, treatment, or instruction. When you answer this survey please think of these people as recipients of the service you provide, even though you may use another term in your work.

Please read each statement carefully and decide if you ever feel this way about your job. If you have never had this feeling, write a "0" (zero) before the statement. If you have had this feeling, indicate how often you feel it by writing the number (from 1 to 6) that best describes how frequently you feel that way.

How Often:	0	1	2	3	4	5	6
	Never	A few times a year	Once a month or less	A few times a month	Once a week	A few times a week	Every day

I. Depersonalization
5. I feel I treat some recipients as if they were impersonal objects.

II. Personal Accomplishment
9. I feel I'm positively influencing other people's lives through my work.

III. Emotional Exhaustion
20. I feel like I'm at the end of my rope.

low personal accomplishment. Here the burned-out workers feel a sense of frustration and helplessness. They begin to believe that their work efforts fail to produce the desired results, and they may quit trying (Jackson et al., 1986). Table 9.4 presents sample items from the Maslach Burnout Inventory Human Services Survey (MBIHSS; Maslach & Jackson, 1986), an instrument that assesses the three hypothesized components of burnout.

Research has shown that burnout is especially high in human service professions that involve helping others, such as health-care providers (physicians, nurses, counselors), teachers, social workers, and police officers (Carlson & Thompson, 1995). This was certainly the case for health-care workers during the COVID-19 pandemic.

A study on the effects of burnout on teachers includes insensitivity toward students, lower tolerance for disruption in the classroom, inadequate preparation for classes, and the feeling that they are no longer able to help students learn (Figure 9.4; Byrne, 1993). A longitudinal study of social welfare workers found that the emotional exhaustion component of Maslach's Burnout Inventory was related to both voluntary turnover and declines in job performance over a 1-year period (Wright & Cropanzano, 1998). Although much of the research on burnout focuses on the "helping professions," there is evidence that burnout can occur in many different occupations (Sonnentag et al., 1994). Clearly, however, the emotional labor of providing services to clients, customers, and patients plays a big part in causing burnout (Brotheridge & Grandey, 2002).

⏱ **Stop** & Review
Discuss four ways of measuring worker stress.

Figure 9.4 Research indicates that job burnout is particularly high in the human service professions, including teachers.

Source: Photo by Taylor Wilcox, on Unsplash (https://unsplash.com/photos/4nKOEAQaTgA).

It is important to note that there is some debate among researchers about the definition and the complexity of the burnout phenomenon. For instance, researchers have disagreed about the number of components that comprise the burnout syndrome (Demerouti et al., 2001). Yet burnout is a serious problem and illustrates some of the long-term psychological and behavioral effects of work-related stress.

Coping with Worker Stress

The tremendous variety of strategies and techniques designed to cope with work stress can all be categorized into two general approaches: individual strategies and organizational strategies. Individual strategies are those that can be used by individual employees to try to reduce or eliminate personal stress. Organizational strategies are techniques and programs that organizations can implement to try to reduce stress levels for groups of workers or for the organization as a whole.

Individual Coping Strategies

Individual coping strategies are behavioral or cognitive efforts made in an attempt to manage internal demands and conflicts that have exceeded an individual's usual coping resources (Sethi & Schuler, 1984). The most obvious of such techniques are programs developed to improve the individual's physical condition, such as exercise and diet plans. The primary rationale behind such health programs is to make the body more resistant to stress-related illnesses. Some claim that exercise itself may directly reduce the anxiety associated with stress or that it may have a certain tranquilizing effect on stressed individuals (Jette, 1984). However, it is unclear whether it is the exercise that directly alleviates the physiological symptoms of stress or simply that an individual "feels good" after exercising because of positive psychological factors. For instance, because exercising and keeping physically fit are valued highly by our culture, it may be that physically active persons feel better about themselves and, thus, psychologically reduce perceived stress. More rigorous evaluation is needed to determine the precise physiological and psychological influences of exercise and diet programs in alleviating stress.

Another individual coping strategy is the inducement of states of relaxation to reduce the negative arousal and strain that accompany stress. A variety of techniques have been used to achieve this, including systematic relaxation training, meditation, and biofeedback (Stein, 2001). In systematic relaxation training, individuals are taught how to relax all the muscles of the body systematically, from the feet to the face. Meditation is a deep relaxed state that is usually brought on by intense concentration on a single word, idea, or object. Supposedly, meditative states are free of anxiety, tension, or distress (Sethi, 1984). Biofeedback uses some measure

Individual Coping Strategies
techniques such as exercise, meditation, or cognitive restructuring that can be used to deal with work stress

of physiological activity, typically brain waves or muscle tension, that is associated with relaxed states. When the person is in the state of relaxation, the measurement machinery provides some sort of feedback, such as a tone. The individual then learns through practice how to enter into the relaxed, stress-free state. Although relaxation, meditation, and biofeedback are intended principally to reduce the physiological arousal associated with stress, they may also induce positive psychological reactions to stress.

These various methods of coping with stress through relaxation processes are widely touted, but there has been very little systematic investigation of their effectiveness. In fact, some findings indicate that such programs are not very effective at all (Sallis et al., 1985).

One possible reason why systematic relaxation coping strategies may not be effective is that most of the relaxation techniques require quite a bit of dedication and practice to be used effectively. Not all persons find it easy to induce a deeply relaxed state; others may not be able to adhere to a regular program of systematic relaxation or meditation. Also, many of these programs last only a few hours, which may not be enough time to teach someone difficult relaxation techniques. The timing of the relaxation technique is another problem. Many people would find it difficult (and perhaps inappropriate) to meditate at work, and relaxing before or after work may or may not significantly reduce stress while at work. The same argument can be made for exercise programs—the benefits will only occur if people adhere to their exercise regimens (see Erfurt et al., 1992). In short, although any and all of these techniques may be good in theory, they may not function well in practice.

Other individual coping strategies include a variety of techniques to try to fend off work stress through better, more efficient work methods. Courses in time management are often advertised as methods of reducing stress caused by overwork and inefficiency (Sethi & Schuler, 1984). For example, learning to approach work tasks systematically by budgeting and assigning parcels of time to specific tasks and by planning ahead to avoid last-minute deadlines may be quite effective in helping reduce stress for some workers. Again, however, these strategies depend on the individual's commitment to the technique, and willingness and ability to use it regularly (Shahani et al., 1993). (See "Applying I/O Psychology" for guidelines on how organizations should implement stress management programs.)

Individuals may also try to cope with stress by removing themselves, temporarily or permanently, from the stressful work situation (Fritz et al., 2013). It is not uncommon for workers to exchange a stressful job for one that is less stressful (although many do seek more challenging and more stressful jobs). Although a vacation may temporarily eliminate work stress, certain trips, such as intense tours of eight European countries in 7 days, may create a different kind of stress themselves (Lounsbury & Hoopes, 1986). Research indicates that, although vacations do indeed reduce work stress and feelings of burnout, the effects are temporary. In fact, levels of stress and burnout are reduced immediately before, during, and immediately after the vacation, but may go back to original levels a few weeks after the vacation (Etzion, 2003; Westman & Eden, 1997).

It is interesting to note that workers might use absence from work—voluntarily taking a day off—as a coping strategy. If absence is used as an attempt to cope with a particularly stressful job, then the lost work time must be balanced against the possible gains in terms of the employee's long-term performance and well-being (Hackett & Bycio, 1996).

Another strategy uses cognitive efforts to cope, which may include cognitive restructuring, which entails changing the way one thinks about stressors (Wright et al., 2015). For example, instead of thinking negative thoughts when faced with a stressor, the individual practices thinking neutral or positive thoughts (e.g., "this is not important," "this is, in actuality, a challenge"). Studies of teachers and nurses who used cognitive restructuring found that it reduced their perceptions of stress and stress-related illnesses (Gardner et al., 2005). Cognitive restructuring is often used to treat post-traumatic stress disorder in workers and others who have experienced severe trauma (Mueser et al., 2009).

The fact that there are individual differences in resilience to stress has led to programs designed to increase employees' resiliency. These programs take different forms, but many of them involve some sort of cognitive training, including mindfulness training, improving emotional awareness and regulation of emotions, and developing a sense of self-efficacy. Resilience training programs range from a few hours to multiweek programs. Meta-analyses of resilience training programs' effectiveness have concluded that they have small, but significant, beneficial effects in reducing stress and, in some cases, lead to improved performance (Vanhove et al., 2016). As you might expect, resilience training programs work best when they are conducted at the individual, as opposed to the group, level and when the amount of training time is extensive.

Individual coping strategies may be effective in combating stress if they increase an individual's self-efficacy for coping with stress. Research shows that self-efficacy can help cope with work demands, such as work overload, but only if the person has the resources to help reduce the job demands (Jex et al., 2001). On the downside, individual coping strategies can be expensive and labor-intensive. In addition, success is dependent on the individual's motivation and ability to learn coping strategies.

Organizational Coping Strategies

Individual coping strategies are steps that workers themselves can take to alleviate personal stress, and **organizational coping strategies** are steps that organizations can take to try to reduce stress levels in the organization for all, or most, employees (Burke, 1993). Because work stress can come from a variety of organizational sources, there are many things that organizations can do to reduce situational stressors in the workplace. These strategies include the following:

Improve the person–job fit—We have already seen that work stress commonly arises when workers are in jobs they dislike or jobs for which they are ill suited (French & Caplan, 1972).

Organizational Coping Strategies
techniques that organizations can use to reduce stress for all or most employees

APPLYING I/O PSYCHOLOGY

Designing Effective Work Stress Management Training Programs

A wide range of programs are used to help employees manage work stress. According to leading researchers, such programs must follow certain guidelines to ensure their effectiveness: they must be systematic; they must teach knowledge, skills, or attitudes that are useful in coping with stress; and their success must be evaluated and documented (Munz & Kohler, 1997).

The first step in designing a stress management program is the same as in designing any sort of training program: an assessment of training needs. An organizational stress analysis is needed and might include answering such questions as: What are the major producers of stress in the organization? Do these stressors necessarily detract from the accomplishment of organizational goals? (In other words, are they "bad"?) What sort of resources will be committed to the training program?

According to Matteson and Ivancevich (1987), most stress management programs take one of two forms: knowledge acquisition programs or skill training programs. Knowledge acquisition programs provide participants with some information about stress and a number of coping techniques. An outline of a sample four-part stress knowledge acquisition program is presented next:

1 *Overview of stress and its potential consequences (3 hours)*—This might include a lecture and readings on facts and myths about stress, the impact of stress on physical and psychological health and on work performance, and potential sources of stress.
2 *Self-analysis: Learning about your personal stress (3 hours)*—This section can include assessments of personal stressors using instruments such as the stressful life events scale or workers' self-reports.

3 *Methods of coping with work stress (3 hours)*—Here, various individual coping strategies are presented and perhaps demonstrated.
4 *Developing a personalized coping plan (3 hours)*—In this final part, participants work on developing customized programs for managing stress, including setting personal stress management goals and finding means to assess their attainment.

The major advantages of knowledge acquisition programs are that they are relatively inexpensive, do not require a lot of time, and do not place heavy demands on participants. Unfortunately, these "one-shot" training programs may not be as effective as the more involved skill training programs in alleviating work stress (Hemingway & Smith, 1999).

Skill training programs are designed to improve specific coping skills in areas such as problem solving, time management, communication, social interaction, cognitive coping, or strategies for making changes in lifestyle. An example of a step-by-step problem-solving skill program developed by Wasik (1984) is illustrated next:

1 Identify problem (What is my problem?)
2 Select goals (What do I want to accomplish by solving the problem?)
3 Generate alternatives (What else can I do?)
4 Review the consequences (What might happen?)
5 Make a decision (What is my decision?)
6 Implement the decision (Did I do what I decided?)
7 Evaluate the decision (Does it work?)

This step-by-step program would be conducted in a series of 1–2-hour sessions over many weeks. Participants learn each of the steps, practice them using role-playing, and receive feedback concerning their skill

APPLYING I/O PSYCHOLOGY

(Continued)

development. They are also encouraged to use the skills to deal with actual work problems and then report back to discuss the success or failure of the strategy. The key to these programs is to practice using the coping strategies and applying them to real and simulated stressful situations.

The final stage in any stress management program is to evaluate its effectiveness. Too often, stress management programs are not properly evaluated (Loo, 1994). It has been suggested that an assessment should consider trainees' reactions; how well the program accomplished its immediate objectives; actual behavioral changes; the impact of the program on organizational outcomes such as productivity, absenteeism, morale, and employee health; and the cost-effectiveness of the program (Kirkpatrick, 1978).

A mismatch between a worker's interests or skills and job requirements can be very stressful. By maximizing the person–job fit through the careful screening, selection, and placement of employees, organizations can alleviate a great deal of this stress.

Improve employee training and orientation programs—Perhaps the most stressed groups of workers in any organization are new employees. Although they are usually highly motivated and want to make a good impression on their new bosses by showing that they are hardworking and competent, their lack of certain job-related skills and knowledge means that new employees are often unable to perform their jobs as well as they would like. This mismatch between expectations and outcomes can be very stressful for new workers. Moreover, they feel a great deal of stress simply because they are in a new and unfamiliar environment in which there is much important information to be learned. Companies can help eliminate some of this stress by ensuring that new workers receive proper job training and orientation to the organization. Not only does this lead to a more capable and productive new workforce, but it also helps to reduce the stress-induced turnover of new employees.

Increase employees' sense of control—We have previously mentioned that the lack of a sense of control over one's job can be very stressful. By giving workers a greater feeling of control through participation in work-related decisions, more responsibility, or increased autonomy and independence, organizations can alleviate some of this stress (Jimmieson & Terry, 1993). Programs such as job enrichment, participative decision making, and systems of delegating authority all help increase employees' sense of control over their jobs and the work environment.

Eliminate punitive management—It is well known that humans react strongly when they are punished or harassed, particularly if the punishment or harassment is believed to be unfair and undeserved. The very act of being threatened or punished at work can be very stressful. If organizations take steps to eliminate company policies that are perceived to be threatening or punitive, a major source of work stress will also be eliminated. Training supervisors to minimize the use of punishment as a managerial technique will also help control this common source of stress.

Remove hazardous or dangerous work conditions—In some occupations, stress results from exposure to hazardous work conditions, such as mechanical danger of loss of limb or life, health-harming chemicals, excessive fatigue, or extreme temperatures. The elimination or reduction of these situations is another way of limiting organizational stress.

Provide a supportive, team-oriented work environment—There is considerable research evidence that having supportive colleagues—people who can help deal with stressful work situations—can help reduce worker stress (Lim, 1996). This is particularly true for workers involved in the emotional labor of service work (Korczynski, 2003). Meta-analyses suggest that social support in the workplace reduces perceptions of threat, lessens the perceived strength of the stressors, and helps in coping with work-related stress (Viswesvaran et al., 1999). The more organizations can foster good interpersonal relationships among coworkers and an integrated, highly functioning work team, the more likely that workers will be able to provide support for one another in times of stress (Heaney et al., 1995). We will look at work group processes and teamwork in more depth in Chapters 11 and 12.

Improve communication—Much of the stress at work derives from difficulties in interpersonal relations with supervisors and coworkers. The better the communication among workers, the lower the stress created because of misunderstandings. In addition, stress occurs when workers feel cut off from or uninformed about organizational processes and operations. In one study, merely providing more job-related information helped in reducing stress caused by task overload (Jimmieson & Terry, 1999). Proper organizational communication, which will be examined in Chapter 10, can prevent workers from experiencing stress from job uncertainty and feelings of isolation.

 Stop & Review

List and describe five organizational coping strategies.

 CLOSE   **Stress Levels and Stress Sources of Executives around the World**

A common stereotype in the U.S. is the highly stressed, top-level business executive (Friedman et al., 1985). Is this characterization accurate, and, if so, are high-level managers in other nations similarly stressed? The first question—"Are executives highly stressed?"—does not have an easy answer. For example, many executives constantly work under such stressful conditions as work overload, high levels of responsibility, and inter-role conflict (e.g., being required to travel extensively on business, which interferes with family and personal commitments). The finding that executives have a higher rate of certain types of ulcers than certain blue-collar workers attests to the existence of executive stress (Hurrell et al., 1988). On the other hand, executives have the benefit of some working conditions that are believed to moderate stress, such as control over the job.

The answer to the question of whether executives worldwide experience similar stressors is also not completely clear. There is some indication, however, that executives in different nations experience different types or sources of stress. For example, executives in less-developed countries such as Nigeria and Egypt seem to experience a great deal of stress owing to lack of autonomy, whereas those from more developed countries, such as the U.S., the United Kingdom, the Netherlands, and Japan, experience greater stress from work overload (Carayon & Zijlstra, 1999). Workers in India rated lack of job structure, not workload, as their greatest source of stress (Narayanan et al., 1999). One study found that executives in New Zealand experience less job-related stress than executives in nine other countries (McCormick & Cooper, 1988). These researchers mention that this may be owing to the more relaxed lifestyle in New Zealand and the fact that many of these executives worked for rather small organizations.

An interesting study by Kirkcaldy and Cooper (1993) found some evidence that work stress for executives may be modified by preference for leisure activities—and that preferred leisure activities may be related to culture. For example, managers from Germany, who tend to prefer nonaggressive leisure activities, experienced less job stress than British managers, who typically prefer aggressive leisure activities.

Overall, such studies seem to indicate that, although executive job stress is universal, the amount of stress experienced and the sources of the stress may vary depending on country or culture.

One Outcome of Stress: Alcohol and Drug Use in the Workplace

A problem that is of great concern to businesses and to industrial/organizational psychologists is an employee's use and abuse of alcohol and drugs (Frone, 2011). No doubt a certain percentage of industrial accidents occur because of worker intoxication. The combination of alcohol or drugs and heavy machinery or motor vehicles can be deadly. Drug and alcohol abuse can also be responsible for decreased productivity and increased absenteeism and turnover, not to mention all the problems that it can cause in the home lives of workers. The costs of all of this are staggering. One estimate is that substance abuse costs U.S. employers about $160 billion a year, and substance abuse is a worldwide problem.

A study of young workers found that workers who reported problems with alcohol and drugs had greater job instability and reduced job satisfaction in comparison with their peers who did not abuse drugs (Galaif et al., 2001). Moreover, this is likely a cyclical process. Studies suggest that workers who are under severe stress, such as heavy job demands or the stress of job loss, may turn to alcohol or drugs (Murphy et al., 1999). This, in turn, leads to problems on the job, and the cycle continues.

There is some evidence that organizational policies that ban substance abuse in the workplace and advocate against illicit drug use reduce employees' use of drugs both

Employee Assistance Programs (EAPs)
counseling provided for a variety of worker problems, particularly drug and alcohol abuse

on and off the job (Carpenter, 2007). A number of programs have been used to try to deter drug use by employees (Ghodse, 2005).

In an effort to combat substance abuse, many companies have **employee assistance programs (EAPs)** that offer counseling for a variety of employee problems. Of particular concern is counseling for drug and alcohol abuse, although EAPs also help employees deal with work stress and personal problems that may adversely affect their performance and well-being (Cooper et al., 1992). Although employee counseling has long been offered by companies, only in the past 20 years have comprehensive EAPs become commonplace in large organizations. This increase is likely due to the growing concern over the devastating consequences of substance abuse in terms of harming worker health and organizational productivity. The majority of large American companies today have some type of formalized employee assistance program.

Although I/O psychologists are greatly concerned about the negative impact of substance abuse and work stress on employee productivity and well-being, clinical and counseling psychologists, social workers, and drug rehabilitation counselors, rather than I/O psychologists, typically staff EAPs. However, I/O psychologists may have a hand in the design, implementation, and evaluation of EAPs.

Employee assistance programs usually take one of two forms. External programs are those where the company contracts with an outside agency to provide counseling services for its employees. Internal EAPs offer services at the work site. The advantage of an internal program is its convenience for the employees, although they are expensive to maintain. Usually only large organizations can afford internal EAPs. The main advantages of external programs are the lower costs and the increased employee confidentiality.

Despite the increasing popularity of employee assistance programs, there has been surprisingly little research on their effectiveness (Kirk & Brown, 2003). The problem results partly from the difficulty of evaluating any counseling program, because it is not always clear which variables will best determine a program's "success" (Mio & Goishi, 1988). For example, some programs measure success by the number of workers treated, whereas others may use some standard of recovery or "cure." Furthermore, it is difficult to determine how EAP counseling affects bottom-line variables such as employee performance. It is also difficult to determine the effectiveness of EAPs, because the large number of external agencies that offer counseling services for businesses usually conduct their own evaluations, and it is unclear how objective and accurate these self-assessments are. Although there are questions about the effectiveness of employee assistance programs in general, it is likely that even a few cases of employee recovery would lead an employer to label an EAP a success because of the severity of drug and alcohol addiction. Moreover, there is some evidence that EAPs do help reduce long-term health-care costs for employees (Cummings & Follette, 1976). One critic of substance abuse EAPs argues that they focus primarily on treating alcohol and drug problems after they have reached the problem stage, but give little attention to their prevention (Nathan, 1983). Despite the uncertainty of the effectiveness of employee assistance programs, it is likely that they will become a mainstay in most work organizations and another service that will be considered an essential part of any employee benefit package.

Summary

Although there is a great deal of disagreement over definitions of stress, *worker stress* can be defined as physiological or psychological reactions to an event that is perceived to be threatening or taxing. Stress is actually a perception, so there is tremendous individual variation in what one perceives to be stressful. Negative stress, or distress, can cause stress-related illness, and it can affect absenteeism, turnover, and work performance.

Certain occupations, such as air traffic controller and health-care provider, are stereotypically associated with high levels of stress. Worker stress can also come from either organizational sources or individual sources, which are commonly classified as *situational* or *dispositional sources*, respectively. Organizational sources may include having too much to do—*work overload*—or too little to do—*underutilization. Job ambiguity*, which occurs when job tasks and responsibilities are not clearly defined or from inadequate performance feedback or job insecurity, and *interpersonal stress*, including bullying and harassment, which arises from relations with coworkers are other organizational sources of stress, as is *organizational change*. Individual sources of work stress include the worker's experience of traumatic *life events*; susceptibility to stress, such as the lack of *hardiness*, or resistance to stress-related illnesses; and certain personality characteristics such as the *Type A behavior pattern*, which is the coronary-prone personality.

Attempts to measure stress have included physiological measures, self-report assessments, the measurement of stressful life events, and the match between worker characteristics and the demands of the work situation, referred to as the *person–environment fit* approach. Stress has been shown to be related to certain physical illnesses such as ulcers, high blood pressure, and heart disease. These stress-related illnesses as well as stress itself are tied to rates of employee absenteeism and turnover and to job performance, although the relationship between stress and performance is complex. Long-term stress can lead to *job burnout*, a multidimensional construct that relates to one's tendency to withdraw from work.

Strategies for coping with work stress can be divided into *individual coping strategies* and *organizational coping strategies*. Individual strategies include programs of exercise, diet, systematic relaxation training, meditation, biofeedback, time management, work planning, and cognitive coping strategies. Organizational strategies include improving the person–job fit, offering better training and orientation programs, giving workers a sense of control over their jobs, eliminating punitive management styles, removing hazardous work conditions, and improving organizational communication.

Study Questions and Exercises

1 List the sources of stress in your own life. Ask a friend to do the same. Are there implications for defining and understanding important differences in your two

lists, or are they quite similar? What are the implications for defining and understanding stress?

2 Consider how the work world will be changing in the next several years. What are the implications for worker stress? Will there be more of it or less?

3 Consider the various means of assessing stress. Which seems most accurate, and why?

4 Based on the material in the chapter, design a stress management program for use in an organization.

5 What experiences have you had in the workplace with harassment or bullying? What can organizations do to stop those events from happening?

Web Links

www.jobstresshelp.com
A site offering information on job stress.

www.eapweb.com
A site designed to help workers deal with stress and trauma.

Suggested Readings

Bowling, N. A., & Schumm, J. A. (2021). The COVID-19 pandemic: A source of post-traumatic growth? *Industrial and Organizational Psychology, 14*(1–2), 184–188.

Fu, S. Q., Greco, L. M., Lennard, A. C., & Dimotakis, N. (2020). Anxiety responses to the unfolding COVID-19 crisis: Patterns of change in the experience of prolonged exposure to stressors. *Journal of Applied Psychology.* https://doi.org/10.1037/apl0000855

Min, H., Peng, Y., Shoss, M., & Yang, B. (2021). Using machine learning to investigate the public's emotional responses to work from home during the COVID-19 pandemic. *Journal of Applied Psychology, 106*(2), 214.

Reindl, G., Lang, J. W., & Runge, J. M. (2021). Work event experiences: Implications of an expanded taxonomy for understanding daily well-being. *Journal of Occupational Health Psychology.* https://doi.org/10.1037/ocp0000276

PART IV

Work Group and Organizational Issues

CHAPTER 10

Communication in the Workplace

Inside Tips
COMMUNICATION: A COMPLEX PROCESS IN WORK ORGANIZATIONS

Communication is a constant, ongoing process involving all members of the organization. As a result, it is extremely complex and difficult to study. In contrast to the previous chapters, this chapter is more general. The theories and models tend to represent general aspects of communication, and relatively little new terminology is introduced. In this chapter, rather than concentrating on learning new terms or specific theories, think about the complexity of organizational communication and the difficulties encountered in trying to measure and understand this important, ongoing process. Consider the number and types of communication you send and receive each day, the various ways that messages are communicated, and the different settings in which these occur.

Most of us do not work alone, but rather work with others in the context of small groups. In large organizations, these groups are in turn members of larger work groups or departments, which in combination make up the work organization. Depending on the size of the organization, our coworkers may number in the tens, hundreds, or even thousands. Much energy in organizations, particularly from the management perspective, involves coordinating the activities of the various members. In the next few chapters, we will examine work behavior in terms of this organizational interaction. We will investigate the dynamics of work groups—how they coordinate activities and make decisions—as well as the very factors that hold them together. We will see how workers differ in terms of their power and status within the organization, paying particular attention to the relationship between those persons designated as leaders and other workers. We will examine the politics within work organizations and the structure of work groups and larger work organizations. However, before we begin to explore these topics, we must understand one of the most basic processes that occurs among workers in organizational settings: communication.

DOI: 10.4324/9781003143987-14

You return from vacation. On your desk is a foot-high stack of mail, memos, and reports, and you have a dozen voice mail messages. Logging on, you find that you have 312 e-mail messages and wonder if the company's spam filter is working. A colleague stops by, reminds you that you have an important staff meeting in 5 minutes, and gives you an odd look—sort of a scowl—and you start to wonder what it means. You have always felt a sense of "communication overload" at work, but this is definitely too much.

The Communication Process: A Definition and a Model

Communication
the passage of information between one person or group to another person or group

Communication can be defined as the transmission of information from one person or group to another person or group. In work settings, communication takes many forms, such as written or spoken orders, informal chatter, electronic messaging, printed reports or procedure manuals, videoconferences, discussion among executives in a corporate boardroom, and announcements posted on bulletin boards or on social media. Communication is an ongoing process that serves as the lifeblood of the organization. Communication is also extremely complex and can occur in a variety of ways: through the written or spoken word; through nonverbal means such as gestures, nods, or tone of voice; or through a picture or diagram. We can also communicate in a number of contexts, including face-to-face conversation, telephone, text messaging, letters or memos, e-mail, charts and diagrams, a videoconference, or a public address. We also communicate to people at different levels in the organization—to superiors, subordinates, peers, and customers—and alter our communication to fit the audience. This complexity, coupled with its almost continuous nature (even our silence can communicate), makes communication very difficult to study.

Sender
the originator of a communication who encodes and transmits a message; also known as the encoder

Receiver
the recipient of a communication who decodes the message; also known as the decoder

Communication involves the process of the exchange of information among two or more parties, which is best represented by a simple model of communication between two persons: the sender and the receiver (see Figure 10.1). The **sender** (also known as the *encoder*) is the originator of the communication; the **receiver** (also called the *decoder*) is the recipient. Communication begins with some information—a message—that the sender wishes to transmit to a receiver. The sender's task is to take the information and put it into some form in which it can be communicated to the receiver. This process of preparing a message for transmission is referred to as **encoding**, because the sender chooses some sort of shared code as a means of communication. In work settings, this code is usually the shared verbal language, but it might also consist of some common nonverbal code, or "body language."

Encoding
the process of preparing a message for transmission by putting it into some form or code

Channel
the vehicle through which a message flows from sender to receiver

The next step is for the sender to select a **channel**, the vehicle through which the message will flow from the sender to the receiver (Figure 10.2). The sender may choose the spoken word, confronting the receiver face-to-face or through the

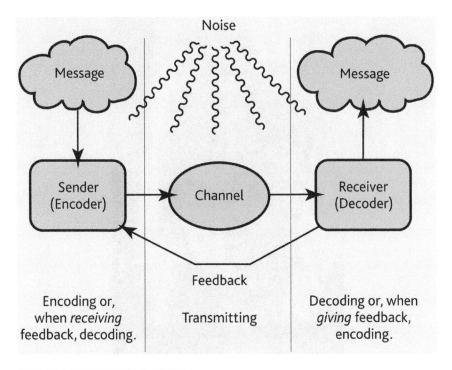

Noise

Message

Message

Sender
(Encoder)

Channel

Receiver
(Decoder)

Feedback

Encoding or,
when *receiving*
feedback, decoding.

Transmitting

Decoding or, when
giving feedback,
encoding.

Figure 10.1 The communication process.

telephone, or the written word, using a memo, or a typed message sent through a text or e-mail. Different methods of communication have various advantages and disadvantages (see Table 10.1). For example, face-to-face, text messaging, or telephone communication is typically quick and convenient, whereas formal reports or detailed memos can be time-consuming to prepare. However, the more formal, written channels of communication are less likely to be misunderstood or misinterpreted because of their length, detail, and careful preparation. Importantly, the sender must also choose the channel of communication that is appropriate for the situation. For example, personal information is usually conveyed verbally, face-to-face, whereas an important directive concerning a project deadline might be put in the form of a detailed, typed memo or e-mail that is distributed to all relevant parties, with follow-up reminders sent as the deadline nears.

In the two-person communication model, the receiver picks up the message and is responsible for **decoding** it, or translating it, in an effort to understand the meaning intended by the sender. Of course, in many communications, some of the original message—that information drawn from the thought processes of the encoder—will be lost or distorted, whether through the encoding process, through transmission, or in decoding. (That is why the second, received "message" in the communication model is not identical to the original message.)

Decoding
the process of translating a message so that it can be understood

Figure 10.2 A channel is any vehicle of communication, such as the spoken word, text message, direct message, e-mail, or phone.

Source: Photograph by Erik Brolin, found on Unsplash (https://unsplash.com/photos/8WnxVCXboKg).

Feedback
an acknowledgment that a message has been received and understood

Typically, when the receiver has decoded the message, **feedback**, or a response, is transmitted to the sender. The receiver acknowledges receipt of the message and either tells the sender that the message is understood or requests clarification. In the feedback stage of the process, the communication model actually reverses, with the receiver becoming the sender, and vice versa. Feedback can be as simple as a nod of the head, a text saying "ok," or as formal as a letter of receipt or the initializing of a memo that is returned to the sender.

Although this model represents communication as a simple and relatively fool-proof process, the effective flow of information from sender to receiver can break down at many points. The sender can have difficulty in encoding the message, making comprehension by the receiver difficult. For example, a supervisor might tell an employee, "I would really like you to try to make this deadline," when what she really means is that the deadline must be met, with no exceptions. On the other side, the receiver may inaccurately decode the message and interpret it in a way wholly different from what the sender had in mind. For example, the employee might interpret the "deadline" statement to mean that the supervisor has now turned entire responsibility for the project over to him and will no longer be available to help meet the deadline. A poor choice of channel may also result in a breakdown of effective communication. For example, giving a coworker lengthy and detailed instructions about a work task over the telephone rather than in writing may lead to inadequate performance of the job. Furthermore, the work environment may provide any number of distractions that can disrupt the communication process, such as competing conversations, loud machinery, or inconsistent or contradictory messages. Such distractions are collectively called **noise**. Noise may also refer to psychological factors such as biases, perceptual differences, or selective attention, all of which make it difficult for persons to communicate with and to understand one another. For example, psychological noise can occur when the receiver ignores the sender because of a belief that the sender "has nothing important to say."

Noise
physical or psychological distractions that disrupt the effective flow of communication

Research on the Communication Process

Much of the research on the communication process in work settings has focused on factors that can increase or decrease its effectiveness. Among the factors that can affect the flow of communication from sender to receiver are source factors, channel factors, and audience factors.

Source Factors

Source factors are characteristics of the sender—the source of the message—that can facilitate or detract from the effective flow of communication. One such factor is the status of the source, which can affect whether potential receivers attend to a message. Generally, the higher the organizational status of the sender, the more likely the communication will be listened to and acted on. For example, messages from the president or owner of a company are usually given top priority ("When the boss talks, people listen").

Source Factors
characteristics of the sender that influence the effectiveness of a communication

Another source factor is the credibility, or believability, of the sender. If the source is trusted, particularly if someone is in a supervisory or leadership role, it is more likely that the message will receive proper attention (Mackenzie, 2010). Variables such as the expertise, knowledge, and reliability of the source (e.g., Has this person provided truthful information in the past?) contribute to the credibility of the sender (O'Reilly & Roberts, 1976). Employees learn which sources can be trusted

Table 10.1 Advantages and Disadvantages of Communication Channels

Channel	Advantages	Disadvantages
Telephone	Verbal	Less personal
	Permits questions and answers	No record of conversation
	Convenient	Message might be misunderstood
	Two-way flow	Timing may be inconvenient
	Immediate feedback	May be impossible to terminate
Face-to-face	Visual and verbal	Timing may be inconvenient
	Personal contact	Requires spontaneous thinking
	Can "show" and "explain"	May not be easy to terminate
	Can set the mood	Power or status of one person may cause pressure
	Immediate feedback	
Meetings	Can use audiovisuals	Time-consuming
	Involves several minds at once	Time may be inconvenient
	Two-way flow	One person may dominate the group
Memorandum	Brief	No control over receiver
	Provides a record	Less personal
	Can prethink the message	One-way flow
	Can disseminate widely	Delayed feedback
Formal report	Complete; comprehensive	Less personal
	Can organize material at writer's leisure	May require considerable time in reading
	Can disseminate widely	Language may not be understandable
		Expensive
		One-way flow
		Delayed feedback
Teleconference	Saves time for travel	No face-to-face interpersonal contact
	Visual	Not good for initial brainstorming sessions
	Lessens impact of power/makes users be better prepared	Expensive
E-mail and text messaging	Convenient	Ease can lead to message "overload"
	Messages sent/received at all hours	No nonverbal communication
	Extremely fast compared with other written messages	Others may be able to get access to messages
	Can be sent to multiple parties simultaneously	
Web-based/social media	Convenient	Ease can lead to message "overload"
	Can interact in real time	Difficult to control flow of messages (e.g., turn-taking)
	Can communicate with multiple parties simultaneously	
	Can present drawings, figures, pictures, and videos easily	

Source: Adapted from Lewis, 2002. © reprinted by permission of Pearson Education, Inc., Upper Saddle River, NJ.

and pay closest attention to their messages. Research suggests that a sender's communication style is also important. For instance, more expressive and more organized trainers tended to do a better job of imparting learning to trainees (Towler & Dipboye, 2001).

A final source factor is the encoding skills of the sender, or the source's ability to translate an abstract message into some sort of shared code, usually the written or spoken language, so that it can be clearly conveyed to the receiver. For example, the communication skills of a CEO may be critical when she or he is trying to articulate the company's vision or goals for the future. In short, these skills include the abilities to speak and write clearly and to select the appropriate channel for transmitting information. Generally, the better the encoding skills of the sender, the smoother and more effective the flow of communication.

Channel Factors

Channel factors, which are positive or negative characteristics related to the vehicle through which the message is communicated, can also influence the effectiveness of the communication process. Selection of the proper channel can have an important effect on the accurate flow of communication. For example, using a visual device such as a chart or graph to present complex information on sales and profit figures is likely to be a more effective channel than the spoken word. The channel selected can also affect the impact of the message. For example, a face-to-face reprimand from a supervisor might carry more weight than the same reprimand conveyed over the telephone. Whenever possible, using multiple channels to present complicated information will increase the likelihood that it will be attended to and retained. Research on organizational communication has focused on specific types, or "genres," of messages, such as business letters, memos, or group meetings (Yates & Orlikowski, 1992). In one study, it was found that persons higher in the organizational hierarchy had a preference for more formal modes of written communication (word-processed letters and memos) over more informal, handwritten messages (Reinsch Jr & Beswick, 1995). Another study has found that managers are indicating a growing preference for using e-mail or texting to communicate messages, even in situations such as responding to another's telephone message or when the recipient is in an office just down the hall (Markus, 1994).

Semantic problems are common channel factors that can lead to a breakdown in communication. These difficulties occur because different people may interpret the meanings of certain words differently. For example, if your work supervisor tells you that you are doing a "good" job, you may infer that your performance is well above average. However, if the supervisor defines "good" as work that is barely passable (but really expects "excellent," "superior," or "outstanding" performance), you may be missing the meaning of the message. Semantic problems may arise through the use

⏱ Stop & Review

Explain each of the steps in two-person communication.

Channel Factors
characteristics of the vehicle of transmission of a message that affect communication

Jargon
special language developed in connection with certain jobs; also called technical language

of technical language, or **jargon**, the special language that develops within a specific work environment. Jargon is typically filled with abbreviated words, acronyms, special vocabularies, and slang. For example, industrial/organizational psychology could be abbreviated as "I/O Psych" and might be described as the field in which topics such as RJPs, BARS, and validity generalization are studied.

Although jargon serves the purpose of speeding up communication between those who speak the language, it can create problems when the receiver is not "fluent" in its use. The use of jargon can also create problems when a team of workers is composed of members from different professional disciplines, all of whom may use different jargon (Cooley, 1994). For example, imagine the communication breakdowns that might have occurred during some of the NASA space projects, where decision-making teams were made up of aerospace engineers, military officers, and research scientists, each using their own technical jargon.

The type of channel used to communicate can affect important work-related outcomes, such as job satisfaction. Research suggests that the frequency and quality of face-to-face communication between supervisors and subordinates is positively related to workers' job satisfaction (Muchinsky, 1977). The type of channel may also have some influence on work performance and efficiency. For example, a company policy of keeping written documentation of all orders and directives, rather than simply relying on spoken orders, may decrease the likelihood that workers will forget what they are supposed to be doing, which in turn may have positive effects on the productivity and efficiency of the work unit.

A topic of great interest has been the use of computer-mediated meetings (Figure 10.3), where workers interconnect and hold meetings at their individual computer workstations, or teleconference via the web (Sadowski-Rasters et al., 2006). The relevance of this topic became extremely clear in 2020 when the vast majority of workers began working from home. During this time, the reliance on computer-mediated technology, including Zoom, Microsoft Teams, Google Meets, and others, greatly increased. Although there is still very little information about the impact of this change on outcomes, some research shows that people who work from home (telework) tend to be more satisfied with their jobs than others (Fonner & Roloff, 2010), although there is also evidence that virtual workplace incivility can be particularly damaging for employees (Zivnuska et al., 2020), but more work needs to be done in this area (Ezerins & Ludwig, 2021).

Interestingly, there is some evidence that virtual meetings elicit greater equality in participation than occurs in face-to-face meetings (Weisband et al., 1995). Low-status or shy members may be more willing to share information in computer-mediated meetings. However, the lack of "social dynamics," including the loss of nonverbal cues available in face-to-face interactions, tends to lead members of computer-mediated meetings to engage in more extreme or "risky" decisions. Members communicating via computer may also be more outspoken, and members may engage in "rude" behaviors, including "put-downs" of other participants, because the members do not have to face the disapproving looks of other participants (Kiesler & Sproull, 1992). There may also be some difficulties in coordinating the flow of communication and

Figure 10.3 Videoconferencing offers instantaneous, face-to-face communication over long distances.

Source: Photograph by Christina Wocintechchat, found on Unsplash (https://unsplash.com/photos/vpa6e3Hqy9U).

in taking turns—actually causing electronic meetings to be longer than face-to-face ones (Carey & Kacmar, 1997)—and the camera use associated with video meetings can create fatigue (Shockley et al., 2020).

Computer-mediated meetings are really only one of the many changes in communication that have occurred with increased technology use. Companies are also using social media, such as Twitter and Instagram, to communicate with customers, employees, and other constituents (Islam et al., 2021). Although these alternative modes of communication have been studied for over a decade in other disciplines (e.g., García-Morales et al., 2011), industrial/organizational psychologists have only recently started to examine the effects of them on workplace outcomes (see McFarland & Ployhart, 2015, for an exception).

Audience Factors

Audience factors are elements related to the receiver, such as the person's attention span and perceptual abilities, which can facilitate or impair the communication process.

Audience Factors
characteristics of the receiver that influence the effectiveness of a communication

For example, it is important that training information be presented at a level that matches the audience's ability to perceive and process that information, or much of the communication may be lost. Moreover, it is critical to consider the attention span of the target audience. Although all-day classroom training sessions might be appropriate for management trainees who are used to such long sessions, the attention of assembly-line workers might be lost after a 1-hour lecture because of their unfamiliarity with this format.

The receiver's relationship to the sender can also affect the communication process. For example, if the receiver is subordinate to the sender, the message may be better attended to because the receiver is supposed to listen to superiors. If, however, the situation is reversed, a message from a lower-ranking organizational member may not receive much attention from a higher-ranking employee.

Finally, the decoding skills of the receiver can influence the effectiveness of communication. Workers vary greatly in their ability to receive, decode, and understand organizational messages. Although managers are often considered the source rather than the audience of much organizational communication, research has shown that effective managers have good decoding skills in listening and responding to the needs and concerns of their subordinates (Baron, 1986). In fact, because much of the communication in work settings involves spoken communication, oral decoding skills, often referred to as listening skills, are considered to be the most important decoding skills of all (Hunt, 1980).

Research suggests that "active listening"—where the decoder asks clarifying questions, repeats the encoder's words, and provides feedback ("Yes, I see," "Uh-hum," etc.)—has positive effects on the effectiveness of the communication flow in terms of greater comprehension, mutual understanding, and participant satisfaction (Rao, 1995). There is some evidence that active listening is important for effective management of employees (Van Dun et al., 2017). Bays (2007) argues that college students should be taught *both* speaking *and* listening skills in order to prepare them for the workplace.

Nonverbal Communication in Work Settings

We commonly think of communication in work settings as taking one of two forms, either written or spoken. However, people can and do use a great deal of **nonverbal communication**, which is sent and received by means other than the written or spoken word. Broadly defined, nonverbal communication can occur through facial expressions, gesture, tone of voice, body movements, posture, style of dress, touching, and physical distance between sender and receiver (Bonaccio et al., 2016). We use nonverbal communication to convey a wide range of feelings and attitudes.

To understand the role of nonverbal communication in work settings, we can examine its use from both the sender's and the receiver's perspective. For the sender,

Nonverbal Communication
messages sent and received through means other than the spoken or written word

nonverbal communication can be used in three ways. First, nonverbal cues can be substituted for verbal communication. Nodding to show approval, shaking your head in disagreement, or gesturing for a person to come closer or to go away are all ways of sending clear, unspoken messages. In particular, noisy work environments or situations in which coworkers are positioned out of hearing range may necessitate the use of a set of nonverbal signals, which decreases the reliance on verbal communication. The hand signals used by ground crews to guide airline pilots or the gestures used by land surveyors are examples of the use of nonverbal communication.

Second, nonverbal cues can also be used to enhance verbal messages. We often use our tone of voice, facial expressions, and body movements to emphasize what we are saying. If you want to compliment a subordinate for doing an outstanding job, the words will have greater impact if they are accompanied by an enthusiastic tone of voice and an approving smile. A board member who pounds her fist on the table while voicing disagreement with a proposal is going to command greater attention by including this nonverbal emphasizer.

Stop & Review

List several source and audience factors that affect communication flow.

ON THE *CUTTING* EDGE

On the *Cutting* Edge: Communicating in a Diverse, Multicultural Work Environment

The world of work is becoming more and more diverse. The workforce in most organizations is made up of people from various cultural backgrounds, many of whom are non-native speakers of the dominant language (Offermann, Matos & DeGraaf, 2014). Moreover, many companies are engaged in international business and interact with workers from a variety of nations and cultures, making the study of cross-cultural communication highly important (Szkudlarek et al., 2020).

Cultural diversity has many advantages: diverse workforces tend to be more creative, more adaptable, and more tolerant of others (Adler, 1991). As you can imagine, however, cultural and language differences can present challenges to the effective flow of communication within organizations (Shachaf, 2008). Moreover, cultural differences can threaten a common, shared

commitment to organizational goals (Granrose, 1997). Culturally based communication differences can also affect the ability of companies from different nations and cultures to work with one another. For example, the communication style of most North American managers tends to be direct and "confrontation-centered." The Japanese business communication style, however, tends to be indirect and "agreement-centered" (Kume, 1985). Such differences can lead to serious communication breakdowns.

Realizing the need to prevent cross-cultural communication breakdown, organizations have taken several steps to facilitate intercultural organizational communication. For example, many organizations have developed multicultural awareness and training programs (Gelfand et al., 2017; Kossek & Zonia, 1993).

ON THE *CUTTING* EDGE (*continued*)

One model of preparing managers for working with culturally diverse and multinational work groups suggests that general communication competence, proficiency in other languages, an awareness of cultural differences, and an ability to negotiate with people of diverse backgrounds are the keys to success (Tung, 1997). In short, the issues of multicultural and cross-cultural communication are going to be important ones in the world of work as we move into the future (Rost-Roth, 2010).

Given the increase in electronic communication, including team collaboration channels (such as Slack and Trello) and e-mail, one problem is the absence of nonverbal cues in electronic text messages. It is very difficult to convey emotional meaning, sarcasm, and the like. As a result, savvy e-mail users (and programmers) have developed symbols, typically called "emoticons" or "emojis" (the little smiley faces, etc.), to help compensate and put some "nonverbal" into these verbal interactions.

Third, nonverbal cues are also important for conveying certain impressions in organizations (Darioly & Mast, 2014). For example, it is often important that persons in positions of leadership or authority convey their power and authority nonverbally if they want to get others' attention and be persuasive (Riordan, 1989). Similarly, customer service representatives, such as salespersons or waitpersons, who display authentic, positive nonverbal behaviors elicit greater customer satisfaction and rapport (Bonaccio et al., 2016).

Nonverbal cues can be used to convey underlying feelings. In some situations, when a person is restricted in what can be said verbally, the verbal message may be accompanied by a nonverbal "disclaimer" in order to get the true message across (see Mehrabian, 1981). For example, at a new employee orientation, the trainer may verbally praise the company but, with her tone of voice, she may convey that things are not really going as well as they seem.

Pygmalion Effect
when a sender nonverbally communicates expectations to a receiver, influencing his or her behavior

A sender's nonverbal communication can also subtly communicate his or her expectations to other workers and influence the workers' behaviors in line with those expectations, in what is called the **Pygmalion effect** (Rosenthal, 1994). An example of the Pygmalion effect would be a supervisor who expects a team to perform very well (or very poorly), who nonverbally communicates those expectations to the team members, perhaps through an enthusiastic (or unenthusiastic) tone of voice, actually spurring the team to better (or worse) performance (Eden, 1990). A meta-analysis suggests that the Pygmalion effect does indeed occur in work organizations, but is stronger in initially low-performing groups and in the military, presumably because of the strong influence leaders have on followers in the armed forces (Kierein & Gold, 2000).

From the perspective of a receiver, nonverbal cues serve two important functions. First, they provide additional information. When verbal communication is limited or when the receiver has reason to mistrust the verbal message, the receiver will look to nonverbal cues as a source of more data. This is particularly likely when the receiver feels that the verbal message may be deceptive, although research has shown that most people do not read the nonverbal cues of deception very accurately (O'Sullivan, 2005).

Nonverbal cues are also used by receivers in person perception—that is, in making judgments about a person's attitudes, personality, and competence (see Bonaccio et al., 2016, for a review). For example, it has been found that persons exhibiting more expressive nonverbal behaviors, such as more smiling and greater eye contact, are more favorably evaluated in hiring interviews than are nonexpressive individuals (Bonaccio et al., 2016). This is particularly important in personnel decisions such as in performance feedback sessions or in hiring (Riggio, 2005). Other nonverbal cues, such as style of dress, physical attractiveness, and indications of dominance, may likewise play an important role in how people are perceived in work settings (Riggio & Throckmorton, 1988). Style of dress can impact impressions of others in the workplace. For example, women who dress in an overly feminine way can be seen as unsuitable for certain jobs, whereas those who dress in too masculine a way can be seen as violating their gender role (Peluchette & Karl, 2018).

Although nonverbal communication sometimes facilitates the flow of communication in work settings, misinterpreting such messages can also lead to considerable confusion and may disrupt work operations. Although there are well-known rules and techniques for learning to use appropriate written and spoken language, there are no firm guidelines governing nonverbal communication. Often, the misunderstandings that occur in organizational communication, verbal and nonverbal, are related to the inadequate skills of the sender or receiver, or both. A great deal of attention is paid to trying to improve the verbal and writing skills of employees, and less concern is focused on nonverbal communication skills, even though they may represent a great deal of the critical communication that occurs in work settings. The ability to decode subtle nonverbal cues is particularly important for work supervisors, not only in helping to understand the subtle messages sent by supervisees, but also in building rapport and in helping the supervisor be responsive to the legitimate needs of workers (Riggio, 2001; Uhl-Bien, 2004).

The Flow of Communication in Work Organizations

Just as blood flows through the arteries, giving life to the body, messages flow through communication lines and networks, giving life to the work organization. If you look at the organizational chart of most organizations, you will see positions arranged in a pyramid-like hierarchy. Although this hierarchy is most commonly thought of as representing the lines of status and authority within the organization, it also depicts the lines of communication between superiors and subordinates. Formal messages travel back and forth along these routes between the top levels and the lower levels of the organization.

Downward, Upward, and Lateral Flow of Communication

The communication flow in work organizations is usually classified into three types: it can flow downward, through the organizational hierarchy; upward, through the same chain of command; or laterally, from colleague to colleague. Typically, each type of communication flow takes different forms and tends to contain different kinds of messages.

Downward communication consists of those messages sent from superiors to subordinates. Most commonly, they are one of several types: (a) instructions or directions concerning job performance, (b) information about organizational procedures and policies, (c) feedback to the supervisee concerning job performance, or (d) information to assist in the coordination of work tasks (Katz & Kahn, 1966). As you might guess, much of the formal communication that occurs in work organizations involves this downward flow, which makes sense, because the top levels are involved in making important decisions that must be communicated to the lower levels.

Although much formal communication in organizations is downward, research indicates that most organizations still do not have enough of this communication. A number of studies have found that workers would like more information from their superiors about work procedures and about what is happening elsewhere in the organization. Certain types of downward communication may be particularly limited, such as feedback concerning work performance (Baird, 1977). This is especially true in companies that fail to conduct regular performance appraisals. Also, organizations that neglect to provide workers with job descriptions and adequate orientation and training may experience a shortage of downward communication involving proper work procedures and company policies.

Research has shown that the frequency and quality of superior–subordinate communication influences important organizational outcomes (Bambacas & Patrickson, 2008). At least on work teams, meta-analytic evidence shows that quality of communication has stronger effects on team performance than frequency of communication (Marlow et al., 2018). Research also suggests that supervisors need to be fair and consistent in their communication with subordinates, or workers can become concerned that supervisors are "playing favorites" (Sias & Jablin, 1995). Analysis of leader communication suggests certain critical elements: for example, leaders should communicate that they are supportive of followers and that they are confident and assured in their leadership, and leaders should be precise in their communications (de Vries et al., 2010).

Downward Communication
messages flowing downward in an organizational hierarchy, usually from superiors to subordinates

Upward communication is the flow of messages from the lower levels of the organization to the upper levels. It most typically consists of information managers need to perform their jobs, such as feedback concerning the status of lower-level operations, which could include reports of production output or information about any problems. The upward communication of feedback is critical for managers, who must use this information to make important work-related decisions. Upward communication can also involve complaints and suggestions for improvement from lower-level workers and is significant because it gives subordinates some input into the functioning of the organization. Research suggests that supervisors are more accepting of that feedback if they believe it is motivated by a desire for better performance/productivity (Lam et al., 2007). Finally, an important form of upward feedback concerns subordinates' evaluations of the particular supervisor's effectiveness as a leader/supervisor (Smither et al., 1995; as we saw in Chapter 5 during our discussion of subordinate performance appraisals). Research indicates that the upward flow of suggestions for improvement can be increased when workers feel highly engaged in their jobs and they have a sense of self-efficacy (e.g., a sense that their suggestions will actually be considered and implemented; Axtell et al., 2000).

In recent years, I/O psychologists and management scholars have begun investigating employee *voice*. Voice has been conceptualized as a willingness of employees to communicate concerns to superiors and has also been defined as the ability to engage in decision-making (see Mowbray et al., 2015, for a review). In each case, the communication of voice can occur through either formal methods such as scheduled feedback sessions or informal methods such as one-off comments (Kwon & Farndale, 2020). In one study, Farh and Chen (2018) found that leadership behaviors can promote follower voice behavior in surgical teams. Unfortunately, in many organizations, there is simply not enough upward communication (see the box "Applying I/O Psychology"). The upward communication of feedback about problems or difficulties in operations may be restricted because lower-level workers fear that the negative information might reflect poorly on their abilities, because managers neglect to ask for it, or because subordinates believe that management will not really listen to their suggestions and concerns. One study showed that employees tend not to voice concerns unless (a) the issue is important, (b) managers are open to hearing employees' voice, and (c) managers are in a good mood (Xu et al., 2020). However, interventions to increase voice have been developed (O'Donovan & McAuliffe, 2020).

Lateral communication flows between people who are at the same level in the organizational hierarchy are particularly important when coworkers must coordinate their activities to accomplish a goal (Figure 10.4). Lateral communication can also occur between two or more departments within an organization. For example, effective lateral communication between the production and quality control departments in a television manufacturing plant can help the two departments to coordinate efforts to find and correct assembly errors. Lateral communication between departments also allows the sharing of news and information and helps in the development and maintenance of interpersonal relationships on the job (Hart, 2001). Although

Upward Communication
messages flowing upward in an organizational hierarchy, usually taking the form of feedback

Lateral Communication
messages between two parties at the same level in an organizational hierarchy

Figure 10.4 When two individuals at the same level of an organization communicate to complete tasks we call it lateral communication.

Source: Photograph by Airfocus, found on Unsplash (https://unsplash.com/photos/8k1R1BngPxY).

it can help in coordinating worker activities within or between departments, thereby leading to increased productivity, "unauthorized" lateral communication, such as too much socializing on the job, can detract from effective job performance (Katz & Kahn, 1966).

Barriers to the Effective Flow of Communication

The upward, downward, and lateral flows of communication within an organization are subject to various types of information distortion that disrupt communication effectiveness by eliminating or changing key aspects of the message, so that the message that should be sent is not the one that the recipient receives. We will look closely at two types of distortion that affect communication flow in work organizations: filtering and exaggeration (Gaines, 1980).

Filtering is the selective presentation of the content of a communication—in other words, certain pieces of information are left out of the message. In downward communication, information is often filtered because it is considered to be unimportant to lower-level employees. Often, messages are sent telling workers what to do but not telling them why it is being done. Information from upper levels of

Filtering
the selective presentation of the content of a communication

the organization may also be filtered because management fears the impact of the complete message on workers. For example, management may send a memo to workers about proposed cost-cutting measures, telling them that these actions are needed to increase efficiency and productivity. However, the fact that these cost-cutting measures are needed for the company to stay financially solvent is filtered out, because management is afraid that this information might cause workers to anticipate layoffs and thus begin to look for jobs elsewhere. Filtering of content in upward communication can occur if the information is unfavorable and the communicator fears incurring the wrath of the superior. In such cases, the negative information might be altered to make it appear less negative. Filtering in lateral communication can occur when two employees feel that they are in competition with one another for important organizational rewards, such as promotions and recognition from superiors. In such cases, workers continue to communicate, but may filter out any important information that is seen as giving the other person a competitive edge.

Sometimes, there is purposeful omission of a message to a receiver when a sender believes that the receiver does not need the information because it is unimportant or would be disruptive to the receiver. Davis (1968) examined this sort of selective omission of information in the downward communications in a large manufacturing company. In this study, top management presented middle-level managers with two messages that were to be sent downward. The first message was important and concerned tentative plans for laying off workers. The second message was relatively unimportant, dealing with changes in the parking situation. The results of the study indicated that the middle managers altered the messages as a function of who was receiving the information. The important layoff information was passed on to 94% of the supervisors, who in turn presented it to only 70% of the assistant supervisors. The unimportant message about the parking changes was rarely communicated, with only 15% of the assistant supervisors eventually getting the message. In this case, the message was believed to be irrelevant to lower-level workers.

APPLYING I/O PSYCHOLOGY

Increasing the Upward Flow of Organizational Communication

Most communication problems in work organizations relate to the insufficient flow of information that results from a shortage in either downward communication or upward communication. However, because downward communication predominates in most work settings, and because it originates from those who have the most power and control over the organizational environment, attention must be given to increasing the flow of communication from those individuals at the bottom of the organization to those at the top, for a shortage of this

APPLYING I/O PSYCHOLOGY

(*Continued*)

communication has been associated with employee dissatisfaction and feelings that management is out of touch with employee needs and concerns. Several strategies that can increase upward communication follow.

Employee Suggestion Systems

There are a variety of procedures by which workers can submit ideas for improving some aspect of company operations. The suggestions are then reviewed by company decision makers, and beneficial ideas are implemented. Usually, suggestions are encouraged by some sort of incentive, such as recognition awards or cash prizes that are either fixed monetary amounts or amounts based on percentages of the savings that the suggestion produces. This form of upward communication can lead to innovations and improvement in company operations and can increase lower-level employees' feelings that they can indeed have some influence in the organization. One potential problem with suggestion systems is that employees may use it to voice complaints about conditions that management is unable to change.

Grievance Systems

A related concept is the establishment of formal complaint or grievance procedures. Whereas suggestion systems focus on positive changes, grievances are designed to change existing negative situations and, thus, must be handled more delicately to protect the employee from the retribution that can result when the complaint concerns mistreatment by someone higher in the organizational hierarchy. Also, to keep communication open and flowing, company officials must acknowledge the receipt of grievances and make it

clear what action is to be taken (or why action will not or cannot be taken).

Subordinate Appraisals of Supervisory Performance

As we saw in our discussion of performance appraisals in Chapter 5, upward, subordinate appraisals of managerial performance can provide valuable feedback to improve supervisors' job performance, air the concerns of subordinates, and provide a starting point for the eventual improvement of supervisor–subordinate relationships.

Open-Door Policies

The bottom-to-top flow of organizational communication can also be stimulated if upper-level managers establish an open-door policy, which involves setting aside times when employees can go directly to top-level managers and discuss whatever is on their minds. This procedure bypasses the intermediate steps in the upward organizational chain, ensuring that important messages do indeed get to the top intact. The obvious drawback to the open-door policy is that a lot of the manager's time may be taken up in dealing with trivial or unimportant employee concerns.

Employee Surveys

Conducting an employee survey is an efficient and quick way to measure employees' attitudes about any aspect of organizational operations in an effort to target particular problem areas or solicit suggestions for improvement. (We discussed employee job satisfaction surveys in Chapter 8.) Because surveys offer the added benefit of anonymity, workers can respond honestly without fear of reprisal from management. As in all methods,

APPLYING I/O PSYCHOLOGY

(Continued)

feedback from management, in the form of either action taken or justification for not taking action, is critical for the program to operate effectively. Many times, companies will conduct an employee survey, look at the results, and do nothing. If feedback is not given, respondents will begin to see the survey as a waste of time, and future efforts will not be taken seriously.

Participative Decision Making

A number of strategies based on democratic or participative styles of management facilitate the upward flow of communication by involving employees in the process of making important decisions (Harrison, 1985). In participative decision making, employees can submit possible plans and discuss their benefits and drawbacks. They are then allowed to vote on the courses of action the company or work group will take. This strategy covers a wide range of programs and techniques that we will be studying in later chapters on group and team processes (Chapters 11 and 12) and leadership (Chapter 14). However, any management technique that solicits employee input serves to increase the upward flow of communication.

A potential sender may not forward a message when it involves bad news. This has been labeled the "MUM effect" (Zanin et al., 2016). The MUM effect can be particularly detrimental to organizational functioning and effectiveness. For example, during the building of the U.S. Air Force's stealth bomber, the MUM effect was in operation as officers systematically suppressed bad news about the project's many problems from reaching higher-level officers. As a result, Pentagon officials continued to fund the project, because they were uninformed about the project's many technical problems and errors (Lee, 1993). In the space shuttle *Challenger* disaster, it was found that engineers believed that there was a reasonable probability that an O-ring might fail and cause the rocket to explode, but they did not allow this to be conveyed to upper-level managers owing to the MUM effect.

Exaggeration is the distortion of information, which involves elaborating or over-emphasizing certain aspects of the message. To draw attention to a problem, people may exaggerate its magnitude and impact. In downward communication, a supervisor might emphasize that, if performance does not improve, subordinates may lose their jobs. In upward communication, workers might present a problem as a crisis to get management to react and make some quick decisions. On the other hand, exaggeration may occur through the minimization of an issue, which involves making it seem like less of a problem than it actually is. This can happen, for example, when a worker wants to give the impression of competence and thus says that everything is under control when it is not (see the "Up Close" box).

Certain factors increase or decrease the likelihood of distortion taking place in organizational communication. For example, spoken messages are more prone

⏱ Stop & Review

Describe the three directions in which organizational communication can flow. What form does each typically take?

Exaggeration
the distortion of information by elaborating, overestimating, or minimizing parts of the message

to distortion than are written messages. Regardless of form, a downward-flowing message from a high-status source is less likely to be intentionally altered than a communication originating from a low-status member. O'Reilly (1978) studied several factors related to communication distortion and specifically found a tendency for the greater distortion of upward messages that are unfavorable in content and less distortion of upward-flowing positive information. He also discovered that low trust in the receiver of a message resulted in a tendency toward distortion, particularly if the information reflected unfavorably on the sender.

UP Close Why Are Communication Breakdowns So Common in Organizations?

In many ways, the success of an organization depends on the efficient and effective flow of communication among its members. Even in very efficient and productive organizations, however, miscommunication seems to occur almost daily. Why are such breakdowns so common?

One answer is that many informal rules (or norms) in organizations appear to work against open and honest communication. Organizational members learn that it is important to engage in impression management—that is, to present oneself in a favorable light to get ahead in the company. It is not considered wise to admit to personal faults or limitations. Likewise, it is seen as important to project an air of self-confidence and competence. This may lead to a worker trying to tackle a very difficult task or problem alone, rather than asking for assistance. As we saw in studying hiring interviews, job applicants are particularly concerned with impressing management. The resulting restricted communication may lead to a total mismatch between a worker's skills and abilities and the job requirements.

In competitive organizational settings, an air of mistrust of others may arise. As a result, verbal messages may not be entirely believed or may be seen as containing underlying alternative meanings ("What was he really saying to me?"). Mistrust is often present in organizations that have a history of not dealing honestly and openly with employees. This lack of trust may lead to limited communication, which is a serious problem for organizations whose lifeblood is the open flow of messages.

Another reason for communication breakdowns is employees' feelings of defensiveness, which often develop when their performance is criticized or questioned. Defensive postures by one participant are often followed by a defensive stance in another (Gibb, 1961). For example, when a work group has failed at some task, one group member might act defensively—"It wasn't my fault"—which then causes others to act in the same way. When employees become overly defensive, a communication breakdown can result. This defensiveness can also stifle employee creativity, as workers become afraid to take chances or to try new things for fear of being criticized.

Organizational communication breakdowns can also be caused by the tendency for people to undercommunicate. Workers generally assume that everyone in the work setting has access to the same information

UP CLOSE *(continued)*

and possesses the same knowledge. Therefore, to avoid redundancy, a communicator may neglect to convey some important information to coworkers, assuming that they already know it. In reality, the other workers may not have the information or may have forgotten it and thus need to be reminded. Supervisors and managers are particularly prone to undercommunicate, believing that subordinates do not need to be (or should not be) given certain information. This lack of communication flow can seriously disrupt productivity and may cause dissatisfaction among workers who feel as if they are left in the dark.

Communication Networks

In our discussion of the communication model and the downward, upward, and lateral flow of communication, we have been focusing on communication between two individuals, such as superior-to-subordinate or colleague-to-colleague. When we look beyond two-person communication to the linkages among work group, departmental, or organizational members, we are concerned with **communication networks**, which are systems of communication lines linking various senders and receivers.

The flow of organizational communication is regulated by several factors: the proximity of workers to one another, the rules governing who communicates with whom, the status hierarchy, and other elements of the work situation, such as job assignments and duties (Zahn, 1991). Thus, communication usually follows predictable patterns, or networks. Considerable research has been conducted on these networks and the properties associated with each. Five major types of communication networks have been studied in depth (Shaw, 1978; see Figure 10.5). The first three are termed **centralized networks** because the flow of information is centralized, or directed, through specific members. The next two are called **decentralized networks** because the communication flow can originate at any point and does not have to be directed through certain central group members. Centralized networks are governed by members' status within the organization; decentralized networks typically are not. Often, decentralized networks are controlled by factors such as proximity of members to one another or the personal preferences of the sender.

Centralized Networks

The first centralized communication network, which is known as the *chain*, represents a five-member status hierarchy. A message typically originates at the top or at

Communication Networks
systematic lines of communication among various senders and receivers

Centralized Networks
communication networks in which the flow of communication is directed through specific members

Decentralized Networks
communication networks in which messages can originate at any point and need not be directed through specific group members

⏱ Stop & Review

List and describe four strategies for improving the upward flow of communication in organizations.

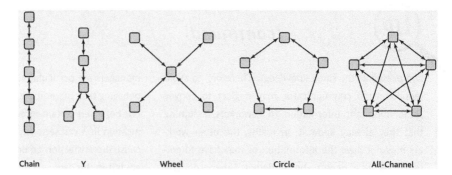

| Chain | Y | Wheel | Circle | All-Channel |

Figure 10.5 Communication networks.

the bottom of the chain and works its way upward or downward through the different links. An example might be a message concerning some changes in the formula for payroll deductions. The director of human resources is the source of the message, which is then passed to the payroll manager, who in turn gives the instructions to the assistant payroll manager, who then tells the payroll supervisor. Finally, the payroll supervisor passes the message along to the clerk who will implement the changes. A message that is to go from the clerk to the human resources director must follow the same pattern. As you might guess, the chain is a relatively slow process, but it is direct, with all levels of the hierarchy being made aware of the message because it must pass through each link.

A related communication network is the *Y* (which is actually an upside-down Y). The Y is also a hierarchical network, representing four levels of status within the organization, but its last link involves communication to more than one person. The inverted Y is a model of the communication network typically involved in a traditional, pyramid-shaped organization. The president issues an order to the chief of operations, who then tells the work supervisor. The work supervisor then gathers the bottom-line workers and gives them the order. In the other direction, the front-line supervisor is responsible for gathering information from bottom-line workers that must be sent upward. The chain and the Y networks are very similar in terms of speed of transmission and the formality of who communicates with whom.

The *wheel* network involves two status levels: a higher-status member (usually a work supervisor) and four lower-level members. The higher-status member is the hub, or center, through which all communication must pass. In the wheel network, there are no direct communication links between the lower-level members. An example might be a sales manager and four salespersons out in the field, each of whom receives instructions directly from the manager and then sends information about sales activities back to the manager. However, the salespersons do not have any direct contact with one another, only indirect contact, as information is relayed through the supervisor.

Decentralized Networks

The *circle* network, the first of the two decentralized networks, represents communication between members who are immediately accessible to each other, such as workers positioned side by side on an assembly line or in adjacent cubicles. Because any member can initiate a communication and no rules govern the direction in which it is sent, it can be difficult to trace the original source of the message in a circle network. Also, because the message can travel in two or more directions, the circle network has a fairly quick rate of transmission.

The *all-channel*, or *comcon*, network allows complete freedom among communication links. Any member can freely communicate with any other, and all members are accessible to each other. In all-channel networks, communication can be rapid, and there is maximum opportunity for feedback. Boards of directors, problem-solving task forces, and employees working as a team are examples of these networks.

There has been extensive research on communication networks, most of which has been conducted in laboratory settings. The results of these studies indicate that each of the different networks has different strengths and weaknesses. For example, the centralized networks (the chain, Y, and wheel) are faster and make fewer errors in dealing with simple, repetitive tasks than do decentralized networks. This makes sense because the central person through whom all messages must pass can coordinate group activities, as that individual has all the information needed to perform the simple tasks. Decentralized networks (circle and all-channel), on the other hand, are better at dealing with complex tasks, such as abstract problem solving (Shaw, 1964). In general, straightforward, repetitive tasks, such as assembly or manufacturing work, tend to operate well with a centralized communication network, whereas creative tasks, such as a group working on a product advertising campaign, are best accomplished using a decentralized network. One reason why centralized networks may have difficulty in solving complex problems is because the central people may be subject to information overload: they may have too much information to deal with efficiently. Because all the messages cannot be passed on intact to the various network members efficiently and quickly, group performance suffers.

The type of communication network used can also affect the satisfaction of network members. Generally, because of the restrictions on who can initiate communication and on who can communicate with whom, members in centralized networks have lower levels of satisfaction than those in decentralized networks (Shaw, 1964). More specifically, in the centralized networks, the persons holding the central positions tend to have high levels of satisfaction owing to their role, whereas the non-central members have lower satisfaction and organizational commitment and higher turnover (Erdogan et al., 2020).

Some of the research on communication networks has been criticized for oversimplifying the communication process. Evidence suggests that the differences in speed and efficiency among the various networks may disappear over time as the group involved learns to adjust to the required communication patterns (Burgess, 1968).

Stop & Review

Define and give examples of the two barriers to effective communication.

For example, members of decentralized networks may learn to cut down on the amount of member discussion to speed up the decision-making process. Because most of the research on communication networks has been conducted in controlled laboratory settings, there is some concern about whether the results of these studies will generalize to communication networks in actual work settings, although the findings do indeed allow us to model (although simplistically) the communication patterns in work organizations.

Formal and Informal Lines of Communication: The Hierarchy versus the Grapevine

Organigram

a diagram of an organization's hierarchy representing the formal lines of communication

So far, we have been discussing the formal lines of communication, or how organizational members are supposed to communicate with one another. We have also seen that the official lines of communication in an organization are illustrated in the company's organizational chart, or **organigram**, which is a diagram of the hierarchy. When official messages must be sent up or down the hierarchy, they typically follow the lines shown in the organigram. The formal lines of communication are usually governed by the organizational status or authority of the different members. However, although every organization possesses formal lines of communication, each also has informal communication lines, known as the **grapevine**. Just as a real grapevine twists and turns, branching out wherever it pleases, the organizational grapevine can follow any course through a network of organizational members. Throughout the workday, messages are passed from one worker to another along the grapevine. Because much of the daily communication that occurs in work organizations is informal, the organizational grapevine is an important element for I/O psychologists to study.

Grapevine

the informal communication network in an organization

Whereas formal communication lines are represented by the organigram, the informal lines of communication among work group or organizational members are illustrated by the **sociogram**. In effect, the sociogram is a diagram of the organizational grapevine. Sociograms are used to study the informal contacts and communications occurring among organizational members (see Figure 10.6). When informal communication networks are studied, workers are surveyed to determine which other organizational members they typically interact with (Stork & Richards, 1992). A new approach to studying informal communication networks uses a "badge" with a Bluetooth sensor that can record the number and length of face-to-face interactions between workers (Orbach et al., 2015).

Sociogram

a diagram of the informal lines of communication among organizational members

Baird (1977) suggested that three factors determine the pattern of communication links that form the grapevine: friendship, usage, and efficiency. In the informal communication network, people pass information to their friends, which is only natural. We communicate with those people we like and avoid communicating informally with those people we do not like. Friendship is thus perhaps the most important factor that holds the grapevine together. In addition, persons who are used as communication links for other purposes will also be used as links in the grapevine. For

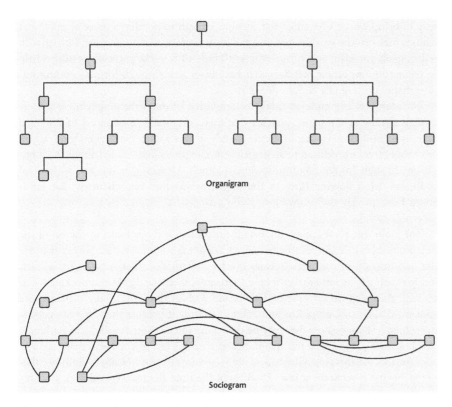

Figure 10.6 The organigram versus the sociogram.

example, workers who often come into contact with one another for job-related reasons are more likely to start sharing information informally. Finally, the grapevine sometimes develops because it is easier and more efficient for workers to follow their own informal networks rather than the formal lines of communication. An organizational member who needs to communicate something immediately may try to get the message through via the grapevine rather than by using the slow and cumbersome formal communication lines. For example, a low-ranking organizational member who wants to get a message to somebody high up in the organizational hierarchy may find it quicker and more efficient to rely on the grapevine to transmit the message rather than going through the formal organizational channels that involve relaying the message through a successive chain of higher-status managers.

In addition to being a substitute network for formal lines of communication, the grapevine serves a vital function in maintaining social relationships among workers. Because most formal communication tends to be task-oriented, focusing on jobs and job outcomes, the grapevine helps to meet the social communication needs of workers (which Mayo and his associates in the human relations movement long ago determined were so important to workers). Through informal communication contacts and the subsequent development of strong work friendships, the grapevine can help to bring workers together and encourage them to develop a sense of unity and commitment to the work group and the organization, which can play a big part in reducing absenteeism and turnover rates (Baird, 1977). The grapevine can also help in reiterating important messages that have been sent through formal communication channels (Tenhiälä & Salvador, 2014).

For example, an employee might be reminded through the grapevine of important deadlines or company policies that were originally announced in e-mailed memos or bulletins. In one interesting study, it was found that, when innovations or changes were introduced to an organization, workers first learned about the innovation through formal communication channels. However, it was the amount of communication flowing through the organization's informal channels that influenced how quickly the innovation would actually be adopted by the work groups (Weenig, 1999).

The grapevine serves many important functions for the smooth operation of the organization, but it can also be perceived as having a somewhat negative function: the transmission of rumors. **Rumors** involve information that is presented as fact, but may actually be either true or false (Aertsen & Gelders, 2011). Rumors are based on such things as employee speculations and wishful thinking. Many managers are concerned about the grapevine and attempt to stifle it because they believe that it is the source of false rumors that may be damaging to the company and the workforce (Mishra, 1990). However, research indicates that this is a myth. The transmission of false rumors via the grapevine is actually relatively rare, and estimates indicate that the grapevine is accurate at least 75–80% of the time (Langan-Fox, 2001). In comparison, remember that the messages sent through formal communication lines may not always be 100% accurate.

A false rumor usually results when organizational members lack information about a topic that concerns them. When false rumors do occur, the best strategy for combating them may be to provide accurate information through formal channels of communication and through the grapevine, if management is tapped into it (DiFonzo et al., 1994).

Organizational Communication and Work Outcomes

The effective flow of communication is crucial to an organization's ability to operate smoothly and productively. Although I/O psychologists and organizations themselves believe this to be true, very little research historically has directly examined the impact of communication on organizational performance (Porter & Roberts, 1976). In 12 district offices of a state social services agency, one comprehensive study looked at the relationships between reported organizational communication effectiveness and five independent measures of organizational performance, including the number of clients served, the costs of operation, and the costs of operation per client served (Snyder & Morris, 1984). Questionnaires administered to more than

Rumors
information that is presented as fact, but may actually be true or false

500 employees assessed perceptions of different types of organizational communication, which included two forms of downward communication—the adequacy of information provided concerning organizational policies and procedures, and the skills of supervisors as communicators. One form of lateral communication—the information exchange within the work group—and one type of downward communication—the feedback given about individual performance—were also measured. The results indicated that the amount of communication, particularly the lateral communication within work groups, and the communication skills of supervisors were related to more cost-effective organizational performance. In another study, it was found that communication about how and why layoffs were conducted impacted employee perceptions of fairness (Wanberg et al., 1999). A laboratory study found that group performance on a manual task—assembling a complex toy—was related to the quality of communication. Specifically, if the groups engaged in high-quality "cycles" of communication, including interactions that involved orienting the group to the task, planning how the work would be done, and evaluating the outcomes, then the groups outperformed those who did not have systematic cycles of communication (Tschan, 1995). Finally, it is clear that communication technology, such as e-mail, cell phones, and web-based communications, have had an important impact on increasing worker productivity, although workers can waste their valuable work time on personal e-mail communications and non-work-related web surfing (Langan-Fox, 2001).

Although effective communication can lead to bottom-line payoffs in terms of increased productivity, it can also create increased levels of employee satisfaction. Research suggests positive relationships between the amount of upward communication in an organization and feelings of satisfaction in lower-level workers (Koehler et al., 1981). It has also been demonstrated that employees who receive a great deal of information about the organization in the form of downward communication tend to be more satisfied and have higher organizational commitment than those who do not (Ng et al., 2006).

In addition to job performance and job satisfaction, effective communication may have an impact on employee well-being, reducing stress, which may, in turn, affect absenteeism and turnover rates. Although research has not directly addressed this relationship, one study found that open and supportive downward communication helped one organization retain its "surviving" workers after a companywide downsizing. Moreover, communication seemed to be very important in reducing worker stress and maintaining job satisfaction during the downsizing (Johnson et al., 1996). Keeping downward and upward communication flowing is considered to be crucial best practice when effectively managing a major organizational change such as downsizing or organizational restructuring (Marks & Mirvis, 2010).

Although it makes sense that organizations with free and open lines of communication would tend to have more satisfied workers, leading to lowered rates of absenteeism and turnover, open communication among workers can also have some drawbacks. For example, researchers who examined the patterns of turnover among workers in three fast-food restaurants found that workers tended to quit their jobs in

⏱ Stop & Review

List the five communication network types and give examples of each.

clusters. Most importantly, the clusters tended to be among workers who communicated freely with one another, a phenomenon that has been termed the "snowball effect" (Krackhardt & Porter, 1986).

All in all, when dealing with organizational communication, more is usually better, although there may be a few exceptions, as when workers engage in so much non-work-related communication or are so deluged with messages and other information that job performance is impaired. Although much evidence indicates that it is usually better to keep communication flowing, open, and honest, some researchers claim that, because of organizational politics, at times organizational members might want to close some communication lines and keep certain types of information to themselves (see, e.g., Eisenberg & Witten, 1987).

In summary, it appears that many organizations can benefit from greater amounts of communication, and that companies can work to make organizational communication more accurate and effective. Top-level managers need to be aware of employees' needs for information and must open the flow of downward communication to provide for these needs. On the other hand, there needs to be a greater upward flow of communication to make management aware of what is going on at the lower levels of the company and to increase employee participation in and commitment to the organization. It also appears that increased lateral communication plays an important role in the ability of work groups to get the job done and in the development and maintenance of interpersonal relationships on the job. All of this can lead to more positive outcomes for the individuals, work groups, and organizations involved.

Summary

Communication is crucial for effective organizational performance. The basic communication model begins with the *sender*, who is responsible for *encoding* the message, which involves choosing some mutually understood code for transmitting the message to another person. The sender also selects a vehicle for communication, or the *channel*. The task of the *receiver* is to *decode* the message in an effort to understand its original meaning. The receiver also sends *feedback* to indicate that the message was received and understood. Any factors that disrupt the effective flow of communication from sender to receiver are referred to as *noise*.

Research on the communication process has examined the factors that can influence communication effectiveness. *Source factors* are variables related to the sender, such as status, credibility, and communication skills, which can influence the effectiveness of communication. *Channel factors* are variables related to the actual communication vehicle that can enhance or detract from the flow of communication from sender to receiver. In verbal communication, semantic problems, or the use of technical language termed *jargon*, can sometimes disrupt the communication flow. *Audience factors*, such as the decoding skills and attention span of the receiver, can also play a role in the communication process.

Nonverbal communication has a subtle but important effect on communication in work settings. It can be used as a substitute for verbal communication, to enhance verbal messages or to send true feelings. Receivers may also use nonverbal cues as an additional information source or as a means of forming impressions about people. A *Pygmalion effect* can occur if a sender holds positive expectations about a worker's performance and subtly influences that worker's performance via nonverbal communication.

Communication can flow in three directions through the organizational hierarchy: upward, downward, or laterally. *Downward communication* typically involves messages sent from superiors to subordinates, *upward communication* flows from the lower levels of the organization, and *lateral communication* occurs between persons at the same status level. *Filtering* and *exaggeration* are two types of distortion that often disrupt the effective flow of organizational communication.

Much of our knowledge of organizational communication patterns comes from research conducted on *communication networks*, which can be grouped into two types: *centralized*, in which messages move through central members, and *decentralized*, in which communication paths are not directed through specific network members. The formal communication patterns in organizations are represented in the organizational chart, or *organigram*. The informal lines of communication, or *grapevine*, are illustrated in a *sociogram*. The formal lines of communication carry messages that are sanctioned by the organization, whereas the grapevine is an informal network through which messages are passed from worker to worker. Managers are sometimes wary of the grapevine because they see it as a source of *rumors*, although research indicates that the grapevine can be a highly accurate and important information network.

Research suggests that greater and more effective organizational communication is linked to improved levels of performance and job satisfaction. Moreover, there may be links between open, flowing organizational communication and rates of employee absenteeism and turnover.

Study Questions and Exercises

1. List the steps in the basic communication model. Which factors influence the effective flow of communication at each of the steps?
2. In what ways can nonverbal communication affect the interaction between a supervisor and a subordinate? Between two same-status coworkers?
3. Think of an organization with which you have had some contact, such as a work organization, a club or social group, or your college or university. What forms of downward, upward, and lateral communication take place in this organization? How could the flow of each direction of communication be improved?
4. Consider the five types of communication networks. What are the characteristics of each? Can you think of any special work groups that illustrate each network?

5. In what ways will the sources, channels, and audiences of the formal lines of communication and the informal lines of communication (grapevine) in an organization differ?

Web Link

https://ocis.aom.org/home
Site for the Academy of Management's Division of Organizational Communication and Information Systems.

Suggested Readings

Management Communication Quarterly and *Journal of Business and Technical Communication*, both published by Sage Publications, and *The Journal of Business Communication*, published by the Association for Business Communication. *These journals contain articles on the theory and practice of management and business communication. Recent topics include intercultural communication, computer-mediated communication, and state-of-the-art communication technology.*

Armstrong, B., Schmidt, G. B., Islam, S., Jimenez, W. P., & Knudsen, E. (2020). Searching for IO psychology: How practitioners, academics, and laypeople engage with the IO brand online. *The Industrial-Organizational Psychologist, 57*(3), 62–68.

Kilcullen, M., Feitosa, J., & Salas, E. (2021). Insights from the virtual team science: Rapid deployment during COVID-19. *Human Factors*, 0018720821991678.

Strawser, M. G., Smith, S. A., & Rubenking, B. (2021). *Multigenerational Communication in Organizations: Insights from the Workplace.* Routledge.

CHAPTER 11

Socialization and Working in Groups

Inside Tips

GROUP ROLES AND PROCESSES: LEARNING TO WORK IN GROUPS

A knowledge of group dynamics, or the processes by which groups function, is central to understanding how work organizations operate because they are made up of smaller work groups. This chapter builds on Chapter 10's discussion of workplace communication, for it is communication that holds people together in work groups and sets the stage for the next four chapters on organizational processes. Chapter 12 focuses on a different aspect of working in groups—group decision making. Chapter 13, which examines influence, power, and politics, continues the discussion of group processes presented in this chapter by considering how these three social processes operate in work groups and larger work organizations. Chapter 14, on leadership, studies a very important ongoing process in work groups: the relationship between the leader and the other members of the group. Chapter 15 moves to the next level—the design and structure of work organizations—to explore how work groups link to form larger organizations.

You may already be familiar with some of the concepts presented in this chapter. For example, roles, norms, and conflict are central not only in industrial/organizational psychology but also in other specialty areas of psychology and in other behavioral sciences. Here, however, we will be applying these concepts specifically to the study of behavior in work settings. Other topics, such as organizational socialization and organizational conflict, are more particular to I/O psychology. This chapter represents a blending of some older, traditional concepts with some newer ones.

You have been working for some time with the same group of coworkers. At first, you felt like an outsider, but you soon learned your way around and began to feel like an accepted team member. You have noticed, however, that, although group members often cooperate with one another, they don't always. Moreover, when the pressure is on, group members can engage in some very interesting (and seemingly bizarre) behavior. There is an important and much anticipated meeting of the entire department where crucial issues will be discussed and important decisions made. As you enter the room, with a mixture of anticipation and trepidation, you wonder how it will all go.

Work organizations are made up of individuals, but typically these individuals are tied together by their membership in particular work groups. A work group might be a department, a job classification, a work team, or an informal group of coworkers who socialize during lunch and after work to discuss work-related problems and issues. Groups are very important to the functioning of work organizations, for the members of a group can pool their talents, energy, and knowledge to perform complex tasks. Work groups also help provide professional identities for members and satisfy human needs for social interaction and the development of interpersonal relationships on the job. Finally, groups help establish rules for proper behavior in the work setting and play a part in determining the courses of action that the work group and the organization will follow. The study of work groups is an important topic in I/O psychology.

In this chapter, we will examine work groups and their processes. We will begin by defining groups, looking at the different roles within groups, and examining the socialization process for groups and organizations. Then, we will cover the four Cs related to group processes: cooperation, competition, conflict, and cohesion.

Defining Work Groups and Teams

Group
two or more individuals engaged in social interaction to achieve some goal

A **group** can be defined as two or more individuals, engaged in social interaction, for the purposes of achieving some goal. In work settings, this goal is usually work-related, such as producing a product or service. However, groups at work may form merely to develop and maintain social relationships. Work groups can be either formal—put together by the organization to perform certain tasks and handle specific responsibilities—or informal, developing naturally. Informal work groups might include groups of workers who regularly get together after work to discuss their jobs.

Team
interdependent workers with complementary skills working toward a shared goal

Whereas groups are individuals working toward a goal, a **team** consists of interdependent workers with complementary skills working toward a shared goal or outcome. We will be discussing historical and recent research on group processes, and the term "group" is typically used, but some of these groups are clearly "teams," with interdependency and shared goals. In the next chapter, we will focus more specifically on research that involves clearly defined teams.

Roles

Roles
patterns of behavior that are adopted based on expectations about the functions of a position

Within work groups (and organizations), members can play various **roles**, or patterns of behavior, that are adopted on the basis of expectations about the functions of a particular position. Group roles are important because they help provide some specific plan for behavior. When a worker is playing a particular role within a group, that person usually knows something about the responsibilities and requirements of the role, or the **role expectations**. In most work groups, members are quite aware of the various expectations associated with each of the different positions within the group.

As a work group develops, the various members learn to become responsible for different aspects of its functioning. In other words, members begin to play different roles within the work group. This process whereby group members learn about and take on various defined roles is called **role differentiation**. For example, a new worker who enters a work group may immediately fall into the role of novice worker. However, that person may later develop a reputation for having a good sense of humor and thus begin to play the role of jokester, providing levity when situations get too tense or when boredom sets in.

The various roles in work groups are often created based on factors such as position or formal job title, status within the group, the tasks to which a member is assigned, or the possession of some particular work skill or ability. For example, employees who are designated as assistant supervisor, senior mechanic, or communications specialist perform specific roles and engage in certain behaviors consistent with these job titles. Although workers can be designated as playing certain usual roles within the work group, they can perform different functional roles at different times. Two early researchers outlined a wide range of work roles, which they

Role Expectations
beliefs concerning the responsibilities and requirements of a particular role

Role Differentiation
the process by which group members learn to perform various roles

Figure 11.1 This woman plays a clearly defined role on this team of chocolate makers.

Source: Photograph by Walter Otto, found on Unsplash (https://unsplash.com/photos/PT70 CT6mATQ).

grouped into three categories (Benne & Sheats, 1948; see Table 11.1). The first category, *group task roles*, is related to getting the job done. Group task roles are given such titles as information giver, procedural technician, and evaluator-critic. For example, a machinist in a cardboard container factory who outlines the steps

Table 11.1 The Various Roles Individuals Play in Work Groups.

Group Task Roles

Initiator-contributor: Recommends new ideas about, or novel solutions to, a problem
Information seeker: Emphasizes getting facts and other information from others
Opinion seeker: Solicits inputs concerning the attitudes or feelings about ideas under consideration
Information giver: Contributes relevant information to help in decision making
Opinion giver: Provides own opinions and feelings
Elaborator: Clarifies and expands on the points made by others
Coordinator: Integrates information from the group
Orientor: Guides the discussion and keeps it on the topic when the group digresses
Evaluator-critic: Uses some set of standards to evaluate the group's accomplishments
Energizer: Stimulates the group to take action
Procedural technician: Handles routine tasks such as providing materials or supplies
Recorder: Keeps track of the group's activities and takes minutes

Group Building and Maintenance Roles

Encourager: Encourages others' contributions
Harmonizer: Tries to resolve conflicts between group members
Compromiser: Tries to provide conflicting members with a mutually agreeable solution
Gatekeeper: Regulates the flow of communication so that all members can have a say
Standard setter: Sets standards or deadlines for group actions
Group observer: Makes objective observations about the tone of the group interaction
Follower: Accepts the ideas of others and goes along with group majority

Self-Centered Roles

Aggressor: Tries to promote own status within group by attacking others
Blocker: Tries to block all group actions and refuses to go along with group
Recognition seeker: Tries to play up own achievements to get group's attention
Self-confessor: Uses group discussion to deal with personal issues
Playboy: Engages in humor and irrelevant acts to draw attention away from the tasks
Dominator: Attempts to monopolize the group
Help seeker: Attempts to gain sympathy by expressing insecurity or inadequacy
Special interest pleader: Argues incessantly to further own desires

Source: Benne & Sheats, 1948.

necessary for the work group to construct and assemble a new type of box is playing the procedural technician role.

The second category of functional roles is *group building and maintenance* roles. These deal with the maintenance of interpersonal relations among group members and include such roles as encourager, harmonizer, and compromiser. A worker who plays an active part in settling an argument between two coworkers may be taking on the harmonizer role. The third category, called *self-centered roles*, involves satisfying personal rather than group goals. Titles of these roles include recognition seeker, aggressor, and help seeker. Employees who look to others for assistance in completing their own work assignments are playing the help-seeker role. It has been suggested that workers may or may not define prosocial behaviors—the organizational citizenship behaviors that we discussed earlier—as part of their defined work role, rather than viewing OCBs (organizational citizenship behaviors) as "extrarole" behaviors (Tepper et al., 2001). The fact that there are so many different roles that members can play in work group functioning illustrates the complexity of the processes that occur daily in work groups.

It is important to mention that sometimes workers are unclear about the requirements of the various roles they are expected to play in the workplace. This can lead to **role ambiguity**, or a sense of uncertainty over the requirements of a particular role an individual is expected to play. Role ambiguity, like **job ambiguity**, is an important source of workplace stress.

In organizations, persons often are expected to play more than one role at a time. In some cases, the behaviors expected of an individual owing to one role may not be consistent with the expectations concerning another role. Instances such as these give rise to **role conflict**. Role conflict is quite common, particularly in positions that require workers to be members of different groups simultaneously. For example, imagine that you are the supervisor of a work group. One of your roles involves holding the group together and protecting the interests of its members. However, you are also a member of the organization's management team and, in this role, you are ordered to transfer a very talented and very popular work group member, against her wishes, to another department. Because you cannot satisfy the two incompatible goals of holding the team together while carrying out the organization's plan to transfer the worker, you experience role conflict, another form of stress that can have negative effects on job satisfaction, performance, and mental and physical well-being.

One specific type of role conflict is work–family conflict, which results from efforts to balance the often-competing demands of work roles and family roles. I/O psychologists have argued for the importance of this area of study to the field and to workers in organizations for the last decade (Kossek et al., 2011; Wells, 2011). Almost 72% of women with children under the age of 18 are working moms. Although work–family conflict is often thought about in terms of working mothers, the reality is that all individuals can experience work–family conflict, making it a social issue rather than just a women's issue (Leslie & Manchester, 2011). Work–family conflict can also impact men and non-binary individuals. Realistically, individuals without

Role Ambiguity
a sense of uncertainty over the requirements of a particular role

Job Ambiguity
a source of stress resulting from a lack of clearly defined jobs and/or work tasks

Role Conflict
conflict that results when the expectations associated with one role interfere with the expectations concerning another role

children can still face work–family conflict because we all have nonwork roles. Individuals with older parents, those with pets, and even individuals who are just trying to balance their hobbies, fitness goals, or social lives can experience this type of push and pull when it comes to work and life. Although the term work–family conflict (or work–family balance) is the most common, a better conceptualization of the experience might be work–life balance.

Work–Family Conflict
cumulative stress that results from duties of work and family roles

Work–family conflict (or work–life conflict) is an organizational issue because it impacts job satisfaction, just as it impacts family and life satisfaction (Allen et al., 2020). Organizations that want to retain the best talent and those that want to create environments where anyone can thrive should consider work–family concerns. Despite that, most research suggests that work–family conflict is on the rise because of the increased demands of work (Rantanen et al., 2011). Some of this change relates to the increase in mobile technology—smartphones allow you to answer work messages at any time of day or night. But, just because you *can* do it, does not mean you should. Indeed, the need to respond to e-mail at all hours negatively impacts a variety of outcomes, such as work–family conflict (Belkin et al., 2020).

Beyond the increased demands of the workplace, external influences can also impact work–family balance. For example, after the collapse of the U.S. housing market in 2008, workers who were fearful of losing their homes reported increased stress in the workplace (Ragins et al., 2014). Similarly, work–family conflict became particularly challenging amidst the COVID-19 pandemic as childcare centers and schools were closed across the globe, but parents continued to need to work (Shockley et al., 2020). Parents who experienced increased work–family conflict during the pandemic had corresponding reductions in job satisfaction and job performance and increased turnover intentions (Vaziri et al., 2020). One estimate is that individuals worked an extra 3 hours a day during the COVID-19 pandemic (Davis & Green, 2020).

Another environmental factor that impacts work–family conflict is federal support for new parents. The United States and Papua New Guinea are the only two countries that do not require paid parental leave (Mills & Culbertson, 2017). As covered in Chapter 1, the Family and Medical Leave Act (FMLA) provides workers with 12 weeks of leave, but that leave is unpaid, and so many employees cannot afford to take their full leave. Certain states such as California, New Jersey, Rhode Island, and New York do offer paid leave (Mills & Culbertson, 2017). The city of San Francisco, within California, takes the measure further, requiring employers to offer 12 weeks of paid leave. Of course, many companies have made efforts to help reduce work–family conflict (see "Applying I/O Psychology" box).

It is also worth noting that the combination of work and family is not only a conflict. Most people also experience benefits from combining work and family that have been conceptualized as work–family integration, enrichment, or positive spillover (see Bear, 2019, for a review). Others offer the concepts of work–family interaction (Halpern & Murphy, 2005) or work–family integration (Kossek & Lambert, 2005).

APPLYING I/O PSYCHOLOGY

D&I INSIGHT

Making Workplaces Work for Working Parents

Because of the pervasiveness of work–family conflict and the need to support parents with young children, the best companies have designed unique and creative ways of supporting parents. Even before children, some companies offer assistance with helping employees become parents. General Mills offers $10,000 in adoption aid, while Abbott Laboratories offers $20,000 in adoption aid. Avon offers $10,000 in adoption aid and $114,000 for fertility treatments. Ernst & Young (EY) offers $25,000 for fertility treatments (or egg freezing), surrogacy, or adoption. For those who have just had children, Facebook offers "baby cash" of $4,000. Google also offers some baby dollars. That helps with all of those diapers and childcare expenses that can be so stressful for new parents.

More commonly, many organizations offer some type of paid leave immediately following birth or adoption. At the time this was published, Virgin was among the most generous companies when it comes to leave, offering a year of paid parental leave. Etsy and Deloitte offer 6 months, and American Express and Twitter offer 5 months paid leave. EY and Bank of America offer 4 months. In addition, some companies offer resources for nursing mothers. Abbott Labs provides discounts on

breast pumps and lactation specialists. EY, Wegmans, and many other companies provide lactation rooms and milk delivery services for moms who are on the road traveling. Companies such as Intel, CA Technologies, EY, MetLife, and Etsy all have post-maternity leave integration programs and coaching.

As children get older, many organizations provide options to help care for children. For example, Boston Consulting Group and Salesforce offer emergency backup childcare in the case that childcare arrangements fall through. Wegmans offers paid leave when parents' kids are sick. Campbell Soup offers on-site after-school programs, kindergarten classes, and summer programs for kids. Ultimate Software offers $300 a year to pay for kids' extracurricular activities, while Kimley-Horn offers tutoring assistance for children. Another common way that companies such as Salesforce, Boston Consulting Group, and Kimley-Horn help to reduce work–family conflict is by offering flexible work hours or compressed work weeks. Deloitte says that 90% of its employees have flexible work schedules. The reality is, however, that there can be a gap between the availability of policies and the use of policies if the organizational culture or supervisor does not support the use of flexibility.

Norms

Work groups contain various members, each playing different roles, but all members, regardless of their role, must adhere to certain group rules. **Norms** are the rules that groups adopt to indicate appropriate and inappropriate behavior for members. Group norms can be formalized as written work rules, but are most commonly informal and unrecorded. Norms can govern any work activity, including the speed with which a person should perform a job, proper modes of dress, acceptable topics for

Norms
rules that groups adopt governing appropriate and inappropriate behavior for members

group conversation, and even who sits where in the employee lunchroom. According to Feldman (1984), norms develop in a number of ways. They can come from explicit statements made by supervisors or coworkers. For example, a supervisor might tell group members, "No one goes home until the work area is spotlessly clean." This leads to a norm that all workers stop working 15 minutes before quitting time to clean up the work area. Group leaders or powerful group members often play an important role in such norm formation. Norms can also evolve from the group's history. For example, if a certain work procedure leads to a disastrous outcome, the group may place a ban on its use. In other instances, norms may be carried over from past situations. When a member changes groups, norms from the old group may be imported to the new one. For example, a sales supervisor was transferred from the corporate office to a regional sales office. On her first day in the new office, she commented on the casual dress of employees by saying, "At the corporate office, men always wear suits and ties and women always wear skirts or dresses." From the next day on, a new dress code of more formal attire developed.

Norms serve many important purposes for groups. First and foremost, they are established to help the group survive. A group must be able to produce enough to ensure the economic success of the group and the organization. Therefore, some norms will develop to facilitate group production. On the other hand, if members feel that production rates are too high and will possibly lead to layoffs, norms to restrict group output (called "rate setting") may arise. Work groups can develop norms that result in high levels of positive work behaviors, such as engagement (Griffin, 2015), or safety behaviors (Silva & Fugas, 2016), but norms encouraging counterproductive work behaviors can also occur (Fox & Spector, 2005).

Norms also help increase the predictability of members' behavior. For example, there are norms regarding lateness for meetings (van Eerde & Azar, 2020) and who should speak for how long in meetings (Niederman & Volkema, 1999). Researchers have even studied the norms that evolve in online communication and chat networks (Dietz-Uhler et al., 2005). Finally, norms provide a sense of identity for the group by giving members a chance to express their shared values and beliefs. For example, if an advertising agency believes that it is responsible for setting advertising trends, a norm for producing advertisements that are unique or novel may develop.

In summary, both roles and norms help provide a structure and plan for group members' behavior. They play an important part in regulating group activities and in helping group members to achieve shared goals. In addition, norms and, to some extent, roles provide some of the foundation of a company's organizational culture (a topic we will consider in Chapter 15).

Organizational Socialization: Learning Group Roles and Norms

A critical area of research that has received a great deal of attention from I/O psychologists is **organizational socialization**, or the process by which new employees

Organizational Socialization
the process by which new employees learn group roles and norms and develop specific work skills and abilities

become integrated into work groups. Companies today often refer to organizational socialization as the "onboarding process" (Bauer & Erdogan, 2011). Organizational socialization includes three important processes: (a) the development of specific work skills and abilities, (b) the acquisition of a set of appropriate role behaviors, and (c) adjustment to the work group's norms and values (Anakwe & Greenhaus, 1999). The first process—learning specific work skills and abilities—is the main goal of personnel training, which was discussed in depth in Chapter 6.

The other two processes—the acquisition of roles and role behaviors and the learning of group norms—are of particular interest here. New employees learn about group roles and norms in the same way that they learn new job skills, specifically by observing and imitating the behaviors of others. Newcomers may look to established workers as role models and try to copy their successful work behaviors (Louis et al., 1983). For example, a novice trial attorney may watch the way that a seasoned senior partner handles herself in court and at firm meetings to learn about the expected role behaviors for the firm's successful attorneys. New employees may also learn about group norms by being reinforced for performing appropriate behaviors and being punished for inappropriate actions. A new salesperson in a busy clothing store may learn about norms for appropriate employee dress and the usual procedures for handling impatient customers by receiving either a reinforcing smile and nod or a disapproving frown from the sales manager.

Typically, organizational socialization occurs in stages as one moves from being a newcomer to a fully functioning and contributing member of the work group (Wanous et al., 1984). One model outlines three stages in the socialization of new employees (Feldman, 1976). The first is *anticipatory socialization*. Here, newcomers develop a set of realistic expectations concerning the job and the organization and determine if the organization will provide the right match with their abilities, needs, and values. The second stage in the process is *accommodation*. In this stage, new employees learn about the various roles that work group members play and about their own specific roles in the group. They also begin to "learn the ropes" as they discover important work group norms and standards. In this second stage, the newcomers begin to develop interpersonal relationships with other group members. In the third stage, *role management*, newcomers make the transition to regular members or insiders, mastering the tasks and roles they must perform. As they move through this stage, they eventually have a thorough knowledge of all facets of work group norms and operations.

Although all new employees are likely to pass through the same stages in the organizational socialization process, research indicates that employees may be socialized at different rates, depending on the characteristics of the workers and of the work environment (Taormina, 2009). For example, workers who are forced to move from an old, established work group or organization to a new setting because of layoffs or geographical moves may have a more difficult time becoming socialized than workers who voluntarily make the move. Research has clearly shown that supervisors and coworkers play an important part in the successful socialization of new employees by establishing positive relationships and mentoring newcomers (Ostroff & Kozlowski, 1993). Research suggests that structured and regular socialization

Stop & Review

Describe the three stages of organizational socialization.

that focuses on employees' job learning and career progression is better than less systematic socialization processes (Cable & Parsons, 2001).

Workers can also play an active part in their own socialization (Cooper-Thomas, 2009). One study showed that new employees who engage in more proactive behaviors such as greater information seeking, feedback seeking, socializing, and relationship building over the first 6 months on the job enhanced their own socialization and job satisfaction (Bauer et al., 2019). Not surprisingly then, employee personality characteristics such as having a proactive personality positively predict socialization (Bauer, Erdogan et al., 2020). According to another study on salespeople in a financial services organization, high-performing employees may also be more willing to put effort toward socialization than low-performing employees (Stan et al., 2021). It may also be the case that prior work experience and personality characteristics of workers affect socialization rates (Ostroff & Kozlowski, 1992).

APPLYING I/O PSYCHOLOGY

Training as Part of the Onboarding Process

An important source of socialization (or onboarding) involves the interaction between newcomers and insider employees because it allows employees to make sense of their new role (Harris et al., 2020). Similar to the mentoring concept discussed in Chapter 6, insiders can teach new employees the ropes and accelerate socialization (Cooper-Thomas, 2009). Multiple studies support the importance of connection to insiders and becoming integrated into social networks to new employee socialization (Hatmaker & Park, 2014). Importantly, one study showed the importance of effectively communicating the types of programs that are available, which can impact whether employees use the programs and their eventual satisfaction with socialization and job satisfaction (Stan et al., 2021).

Organizations can also greatly facilitate the socialization of new employees (Kammeyer-Mueller et al., 2013). An interesting study of employees on their first day at work showed that simple efforts such as having their work station set up and ready and meeting with their supervisor on their first day at work predicted socialization outcomes (Bauer, Erdogan et al., 2020). Employee orientation and training programs are essential to the process, as are the work group's openness and willingness to welcome new members. One study on post-merger socialization showed that training had the most positive effect on employee socialization, whereas other socialization practices, such as manager and HR efforts, had little effect (Yalabik, 2013).

Socialization and Person–Environment Fit

Person–Environment (P–E) Fit
the match between a worker's abilities, needs, and values and organizational demands, rewards, and values

During socialization, employees start to realize the extent to which they fit in their new organization's environment. **Person–environment (P–E) fit** refers to the match between a worker's abilities, needs, and values and organizational demands, rewards, and values. P–E fit has been found to have a positive correlation with

---

BEFORE YOU START
- ☐ Return a signed contract
- ☐ Complete New Employee Packet
- ☐ Sign up for health insurance, etc.

DURING YOUR FIRST TWO WEEKS
- ☐ Obtain employee identification card
- ☐ Obtain access key card
- ☐ Complete benefits worksheet, etc.

AFTER YOUR FIRST THREE MONTHS, YOU SHOULD KNOW. . .

ABOUT YOUR JOB
- ☐ Department's goals and mission
- ☐ Department organization and personnel
- ☐ Your reporting lines
- ☐ Your duties and responsibilities, etc.

ABOUT YOUR WORK ENVIRONMENT
- ☐ Your work area and office
- ☐ Your colleagues and their job functions
- ☐ How to use e-mail and phones
- ☐ How to obtain/order office supplies and resources, etc.

ABOUT YOUR PAY
- ☐ Your pay rate
- ☐ Overtime policies and regulations
- ☐ Travel reimbursement procedures
- ☐ Accrual policies for sick and vacation days, etc.

ABOUT YOUR RIGHTS AND RESPONSIBILITIES
- ☐ Benefits available to you and your family
- ☐ Organizational policies on equal employment opportunities, sexual harassment, etc.
- ☐ Formal training available to you
- ☐ Policies on discipline and procedures governing your employment, etc.

Figure 11.2 Example of a new employee orientation checklist.

organizational commitment and well-being and a negative correlation with turn-over (Ostroff, 1993; Verquer et al., 2003; Yang et al., 2008). According to the P–E fit approach, a mismatch between the worker and the work organization/environment is believed to be a primary cause of worker stress. For example, imagine a worker who has a high need for job clarification, job structure, and feedback and who accepts a job with a small, fast-growing company where jobs are neither well defined nor structured and where supervisors have little time for feedback owing to constant production demands. In such a case, there would be a poor person–environment fit.

The Four Cs: Cooperation, Competition, Conflict, and Cohesiveness

We have mentioned that the main purpose of work groups and teams is to facilitate the attainment of personal and organizational work goals. This often requires that people work together, coordinating their activities, cooperating with one another, and sometimes helping each other. Yet work groups are also rife with competition as workers try to outperform one another to attain scarce bonuses, raises, and promotions. Competition may also be encouraged when one employee's performance is compared with that of others. Incentive programs are specifically designed to increase motivation by inducing competition—pitting one worker against another. These two seemingly incompatible processes, cooperation and competition, exist simultaneously in all work groups (Tjosvold et al., 1999). Two related processes—conflict, purposely trying to reduce others' attainment of goals, and cohesion, which is the "social glue" that holds groups together—begin to emerge over time. We will discuss each of these four processes in greater depth as they relate to groups and organizations more broadly.

Cooperation

Cooperation is critical to the effective functioning of work groups/teams and organizations. Consider three employees in a college bookstore as an example. The employees take turns performing the tasks that their jobs require. At any time, two are at the front desk, serving customers. The third worker is opening boxes of books, pricing them, and putting them on the appropriate shelves. The workers are coordinating their efforts in an attempt to meet the organizational goals of selling books and providing good customer service. If one of the workers at the front desk goes on a lunch break, the person stocking shelves moves to the front to help customers. If an employee does not know the answer to a customer's question, he may turn to a more knowledgeable and experienced coworker for assistance. The store employees also coordinate their time off, developing a mutually agreeable vacation schedule.

For the most part, such cooperation among work group members is the rule rather than the exception, chiefly because it is often difficult to achieve work goals alone. As long as workers hold to the same goals, they will usually cooperate with one another. Employees might also go out of their way to help each other because of the **reciprocity rule** (Gouldner, 1960), which is illustrated by the sayings "One good turn deserves another" and "Do unto others as you would have them do unto you." Thus, workers help each other because they believe that, when they need assistance, they will be paid back in kind. The reciprocity rule is very strong, and people do indeed tend to reciprocate helping behaviors (Eisenberger et al., 2001).

Reciprocity Rule
the tendency for persons to pay back those to whom they are indebted for assistance

One element that helps increase cooperation among work group members is the degree of **task interdependence**, or the degree to which an individual worker's task performance depends on the efforts or skills of others (Somech et al., 2009). In large part, it is task interdependence that differentiates work "groups" from work "teams." Research has shown that task interdependence fosters positive feelings about coworkers and increases cooperative behavior in work groups and teams (Wageman & Baker, 1997).

Group members also cooperate because achieving organizational goals can lead to payoffs for the individual workers in terms of raises, bonuses, and promotions. This, in turn, can increase group member satisfaction and subsequent performance (consistent with the Porter–Lawler model introduced in Chapter 8; Alper et al., 2000). Moreover, when work-related rewards are based on effective group performance, such as in the gainsharing programs also discussed in Chapter 8, it helps foster cooperation among work group members.

Finally, group or organizational norms can serve to facilitate cooperation ("we help one another at this organization") or hinder it ("Look out for #1"; Gonzalez-Mulé et al., 2014). The organizational culture or climate, and its history, can also work to encourage or discourage cooperation (Salas et al., 2014).

Although the presence of cooperative group members often helps facilitate work performance, there are instances where work group members refuse to cooperate and "pull their load." **Social loafing** is the name given to the phenomenon whereby individuals working in a group put forth less effort than when working alone (Latané et al., 1979). Research has shown that social loafing occurs most frequently when workers believe that their individual performance or contribution will not be measured and when working on simple, additive tasks, rather than complex, interdependent tasks (Karau & Williams, 1993). Social loafing has also occurred in virtual teams (Suleiman & Watson, 2008). In addition, social loafing is more likely to occur in groups that are low in cohesiveness (Liden et al., 2004).

Research suggests what some of us have believed all along—that some individuals may be more prone to social loafing than others (Hoon & Tan, 2008). Another study (Robbins, 1995) found that, if group members perceived others as engaging in social loafing, it increased their tendency to loaf—good evidence for the equity theory of motivation (see Chapter 7; "If they're going to slack off, I'll slack off, too").

Competition

Like cooperation, **competition** is also a natural behavior that commonly arises in group dynamics (Tjosvold et al., 2008). Whereas cooperation involves group members working together toward shared common goals, competition within groups involves members working against one another to achieve individual goals, often at the expense of other members. For example, in a sales competition, all members of a sales group compete with one another, but only one can be named top salesperson. Most work groups are rife with competition as members struggle to get ahead. One

Task Interdependence
the degree to which an individual's task performance depends on the efforts or skills of others

Social Loafing
the phenomenon whereby individuals working in groups exert less effort than when working alone

 Stop & Review

Name five factors that increase group cohesiveness.

Competition
the process whereby group members are pitted against one another to achieve individual goals

study by Campbell and Furrer (1995) found evidence that the introduction of competition in a work situation where goals were already set actually led to a decrease in performance, and so managers should be cautious in their use of competition as a motivational strategy, as we will see shortly in our discussion of conflict.

Because both cooperation and competition are natural human processes, they often exist side by side in work groups, and work organizations and work culture actually encourage both. The very fact that work organizations exist indicates that there must be some advantage in having workers cooperate by pooling their efforts to perform some complex tasks. At the same time, the compensation systems adopted by U.S. organizations, and companies in most Western countries, emphasize the rewarding of individual efforts, which breeds competition. Much of this competition is viewed as healthy because it often motivates people to improve their work performance. Indeed, in the U.S. and many other industrialized Western nations, being competitive is a highly valued characteristic that is considered imperative for individual and organizational success. On the other hand, competition in a work environment that requires sharing of knowledge, such as in high-tech industries, may lead to less creativity and synergy and work against the organization's goals (He et al., 2014).

Conflict in Work Groups and Organizations

Conflict

behavior by a person or group intended to inhibit the attainment of goals by another person or group

Whereas competition refers to a motivating state, conflict is used to describe competitiveness of individual workers or work groups that becomes exposed. **Conflict** is behavior by a person or group that is purposely designed to inhibit the attainment of goals by another person or group (Greer & Dannals, 2017). There are many typical instances of conflict between members of an organization, such as two delivery persons arguing over who gets to drive the new company truck, union and management representatives in heated negotiations over a new contract, or two applicants competing for a single job. Conflict in work organizations and in other areas of everyday life is indeed a common state of affairs.

The key element in the definition of conflict is that the conflicting parties have incompatible goals (Tjosvold, 1998). Thus, both delivery persons cannot drive the same truck, the union cannot attain its goals unless management is willing to give up some of its goals, and two people cannot hold the same job. Because, in extreme cases, conflict can lead to a variety of negative behaviors, such as shouting, name calling, and acts of aggression, and perhaps because there is often a "loser" in conflict outcomes, it is commonly believed that conflict is bad. However, this is not necessarily true. Conflict is a natural process that occurs in all work groups and organizations. It can have negative, destructive consequences, but it can also be constructive and lead to positive outcomes for work groups and organizations, but only under specific and controlled circumstances (De Dreu, 2008). Generally, the only way to be certain when conflict is bad or good is to examine whether it has positive or negative consequences for the conflicting parties and for the work group or organization as a whole. Although the consequences of conflict are very important, we must first examine the different levels of conflict that occur in organizations and the potential sources of conflict.

Sources of Conflict

Conflict in work groups and organizations comes from many sources. Sometimes it is caused by the organizational structure. For example, status differences are a common source of conflict. Sometimes conflict results because of simple disagreements between two parties over the appropriate work behavior or course of action. Although it would be difficult to list all potential sources of conflict, we will examine some of the more common causes.

A scarcity of important resources—money, materials, tools, and supplies—is perhaps the most common source of conflict in work organizations (Greenberg & Baron, 1997). It is a rare organization that has enough resources to satisfy the needs of all of its members. When members are forced to compete with one another for these resources, conflict usually follows.

Individuals and work groups usually must rely on the activities of other persons and groups to get their own jobs done. Therefore, individual and group interdependence is an important source of conflict (Lee et al., 2015). Generally, the greater the interdependence of work activities, the greater the potential for conflict (Walton & Dutton, 1969). For example, in the airline industry, flight crews must depend on the maintenance crews, luggage handlers, and passenger boarding personnel to do their jobs in servicing and loading the aircraft before they can do their job. Intergroup conflict can result if one group does not feel that another is doing its job. If the flight crew feels that the luggage handlers are too slow, causing delays in takeoff, the fact that the flight crew may be blamed for the delays creates a potential conflict situation.

Nothing can draw a group together better than having a common enemy to fight. However, a problem occurs when the "enemy" is within your own organization. This is what often causes the conflict in wage negotiations between workers and managers. The workers ask for a wage increase, whereas management, in an effort to keep costs down, rejects the request. What commonly results is that each group views the other as an enemy blocking its goal attainment. Although the common enemy helps draw the members together within their respective groups, it also tends to draw the two groups further away from each other.

One of the most common sources of conflict results from the fact that certain individuals simply do not get along with each other (Gilin Oore et al., 2015). This important source of conflict thus comes from interpersonal sources. Two organizational members who dislike each other may refuse to cooperate. This sort of interpersonal conflict can be highly disruptive to the larger work group and the organization in general, especially if the problem is between two powerful people, such as two department heads, who may turn their supervisees against members of the other department. What was once a conflict between two persons can thus escalate into conflict between two groups.

Interindividual Conflict
conflict that occurs when two people are striving to attain their own goals, thus blocking the other's achievement

Research evidence also suggests that some people are more conflict prone than others. Differences in personality and temperament mean that certain persons may be likely to engage in conflict. Indeed, studies have shown that some people try to stir up **interindividual conflict** because of their desire to gain at others' expense (Wertheim & Donnoli, 2012). Inability to deal effectively with negative emotions may also make certain people more conflict prone (Yang & Mossholder, 2004).

A final characteristic that can be a potential source of conflict is age. A good deal of evidence indicates that younger workers are more conflict prone than older workers, presumably because they have less to lose and more to gain from the outcomes of conflict situations (Williams, 2016). Some research also suggests that young workers, particularly those who are trying to balance work and school, are more negatively influenced by interpersonal conflict, experiencing greater job dissatisfaction and stress than older workers (Harvey et al., 2006).

Conflict Outcomes

It has been stated that conflict in work settings can produce both positive and negative outcomes for the organization. Attention is usually given to how conflict affects the important organizational outcomes of job performance or productivity, job satisfaction, and employee attendance. First, we will examine the positive outcomes of conflict.

Figure 11.3 Most organizational conflict occurs behind the scenes, but in extreme instances the dispute becomes public.

Source: Photo by Afif Kusuma on Unsplash (https://unsplash.com/photos/mv38TB_Ljj8).

A primary question is how conflict within a work group or organization relates to performance. One way that conflict can indirectly affect performance is by increasing the motivation and energy level of group members. A little bit of conflict seems to energize members, which in turn may increase their motivation to perform their jobs. The complete absence of conflict in work groups can cause workers to become complacent and unmotivated. (It can also be very dull.)

Another positive outcome of conflict is that it can stimulate creativity and innovation (Jung & Lee, 2015). When people challenge the existing system, a form of conflict results. But out of this type of conflict come new, and often better, ideas. For example, in many groups, workers continue to use the same old "tried and true" work procedures. When a worker suggests a new, improved method, there may be some initial conflict as members resist having to learn a new technique. However, if the new procedure is effective, group productivity may increase. Thus, although people tend to resist changes, when change is for the better, the organization and its members benefit.

Another positive, performance-related outcome of conflict occurs when conflict improves the quality of decisions (Hamilton et al., 2014). Giving all members of a group some input into the decision-making process leads to conflict because the group must consider a wide range of opposing views and opinions. Conflict occurs as each member tries to be heard and pushes for what he or she thinks is right. The positive result of all of this, however, is that decisions made are usually of high quality, being the result of a very critical process. (We will return to a discussion of group decision-making processes in the next chapter.)

Being able to communicate freely with coworkers, having a voice in decision making, and being allowed to make suggestions or criticize group or organizational operations are all ways in which workers can have some impact on group processes. Although some conflict is likely to arise every time workers are allowed to introduce their own opinions, the fact that they can take part in this positive, productive type of conflict is associated with greater group member satisfaction. Therefore, some forms of conflict can be directly associated with member satisfaction and commitment to the work group.

Among the various negative outcomes of conflict, one of the most obvious is the reduction of group cohesiveness—a topic that we will discuss next. Although a little bit of conflict can energize group members, too much can erode cohesiveness and, in extremes, diminish the members' abilities to work with each other. This may contribute to increased voluntary absenteeism and, eventually, employee turnover.

Conflict can also hamper effective group performance when it retards communication. People who are in conflict may avoid communicating with each other, making it difficult to work together. Conflict can also be destructive to group member satisfaction when conflicting parties begin to send misleading or deceptive messages to one another or when false and disparaging rumors are started. Evidence also suggests that, when a great deal of interpersonal conflict occurs among work group members, supervisors may begin to avoid allowing subordinates to participate in decision-making processes, thus shutting down this type of communication, presumably in an effort to avoid further conflict (Fodor, 1976). Conflict is especially damaging to performance when it allows group goals to become secondary to the infighting. Sometimes members direct so much energy to the conflict situation that they neglect to perform their jobs (Robbins, 1979). A meta-analysis suggests that conflict can have negative impacts on both team productivity and job satisfaction (De Dreu & Weingart, 2003).

In summary, neither too much nor too little conflict is beneficial for the work group members and the organization. This means that there must be some optimal level of conflict. Because conflict is so pervasive in work groups and organizations, it would be very difficult to assess whether all forms of conflict were at their optimal levels at any given time. Because some excess or shortage of conflict is inevitably going to exist, the smart thing to do at all times in all work groups is to learn to manage conflict.

Managing Conflict

To manage conflict—to keep it at an optimal level—one of two things must be done. If the conflict becomes too great, leading to severe negative outcomes, it must be resolved. If, on the other hand, the level of conflict is too low, conflict stimulation is needed.

There is little doubt that too much conflict can have devastating consequences for both the work group and the organization. Therefore, a great deal of attention has been given to the development and application of various conflict resolution strategies, which can be of two types. Individual conflict resolution strategies are those that the conflicting parties can use themselves to try to resolve the conflict; managerial conflict resolution strategies are steps that managers or other third parties can take to encourage conflict resolution. Thomas (1976) has identified five individual conflict resolution strategies, in what is often referred to as the Thomas–Kilmann model of conflict resolution:

Dominating (Forcing)
a conflict resolution strategy of persisting in a conflict until one party attains personal goals at the expense of the other's

Accommodation
a conflict resolution strategy of making a sacrifice to resolve a conflict

Compromise
a conflict resolution strategy in which both parties give up some part of their goals

1 **Dominating (forcing)**—Persisting in the conflict until one party's goals are achieved at the expense of those of the other. This can be labeled a win–lose strategy: one party wins, the other loses.

2 **Accommodation**—Giving in or acting in a self-sacrificing manner to resolve the conflict. This is a lose–win strategy. Often, this strategy of appeasement is done to cut losses or in an effort to save the relationship between the conflicting parties.

3 **Compromise**—Each party must give up something. This is a lose–lose strategy. Compromise is typical in bargaining situations. For example, in union–management negotiations, management may offer a $2.50 an hour raise, whereas the union wants a $4.00 raise. They compromise at $3.00, but neither group has achieved its complete goal. They have each lost something from their original position: a lose–lose outcome. Compromise is not an appropriate strategy if both parties cannot afford to yield part of their goals (Harris, 1993).

4 **Collaboration**—The parties try to cooperate and reach a mutually beneficial solution. This is a win–win situation. Unfortunately, this is not always possible, particularly when the conflict is over scarce resources, and there is not enough to satisfy both parties' needs. It has been suggested that, if both parties work at it, many conflicts can be resolved collaboratively (Ury et al., 1988).

5 **Avoidance**—Suppressing the conflict, not allowing it to come into the open, or simply withdrawing from the situation. Although this strategy avoids open conflict, the differences between the two parties still exist and will likely continue to affect their ability to work with one another. Avoidance can be appropriate if the timing for open conflict is not right or if the conflicting parties need a "cooling-off" period.

The Thomas–Kilmann model assumes two things: (1) that the conflicting parties can manage the conflict themselves and (2) that there is willingness between the parties to move forward in resolving the conflict (except in the case of avoidance). However, this model may not be applicable if there are very bad relationships between the conflicting parties, including resentment, and an inability to engage (Trippe & Baumoel, 2015). Under these conditions, others may need to step in.

Managers, because of their status and power in the organization, can play a major role in resolving conflict between subordinates (Pinkley et al., 1995). Managers may try to force an end to the conflict by deciding in favor of one or the other party. Although this may end the conflict, resentment may be built up in the losing person that may surface later in actions against the manager or the coworker (van de Vliert et al., 1995). Managers can also act as arbitrators or mediators to resolve conflict in a way that may satisfy both parties (Kozan et al., 2014). For example, two graphic artists were constantly fighting over use of a computer scanner needed to perform their jobs. When one worker needed the scanner, it always seemed that the other person was using it, which led to constant arguments. When the manager became aware of the problem, he instantly resolved it by simply purchasing another scanner. In other circumstances, outside consultants or arbitrators may be called in specifically to resolve internal conflicts in organizations (Thomas, 1992).

One managerial conflict resolution strategy, outlined in a series of studies by Sherif and his colleagues (Sherif et al., 1961), deals with resolving **intragroup conflict** by stimulating intragroup cohesiveness through the introduction of a common, **superordinate goal** that is attractive to both parties. When a group is split over some minor issue, introducing a more important superordinate goal may draw the two sides together as they strive to attain the common end. For example, commissioned salespersons in the men's clothing section of a large chain department store were constantly fighting over who would be the first to grab a customer who walked into the area. The manager helped to resolve much of this conflict by introducing a bonus program that pitted the department's overall sales against those of men's departments in other stores. By focusing on pooled sales figures, the employees became oriented toward beating the other stores rather than beating each other.

Managers can also help resolve conflict in group decision making (Conlon & Ross, 1993). For example, they may use their authority to call an issue to a vote,

Collaboration
a conflict resolution strategy in which the parties cooperate to reach a solution that satisfies both

Avoidance
withdrawing from or avoiding a conflict situation

 Stop & Review
Define the five individual conflict resolution strategies.

Intragroup Conflict
conflict that arises when a person or faction within a group attempts to achieve a goal that interferes with the group's goal attainment

Superordinate Goal
a goal that two conflicting parties are willing to work to attain

which means that the majority of workers will win the conflict situation. However, there may be a disgruntled minority of losers, who may then carry on the conflict by refusing to follow the elected plan or by some other means. The manager will need to deal with this residual conflict if it is deemed serious enough to require resolution.

The key to successful conflict resolution from the managerial perspective is to maintain a broad perspective, trying to find a workable solution and considering the potential side effects, such as disgruntled losers, that may result from the resolution process.

In certain situations, such as when group members appear to have become complacent and disinterested in work activities, managers may feel that some specific types of conflict are needed. A number of strategies can be used to stimulate conflict. One tactic is simply to ask for it. Asking employees for their suggestions or for complaints about the organization and its policies may lead to some conflict as employees critically evaluate the organization and management. However, it is hoped that this type of conflict will lead to constructive change and improvement. When top management feels that work groups have become too cohesive, to the detriment of the groups' energy and motivational levels, they may decide to break up that cohesiveness and inject a little stimulating conflict by making personnel changes such as bringing in new employees or rotating workers to different departments or work sites. Restaurant and retail chains use this strategy when they rotate managers among stores.

Sales or performance competition programs are another way of stimulating some positive group conflict. The key to a successful competition program, however, is to ensure that members do not engage in dysfunctional behaviors, such as sabotaging others' work activities, in an effort to win the competition. Ideally, a good program should allow all participants to achieve a goal. For example, a bonus should be given to each employee who reaches a certain performance level, instead of only to the top performer (Blake et al., 1964).

A widely used conflict stimulation strategy that can often lead to positive outcomes is to move from centralized decision-making procedures to a group decision-making process, in which all group members have a say in certain work-related issues. Although this automatically increases conflict by allowing each worker to state his or her opinion and argue for a particular course of action, it is presumed that this type of conflict will yield positive results because it allows for consideration of a wider range of plans and greater critiquing of the various possible decisions.

Stop & Review

Compare and contrast competition and conflict.

Cohesiveness

Cohesiveness
the degree of attraction among group members

Cohesiveness refers simply to the amount or degree of attraction among group members. Cohesiveness is like the social "glue" that holds people together in groups. It is cohesiveness that explains the team spirit that many work groups possess. It is generally assumed that cohesive groups are more satisfied and more productive than noncohesive groups because their members tend to interact more, participate more fully in group activities, and accept and work toward the groups' goals (Rios & Mackey, 2020). In fact, however, although cohesive groups are usually more satisfied than noncohesive groups, the relationship between cohesiveness and productivity is rather weak (Gully et al., 1995). That is because, typically, for a cohesive group to be productive, the reason for the cohesiveness must be work-related (Klein & Mulvey, 1995). For example, groups with strong, work-related norms, such as willingness to work overtime and workers taking personal responsibility for doing a good job, had higher group performance than work teams without such strong work-related norms (Langfred, 1998). However, a group may be cohesive yet have as a goal to do as little work as possible. In this case, cohesiveness is high, and group satisfaction may be high, but productivity is likely to be very low (Tziner, 1982). For example, one study found that workers who were highly cohesive spent a great deal of time maintaining their interpersonal relationships, presumably resulting in a loss of productivity (Wise, 2014).

Because group cohesiveness is theoretically linked to member satisfaction and, under certain circumstances, productivity, there has been considerable research on the factors that increase group cohesiveness. The most important of these factors are the size of the group, the equality of status of members, member stability, member similarity, and the existence of a common threat or enemy.

Generally, the smaller the group, the more cohesive and the more satisfied its members. This makes sense, because small groups offer many more chances to interact with members and to form closer ties than do large groups (Forsyth, 2006). As smaller businesses become larger, gaining more and more employees, cohesiveness often declines. Older workers often lament the strong cohesiveness of the earlier, smaller work group ("In the old days it used to be like a family around here"). Therefore, one way to regain some of the cohesiveness would be to break the large group into smaller work teams.

The more equivalent the status of group members, the greater the cohesiveness generally (Cartwright, 1968). When a status hierarchy exists, the lower-status members may feel resentful of those of higher status, which leads to disharmony. Conversely, the higher-status members may try to use their authority to direct or control the activities of the lower-status members, which can also erode group cohesiveness. Many team approaches, such as job enrichment, attempt to eliminate status differences in groups to increase cohesiveness. For example, in many job enrichment programs, team members are all given the same work classification and job title.

The stability of group membership can also have positive effects on cohesiveness (Forsyth, 2006). Generally, the more stable the membership, the more time members have to develop strong ties with one another. New members may often disrupt group harmony because they are unaware of group norms and may unwittingly violate them as they try to learn the ropes. Thus, high rates of member turnover and the presence of many new members can be detrimental to group cohesiveness (Figure 11.4).

Another factor that affects group cohesiveness is the similarity of group members. The more similar the characteristics of the group members, the more cohesive the

Figure 11.4 Groups, like this trio of engineers, that are smaller in size and have equivalent status and stability among group members are more cohesive.

Source: Photograph by ThisisEngineering RAEng, found on Unsplash (https://unsplash.com/photos/5W43yn8z2-A).

group is likely to be. If members have similar backgrounds, education, and attitudes, it is reasonable to assume that they will develop closer ties to one another. Years of research on group processes indicate that member similarity is a very powerful force in determining social ties: we tend to be attracted to, and establish close relationships with, persons who are similar to us (Forsyth, 2006; Jackson et al., 1991). It is important to emphasize, however, that similarity of group members can limit a group's potential to be creative and to innovate, as similar members may tend to "think alike." Research has emphasized that group member diversity can lead to more creative, innovative, and perhaps more productive work groups (Rogelberg & Rumery, 1996).

The presence of an external threat or enemy can likewise increase the cohesiveness of a work group (Shaw, 1981). When a group perceives itself as under attack, the members tend to pull together. Cohesiveness of this type is often referred to as the **we–they feeling** ("We're the good guys, they're the bad guys"). Often, small, up-and-coming companies will characterize large competitor companies as "threatening" or even "evil," in an effort to increase cohesiveness of workers as they try to overcome the ominous giant company that threatens the smaller company's, and its workers', very existence. The smaller company is hoping that the increased cohesiveness will result in greater productivity as the workers pull together in an effort to beat the competition. Unfortunately, within organizations, this we–they feeling often develops between the workers and management. This can lead to increased cohesiveness within the work group but can be disruptive in coordinated efforts to achieve organizational goals if the workers perceive management as the enemy.

In sum, all these factors tend to increase group cohesiveness, which can in turn be related to improved work outcomes, particularly increased levels of member satisfaction and organizational commitment and reduced rates of absenteeism and turnover (Wech et al., 1998). Moreover, regardless of the actual relationship between group cohesiveness and group productivity, many managers believe that cohesiveness is critical for work group success. And, if part of the reason for the work group's cohesiveness is task-related, then cohesive groups are usually high-performing groups (Carless & De Paola, 2000).

We–They Feeling
intragroup cohesiveness created by the existence of a common threat, which is typically another group

Summary

A *group* is two or more individuals engaged in social interaction to achieve some goal. *Teams* consist of interdependent workers with complementary skills working toward a shared goal or outcome. Within work groups, members play various *roles*, which are patterns of behavior adopted based on expectations held about the function of a position. Individuals may experience *role conflict*, including *work–family conflict*. Work groups also develop *norms*, or rules, to help govern member behavior. The process of *organizational socialization* refers to the **integration** of individuals into work groups and organizations through learning work procedures, work roles, and organizational and group norms. Individuals play a part in their own socialization, as do coworkers. Organizations also aid in the socialization process. *New employee orientation* is an important part of the socialization process.

Certain basic processes occur in all work groups. Two common yet opposing forces that are evident in all groups are cooperation and competition. *Cooperation* is critical to coordinating the activities of work group members. However, *social loafing* can occur when workers in groups put in less effort than they would when working alone. *Competition* can lead to *conflict*, which is behavior by one party that is designed to inhibit the goal attainment of another party. It can arise from various sources, most notably from a scarcity of desired resources and from individual and group interdependence. The effect of conflict can be both positive and negative: it is positive when it motivates workers or stimulates them to be creative or innovative and negative

Integration
the amount and quality of collaboration among the divisions of an organization

when it disrupts group work activities and social relationships. Managing conflict involves regulating the level of conflict, resolving it when it is negative, and stimulating it when it is positive or productive. A number of conflict resolution and conflict stimulation strategies are used in organizations.

Another basic process, *cohesiveness*, is the degree of attraction among group members. A number of factors, such as group size, member status, member stability, and member similarity, can influence group cohesiveness.

Study Questions and Exercises

1 Consider a work or social group of which you are a member. What are the various roles that members play? What roles have you played? What are some of the norms that are particular to this group?
2 Think about what you have felt like when you first started a new job and how important employee socialization can be. What are the elements that are going to lead to better organizational socialization for new employees?
3 In what ways can group cohesiveness facilitate goal attainment in work groups? How might cohesiveness hinder goal attainment?
4 Discuss the ways in which cohesiveness and conflict can be seen as opposite forces in work groups.
5 What are some of the potential positive and negative outcomes of conflict? Using a work or social group with which you have had contact, think of examples of conflict that led to negative outcomes. How might these situations have been managed to reduce their negative impact?

Web Link

https://donforsythgroups.wordpress.com/
A group dynamics site designed to accompany Forsyth's text on group dynamics.

Suggested Readings

Coleman, P. T., Deutsch, M., & Marcus, E. C. (2014). *The handbook of conflict resolution: Theory and practice* (3rd ed.). San Francisco: Jossey-Bass. *An accessible, but scholarly review of research on conflict and its resolution that also has implications for practice.*

Ellis, A. M., Nifadkar, S. S., Bauer, T. N., & Erdogan, B. (2017). Newcomer adjustment: Examining the role of managers' perception of newcomer proactive behavior during organizational socialization. *Journal of Applied Psychology, 102*(6), 993.

Gardner, D. M., & Alanis, J. M. (2020). Together we stand: Ally training for discrimination and harassment reduction. *Industrial and Organizational Psychology, 13*(2), 196–199.

Kossek, E. K., Odle-Dusseau, H. N., & Hammer, L. B. (2018). Family-supportive supervision around the globe. In K. M. Shockley, W. Shen, & R. C. Johnson (Eds.), *The Cambridge handbook of the global work–family interface* (pp. 570–596). Cambridge: Cambridge University Press.

CHAPTER 12

Decision Making in Groups

Inside Tips

DECISION MAKING IN GROUPS

This chapter is an extension of Chapter 11's discussion of decision making as individuals and groups. Keep in mind the fact that interdependence is a key factor that differentiates a team from a group. Many of the issues involved in group decision making are complex. Groups can sometimes make errors in decision making that result in more extreme outcomes than those made by individuals. Further, the concept of groupthink, with its many interrelated symptoms, merits attention—it is quite complicated, but pulls from the work on groups discussed in the previous chapter. In addition to these two forms of decision-making errors, we will examine errors related to conformity and how conformity can result in unethical decision making. Finally, we will dive into the very important topic of ethical decision making, whether it be in groups or individuals.

You have been working with your colleagues for several years and you really feel like a cohesive team—you all get along, often socialize together, and share a common sense of purpose and dedication to the company. But recently, some of your team members have become upset with management and they want to send it a message. You show up for work on a Wednesday and find out that your team has made a decision to purposely slow down their work output so that management will realize how important they are. You wonder how and when this decision was made because you have always been in the loop on other team decisions. You start to ask around about the decision-making process and why the decision was made and you worry that the team might be doing the wrong thing.

DOI: 10.4324/9781003143987-16

Decision Making

Every day we are faced with the task of making a multitude of decisions. Some of these we will make as individuals. Others we will make as part of a group. Here, we discuss both individual and group decision making. There is a great deal of research in psychology, more generally, on how decisions get made, but we, as industrial/organizational psychologists, are more focused on the decision making that takes place in actual work settings (Bonaccio et al., 2010). Decision making is a critical part of nearly all organizational practices, whether it be deciding which employee to hire, what training to deliver, or when and how to evaluate employees' performance. What makes the study of decision making in organizations particularly challenging is the gap between how employees *should* make decisions and how they are typically made.

A recent review of the decision-making literature highlights some of the key dichotomies in making decisions (Adinolfi, 2021). For example, the rational decision-making model provides the steps that individuals should take to make a logical decision including: identifying the problem, establishing decision criteria, weighing the criteria, generating decision alternatives, evaluating those alternatives, and selecting the best decision based on the decision criteria you established. This is often the approach used by economists; psychologists, however, do not assume that this is the reality of how decisions are made. If you think about how you selected a college or graduate program, you can imagine going through these steps using some type of spreadsheet. In the end, however, which college do most people attend? The one that feels right. In contrast to the rational decision-making model, this would be considered the intuitive approach to decision making.

In addition to the fact that we often just want to "go with our gut" (i.e., follow the intuitive approach), heuristics and biases can cloud our judgment. In this text, we talk about many heuristics and biases that introduce gender and racial biases into organizations. However, there are many other biases that shape our decisions. As Adinolfi (2021) covers in her review, the seemingly irrational decisions that people make can often be explained by well-established theories of decision making. For example, we know that individuals are vulnerable to escalation of commitment and a desire to appear consistent in their decision making, so that we often stick with poor decisions long after we know that they are problematic. We are also extremely loss averse, so that, in many circumstances, we would rather avoid loss than experience gain. Imagine if you randomly chose a seat in a classroom and another student approached you and asked if they could have your seat. For most people, the immediate reaction would be to hold on to your seat, fearing that it has some inherent value that you absentmindedly acquired but don't want to lose. If the person offered you a dollar for the seat, you may see the seat as even more valuable and refuse to move. On the other hand, if this same student approached you before you sat and asked you if you would rather have seat A (the seat you chose) or seat B (an adjacent seat), most people would respond with, "I don't care."

These are all considered unprogrammed decisions—those for which there is no well-defined course of action. In organizations, however, many of the decisions we make are programmed, which means we are following outlined procedures for what we are supposed to do in a certain circumstance. Three dimensions define the characteristics of each strategy. The *routine–nonroutine* dimension describes whether the decision is common or unusual. The *recurring–nonrecurring* dimension describes whether the decision happens often or infrequently. The *certainty–uncertainty* dimension describes the degree of predictability of the decision. Organizations establish formal policies and procedures that are intended to make decisions easier by providing a programmed course of action.

So, what can be done to improve decision making? In addition to the ideas covered in this chapter for how to improve decision making in groups, Dalal et al. (2010) offer these evidence-based suggestions for making better decisions.

1 When deciding between alternatives, consider the benefits of your less-favored choice rather than your implicit favorite.
2 Identify similarities and differences between different alternatives rather than acting as if they are opposite ends of the decision-making spectrum.
3 Take the average judgment of a diverse group of experts (see the "wisdom of the crowd" discussion later in this chapter).
4 Use simple statistical models based on experts to make decisions, rather than having the actual experts make decisions.

Group Decision-Making Processes

Just as individual decision making is important, decision making is one of the most important tasks that groups accomplish. Group decision making includes establishing group goals, choosing among various courses of action, selecting new members, and determining standards of appropriate behavior. The processes by which groups make these decisions have been of interest to I/O psychologists for many years. We will examine the different types of decision-making processes here (see Figure 12.1).

Groups can make work-related decisions in a number of ways. The simplest and most straightforward strategy, known as **autocratic decision making**, is when the group leader makes decisions alone, using only the information that the leader possesses. The major advantage of autocratic decision making is that it is fast. Decisions are made quickly by the leader and are then expected to be carried out by group members. However, because the decision is made based only on what the leader knows, the quality of the decision may suffer. For example, suppose a leader of a group of accountants has to decide which accounting software to order. If the leader actually knows which program is the best for the group, there will be no drawback to

Autocratic Decision Making
a process by which group decisions are made by the leader alone, based on information the leader possesses

Figure 12.1 Although consensus decision results are effective for ensuring that all group members agree with the final decision, it can be slower than democratic decision making, which is slower than autocratic decision making.

Source: Photograph by Hello I'm Nik, found on Unsplash (https://unsplash.com/photos/73_kRz s9sqo).

the autocratic approach. If, however, the leader cannot make an informed choice, the decision may be faulty. In this case, input from the group members would be helpful. A variation on the strict autocratic decision-making approach occurs when the leader solicits information from group members to assist in reaching a decision, but still holds the final say. This is sometimes referred to as *consultative decision making*. In the software decision, soliciting input from group members about which systems they favor might lead to a higher-quality decision (and to greater acceptance of the decision by the group members).

A very different strategy is **democratic decision making**, in which all group members are allowed to discuss the decision and then vote on a particular course of action. Typically, democratic decision making is based on majority rule. One advantage of this approach is that decisions are made using the pooled knowledge and experience of all the group members. Moreover, because all members have a chance to voice an opinion or suggest a different course of action, a greater number of alternatives are considered. Also, because group members have a role in the decision making, they are more likely to follow the chosen course.

The most obvious drawback to democratic decision making is that it is time-consuming. Because it encourages conflict, it can also be inefficient. Although the democratic, majority-rule approach results in a satisfied majority who will back the decision, there may be a disgruntled minority who resist its implementation.

Democratic Decision Making
a strategy by which decisions are made by the group members based on majority-rule voting

Consensus

decision making based on 100% member agreement

A strategy that overcomes some of the weaknesses of democratic decision making is to make decisions based on **consensus**, which means that all group members have agreed on the chosen course of action. Because consensus decision making is especially time-consuming, it is usually used only for very important decisions. For example, juries use this strategy because the decision affects the freedom and future of the accused. Some company executive boards may strive for a consensus when making major decisions about changes in the direction of the organization or in organizational structure or company policy. As you might imagine, the outcome of consensus decision making is usually a high-quality, highly critiqued decision, backed by all members of the group.

The obvious drawback is the tremendous amount of time it may take for the group to reach a consensus. In fact, in many situations, arriving at a consensus may be impossible, particularly if one or more group members are strongly resistant to the majority's decision (the courtroom analogy would be a "hung" jury). Of course, in some situations, it may appear that the group has reached a consensus, but not all members have completely agreed and may have lingering doubts—a sort of "false consensus" (Haug, 2015).

Effectiveness of Group Decision Making

Organizations often rely on group strategies for making important work-related decisions. Part of this is fueled by beliefs in the inherent advantages of group over individual decision making. However, although group decision making has many positive aspects, it also has some drawbacks (see Table 12.1). The key is to know not only how group-made decisions can be more effective than those made by individuals, but also when group decision making is superior.

As mentioned, the major advantage of group decision making is that it offers increased knowledge and experience on which to base the decision. But do groups actually make better decisions than individuals? Decades of research do give the edge to group decision making, on the average. The average group will make a higher-quality decision than the average individual. However, some research indicates that the best decision-making individual—one who possesses all the information needed to make a high-quality decision—will be able to perform as well as or better than

Table 12.1 Advantages and Disadvantages of Group Decision Making.

Advantages	Disadvantages
Works from a broad knowledge base	Slow (can be a problem in crisis situations)
Decision is accepted by members	Creates intragroup conflict
Decision is highly critiqued	Potential for groupthink and group polarization
Aspects of the problem can be divided among group members	Certain members, such as leaders, may dominate the decision-making process

a group (Hill, 1982). In other circumstances, groups may arrive at decisions that are superior to even those made by the group's best decision maker (Michaelsen et al., 1989). Moreover, certain members, such as a group leader or respected individual, may have more influence in affecting the outcome and may be able to sway a group toward accepting a particular course of action. If the influential member is not knowledgeable or well informed about the alternatives, however, the group may be led to make a poor decision.

We have also seen that group decision making tends to be slower than individual decision making, which can be a problem in situations such as an emergency or crisis.

At these times, it may be better for an individual to take charge and make decisions for the group (Tjosvold, 1984). However, if a problem is complex and multifaceted, with many steps required to arrive at a decision, a group may make the decision faster than an individual, because the various aspects of the problem can be divided among group members.

Perhaps the strongest argument in support of group decision making is that it tends to lead to increased member satisfaction and greater member commitment to the course of action than does individual decision making. But what happens if the group-made decision is a bad one? Research indicates that, when this occurs, members may increase their commitment to the poor decision (Bazerman et al., 1984). If the poor decision was made by an individual, group members will not be as committed and may be more likely to see its faults and try another course of action.

Group members may also be widely distributed geographically. As a result, there has been an increase in electronic decision-making meetings (Askew & Coovert, 2013), and this was especially true in 2020 amidst the COVID-19 pandemic. A meta-analysis that compared decision making in face-to-face versus computer-mediated groups suggested that face-to-face groups were perceived as more effective and more efficient, with group members feeling more satisfied than the computer-mediated decision-making groups (Baltes et al., 2002).

ON THE *CUTTING* EDGE

Virtual Teams

As mentioned earlier, the COVID-19 pandemic shut down businesses across the globe, causing many employees to start working from home (Figure 12.2). This meant that those who used to work in a face-to-face environment got a crash course in how to work on a virtual team. Even though the use of virtual teams has been slowly increasing over the last several decades, Newman and Ford (2021) reported that 67% of people were working from home for the first time during the pandemic. They also offered several suggestions on how to most effectively manage a virtual team.

Step 1: Recognize that things have changed. This requires greater empathy and understanding for the fact that not only are individuals learning to do something new (working from home), but they are doing so amidst a

ON THE *CUTTING* EDGE (*continued*)

host of other demands. Managers should set weekly one-on-one calls with each direct report and a weekly call with the team as a whole. In addition, new norms for communication should be established, and new goals should be set. Each meeting should start with two questions: "How's everyone doing?" and "Are you having any problems I can help you with?"

Step 2: Build trust. Effort should be taken to maintain and build trust and sustain the team's culture. The first step here is ensuring employees have needed technology and technology support. Organizations may consider offering additional support for work–family conflict. Teams should work to help team members feel included and that it is safe to learn, contribute, and suggest changes. In addition, consider creating some cultural rites and rituals (such as social events or celebrations) adapted to a virtual environment.

Step 3: Improve communication. Leader communication should be increased—ideally to once a day. This could be done by conversations, instant messaging, e-mail, blogs or newsletters, or business social media applications such as Yammer or Slack. Communication should also be predictable so that employees know what to expect by responding quickly and clearly.

Step 4: Share leadership. Leaders should empower employees to take on more leadership, similar to a self-managed work team. This might require team members to receive training on how to do leadership tasks and does require that the manager understands the strengths and skills of each team member so the right roles are assigned to each member. Collaboration and shared responsibility for work outcomes are keys to the success of virtual teams.

Step 5: Survey success. Finally, leaders should periodically survey employees or conduct audits to ensure that the above practices are being followed and are being received as intended, and that the team is healthy.

Creating effective teams can be challenging in the best of circumstances. Creating effective virtual teams might be a bit more challenging. Creating effective virtual teams overnight during a pandemic was indeed a crisis. But the steps above are really helpful in creating more effective teams in any circumstance.

In summary, although group decision making has certain limitations, it offers many advantages over individual decision making, particularly in improving the quality of decisions and increasing the commitment to decisions once they are made. Trends toward greater use of teams and encouraging greater involvement of workers in organizational processes mean that group decision making is likely to increase in the future (De Dreu & West, 2001).

Group Decision Making Gone Awry: Groupthink and Group Polarization

When making important work decisions, particularly those that have a major impact on the work procedures or working lives of group members, group decision making may be preferred over decision making by high-ranking members of the organization.

Figure 12.2 During the COVID-19 pandemic, most employees worked virtually, and those who met in person were required to wear masks and stay 6 feet apart.

Source: Photograph by Cherrydeck, found on Unsplash (https://unsplash.com/photos/PH8Ccg q3mvk).

This is done in an effort to increase the amount of relevant information available and to encourage member commitment to the eventually chosen course. However, psychologists have discovered two situations in which the usual advantages of group decision making may not be forthcoming: one is known as group polarization and the other is groupthink.

Group Polarization

The quality of group decisions may also be adversely affected by **group polarization**, or the tendency for groups to make decisions that are more extreme than those made by individuals (Myers & Lamm, 1976). Early research found evidence of the effects of group polarization when decisions carried a high degree of risk. In these studies, individuals were asked to make a decision between an attractive but risky course of action and one that was less attractive but also less risky. After making the decision, the respondents were put into groups and asked to come up with a group decision. It was found that the groups tended to make riskier decisions than the average individual (Wallach et al., 1962). This effect became known as the "risky shift" and was the topic of much research and theorizing. It had major implications for the making

Group Polarization
the tendency for groups to make decisions that are more extreme than those made by individuals

of important decisions in business and government because it suggested that group decisions might be more dangerous than decisions made by individuals. However, subsequent research began to challenge these early findings, failing to find a risky shift in some decision-making groups and occasionally finding evidence of a cautious shift. What we now know is that group discussion often leads individuals to become more extreme in their opinions about the topic.

The attitudes and opinions of individuals who favor an idea tend to become even more positive after group discussion, whereas those who do not favor an idea tend to develop opinions that are even more negative (Isenberg, 1986).

How does group polarization relate to decisions made in work situations, and why does it occur? Imagine that a company must choose which of several new products it should introduce. Some of the products are costly to develop and market, but, if successful, they could bring large profits. Other products are less costly but will lead to smaller financial gains. An individual who makes the decision might choose to introduce a product of medium-level risk and payoff. However, if the person is put into a group that is leaning toward marketing a risky product, the group's decision would be more extreme than the individual's decision. If, on the other hand, the group is leaning toward the side of caution, the group might shift to a more cautious choice than the typical individual would choose. One study suggests that board of directors' decisions to give high chief executive officer (CEO) compensation may be due to a group polarization effect (Zhu, 2014). Additional research suggests that virtual groups may be even more prone to group polarization than face-to-face groups (Sia et al., 2002).

Two explanations for group polarization have been offered. The first is that, in the group, the individual is presented with persuasive arguments by other members that bolster the individual's original positive or negative stance on an issue. After hearing others in the group argue for a decision that coincides with the individual's opinion, he or she becomes more certain that his or her opinion is correct, and there is a tendency for the group as a whole to become more extreme in its final decision. The other explanation is that individuals adopt the values of the group. If the group presents a positive opinion on an issue, the individuals go along with the group, becoming even more positive (or negative) about an idea than they would be alone. Individuals may support the viewpoint of the group to demonstrate that they endorse the group's values.

Regardless of why it occurs, the fact that some group decisions may be more extreme than those of individuals is a reason for some concern, particularly when a decision involves risks that may compromise the goals of the group, or when extremely cautious decisions inhibit the attainment of group goals.

Despite the persistence of group polarization, there are potential safeguards that may minimize its effect on decision making. Evidence has indicated that groups composed of individuals who all initially agree on an issue, before any group discussion has taken place, tend to make decisions that are the most extreme. That is, these decisions tend to be even more extreme than decisions made by groups composed of members who do not initially agree with one another (Williams & Levy, 1992). Thus, when groups include members who have varying original opinions on an issue, the decisions made by those groups may be more resistant to the effects of group polarization and, thus, less extreme. The presence of even a single dissenting member

Stop & Review

Describe the advantages and disadvantages of group decision making.

in a group may help to combat group polarization, just as a "devil's advocate" can help combat groupthink, as we will see.

Groupthink

Groups generally arrive at high-quality decisions because the alternative courses of action have been subjected to critical evaluation. This is particularly true in consensus decision making, because even one dissenting member can argue against a plan favored by all the rest. There is, however, an exception to this rule. A complex set of circumstances can sometimes occur in consensus decision making that retards the critical evaluation process. What results is a complete backfiring of the normal, critical decision making that results in a premature, hasty, and often catastrophic decision. This situation is termed **groupthink**. Groupthink is a syndrome that occurs in highly cohesive decision-making groups, where a norm develops to arrive at an early consensus, thereby reducing the effectiveness of the group's ability to make high-quality, critical decisions.

Groupthink
a syndrome characterized by a concurrence-seeking tendency that overrides the ability of a cohesive group to make critical decisions

The concept of groupthink was researched by psychologist Irving Janis (1972). According to Janis, groupthink usually occurs only in highly cohesive groups in which the members' desire to maintain cohesiveness overrides the sometimes uncomfortable and disruptive process of critical decision making. A course of action is laid out on the table, and, without it being adequately critiqued, the members rapidly move toward a consensus to adopt the plan. Despite Janis's assertion that groupthink usually only occurs in highly cohesive groups, research suggests that it is groups whose cohesiveness is "relationship-based" that are more prone to groupthink than groups whose cohesiveness is "task-based," or related to the decision-making and performance goals of the group (Bernthal & Insko, 1993).

In developing his theory of groupthink, Janis studied a number of poor decisions made by high-level decision-making groups, such as U.S. presidential administrations and boards of directors of large companies, the consequences of which were so bad that Janis labeled the outcomes "fiascoes." Janis investigated a number of historical fiascoes, such as the Kennedy administration's failed Bay of Pigs invasion, the Truman administration's decision to cross the 38th parallel in the Korean War, and the Johnson administration's decision to escalate the Vietnam War. He also studied catastrophic business decisions, such as the decision to market the drug thalidomide, which led to thousands of birth deformities; the Buffalo Mining Company's decision about dam construction, which caused the deaths of 125 people; and the Ford Motor Company's decision to market the Edsel, one of the greatest failures in U.S. automotive history (Wheeler & Janis, 1980). In more recent history, researchers have studied NASA's catastrophic decision to launch the *Challenger* space shuttle (Esser, 1998), the Bush administration's decision to invade Iraq (Mitz & Wayne, 2014), and the torture of Iraqi prisoners by the U.S. military in Abu Ghraib (Post & Panis, 2011). By studying the decision-making processes in each early case of groupthink, Janis noticed certain similarities that he has termed the "symptoms of groupthink"—specific group factors that work toward preventing the critical evaluation usually present in decision-making groups (see Table 12.2).

To understand how the symptoms of groupthink interfere with critical decision-making processes, consider the following example. A board of directors of an international air freight service must decide whether the company should enter a cost-cutting war with its competitors. The board begins its decision-making meeting with the chairperson's loaded question, "Should we enter into this foolish price war, or just keep rates the way they are?" By labeling the price war as "foolish," the chairperson has already indicated her preferred course of action: keep the rates as they are. Normally, the critical decision-making process would involve a great deal of discussion about the relative strengths and weaknesses of the various alternatives, and the decision that would result should be of high quality. However, in groupthink situations, this does not occur. The symptoms of groupthink, themselves manifestations of such basic group processes as cohesiveness, stereotyped and rationalized views, and conformity, can counteract the critical evaluations that should be made. If groupthink does indeed occur, the consequences may be devastating, particularly because the group believes that the chosen action is the result of a critical and well-conducted decision-making process, when it is not.

If groupthink takes place at the air freight company, the board of directors would likely manifest three symptoms—the *illusion of invulnerability*, the *illusion of morality*, and the presence of *shared negative stereotypes*—that result from the we–they feeling that is typically present in highly cohesive groups. The members believe that they and

Table 12.2 The Eight Symptoms of Groupthink

---

1 *Illusion of invulnerability*—The highly cohesive decision-making group members see themselves as powerful and invincible. Their attraction to and faith in the group leads them to ignore the potential disastrous outcomes of their decision.

2 *Illusion of morality*—Members believe in the moral correctness of the group and its decision; related to the first symptom. Derived from the we–they feeling, members view themselves as the "good guys" and the opposition as bad or evil.

3 *Shared negative stereotypes*—Members have common beliefs that minimize the risks involved in a decision or belittle any opposing viewpoints.

4 *Collective rationalizations*—The members explain away any negative information that runs counter to the group decision.

5 *Self-censorship*—Members suppress their own doubts or criticisms concerning the decision.

6 *Illusion of unanimity*—Members mistakenly believe that the decision is a consensus. Because dissenting viewpoints are not being voiced, it is assumed that silence indicates support.

7 *Direct conformity pressure*—When an opposing view or a doubt is expressed, pressure is applied to get the dissenter to concur with the decision.

8 *Mindguards*—Some members play the role of protecting or insulating the group from any opposing opinions or negative information.

---

their organization are powerful and good. Negative stereotypes about nonmembers or other groups (the enemy) also stem from the we–they feeling. Examples of these three symptoms might be seen in the board members' statements that they believe the group and the company are invulnerable ("We're the number one company in this business") and morally good ("We always provide the best possible service to our customers"). Other comments suggest that they hold shared negative stereotypes about the competition ("With their inept management and poor equipment, they will never be able to offer the kind of service that we do"). These three groupthink symptoms thus begin a tendency toward seeking concurrence, as the members strive to stick together and agree with one another (Janis, 1972).

Additional groupthink symptoms—*collective rationalizations* of opposing viewpoints, a tendency for members to engage in *self-censorship*, and the *illusion of unanimity*—lead the group to arrive at a premature consensus. Suppose that one of the board members suggests an alternative to the plan to keep rates as they are that the board is moving toward adopting. The dissenter wants to keep rates the same while starting an advertising campaign that tells customers, "You get what you pay for," thus emphasizing the company's higher quality of service. Collective rationalizations of members immediately put down the alternative plan ("People never listen to advertisements anyway" and "That will cost us more than lowering our rates!"). Other board members may see the merit in the alternative plan, but, because it appears that most of the others, because of their silence, do not like it, they engage in self-censorship and keep their opinions to themselves. The fact that no one speaks up leads to the illusion of unanimity, the misconception that everybody is for the original plan.

If dissenters do speak up, two additional groupthink symptoms operate to stifle the critical decision-making process even further. *Direct conformity pressure* might be applied to force dissenters to keep their opinions to themselves and not break up the group's agreement. Some members may even play the role of *mindguards* by taking it on themselves to keep dissenting opinions from reaching the ears of the group leader and other members. The member advocating the advertisement plan, for example, might be told by a self-appointed mindguard to not bring the plan up again, "for the good of the group."

Janis believes that groupthink can be combated by breaking up some of the cohesiveness of the group through the interjection of productive conflict. This might involve using strategies such as bringing in outsiders to offer different viewpoints or having some members play the role of critical evaluators—"devil's advocates"—who are highly critical of any plan of action that is brought before the group (Schweiger et al., 1986). Similarly, a group norm that encourages critical evaluation will help prevent groupthink (Postmes et al., 2001). Also, because groupthink is partly brought on by a sense of time urgency, if the group begins with the idea that they need to come up with the best possible decision, regardless of how long it takes, groupthink may be avoided (Chapman, 2006). Härtel (1998) suggested that holding individual group members accountable and reducing pressures to conform will help combat groupthink. Baron (2005) suggested that groupthink may occur quite frequently in all sorts of decision-making groups.

⏱ Stop & Review

List and define six symptoms of groupthink.

Conformity

Conformity
the process of adhering to
group norms

A concept closely related to groupthink is conformity. **Conformity** is the process of adhering to group norms (which we discussed in the last chapter). Because these norms are so important to a group's identity and activities, groups exert considerable pressure on members to follow them. Violation can result in subtle or overt pressure to comply with the rules, which can take the form of a look of disapproval, verbal criticism, or isolation of the offending individual (giving the person the "silent treatment"). Once the violator conforms to the norm, the pressure is removed, and the person is again included in normal group activities. Generally, conformity to norms is very strong and helps maintain order and uniformity in the group's behavior.

Because pressure to conform to group norms is so strong, we need to consider the circumstances in which an individual might choose to violate a norm. Usually, someone will not conform to a group norm if the individual's goals are different from those of the group. For example, imagine that a manufacturing group has a norm of steady but less-than-optimal production. If a worker within the group wants to be noticed by management as an exceptionally hard worker who would be a good candidate for a promotion to a supervisory position, that person might break the group's production rate norm. Of course, the group will exert pressure in an effort to get the "rate buster" to conform. Extreme and repeated cases of norm violation may eventually lead to ostracism from the group (Rudert et al., 2020). Even individuals who are trying to do the right thing by whistleblowing (going outside of the organization to try to stop bad corporate behavior) can be ostracized if they are seen as violating norms (Curtis et al., 2020). Generally, members who have more power and influence in the group, such as the leader, will have a better chance of resisting the group's conformity pressure and persuading the group to change or eliminate the norm. Also, if the violator has a past history of being a "good," conforming member, the nonconformity will be tolerated more and have a better chance of being accepted by the group than if it is done by a member known for repeated norm violations (Feldman, 1984).

Although conforming to group norms is typically functional in a work setting, conformity can also give rise to poor decision making such as evidenced in groupthink. Moreover, conformity pressure may attempt to get members to engage in undesirable, counterproductive, or even unethical behavior (see the section on ethical decision making later in this chapter). Conformity has been blamed for many unethical decisions where high-profile individuals have gotten away with horrible crimes. In addition, there is evidence that conformity among work group members can sometimes stifle individual innovation and creativity (Madjar et al., 2011), although diversity and brainstorming can diminish those negative effects.

Conformity and Unethical Decisions

Although there are many benefits of conformity for helping groups function, conformity carries the risk of promoting bad behavior. High performers and high-status individuals are often given freedom to deviate from norms of behavior—sometimes called *idiosyncrasy credits*. Bailey and Ferguson (2013) argue that the concept of idiosyncrasy credits provides an explanation for why extremely unethical behavior can go overlooked, such as the Sandusky scandal. In November 2011, Penn State assistant football coach Jerry Sandusky was accused and convicted of sexual abuse against young boys (Drape, 2012). Although many people had some insight into the crimes, Bailey and Ferguson (2013) argue that Sandusky had earned idiosyncrasy credits because of his success and prestige, so that, even when Sandusky's behavior came to light, many people tolerated the behavior and others conformed to that norm of silence. The authors specifically point to head coach Joe Paterno's reframing of the evident abuse as a "mental health issue." Thoroughgood and Padilla (2013) further add that, in addition to conformity, idiosyncrasy credits can also bring about colluders. Although conformers comply with a norm of silence, they do not actually engage in destructive behavior. In contrast, colluders engage in illegal actions to protect the perpetrator. This same type of protective behavior was evident in the #MeToo scandal, as certain known perpetrators such as movie producer Harvey Weinstein, who was eventually convicted of first-degree rape (Grady, 2020), were allowed to continue exhibiting illegal behavior while those around them turned a blind eye to or actively supported sexual crimes. Later in the chapter, we will discuss the importance of ethical decision making to avoid crimes such as those perpetrated by Sandusky, Weinstein, and many others.

Group Characteristics that Impact Decision Making

You may have heard the phrase that a team is more than the sum of its parts. Bringing people to work together creates dynamic processes that can be effective, or can result in poor decision making. We will review three group characteristics that impact decision making: the composition of individual team members, shared team mental models, and team diversity.

Team Composition

One factor that can impact the way teams make decisions is the composition of those on a team. Team composition involves the mix of traits, characteristics, and expertise among people on a team. Earlier in this text, we talked about how individual differences such as trait affectivity (the likelihood that one experiences positive or negative moods and emotions) and personality characteristics such as in the Big Five model (conscientiousness, extraversion, openness to experience, emotional stability, agreeableness) relate to job performance. Team composition researchers have examined how the homogeneity or heterogeneity of deep-level characteristics (such as personality) and surface-level characteristics (such as race and gender) impact team outcomes. Consider personality: you might imagine that a team full of extraverts might get off task owing to socializing. Teams that are full of agreeable members might be more likely to suffer from groupthink.

Another factor that is specific to teams is that team-level state can emerge based on the composition of team members (see Bell et al., 2018, for a review). Having one team member with high positive affect, for example, can actually increase other team members' positive affect, because moods and emotions can be contagious. Team affect is important as it can impact decision making (Brown & Stuhlmacher, 2020). Likewise, even if all members of the team are not high on conscientiousness, having at least one conscientious member on a team can help the team stay on track and meet deadlines.

When it comes to skills, however, the best teams have members whose skills complement one another's rather than just cloning the best team member. The same is true for perspectives and backgrounds, which is why surface-level diversity (such as race and gender) relates to improved team decision making. We will discuss diversity on teams later in this chapter.

Team Mental Models

Team Mental Models
team members' shared understanding of important aspects of common work goals

Team mental models reflect the extent to which team members are "on the same page" when it comes to their understanding of the team (Mohammed et al., 2010). These models include things such as work goals, performance requirements, teamwork norms, what needs to be accomplished, and how it should be accomplished. **Team mental models** explain how teams coordinate their efforts even when having to function in a complex, dynamic, and uncertain world (Cannon-Bowers et al., 1990). If you think of how athletes who play on a team know exactly where to stand to receive a pass or how surgical teams are able to effortlessly deal with crises, they clearly have team mental models that guide what needs to be done.

Not surprisingly, having a shared understanding positively impacts group performance (DeChurch & Mesmer-Magnus, 2010). One study examined 735 individuals on 161 teams who were participating in a management simulation. They found that shared mental models were related to lower conflict and higher creativity, which resulted in better team performance and team satisfaction (Santos et al., 2015).

However, much like concerns about conformity, scholars have argued that too much similarity on teams can result in a groupthink-type outcome where inaccurate views are accepted and mistakes are made. Converse and associates (Converse et al., 1993) ask, "at what point do team members' knowledge and expectations overlap so much that the uniqueness of their individual contributions is lost?" (p. 236). Likewise, research has suggested that team mental models are a "mixed blessing" for decision making, sometime causing declines in decision quality (Kellermanns et al., 2008).

Strategies to Improve Team Decision Making

With so many organizations using teams, and the risks associated with making poor decisions, there are steps to ensure team decision making is as effective as possible. Three themes for how to improve team decision making are: (1) structuring the decision-making process, (2) ensuring that teams have a diverse set of members, and (3) stressing the importance of ethical decision making. These efforts may not only improve the quality of decision outcomes to some extent, but also have other positive benefits such as improved employee attitudes (see "Up Close" box).

UP CLOSE How to Keep Teams Effective

Jay Galbraith (2008) provided a set of recommendations for creating effective teams that still holds true today:

1 *Team members should perceive their participation as important and personally rewarding*—To build commitment to the team, members must view their work as beneficial. One way to do this is to offer some sort of formal reward for contributions to the team.

2 *The work team should include some persons of organizational power who will be responsible for helping to implement any decisions made by the group*—If a team is to develop innovative strategies, it is important that these efforts are implemented. A key is to have some managers with organizational power as part of the work team to make sure that team suggestions are listened to and implemented.

3 *Team members should have knowledge and information relevant to the decision*—In any problem-solving work team, it is critical that members have job-related knowledge relevant to the decisions that are being made. This involves including lower-level workers who have firsthand experience with the job.

4 *Team members should have the authority to commit their respective departments to the decision*—The work team participants must be able to commit valuable resources (human and otherwise) to help in the successful implementation of the strategies developed by the team.

5 *Team members should represent and inform non-team workers*—If the problem-solving work team or committee is a select group of a larger body of workers, it is crucial that the team members inform nonteam members about the committee tasks and decisions.

6 *The influence of team members on decisions should be based on expertise*—This is especially important when members come from various levels in the organization. Work-related decisions should be based on relevant knowledge, not on organizational politics.

7 *Work team conflict should be managed to maximize the problem-solving process*—The conflict that arises in problem-solving committees should be functional and help to develop a high-level and highly critiqued course of action. It is important that such conflict be controlled to avoid dysfunctional outcomes.

UP CLOSE *(continued)*

8 *Team members should have good interpersonal skills and adequate leadership*—The success of a work team is going to be directly related to the smooth flow of communication among members. The better their interpersonal skills, the better the group's ability to reach high-quality decisions. It is also important for the team leader to take an appropriate but not too dominant role to facilitate team interaction and to help resolve nonproductive conflicts.

Utilize Brainstorming

Brainstorming
a group process generating creative ideas or solutions through a noncritical and nonjudgmental process

One common approach to improve decision making is **brainstorming**. In the 1950s, an advertising executive developed a technique to encourage groups to come up with creative ideas (Osborn, 1957). The technique, termed brainstorming, involved six to ten group members throwing out ideas in a noncritical and nonjudgmental atmosphere as a means of trying to generate as many creative ideas or solutions to a problem as possible. Since its invention, brainstorming has become quite popular, and tremendous claims have been made regarding its success. The basic rules in brainstorming sessions are as follows:

- No idea is too far out
- Criticism of any idea is not allowed
- The more ideas the better
- Members should try to build on each other's ideas.

The technique has been widely used in a variety of businesses, but does it work? Evidence from nearly 60 years of research indicates that, despite its popularity, brainstorming is not as effective as its proponents might lead one to believe (Kuhn, 2010). The problem is that, despite the rules, group dynamics are too powerful; the creativity of people in the brainstorming groups is often inhibited (Brown & Paulus, 1996). Research indicates that individuals are equal to or better than brainstorming groups in generating creative ideas. Asynchronous electronic brainstorming has been suggested as an alternative to reduce these concerns, but research has not supported the idea that electronic brainstorming is any more effective than normal brainstorming (Dornburg et al., 2009), and it is not always feasible to use it (Kuhn, 2010). What is extremely interesting, however, is that members of brainstorming groups firmly believe that the group brainstorming was more productive than individual brainstorming in terms of both the number and the quality of the ideas generated (Paulus & Dzindolet, 1993). In this way, group brainstorming may offer alternative benefits to teams, even if it does not always improve decision making (Kuhn, 2010).

Ensuring Adequate Team Diversity

As work groups become increasingly diverse, how might this diversity—in cultural and ethnic background, gender, and perspectives—influence group and team processes? As we might also expect from research on group dynamics and **personnel psychology**, gender and ethnic diversity can lead to the development of factions, such as when same-sex or same-race subgroups develop and impede the overall functioning of the group and discriminate against members of the other factions (Williams & O'Reilly III, 1998). Research shows that work groups that were more diverse in terms of gender, age, status, and work background/experience were evaluated as more effective groups, but were also more prone to conflict (Devine et al., 1999). Moreover, the ability of the group and the organization to effectively manage diversity by creating a culture that accepts, supports, and values diverse individuals and diverse perspectives is critical, as is ensuring equitable treatment of all group members and creating an environment where team members learn from one another (Ely & Thomas, 2001). It is not only diversity that matters, but also inclusion (which we discussed in Chapter 1). According to Berson (2014), research by Deloitte shows that teams that have higher inclusion outperform other teams 8:1.

When it comes to decision making, most evidence suggests that diversity positively impacts decision making in groups. Diversity is particularly important when the task is complex and involves creativity, primarily owing to the differing opinions and points of view of the diverse members. However, along with these differing viewpoints, there is an increase in potentially disruptive intragroup conflict. One study asked college students to solve a murder mystery problem in a group of three students from their same sorority or fraternity (Phillips et al., 2009). After 5 minutes, a fourth person joined the group who was either from the same fraternity or sorority or not. When the newly added member was *not* from the same fraternity or sorority, the team's chance of arriving at the correct solution more than doubled from 29% to 60%. Another study showed that members of racially diverse groups share more information with one another, which leads to better performance (Phillips et al., 2006).

Diverse groups are also less likely to suffer from conformity. Psychology students will most likely remember the classic study on conformity done by Solomon Asch in the 1950s. The study involved having three students who were confederates (they were in on the research project) purposely give the wrong answer to a question. Then, the actual participant would be asked the same question, and conformity was measured as the percentage of people who would give the wrong answer. The question was simple. Which line is the same length as line X?

Personnel Psychology
the specialty area of I/O psychology focusing on an organization's human resources

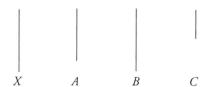

X A B C

This study was redone by researchers in 2018, and they added an additional twist (Gaither et al., 2018). In one condition, the three confederates were racially diverse, and, in the other condition, the confederates were racially homogeneous. In the homogeneous condition, 35% of the actual participants conformed by knowingly giving the wrong answer, but, in the diverse condition, only 20% conformed.

Finally, diverse teams make better decisions because they are less likely to suffer from the same decision-making errors, a concept referred to as the **wisdom of the crowd**. The wisdom of the crowd essentially shows that diverse novices can make better decisions than homogeneous experts, because homogeneous experts tend to suffer from the same errors in judgment. Diverse novices are equally likely to have errors in their decision making, but, because their errors are more varied, other novices are likely to point the errors out. In a study using a computer simulation, scientists programmed fake "agents" to solve problems in groups of 20. The simulation created groups of the 20 smartest agents or 20 randomly selected agents. The randomly selected agents outperformed the smartest agents (Hong & Page, 2004).

Wisdom of the Crowd
the phenomenon by which a diverse group of novices can outperform a homogeneous group of experts because they can identify each other's errors in judgments

Ethical Decision Making

In the 21st century, there has been increasing concern about companies committing horrendous ethical violations. In the early part of the century, energy company Enron was synonymous with engaging in unethical business practices, but there were many more. More recently, Wells Fargo bank has committed a series of ethical violations, with employees opening unauthorized accounts for customers and trying to rip off pandemic assistance funds. As I/O psychologists, we are always concerned with issues of ethics, and there has been considerable research into how organizations and teams should avoid ethical violations and make more ethical decisions.

One model for ethical decision making breaks it down into four steps (Rest, 1986). The first step is *recognizing* the ethical issue. Leaders and team members need to be aware of moral issues and be able to determine that there is a potential to make an unethical decision. Second is the step of choosing to make the correct, *moral judgment*. The decision-making team members need to simply choose to do the right thing. The third step involves the team making a commitment to *place moral concerns above other concerns*—for example, choosing the ethical path rather than focusing on success or profits. An example would be a company deciding between suppliers from two countries and avoiding choosing the cheaper supplier because of their ethical violations—putting moral concerns over profit. The final step in this model is *acting* on the moral concerns—for example, making the correct, ethical decision and, perhaps, creating policies that will prevent future unethical decisions (Rest, 1986).

Teams and organizations that commit ethical violations are subject to lawsuits, from both government regulators and persons affected by the malfeasance, but the damage to reputation, particularly for high-profile companies, is also a major factor. Moreover, the team's or company's ability to attract talented employees may also suffer, along with their tainted reputation.

When to Use Teams

Early on, we differentiated between work groups and work teams, although in many instances the two terms are synonymous. We have already seen that the use of work teams is on the rise, with well more than half of U.S. workers reporting working in some sort of team, as opposed to only 5% of workers in the early 1980s. Although some scholars have touted the use of teams as the solution for improving productivity, we can draw on research on group processes and research on work teams to determine under what conditions teams and teamwork are most appropriate (Hackman, 1998).

Teams are most appropriate when the task is complex, requiring individuals with varied skills and competencies to work together. In today's world, that is likely the majority of tasks, from construction, to surgery, to software engineering and design. That is why some researchers emphasize the importance of selecting the right individuals, based on members' knowledge, skills, abilities, and other characteristics (KSAOs), for a particular team and team task (LePine et al., 2000). It has been suggested that a common mistake is assigning a task to a team that is better done by individuals working alone. A simple example might be using a team to write a complex report that might be done more easily and more effectively by an individual author (Hackman, 1998). Teams are appropriate for complex decision-making tasks or for tasks requiring innovation or creativity. Teams are also appropriate when the situation is variable, requiring the team to adapt to changing external conditions (Kozlowski & Ilgen, 2006).

In addition to team members possessing the required KSAOs to complement one another, effective team members should possess the kinds of characteristics that will make them highly functioning team members, such as good communication, problem-solving, and conflict management skills, and they should be self-motivated and committed to the team (Stevens & Campion, 1994). Because team members may not possess some of these characteristics, and because team members may come and go, I/O psychologists have advocated training for team members, as well as cross-training, so that members have overlapping competencies in the event that a member leaves the team (Marks et al., 2002).

Teams as Parts of Organizations

In the rest of this chapter, we will discuss how teams operate within organizations. Teams can take many forms, including a project task force and teams that govern themselves (called self-managing work teams). In addition, organizations can create their entire structure around teams. With the increased responsibilities of teams, organizations must work to apply basic human resource practices such as team training, team building, and performance appraisals to the team level.

The Project Task Force

Project Task Force
a nontraditional organization of workers who are assembled temporarily to complete a specific job or project

A **project task force** is a temporary, nontraditional organization of members from different departments or positions within a traditional structure who are assembled to complete a specific job or project. Traditional lines of status or authority do not usually operate in such a task force, the structure of which is more like a "temporary" team organization (Ford & Randolph, 1992; Soderlund, 2015). All members are viewed as professionals who will contribute collaboratively to the group's output.

Conference
an unstructured management training technique in which participants share ideas, information, and problems; also called a group discussion

A project task force might be created in an organization that is suddenly faced with hosting the annual 2-day **conference** of executives from all the divisions and affiliates. A task force is put together to handle all facets of the meeting, including obtaining space, arranging accommodations for out-of-town participants, assembling the program, mailing information, and conducting the sessions. In creating the task force, persons with varied skills and expertise are selected, including budgeting specialists to handle finances, graphic artists to produce designs for printed programs, and clerical workers to deal with correspondence. All members work together until the task is completed and then return to their original positions. Some companies may even have standing task forces that, like volunteer fire departments, assemble ready for action whenever special projects arise.

Self-Managing Work Teams

Self-Managing Work Teams
teams that have complete responsibility for whole tasks

Teams have been making dramatic shifts in how they function. For example, it is now far more common to have teams that are self-governing than it has been in the past (Wageman et al., 2012). Many of today's work groups and teams, in areas that involve creative output (e.g., software development teams, research and development groups) or high levels of interdependency, require that group members share the load of leadership. Teams that have complete responsibility for whole tasks, products, or service lines are referred to as **self-managing work teams** (Cohen et al., 1996). Self-managing work teams often operate without a formal supervisor or leader.

If not completely self-managing, many teams engage in **shared leadership**, which is "a dynamic, interactive influence process among individuals in groups for which the objective is to lead one another to the achievement of group or organizational goals" (Pearce & Conger, 2003, p. 1). Leadership is shared in many work groups (Wang et al., 2014). The concept of leadership will be explored in greater depth in the next chapter.

One benefit of self-managing work teams is they reduce the feeling of a **lack of control** that often causes stress for employees. Lack of control is particularly common in lower-level jobs or in highly structured organizations. Jobs that are so constrained and so rule-driven that employees are unable to have any sort of input in work decisions and procedures are likely to be stress inducing, particularly for those workers who want to have some input (see Dwyer & Ganster, 1991).

Research indicates that providing workers with a sense of control over their work environment, through techniques such as giving them a voice in decision-making processes or allowing them to plan their own work tasks, reduces work stress and fatigue and increases job satisfaction (Sonnentag & Zijlstra, 2006). On the other hand, some studies suggest that a sense of a lack of control over one's job may not be stressful for many workers (see Carayon, 1994). It may be the case that different types of workers are more or less concerned with having a sense of control over their jobs (recall our discussion in Chapter 8 on the job characteristics model and individual differences in workers' desire for autonomy).

Team Organization

Teams can also become the main structure of an organization. In **team organizations** (Figure 12.3), workers have broadly defined jobs, not the narrowly specialized positions common to traditionally structured organizations. Workers in a team structure thus know a great deal about the product or goals of the organization and tend to possess a variety of work-related skills. This enables both the workers and the organization to adopt new technology readily, to take on new projects, and to develop innovative work strategies. A second characteristic of team organizations is the collaboration among workers. Rather than each worker independently contributing a "piece" to the final product, as in a traditional organization, employees in team organizations share skills and resources, working collaboratively to get the job done. Many entrepreneurial "start-up" organizations employ a team organization structure, with relatively few members engaging in a variety of different tasks—all with strong commitment to the primary mission and goals of the company.

Team organizations also place much less emphasis on organizational status than do traditional structures. Although team organizations may have a formal project leader and supervisors or managers, these workers do not typically possess the "ultimate" authority that leaders or managers have in traditional organizations. Each worker

Shared Leadership
where leadership is shared among the group members rather than being centralized in one person

Lack of Control
a feeling of having little input or effect on the job and/or work environment; typically results in stress

Team Organization
a nontraditional organizational structure consisting of a team of members organized around a particular project or product

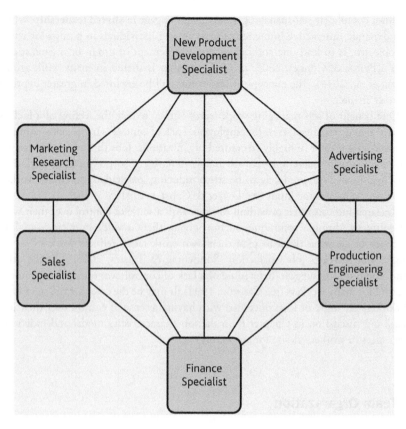

Figure 12.3 A simple team organization.

is viewed as a knowledgeable and skilled professional who is expected to be self-motivated and committed to the goals of the organization.

A final characteristic of team organizations is the tendency toward group decision making. Often, team organizations make important decisions by consensus. The lack of both hierarchy and formally designated roles means that the structure of a team organization is radically different from the pyramidal shape of traditional organizations. We will talk much more about other organizational structures in Chapter 15.

HR Processes Applied to Teams

Team Training

As organizations rely more and more on work teams, I/O psychologists and HR professionals have begun to realize the importance of training aimed at developing the team as a group, rather than the individual focus that is common to most employee training programs (Bisbey et al., 2019). There is an increase in team training and team building, which is distinct from team training and covered in the next section (Lacerenza et al., 2018). Team training programs typically have several components (Lacerenza et al., 2018). Team training should involve setting goals at the team level, evaluating team processes and outcomes, and ensuring psychological safety. Additionally, there are some important areas to focus on that would fall more under the umbrella of team building but are, nonetheless, important for improving team functioning. The key areas of opportunity that need improvement should be identified. Team members should also engage in discussion over concerns that may hurt team effectiveness and develop action plans and accountability to ensure change. As you might imagine, team training is critical to certain groups, such as airline cockpit crews (Bisbey et al., 2019) and health-care teams (Hughes et al., 2016). Cannon-Bowers and Salas (1997) suggested that successful team training should measure both team and individual performance, with feedback provided so that team members can learn to diagnose and evaluate their own performance within the team. Meta-analytic evidence shows that team training has positive effects on team performance (Salas et al., 2008).

Team Building

Team building is similar to team training but also encourages workers to discuss ways to improve their performance by identifying strengths and weaknesses in their interaction with one another (Liebowitz & De Meuse, 1982). Although some emphasis is put on improving members' abilities to communicate with one another, greater stress is placed on helping the team to achieve performance-related goals. Because of the increase in work teams, and because of its focus on improving team dynamics and performance, team building is very popular.

Team building can use existing groups of workers or construct new work teams. The first session is a diagnostic meeting (Figure 12.4). Often a consultant serves as moderator, while the team discusses its current level of functioning in an unstructured setting. Each team member is allowed to present personal views and suggestions for improving the team's performance. Through this process, the group should eventually agree on strategies for implementing positive changes. Subsequent sessions involve evaluating and "fine-tuning" new procedures or suggesting alternative approaches. Compared with other similar interventions, team building has the largest and most consistent positive effects on increasing employee job satisfaction and morale (Neuman et al., 1989). Two meta-analytic evaluations of the effects of team building found positive relationships between team building and team performance; however, team building worked better when the focus of team building was on the skills and roles of team members than when it was focused on goal setting or on improving interpersonal relationships within the team (Salas et al., 1999; Svyantek et al., 1999). It has been suggested that team building may be particularly popular and effective in nonprofit organizations to build commitment to the shared mission (Lefkowitz, 2016).

Team Building
a type of team training focused on how to improve team performance by analyzing group interaction

Figure 12.4 In team building, groups of employees discuss methods of improving their work.

Source: Photograph by Jason Goodman, found on Unsplash (https://unsplash.com/photos/Oalh2 MojUuk).

With the increase in virtual teams—interdependent work groups that rarely meet face-to-face—team building might be a good strategy for bringing team members closer together, although evaluation of the team-building program should be done to ensure that it is having a positive impact.

Team Appraisals

The increase in team-based work groups has important implications for the use of performance appraisals. It has been argued that true work teams, where workers complete highly interdependent tasks with shared team goals, should be appraised as a team, rather than using traditional individual appraisals (Wildman et al., 2011). One model suggests that a good appraisal of team performance should assess team members' competencies (knowledge, skills), their team behaviors (effective communication, collaboration, decision making), and the total team performance (output, quality; Reilly & McGourty, 1998). Often, team performance appraisals may require team members to evaluate one another, as well as be evaluated by the supervisor or leader of the team as a unit.

The shift toward team approaches, as well as the fact that the nature and structure of many jobs change quickly over time, presents special challenges to performance appraisal. Performance appraisal systems, therefore, need to be subject to constant review and revision. Performance appraisal should not be an end product, but should be integrated into day-to-day performance, employee development, and the greater goals of the organization. Employees need to be active participants in the appraisal process if they are to perceive it as fair and have a positive, constructive reaction to the appraisals (Meinecke et al., 2017).

Summary

An important function in work groups is group decision making, which has several advantages and disadvantages over individual decision making. Even as individuals, making decisions can be difficult as we are often plagued by decision-making heuristics or the tendency to go with our gut rather than following the rational decision-making model. This concern is more for unprogrammed decisions—those without a pre-existing plan or process—rather than structured decisions for which we simply follow the organization's outlined processes and procedures. When it comes to working with others, decisions can be made unilaterally, such as a top–down or *autocratic* decision, by vote, as in a *democratic* decision, or with full agreement, as in a *consensus* decision.

Although group decision making is slow and conflict-ridden, it can lead to high-quality decisions and greater member satisfaction with and commitment to the decision. Decisions in groups can be autocratic, democratic, or consensus-based. A type of breakdown in the effectiveness of decision-making groups is termed *group polarization*. It is the tendency for groups to make more extreme decisions, either more risky or more cautious, than individuals. *Groupthink* is a concurrence-seeking tendency that overrides the ability of a cohesive group to make critical decisions. Related to groupthink, team decision making can also suffer from conformity, which can lead to poor and maybe even unethical decisions being made because of the tendency to conform. A variety of characteristics impact group decision making, including the composition of the team and the formation of team mental models. Tips for improving group decision making include the use of brainstorming, ensuring the team has adequate diversity, and stressing the importance of ethical decision making.

Teams are really situated within organizations and take a couple of common forms including project task forces, which are temporary groups designed to solve a specific problem, and self-managing work teams, which are usually long-lasting work teams who govern their own work or at least share leadership. Teams can even be used as an overall organizational structure. Many of the personnel practices we covered at the start of the book are specifically adapted for teams. We do not cover selection into teams, but discuss team training, team building, and team-based performance appraisals.

Study Questions and Exercises

1 What is the difference between the rational decision-making model and the intuitive model?
2 How do the approaches to team decision making (autocratic, democratic, consensus) differ in terms of the amount of time they take, the quality of the decision they achieve, and the buy-in of team members?
3 What is meant by group polarization?
4 Consider the eight symptoms of groupthink. What steps can decision-making groups take to try to avoid each of them?
5 How are self-managing teams different from project-task forces?
6 What is the difference between team training and team building?

Web Link

https://donforsythgroups.wordpress.com/
A group dynamics site designed to accompany Forsyth's text on group dynamics.

Suggested Readings

Group Dynamics: Theory Research and Practice. First published in 1997, this journal focuses on research in group processes, much of which has to deal with work groups.

Chen, A., Treviño, L. K., & Humphrey, S. E. (2020). Ethical champions, emotions, framing, and team ethical decision making. *Journal of Applied Psychology, 105*(3), 245.

Lacerenza, C. N., Marlow, S. L., Tannenbaum, S. I., & Salas, E. (2018). Team development interventions: Evidence-based approaches for improving teamwork. *American Psychologist, 73*(4), 517–531. *An excellent review of research on strategies and programs for developing more highly effective teams.*

Lorscheid, I., & Meyer, M. (2021). Toward a better understanding of team decision processes: Combining laboratory experiments with agent-based modeling. *Journal of Business Economics, 91*(9), 1431–1467.

CHAPTER 13

Influence, Power, and Politics

Inside Tips

DEFINING AND DIFFERENTIATING INFLUENCE, POWER, AND POLITICS

This chapter presents and discusses three topics: influence, power, and organizational politics. Although each is a distinct concept, they are also three facets of the same general process, for all involve one party trying to affect the behavior of another. However, it is important to be able to distinguish between the three. The differences are subtle.

Influence, power, and politics are extremely significant and pervasive processes in all work groups and organizations. Power and influence in particular are important aspects of leadership (see Chapter 14) because leaders use their power and influence to help work groups attain their goals. Influence, power, and politics are also important factors in group and team processes, which we discussed in Chapters 11 and 12. For example, conformity to group norms will occur only if the group can influence members to follow the rules. Also, managers can use their power and authority to help resolve conflicts among group members. Furthermore, group decision making, by its very nature, is a political process. Finally, because certain forms of power are linked to the very structure of the organizational hierarchy, our discussion in this chapter will provide some groundwork for examining organizational structure and culture in Chapter 15.

As you reflect on your work organization, you marvel at how people use their power and influence in their efforts to perform their jobs and to get ahead. You have noticed that some high-level executives seem to enjoy the power and control that they have over others, and some are very low key in using their power and authority. You notice that two managers at the same level in a company still may not be equal in terms of their power and influence. One is more powerful because she is well liked and respected by subordinates and superiors and because she understands the politics of the company and knows how to "play the game." And you don't even want to get started thinking about organizational politics—that's a whole game unto itself.

Although influence, power, and politics are ongoing processes in the day-to-day life of any work organization, with important implications for organizational performance and employee satisfaction, social scientists only began to study them in the past several decades (Ferris & Hochwater, 2011). The concepts of influence, power, and politics are also closely intertwined with the topics of group processes and leadership that were discussed earlier. For example, individuals in work groups use influence and power to affect and alter the behavior of other members. Leaders also use their power and influence to achieve group goals. Moreover, they must often act politically to gain and hold their powerful leadership positions, and individuals may also engage in politics to improve their positions in organizations.

Influence, power, and politics likewise play major roles in group decision-making processes. For example, a powerful, influential member can have an important impact in deciding the courses of action a group will take. Democratic decision making, by its very nature, involves political behaviors, such as lobbying for and voting on particular plans. Moreover, because influence, power, and politics affect the behavior of others, they can help determine the amount of conflict and coordination within work groups.

Influence: The Use of Social Control

People often attempt to persuade, cajole, convince, or induce others to provide assistance, change an opinion, offer support, or engage in a certain behavior in both work organizations and in everyday social life. A study by Kipnis et al. (1980) attempted to classify the various influence tactics used in the workplace by having 165 lower-level managers write essays describing incidents in which they influenced either their superiors, coworkers, or subordinates. The 370 tactics were put into eight categories: assertiveness, ingratiation, rationality, sanctions, exchanges, upward appeals, blocking, and coalitions (see Table 13.1; it is important to note that this classification includes behaviors that, by our definitions, would include both influence and power tactics).

Ingratiation
influencing others by increasing one's personal appeal to them

Ingratiation is a widely used influence tactic that involves increasing your appeal to another person, often by praising or flattering them. There is some evidence that interviewees use ingratiation in their resumes and job interviews and that it can actually increase hireability (Peck & Levashina, 2017; Waung et al., 2017). Of course, it is important to be subtle and nonobvious when using influence tactics such as ingratiation—skill in social influence matters (Liu et al., 2014). Other categories of influence include offering exchanges of favors or threatening the other person with negative sanctions, such as a demotion or firing. The final three categories of influence are making appeals to persons higher in the status hierarchy; engaging in behaviors that block, interfere with, or prohibit the others' work activities;

Table 13.1 Categories of Influence Tactics

Assertiveness	**Exchanges**
Making orders or demands	Offering an exchange of favors
Setting deadlines and making sure they are met	Reminding another of past favors
Emphasizing rules that require compliance	Offering to make some personal sacrifice in exchange for a favour
Ingratiation	**Upward Appeals**
Using praise or making the other person feel important	Obtaining the support of superiors
Showing a need for the other person's help	Sending the target person to see superiors
Being polite and/or friendly	Filing a report about the target person to superiors
Rationality	**Blocking**
Using logic to convince someone else	Threatening to stop working with the other person
Writing a detailed justification of a plan	Ignoring the other person or withdrawing friendship
Presenting information to support a request along with the request	Engaging in a work slowdown
Sanctions	**Coalitions**
Withholding salary increases	Obtaining coworkers' support for a request
Threatening to fire someone or to give a poor performance evaluation	Making a request at a formal conference
Promising or giving a salary increase	Obtaining subordinates' support for a request

Source: Kipnis et al., 1980, pp. 445–448.

or building coalitions by getting the support of coworkers or subordinates. Which influence tactics are the most effective? In terms of upward influence tactics, subordinates' use of reasoning, assertiveness, and favor rendering are positively related, but bargaining and self-promotion are negatively related to manager reactions (Wayne et al., 1997).

An interesting question about influence tactics is whether certain tactics work differently for women and people of color compared with White men. In fact, the data do suggest that there are some differences between the effectiveness of certain influence tactics for men and women. Lex Smith and her colleagues reviewed the research on the topic using meta-analysis to answer this question (Smith et al., 2013). They categorized certain tactics as agentic and others as communal. Agentic characteristics are those that are consistent with the male gender role such as independence, assertiveness, and confidence. Communal characteristics are associated with the female gender role and include collaboration, kindness, and empathy. As such, tactics such as assertiveness, sanctions, intimidation, self-promotion, and legitimating are agentic. Ingratiation, personal appeals, consultation, and collaboration are categorized as communal. There were also gender-neutral tactics including rationality, apprising, upward appeals, exchange, coalitions, and inspirational appeals.

The results show that there are some differences, but probably not as many as one would expect. Not surprisingly, the research found that men tend to use agentic influence tactics more than communal tactics. But women did not seem to favor communal tactics over agentic, using both equally. When it comes to the effectiveness of different tactics, women who used communal tactics had higher advancement and overall effectiveness compared with women who used agentic tactics (Smith et al., 2013). This finding is quite consistent with what we find for leadership. However, men's use of agentic and communal tactics were seen as equally effective (Smith et al., 2013). There were no differences on the neutral tactics. In sum, although men use more agentic tactics, they are equally effective, regardless of tactics used. Women use agentic and communal tactics to an equal extent, but are seen as less effective when they use agentic characteristics. Another study showed that more feminine women are less likely to use any influence tactics than masculine women, but both masculine and feminine individuals who use agentic influence tactics received lower performance appraisal scores (Cheung et al., 2016).

Do we also see differences in the effectiveness of tactics when it comes to race? There is much less work on this topic than gender, but there is some evidence that the effectiveness of certain influence tactics may be different for Black employees compared with White employees (Houston & Grandey, 2013). This research suggests that Black men can be stereotyped as angry, unless they use influence tactics that mitigate that stereotype. These additional requirements to avoid racial stereotyping can tax emotional resources for employees of color (Grandey et al., 2019). Drawing from perspectives on leadership, agentic influence tactics may be particularly risky for Black women because they are already stereotyped to be particularly high on the dominance dimension of agentic (Livingston et al., 2012; Rosette et al., 2016). In contrast, Asian women are stereotyped to be particularly low on the dominance dimension of agentic, although quite high on the competent dimension (Rosette et al., 2018; Sanchez-Hucles & Davis, 2010). Asian women, too, can be viewed negatively for using agentic influence tactics because it violates expectations for their race and gender.

Research has suggested some cross-cultural differences in the use of influence tactics. One study showed that conformity may be a low-risk influence tactic to use when interviewing in a cross-cultural context (Derous, 2017). Another study showed that U.S. managers rated rational persuasion and exchange as more effective influence tactics, whereas Chinese managers believed that coalition tactics, upward appeals, and gifts would be more effective (Fu & Yukl, 2000). However, few differences in preferences for influence tactics were found between Asian American and Caucasian American managers (Xin & Tsui, 1996). And differences are not only observed between Asians and Whites. Qiadan et al. (2012) found that Arab employees viewed ingratiation, pressure, and coalition as more favorable than Jewish employees. The only influence tactic that was seen as more effective by Jewish employees than Arab employees was rational persuasion.

Defining Influence, Power, and Politics

In one sense, influence, power, and politics are similar, because all three involve getting others to do something. There are, however, some important differences between them.

Influence can be viewed as a form of social control or social power. It is an individual's ability to get another person to perform a certain action. Usually, influence is exerted by using informal strategies such as persuasion, peer pressure, or compliance techniques. For example, an individual might use persuasive influence in trying to obtain a loan from a friend or when attempting to persuade a coworker to help complete a work task. Peer pressure influence might take the form of a worker's plea to a colleague to break a company rule because "everybody does it." Influence might also involve the use of compliance techniques. For example, an executive might use flattery or the offer of a favor to get a clerical assistant to work overtime to finish producing a report. In this definition, the term might be called "social influence," which is a more restricted usage than the more general notion of influence, which is defined as any process of effecting behavioral change in others (Allen & Porter, 1983).

Power in the workplace is a more formal process that can be defined as the use of some aspect of a work relationship to force or compel another person to perform a certain action despite resistance. For example, a company president can give an order to a vice president and expect it to be carried out because of the power associated with the status relationship. A safety inspector may be able to demand that operators shut down a piece of machinery that has a potentially dangerous malfunction by virtue of the person's position as an acknowledged safety expert. Although influence resides primarily in the individual, power usually derives from the relationship between two parties. For example, a coworker might use persuasion skills—a form of influence—to try to get an unmotivated worker to increase work output by appealing to the worker to "pull his own weight." However, a supervisor, by virtue of the status relationship that gives the person authority over the worker, can use power to order the worker to improve productivity or face the consequences. Thus, power resides in the relationship between parties or in their positions, rather than in the individuals themselves.

Organizational politics is a very different process that involves any actions taken to influence the behavior of others to reach personal goals. The one thing that distinguishes political behaviors from power and influence is the fact that organizational politics are always self-serving, whereas power and influence are not necessarily self-serving.

The following example shows how a person might use influence, power, and politics to achieve a certain outcome: Marilyn James has a problem. The vacation schedules at her company, Mackenzie Electronics, have been set up for several months. However, she has just found out that her husband's vacation will come 2 weeks earlier than they had anticipated. She now needs to exchange her vacation time with Dan Gibbons, who will be taking his vacation during the 2 weeks she needs. Marilyn could use influence by trying to persuade Dan to change his plans; she might

Influence
the ability to use social forces to affect the behavior of others

Power
the use of some aspect of a work relationship to compel another to perform a certain action despite resistance

Organizational Politics
self-serving actions designed to affect the behavior of others to achieve personal goals

promise to do him a favor, or she might simply make an appeal to Dan's generous nature and willingness to help. Marilyn would be using power if she ordered a change in the vacation schedule, which she could do because she is assistant manager of the marketing department, and Dan is a newcomer, far down in the departmental hierarchy. Finally, she might use politics to get what she wants. Marilyn could encourage the marketing director to assign an important project to Dan, saying, "He's a real hard worker, and he deserves to handle this assignment." The project would require that Dan make a formal presentation on August 24, right in the middle of his vacation. Later, when Dan mentions that he needs to trade vacation times to work on the assignment, Marilyn would be ready to jump right in and offer to switch. In short, Marilyn could use any one of these methods—influence, power, or politics—to affect Dan's behavior.

Influence, power, and politics are pervasive processes in all work organizations that involve efforts by some organizational members to control the actions of others. However, the means exerted in using each process are quite different and, thus, will be examined separately.

Power: A Major Force in Work Organizations

Power, in contrast to influence, is a more formal force in work organizations that derives from an individual's role or position or from some specific characteristics of the individual, such as work-related expertise or admirable leadership qualities. Whereas influence depends on the skill of the influencer in affecting another person at a particular place or time, power is a consistent force that is likely to work across situations and time. In organizations, power is a fairly stable capacity or potential that can consistently affect the behavior of others, as long as the power remains with the individual (Hocker & Wilmot, 1985). In other words, the use of influence strategies to affect the behavior of others is sometimes successful, but the use of power is almost always successful.

Power Sources

Power can take many forms and is derived from a variety of sources that are of two main types (Yukl & Falbe, 1991). Most often, power comes from the organization. **Organizational power** comes from an individual's position in the organization and from the control over important organizational resources conveyed by that position. These organizational resources can be tangible, such as money, work assignments, or office space, or more intangible, such as information or communication access to other people. **Individual power** is derived from personal characteristics, such as particular expertise or leadership ability, that are of value to the organization and its members.

Organizational Power
power derived from a person's position in an organization and from control over important resources afforded by that position

Individual Power
power derived from personal characteristics that are of value to the organization, such as particular expertise or leadership ability

Stop & Review

Describe the eight categories of influence tactics and give examples of each.

CLOSE   How to Resist Social Influence Tactics

Social psychologist Robert Cialdini (2008) has discussed the various uses of social influence tactics by "compliance professionals," such as salespersons, advertisers, and con artists, who are those people whose job it is to get others to do something. Using the technique of participant observation, he infiltrated such groups by posing as a door-to-door vacuum cleaner salesman, a car dealer, and a telephone fundraiser. Through his research, Cialdini (2008) was able to identify the most frequently used influence tactics. Three of the more common strategies are the reciprocity rule, the rule of commitment and consistency, and the scarcity principle. With the reciprocity rule, a "favor" is done to get something in return. The rule of commitment and consistency is used to get people to commit to a small initial request and then hitting them with a larger request. The most infamous example of this is the "foot-in-the-door" tactic used by salespersons or people seeking donations. The compliance professional might begin with the question, "You are concerned about the plight of the whales, aren't you?" Answering affirmatively commits you to agreeing with the next question: "Then you would like to make a donation to the Save the Whales Fund, wouldn't you?" The scarcity principle is used to create the illusion of a limited supply, as is done by advertisements that read, "Act now, supply is limited."

A fourth influence tactic identified by Cialdini (2008) seems to involve the use of guilt in getting individuals to comply with requests. This additional tactic, called the "door-in-the-face" technique, is a two-step compliance technique that is like using the foot-in-the-door tactic in reverse. In using the door-in-the-face technique, the influencer prefaces the real request with a first request that is so large that it is certain to be rejected. For example, an influencer who wants to borrow $10 from a friend will start out asking for a loan of $100. When the exorbitant request is denied, the second request, for $10, is made, and it seems reasonable by contrast, making the friend more likely to grant the $10 loan than he or she would have been if the smaller request had been made alone.

Finally, Cialdini (2008) also emphasized the importance of liking in influence attempts—we are more easily influenced by people we like—and what better way for influence "peddlers" to get you to like them but by ingratiation. Research has demonstrated that ingratiation is not only used by salespersons, but is often used in the workplace by supervisors to influence supervisees (Aguinis et al., 1994) and by subordinates to try to influence the promotion process (Thacker & Wayne, 1995).

As you can see, all the tactics of influence mentioned by Cialdini (2008) can be used by coworkers or bosses to influence people to do what they might not otherwise do. For example, reciprocity is often invoked by management after workers are given a cost-of-living raise. Workers, feeling as if management has just done them a favor, may be more compliant than usual, even though the raise was tied to some factor other than management's generosity. A company may try to use the commitment and consistency rule to increase company loyalty and cut down on voluntary turnover. For example, each month the company might hold a contest in which employees submit essays about why the company is a great place to work. Winning essays could be published in the company newsletter. This may make it tougher for employees to consider leaving for work elsewhere, as they have made such a public act of loyalty. An organization might employ the scarcity principle in performance incentive programs by

UP CLOSE *(continued)*

encouraging employees to work hard to obtain one of a very few rewards.

Cialdini (2008) maintains that the best way to combat unethical use of influence tactics is to be able to recognize them. By understanding that people are trying to use these strategies to take unfair advantage of you, you may be able to resist them simply by seeing such obvious exploitation attempts for what they really are.

Power Bases
sources of power possessed by individuals in organizations

French and Raven (1959) looked at different types of power that they called **power bases**, which are the sources of a person's power over others in the organization. They specified five important power bases: coercive power, reward power, legitimate power, expert power, and referent power.

Coercive Power
the use of punishment or the threat of punishment to affect the behavior of others

Coercive power is the ability to punish or to threaten to punish others. For example, threatening to fine, demote, or fire someone are all means of exercising coercive power, as is assigning a person to an aversive work task. An individual may possess coercive power by holding a position in the organization that allows the person to punish others. However, any individual, regardless of position, can use coercive power by threatening to harm someone either physically or psychologically with tactics such as damaging a reputation by spreading false rumors.

We have seen that the use of coercive power, with its punishment and threats of punishment, carries certain risks, because it may create anger and resentment in the subject. Coercive power must be exercised carefully, with awareness of the potential strengths and weaknesses of punitive strategies. For example, although coercive threats may get quick action, the threatened person may try to retaliate later. Raven (1992) said that, if a leader is to use coercive power, the leader must be ready and willing to follow through on threats, regardless of the costs involved. Moreover, the leader who uses coercive power must be ready to maintain surveillance over the target, to ensure that the target is behaving appropriately. Thus, when used effectively, coercive power can put a drain on the manager who uses it, because the manager must constantly watch subordinates to apply sanctions quickly when undesirable work behaviors occur.

Reward Power
power that results from having the ability to offer something positive, such as money or praise

In many ways, **reward power** is the opposite of coercive power, for, whereas coercive power is the ability to do harm, reward power is the ability to give something positive, such as money, praise, promotions, and interesting or challenging work assignments. The ability to reward others is a common source of power in work organizations, where it often derives from having control over the resources that others value. Having the ability to administer pay raises, bonuses, or promotions or assign coveted work tasks can be an extremely strong power base.

Legitimate Power
the formal rights or authority accompanying a position in an organization

Legitimate power involves the formal rights or authority that an individual possesses by virtue of a position in an organization. Titles such as manager, shift supervisor, director, or vice president are all bases for legitimate power. When employees carry out a request simply because "the boss" asked them to do it, they are responding to such power. In work organizations, legitimate power is typically combined with the reward and coercive power bases. That is, most persons with legitimate authority also have the power to reward or punish subordinates. These three power bases are usually, although not always, tied together. There can be some rare instances in which persons are given some formal position that is not accompanied by reward and coercive power—a position of power in name only. Such is the case of the vice president for public affairs in a relatively small insurance company. The organizational chart for this company reveals that this vice president probably lacks much reward or coercive power to back up his legitimate title because he is the sole employee in the department with no subordinates! Yet there is good evidence that workers respond well to persons who possess legitimate power (Hinkin & Schriesheim, 1994; Yukl & Falbe, 1991), perhaps because most individuals are taught from an early age to respect those in authority.

Expert power is one of the strongest power bases an individual can possess because it results from the possession of some special, work-related knowledge, skill, or expertise (Figure 13.1). In high-tech organizations or companies that are based on knowledge and ideas, such as software development, the development of complex drugs and medical devices, and the like, knowledge and expertise are valuable commodities. Research has shown that the possession of work-related expertise was found to be strongly related to supervisors awarding subordinates pay raises (Bartol & Martin, 1990). Expert power is also the source of power behind many health-care professionals. For example, you are willing to take the advice of

Expert Power
power derived from having certain work-related knowledge or skill

Figure 13.1 To be effective, members of a race-car pit crew must be high in expert power.

Source: Photograph by Andrew Roberts, found on Unsplash (https://unsplash.com/photos/6lqk_bNnw_c).

Referent Power
power resulting from the fact that an individual is respected, admired, and liked by others.

a physician because you believe that this individual has some special knowledge concerning your health.

A very different type of power base is **referent power**, which develops because an individual is respected, admired, and liked by others. Because the person is liked or admired, workers respond to the person's wishes in an effort to please the person and to gain favor. The most dramatic illustration of referent power is the charismatic political leader who can spur an entire population to action merely because of their admiration and respect for that person (see Chapter 14). Certain leaders in work settings may also have a strong referent power base and thus be very influential in controlling the activities of others.

Because of the renewed interest in studying organizational power, researchers have developed a number of scales to measure the different French and Raven power bases (Schriesheim et al., 1991).

One such instrument is presented in Table 13.2; it is designed to be administered to workers to assess which power bases are used by their supervisors and helps further illustrate these power bases.

Table 13.2 A Measure of Power Bases

Instructions: Following is a list of statements that may be used in describing behaviors that supervisors in work organizations can direct toward their subordinates. First, carefully read each descriptive statement, thinking in terms of your supervisor. Then decide to what extent you agree that your supervisor could do this to you. Mark the number that most closely represents how you feel. Use the following numbers for your answers:

(5) = strongly agree
(4) = agree
(3) = neither agree nor disagree
(2) = disagree
(1) = strongly disagree

My supervisor can:
(reward power):
• increase my pay level
• influence my getting a pay raise
• provide me with special benefits
• influence my getting a promotion

(coercive power):
• give me undesirable job assignments
• make my work difficult for me
• make things unpleasant here
• make being at work distasteful

(legitimate power):
• make me feel that I have commitments to meet
• make me feel like I should satisfy my job requirements
• give me the feeling I have responsibilities to fulfill
• make me recognize that I have tasks to accomplish

(expert power):
• give me good technical suggestions
• share with me his or her considerable experience and/or training
• provide me with sound, job-related advice
• provide me with needed technical knowledge

(referent power):
• make me feel valued
• make me feel like he or she approves of me
• make me feel personally accepted
• make me feel important

Source: Hinkin & Schriesheim, 1989.

In sum, the different power bases indicate that power can indeed take many forms and arise from many sources. For example, expert power and referent power reside within the individual and, thus, are forms of individual power. More often than not, legitimate, reward, and coercive power are derived from organizational rather than personal sources and, thus, are types of organizational power. As you might expect, the various power bases can combine to further increase an individual's power in an organization. At the same time, possession of certain power bases, coupled with the effective use of influence tactics (e.g., assertiveness, ingratiation, upward appeals), can even further increase the power an individual wields in a group or organization (Brass & Burkhardt, 1993). A great deal of research has been conducted on power dynamics, or on how the different power bases operate in work settings and how they affect work outcomes. Let's explore power dynamics in work organizations.

Stop & Review

Name and describe three influence tactics identified by Cialdini.

Power Dynamics in Work Organizations

The topic of power in work settings is an important one, and research on the topic has increased, particularly on the dynamics of power in work organizations (Tarakci et al., 2016). For example, researchers have investigated such issues as the distribution of power in organizations, the attempts of organizational members to increase power, power and dependency relationships, and the effects of power on important organizational outcomes, specifically job performance and satisfaction.

Differences in Power Distribution

We know that power, because of its many forms, is unevenly distributed in work settings. Usually, organizations are arranged in a power hierarchy, with people at the upper levels possessing great power and those at the bottom having relatively little power. However, individual differences in the expert and referent power bases ensure that no two people, even those at the same status level, have exactly equal power. Therefore, although persons high in the hierarchy tend to possess more power than those at lower levels, even a low-ranking member can wield considerable power because of personal sources of power, such as expert power and referent power.

McClelland (1975) and others (Winter, 1973) have shown that people place different values on the gain and use of power, with some people being high in the need for power and others having a low need for power (see Chapter 7). Thus, organizations may have some individuals who are "power hungry" and others who have little interest in gaining much power. However, although people may differ in their needs for power, once individuals have obtained power, they are usually reluctant to give it up (Kipnis, 1976). Perhaps this is what underlies the common notion that power can be "intoxicating" or "addicting." This makes sense, because it is power that enables organizational members to satisfy their various work-related goals. Does possession of power "corrupt"? Evidence suggests that, when people are given more power, they may tend to behave in self-serving ways (Mitchell et al., 1998).

Ways to Increase Power

One way for an organizational member to increase power is to gain work-related expertise or knowledge (Tarakci et al., 2016). Learning to solve complex problems, being able to operate or repair sophisticated machinery, and knowing complicated procedures are all linked to an expert power base. Low-power individuals may also increase their organizational power by developing a relationship with a higher-ranking member (Bartol & Martin, 1988). Protégés often benefit from their association with a mentor, leading to greater organizational status and power (see Chapter 6). In fact, it has been shown that networking within the organization, and even simply possessing knowledge of important social networks in the organization, are related to an individual's possession of power (Krackhardt, 1990).

Low-ranking members may also gain power by forming a **coalition**, which involves a group of workers banding together to achieve common goals (Bacharach & Lawler, 1998). A coalition can be a powerful force because of its ability to slow or shut down organizational operations. A group of low-level workers acting together as a unit can become powerful by sheer virtue of their numbers. In other words, a few workers may be easily replaced, but an entire line of workers cannot. A strong coalition can be created when employees join a union, which can exercise its power by threatening to strike or by actually striking. Generally, the larger the coalition, the greater its power. There can indeed be "power in numbers."

Coalition
a group of individuals who band together to combine their power

Stop & Review

Name and describe the five French and Raven power bases.

Power and Work Outcomes

The possession and use of power bases can be directly related to important organizational outcomes such as performance and job satisfaction. For example, expert power is generally related to effective job performance (Bachman et al., 1968) because expert power is based on knowing how to do the job. Greater leader expert power is also related to higher levels of organizational citizenship behaviors (OCBs; Reiley & Jacobs, 2016). Referent power, on the other hand, is consistently linked to member satisfaction with the person wielding the power (Carson et al., 1993). This should not be surprising, because referent power results from subjects' willingness to submit to the power of someone they admire and respect. In contrast, coercive power tends to decrease the attractiveness of the power wielder and may lead to decreased job satisfaction in work group members. The use of coercive power by supervisors may also inhibit employee creativity and innovation (Rousseau & Aubé, 2018). Moreover, the use of coercive power may erode the individual's referent power base. In other words, we lose respect for people who consistently punish or threaten us. In practice, the exercise of coercive power more often involves threats of punishment rather than actual punishment. Although drastic threats can be effective means for gaining compliance, the person who makes such threats runs the risk of having someone "call their bluff" and refuse to comply. The exerciser is now faced with a dilemma: if the person does not follow through with the punishment, some coercive power will be lost, because the subject learns that it is an empty threat.

On the other hand, the exerciser who administers the punishment risks infuriating or, in the case of threats of dismissal, losing the employee. In many instances, the use of coercive power is a no-win situation. Although it may be used to threaten workers into higher levels of performance, satisfaction is likely to decrease, and the organization may lose in the long run through increases in voluntary absenteeism and turnover in the dissatisfied workforce. It is probably for these reasons that studies of practicing managers indicate that coercive power is the least used of the five power bases (e.g., Stahelski et al., 1989).

The Power Corollary

One aspect of power dynamics is known as the **power corollary** (Robbins, 1979), which states that, for every use of power, there is a tendency for a corollary use of power—a return power play by the subject ("for every action there is a reaction"). In other words, when people are the subject of an obvious power play, they tend to try to assert their own power. According to French and Raven (1959), this is why it is important to possess a legitimate power base when exercising other power bases, particularly coercive power, for the combination will limit the form a corollary use of power can take. For example, if a coworker tries to use coercive tactics on you, you might respond in kind, with threats of your own. However, if the person using coercive power is your supervisor, your response options are limited. In other words, it is unlikely that you will directly threaten someone who has legitimate authority.

Power Corollary
the concept that, for every exercise of power, there is a tendency for the subject to react with a return power play

Power and Leadership

The concepts of power and leadership are closely intertwined. Leaders use their power to help followers attain desired goals. Ideally, to be effective, a leader should possess a number of power bases. Having high levels of all five would be ideal (although it may often be rare), because the various power bases often complement one another (Raven et al., 1998). As we have seen, legitimate power tends to validate the use of reward and coercive power. Expert power should also exist in legitimate power positions, because the most qualified persons are usually the supervisors. If a work group is committed to doing a good job, and if it has a leader who is high in legitimate and reward power and who has the expert power to lead a group to high levels of productivity, the leader is likely to develop a strong referent power base as well. Conversely, because of their strong admiration for a leader with referent power, followers may also assume the leader has expertise (Podsakoff & Schriesheim, 1985).

Power and Teams

In the same way that power is inherent in leadership (see the "Applying I/O Psychology" box), power always exists in groups and teams. In some teams, there is a clear leader who holds more power than the rest of the team members. In other types of teams, such as self-managing work teams, power is supposed to be shared among the team members. A team, as a whole, also holds a certain amount of power in the organization compared with other teams. Interestingly, unlike leadership, most research suggests that power corrupts teams. Greer and her colleagues have shown that teams that control more resources (a source of power) end up with more team conflict, and, as a result, high-power teams perform worse than low-power teams (Greer et al., 2011).

Power distribution on the team can also create concerns such that teams with an unequal distribution of power among team members tend to have lower team performance (Greer et al., 2017). Teams with unequal dispersion of power tend to have

Figure 13.2 Teams with more equal power and shared leadership tend to be more effective and have greater gender equality.

Source: Photograph by Windows, found on Unsplash (windows-p74ndnYWRY4-unsplash).

power struggles and are less effective at engaging in conflict resolution (Greer & van Kleef, 2010). The increased conflict on teams with unequal power results in lower team effectiveness. This negative relationship between power dispersion and team outcomes is affected by other aspects of the team. For example, teams that have unequal power distribution and also have membership instability and skill differentiation are more likely to have conflict (Greer et al., 2018). So, what is a team to do? The simple answer is to create teams that have more equal distributions of power (Figure 13.2). Not only does shared leadership in teams make teams more effective, but it has been argued that it can also create greater gender equality (Lacerenza et al., 2018).

Empowerment
the process by which organizational members can increase their sense of power and personal control in the work setting

APPLYING I/O PSYCHOLOGY

The Empowerment Process: A Key to Organizational Success

A major focus of research in the past two decades has centered on the notion of **empowerment**, which is the process by which organizational members are able to increase their sense of power and personal control in the work environment. Workers can be empowered by managers or other persons in authority positions or by increasing important work-related skills or responsibilities. A manager can empower subordinates by giving them some decision-making power or assigning some legitimate power, but workers can also be empowered when conditions in the work environment that make them feel powerless are removed. Individual workers can also become empowered by developing a sense of self-efficacy, which is, as we saw earlier, a belief in one's abilities to engage in courses of action that will lead to desired outcomes. Other ways in which leaders can empower workers include the following:

Express confidence in subordinates' abilities and hold high expectations concerning their performance—Considerable evidence suggests that supervisors who have high expectations about their work group's performance may subtly communicate these feelings to the workers and thus positively influence their behavior (Eden & Shani, 1982). We saw this in Chapter 10 in the discussion of the Pygmalion

effect, and there is good evidence that leaders can significantly affect followers' performance by holding and communicating positive expectations about their performance (Avolio et al., 2009).

Allow workers to participate in decision-making processes—Workers who share in decision making are more committed to the chosen courses of action (see Chapter 12).

Allow workers some freedom and autonomy in how they perform their jobs—For example, let workers be creative or innovative in work methods. The job enrichment programs discussed in Chapter 8 can empower workers by giving them increased responsibility over how their jobs are performed and evaluated.

Set inspirational and/or meaningful goals—Again, there is considerable evidence that goal setting is an important motivational strategy (see Chapter 7).

Use managerial power in a wise and positive manner, such as limiting the use of coercive tactics—Our discussion of the use of different power bases emphasized that coercive power can lead to dissatisfaction in the targets of the power and a reduction in the power user's referent power base. By contrast, reward, expert, and referent power bases allow workers greater choice and flexibility in following

APPLYING I/O PSYCHOLOGY

(Continued)

the power user. They can decide to strive for the reward, or they can choose to follow someone who is knowledgeable or admired. These are generally more effective strategies for achieving positive work group outcomes.

The empowerment process can have positive effects on organizational outcomes. For example, empowering workers can help lessen the impact of demoralizing organizational changes. If workers feel that they have some sort of personal control over aspects of the work environment, and if they have had a say in some of the organizational changes, they can more easily adapt to and accept the changes (Greenberger & Strasser, 1986). Empowered workers may be more satisfied, less prone to leave the organization (Dewettinck & Van Ameijde, 2011), and better able to deal with certain types of organizational stress (Spreitzer, 1996), particularly stress that results from a sense of lack of control or from job uncertainty. There is considerable evidence that empowerment and feelings of self-efficacy play an important role in motivating workers to achieve challenging work-related goals (Gist, 1987), especially if they have a hand in setting the goals and feel that the goals are within reach. In addition, empowered workers are more likely to persist at a task despite difficult organizational or environmental obstacles (Block, 1987). Empowered workers are also more creative and innovative (Shin, 2015). Finally, empowerment may be related to future career development and career success of workers (London & Beatty, 1993).

Organizational Politics

The use of politics occurs daily at all levels of all organizations (Ferris & Treadway, 2012). For example, a qualified individual is passed over for a promotion that goes to a coworker who is clearly less qualified; organizational members say that it was a political decision. Two office workers who have a history of never getting along suddenly file a joint formal complaint about a mutually disliked supervisor; observers explain that their collaboration is due to office politics. A junior-level manager gives up a planned weekend trip to stay at home and take care of the boss's dog while the executive is out of town. The manager's motivation? Obviously political. Anyone who has had the chance to observe the operations of an organization has seen organizational politics in action.

Although the study of organizational politics is relatively new in industrial/organizational psychology, research interest in the topic is growing rapidly (Chernyak-Hai & Rabenu, 2018). This makes sense because politics in organizations is quite common, occurs at all levels, and can have serious effects on job performance, satisfaction, and turnover (Munyon et al., 2015). However, before we begin to explore the effects of organizational politics, we must start by clearly defining the term.

⏱ Stop & Review

Outline three strategies for increasing power in organizations.

Defining Organizational Politics

Earlier definitions stated that organizational politics involved the self-serving, or selfish, use of power or influence to achieve desired outcomes. This covers a very wide range of behaviors; in fact, just about any behavior can be interpreted as being political. Typically, the types of political behaviors in which we are interested involve the use of power or influence that is not a part of one's position or role within the organization (Mayes & Allen, 1977). Because political behaviors are not "sanctioned" by the organization, it is assumed that organizational politics are bad or harmful to the organization's functioning, but this is not always true. Although a worker may act politically to satisfy selfish goals, using means that are not considered to be acceptable organizational procedures, the outcome might actually be favorable to the organization (Cropanzano & Grandey, 1998). In other words, political behaviors sometimes lead to successful organizational outcomes. Such behavior might be called **functional politics**—behaviors that assist the organization in attaining its goals. On the other hand, political behavior that inhibits the attainment of organizational goals is **dysfunctional politics**. The same political behavior may be either functional or dysfunctional, depending on how it affects the goals of the organization.

Ideally, if political behavior is going to occur in organizations (and it is), it should be functional. However, in any organization, some of the political behavior will be functional and some will be dysfunctional. Figure 13.3 shows how political behavior that operates in the individual's self-interest can sometimes overlap with the organization's goals. The political behavior that satisfies the goals of both is functional; the behavior that satisfies the goals of the individual but not those of the organization is dysfunctional.

Although some of the political behavior that takes place in government and work organizations is dysfunctional, oriented toward achieving personal goals to the detriment of organizational goals, much political behavior is actually functional, helping both the individual and the organization achieve respective goals.

Functional Politics
political behaviors that help the organization to attain its goals

Dysfunctional Politics
political behaviors that detract from the organization's ability to attain its goals

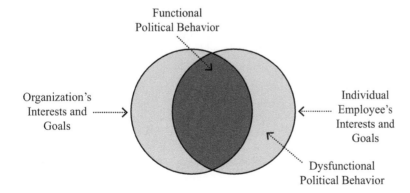

Figure 13.3 Political behaviour.

Source: Sourced from Robbins, 1979, p. 404.

However, it is the dysfunctional politics that often gain the most attention, because they sometimes violate the organization's codes of ethical and moral behavior. For example, in one organization, reporting negative information about another worker to management might be considered a breach of ethics, whereas, in another organization, such political behavior might be more accepted. In one company, management might view workers' unionization as an acceptable political practice, whereas the management of a rival organization might see it as mutiny.

Employee Perceptions of Organizational Politics

Research has examined how organizational politics and the political "climate" at work are perceived by workers and work teams. First, it is important to emphasize that employees tend to view organizational politics negatively—often as a sort of necessary "evil," likely because of its self-serving nature. As a result, perceptions of high levels of organizational political behavior, or a climate that seems to tolerate politicking, are associated with negative employee outcomes. For example, a meta-analysis found that perceptions of politics led to decreased levels of job satisfaction, commitment, task performance, and organizational citizenship behaviors. There were also increased employee perceptions of "strain" and intention to turnover (Chang et al., 2009). Figure 13.4 shows a model of how employee perceptions of negative politics impact stress/strain and morale, which in turn lead to negative work outcomes.

As the meta-analysis suggests, for many workers, organizational politics is seen as a significant source of stress, and highly political organizations can experience high levels of turnover and job dissatisfaction (Poon, 2003).

Other workers seem to truly enjoy engaging in organizational politics. Although lower-level employees may view politics as an additional burden, managers tend to view organizational politics as "part of the job" (Ferris et al., 1996). Employees at different levels of the organization also seem to perceive politics differently. One study found that top-level managers and lower-level employees believed that there was less politicking going on in their organizations than did managers at the middle levels (Parker et al., 1995). In addition, there may be cultural variations

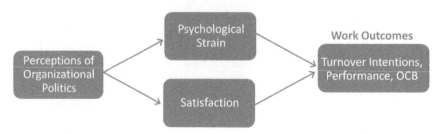

Figure 13.4 Model of effects of perceptions of politics on employee outcomes.

in reactions to organizational politics. For example, Israeli workers appear to be more tolerant of high levels of organizational politicking than British workers (Vigoda, 2001).

Types of Political Behaviors

Political behavior was defined as any self-serving behavior. This means that politics includes many different types of behaviors. To better understand organizational politics, it is important to have some scheme for classifying political behaviors. Farrell and Petersen (1982) have suggested that political behaviors can be grouped along three dimensions: *internal–external*, *lateral–vertical*, and *legitimate–illegitimate*.

The *internal–external* dimension refers to whether political behavior involves only members of the organization or if it extends beyond the boundaries of the organization to include outside people and resources. Examples of external political behaviors would be bringing a lawsuit against an organization or an organizational member, consulting with members of competitor organizations, or leaking secret company information to the press. The *lateral–vertical* dimension concerns whether the political behavior occurs between members of the same status within the organization or if it crosses vertical status levels. Political behaviors involving superiors and subordinates would be an example of vertical politics, whereas two coworkers campaigning for the same promotion are engaging in lateral politics. If a subordinate bypasses the typical chain of command and goes to someone higher in the organization to complain about an immediate supervisor, this is vertical politics. Several coworkers of the same status who form a coalition are engaging in lateral politics. The third dimension is whether a particular political behavior is legitimate or illegitimate. This *legitimate–illegitimate* dimension concerns whether the behavior is "normal everyday" politics or some extreme form of political behavior that violates the generally accepted "rules of the game." As mentioned earlier, organizations and work groups establish their own codes of what is appropriate, or legitimate, and what is unacceptable, or illegitimate. Illegitimate political behavior is most likely to be used by alienated members of the organization who feel that they have no other alternatives and nothing to lose, such as a worker who is about to be fired. For example, slowing down work output—rate setting—may be a legitimate form of political behavior in many organizations, whereas sabotage, such as purposely breaking an important piece of work equipment, will always be considered illegitimate.

Interestingly, the distinction between whether a particular political behavior is legitimate or illegitimate, acceptable or unacceptable, good or bad is in large part a value judgment. The same type of behavior may be considered unacceptable in one situation, but acceptable when performed in another. The same basic process can thus be perceived as either good or bad, depending on the timing, the circumstances, and the people involved (see Table 13.3 and the "On the Cutting Edge" box).

Table 13.3 Organizational Political Behaviors: The Good, The Bad, and The Ugly

Good	Bad	Ugly
Forming coalitions	Striking	Rioting
Blame placing (pointing out who is legitimately at fault)	Passing the buck (avoiding personal blame)	Scapegoating (blaming an individual who is likely not at fault)
Image building (making yourself look good by emphasizing your positive attributes)	Discrediting others (pointing out others' faults so that you look good in comparison)	Mudslinging (bringing up negative and possibly false information about another person)
Making demands and bargaining	Blackmailing	Sabotaging
Limiting communication	Withholding information	Lying
Refusing to comply	Stalling	"Stonewalling"
Forming alliances	Displaying favoritism	"Brown-nosing"

ON THE *CUTTING* EDGE: HOW TO SELL YOUR ISSUES

Application of Influence and Politics: Learn to Sell Your Ideas

An understanding of influence tactics can be useful if you have a great idea at work and you want to persuade others to buy in to your idea—a process called issue-selling (Dutton & Ashford, 1993). Jane Dutton, Sue Ashford, and their colleagues have done multiple qualitative studies on the ways that individuals successfully sell their ideas in organizations. Through interviews, they have identified several factors that are often considered when individuals try to sell their ideas. For example, individuals may consider whether selling an issue would make them politically vulnerable, such as when an issue might imply criticism of leadership (Dutton et al., 1997). If you are unsuccessful in selling your issue and have just publicly criticized your boss, you could elicit retaliation.

In addition, they learned the types of strategies that are most likely to be effective in persuading others. One important finding from their research is that packaging and presentation greatly affect the success of ideas. More successful sellers often tie their ideas to other strategic imperatives in the organization (Dutton et al.,

2001). Further, they might bundle one issue with others to make it more appealing (Dutton & Ashford, 1993). Another important piece of advice is that selling ideas requires preparation, preparation, and more preparation (Dutton et al., 2001). But, in order to prepare, you have to understand what to prepare.

This can be grouped into three categories: (1) strategic issues, such as how to link your idea to larger organizational goals; (2) relational issues, such as who is affected by the issue, who else might back the idea, or who is likely to object; (3) normative issues, such as the preferred types of data or modes of communication typically used in your team or organization. Ashford and Detert (2015) offer seven practical tips to get others to buy into your idea:

1 **Consider your audience**

When it comes to selling your ideas, this can be one of the most important steps. What are the goals and values of the person you are trying to persuade? When choosing how to pitch an idea to someone,

ON THE *CUTTING* EDGE: HOW TO SELL YOUR ISSUES (CONTINUED)

focus on the arguments that would be most appealing to that audience.

2 Align with strategy

Organizations have many competing priorities. How can you be sure that yours rises to the top? Tie your issue to the organization's top strategic imperatives. Frame your issue by starting with the strategic goal it relates to and then explain how your idea fits with that goal.

3 Keep emotions in check

Issue sellers can use their own emotions to increase the impact of their argument. However, be careful how your emotions are perceived. You want to sound passionate about your idea, rather than angry with the current situation. If you let your emotions get away from you, they can make you less influential. Consider that your appeal may also affect the emotions of decision makers. So, think about what emotions you do and don't want to elicit in them.

4 Time it right

A great idea can be rejected if there are more pressing issues at the moment. Or there may be certain employees who you know will block the idea, so you can consider whether you want to wait until those individuals have left the organization. Notice when other people are starting to care about your issue and use that timing to increase your effectiveness.

5 Involve others

More often than not, there is strength in numbers, so consider the ideas shared earlier in this chapter about coalition building. Having more people backing your ideas can create energy around your idea and communicate that this issue is important to many people. Consider bringing experts into your coalition to increase your credibility.

6 Remember group norms

Every organization is different in terms of how it prefers to receive information or how it reacts to different influence techniques. Does your organization tend to be formal? Or are you better off proposing your idea in casual conversation? Understanding these norms can help you come up with the best approach to selling your idea.

7 Provide solutions

Rather than approaching a decision maker with more problems for them to solve, consider focusing on the solutions that you bring. Where will you get the money for your idea? How will you find time to make it happen? If you don't have the solution, consider suggesting that a task force is formed to solve the issue.

One particular political behavior that has received a great deal of attention is termed "whistle-blowing." **Whistle-blowing** is when employees convey criticisms about their organization's policies and practices to persons or authorities outside the organization (Perry, 1998). (Note that, in Farrell and Petersen's scheme, whistle-blowing is external political behavior.) Typically, whistle-blowers believe that the organization's practices are illegal, immoral, or illegitimate, regardless of whether the criticisms are indeed valid (Johnson, 2003). Well-known instances of whistle-blowing include employees of chemical companies who have reported instances of dumping of hazardous waste; Enron employees who exposed the company's financial

Whistle-Blowing
political behavior whereby an employee criticizes company policies and practices to persons outside the organization

scandals; a staffer who exposed the FBI's slow actions in dealing with terrorists prior to the 9/11 attacks; and exposures of the criminal activities of politicians by members of their office staffs.

Whistle-blowing is a particularly complicated form of organizational politics. The whistle-blower may face an ethical dilemma between doing what he or she believes to be right and hurting a company toward which the worker may feel a sense of loyalty and commitment by exposing the company to possible fines, sanctions, and costs (Jubb, 1999). Moreover, there is the possibility that the organization will retaliate against the whistle-blower. For this reason, in the U.S., the United Kingdom, Canada, and India, there are laws that partially protect whistle-blowers. Of course, disgruntled employees may file false complaints as a way of getting back at the company that they feel has wronged them.

Not surprisingly, it has been found that employees in organizations that have policies encouraging whistle-blowing and workers whose supervisors support their whistle-blowing have greater instances of reporting inappropriate company practices to external agencies (Kaptein, 2011a, 2011b). In addition, workers who have strong values are more likely to whistle-blow (Sims & Keenan, 1998). One author has advised HR departments to have whistle-blowing policies and procedures in place for the benefit of all concerned (Lewis, 2002).

Whistle-blowing is only one type of organizational politics, but it is one that receives a great deal of attention because it involves parties outside the organization (often the press or consumer protection agencies) and because of the ethical and loyalty implications of whistle-blowing. Interestingly, many organizational political behaviors, such as whistle-blowing, are labeled using slang terminology (see Table 13.3).

⏱ Stop & Review

Distinguish between functional and dysfunctional political behavior and give examples of each.

Consequences of Organizational Politics

Because organizational politics can be functional or dysfunctional—either helping the organization achieve its performance-related goals or hindering it—connections between politics and productivity are not straightforward (Figure 13.5). Clearly, if too much dysfunctional politicking is occurring in an organization, it will have a negative effect on work group productivity. In extreme cases, employees may spend so much time politicking that they spend little time doing their work. However, at least one study suggests that organizational politics are positively related to work performance if workers and supervisors share similar goals (Witt, 1998).

The relationship between organizational politics and job satisfaction is a bit clearer. Research has shown a fairly consistent negative relationship between political behaviors and job satisfaction (Larwood et al., 1998). In addition, organizational politics is negatively related to commitment and to the incidence of organizational citizenship behaviors (Shore & Wayne, 1993). Low levels of organizational politics are also associated with better organizational communication (Rosen et al., 2006). Finally, organizational politics may be positively related to

Figure 13.5 Organizational politics can lead to employee stress.

Source: Photograph by JeSHOOTS, found on Unsplash (https://unsplash.com/photos/-2vD8 llhdnw).

both absenteeism and turnover, as workers in highly political work environments get tired of the "political games" and call in sick or begin to look for work elsewhere (Cropanzano et al., 1997).

Individual Differences in Political Behavior

It is clear that politics can be stimulated by a number of factors in work organizations and that political behaviors take many forms. First, there is little doubt that there are individual differences in workers' tendencies to engage in organizational politicking, as well as their tolerance for it (Kacmar & Baron, 1999). It has been suggested that, given the fact that political behavior is so common in organizations, wise employees need to develop their "political skill" (Ferris et al., 2000). In fact, with increased use of teams, the overlapping and interdependent nature of jobs, as well as increasing job ambiguity and the great mobility of workers today, it is likely that political skill is even more important today than it was when jobs and organizations were more stable and predictable. A review and meta-analyses suggest that employee political skill is related to job satisfaction, organizational commitment, work productivity, organizational citizenship behaviors, and career success (Munyon et al., 2015).

What are the elements of political skill? It has been suggested that social intelligence, emotional intelligence, and self-efficacy—all constructs that we looked at earlier—are important elements of political skill. Another important component of political skill is called "tacit knowledge" and refers to what one needs to know to succeed in a given environment (Sternberg, 2002). Tacit knowledge is related to political "savvy" and is often unspoken and needs to be acquired on the job. Scholars have developed a measure of political skill, and their research suggests that political skill helps people cope with some aspects of work stress and is advantageous for leaders to possess (Perrewé et al., 2005).

Managing Organizational Politics

An important concern is how to manage organizational politics. In many ways, the management of organizational politics is much like the management of conflict that was discussed earlier: the first step is simply to know when it occurs. Learning the causes of political behavior—particularly factors that are likely to lead to dysfunctional political behavior, such as inappropriate performance measures, inadequate job descriptions and procedures, or poor training for new employees—can help to ensure that conditions do not encourage too much political behavior. On the other hand, a certain amount of politics is natural and may even lead to functional outcomes for the organization. Group decision-making processes, workers' critiques of established work procedures and suggestions for alternatives and improvements, and competition among workers may all result in functional political behaviors and improved organizational outcomes.

One model suggests five strategies for managing organizational politics (Mayes, 1995):

1 *Remove ambiguity and uncertainty*—Written job descriptions and procedures manuals can help clarify jobs and organizational procedures and help eliminate some dysfunctional politicking.
2 *Provide "slack" resources*—Giving managers slightly more than minimal resources (e.g., discretionary funds, extra positions) means that they will not have to trade political favors to meet goals.
3 *Create a positive and ethical organizational climate*—From the top levels of the organization down, executives and managers should encourage a climate that discourages negative political behavior. If top-level management is engaging in dysfunctional political behavior, lower-level workers will follow their example, and vice versa.
4 *Clarify personnel selection and appraisal processes*—All personnel decisions should be made devoid of politics.
5 *Reward performance, not politics*—Workers should not be able to succeed in the organization through politics alone.

A Contingency Approach to Organizational Power and Politics

The use and effectiveness of organizational power and politics depend on a number of factors. We have seen that individuals vary in their tendencies, abilities, and willingness to use power and politics. Moreover, organizations and work groups differ in the extent to which they will allow certain types of power and political maneuvering by members (e.g., Near et al., 1993). All of this indicates that power and politics in work organizations are extremely complex phenomena that are best explained and understood through a contingency approach, which looks at the interaction of characteristics of the individual or group and factors related to the situation in which the individual or group is behaving.

Researchers have attempted to put power and politics into contingency frameworks. Gray and Ariss (1985) proposed that politics varies across the stages of an organization's "life cycle." That is, the political behaviors observed in a very new organization (termed the "birth and early growth stage") are very different from those occurring in a more "mature," established organization. According to this model, appropriate political behaviors are critical for success in managing an organization effectively. The manager must be able to adapt political strategies to those appropriate to the organization and its particular life cycle stage (see also Mintzberg, 1984; Salancik & Pfeffer, 1977). For example, in the earliest stages of an organization, the manager is actually the entrepreneur who founded the organization. At this point, the manager should wield absolute power, controlling and distributing resources as the manager sees fit. The entrepreneur-manager also controls decision-making power and aligns the organization's goals with the manager's self-interest. In other words, the organization is created in the image and likeness of the manager. As the organization moves toward maturity, the manager will switch to more of a "bargaining" political strategy of exchanging resources for favors.

In another contingency approach, Cobb (1984), building on the work of Porter et al. (1981), proposed an "episodic model of power" that examines power episodes, or the use of power in actual work settings (see Figure 13.6). The episodic model includes consideration of aspects of the exerciser, or agent, of power and the subject, or target, as well as elements of the power situation. For example, in trying to understand the use of power, this model looks at three factors related to the agent of power.

The first, psychological orientation, is the motivation to use power. The second, political skills, is the agent's understanding of organizational politics and her or his ability to act politically. Finally, personal power base is the amount and type(s) of power a person possesses. The model also considers two factors related to the target of power: the readiness to act and the ability to act. Readiness is defined as the extent to which the target is inclined to act in a manner consistent with the agent's desires. Ability is whether the target can indeed perform the act the agent desires. Finally, this model looks at the power situation, examining whether the "power episode" occurs in the context of the formal organization, the informal organization, or both.

Factors Considered in Cobb's Episodic Model of Power

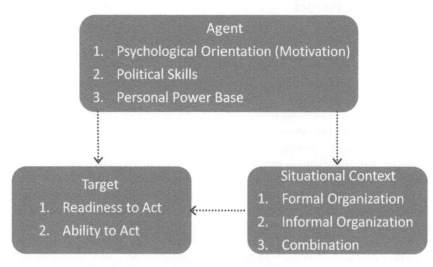

Figure 13.6 Factors considered in Cobb's episodic model of power.

Source: Found in Cobb, 1984. Reprinted by permission of the Academy of Management.

Stop & Review

Name and define the three power agent factors that affect the use of power in the episodic model of power (Cobb, 1984).

If the power episode is a formal situation, the agent's legitimate power and authority will likely play a greater role in influencing the target than will the agent's political skills. However, if the situation is informal, the agent's influence skills may be more important than legitimate power bases. This model thus attempts to integrate the scattered research on power in organizations to offer a broad and complex approach to understanding power dynamics.

In sum, the topics of power and politics are very important to understanding the dynamics of work groups, and particularly the relationships between leaders and followers. Power and politics are complex, but they are ongoing and critical processes in helping us to understand human behavior in organizations.

Summary

Influence, power, and politics are important processes in work groups and organizations. *Influence* is the use of informal social strategies to get another to perform specific actions. *Power* is the use of some aspect of a social relationship to compel another to perform an action despite resistance. *Organizational politics* is the use of power to achieve selfish, or self-serving, goals. A wide variety of influence tactics are commonly employed in work organizations. One such strategy, *ingratiation*, occurs when an individual tries to influence others by increasing personal appeal through doing favors or through flattery.

There are five major power bases, or sources of power: *coercive power*, which involves the use or threat of punishment; *reward power*, which is the ability to give organizational rewards to others; *legitimate power*, which involves the formal rights and authorities that accompany a position; *expert power*, which derives from an individual's work-related knowledge, skill, or expertise; and *referent power*, which comes from the fact that an individual is respected and admired by others. Research indicates that the various power bases have different effects on important organizational outcomes, such as work performance and job satisfaction.

Organizational political behaviors can be divided into two categories. The first, *functional politics*, is political behavior on the part of an organizational member that helps the organization to attain its goals. The second, *dysfunctional politics*, inhibits the organization's goal attainment. Organizational politics arise from a variety of sources, including competition for power and resources, subjective performance appraisals, delay in measurement of work outcomes, compensation for inadequacies, and increased group decision making. Research has attempted to categorize political behaviors and recognize conditions under which they are likely to occur. One goal of management is to try to eliminate dysfunctional political behavior by eliminating conditions that give rise to it. The most recent approaches to studying organizational power and politics take a contingency approach, examining the interaction of individual power characteristics, the target of the power play, and the situational context.

Study Questions and Exercises

1 In what ways are influence, power, and organizational politics different? In what ways are they similar?
2 Consider the five power bases described by French and Raven (1959). Give examples of how a manager might use each to increase work group productivity.
3 Recall some instances in which you observed power used in a work or social group. Which power bases were used in each case? How effective were they in influencing others' behavior?
4 What is the distinction between functional and dysfunctional political behavior? Give examples of each.
5 List some of the potential causes of political behaviors.

Web Link

www.influenceatwork.com
A site based on Cialdini's research on social influence.

Suggested Readings

Cialdini, R. B. (2008). *Influence: Science and practice* (5th ed.). Boston, MA: Pearson. *An enjoyable explanation of how social influence is used by compliance professionals to affect the behavior of others.*

Ferris, G. R., Perrewé, P. L., Ellen, B. P., McAllister, C. P., & Treadway, D. C. (2020). Political skill at work: How to influence, motivate and win support. Boston, MA: Nicholas Brealey. *Several leading researchers in the area of politics and influence provide strategies for the effective use of politics and power in organizations.*

Kovach, M. (2020). Leader influence: A research review of French & Raven's (1959) power dynamics. *The Journal of Values-Based Leadership*, *13*(2), 15.

Upchurch, D. F. (2021). The usage of personal power when collaborating with black male scholars at a historically black college and university. In G. B. Crosby, K. A. White, M. A. Chanay, & A. A. Hilton (Eds.), *Reimagining historically black colleges and universities* (pp. 161–171). Bingley, UK: Emerald.

CHAPTER 14

Leadership

Inside Tips
UNDERSTANDING LEADERSHIP THEORIES

This chapter presents some of the many theories of leadership in work organizations in more or less chronological order, beginning with the earliest (and simplest) theories and progressing to the more current (and usually more complex) models. Although each of these theories takes a somewhat different perspective in examining work group leadership, you will find common threads. Later theories tend to build on earlier theories and so contain some of the same elements, but they are enhanced or looked at in different ways. You might also notice that different theoretical approaches sometimes lead to very different interventions to develop leadership.

The theories of leadership introduced in this chapter are directly related to topics discussed previously. Specifically, the topic of leadership follows the discussion of group processes in Chapters 11 and 12, as the relationship between leaders and other members of the work group is itself an important group process. Leadership and the leadership role are also linked to organizational communication (Chapter 10), particularly the downward flow of communication in organizations. And this chapter also links to our prior discussion of influence, power, and politics (Chapter 13), for it is clear that the most influential and powerful members of work groups are usually the leaders.

What Is Leadership?

Following your recent promotion, you reflect and realize that for the first time you feel like you are truly a leader in your organization. Your elation is tempered by the fact that with your leadership position come many new responsibilities. Your supervisees and others will look to you for guidance, to make decisions, and to settle disputes. As you ponder all of this, you wonder, "How can I be the best possible leader for my work group and for my company?"

In Chapter 11, we saw that individuals play various roles in work groups and organizations. One of these roles is that of leader, which in many groups is viewed as the key position. Rightly or wrongly, many people believe that the success or failure of a particular group is largely dependent on the leader and the type of leadership demonstrated. The importance placed on leadership has made it a major topic in politics, the military, and work organizations. Organizations spend millions of dollars annually trying to select managerial personnel who possess the qualities necessary to be effective leaders of work groups. Many millions more are spent on training employees to be more effective leaders and to develop important leadership characteristics, as we saw in Chapter 6 in our discussion of management training. Before we can study the qualities of leaders, however, we must first define and understand leadership.

Defining Leadership

Leadership
ability to guide a group toward the achievement of goals

There are many definitions of leadership, but most of these definitions involve the leader using his or her influence to assist groups in attaining goals. Therefore, for our purposes, we will define **leadership** as the ability to help direct a group toward the attainment of goals. It is important to realize, however, that the process of leadership involves leaders and others working together. Often, the leader of a work group is the person who holds a particular position or title, such as supervisor, manager, vice president, or lead person. But there are such things as informal leaders. Thus, a work group leader can be a person with no official title or status. These informal leaders emerge because they have some characteristics that the group members value.

Regardless of whether a leader holds a formal leadership role or emerges informally, a true leader should work with followers, because, together, they strive to attain shared goals. Consequently, the fact that a manager or supervisor holds a position of responsibility does not necessarily make that person a true leader. Of course, in work organizations, a powerful position or title can provide a strong starting point for a person to become an effective leader, but a position or title alone will not make an effective leader. Therefore, our definition deals with effective leadership. We may all know (or have worked under) managers who were not effective leaders. They may actually have done nothing to help the group achieve work goals, or they may have even hindered the group's work. Such leaders are "leaders" in name only. This chapter will concentrate on theories of effective leadership.

There has been a long history of research on and theorizing about leadership, and today leadership is one of the most widely studied areas of I/O psychology and management. Leadership theories tend to build on one another, with later theories using components of earlier models and expanding on or using them in new ways. The discussion will begin with the earliest theories, which are known as universalist theories because they were attempts to uncover the universal characteristics of effective leaders. The second category consists of behavioral theories, which focus on the behaviors of effective leaders. The largest category contains the more complex contingency theories, which examine the interaction between leader characteristics and elements of the work situation. Finally, we will examine theories that focus on leaders and their relationships with followers. For example, we will discuss charismatic and transformational individuals who affect followers and organizations in profound ways. Throughout the discussion, relevant research and applications of the theories will also be presented. In particular, we will compare and contrast the various theories. At the end of the chapter, we will discuss how leadership theories can be used to improve the effectiveness of leadership in work organizations.

Universalist Theories of Leadership

Universalist theories of leadership search for the one key characteristic or a cluster of key characteristics held by effective leaders, arguing that leaders with these traits will be successful regardless of the situation. Universalist theories represent the earliest and simplest approaches to the study of leadership. We will briefly discuss two of these theories, the great man/woman theory and the trait theory. The predominant theory here is the great man/woman theory, which suggests that great leaders are born, and the broader trait theory seeks to identify traits (born or not) that are related to effective leadership.

Universalist Theories
theories that look for the major characteristics common to all effective leaders

Great Man/Woman Theory

The **great man/woman theory**, which is much older than any of the formal social science disciplines, reflects the adage that "great leaders are born, not made." Rather than being a formal theory, this is a belief that personal qualities and abilities make certain great persons natural leaders.

Proponents of the great man/woman theory would state that, if important historical leaders such as Julius Caesar, Alexander the Great, or Joan of Arc were alive today, they would again rise to positions of leadership because of their natural abilities (Figure 14.1). Of course, this is mere speculation, and there is little evidence to support the theory, but this does not mean that people do not still believe in it. The fact that in certain countries the relatives of great leaders are also put into positions of power may indicate that there is some general faith in this notion of inborn leadership ability.

Great Man/Woman Theory
a universalist theory of leadership that maintains that great leaders are born, not made

Trait Theory

In the early part of the 20th century, psychologists made many attempts to isolate the specific **traits**, or consistent and enduring physical and personality attributes, that are

Traits
enduring attributes associated with an individual's makeup or personality

Figure 14.1 Does the fact that generations of Kennedys have held leadership positions suggest a belief in the great man/woman theory?

Source: Photograph by Rob Crandall, found on Shutterstock.com

Trait Theory
attempts to discover the traits shared by all effective leaders

associated with leader success. The **trait theory** of leadership refers to several of these investigations. Much of this research involved identifying certain physical characteristics, including height, appearance, and energy level; other characteristics, such as intelligence; and personality traits, such as extraversion, dominance, or achievement, that were associated with effective leaders (Hollander, 1985; Yukl, 1998). It was presumed, for example, that those who were more intelligent, extraverted, or dominant would be more likely to do well as leaders. Unfortunately, the results of these early studies were inconclusive and showed no solid evidence of any single trait common to all effective leaders (Hollander, 1985; Stogdill, 1948).

However, interest in leadership traits has come back into favor (Dinh et al., 2014). This newer work suggests that leadership traits are indeed important. For instance, meta-analytic studies of what are called the *Big Five* core personality traits (the Big Five are extraversion, conscientiousness, openness to experience, agreeableness, and emotional stability) show that, in combination, these five traits correlate fairly strongly with measures of leadership emergence and effectiveness (Bono & Judge, 2004). Furthermore, research on more complex "constellations" of leader characteristics, such as flexibility, charisma, or social intelligence, also suggests that possession of some of these complex traits are important for leadership. For example, Kenny and Zaccaro (1983, p. 683) described flexibility as "the ability to perceive the needs and goals of a constituency and to adjust one's personal approach to group action accordingly." As such, leader flexibility may not be a single trait but instead a very complex set of abilities to perceive and understand social situations, to communicate effectively, and to act wisely in a variety of social settings (Hall et al., 1998; Riggio & Reichard, 2008) that might be better termed "social intelligence" or "social competence" (Hollander, 1978). Certain characteristics, such as a leader's flexibility or social intelligence, may be significant in predicting leader success, although these key leader qualities are probably more complex and multifaceted than those investigated in early leadership research (Riggio et al., 2002).

The major problem with the original trait approach to leadership was that it was too general. It is unlikely that any one trait will be associated with effective leadership in all situations, with all kinds of tasks, and among all groups of followers. The world of work, with the variety of workers and work settings, is much too complex and diverse for any one type of leader to be universally successful. On the other hand, complex constellations of leader characteristics, such as "flexibility" or "charisma," may be related to leader effectiveness, but these complex leader characteristics involve leaders adapting their behavior to the leadership situation. We will examine this approach of looking at the interaction of leader characteristics and the leadership situation in later theories of leadership.

Behavioral Theories of Leadership

The early failure of the universalist theories to isolate the characteristics associated with leader effectiveness led to a change in focus. Rather than trying to measure characteristics in the leader's orientation or personality, researchers began to examine the actual behavior of effective leaders to determine what kinds of behavior led to success. In the late 1940s and throughout the 1950s, two research projects, one conducted at Ohio State University and the other at the University of Michigan, investigated the behaviors exhibited by effective leaders. Both projects arrived at some very similar conclusions concerning leaders, their behavior, and effective leadership. Theories based on these studies and focusing on the particular behaviors that related to effective leadership are called **behavioral theories of leadership**.

These theories include the basic **differentiation** between task-oriented and relationship-oriented leadership theories (developed by the Ohio State and University of Michigan leadership studies).

Behavioral Theories of Leadership
theories derived from studies at Ohio State and University of Michigan that focus on the behaviors common to effective leaders

Ohio State Leadership Studies

Using self-reports and detailed observations of leader behavior from both the leaders themselves and their subordinates, researchers at Ohio State University accumulated a list of hundreds of leader behaviors. Using a statistical process called factor analysis, they found that these hundreds of behaviors could all be narrowed into two general categories: initiating structure and consideration (Halpin & Winer, 1957).

Differentiation
the complexity of an organization's structure that is based on the number of units, the orientations of managers, and the goals and interests of members

Initiating Structure
leader behaviors that define, organize, and structure the work situation

Consideration
leader behaviors that show a concern for the feelings, attitudes, and needs of followers

Stop & Review

Discuss the limitations of universalist theories of leadership.

(Recall from the appendix on statistics in Chapter 2 that factor analysis examines how variables are related to each other and clusters them together to form meaningful categories, or factors.) **Initiating structure** includes leader activities that define and organize, or structure, the work situation, such as assigning specific tasks, defining work group roles, meeting deadlines, making task-related decisions, and maintaining standards of work performance. **Consideration** describes behaviors that show a genuine concern for the feelings, attitudes, and needs of subordinates by developing rapport with them and showing them mutual respect and trust. Such activities include asking subordinates for their opinions and input, showing concern for the feelings of workers, encouraging communication from and between subordinates, bolstering workers' self-confidence and job satisfaction, and implementing their suggestions.

The Ohio State researchers concluded that these two dimensions, initiating structure and consideration, were independent of each other. That is, a leader's score on one did not relate to the score on the other. This means that both categories of leader behavior are associated with effective leadership, but that they do not necessarily coexist. In other words, some effective leaders are high on initiating structure alone, others display only consideration behaviors, and still others exhibit both.

A great deal of research has been conducted to test the soundness of the initiating structure and consideration dimensions. Generally, the results show that most leader behavior can indeed be grouped into one of the two categories (Bass & Bass, 2008). Additional studies have looked at how the two categories are related to the important outcome variables of work performance and job satisfaction (Lambert et al., 2012). Meta-analysis of many studies over a long period suggested that both initiating structure and consideration are related to both performance and group member satisfaction in the expected relationships. That is, consideration was more strongly related to satisfaction, and initiating structure was more strongly related to performance (Judge et al., 2004).

Although the Ohio State behavioral approach stimulated a great deal of research on effective leader behaviors, it, like the universalist theories, is too simplistic. The Ohio State investigations leave us with two categories of leader behavior, both of which may or may not be related to certain indicators of leader effectiveness. Although the results had the positive effect of stimulating research on leader behaviors, it is clear that the Ohio State studies fall short when it comes to making firm predictions about the relationships between leader behaviors and specific work outcomes in all types of working situations.

University of Michigan Leadership Studies

At about the same time as the Ohio State studies were being conducted, researchers at the University of Michigan were also focusing on the behaviors characteristic of effective leaders and came up with quite similar results. Studying leaders in a number of large industrial organizations, the Michigan researchers found that successful leaders tended to exhibit patterns of behavior that were labeled task-oriented—sometimes also called production-oriented—and relationship-oriented, also referred to as employee-oriented (Kahn & Katz, 1960). **Task-oriented behaviors** are concentrated on performing the job that the work group faces and are thus similar to those of the initiating structure factor. The leader is concerned with setting work standards, supervising the job, and meeting production goals. **Relationship-oriented behaviors** include showing concern for employees' well-being and involving them in decision-making processes. The primary difference between the Ohio State and University of Michigan studies was that the Michigan results tended to consider relationship-oriented leader behaviors to be more effective than task-oriented behaviors (Likert, 1967). One of the most famous Michigan studies examined the behavior of leaders in a large insurance company. The findings indicated that both task-oriented and relationship-oriented leadership behavior patterns were positively related to work group performance. However, subordinates of relationship-oriented leaders tended to be more satisfied and had lower turnover rates than employees who were managed by task-oriented leaders (Morse & Reimer, 1956; see also the "Up Close" box).

Task-Oriented Behaviors
leader behaviors focused on the work task

Relationship-Oriented Behaviors
leader behaviors focused on maintaining interpersonal relationships on the job

UP CLOSE   How to Be an Effective Leader

It is very likely that sometime in the near future you will find yourself in a leadership role. You may serve as a formal manager of a work group, you may be elected to serve as a leader of a club or civic organization, or you may be appointed head of some work task force. In any case, the research on leadership, as well as other findings that we have studied in the areas of communication and group dynamics, can help you to do a better job. Of course, as you should know by now, there is no one best way to lead. There are, however, some general principles that you can follow to increase your chances of success:

Become a More Effective Communicator

It has been estimated that as much as 80% of a manager's job involves communication (Mintzberg, 1973). As

we saw in Chapter 10, communication is essential for the effective functioning of work groups, teams, and organizations. The better the channels of communication between the leader and followers, the more likely it is that the two will be able to cooperate to get the task done. It is particularly important to listen to supervisees and be sensitive to their needs and concerns. In fact, effective listening may be a leader's most important skill (Lloyd et al., 2017). The leader who steals away behind closed doors will be unable to meet these needs, which may lead to breakdowns in productivity and in work group satisfaction.

Be Both Task-Oriented and Relationship-Oriented

As the research indicates, both task-oriented and relationship-oriented behaviors are related to leader

effectiveness (Lambert et al., 2012). Therefore, leaders who are able to display concern for both the task and the people are more likely to be successful. In general, having a larger "repertoire" of leadership behaviors is a good thing (Lambert et al., 2012). Gaining insight into your own leader behavior patterns will help you to realize if you have a deficit in either area.

Develop Leadership Self-Efficacy

Leadership self-efficacy is belief in one's ability to play a leadership role. Self-efficacy is important because leaders with higher levels of self-efficacy (e.g., who seem confident in their leadership abilities) are seen as more effective leaders. In addition, they are more persistent under stressful working conditions and they enhance their followers' self-efficacy (Murphy, 2002).

Give Careful Attention to Decision Making

One of the leader's most important tasks is decision making. As we have seen, in addition to reaching a good and workable solution, the process itself is also important. Certain decisions may call for more autocratic decision making; others demand a participative approach (Leana, 1985). Being able to determine what process to use in what situation is the key. However, because evidence indicates that supervisees are generally satisfied with participative decision making, when in doubt it may be wise to use this style.

Monitor Followers' Performance, Set Challenging Goals, and Give Constructive Feedback

Field studies of work groups from a variety of settings indicate that effective leaders keep tabs on what work group members are doing and provide constructive feedback to help them improve performance and correct errors (Komaki, 1986; Komaki et al., 1989). In addition, effective leaders use effective goal setting to motivate followers (see Chapter 7), to help monitor performance, and to provide a forum for providing constructive feedback.

Remember That Leadership Is a Two-Way Street

Although leaders influence their followers, followers also influence their leaders. A leader can be truly effective only if that person has the support of followers (Riggio et al., 2008). An effective leader knows what his or her own needs are and works to satisfy those needs, but the effective leader is also in tune with, and responsive to, the needs of followers.

Be Flexible and Ethical

Effective leadership means doing the right thing in the right situation. Effective leaders are thus flexible or adaptable (Zaccaro & Banks, 2004). One way to be more flexible is to step back and objectively analyze a situation before you act. Leaders should also be objective about their own feelings, behaviors, attitudes, and biases, and how they may negatively affect leadership ability. Sometimes, leaders fall into comfortable patterns of behavior, using the same leadership style in all situations simply because it is easier than adapting behavior to fit the situation. However, it is the objective, adaptable leaders who are successful. Doing the right thing—ethical leadership—is also critically important for leader success.

CLOSE *(continued)*

Learn to Delegate

Effective leaders learn to delegate certain challenging and responsible tasks to followers, which often not only develops their work skills and abilities, thus making them more valuable to the leader and to the organization, but also gives the leader more time to work on other duties, leading to higher levels of productivity.

Hughes et al. (1996) provided guidelines for effective delegation. These include choosing what to delegate and to whom; making the assignment clear and specific; allowing follower autonomy, but monitoring performance (after all, the leader is ultimately responsible for the task being completed); and "giving credit, not blame."

Evaluation of the Behavioral Theories of Leadership

Although initiating structure (task orientation) and consideration (relationship orientation) seem to be reliable dimensions describing leader behavior, the behavioral approach has one major shortcoming: the two dimensions represent very different types of leader behavior, yet both have been linked to effective management (Bass, 1981). If we believe the universalist contention that there is one set of effective leader characteristics or one best leadership style, such divergent leader behaviors simply cannot represent a single, effective leader. The most likely explanation is that other variables, particularly those related to the types of tasks or the characteristics of the work group, determine whether certain leadership behaviors will be effective. In other words, a task-oriented leader might be effective in certain situations under specific circumstances, whereas a relationship-oriented leader might be effective in another situation.

Contingency Theories

The next stage in the evolution of leadership theories produced **contingency theories**, which examine the interaction of characteristics of the leader and the situation, stating that effective leadership depends on the proper match between the two. Many of the contingency theories do, however, build on the behavioral theories, using the leader behavior dichotomies—task-oriented/initiating structure and relationship-oriented/consideration—as a starting point. However, contingency theories recognize no one best style of leadership behavior. Rather, leader effectiveness depends, or

Contingency Theories
theories that look at the interaction of characteristics of both the leader and the situation

is contingent on, the interaction of leader behavior and the situation. We will examine three of these contingency theories of leadership: Fiedler's contingency model, the path–goal theory, and the decision-making model.

Fiedler's Contingency Model

Fiedler's Contingency Model
a leadership theory that maintains that effective leadership depends on a match between the leader's style and the degree to which the work situation gives control and influence to the leader

Least Preferred Coworker (LPC)
a measure that assesses leaders' task or relationship orientation by having them rate their most difficult fellow worker

The leadership theory proposed by psychologist Fred Fiedler (1967) is so well known that it is often simply referred to as *the* contingency model. But, as outlined, the term *contingency model* actually specifies a certain category of theory. **Fiedler's contingency model** argues that effective leadership depends on a match between a leader's behavioral style and the degree to which the work situation gives control and influence to the leader. In other words, the leader's style of behavior must fit with the amount of control and power the leader will have in the work situation.

Building on the Ohio State and University of Michigan behavioral approaches, Fiedler's theory divides leaders based on their primary motivation—task-oriented or relationship-oriented—which he sees as relatively fixed and stable. According to Fiedler, certain leaders may be primarily concerned with getting the job done (task-oriented), although they are also concerned with maintaining good group relations. Other leaders focus primarily on relationships and give "secondary" concern to the task. In other words, leaders differ on which motivation takes precedence in most situations. A task-oriented leader will attend less to the group, and the relationship-oriented leader will tend to focus on the group at the expense of the task.

To measure a leader's orientation, Fiedler developed a self-report measure referred to as the **LPC** measure, which stands for **least preferred coworker**. The LPC requires leaders to rate the person with whom they had worked least well— "the person with whom you had the most difficulty in getting a job done." These ratings are done using bipolar adjective rating scales, such as pleasant–unpleasant and friendly–unfriendly (see Figure 14.2). The LPC is scored by summing the ratings on the scales. This total score indicates whether a person is a task-oriented or relationship-oriented leader. Persons scoring relatively low on the LPC measure, giving their least preferred coworkers very harsh ratings, are task-oriented leaders. Individuals who rate their least preferred coworker somewhat leniently, leading to relatively high LPC scores, are considered to be relationship-oriented. Scores from normative populations help determine what are low and high LPC scores. The rationale behind this scoring system is that task-oriented leaders will be very critical of a poor worker because they value task success. A relationship-oriented leader, on the other hand, values interpersonal relationships and is likely to rate the least preferred coworker more leniently (Rice, 1978). According to Fiedler, task-oriented leaders with low LPC scores link a worker's poor performance with undesirable personality characteristics, whereas relationship-oriented leaders with high LPC scores can separate the least preferred coworker's personality from the individual's work performance (Fiedler, 1967).

Determining a leader's task or relationship orientation with the LPC is only the first part of Fiedler's contingency model. The next step is defining characteristics of the work situation to find the proper match between leadership style and the situation. The characteristics of a work situation are defined using three variables—leader–member relations, task structure, and position power—that combine to create circumstances that are very favorable, very unfavorable, or neither favorable nor unfavorable for the leader.

Stop & Review
Compare and contrast the findings of the Ohio State and University of Michigan behavioral studies of leadership.

NAME _____

People differ in the ways they think about those with whom they work. This may be important in working with others. Please give your immediate, first reaction to the items on the following two pages.

Below are pairs of words which are opposite in meaning, such as "Very neat" and "Not neat." You are asked to describe someone with whom you have worked by placing an "X" in one of the eight spaces on the line between the two words.

Each space represents how well the adjective fits the person you are describing, as if it were written.

Very neat └─┴─┴─┴─┴─┴─┴─┴─┘ Not neat
    8 7 6 5 4 3 2 1

Very Quite Some- Slightly Slightly Some- Quite Very
neat neat what neat untidy what untidy untidy
         neat   untidy

FOR EXAMPLE If you were to describe the person with whom you are able to work least well, and you ordinarily think of him or her as being *quite neat*, you would put an "X" in the second space from the words Very neat, like this

Very neat └─┴─X─┴─┴─┴─┴─┴─┘ Not neat
    8 7 6 5 4 3 2 1

Very Quite Some- Slightly Slightly Some- Quite Very
neat neat what neat untidy what untidy untidy
         neat   untidy

If you ordinarily think of the person with whom you can work least well as being only *slightly neat*, you would put your "X" as follows

Very neat └─┴─┴─X─┴─┴─┴─┴─┘ Not neat
    8 7 6 5 4 3 2 1

Very Quite Some- Slightly Slightly Some- Quite Very
neat neat what neat untidy what untidy untidy
         neat   untidy

If you think of the person as being *very untidy*, you would use the space nearest the words Not Neat

Very neat └─┴─┴─┴─┴─┴─┴─X─┘ Not neat
    8 7 6 5 4 3 2 1

Very Quite Some- Slightly Slightly Some- Quite Very
neat neat what neat untidy what untidy untidy
         neat   untidy

Look at the words at both ends of the line before you put in your "X." Please remember that there are *no right or wrong answers*. Work rapidly, your first answer is likely to be the best. Please do not omit any items, and mark each item only once.

LPC

Think of the person *with whom you can work least well*. He or she may be someone you work with now or someone you knew in the past.

He or she does not have to be the person you like least well, but should be the person with whom you had the most difficulty in getting a job done. Describe this person as he or she appears to you.

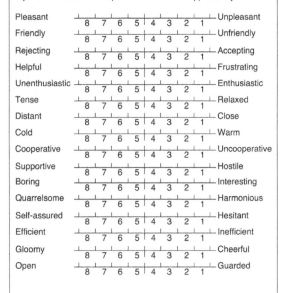

Pleasant	8 7 6 5 4 3 2 1	Unpleasant
Friendly	8 7 6 5 4 3 2 1	Unfriendly
Rejecting	8 7 6 5 4 3 2 1	Accepting
Helpful	8 7 6 5 4 3 2 1	Frustrating
Unenthusiastic	8 7 6 5 4 3 2 1	Enthusiastic
Tense	8 7 6 5 4 3 2 1	Relaxed
Distant	8 7 6 5 4 3 2 1	Close
Cold	8 7 6 5 4 3 2 1	Warm
Cooperative	8 7 6 5 4 3 2 1	Uncooperative
Supportive	8 7 6 5 4 3 2 1	Hostile
Boring	8 7 6 5 4 3 2 1	Interesting
Quarrelsome	8 7 6 5 4 3 2 1	Harmonious
Self-assured	8 7 6 5 4 3 2 1	Hesitant
Efficient	8 7 6 5 4 3 2 1	Inefficient
Gloomy	8 7 6 5 4 3 2 1	Cheerful
Open	8 7 6 5 4 3 2 1	Guarded

Figure 14.2 Least preferred coworker (LPC) measure.

Source: Found in Fiedler, 1967, pp. 40–41.

Leader–Member Relations
the quality of the relationship between leader and followers

Task Structure
an assessment of how well elements of the work task are structured

Position Power
a leader's authority to punish or reward followers

Leader–member relations represent the relationship between the leader and followers—in other words, how well liked, respected, and trusted the leader is by subordinates. According to Fiedler, this dimension can be measured on a scale involving good and poor ratings by having group members indicate their loyalty for and acceptance of the leader (Figure 14.3).

The second dimension, **task structure**, assesses how well a job is structured by considering such factors as whether the group's output can be easily evaluated, whether the group has well-defined goals, and whether clear procedures for reaching those goals exist. Tasks can be defined as "structured" or "unstructured."

The third dimension that Fiedler uses to define the situation is **position power**, or the leader's authority over subordinates, which is usually defined as the strength of a leader's ability to hire, fire, discipline, and reward. Position power is assessed as either strong or weak. It is usually easy to determine position power, because it is clearly outlined in company policies.

Recall that, according to Fiedler's contingency model, the key to effective leadership is the leader's control and influence in a specific situation. Obviously, the situation that is going to be most favorable for the leader is one in which the leader–member relations are good, the task is structured, and the leader has strong position power. The least favorable situation for the leader is one where leader–member relations are poor, the task is unstructured, and the leader has weak position power. Research indicates that task-oriented leaders with low LPC scores are most effective in situations that are

Figure 14.3 According to Fiedler, leader–member relations reflect the respect workers have for their leader.

Source: Photo by krakenimages, found on Unsplash (https://unsplash.com/photos/376KN_ISplE).

either highly favorable or highly unfavorable for the leader—the two extremes of the continuum. Relationship-oriented leaders are more effective in "middle situations" in which the leader's control and influence are neither low nor high.

According to Fiedler, task-oriented leaders with low LPC scores are successful in very unfavorable situations because their take-charge style puts some structure into the circumstances and may encourage the group to perform the job. In other words, in an extremely unfavorable situation, the task-oriented leader has nothing to lose. Taking a firm hand and focusing on task performance and task-related goals may produce results, which is what is needed in such a crisis. At these times, followers might walk all over a relationship-oriented leader. In very favorable situations, groups are already likely to be productive because the task is straightforward and structured, relations between leader and members are good, and the leader has the power to reward for good performance.

Relationship-oriented leaders are more successful when their situational control and influence are neither very high nor low. In these "middle" circumstances, it is important that leaders be well equipped to deal with the interpersonal conflicts that inevitably arise. This is the specialty of the high-LPC, relationship-oriented leaders. Because such situations may lack one of the three situational variables, a leader who shows increased concern for workers and allows them to voice opinions may increase group member satisfaction levels and even job performance. By contrast, being task-oriented in these situations may be counterproductive, alienating members and decreasing levels of satisfaction, because the leader appears to care only about the task. Fiedler also argued that high-LPC leaders may be more cognitively complex, or better able to deal with complex situations. Situations that are neither clearly favorable nor clearly unfavorable for the leader are complex and are best handled by such a person.

Figure 14.4 is a graphic representation of the predictions made by the Fiedler model. The graph shows that task-oriented leaders (solid line) have higher group performance when in very favorable or very unfavorable situations. Relationship-oriented leaders (dotted line) lead higher-performing groups in situations of moderate favorability.

Although some studies have failed to find the predictions made by Fiedler's theory, others have generally supported the model (see Ayman et al., 1995, for a review). Critics have focused primarily on the use of the LPC measure, arguing that it is not clear exactly what it measures because it only infers a leader's orientation from feelings about a coworker rather than directly assessing task and relationship orientation. Another weakness in Fiedler's predictions concerns the assessment of situations, for it is not clear how actual work situations would break down in terms of their favorableness for the leader. In other words, we do not know how many real-world situations would be favorable or very unfavorable for the leader and thus demand a task-oriented leader. Nor do we know how many situations are moderately favorable for the leader or what distinctions there are between moderately favorable situations (e.g., are there "low moderate" and "high moderate" favorable situations?).

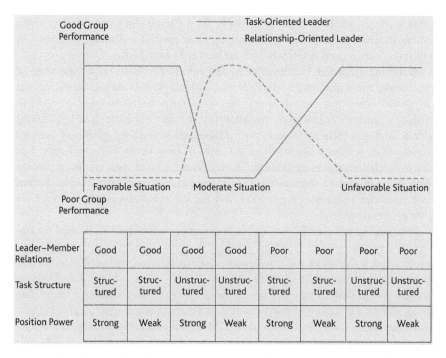

Figure 14.4 Fiedler's contingency model predictions.

Despite these criticisms, and the fact that it is somewhat outdated, the Fiedler contingency model is important for many reasons. First, it was the first highly visible leadership theory to present the contingency approach. Second, its detailed attention to the situation emphasized the importance of both situation and leader characteristics in determining leader effectiveness (an issue we will return to later). Third, Fiedler's model stimulated a great deal of research, including tests of its predictions and attempts to improve on the model, and inspired the formulation of alternative contingency theories.

In sum, Fiedler's contingency model was one of the first detailed theories of leadership. It makes certain predictions about the situations in which certain types of leaders will be effective and has been a straightforward and widely used intervention for improving leader effectiveness.

The Path–Goal Theory

Path–Goal Theory
states that a leader's job is to help the work group achieve its desired goals

Expanding on the definition of leadership presented at the start of this chapter, the **path–goal theory** states that a leader's job is to help the work group attain the goals that it desires (House, 1971). The leader is accordingly seen as a facilitator, or guide, who helps the group overcome the various barriers and roadblocks it may encounter on the way to achieving its goals. Usually, these goals involve increasing worker motivation to perform the job and attempting to gain increases in worker satisfaction. As is reflected in its emphasis on worker motivation, the expectancy theory of motivation (see Chapter 7) was used as the foundation for the path–goal theory (Yukl, 1998).

To help the group reach its goals, the leader may adopt one of four categories of behavior—directive, achievement-oriented, supportive, and participative—the selection of which depends on the characteristics of the situation. **Directive behavior** provides instructions and suggestions for getting the job done. Examples include giving workers specific guidelines and procedures, setting up schedules and work rules, and coordinating work group activities.

Achievement-oriented behavior focuses on specific work outcomes and may involve setting challenging goals for the group and measuring and encouraging improvements in performance. **Supportive behavior** concentrates on the interpersonal relations among group members by showing concern for workers' well-being and providing a friendly work environment. Finally, **participative behavior** encourages members to take an active role in work group planning and decision making through actions such as soliciting information from workers about how to do the job and asking for opinions and suggestions. These four types of leader behaviors outlined in the path–goal theory offer a more detailed breakdown of the initiating structure (task-oriented) and consideration (relationship-oriented) behaviors. Directive and achievement-oriented behaviors are two kinds of initiating structure behavior, whereas the supportive and participative behaviors are two kinds of consideration behaviors.

The choice of leader behavior is contingent on the type of work task and the characteristics of the followers. For example, if a task is routine and easy to understand and if the work group is made up of experienced, self-motivated individuals, the directive style of leadership would probably not be needed because followers can perform the job without much supervision. Instead, supportive behavior might be called for to maintain a harmonious work setting, or participative behavior may be necessary to encourage employees to suggest ways to improve work procedures and the work environment. On the other hand, if the task is fairly complex and the workers are somewhat inexperienced, a directive style might be appropriate.

Although there has been some support for the model (Dixon & Hart, 2010), its general approach and its inability to make specific and precise predictions in actual work settings have been criticized (Yukl, 1998). The theory does offer some idea of how leaders must change their behavior to fit the situation and offers a rather detailed assessment of the situation in an effort to relate the leader's behavior to the characteristics of a specific situation. It also goes a step beyond the simple dichotomy of task orientation and relationship orientation in defining leader behavior.

Directive Behavior
leader behavior that provides instructions and suggestions for performing a job

Achievement-Oriented Behavior
leader behavior concentrated on particular work outcomes

Supportive Behavior
leader behavior focusing on interpersonal relationships and showing concern for workers' well-being

Participative Behavior
leader behavior that encourages members to assume an active role in group planning and decision making

The Decision-Making Model

As seen in Chapter 13, one of the major tasks of a work group leader is to preside over important work-related decisions. Vroom and his colleagues (Vroom &

Table 14.1 Five Decision-Making Strategies: The Model

Decision-Making Strategy Process

1 Autocratic decision I: The leader makes the decision alone, using information available only to the leader

2 Autocratic decision II: The leader obtains information from subordinates and then makes the decision alone

3 Consultative decision I: The leader shares the problem with relevant subordinates and gets their ideas and input individually but makes the decision alone

4 Consultative decision II: The leader shares the problem with subordinates as a group and gets their collective input, but makes the decision alone

5 Group decision: The leader shares the problem with subordinates as a group, and together they make a consensus decision

Source: Vroom & Yetton, 1973, p. 13.

Decision-Making Model
a theory that matches characteristics of the situation with leader decision-making strategies

Jago, 1988) have developed a contingency theory of leadership called the **decision-making model** that is based on the premise that leaders are basically decision makers. This theory is somewhat unique in that it not only makes predictions about proper leader behavior in making decisions but also actually gives "prescriptions" for the decision maker to follow. The decision-making theory holds that a leader can make work decisions using a number of strategies, ranging from acting alone (purely autocratic decision making) to arriving at a decision on the basis of group consensus (completely participative decision making). In the latter type of decision making, the leader is just another group member. The five decision-making styles used in the decision-making model are presented in Table 14.1.

To define the decision-making situation, the theory provides a series of yes/no work-related questions that a leader must ask before adopting a particular strategy. For example, the first question is whether or not a high-quality decision is needed. If the leader answers "yes," it is likely that a more participative style is needed; if the answer is "no," it is likely that a more autocratic style is appropriate. Of course, the decision-making style chosen is a composite of all questions.

The decision-making model presents a decision tree framework for the leader to follow, with each of the seven questions representing a choice point that eventually leads to the correct behavior for the decision that needs to be made (see Figure 14.5). Consider, for example, the manager of the parts department of an automobile dealer who must purchase a computer software inventory system for the department. A number of systems are available, each with its own advantages and drawbacks. The leader answers each of the questions on the decision tree as follows:

(A) Yes, there is a need for quality—a system that will work best in our department.
(B) No, the leader doesn't have enough information to make a quality decision alone.
(C) No, the problem is not structured, because there is no clear-cut way to decide among the various systems.
(D) Yes, subordinates will be using the system and need to accept it.

(E) No, if subordinates did not like the system, they might avoid using it.
(F) Yes, workers do share organizational goals (they want a system that will do the job).
(G) Not applicable.

This framework suggests that the leader should use a group strategy to arrive at a consensus. Because the department is small and the workers are involved in their jobs, they can contribute a great deal to the decision-making process, and it is critical that they accept the decision.

Research has largely supported this decision-making model, showing that effective strategies used by actual managers to solve important work-related decisions were consistent with the theory's prescriptions (Vroom & Jago, 1978). Because of the normative nature of the model, it is also a unique combination of theory and application. As a contingency model, it is effective because it considers how a leader's individual behavior fits with the dynamics of a specific situation. Moreover, it provides a highly detailed definition of the situation, as outlined by the decision-related questions.

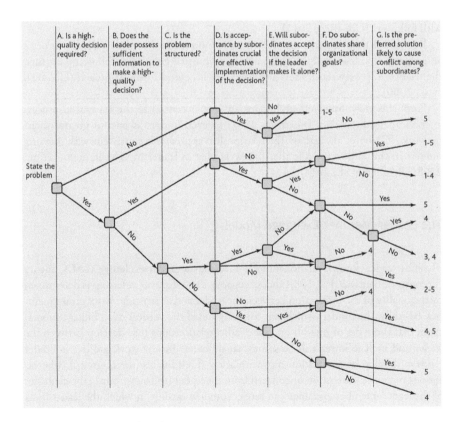

Figure 14.5 Decision tree flow chart.

Note: See Table 14.1, for decision-making strategies.

Stop & Review

Define the three situational characteristics in Fiedler's contingency model.

The major problem with the model is its complexity, which may make it difficult for managers to understand and to learn to use. (In fact, revisions to the decision-making theory have further refined it and made it even more complex and precise than what is presented in Figure 14.5; Vroom & Jago, 1995).

This occurs to theories in general: as they get closer to modeling real-world complexity, they may also become harder to apply. There is a general tendency for people to look for relatively simple solutions to problems. Thus, although complex contingency models, such as the decision-making model, might be sound and accurate, they may not be widely used or accepted in actual work settings owing to their complex nature.

Relational Theories

Relational Theories
theories that look at the relationship between leaders and followers as central to the leadership process

Next, we will examine relational theories of leadership that focus on the relationships between leaders and followers. Relational theories of leadership focus on the attributes important to leaders' effectiveness and the process of building relationships with followers (Uhl-Bien, 2011).

Relational theories consider followers as more central to the leadership process and suggest that leadership is about achieving mutual goals with followers. Further, the relationship between leaders and followers is central to the approach (Uhl-Bien et al., 2000).

From this view, followers and teams are just as central to the leadership process as the leaders themselves (Hosking, 2007) or even leaders as part of greater social networks (Carter et al., 2015). The relationship approach is consistent with growing interest in the important role that followers play in leadership (Kellermanns et al., 2008; Uhl-Bien et al., 2014).

The Leader–Member Exchange Model

Leader–Member Exchange Model (LMX)
a theory that effective leadership is determined by the quality of the interaction between the leader and particular group members

The most widely known relational model is **leader–member exchange (LMX)** theory (Erdogan & Bauer, 2014). LMX theory suggests that effective leadership is determined by the quality of the interaction between the leader and a particular work group member. Basically, the model (which was formerly called the vertical dyad linkage model) states that the types of one-on-one, or dyadic, relationships that develop between the leader and each follower will be somewhat different. In any work group, the leader tends to develop better relationships with a few subordinates (the in-group), whereas the rest receive less attention or concern from the leader (the out-group). The character of the leader–member exchange can range from low quality, in which the leader has a negative image of the subordinate, and the subordinate does not respect or trust the leader, to high quality, in which the leader has a positive view of the worker, and the worker feels that the leader is supportive and provides encouragement.

Having a positive LMX relationship with one's supervisor is related to job satisfaction, and job satisfaction reinforces positive LMX relationships (Volmer et al., 2011). Strong LMX relationships also affect employee work performance, employee loyalty, and attendance (Howell & Hall-Merenda, 1999). As one might expect, in high-quality leader–member relations, there is frequent communication between the leader and subordinate, and these interactions are generally positive. In low-quality LMX relationships, communication is infrequent and/or less positive in tone (Kacmar et al., 2003). Leaders and followers are likely to form positive LMX relationships when, among other things, they share similar personalities and levels of competence (Goodwin et al., 2009).

The notion that leaders develop different types and qualities of relationships with subordinates makes sense. For example, the president of a large company may have to interact with a number of department managers. Some of them may be the trusted advisors with whom the president interacts quite frequently and to whom he gives an important role in establishing company policy. The president's relationships with other managers may not be close at all, and they may in fact have very little actual contact with the president. Naturally, and as the LMX model predicts, the motivation to perform and the levels of satisfaction of the in-group managers are likely to be high, whereas the out-group managers may not be very motivated or satisfied.

Not surprisingly, then, studies show that the central idea behind LMX theory—namely, that leaders form relationships of differing quality with followers—can have deleterious outcomes for teams (Le Blanc & González-Romá, 2012). One study analyzed 162 soldiers from the Canadian Forces grouped into 35 teams (Boies & Howell, 2006). The study showed that leaders who had, overall, more positive relationships with all team members had higher team-level self-efficacy and lower team conflict. However, leaders who tended to form more differentiated relationships with different followers had negative team outcomes unless the overall average level of LMX was high. The study provides an important warning to differentiating, suggesting that the best-case scenario would be to form high-quality, undifferentiated relationships with all followers.

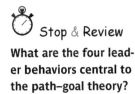

Stop & Review

What are the four leader behaviors central to the path–goal theory?

The authors of the LMX theory claim that their approach is an improvement over other leadership theories because previous models assume that leaders act in a relatively uniform way toward all subordinates. A number of improvements have been made to the theory, including in measuring in-group/out-group membership and the quality of leader–member exchanges (Bauer & Erdogan, 2016).

The strategy for applying LMX to improve leader effectiveness seems relatively straightforward: improve the quality of leader–member relationships. Tests of leadership training programs aimed at this goal have been encouraging. For example, in one study of 83 computer-processing employees of a large service organization, a program that trained leaders to listen and communicate their expectations to subordinates led to a 19% increase in work group productivity and significant increases in subordinates' job satisfaction (Scandura & Graen, 1984). In another study, the quality of leader–member exchanges between supervisors and newly hired employees in the newcomers' first 5 days on the job predicted the quality of leader–member exchanges at 6 months, indicating the importance of developing good-quality supervisor–subordinate interactions early on (Liden et al., 1993).

Inclusive Leadership Theory

Inclusive Leadership Theory
a theory that effective leadership encourages belonging while recognizing the uniqueness of all group members

A second relational theory is **inclusive leadership theory** (Booysen, 2014). As the workplace becomes more diverse, the active inclusion of women, women of color, persons with disabilities, the LGBTQ+ community, and other marginalized groups becomes increasingly important. Emerging theory related to how leaders can be more inclusive helps explain how leaders can increase inclusion in their teams, cultures (we will cover this in Chapter 15), and organizations (Ferdman et al., 2020). In Chapter 1, we covered a definition of inclusion, but, essentially, individuals feel included when they feel that they can be themselves while still being an essential and valued member of their team. Booysen (2014, p. 306) defines inclusive leadership as,

> an ongoing cycle of learning through collaborative and respectful relational practice that enables individuals and collectives to be fully part of the whole, such that they are directed, aligned, and committed toward shared outcomes, for the common good of all, while retaining a sense of authenticity and uniqueness.

To achieve this goal, leaders must demonstrate behaviors related to effective collaboration, consensus building, and engagement (Ferdman, 2010; Mor Barak, 2011).

One approach that has received increasing attention was proposed by Shore and colleagues and focuses on how leaders can meet employees' two most basic and essential needs: the need to be unique and the need to belong (Randel et al., 2018; Shore et al., 2018). The goal of inclusive leaders is to create an environment where people feel safe to share their unique ideas and perspectives. This requires that leaders engage in behavior to build trust, ensure that people are treated fairly, create actual connections with people so they feel they belong, and truly work to elicit and use insights from everyone. Research based on interviews with Fortune 500 CEOs isolated specific leader behaviors that achieve these outcomes: supporting diversity, increasing transparency, and ensuring fairness; making the effort to learn all employees' perspectives and empowering employees to do work in their own ways; and building connection by having empathy and increasing motivation and alignment around diversity and inclusion (Johnson, 2020; Johnson & Lambert, 2020).

Shore's model shows that followers who experience both uniqueness and belonging report higher levels of justice, diversity climate, leader inclusiveness, helping, and health, and lower intentions to quit (Chung et al., 2020). Another study that was done during the COVID-19 pandemic further showed that inclusive leadership reduced psychological distress and increased engagement among a sample of 496 nurses across five hospitals (Ahmed et al., 2020). The outcome that has received the most interest is the idea that inclusive leadership increases innovation (Javed et al., 2019). Inclusive leadership presumes that there is diversity in the group, and diversity brings in different perspectives, as we saw in our discussion of decision making. Inclusive leadership makes teams more creative by increasing psychological safety, but it may also decrease creativity by diminishing motivation (Zhu et al., 2020). As we discussed in Chapter 9, some stress can be beneficial for performance, but too much stress is detrimental.

Gender and Leadership

The focus on relational leadership has obvious implications for women in leadership roles. Stereotypical views of leadership tend to be highly agentic and masculine. This is important to women in leadership roles because role congruity theory (Eagly & Karau, 2002) posits that we hold gender roles for men and women. Men are expected to be strong, confident, and independent (agentic), whereas women are expected to be caring, kind, and understanding (communal). **Role congruity theory** shows that, when women behave in a way that is non-communal and highly agentic, they are viewed negatively because of this violation of their gender role (Johnson et al., 2008). However, meta-analytic evidence shows that women's communal behavior and lack of agentic behavior still reduce the likelihood that they will emerge as leaders (Badura et al., 2018).

Stereotyped expectations of women are further influenced by race such that the agentic expectations for Black women differ from those for Asian women or White women (Rosette et al., 2016). A more nuanced examination of agency is needed when examining female leaders of color. Agency includes two separate dimensions— there is agency as dominance and agency as competence. Black female leaders are stereotyped to be particularly high on the dominance dimension of agentic behavior, but lower on the competence dimension of agentic behavior (Livingston et al., 2012; Rosette et al., 2016). In contrast, Asian women are stereotyped to be particularly low on the dominance dimension of agentic behavior, but high on the competence dimension (Rosette et al., 2018; Sanchez-Hucles & Davis, 2010). These additional factors make navigating the leadership tightrope particularly difficult for women of color, who face the competing demands of appearing competent but not overly dominant, while still maintaining their communal gender role. In reality, it should not be female leaders and female leaders of color who need to circumvent such stereotypes. Instead, effective performance evaluations should ensure that women and women of color are evaluated without bias.

In fact, the evidence suggests that it is the inconsistency in gender role expectations that creates the difference between male and female leaders, rather than true differences in leadership behavior. In 1990, Eagly and Johnson (1990) reviewed 162 studies to compare how men and women led. There were only small differences, such that women led more democratically and participatively than men, and men were more directive or autocratic than women. A later meta-analysis by Eagly and

Role congruity theory
a theory explaining the gender–leadership gap by the inconsistency between the female gender role of being communal and the stereotype that leaders are expected to be agentic, which is consistent with the male gender role

colleagues (Eagly et al., 2003) showed that female leaders were more transformational than male leaders (we will discuss transformational leadership in the next section). More recent meta-analyses show that women are rated as more effective leaders than men, although the opposite used to be true (Paustian-Underdahl et al., 2014). In addition, a study of national opinion polls ranging from 1946 to 2018 and comprising over 30,000 adults showed that men used to be seen as more competent than women, but most people today see the two genders as equally competent (Eagly et al., 2020). Among those who do not see them as equally competent, more people believe women are more competent than men than the other way around.

So, what explains the differences? It is unlikely that women are just better leaders. Instead, the differences can be explained by a selection bias such that the relatively small percentage of women leaders who make it to the top had to be particularly effective to get there. Indeed, research by Rosette and Tost (2010) suggests that women may actually be seen as more effective than equally well-qualified men when they achieve leadership success because of the presumption that they must have been particularly talented to get there.

The differences over time can further be explained by the fact that the stereotypes of leaders are changing. According to another meta-analysis, stereotypes of leaders from the 1970s through 2010 became more relational over time (Koenig et al., 2011). The authors state that leadership stereotypes now include more "feminine relational qualities, such as sensitivity, warmth, and understanding" (p. 634). Possibly as a result of shifting expectations for leaders, 2021 marked a year of progress for top female leaders. Kamala Harris was sworn in as the first woman (and first woman of color) to serve as vice president of the United States alongside President Joe Biden on January 20, 2021. Other high-ranking women leaders in the Biden administration include: Deb Haaland, secretary of the interior; Janet Yellen, treasury secretary; and Linda Thomas-Greenfield, ambassador to the United Nations.

We will discuss the benefits of more relational leadership in the "Cutting Edge" box.

Change-Oriented Leaders

Whereas contingency theories of leadership focus on the interaction between a leader's behavior or style and elements of the situation, and relational theories consider the importance of the follower in determining overall leader effectiveness, change-oriented leadership theories do both of those things to conceptualize truly exceptional leadership. For example, when we think of exceptional leaders throughout history and the truly great leaders of today, they seem to do more than simply adapt their behavior to the situation. These leaders seem to have the ability to inspire or "energize" followers toward organizational goals. They often are able to "transform" groups of workers into highly effective teams. Great leaders, in effect, inspire followers to become leaders themselves. We will briefly examine two additional theories of

Figure 14.6 Former U.S. President Barack Obama is considered by many to be a charismatic leader.

Source: Photograph by Library of Congress on Unsplash.

leadership that deal with these exceptional types of leaders: charismatic leadership theory and transformational leadership.

Charismatic Leadership Theory

We can all think of great political and social leaders who possessed charisma: Barack Obama, Winston Churchill, Martin Luther King Jr., Eleanor Roosevelt, John F. Kennedy, Mahatma Gandhi. There are also charismatic business leaders who seem to inspire and captivate their employees—Jeff Bezos, CEO of Amazon; Elon Musk of Tesla and SpaceX; and Sheryl Sandberg, COO of Meta (formerly Facebook). **Charismatic leadership theory** focuses on such exceptional leaders and tries to

Charismatic Leadership Theory
states that leaders possess some exceptional characteristics that cause followers to be loyal and inspired

Stop & Review

Describe the strengths and weaknesses of the decision-making theory of leadership.

identify and define the characteristics that these leaders possess that inspire followers to identify with and be devoted to them and also outlines the nature of the relationship charismatic leaders have with followers (Klein & House, 1995). According to House (1977), charismatic leaders have the ability to communicate shared group goals and they convey confidence in their own abilities as well as those of their followers. Elements of the situation also come into play, however, because charismatic leaders are often most effective in situations where goals are unclear and environmental conditions are uncertain or unstable, presumably because charismatic leaders are able to provide some vision of where the group should be headed (Mhatre & Riggio, 2014).

There is some speculation that the "exceptional" characteristics or qualities of charismatic leaders are related to the possession of exceptionally high social skills and an ability to relate to (and inspire) followers at a deep, emotional level (Riggio, 1987). Conger and Kanungo (1987, 1988) propose that the key characteristics of charismatic leaders include sensitivity to followers and the situation/environment, ability to inspire, and a desire to change the status quo. It has also been suggested that follower characteristics, such as identification with the leader, susceptibility to the leader's emotional messages, and a willingness to follow, are components of charismatic leadership. Thus, charismatic leadership is indeed an interaction of leader, follower, and situation, as shown in Figure 14.7.

Many studies on charismatic leadership have focused on the communication style of charismatic leaders, which is characterized by a highly expressive tone and visionary language (Johnson & Dipboye, 2008). This often includes the expression of positive affect that can be contagious to followers, improving their affective states and performance (Johnson, 2008, 2009). As analysis of presidential speeches shows that more charismatic presidents used greater imagery and references to inclusion in their speeches (Seyranian & Bligh, 2008). Another study suggests that Barack Obama's

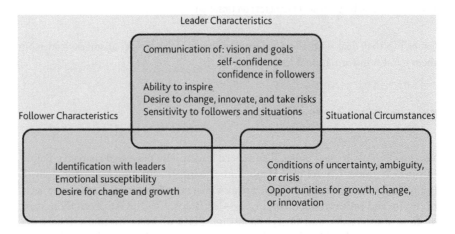

Figure 14.7 Charismatic leadership theory is an interaction between leader characteristics, follower characteristics, and elements of the situation.

charismatic communication style and the emerging social crisis contributed to his 2008 presidential win (Bligh & Kohles, 2009). In a study with similar findings, Bligh and colleagues (2004) found that President George Bush used charismatic rhetoric following the September 11 terrorist attacks in 2001.

ON THE *CUTTING* EDGE

On the *Cutting* Edge: Women's Leadership in the Pandemic

Earlier in this text we have discussed the extraordinary changes surrounding the COVID-19 pandemic. When it comes to leadership, the story that dominated the headlines was how women leaders used their relational leadership style to ensure more positive outcomes in the pandemic. The countries who were faring the best in the face of the pandemic included New Zealand, Germany, Finland, Iceland, Denmark, Norway, and Taiwan—all countries led by women. A qualitative study (Dada et al., 2021) showed that male leaders used more war analogies and fear-based tactics in their communication than their female counterparts. In contrast, female leaders tended to focus on people first, including families, children, and vulnerable groups (such as refugees, persons with mental health concerns) in their rhetoric. The authors state:

> The empathetic and personal appeals that women made focused on compassion and social cohesion, such as Chancellor Merkel's comment, "these are not just abstract numbers in statistics, but this is about a father or grandfather, a mother or grandmother, a partner—this is about people."
>
> (p. 10)

A similar study in the U.S. showed that female governors in the United States showed greater empathy and optimism in the face of the pandemic (Sergent & Stajkovic, 2020). Analyzing speeches from 251 briefings between April 1, 2020 and May 5, 2020, the authors found that women showed greater empathy through their awareness of others' feelings and outward emotional support for followers' welfare. They also found that women governors expressed greater confidence that the COVID-19 situation would improve. They highlight a quote from an April 27, 2020 speech by Governor Gretchen Whitmer in which she said, "We are not out of the woods yet, but we are seeing signs to give us reason to be feeling optimistic; cautiously, but optimistic nonetheless."

The evidence is consistent with other studies of crisis leadership, showing that people prefer more relational leadership in times of extraordinary stress and crisis (Vongas & Al Hajj, 2015).

Transformational Leadership Theory

Another prominent leadership theory distinguishes between transactional and transformational leadership (Burns, 1978). **Transactional leadership** occurs when

Transactional Leadership
leadership based on some transaction, such as exchanging money for work

Transformational Leadership
focuses on the leader's ability
to provide shared values and
a vision for the future for the
work group

the relationship between leader and followers is based on some sort of exchange or "transaction," such as exchanging money or praise for work, or exchanging leader consideration behaviors for employee loyalty and commitment. **Transformational leadership** involves the leader changing the values, beliefs, and attitudes of followers. In other words, in transactional approaches, the leader and followers can be seen as involved in an implicit or explicit agreement whereby followers devote time and energy to pursuing organizational goals, and the leader, in exchange, provides rewards and job security. The transformational leader, however, inspires followers by providing a vision of where the group is headed and developing a work culture that stimulates high-performance activities (Bass & Riggio, 2006). Transformational leaders are viewed as responsible for performance beyond ordinary expectations as they transmit a sense of mission, stimulate workers' learning experiences, and inspire new and creative ways of thinking. Both charismatic and transformational leadership may be particularly important for leading organizations through significant change processes (Eisenbach et al., 1999).

Four components make up transformational leadership and can be referred to as the four "Is." These are:

- *Idealized Influence*—refers to the transformational leader being a positive role model for followers. Transformational leaders "walk the talk" and would not behave in a manner inconsistent with their beliefs or values. As a result, transformational leaders are respected and admired by followers.
- *Inspirational Motivation*—Like charismatic leaders, transformational leaders are able to arouse and inspire followers by providing a compelling vision of a positive future and important and meaningful outcomes.
- *Intellectual Stimulation*—Transformational leaders stimulate followers' curiosity and their innovation and creativity. This is done in an intellectually challenging way, allowing followers to have input into brainstorming sessions and in decision making.
- *Individualized Consideration*—involves the leader's personalized attention to each follower's feelings, needs, and concerns. Through this individualized attention, each follower is developed to his or her full potential.

The results of a great deal of research suggest that both transactional and transformational leadership are associated with leader effectiveness (Judge et al., 2004), but transformational leaders have extraordinarily successful work groups (Bass & Riggio, 2006). For example, meta-analyses demonstrate that groups led by transformational leaders have moderately higher performance than groups led by nontransformational leaders (Lowe et al., 1996). Moreover, followers of transformational leaders are much more satisfied than those led by other types of leaders (Dumdum et al., 2002).

Research on transformational leadership has grown because of the development of an instrument that measures elements of both transactional and transformational leadership, the Multifactor Leadership Questionnaire (MLQ; Bass & Avolio, 1997). The MLQ surveys the followers of a particular leader who evaluate the leader on the four components of transformational leadership. In addition to the MLQ, alternative measures of transformational leadership have also been developed (Alimo-Metcalfe & Alban-Metcalfe, 2001).

A meta-analysis of more than 20 studies found that transformational leadership was superior to transactional leadership in fostering work group effectiveness (Lowe et al., 1996). Moreover, the positive effects of transformational leadership on group performance hold for groups as varied as student leaders in laboratory experiments (Kirkpatrick & Locke, 1996), nursing and health-care supervisors (Mullen & Kelloway, 2009), and German and Indian bank managers (Majumdar & Ray, 2011).

Led by research on transformational leadership, scholars have begun to pay careful attention to the ethics of leaders. For example, charismatic leaders have been separated into those who are more oriented toward the common good, such as Gandhi and Martin Luther King Jr., and self-serving and corrupt charismatics, such as Hitler and Saddam Hussein. As a result, leaders are being distinguished as "socialized" or "authentic" leaders versus the "personalized" or "inauthentic" types (Howell & Avolio, 1993). This search for authentic or ethical leaders has led to a new wave of research that is trying to distinguish "good" from "bad" or "destructive" leadership (see Lipman-Blumen, 2005).

Comparing and Contrasting Theories of Leadership

Table 14.2 presents a summary of the various leadership theories we have reviewed. The early universalist theories of leadership were limited because they were too simplistic—leadership is too complex a phenomenon to be captured in terms of a single characteristic or group of leader characteristics. The behavioral theories of leadership suggested that two very different sets of leader behaviors—task–oriented and person-oriented—were associated with effective leadership. But this perspective too was limited because different leader behaviors will be more or less successful depending on characteristics of the leadership situation. This brought us to the contingency models.

Each of the contingency theories of leadership presents a different way of examining leader effectiveness by focusing on the leader–situation interaction. To understand better the perspectives that these theories take in predicting leader effectiveness, we need to compare the various models.

One obvious difference between the contingency theories is how they view the leader's primary task. For example, Fiedler's model sees the leader as determining the course the work group should take, the path–goal theory considers the leader as merely a facilitator who helps the group achieve its goals, the decision-making model sees the leader's main job as work-related decision making, and the leader–member exchange theory focuses on the leader's role with subordinates. The models also differ in how they define effective leadership. In Fiedler's contingency model, in contrast to the other models, the leader's style is seen as relatively fixed and unchangeable. Thus, the leader must seek out or create situations that are compatible with the leader's behavioral orientation. All the other contingency models assume that leaders

Table 14.2 Summary of Leadership Theories.

Theory	Elements/Components	Applications
Universalist Theories		
Great man/woman theory	Effective leaders are born, not made	(No direct intervention programs)
Trait theory	Searching for traits common to all effective leaders	(No direct intervention programs)
Behavioral Theories		
Ohio State studies	Two leader behaviors: initiating structure and consideration	(No direct intervention)
University of Michigan studies	Two leader behaviors: task-oriented and relationship-oriented	
Contingency Theories		
Fiedler's contingency theory	Leader style must be matched to situational characteristics	Leader match
Path–goal theory	Leader must play roles to help groups attain goals	(No specific interventions)
Decision-making model	Leader asks situation-related questions before choosing decision-making style	Model contains its own application
Relational Theories		
Leader–member exchange	Focuses on quality of leader–member relationship	Leadership training
Inclusive leadership	Focuses on the uniqueness and belonging of all team members	Leadership training
Charismatic and Transformational Theories		
Charismatic leadership	Followers are drawn to "exceptional" characteristics possessed by leader	Leadership training
Transformational leadership	Leader inspires, provides a "vision," and develops followers	Leadership training

are more flexible and require leaders to change their behavior in accordance with the situation. For example, according to the decision-making model, a leader should be participative and democratic in dealing with decision making in one situation and be more autocratic and directive in another. Likewise, according to the path–goal theory, a leader may change roles from time to time to meet the varying goals of the work group. As we shall see, this notion of the flexibility or stability of leader behavior is very important to the application of leadership theory.

Relational leadership theories emphasize the importance of fostering good relationships with followers through partnering with them and making them feel included and important. After all, leaders don't do leadership alone. True leadership is created by leaders and followers working together.

Finally, charismatic and transformational leadership theories seem, at the same time, to combine and to move beyond both the trait approaches and the contingency approaches to leadership. That is, these newer approaches to leadership focus on characteristics of the leader and how these extraordinary leader characteristics interact with situational elements, including the attitudes, beliefs, and loyalty of the followers. The charismatic and transformational leadership theories, however, go a step beyond contingency models because, in these newer models, the leader's behavior is more than just a simple adjusting or adapting to situational constraints.

Leadership Training and Development

Leadership training programs take a number of forms, although most follow two general approaches. The first approach teaches leaders diagnostic skills—that is, how to assess a situation to determine the type of leader behavior that will work best. The assumption is that a leader who knows the particular behavior that a situation requires will be able to adjust behavior accordingly. The path–goal and decision-making theories emphasize such a diagnosis. The path–goal theory requires leaders to determine the goal expectations of the work group, whereas the decision-making model asks the leader to perform a detailed assessment of a situation before adopting a decision-making strategy.

The second approach teaches leaders specific skills or behaviors that they lack. For example, such programs might train task-oriented leaders to be more relationship-oriented or train transactional leaders to become more transformational (Barling et al., 1996); a combination of both approaches—teaching diagnostic skills plus increasing the leader's behavioral repertoire—is likely to be most effective.

Organizations invest a great deal of time and money in programs designed to train their leaders to be more effective. In fact, a majority of funds in organizational training budgets tend to be allocated to leadership training (Ho, 2016; O'Leonard, 2014). A meta-analysis of leadership training (Lacerenza et al., 2017) showed that leader development has strong and consistent effects on trainee reactions, learning, transfer, and even results. The meta-analysis further suggests that utilizing a needs analysis (see Chapter 6), feedback, multiple delivery methods (especially practice), spaced training sessions, a location that is on-site, and face-to-face delivery that is not self-administered all improve the impact of leader development.

It is also important to consider the leader trainee's openness and acceptance of the training program. This has been termed *leader developmental readiness*—which relates to whether a leader is prepared and motivated to develop and advance his or her leadership skills (Day, 2013). If leaders are to be successful in a program that involves a substantial change in behavior, they must see the merit in learning new leadership behaviors and perhaps abandoning past leadership behaviors. This is a problem with many training programs that managers are "forced" to attend, and the program may fail because of resistance from the participants.

Another important consideration is whether the particular leadership behaviors taught in the training program will be accepted in the work group and organization. In many cases, when the leaders try to use their newly acquired leadership behaviors in the work environment, they meet with resistance from both supervisees and colleagues. The new behaviors may be incompatible with the usual operating procedures within the organization or the work group, and the new leadership style may not fit the expectations of group members. For example, a training program that taught police sergeants to replace task-oriented, authoritarian styles with participative behaviors was a spectacular failure. Although the sergeants accepted the change, it was met with considerable resistance by their subordinates, who felt that the program had made their leaders "soft"—a condition that they perceived as dangerous in the life-and-death situations that police officers often face. Thus, for leadership training to be effective, the organization must accept and support the new leader behavior.

Finally, sound evaluations of leadership training programs must be conducted routinely to determine whether the programs are indeed successful (Hannum et al., 2007). Such evaluations include measuring the effects of leadership training programs on organizational outcomes such as work group productivity, work quality, and member satisfaction. One measure that has been suggested is to estimate the return on investment in leadership development, but looking at the costs of the leader development program and the resulting increases in work group performance (Avolio et al., 2010). Training programs that deal with these various concerns can improve the quality of leadership in work groups and organizations.

APPLYING I/O PSYCHOLOGY

Transcultural Leadership: Training Leaders in the 21st Century

The increasing internationalization of business, with multinational organizations routinely doing business worldwide, coupled with the increasing diversity of the workforce, means that leaders today and in the future must be specially trained for a more complex work world (Rost-Roth, 2010). The majority of large U.S. organizations now routinely do business with companies in other countries. One model of leadership training (Conger, 1993) suggests that future leaders will need, among other things, the following areas of training:

- *Global awareness*—Leaders will need to be knowledgeable of worldwide issues that may affect the

APPLYING I/O PSYCHOLOGY

(Continued)

organization and the organizations and organizational members it must interact with. One approach emphasizes that Westerners need to "let go" of their own cultural perspective and approach new countries and cultures as a "stranger," intent on learning the new culture (White & Shullman, 2012).

- *Capability of managing highly decentralized organizations*—As more and more work is done in independently functioning work teams, leaders will need to play more of a "coaching" or "consultant" role than the traditional authority role of "boss."
- *Sensitivity to diversity issues*—Leaders will be looked to as "diversity experts," so they must be able to deal effectively with groups that have different values and worldviews.

- *Interpersonal skills*—The changing and expanding role of work group leaders (e.g., from "bosses" to "coaches") will require them to become more interpersonally skilled.
- *Community-building skills*—Effective leaders of the future will have to build work groups into cooperating, interdependent "communities" of workers. The leader will need to build group cohesiveness and commitment to goals. More and more, group members will turn to leaders for the "vision" of where the work group and the organization are going.

It appears that, once again, leader flexibility is called for. Leaders of the future will be required to be "culturally" flexible and adaptable if they are going to be effective in leading diverse work groups in an increasingly complex world of work.

Job Redesign and Substitutes for Leadership

Research in redesigning jobs indicates that in certain instances leaders may be unnecessary, leading to a search for "substitutes for leadership" (Hackman, 1990). For example, a group that is cohesive and has highly structured norms for operation may have no need for a leader. Examples of such leaderless groups include some of the job enrichment teams mentioned in Chapter 7, in which all members have equal status and authority, as well as groups of professionals such as physicians or real estate agents, who all have high levels of ability, experience, training, and knowledge. In addition, a leader would be redundant in a situation in which the task is well structured and routine and the work is intrinsically satisfying to workers, because there would be no need for direction or for encouragement. Finally, it has been suggested that a form of self-leadership, or self-management, might substitute for the traditional supervision provided by a formal leader (Spreitzer et al., 1999).

Stop & Review

What are the five needs for transcultural leaders outlined by Conger (1993)?

Stop & Review

Describe three applications of leadership theories.

Summary

Leadership is the ability to direct a group toward the attainment of goals. Leadership theories can be divided into three categories: *universalist theories*, *behavioral theories*, and *contingency theories*. The *great man/woman theory*, a universalist theory, holds that some people are natural, born leaders. The *trait theory* specifies certain personality traits, or characteristics, that are common to all effective leaders. These universalist theories suffer from the facts that they are simplistic and that they focus on individual leader characteristics.

The behavioral theories of leadership are typified by studies conducted at Ohio State and the University of Michigan that looked directly at leader behavior rather than at inferred leader characteristics. Two dimensions of leader behavior emerged: *initiating structure* (also called *task-oriented behaviors*), which focuses on work task production, and *consideration* (also known as *relationship-oriented behaviors*), which emphasizes interpersonal relationships among workers.

Next to emerge were the contingency theories of leadership. *Fiedler's contingency model* states that effective leadership depends on a match between the leader's style and the favorableness of the work situation. Leader style is assessed through the *least preferred coworker (LPC)* measure. Task-oriented leaders are most effective in either very favorable or very unfavorable situations, whereas relationship-oriented leaders do better in moderately favorable situations. The favorability of situations in Fiedler's model is determined by three variables: *leader–member relations*, *task structure*, and the leader's *position power*. The *path–goal theory* asserts that the leader is a facilitator who chooses the type of behavior that will most help the work group to achieve its goals. According to the path–goal theory, the leader can adopt four types of leader behavior: *directive*, *achievement-oriented*, *supportive*, or *participative*.

The *decision-making model* sees the leader's main role as making work-related decisions. This prescriptive model contains a decision tree framework for the leader to follow to decide the appropriate decision-making strategy (ranging from autocratic to democratic) to use in a particular situation. Relational theories, such as the *leader–member exchange (LMX)* model, examine the quality of the relationship between the leader and each subordinate, which leads to a more precise determination of work outcomes. Finally, *transformational* and *charismatic leadership theories* focus on exceptional characteristics or qualities that leaders possess that inspire loyalty in followers and motivate them to achieve extraordinary goals.

The application of leadership theories involves one of two strategies: instituting leadership training programs or redesigning the job to fit the leader. The majority of the theories advocate leadership training, either by teaching specific leader behaviors (e.g., task-oriented or relationship-oriented) or by training leaders to diagnose situations that call for either task-oriented or relationship-oriented behaviors. Job redesign usually involves changing characteristics of the situation to fit the leader's typical style or orientation. However, work situations that are amenable to such job redesigns may be limited.

Study Questions and Exercises

1. Discuss the limitations of the universalist leadership theories. Why do you suppose they had, and continue to have, such popular appeal?
2. Consider the distinction between task-oriented (initiating structure) and relationship-oriented (consideration) leader behaviors. List the roles that they play in each of the various contingency theories.
3. Think of a leader of a work or social group whom you have known. How would you characterize this person's leadership style or orientation? What theory of leadership best describes and explains this person's leadership situation?
4. All contingency theories of leadership measure some characteristics of both the leader and the work situation. How do the different theories—Fiedler's, path–goal, decision-making, leader–member exchange—define characteristics of the work situation?
5. Design a leadership training program for leaders of student organizations. Keep in mind the program characteristics that will maximize the effectiveness of the training program.
6. What sorts of groups might operate efficiently without a leader? How would leadership be shared in these groups?

Web Links

http://kravisleadershipinstitute.org/
Our Kravis Leadership Institute site containing some resources about leadership.

www.ila-net.org/
Website for the International Leadership Association, a professional organization for scholars and practitioners from many disciplines who are interested in the study and practice of leadership.

Suggested Readings

Banks, G. C., Fischer, T., Gooty, J., & Stock, G. (2021). Ethical leadership: Mapping the terrain for concept cleanup and a future research agenda. *The Leadership Quarterly*, *32*(2), 101471.

Bass, B. M., & Riggio, R. E. (2006). *Transformational leadership* (2nd ed.). Mahwah, NJ: Erlbaum. *A comprehensive review of research on transformational and charismatic leadership.*

McCauley, C. D., & Palus, C. J. (2021). Developing the theory and practice of leadership development: A relational view. *The Leadership Quarterly*, *32*(5), 101456.

Roberson, Q., & Perry, J. L. (2021). Inclusive leadership in thought and action: A thematic analysis. *Group & Organization Management*, 10596011211013161.

Sessa, V. (2017). *College student leadership development*. New York: Taylor & Francis/Routledge. *This book is a terrific personal guide to leadership development for college students. It includes exercises and leadership assessments.*

CHAPTER 15

Organizational Structure, Culture, and Development

Inside Tips

ORGANIZATIONAL STRUCTURE, CULTURE, AND DEVELOPMENT: UNIFYING
CONCEPTS IN INDUSTRIAL/ORGANIZATIONAL PSYCHOLOGY

*In this chapter, we view organizations at their most general level: looking at how the orga-
nization, as a whole, can affect the behavior of the typical worker. Take organizational
structure, for example. In rigid, rule-driven, traditional organizations, it is likely that
employees will be expected to adhere closely to strict company regulations and policies.
By contrast, in nontraditional organizations, there is a lack of rigid structure and rules,
which means that workers will have quite a bit of freedom and are expected to take on
responsibility and to demonstrate initiative. Knowing about the structure and culture of
an organization can help us understand and analyze the work behavior that occurs within
the organization.*

*Although this chapter focuses on the organization as a whole, the concepts of organiza-
tional structure and culture have been touched on previously. For example, in Chapter 10,
we saw that the organizational chart, or organigram, illustrates the lines of formal communication within an organization, or the organization's communication structure. In
this chapter, we will focus more on the organization's authority structure, because the
organizational chart also represents the formal lines of status and authority. The general
concept of authority was also discussed in Chapter 13, when the topic of legitimate power
was introduced. There are strong ties between the concept of power and the structure of
organizations because organizations can be viewed as power structures. The concept of
organizational culture has been hinted at in several previous chapters. Organizational
culture is connected to workers' feelings about their jobs and their organization—recall
Chapter 8 and the discussions of job engagement and organizational commitment.*

In addition, the chapter on group processes (Chapter 11) explored the elements that contribute to an organization's total "culture."

The field of organizational development (OD), which is introduced in this chapter, emphasizes that organizations must take steps to keep up with the changing world around them. Organizational development is an eclectic area of I/O psychology, for it draws on many theories and applications from a variety of topics within the broader field and uses them to help organizations adapt and change. In our discussion of OD, you will see many of the concepts and topics from earlier chapters, but here they will be applied in an effort to help organizations change and innovate.

You have begun working for a new organization. You have had experience with several other organizations and noticed that each was hierarchical and somewhat bureaucratic. Your last company had many layers of management. Even your university was structured, with many levels of administration between the students and the president. But this organization is quite different. The employees act more like a team. Everyone is on a first-name basis, and the head of the company is indistinguishable from some of the other, older employees. Most importantly, the climate of the organization is completely different. People seem more "loose," but they are highly motivated, work long hours, and seem to take real pride in their work and the company. You begin to wonder how organizations can vary so greatly.

So far, we have studied work behavior at a number of levels. We looked at work behavior at the individual level, examining the processes by which individual workers are selected and assigned to jobs, trained, and evaluated, and the internal processes that affect the behavior of individual workers, including the factors that influence worker motivation, job satisfaction, and stress. We have also explored work behavior at the group level. It is now time to look at work behavior from a larger perspective: the organizational level. This larger perspective will allow an exploration of how the structure, dynamics, and culture of the organization itself can affect the behavior of its work groups and individuals (Williams & Rains, 2007).

We will begin by studying the structure of organizations, or how they are designed and operate. We will consider how factors both inside and outside the organization affect its structure, focusing on how different structures affect behavior within the organization. We will then look at how organizations develop their own individual cultures, which can influence nearly all aspects of behavior at work. Finally, we will look at how organizations can change and develop to meet the demands placed on them from both within and without. In particular, we will study some of the various techniques used to help organizations change to become more effective and to become better places to work.

Organizational Structure

Organizational Structure refers to the arrangement of positions in an organization and the authority and responsibility relationships among them

Organizational structure refers to the arrangement of positions in an organization and the authority and responsibility relationships among them. This means that every organization is made up of persons holding particular positions or playing certain roles in an organization. The organization's structure is then determined by the interrelationships among the responsibilities of these various positions or roles. Consider, for example, a simple internet retail business that has three positions.

The first is the director of operations, who has authority over the other two positions. The director's responsibilities include selecting and acquiring the products that will be offered through the business and handling the organization's finances. The second position is the marketing specialist, whose responsibilities consist of designing the web-based advertisements for the organization's products and placing the ads in various social media outlets. In terms of authority, the marketing specialist is subordinate to the director but superior to the third position: the shipping clerk. The clerk's responsibilities are solely to package and mail orders. In this very small organization, positions and responsibilities are clearly defined, and the responsibilities are linked in such a way that all functions of the company are handled smoothly and efficiently.

Of course, most work organizations are extremely complex, made up of dozens, hundreds, or thousands of workers. Each has an arrangement of positions and responsibilities that is in some way unique. There are a number of different dimensions of organizational structure. For example, organizations can be classified under a general continuum of structure that ranges from the very formal and traditional to the completely informal and nontraditional. Organizations can also be classified by their size, or by the "shape" of their organizational hierarchy (Josefy et al., 2015). We will begin our discussion by examining some of the dimensions on which organizations can be structured.

Dimensions of Organizational Structure

Traditional versus Nontraditional Organizational Structures

Traditional organizations have formally defined roles for their members, are very rule-driven, and are stable and resistant to change. Jobs and lines of status and authority tend to be clearly defined in traditional structures, which means that much of the work behavior tends to be regulated and kept within organizational guidelines and standards. Sometimes, traditional organizational structures are called "mechanistic" or "bureaucratic" structures (we will discuss bureaucracies shortly).

Nontraditional organizational structures are characterized by less formalized work roles and procedures. As a result, they tend to be rather flexible and adaptable, without the rigid status hierarchy characteristic of more traditional structures. Nontraditional organizational structures are sometimes referred to as "organic." Generally, nontraditional organizations have fewer employees than the traditional structures, and nontraditional structures may also occur as a small organization that is a subunit of a larger, more traditionally structured organization. For example, an organization that manufactures jet airliners may be made up of a nontraditional organizational unit that is responsible for designing new aircraft and a traditional organizational unit that is charged with producing dozens of the new jets.

Traditional organizational structures arose around the turn of the 20th century when advancements in technology had led to the growth of manufacturing organizations and increases in their output. As these manufacturing organizations became larger and larger, there was greater need to establish rules to coordinate the various activities of the growing numbers of workers in each organization. These traditional structures began to replace the small, family-type manufacturing organizations, and today many work organizations, such as major manufacturers and service organizations—including banks, the Internal Revenue Service, the department of motor vehicles, and your college or university administration—are traditional organizational structures.

Nontraditional structures are often organized around a particular project or product line and are responsible for all aspects of the job (Soderlund, 2015). Motion picture production crews are an example of a nontraditional structure. Film crews contain a number of types of experts and professionals—camerapersons, actors/actresses, lighting specialists, editors—who work together, pooling their knowledge and talents to produce a creative, quality product. Nontraditional structures have also been set up in hospitals and health-care agencies, financial institutions, and government (O'Reilly & Tushman, 2004). Nontraditional organizations typically have four important characteristics: high flexibility and adaptability, collaboration among workers, less emphasis on organizational status, and group decision making. We will look at examples of both traditional and nontraditional organizational structures a bit later.

Chain of Command and Span of Control

Chain of Command
the number of authority levels in an organization

Span of Control
the number of workers who must report to a single supervisor

Traditional organizational structures are characterized by an authority hierarchy that is represented in the organizational chart, or organigram. The organigram graphically depicts the various levels of status or authority in a traditional organization and the number of workers that report to each position of authority. The **chain of command** is the number of authority levels in a particular organization. The chain of command follows the lines of authority and status vertically through the organization. The **span of control** is the number of workers who must report to a single supervisor. An organization with a wide span of control has many workers reporting to each supervisor; an organization with a narrow span has few subordinates reporting to each superior. Based on these dimensions of chain of command and span of control, traditional organizations are often described as being either "tall" or "flat" in structure (see Figure 15.1). A tall organizational structure has a long chain of command—many authority levels—and a narrow span of control. A flat organizational structure has a short chain of command but a wide span of control. It is important to note that both dimensions are more descriptive of traditional rather than nontraditional structures. Highly nontraditional organizations may have a very small chain of command or none at all, because they de-emphasize authority levels.

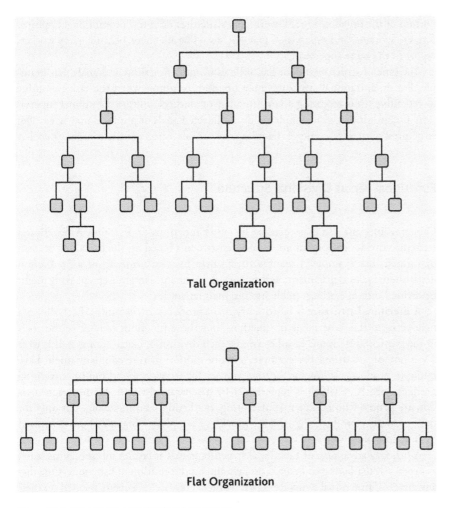

Tall Organization

Flat Organization

Figure 15.1 Tall and flat organizational structures.

An organization's shape, either tall or flat, can have important implications for work life in the organization. For example, in tall organizational structures, workers at the bottom levels may feel cut off from those above, because they are separated by many levels of middle-ranking superiors. On the positive side, tall organizations may offer lower-level employees many different promotional opportunities throughout their careers. Another advantage of such structures is that there is usually adequate supervision because the span of control is narrow: each supervisor is only responsible for a few employees. However, tall organizational structures can become "top heavy" with administrators and managers, because the ratio of line workers to supervisors is very low. Conversely, in a flat structure, few levels separate top-level managers from bottom-level workers, possibly leading to greater interaction between the top and bottom of the organization. However, flat structures offer few promotional opportunities to workers, and supervision may not always be adequate, because many workers report to the same supervisor.

The type of structure, tall or flat, follows from its functions and goals. For example, flat organizational structures may be more common when the task is routine or repetitive, thus requiring a large number of workers who need minimal supervision. Organizations with complex and multifaceted goals or products may have taller structures, with different levels handling the various aspects of the company's goals.

Functional versus Divisional Structure

Functional Structure

an organizational structure that divides the organization into departments based on the functions or tasks they perform

Divisional Structure

an organizational structure that divides the organization according to types of products or customers

Organizations can also be structured by either functions or divisions. A **functional structure** divides the organization into departments based on the functions or tasks performed. For example, a manufacturing firm may be made up of a production department, sales department, and finance department. An amusement park might be divided into operations, publicity, and maintenance.

A divisional structure is based on types of products or customers. Each division may perform the same range of functions, but those functions only serve the goals of the particular division. In other words, each division operates almost as if it were a separate organization. For example, a major motion picture company might have multiple products—films for theatres, movies for television, and online, streaming products—each of which is represented by a separate division. Within each division are people who handle manufacturing, marketing, and financing, but only for their particular product. Figure 15.2 provides examples of organizations structured by function and division.

A primary advantage of functional structure is that it creates job specialists, such as experts in marketing or finance, and eliminates duplication of functions. One disadvantage of functional structure is that workers may become overly focused on their own department and area of specialization, and this may breed interdepartmental rivalry and conflict. Another disadvantage is that work must move from one large department to another to be completed, which may decrease productivity, particularly when work is lost in the shuffle or when one department is particularly slow in accomplishing its functions, thereby creating a bottleneck.

Divisional structure has positive and negative aspects as well. One advantage is that the company can easily expand products or services merely by adding a new division. Also, because each division operates as a separate entity, with its own production goals and profit picture, there is greater accountability. It is easy to determine which units are performing at either exceptional or substandard levels. One of the major drawbacks to divisional structure concerns the duplication of areas of expertise, because each division contains its own departments for production, sales, research, and other functions. Another potential weakness is that workers with similar skills and expertise may not be able to benefit from professional interaction with each other because they are housed in different divisions.

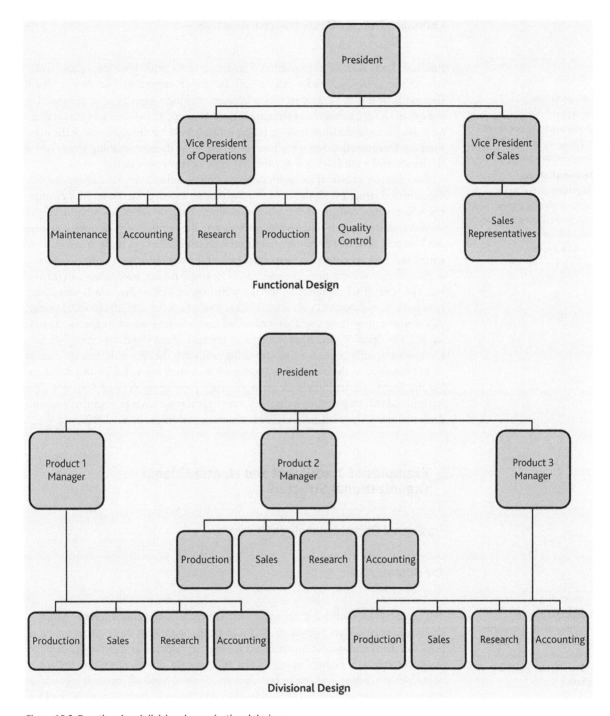

Figure 15.2 Functional and divisional organizational designs.

Centralized versus Decentralized Structure

Centralization

the degree to which decision-making power rests at the upper levels of the organizational hierarchy

Decentralization

the process of taking the decision-making authority away from the top levels of the organization and distributing it to lower levels

Another dimension of organizational structure deals with how important work-related decisions are made, which can be either centralized or decentralized. **Centralization** is the degree to which decision-making authority is concentrated at the top of the organizational hierarchy (Fry & Slocum, 1984). In highly centralized organizations, the decision-making power is firmly held by the top levels of the organization. **Decentralization** is the process of taking the decision-making power out of the hands of the top level and distributing some of it to lower levels.

For example, a chain of ice cream stores could have either a very centralized or a very decentralized structure. In the centralized structure, top-level executives in the corporate office would control all the decision making. They would decide what flavors of ice cream should appear in the stores each month, the number of personnel each store can hire, and how the advertising budget for each store will be spent. In contrast, if the same chain had a decentralized structure, each of the store managers would be allowed to make decisions concerning the selection of ice cream flavors, advertising, and personnel. The centralized organization has the advantage of uniformity, which means that each store should operate with some average level of quality and efficiency. However, this structure may limit the ability of individual stores to adjust to special circumstances. For example, one store manager in the centralized chain may complain that his store has special personnel and advertising needs that the corporate decision makers do not consider. In the decentralized company, each store can make its own decisions, but this could backfire if the store managers make poor or uninformed decisions. One study found that employees felt that they were treated more fairly by organizations with decentralized, as opposed to centralized, structures (Schminke et al., 2000).

Examples of Traditional and Nontraditional Organizational Structures

Traditional Organizational Structures

The Bureaucracy

Bureaucracy

a traditional organizational structure typified by a well-defined authority hierarchy and strict rules governing work behavior

The prototypical traditional organizational structure is the **bureaucracy**, which is characterized by a well-defined authority hierarchy with strict rules governing work behavior. The bureaucratic organization is often represented as a pyramid, with the few members with highest status on the top, leading directly down to the many bottom-level workers who carry out the organization's goal of producing goods or services. The bureaucratic model was developed in the early 20th century by the German sociologist Max Weber, who formulated a theory of organizational structure that was based on formality and authority (Weber, 1947). Weber believed the bureaucracy

Table 15.1 Six Characteristics of a Bureaucratic Organization

Specialization of labor—The complex goals or outputs of the organization are broken down into separate jobs with simple, routine, well-defined tasks. In this way, each person becomes a specialized expert at performing a certain task.

A well-defined authority hierarchy—Bureaucracies are characterized by a pyramid-type arrangement in which each lower position is controlled and supervised by the next higher level. Every position is under the direct supervision of someone higher up so that there is no confusion about who reports to whom (see Figure 15.3).

Formal rules and procedures—In a bureaucracy, there are strict rules and regulations to ensure uniformity and to regulate work behavior. Because of these extensive rules and procedures, there should never be any doubt about what a particular worker is supposed to be doing. Everyone's job is well defined, and procedures for coordinating activities with other workers should be clearly established.

Impersonality—In bureaucracies, behavior is based on logical rather than emotional thinking. This means that personal preferences and emotional factors do not have a place in any work-related decisions. For example, a true bureaucratic service organization would never give preferential treatment to one customer over another.

Employment decisions based on merit—Hiring and promotion decisions are based on who is best qualified for the job, rather than on the personal preferences of those making the personnel decisions. In a true bureaucracy, people who are effective workers should be the only ones advancing to higher-level positions.

Emphasis on written records—To ensure uniformity of action and fair and equitable treatment of employees, bureaucracies keep meticulous records of past decisions and actions. All behaviors occurring in the organization are recorded, which contributes to the image of bureaucrats as compulsive "paper-shufflers."

established order in the work setting and increased productivity by reducing inefficiencies in organizational operations. According to him, a true bureaucratic organization should possess six characteristics, outlined in Table 15.1: the division or specialization of labor, a well-defined authority hierarchy, formal rules and procedures, impersonality, merit-based employment decisions, and an emphasis on written records.

Manufacturing organizations, governmental organizations, and those providing simple customer service are the most likely candidates for bureaucratic structure, which, with its emphasis on job specialization, tends to lead to greater productivity when the manufacturing of goods or the delivery of services is routine. Many of the organizations you deal with on a daily basis, such as the post office, supermarkets, department stores, and fast-food restaurants, are built on the bureaucratic model. And, contrary to popular notions, these bureaucracies are usually efficient organizations. However, the formal nature of the bureaucratic organization, with inflexible rules that stifle individual creativity and initiative, may lead to dissatisfied employees (Adler & Borys, 1996). The bureaucratic model may restrict an organization's ability to grow and innovate.

The Line–Staff Organizational Structure

As organizations grew in complexity, a variation of the traditional bureaucratic model began to emerge. This structure was designated the **line–staff organizational structure** (see Figure 15.4).

Line–Staff Organizational Structure
a traditional organizational structure composed of one group of employees who achieve the goals of the organization (the line) and another group of employees who support the line (staff)

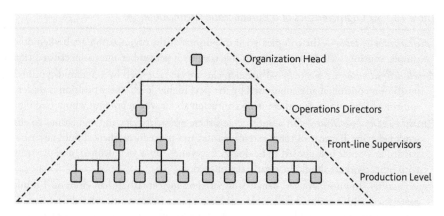

Figure 15.3 A bureaucratic organization is arranged like a pyramid, with decreasing authority levels leading down to the production line.

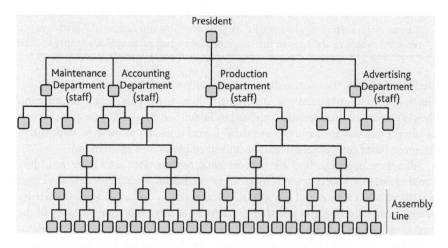

Figure 15.4 Line–staff organizational structure. In a manufacturing organization, the line is represented by production line workers. The staff consists of specialized positions or departments designed to support the line.

Line
employees in an organization who are engaged directly in tasks that accomplish its goals

Staff
specialized employee positions designed to support the line

This traditional structure is made up of two groups of employees, each with different goals. The first group is the **line**, or those workers who are directly engaged in the tasks that accomplish the primary goals of the organization. For example, in manufacturing organizations, line employees are the ones making products on the assembly lines or shop floors. In service organizations, line workers are involved in the distribution of services to customers. The second group of employees is designated as the **staff** and consists of specialized positions designed to support the line. In today's complex organizations, many organizational members hold staff positions that have very little to do directly with the primary goals of the organization. For example, in a computer assembly plant, many employees' jobs involve functions that have nothing to do with assembling computers, such as bookkeeping, plant maintenance, public relations, marketing research, and maintaining employee records (Nossiter, 1979). Recent research suggests that staff managers are, as a group, better at managing relationships and are more open to change and innovation than are line managers. Line managers are more service-oriented than staff managers, but they are less open to change (Church & Waclawski, 2001).

⏱ Stop & Review
Define three dimensions used to classify organizational structure.

Nontraditional Organizational Structures

The Matrix Organization: A Hybrid of Traditional and Nontraditional Organizational Designs

The **matrix organization** is an organizational design that is structured both by product and function simultaneously. This offers the best of both traditional and nontraditional designs. In matrix organizations, workers have two reporting lines: one to a functional manager, a person responsible for the worker's area of expertise (e.g., engineering, marketing), and one to a product manager, who is responsible for the particular product being produced (see Figure 15.5). In manufacturing, matrix organizations are designed to adapt rapidly to changing conditions. They are characterized by high flexibility and adaptability (Larson & Gobeli, 1987).

Matrix organizations will not work well with all types of tasks or workers. They tend to be best suited for projects and products that require creativity and innovation, but are less well suited for routine tasks that can be easily broken down into specialized components.

Routine tasks are better handled in more traditional organizational structures. Matrix organizations tend to have high levels of performance when dealing with complex, creative work products (Ford & Randolph, 1992). Also, because of the amount of interaction among members in matrix structures and the high levels of responsibility they possess, matrix organizations usually have greater worker communication and job satisfaction. The drawbacks to matrix organizations are obvious: reporting to two bosses simultaneously can cause confusion and potentially disruptive conflict.

Matrix Organization

an organizational design that blends functional and product structures

Contingency Models of Organizational Structure

It is clear that no one type of structure is appropriate for all work organizations. Organizations differ in many ways, including the number and type of goods or services they produce, their size, their customers, their employees, and the environment in which they are situated. All these factors can help determine which structure is "best"

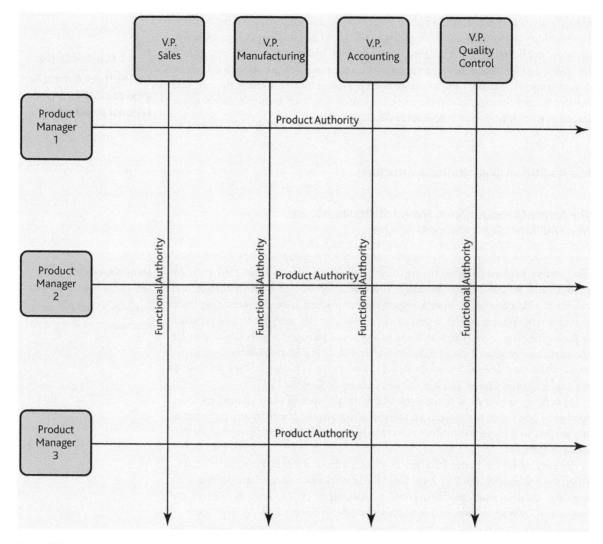

Figure 15.5 A matrix organization is a hybrid of functional and product designs.

⏱ Stop & Review

Compare and contrast traditional and nontraditional organizational structures and give examples of each.

for an organization. Many theorists argue that organizational structure should be addressed with contingency models. Recall that these models look at the interaction of characteristics of the individual—in this case, the organization—and characteristics of the situation—in this case, the setting in which the organization operates.

One of the earliest contingency models of organizational structure was proposed by sociologist Joan Woodward (1965). Focusing solely on manufacturing organizations, Woodward stated that, for maximal performance, the organizational structure needed to match the type of production technology. Woodward classified manufacturers into three types: small-batch production, mass production, and continuous-process production. According to Woodward's model, producers of small batches of specialty products, such as specialized electronic components or construction equipment, required a span of control that was moderate in size, with about 20–30 workers reporting to a supervisor, and a short chain of command. Mass-production organizations, referred to as "large-batch" companies, such as automobile assemblers and manufacturers of household appliances, required a large span of control (40–50 workers per supervisor) and a fairly long chain of command, with several levels in the organizational hierarchy. Finally, continuous-process manufacturing, such as producing chemicals or refining oil, required a small span of control and a very long chain of command.

When organizational structures fit the level of technological complexity, the organizations were productive. When there was a mismatch between technological complexity and the appropriate structures designated by Woodward's model, productivity suffered (Woodward, 1965).

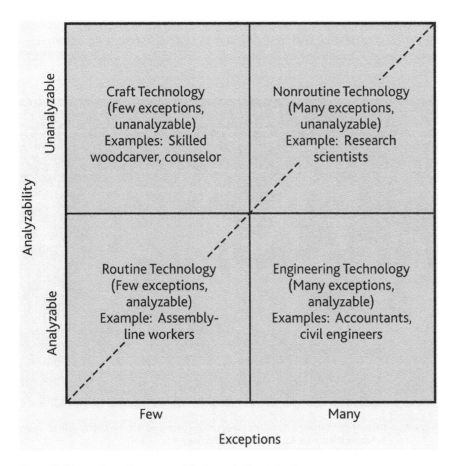

Figure 15.6 Perrow's contingency model of organizational structure.

The one obvious limitation to Woodward's structural contingency model is that it deals only with manufacturing organizations. A theory proposed by Perrow (1970) looked at the relationship between technology and structure in all types of organizations. Rather than focusing solely on production technology, Perrow examined what he called "information technology," which refers to all aspects of jobs, including the equipment and tools used, the decision-making procedures followed, and the information and expertise needed. Perrow classified work-related technology along two dimensions: whether the technology was analyzable or unanalyzable and whether the work contained few or many exceptional work situations requiring creative problem solving. Analyzable work refers to whether the technology can be broken down into simple, objective steps or procedures. Work with few exceptions is predictable and straightforward—presenting few novel problems. Work with many exceptions is "unanalyzable" and has unfamiliar problems turning up often in the work process.

The interaction of these two technology dimensions leads to Perrow's model of four categories of organizational technology: routine, engineering, craft, and nonroutine (see Figure 15.6). Routine technology consists of analyzable work tasks with few exceptions; examples are assembly-line production or the work of grocery store employees. Engineering technology consists of analyzable tasks with many exceptions; examples include the work of lawyers or civil engineers, which involves tasks

Figure 15.7 Because performing artists face many unique problems with no clearly defined steps to follow, they require a nonroutine technology.

Source: Photograph by Michael Afonso, found on Unsplash (https://unsplash.com/photos/nZU76qWy-T8).

that are analyzable but ones that also present workers with novel problems that need to be solved. The lawyer dealing with unique legal cases or an engineer encountering problems in constructing a specific bridge are examples. Craft technology uses technology that is unanalyzable, with no discrete steps, and has few exceptions; examples include the jobs of a skilled woodcarver and a social worker. Both of these jobs involve specialized experience and knowledge, but both present workers with similar types of problems. Finally, nonroutine technology is represented by the work of scientific researchers or professional artists and musicians in which there are no clearly defined steps to follow, yet there are many unique problems to be solved (see Figure 15.7).

According to Perrow's model, the structure of the organization adjusts to the technology. For example, organizations with routine technology tend to be formal, highly rule-driven, and centralized in structure. Nonroutine technology leads to a less formal, more flexible structure, such as a team or matrix organization. The craft and engineering technologies tend to result in structures that are neither completely traditional nor completely nontraditional but rather a combination of both (Gibson et al., 2015).

Stop & Review
List and define the six characteristics of a bureaucracy.

APPLYING I/O PSYCHOLOGY

The Role of Organizational Structure in Computer-Aided Manufacturing

Since the 1980s, there have been profound advances made in manufacturing technology. The greatest impact has been in the area of computer-aided manufacturing (CAM). More and more, product manufacturing is being controlled and monitored by sophisticated computer systems (Cecil, 2001). The changeover to CAM has led to significant organizational restructuring for the purposes of adapting and better integrating state-of-the-art production techniques (Shaiken, 1984).

In a study of nearly 200 U.S. metal-working factories, the impact of CAM technology on organizational structure was explored (Dean Jr et al., 1992). Of particular concern was how CAM affected the decentralization of decision making and the formalization of rules in the organizations. It was found that the use of CAM technology led to increased decentralization, as production

workers took on greater responsibility for making important work-related decisions. A great deal of the increased decision making being done by lower-level workers was related to the increased flexibility offered by CAM technology. Specifically, it was found that the computers could be more quickly and easily reprogrammed by lower-level personnel rather than going through the time-consuming process of going up the chain of command to make reprogramming decisions. Yet, with this increase in decentralization came an increase in the development of rules governing production-related decisions in the factories. The greater decision making of production workers seemed to increase the adoption of specific rules to govern the computer-related decisions they were now shouldered with.

Organizational Culture

Organizational Culture
the shared values, beliefs, assumptions, and patterns of behavior within an organization

Although organizations have a formal structure, "informal" forces also operate to shape the organization and behavior within the organization. A popular approach to viewing these informal aspects of the organization is to refer to them collectively as the "organizational culture." **Organizational culture** can be defined as the shared values, beliefs, assumptions, and patterns of behavior within an organization (Schneider et al., 2013). In many ways, organizational culture is somewhat akin to the organization's "personality" (Kilman et al., 1985). It is differences in organizational culture that cause two companies—similar in most important ways, such as company size, goods produced, and regional location—to "feel" completely different to workers and visitors (Schein, 1992). Organizational culture is different from "organizational climate," with culture being more deeply embedded in the organization (Denison, 1996).

Organizational culture develops from many sources. For example, organizations develop certain assumptions and norms governing behavior through a history of experience concerning what seems to "work" and what "doesn't work" for the organization. Shared norms, values, and goals contribute greatly to an organization's culture (O'Reilly & Chatman, 1996). An organization's culture is also reflected in the stories and "myths" that are told within the organization, and the culture can be communicated and further shaped by those stories (Schneider et al., 2011). The technology used in the organization, the markets it sells its products and/or services to, and the organization's competition all influence organizational culture. Organizational culture can also be affected by the societal culture in which the organization is located and the makeup of its workers. Finally, the organizational culture can be shaped by the personalities of the companies' founders and their most dominant early leaders, as with companies such as Hewlett-Packard (HP), Kellogg's, Walmart, and J. C. Penney (Schneider et al., 1996).

It has been suggested that organizations vary in terms of the strength and influence of their organizational cultures, with some organizations having strong, dominant cultures, and other companies having weaker cultures (O'Reilly, 1989). It has also been suggested that having a strong organizational culture can be beneficial to companies that provide services because it is crucial that representatives of service organizations provide a strong sense of company identity to customers (Chatman & Jehn, 1994). A good example is coffee giant Starbucks, which has a culture focused on customer service and social and environmental responsibility (Gavin, 2013). For these types of customer service-focused organizations, it is important that customers understand what the company "stands for."

In one study, it was found that companies that have a strong commitment to good human resources practices foster a climate that involves mutual trust, cooperation, and a greater sharing of information among organizational members. This very positive organizational culture led to greater company performance (Collins & Smith, 2006). Organizations that gain a reputation for having an exceptional organizational culture are better able to recruit job applicants (Catanzaro et al., 2010).

In many of the earlier chapters, we have touched on elements of organizational culture. For example, in employee selection, particularly in hiring interviews, there are often efforts made to see if a potential employee "fits" with the company's organizational culture (i.e., "Does he or she hold values consistent with our organization?").

For example, Southwest Airlines prefers hiring employees who have a good sense of humor and know how to have fun, consistent with its fun-loving company culture. Initial training and socialization of new employees often include efforts to convey elements of the organization's culture to newcomers. For example, Starbucks makes efforts to impress on new employees the importance of its emphasis on corporate social responsibility. In addition, companies may develop specific norms that help convey corporate culture. For example, at Google, employees are encouraged to eat in the Google café, and there are on-site exercise rooms, washers and dryers, game rooms, and locker rooms to make it easier for employees to work together (and work late).

Organizational culture can, by its very nature, serve as a force that guides behavior within the organization. However, organizational culture can oftentimes make an organization resistant to change and innovation (Bareil, 2013). By understanding and assessing an organization's culture, it becomes easier to predict organizational behavior under different circumstances (Hofstede et al., 1990). For example, studies have found that organizations with strong cultural values that involved flexibility, openness, and responsiveness were more likely to grow,

Figure 15.8 Shared values, beliefs, and behavioral norms make up each company's unique organizational culture.

Source: Photo by Social.Cut, on Unsplash. https://unsplash.com/photos/r0saAQNjEjQ.

expand, and innovate, whereas organizations with a culture that valued consistency and adherence to the company's mission were more productive and profitable (Naranjo-Valencia et al., 2011).

Of utmost importance today is the extent to which organizational culture supports diversity and inclusion. As the workforce becomes increasingly diverse, issues around building cultures that foster diversity and inclusion are more important than ever (Holmes IV et al., 2016). McKay and colleagues define diversity climate as "the degree to which a firm advocates fair human resource policies and socially integrates underrepresented employees" (McKay et al., 2008, p. 352). Diversity climate has been linked to a list of positive outcomes including more positive work attitudes such as higher job satisfaction, better performance, and lower turnover (Holmes IV et al., 2021).

Expanding from the concept of a climate that supports fairness across difference, additional research has shown the importance of inclusive climates, which also promote integrating diverse perspectives and identities (Nishii, 2013). Whereas climates that support diversity might reduce negative treatment of certain team members, inclusive climates create synergies from the different perspectives and identities that employees bring such that the link between inclusive climates and positive outcomes is stronger than that for diversity climate alone (Holmes IV et al., 2021). As we discussed in the chapter on leadership, leaders have a strong impact on inclusion (Bader et al., 2019), but so do peers and other colleagues who have the power to accept or reject us (Wagstaff et al., 2015). Leaders and organizational members play a large part in perceptions of whether an organization's culture is supportive of diversity (Bader et al., 2019).

Societal Influences on Organizational Culture

The larger culture of a nation, society, or ethnic group can have important influences on the development of the organizational culture of a work organization. The most influential work on societal culture is by Hofstede (1980, 1997). According to Hofstede, there are five key dimensions on which societal cultures differ, such as whether the culture has an *individualistic* base, where values are centered on the individual and individual achievements, or a *collectivistic* base, where values are focused on the group or collective. The U.S., for example, is very individualistic in its societal/national orientation, whereas Mexico and Japan are more collectivistic (see Table 15.2 for a description of these five cultural dimensions).

One large study (House et al., 2004), called the Global Leadership and Organizational Behavior Effectiveness project (GLOBE), is looking at cross-national differences in work organizations, in their cultures, and in their leadership. Although societal culture can have a direct influence on a work organization's culture, these cultural influences are also important in organizations whose workers are made up of members from diverse cultural backgrounds. Understanding systematic differences in the society in which a work organization is embedded, and cultural differences in

Table 15.2 Five Dimensions of Societal/National Culture

Individualism versus collectivism—Concerned with the extent to which individual interests and goals are emphasized versus a focus on the larger group, or collective

Power distance—Deals with the extent to which members of the culture accept and expect that there are differences in the way that power is distributed unequally among members

Masculinity versus femininity—Represents the extent to which members of the culture value traits and practices that are stereotypically "masculine," such as assertiveness and competitiveness, or stereotypically "feminine," such as caring for others and being modest in presentation of accomplishments

Uncertainty avoidance—Concerns the extent to which members of the culture avoid or tolerate uncertainty and ambiguity

Long-term versus short-term orientation—This dimension concerns whether members of the culture emphasize long-term orientations, such as perseverance and working hard today for future payoffs, versus short-term fulfillment of immediate needs

Source: Based on Hofstede (1980, 1997).

workers from different nations and societies will help to improve our general understanding of work behavior.

Measuring Organizational Culture

There are a variety of ways of measuring organizational culture. One qualitative strategy is to focus on the "artifacts" of the organization's culture (Rafaeli & Pratt, 2006). These might include important symbols that carry meaning for organizational members, such as employees wearing pins with the word *quality*, suggesting that this is an important focus of the organization. Commonly shared stories about a company, its founders, or heroes might be another type of cultural artifact, as would be certain rituals, such as a company that has a monthly "service day," where employees get together to engage in a joint community service project. One Southern California company has a ritual of employees helping to construct the company's float for the annual Pasadena Tournament of Roses parade.

There are several commonly used measures of diversity and inclusion climate. For diversity climate, McKay and colleagues (2007) and Mor Barak et al. (1998) offer excellent measures that focus on diversity, specific identities, and fair employment practices. For inclusive climate, Nishii (2013) and Chung and colleagues (2020) offer useful measures. An element that is consistent across all of these measures is the sense that individuals are not treated unfairly because of an identity that they hold (such as race or gender). The inclusive measures also assess the extent to which one feels that one's unique perspectives are brought out at work, and the Chung measure also assesses the extent to which one feels a sense of belonging to the organization.

⏱ Stop & Review

Give two examples of contingency models of organizational structure.

One consideration for those who use these measures is to test whether there are differences in the experience of inclusion by race and gender—in other words, are there higher mean scores on inclusion for men than women or the other way around? These types of tests reveal great insights into employees' experience of inclusion in the workplace.

A more general measure of culture is the *Organizational Culture Profile* (OCP) (O'Reilly et al., 1991). The OCP asks organizational representatives to sort 54 "value statements" describing such things as organizational attitudes toward quality, risk taking, and the respect the organization gives to workers into meaningful categories to provide a descriptive profile of the organization. Research using the OCP in a number of different companies indicated that important dimensions of organizational culture include the company's concern with innovation, stability, its leadership, orientation toward people, orientation toward producing results, and team orientation (Chatman & Jehn, 1994)

Another measure is Hofstede et al.'s (1990) *Organizational Practices Scale*. This instrument, designed specifically to measure organizational culture (as opposed to societal culture) assesses the company's culture in terms of dimensions such as whether the organization is "process versus results oriented" or "employee versus job oriented" or has "loose" or "tight" control over employees' behavior, as well as other dimensions. A revised version includes scales of whether an organization is "self-interested versus socially responsible" and "market" versus "internally" oriented (Verbeke, 2000). Other measures of organizational culture are more specific, such as one measure that assesses an organization's culture for quality (Johnson, 2000).

The study of organizational culture is an increasingly popular approach for I/O psychologists studying organizations at a global level (Gelfand et al., 2017). Organizational culture is intertwined with the topics of job satisfaction (Chapter 9) and group processes (Chapter 11) covered earlier.

Organizational Development

Throughout modern history, it has been common for organizations to cease operating because they were unable to change to keep up with the times, such as photo company Kodak or video rental store Blockbuster (Mone et al., 1998). Companies that do not use the latest marketing or production techniques can lose out to competitors who take advantage of state-of-the-art technology. Retail stores and internet companies that are unable to keep pace with changing consumer tastes have gone out of business. Furthermore, organizations have to adapt not only to external conditions but also to internal factors (Mu, 2015). For example, as new generations of workers enter the workforce with different types of skills and different ideas about what they want from their jobs, the organization must adjust to utilize their skills and to meet their demands. Otherwise, the better workers will leave the organization, or disgruntled employees may be able to slow down productivity through costly work stoppages and strikes. In addition, the trend toward downsizing means that many organizations must produce more with fewer organizational members. In short, the ability to change is critical to an organization's survival.

Why is change such a problem for organizations? Even very early research in I/O psychology demonstrated time and time again that individuals, groups, and organizations strongly resist any sort of change (McMurry, 1947). People and organizations get comfortable with the familiar and the "tried and true." Moreover, characteristics of bureaucracies, as we saw earlier, are designed for stability and consistency, and so bureaucratic organizations are particularly resistant to change. It has been argued that the biggest task of today's business leaders is to recognize the need for organizations to change and to manage that change process (Martins, 2011). In fact, an analysis of the reasons given for boards of directors firing chief executive officers (CEOs) found that the most common reason was the failure of the CEO to appropriately manage change (Hempel, 2005).

The study of organizational change is an important topic. In addition to studying organizational change processes, social scientists have made use of certain interventions to help organizations prepare for and manage organizational change (Gallos, 2006). The specific specialty area concerned with helping organizations develop, adapt, and innovate is known as **organizational development (OD)**. Organizational development often involves altering the organization's work structure or influencing workers' attitudes or behavior to help the organization to adapt to fluctuating external and internal conditions.

OD typically takes place in a series of phases. The first phase is usually a diagnosis of the organization to identify significant problems. In the next phase, appropriate interventions are chosen to try to deal with the problems. The third phase is the implementation of the interventions, or OD techniques. Finally, the results of the interventions are evaluated (Burke, 1987). Organizational development does not involve one single theory or approach, but rather a variety of orientations and methods for helping organizations manage change. Although OD is its own subdiscipline, with its own dedicated journals and associations, much of organizational development rests on a foundation created by research in I/O psychology.

Organizational development is an applied, practice-oriented area of the behavioral sciences. The OD practitioner is oriented toward helping the organization design and implement a program for dealing with change-related problems (Jamieson et al., 2016). The OD practitioner is often referred to as a **change agent**—one who coaches or guides the organization in developing problem-solving strategies. The change agent, however, is not a problem solver, but is a behavioral scientist, often an industrial/organizational psychologist, who is expert at assisting organizations in diagnosing problems and skilled in helping organizational members deal with sensitive situations. The change agent works with the various levels of the organization, developing or deciding on problem-solving techniques, and will have some special knowledge of particular OD interventions that may be used to help solve the organization's problems. The change agent also acts as an educator who trains the organization to implement strategies for coping with future problems (Burke, 1987).

Organizational Development (OD)
the process of assisting organizations in preparing for and managing change

Change Agent
name for an OD practitioner, referring to the person's role as a catalyst who helps organizations through the process of change

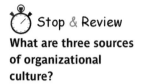

Stop & Review

What are three sources of organizational culture?

Action Research
an OD methodological model that applies social science research methods to collecting relevant organizational data that are used for solving organizational problems

Waclawski and Church (2002) argued that OD is a highly data-driven process, and so the effective OD practitioner should be well steeped in social science research methods and how to apply them.

Organizational development programs usually follow one of several procedural models, all of which typically use an OD consultant, or change agent, and go through the four phases outlined earlier. One popular OD model is **action research**, which is the process of applying social science research methods to collect relevant data within the organization to study the organization and to help it understand and solve its problems (Aguinis, 1993). The application-oriented goal of action research means that it is somewhat different than the traditional hypothesis-testing research discussed in Chapter 2. Whereas hypothesis-testing research attempts to find new knowledge that is applicable to a wide range of organizations, action research tries to solve problems specific to a particular organization. Action research involves some of the same tools used by hypothesis-testing research—namely, objective observation and the collection and analysis of research data. However, their goals and scope are quite different, for action research is oriented toward producing some specific result.

The first step in the action research process is data gathering and problem diagnosis. Here, the OD consultant collects data to diagnose the problem situation (McFillen et al., 2013). In the next step, feedback is given as the data, and the OD consultant's interpretation of the data, are presented to the organization's members. The next step is joint action planning. Here, the OD consultant and the organizational members design a problem-solving program, which might be one of a variety of OD interventions that we will discuss later. Once the program is implemented, the action research process repeats itself. Now, however, the data gathering is an attempt to determine the effectiveness of the OD program. If it is successful, the organization and the OD consultant might discuss ways to make it a regular part of the organization's operations. If unsuccessful, the program might need some alterations, or a different program might be tried. Figure 15.9 graphically depicts the steps in the action research model.

Organizational Development Techniques

In solving organizational problems, OD programs use a wide variety of established techniques (Fagenson & Burke, 1990), some of which we have already discussed. For example, recall from Chapter 7 that job enrichment is a process of increasing the levels of responsibility associated with jobs to improve worker satisfaction and commitment to the work effort. Although job enrichment was presented in Chapter 7 as a motivational technique, it could also be used in OD efforts because it involves the collaboration of workers in work teams that plays an important part in solving change-related problems that may affect the groups' work performance. Organizational behavior modification programs (also presented in Chapter 7), which reinforce desirable work behaviors, can likewise be used as an OD technique.

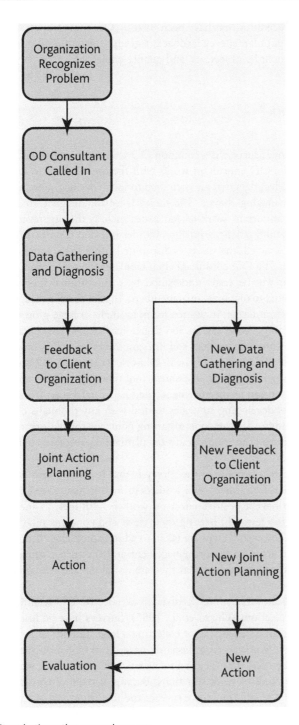

Figure 15.9 Steps in the action research process.

Of the other procedures that have been used by OD practitioners, we will discuss six of the more popular: survey feedback, t-groups, team building, process consultation, management by objectives, and quality circles.

Survey Feedback

Survey Feedback
an OD technique whereby the consultant works with the organization to develop and administer a survey instrument to collect data that are fed back to organizational members and used as the starting point for change

The use of employee surveys is a common OD strategy. **Survey feedback** is the process by which the OD consultant works with the organization to develop a survey instrument to collect data that are then used to solve specific problems or to institute a program for managing change. The survey is usually designed to assess employee attitudes about important work-related issues such as the organization in general, company policies and practices, quality of leadership, and coordination among work units. Once constructed, the survey is distributed either to all workers or to a representative sample. The OD consultant then tabulates the survey data and puts them into a form that will be easily understood by organizational members. Next, the results are presented to organizational members. This feedback can be done in a number of ways: via the internet, in written form, in small- or large-group discussions, or in a general meeting. As we saw in 360-degree feedback, survey data from multiple sources, such as from management and line employees, as well as other constituents, can be very useful. This is also the case in OD-oriented surveys (Church et al., 2002). Because the survey is merely an assessment tool to indicate which areas of the organization need attention or improvement, the final, crucial step in a survey feedback program involves developing strategies to deal with any problems or concerns that arise from the results. The survey is a starting point for solving organizational problems or for instituting future programs for planned organizational change (Born & Mathieu, 1996).

One of the direct benefits of the survey is that it can increase the upward flow of communication from lower-level workers to management (see Chapter 10). The survey may also have a positive effect on workers' attitudes, as they perceive that management is interested in hearing their views and concerns (Gavin, 1984). This will only occur, however, if steps are taken to address problems. If not, workers may develop negative attitudes about management and the survey process. Finally, the survey results can show workers that they are not alone and that others share their attitudes and concerns.

Research indicates that survey feedback is an effective OD technique if followed by some positive actions (Guzzo et al., 1985). Surveys have additional advantages as well. They are an efficient way of collecting a large amount of information from a large number of workers. Also, because surveys can be conducted anonymously, lower-level workers feel that they can safely voice their opinions, which can lead to very honest appraisals of work situations. Because it requires considerable training to create valid and reliable employee surveys and to analyze and interpret the results, I/O psychologists or other social science professionals are most often involved in survey feedback programs.

🕐 Stop & Review

Outline the methods and terms used in organizational development.

T-groups

The OD strategy known as **t-groups** (also called **sensitivity training**) actually refers to the use of unstructured group interaction to help workers gain insight into their motivations and their behavior patterns in dealing with others. T-groups, which stands for "training groups," consists of small groups of workers who meet in a nonwork setting for an unstructured discussion of their attitudes and beliefs concerning their work, the work environment, and their interactions with supervisors and coworkers. The eventual goals of t-groups are for participants to gain insight concerning their own behavior, to develop greater openness, and to improve skills of understanding and dealing with others. Typically, a professional serves as group leader, although the leader usually plays a nondirective role, merely keeping the goals of the session in everyone's minds and keeping the discussion from getting out of hand. An effective leader will usually prevent problems such as "psychological casualties," which occur when the group targets one or more persons for intense criticism or when participants suffer from airing sensitive personal information in a public forum.

T-groups (Sensitivity Training)
an OD technique that uses unstructured group interaction to assist workers in achieving insight into their own motivations and behavior patterns in dealing with other organizational members

Process Consultation

Process consultation is an OD technique in which a consultant helps a client organization to "perceive, understand, and act upon process events which occur in the client's environment" (Schein, 1969, p. 3). In process consultation, the OD consultant helps the organization to learn how to solve its own problems. In many ways, process consultation epitomizes many of the central themes of organizational development. It uses a change agent, the process consultant, who works as a teacher to assist the client-organization in learning how to use objective methods, such as survey instruments, structured interviews, or the collection of relevant performance data, to diagnose and solve its own problems. The consultant also instructs organizational members in how to implement specific OD problem-solving techniques. The goal is for the organization to become self-reliant by knowing how to deal with change-related problems once the process consultant is gone.

Process Consultation
an OD technique in which a consultant helps a client-organization study its problems objectively and learn to solve them

To understand the specific steps in process consultation outlined by Schein (1969), we will use the example of a consultant who is working with CDE company, which produces and sells cosmetics. The first step is the *initial contact* with the client-organization, which is usually initiated by someone in the organization who realizes that problems exist and is willing to try to solve them. In the case of CDE, the vice president of sales called in the process consultant, Dr. Io, because of what he considers to be high turnover of sales personnel and managers.

The second step is *developing the contract*. In initial, exploratory meetings, the vice president of sales meets with top decision makers—the other vice presidents and the company president—to determine the problems, explain the consultant's role, and formulate actions to be taken. A formal contract is drawn up to determine matters such as client time and compensation. A "psychological" contract, which includes the expectations and goals of the organization as well as Dr. Io's goals, is also formulated: the company wants to reduce costly turnover, and Dr. Io wants the organization to take steps not only to reduce turnover, but also to ensure that the company can deal with future turnover problems. In addition, she wants the organization to explore any related problems that the consultation uncovers.

The third step is the *selection of a setting and a method of work*. A site for study is selected collaboratively with the client and is usually a unit near the top of the organization. Those workers who are being observed by the consultant must be made aware of her presence and purpose. Together, Dr. Io and the CDE decision makers choose the largest regional headquarters as the site for study. Because this office is adjacent to corporate headquarters, Dr. Io will have easy contact with the company's top-level executives.

The fourth step is *data gathering and diagnosis*. By using interviews (particularly exit interviews), direct observation, and surveys of employees, Dr. Io tries to obtain an in-depth picture of the organization and its internal processes. She works with certain CDE personnel, instructing them in data collection methods. Through analysis of these data and consultation with relevant CDE personnel and executives, specific problem areas are targeted. The data reveal that turnover is linked to three factors: (a) salespersons perceive their sales commissions rates to be lower than those in other sales positions; (b) salespersons feel they do not receive enough attention from sales managers; and (c) some salespersons are hired without much experience, and CDE provides little specific training of new personnel.

The next step is the *intervention*. A variety of intervention strategies are used in process consultation. Some are as simple as providing feedback of the consultant's observations to workers. Others may involve counseling work groups or individuals or setting agendas to increase a group's awareness of its own internal processes. In the case of CDE, Dr. Io and company executives jointly decide to develop a "sales force improvement task force," composed of both management personnel and salespersons, who will formulate a proposal to improve the hiring and training procedures for new salespersons. Other goals of the task force will be to conduct a survey of sales commission rates in other companies and to develop a program for improving sales managers' supervision.

The final step in process consultation is the *evaluation of results and disengagement*. According to Schein (1969, p. 123), successful process consultation improves organizational performance by "changing some of the values of the organization and by increasing the interpersonal skills of key managers." If these goals are met, CDE should see some changes in the organization's perception of the value of the sales force and in the selection, training, and treatment of sales personnel. There will also likely be some improvement in the interpersonal skills of sales managers. The relationship between consultant and client is terminated by mutual agreement. In the case of CDE, Dr. Io may or may not work with the organization in implementing and evaluating the various new programs. Sometimes, a slow disengagement process is used whereby the consultant gradually lessens involvement with the client-organization.

This is likely in the case of Dr. Io, because the programs for organizational improvement will probably take a long time to design and implement, and their evaluation will likely initially require her assistance.

Process consultation is a detailed OD program involving an extensive and long-term relationship between the consultant and the client-organization, and the process consultant is faced with a challenging role to serve as an expert but not become a problem solver (Lalonde & Adler, 2015). Some authors have likened this technique to the psychotherapeutic process, in which a therapist works with a client over a long period to diagnose and work toward solving the client's problems (Landy, 1989). Unfortunately, there has not been a great deal of research evaluating the effectiveness of process consultation.

Management by Objectives (MBO)

Management by objectives, or **MBO**, is a goal-setting technique that is often used as an OD intervention. In MBO, subordinates work with superiors in jointly setting performance goals. The basic rationales behind the procedure are that work-related goals must be clearly specified and measurable, and that employees should participate in setting them to become committed to their fulfillment. MBO is closely related to the goal-setting techniques of motivation discussed in Chapter 7. Management by objectives can also be used as an alternative to traditional rating methods of performance appraisal, because successful MBO programs must accurately and objectively measure the attainment of performance goals. At the end of the goal period—usually 3–6 months and occasionally 12 months—employees again meet with supervisors and receive feedback concerning the goal attainment. If the goals have not been met, suggestions for improvement are made. If they have been attained, new and perhaps even more challenging goals are set.

The MBO technique actually predates the organizational development movement. Popularized in the 1950s by Drucker and his associates (1954), it has been an often-used method for improving worker performance. Unfortunately, MBO has also been widely misused. Often, any type of goal setting is labeled MBO, even though it does not follow the MBO model (McConkie, 1979). For MBO to be implemented correctly, the following criteria must be met:

▮ *Employees must participate in setting personal performance goals*. A potential weakness of MBO goal setting, however, is that workers may take advantage of the freedom they are afforded and set goals that are much too easy and do not represent a motivating challenge. Alternatively, if the supervisor too strongly influences the setting of goals, MBO may not be effective because employees may feel that they have no real voice in the goal-setting process.

▮ *Feedback concerning goal attainment must be provided*. As in any performance appraisal system, the strength of the appraisal depends on the ability to assess

Management by Objectives (MBO)
a goal-setting OD technique in which supervisors and subordinates jointly set performance goals; at the end of the goal period, their attainment is evaluated, and new goals are set

performance objectively. Objective measurement of goal attainment must take place, and this information must be presented to the employees.

- *Guidelines for improvement must be provided*. In the case of the failure to reach goals, supervisors should provide suggestions for improving work performance. Otherwise, employees may become frustrated and unmotivated by their inability to achieve set goals.
- *Goals must be realistic*. They must be neither too high nor too low. If goals are unrealistically high, the workers will be frustrated. If they are too low, the employees are not challenged.
- *The upper levels of the organization must support the program*. Because MBO is a time-consuming process for supervisors, their efforts must be recognized. The best way to do this is to include effective participation in the MBO program as part of the supervisors' own performance goals.
- *Individual, work group, and organizational goals must be equally emphasized*. If jobs involve cooperation with other employees (and most jobs do), overemphasis on individual goals may inhibit the group's ability to work together. Thus, workers must be oriented toward achieving not only their own goals but also those of the group and the organization as a whole.

Management by objectives is one of the most widely used OD techniques, partly because it can be implemented in just about any work organization and with almost any type of job. MBO is also one of the most successful OD programs. A meta-analysis of 70 studies of MBO programs found that there were productivity gains caused by MBO in 68 of the 70 cases (Rodgers & Hunter, 1991).

Quality Circles

Quality Circles
small groups of volunteer employees from the same work area who meet regularly to solve work-related problems

One OD intervention that is typically associated with Japanese management techniques popularized in the 1980s is the concept of **quality circles**, which are small groups of volunteer employees from the same work areas who meet regularly to identify, analyze, and solve product quality problems and other work-related problems (Adam Jr, 1991). In initial quality circle meetings, members are trained in quality control, work on developing communication skills, and learn problem-solving techniques. They then select a particular problem to study and use a variety of methods to gather information pertinent to the issue. Finally, a recommendation is made to management about how to solve the problem. The goal of quality circles is to get employees more involved in their jobs and to increase their feelings of having some control over their work. This increased employee involvement should lead to greater worker satisfaction, work quality (and perhaps productivity), and worker commitment to the organization (Benson & Lawler, 2016).

Research indicates that quality circles can indeed lead to increased quality and productivity in both Japanese and American manufacturing organizations and may also enhance participants' job satisfaction (Buch & Spangler, 1990). However, in certain instances, U.S. applications of quality circle programs have failed, although analysis suggests that the failures have more to do with poor implementation than with any inherent flaws in the theory underlying quality circles. The failure of quality circle programs, and indeed of other OD programs, can often be traced to a lack of support from management and/or workers or to poor training and preparation of participants (Tang et al., 1996). Moreover, there is evidence, that unless quality circles are maintained and fully integrated into the organizational system, their effectiveness will diminish in 1–2 years (Ledford et al., 1988).

Other "quality-oriented" programs include total quality management (TQM), the implementation of continuous improvement work processes (Coyle-Shapiro, 2000), and Six Sigma, a quality improvement process popularized by former GE CEO Jack Welch (Pande et al., 2000). The success of all quality enhancement programs involves some fundamental changes in organizational climate and culture to get workers committed to improving quality of output. Yet, this is very important, because many organizations have found that, unless they produce high-quality products or services, they cannot compete in the increasingly competitive global market.

The Effectiveness of Organizational Development

A variety of techniques have been used as interventions in organizational development programs. However, the important question is, "Does OD work?" There is no firm answer to this question. A number of factors make it difficult to ascertain the effectiveness of OD programs (Martineau & Preskill, 2002). One difficulty concerns the variety of OD techniques that can be used as part of OD programs. Some of these techniques may simply be better than others. For example, evidence suggests that goal-setting-based programs and survey feedback are moderately successful (Kondrasuk, 1981), whereas there has been some question about the effectiveness of t-groups (Miner, 1983). A second reason lies in the nature of the organization that conducts the OD program. What works in one organization may not be effective in another because of differences in the attitudes of organizational members or in the workers' and management's commitment to OD efforts. Another concern is the abilities of the OD consultants overseeing the intervention—some OD consultants may simply do a better job than others (O'Driscoll & Eubanks, 1993). Furthermore, determining the effectiveness of organizational development is hard because of difficulties in conducting good evaluation research. Because OD interventions usually take place on a large scale, often involving an entire organization, much of the evidence for their effectiveness is based on case studies. The unit of measurement, the "participant," in the evaluation of an OD program is the organization. It is quite difficult to combine the results of a specific OD strategy with those of the same method used in other companies because the circumstances may be different. This often leaves us with only a series of case studies as evidence for the effectiveness of OD programs.

Stop & Review

List and describe five organizational development techniques.

ON THE *CUTTING* EDGE

Fast-Paced and Agile Organizations for the New Millennium

In the ultra-fast modern era, organizations can be created almost overnight and burst into the marketplace with some revolutionary product or service. Think of the startups of the last two decades—Lyft, Airbnb, Slack, Snapchat—companies that burst on the scene and have become household names. Or think of the older, cutting-edge companies—Google/Alphabet, Apple, Facebook, Tesla—that continue to change, adapt, and create new products and services. These fast-paced companies are teaching us a lot about the value of adaptable and organic organizational structures.

One structure or methodology that is gaining notice is what is called *agile management* (or "agile process management"), and it involves project teams that forgo much of the structure and processes that slow down more traditionally structured teams in order to change and adapt quickly. Originally developed for computer software development, the idea is for these teams to try out new ideas and "fail quickly." In other words, new ideas or products are entertained and explored, but, if they do not look promising, the team moves on to another idea. Some of the cornerstones of agile management are ongoing communication in the team, a lack of authority hierarchies (the teams are self-organized, often without a leader), organic and flexible processes, and lots of collaboration. The result is a fast-paced, extremely flexible organizational structure that leads to innovation and highly productive teams (Pirola-Merlo, 2010).

Summary

Organizational structure is the arrangement of positions in an organization and the relationships between them. Organizational structures can be generally classified into traditional and nontraditional forms. Traditional organizational structures tend to be stable and rule-driven, whereas nontraditional structures are characterized by their flexibility, adaptability, and lack of formal authority lines. Important dimensions of organizational structure are the number of authority levels in an organization, or *chain of command*, and the number of workers reporting to a single work supervisor, or the *span of control*. Organizations can also be divided by the kinds of tasks performed—a *functional structure*—or by the types of products produced or customers served—a *divisional structure*. Decision-making power can either be concentrated at the top levels of the organization (*centralization*) or dispersed throughout the organization (*decentralization*).

The *bureaucracy* and the *line–staff organization* typify the traditional structure. The bureaucracy is a structure based on authority relationships among organizational members that operate through a system of formal rules and procedures. The line–staff organization is a formal structure in which the line executes organizational objectives, whereas the staff is designed to support the line. Nontraditional organizational structures are exemplified by the *team organization*, a permanent team of competent workers designed to maximize organizational adaptability, and by the *project task force*, a more temporary structure. A *matrix organization* is a combination of both product and functional organizational designs. The most recent approaches to organizational structure are contingency models, whereby the most effective type of structure depends on the fit between structure and the external or internal environment of the work organization.

Organizational culture refers to the shared values, beliefs, assumptions, and patterns of behavior in organizations. Organizational culture derives from many sources, can be stronger in some organizations than in others, and has important influences on organizational behavior. Societal/national influences on organizational culture can be quite strong. Cultures that support diversity and inclusion create an environment where more people can be successful. Recently, a great deal of attention has been given to developing methods for assessing organizational culture, including the assessment of whether a culture supports diversity and inclusion.

Organizational development (OD) is the process of preparing for and managing change in organizations. OD programs use a consultant who is commonly called a change agent. OD programs usually occur in phases. One model for such a program is *action research*, which involves collecting data, diagnosing organizational problems, and developing strategies to take action to solve them. A variety of interventions are used in OD programs, including *survey feedback*, a technique of using data about organizational members' feelings and concerns as the basis for planned change; *t-groups*, a process of increasing workers' awareness of their own and other members' behavior; *team building*, the development of teams of workers to focus on ways to improve group performance; *process consultation*, a long-term method of helping an organization to develop problem-solving strategies; *management by objectives (MBO)*, a goal-setting technique designed to increase worker commitment to the attainment of personal and organizational goals; and *quality circles*, which are groups of employees who meet regularly to discuss quality-related work problems. Evaluation of OD programs indicates that they can be effective for improving certain aspects of organizational effectiveness, although neither their implementation nor their evaluation is easy.

Study Questions and Exercises

1 Consider an organization with which you have had some contact. Describe the structure of this organization using the dimensions of traditional–nontraditional, functional–divisional, and centralized–decentralized. If you have access to the organization's chart, describe its chain of command and span of control.
2 Based on what you know about traditional and nontraditional organizational structures, contrast the work life of the typical worker in a traditional organization with that of a worker in a nontraditional organization.
3 Compare and contrast the contingency models of organizational structure.

4 Describe the organizational culture of a company or firm you are familiar with. What are some of the sources of this company's organizational culture?

5 Consider a common problem in classrooms, such as a difficulty in communication between professor and students or an unclear grading policy. How might an OD consultant solve this problem? What OD techniques might be used?

6 Drawing on your knowledge of research methods, what are the difficulties in evaluating the success of OD programs?

Web Link

www.odnetwork.org
The OD Network site. A professional network of OD practitioners.

Suggested Readings

Daum, D. L., & Maraist, C. C. (2021). The importance of culture in the era of COVID-19. *Industrial and Organizational Psychology, 14*(1–2), 160–162.

Kuklinski, J. (2021). *Diversity and organizational development*. Emerald.

Perry, S. J. (2020). Changing the narrative on harassment and discrimination training: Building an organizational culture with healthy professional boundaries. *Industrial and Organizational Psychology, 13*(2), 186–190.

Schell, S., & Bischof, N. (2021). Change the way of working. Ways into self-organization with the use of Holacracy: An empirical investigation. *European Management Review.* https://doi.org/10.1111/emre.12457

A number of journals are specifically devoted to organizational development and related topics. These include *Organization Development Journal, Journal of Organizational Change Management, Leadership & Organization Development Journal, OD Practitioner,* and *Action Research.*

GLOSSARY

accommodation   a conflict resolution strategy of making a sacrifice to resolve a conflict.

achievement motivation theory   McClelland's model of motivation that emphasizes the importance of three needs—achievement, power, and affiliation—in determining worker motivation.

achievement-oriented behavior   leader behavior concentrated on particular work outcomes.

action learning   teams assembled to work on a company-related problem or issue to learn by doing.

action research   an OD methodological model that applies social science research methods to collecting relevant organizational data that are used for solving organizational problems.

actor–observer bias   the tendency for observers to overattribute cause to characteristics of the actor and the tendency for the actor to overattribute cause to situational characteristics.

adverse impact   when members of a protected group are treated unfairly by an employer's personnel action.

affirmative action   the voluntary development of policies that try to ensure that jobs are made available to qualified individuals regardless of sex, age, or ethnic background.

apprenticeship   a training technique, usually lasting several years, that combines on-the-job experience with classroom instruction.

assessment center   a detailed, structured evaluation of job applicants using a variety of instruments and techniques.

audience factors   characteristics of the receiver that influence the effectiveness of a communication.

audiovisual instruction   the use of pre-recorded videotapes and other electronic media to convey training material.

autocratic decision making   a process by which group decisions are made by the leader alone, based on information the leader possesses.

avoidance   withdrawing from or avoiding a conflict situation.

behavior modeling training   a training method that exposes trainees to role models performing appropriate and inappropriate work behaviors and their outcomes and then allows trainees to practice modeling the appropriate behaviors.

behavioral observation scales (BOS)   performance appraisal methods that require appraisers to recall how often a worker has been observed performing key work behaviors.

behavioral theories of leadership   theories derived from studies at Ohio State and University of Michigan that focus on the behaviors common to effective leaders.

behaviorally anchored rating scales (BARS)   performance appraisal technique using rating scales with labels reflecting examples of poor, average, and good behavioral incidents.

biodata   background information and personal characteristics that can be used in employee selection.

bona fide occupational qualifications   real and valid occupational needs required for a particular job.

brainstorming   a group process generating creative ideas or solutions through a noncritical and nonjudgmental process.

bureaucracy   a traditional organizational structure typified by a well-defined authority hierarchy and strict rules governing work behavior.

burnout a syndrome resulting from prolonged exposure to work stress that leads to withdrawal from the organization.

case study a research investigation involving a one-time assessment of behavior.

causal attribution the process by which people assign cause to events or behaviors.

central tendency error the tendency to give all workers the midpoint rating in performance appraisals.

centralization the degree to which decision-making power rests at the upper levels of the organizational hierarchy.

centralized networks communication networks in which the flow of communication is directed through specific members.

chain of command the number of authority levels in an organization.

change agent name for an OD practitioner, referring to the person's role as a catalyst who helps organizations through the process of change.

channel the vehicle through which a message flows from sender to receiver.

channel factors characteristics of the vehicle of transmission of a message that affect communication.

charismatic leadership theory a theory that leaders possess some exceptional characteristics that cause followers to be loyal and inspired.

checklists performance appraisal methods using a series of statements about job performance.

coaching a one-on-one relationship where a consultant helps an executive improve performance.

coalition a group of individuals who band together to combine their power.

coercive power the use of punishment or the threat of punishment to affect the behavior of others.

cognitive theories of learning learning theories that emphasize that humans are information processors.

cohesiveness the degree of attraction among group members.

collaboration a conflict resolution strategy in which the parties cooperate to reach a solution that satisfies both.

communication the passage of information between one person or group to another person or group.

communication networks systematic lines of communication among various senders and receivers.

comparable worth the notion that jobs that require equivalent KSAOs should be compensated equally.

comparative methods performance appraisal methods involving comparisons of one worker's performance against that of other workers.

comparison others persons used as a basis for comparison in making judgments of equity/inequity.

compensable factors the job elements that are used to determine appropriate compensation for a job.

competition the process whereby group members are pitted against one another to achieve individual goals.

compressed workweeks schedules that decrease the number of days in the workweek while increasing the number of hours worked per day.

compromise a conflict resolution strategy in which both parties give up some part of their goals.

computer-assisted instruction programmed instruction delivered by computer that adapts to the trainee's learning rate.

conference an unstructured management training technique in which participants share ideas, information, and problems; also called a group discussion.

conflict behavior by a person or group intended to inhibit the attainment of goals by another person or group.

conformity the process of adhering to group norms.

consensus decision making based on 100% member agreement.

consideration leader behaviors that show a concern for the feelings, attitudes, and needs of followers.

construct validity refers to whether an employment test measures what it is supposed to measure.

content validity the ability of the items in a measurement instrument to measure adequately the various characteristics needed to perform a job.

contingency theories theories that look at the interaction of characteristics of both the leader and the situation.

control group   a comparison group in an experimental investigation that receives no treatment.

correlation coefficient   a statistical technique used to determine the strength of a relationship between two variables.

correlational method   a research design that examines the relationship between variables as they naturally occur.

counterproductive work behaviors (CWBs)   deviant, negative behaviors that are harmful to an organization and its workers.

criteria   measures of job success typically related to performance.

criterion contamination   the extent to which performance appraisals contain elements that detract from the accurate assessment of job effectiveness.

criterion deficiency   the degree to which a criterion falls short of measuring job performance.

criterion relevance   the extent to which the means of appraising performance is pertinent to job success.

criterion usefulness   the extent to which a performance criterion is usable in appraising a particular job.

criterion-related validity   the accuracy of a measurement instrument in determining the relationship between scores on the instrument and some criterion of job success.

critical incidents technique (CIT)   a job analysis technique that relies on instances of especially successful or unsuccessful job performance.

decentralization   the process of taking the decision-making authority away from the top levels of the organization and distributing it to lower levels.

decentralized networks   communication networks in which messages can originate at any point and need not be directed through specific group members.

decision-making model   a theory that matches characteristics of the situation with leader decision-making strategies.

decoding   the process of translating a message so that it can be understood.

democratic decision making   a strategy by which decisions are made by the group members based on majority-rule voting.

dependent variable   in the experimental method, the variable that is acted on by the independent variable; the outcome variable.

descriptive statistics   arithmetical formulas for summarizing and describing research data.

***Dictionary of Occupational Titles* (*DOT*)**   a reference guide that classifies and describes over 40,000 jobs.

differentiation   the complexity of an organization's structure that is based on the number of units, the orientations of managers, and the goals and interests of members.

directive behavior   leader behavior that provides instructions and suggestions for performing a job.

divisional structure   an organizational structure that divides the organization according to types of products or customers.

dominating (forcing)   a conflict resolution strategy of persisting in a conflict until one party attains personal goals at the expense of the other's.

downward communication   messages flowing downward in an organizational hierarchy, usually from superiors to subordinates.

dysfunctional politics   political behaviors that detract from the organization's ability to attain its goals.

effect size   an estimate of the magnitude of a relationship or effect found in a research investigation.

emotional intelligence   ability to understand, regulate, and communicate emotions and to use them to inform thinking.

emotional labor   the demands of regulating and controlling emotions in the workplace.

employee assistance programs (EAPs)   counseling provided for a variety of worker problems, particularly drug and alcohol abuse.

employee engagement   a psychological state characterized by vigor, dedication, and absorption in one's work/organization.

employee ownership   a program where employees own all or part of an organization.

employee placement   the process of assigning workers to appropriate jobs.

employee recruitment   the process by which companies attract qualified applicants.

employee screening   the process of reviewing information about job applicants used to select workers.

employee selection   the process of choosing applicants for employment.

employee training   planned organizational efforts to help employees learn job-related knowledge, skills, and other characteristics.

empowerment   the process by which organizational members can increase their sense of power and personal control in the work setting.

encoding   the process of preparing a message for transmission by putting it into some form of code.

Equal Employment Opportunity Commission (EEOC)   the federal agency created to protect against discrimination in employment.

equity theory   a theory that workers are motivated to reduce perceived inequities between work inputs and outcomes.

ERG theory   Alderfer's motivation model that categorizes needs into existence, relatedness, and growth needs.

exaggeration   the distortion of information by elaborating, overestimating, or minimizing parts of the message.

exceptioning   the practice of ignoring pay discrepancies between particular jobs possessing equivalent duties and responsibilities.

expectancy (in expectancy theory)   the perceived relationship between the individual's effort and performance of a behavior.

expectancy theory   a cognitive theory of motivation that states that workers weigh expected costs and benefits of particular courses before they are motivated to take action.

experimental method   a research design characterized by a high degree of control over the research setting to allow for the determination of cause-and-effect relationships among variables.

expert power   power derived from having certain work-related knowledge or skill.

external validity   whether research results obtained in one setting will apply to another setting.

extraneous variables   variables other than the independent variable that may influence the dependent variable.

facet approach   (to job satisfaction) views job satisfaction as made up of several components, or "facets."

faking   purposely distorting one's responses to a test to try to "beat" the test.

false-negative errors   erroneously rejecting applicants who would have been successful.

false-positive errors   erroneously accepting applicants who would have been unsuccessful.

feedback   an acknowledgment that a message has been received and understood.

Fiedler's contingency model   a leadership theory that maintains that effective leadership depends on a match between the leader's style and the degree to which the work situation gives control and influence to the leader.

filtering   the selective presentation of the content of a communication.

fixed-interval schedule   reinforcement that follows the passage of a specified amount of time.

fixed-ratio schedule   reinforcement that is contingent on the performance of a fixed number of behaviors.

flextime   a schedule that commits an employee to working a specified number of hours per week, but offers flexibility in regard to the beginning and ending times for each day.

forced distributions   assigning workers to established categories of poor to good performance, with fixed limitations on how many employees can be assigned to each category.

frequency distribution   a descriptive statistical technique that arranges scores by categories.

functional job analysis (FJA)   a structured job analysis technique that examines the sequence of tasks in a job and the processes by which they are completed.

functional politics   political behaviors that help the organization to attain its goals.

functional structure   an organizational structure that divides the organization into departments based on the functions or tasks they perform.

gainsharing   a compensation system based on effective group performance.

global approach   (to job satisfaction) views job satisfaction as a general, unitary construct.

goal-setting theory   the motivational theory that emphasizes the setting of specific and challenging performance goals.

grapevine   the informal communication network in an organization.

graphic rating scales   performance appraisal methods using a predetermined scale to rate the worker on important job dimensions.

great man/woman theory   a universalist theory of leadership that maintains that great leaders are born, not made.

group   two or more individuals engaged in social interaction to achieve some goal.

group polarization   the tendency for groups to make decisions that are more extreme than those made by individuals.

groupthink   a syndrome characterized by a concurrence-seeking tendency that overrides the ability of a cohesive group to make critical decisions.

growth need strength   the need and desire for personal growth on the job.

halo effect   an overall positive evaluation of a worker based on one known positive characteristic or action.

hardiness   the notion that some people may be more resistant to the health-damaging effects of stress.

Hawthorne effect   changes in behavior occurring as a function of participants' knowledge that they are being observed and their expectations concerning their role as research participants.

human relations movement   a movement based on the studies of Elton Mayo that emphasizes the importance of social factors in influencing work performance.

hygienes   elements related to job context that, when absent, cause job dissatisfaction.

hypotheses   statements about the supposed relationships between variables.

inclusion   the feeling that one can be one's unique self and still belong.

inclusive leadership theory   a theory that effective leadership encourages belonging while recognizing the uniqueness of all group members.

independent variable   in the experimental method, the variable that is manipulated by the researcher.

individual coping strategies   techniques such as exercise, meditation, or cognitive restructuring that can be used to deal with work stress.

individual methods   performance appraisal methods that evaluate an employee by himself or herself, without explicit reference to other workers.

individual power   power derived from personal characteristics that are of value to the organization, such as particular expertise or leadership ability.

industrial/organizational (I/O) psychology   the branch of psychology that is concerned with the study of behavior in work settings and the application of psychology principles to change work behavior.

inferential statistics   statistical techniques used for analyzing data to test hypotheses.

influence   the ability to use social forces to affect the behavior of others.

informed consent   fully informing a research participant of the nature of a study or experiment and informing the individual about the right to refuse participation.

ingratiation   influencing others by increasing one's personal appeal to them.

initiating structure   leader behaviors that define, organize, and structure the work situation.

inputs   elements that a worker invests in a job, such as experience and effort.

instrumentality   the perceived relationship between the performance of a particular behavior and the likelihood of achieving a particular outcome.

integration   the amount and quality of collaboration among the divisions of an organization.

integrity tests   measures of honest or dishonest attitudes and/or behaviors.

interindividual conflict   conflict that occurs when two people are striving to attain their own goals, thus blocking the other's achievement.

internal consistency   a common method of establishing a measurement instrument's reliability by examining how the various items of the instrument are intercorrelated.

internal validity   the extent to which extraneous or confounding variables are removed from a study.

interpersonal stress   stress arising from difficulties with others in the workplace.

intragroup conflict   conflict that arises when a person or faction within a group attempts to achieve a goal that interferes with the group's goal attainment.

intrinsic motivation   the notion that people are motivated by internal rewards.

jargon   special language developed in connection with certain jobs; also called technical language.

job ambiguity   a source of stress resulting from a lack of clearly defined jobs and/or work tasks.

job analysis   the systematic study of the tasks, duties, and responsibilities of a job and the qualities needed to perform it.

job characteristics model   a theory that emphasizes the role that certain aspects of jobs play in influencing work motivation.

job description   a detailed description of job tasks, procedures, and responsibilities; the tools and equipment used; and the end product or service.

Job Descriptive Index (JDI)   a self-report job satisfaction rating scale measuring five job facets.

Job Diagnostic Survey (JDS)   a questionnaire that measures core job characteristics.

job element method   a job analysis method that analyzes jobs in terms of the knowledge, skills, abilities, and other characteristics (KSAOs) required to perform the jobs.

job enlargement   the expansion of a job to include additional, more varied work tasks.

job enrichment   a motivational program that involves redesigning jobs to give workers a greater role in the planning, execution, and evaluation of their work.

job evaluation   an assessment of the relative value of a job to determine appropriate compensation.

job rotation   a method of rotating workers among a variety of jobs to increase their breadth of knowledge.

job satisfaction   the positive and negative feelings and attitudes about one's job.

job specification   a statement of the human characteristics required to perform a job.

lack of control   a feeling of having little input or effect on the job and/or work environment; typically results in stress.

lateral communication   messages between two parties at the same level in an organizational hierarchy.

leader–member exchange model (LMX)   a theory that effective leadership is determined by the quality of the interaction between the leader and particular group members.

leader–member relations   the quality of the relationship between leader and followers.

leadership   ability to guide a group toward the achievement of goals.

least preferred coworker (LPC)   a measure that assesses leaders' task or relationship orientation by having them rate their most difficult fellow worker.

legitimate power   the formal rights or authority accompanying a position in an organization.

leniency error   the tendency to give all workers very positive performance appraisals.

line employees in an organization who are engaged directly in tasks that accomplish its goals.

line–staff organizational structure a traditional organizational structure composed of one group of employees who achieve the goals of the organization (the line) and another group who support the line (staff).

management by objectives (MBO) a goal-setting OD technique in which supervisors and subordinates jointly set performance goals; at the end of the goal period, their attainment is evaluated, and new goals are set.

management games a management training technique using scaled-down enactments of the operations and managements of organizations.

matrix organization an organizational design that blends functional and product structures.

mean a measure of central tendency; also known as the average.

measures of central tendency present the center point in a distribution of scores.

median a measure of central tendency; the midpoint of a distribution of scores.

mentoring a program in which an inexperienced worker develops a relationship with an experienced worker who serves as an advisor.

merit pay a compensation system in which employees receive a base rate and additional pay based on performance.

meta-analysis a technique that allows results from several different research studies to be combined and summarized.

Minnesota Satisfaction Questionnaire (MSQ) a self-report measure of job satisfaction that breaks satisfaction down into 20 job facets.

modeling learning that occurs through the observation and imitation of the behavior of others.

motivation the force that energizes, directs, and sustains behavior.

motivators elements related to job content that, when present, lead to job satisfaction.

multiple cutoff model an employee selection method using a minimum cutoff score on each of the various predictors of job performance.

multiple hurdle model an employee selection strategy that requires that an acceptance or rejection decision be made at each of several stages in a screening process.

multiple regression design examines the relationship between a particular outcome variable and multiple predictors.

multiple regression model an employee selection method that combines separate predictors of job success in a statistical procedure.

narratives open-ended written accounts of a worker's performance used in performance appraisals.

need hierarchy theory a motivation theory proposed by Maslow that arranges needs in a hierarchy from lower, more basic needs to higher-order needs.

needs physiological or psychological deficiencies that an organism is compelled to fulfill.

negative reinforcers events that strengthen a behavior through the avoidance of an existing negative state.

noise physical or psychological distractions that disrupt the effective flow of communication.

nonverbal communication messages sent and received through means other than the spoken or written word.

normal distribution (bell-shaped curve) a distribution of scores along a continuum with known properties.

norms rules that groups adopt governing appropriate and inappropriate behavior for members.

O*NET the U.S. Department of Labor's website that provides comprehensive information about jobs and careers.

objective performance criteria measures of job performance that are easily quantified.

objectivity the unbiased approach to observation and interpretations of behavior.

obtrusive observation research observation in which the presence of the observer is known to the participants.

on-the-job training an employee training method of placing a worker in the workplace to learn firsthand about a job.

operationalized clearly defining a research variable so that it can be measured.

organigram   a diagram of an organization's hierarchy representing the formal lines of communication.

organizational behavior modification   the application of conditioning principles to obtain certain work outcomes.

organizational citizenship behavior (OCB)   efforts by organizational members that advance or promote the work organization and its goals.

organizational commitment   a worker's feelings and attitudes about the entire work organization.

organizational coping strategies   techniques that organizations can use to reduce stress for all or most employees.

organizational culture   the shared values, beliefs, assumptions, and patterns of behavior within an organization.

organizational development (OD)   the process of assisting organizations in preparing for and managing change.

organizational downsizing   a strategy of reducing an organization's workforce to improve organizational efficiency and/or competitiveness.

organizational politics   self-serving actions designed to affect the behavior of others to achieve personal goals.

organizational power   power derived from a person's position in an organization and from control over important resources afforded by that position.

organizational socialization   the process by which new employees learn group roles and norms and develop specific work skills and abilities.

organizational structure   refers to the arrangement of positions in an organization and the authority and responsibility relationships among them.

outcomes   those things that a worker expects to receive from a job, such as pay and recognition.

outsourcing   contracting with an external organization to accomplish work tasks.

overpayment inequity   worker's perception that outcomes are greater than inputs.

paired comparison   performance appraisal method in which the rater compares each worker with each other worker in the group.

parallel forms   a method of establishing the reliability of a measurement instrument by correlating scores on two different but equivalent versions of the same instrument.

participative behavior   leader behavior that encourages members to assume an active role in group planning and decision making.

path–goal theory   a theory that a leader's job is to help the work group achieve its desired goals.

performance appraisals   the formalized means of assessing worker performance in comparison with certain established organizational standards.

performance criteria   measures used to determine successful and unsuccessful job performance.

performance feedback   the process of giving information to a worker about performance level with suggestions for future improvement.

personality tests   instruments that measure psychological characteristics of individuals.

person–environment (P–E) fit   the match between a worker's abilities, needs, and values, and organizational demands, rewards, and values.

personnel psychology   the specialty area of I/O psychology focusing on an organization's human resources.

polygraphs   instruments that measure physiological reactions presumed to accompany deception; also known as lie detectors.

Porter–Lawler model   a theory where the relationship between job satisfaction and performance is mediated by work-related rewards.

Position Analysis Questionnaire (PAQ)   a job analysis technique that uses a structured questionnaire to analyze jobs according to 187 job statements, grouped into six categories.

position power   a leader's authority to punish or reward followers.

positive affect   positive emotions that affect workers' moods in the workplace.

positive reinforcers   desirable events that strengthen the tendency to respond.

posttest-only design   a program evaluation that simply measures training success criterion following completion of the training program.

power   the use of some aspect of a work relationship to compel another to perform a certain action despite resistance.

power bases   sources of power possessed by individuals in organizations.

power corollary   the concept that, for every exercise of power, there is a tendency for the subject to react with a return power play.

predictors   variables about applicants that are related to (predictive of) the criteria.

pretest–posttest design   a design for evaluating a training program that makes comparisons of criterion measures collected before and after the introduction of the program.

problem-solving case study   a management training technique that presents a real or hypothetical organizational problem that trainees attempt to solve.

process consultation   an OD technique in which a consultant helps a client-organization study its problems objectively and learn to solve them.

profit sharing   a plan where all employees receive a small share of an organization's profits.

programmed instruction   self-paced individualized training in which trainees are provided with training materials and can test how much they have learned.

project task force   a nontraditional organization of workers who are assembled temporarily to complete a specific job or project.

Protected Class   characteristics of groups for which discrimination is prohibited, including: sex, race, religion, color, national origin, persons over 40, persons with physical or mental disabilities.

protected groups   groups, including women and certain ethnic and racial minorities, that have been identified as previous targets of employment discrimination.

psychology   the study of behavior and mental processes.

punishment   unpleasant consequences that reduce the tendency to respond.

Pygmalion effect   when a sender nonverbally communicates expectations to a receiver, influencing his or her behavior.

qualitative (categorical or frequency) data   data that measure some category or measurement quality.

quality circles   small groups of volunteer employees from the same work area who meet regularly to solve work-related problems.

quantitative (measurement) data   data that measure some numerical quantity.

quasi-experiment   a study that follows the experimental design but lacks random assignment of participants and/or manipulation of the independent variable.

random assignment   a method of assigning subjects to groups by chance to control for the effects of extraneous variables.

random sampling   the selection of research participants from a population so that each individual has an equal probability of being chosen.

rankings   performance appraisal methods involving the ranking of supervisees from best to worst.

realistic job preview (RJP)   an accurate presentation of the prospective job and organization made to applicants.

receiver   the recipient of a communication who decodes the message; also known as the decoder.

recency effect   the tendency to give greater weight to recent performance and lesser weight to earlier performance.

reciprocity rule   the tendency for persons to pay back those to whom they are indebted for assistance.

referent power   power resulting from the fact that an individual is respected, admired, and liked by others.

reinforcement theory   a theory that behavior is motivated by its consequences.

relational theories   theories that look at the relationship between leaders and followers as central to the leadership process.

relationship-oriented behaviors   leader behaviors focused on maintaining interpersonal relationships on the job.

reliability   the consistency of a measurement instrument or its stability over time.

reward power   power that results from having the ability to offer something positive, such as money or praise.

role ambiguity   a sense of uncertainty over the requirements of a particular role.

role conflict   conflict that results when the expectations associated with one role interfere with the expectations concerning another role.

role congruity theory   a theory explaining the gender–leadership gap by the inconsistency between the female gender role of being communal and the stereotype that leaders are expected to be agentic, which is consistent with the male gender role.

role differentiation   the process by which group members learn to perform various roles.

role expectations   beliefs concerning the responsibilities and requirements of a particular role.

role-playing   a management training exercise that requires trainees to act out problem situations that often occur at work.

roles   patterns of behavior that are adopted based on expectations about the functions of a position.

rumors   information that is presented as fact, but may actually be true or false.

sampling   the selection of a representative group from a larger population for study.

scientific management   begun by Frederick Taylor, a method of using scientific principles to improve the efficiency and productivity of jobs.

self-determination theory   a motivational theory that focuses on the conditions and processes that lead to self-motivation and growth on the job.

self-efficacy   an individual's beliefs in his or her abilities to engage in courses of action that will lead to desired outcomes.

self-managing work teams   teams that have complete responsibility for whole tasks.

self-report techniques   measurement methods relying on research participants' reports of their own behavior or attitudes.

seminar   a common training method in which an expert provides job-related information in a classroom-like setting.

sender   the originator of a communication who encodes and transmits a message; also known as the encoder.

severity error   the tendency to give all workers very negative performance appraisals.

shared leadership   where leadership is shared among the group members rather than being centralized in one person.

simulation training   training that replicates job conditions without placing the trainee in the actual work setting.

situational exercise   assessment tools that require the performance of tasks that approximate actual work tasks.

situational stress   stress arising from certain conditions that exist in the work environment or in the worker's personal life.

skill-based pay   a system of compensation in which workers are paid based on their knowledge and skills rather than on their positions in the organization.

snap judgment   arriving at a premature, early overall evaluation of an applicant in a hiring interview.

social learning theory   learning theory that emphasizes the observational learning of behavior.

social loafing   the phenomenon whereby individuals working in groups exert less effort than when working alone.

sociogram   a diagram of the informal lines of communication among organizational members.

Solomon four-group design a method of program evaluation using two treatment groups and two control groups.

source factors characteristics of the sender that influence the effectiveness of a communication.

span of control the number of workers who must report to a single supervisor.

staff specialized employee positions designed to support the line.

standard deviation a measure of variability of scores in a frequency distribution.

statistical significance the probability of a particular result occurring by chance, used to determine the meaning of research outcomes.

stratified sampling the selection of research participants based on categories that represent important distinguishing characteristics of a population.

stressful life events significant events in a person's recent history that can cause stress.

stressor an environmental event that is perceived by an individual to be threatening.

subject matter expert (SME) an individual who has detailed knowledge about a particular job.

subjective performance criteria measures of job performance that typically consist of ratings or judgments of performance.

superordinate goal a goal that two conflicting parties are willing to work to attain.

supportive behavior leader behavior focusing on interpersonal relationships and showing concern for workers' well-being.

survey a common self-report measure in which participants are asked to report on their attitudes, beliefs, and/or behaviors.

survey feedback an OD technique whereby the consultant works with the organization to develop and administer a survey instrument to collect data that are fed back to organizational members and used as the starting point for change.

task interdependence the degree to which an individual's task performance depends on the efforts or skills of others.

task structure an assessment of how well elements of the work task are structured.

task-oriented behaviors leader behaviors focused on the work task.

team interdependent workers with complementary skills working toward a shared goal.

team building a type of team training focused on how to improve team performance by analyzing group interaction.

team mental models team members' shared understanding of important aspects of common work goals.

team organization a nontraditional organizational structure consisting of a team of members organized around a particular project or product.

test battery a combination of employment tests used to increase the ability to predict future job performance.

test utility the value of a screening test in determining important outcomes, such as dollars gained by the company through its use.

test–retest reliability a method of determining the stability of a measurement instrument by administering the same measure to the same people at two different times and then correlating the scores.

t-groups (sensitivity training) an OD technique that uses unstructured group interaction to assist workers in achieving insight into their own motivations and behavior patterns in dealing with other organizational members.

thematic apperception test (TAT) a projective test that uses ambiguous pictures to assess psychological motivation.

theory/model the organization of beliefs into a representation of the factors that affect behavior.

360-degree feedback a method of gathering performance appraisals from a worker's supervisors, subordinates, peers, customers, and other relevant parties.

time-and-motion studies procedures in which work tasks are broken down into simple component movements and the movements are timed to develop a more efficient method for performing the tasks.

trainee readiness the individual's potential for successful training.

trait theory attempts to discover the traits shared by all effective leaders.

traits enduring attributes associated with an individual's makeup or personality.

transactional leadership leadership based on some transaction, such as exchanging money for work.

transfer of training concept dealing with whether training is actually applied in the work setting.

transformational leadership focuses on the leader's ability to provide shared values and a vision for the future for the work group.

treatment group the group in an experimental investigation that is subjected to the change in the independent variable.

t-test a statistical test for examining the difference between the means of two groups.

turnover intentions workers' self-reported intentions to leave their jobs.

two-factor theory Herzberg's motivational theory that proposes that two factors—motivators and hygienes—are important in determining worker satisfaction and motivation.

Type A behavior pattern a personality characterized by excessive drive, competitiveness, impatience, and hostility that has been linked to greater incidence of coronary heart disease.

underpayment inequity worker's perception that inputs are greater than outcomes.

underutilization a source of stress resulting from workers feeling that their knowledge, skills, or energy are not being fully used.

universalist theories theories that look for the major characteristics common to all effective leaders.

unobtrusive observation research observation in which the presence of the observer is not known to the participants.

upward communication messages flowing upward in an organizational hierarchy, usually taking the form of feedback.

valence the desirability of an outcome to an individual.

validity a concept referring to the accuracy of a measurement instrument and its ability to make accurate inferences about a criterion.

validity generalization the ability of a screening instrument to predict performance in a job or setting different from the one in which the test was validated.

variability estimates the distribution of scores around the middle or average score.

variable-interval schedule reinforcement that follows the passage of a specified amount of time, with exact time of reinforcement varying.

variable-ratio schedule reinforcement that depends on the performance of a specified but varying number of behaviors.

variables the elements measured in research investigations.

vestibule training training that uses a separate area adjacent to the work area to simulate the actual work setting.

webinar an online training method similar to a lecture or seminar.

weighted application forms forms that assign different weights to the various pieces of information provided on a job application.

we–they feeling intragroup cohesiveness created by the existence of a common threat, which is typically another group.

whistle-blowing political behavior whereby an employee criticizes company policies and practices to persons outside the organization.

wisdom of the crowd   the phenomenon by which a diverse group of novices can outperform a homogeneous group of experts because they can identify each other's errors in judgments.

work–family conflict   cumulative stress that results from duties of work and family roles.

work overload   a common source of stress resulting when a job requires excessive speed, output, or concentration.

work sample tests   job skill tests used to measure applicants' abilities to perform brief examples of important job tasks.

worker stress   the physiological and/or psychological reactions to events that are perceived to be threatening or taxing.

REFERENCES

Abdulsalam, D., Maltarich, M. A., Nyberg, A. J., Reilly, G., & Martin, M. (2020). Individualized pay-for-performance arrangements: Peer reactions and consequences. *Journal of Applied Psychology*, Advance online publication.

Adam Jr., E. E. (1991). Quality circle performance. *Journal of Management*, *17*(1), 25–39.

Adams, J. A. (1987). Historical review and appraisal of research on the learning, retention, and transfer of human motor skills. *Psychological Bulletin*, *101*(1), 41–74.

Adams, J. S. (1965). Inequity in social exchange. *Advances in Experimental Social Psychology*, *2*, 267–299.

Adinolfi, P. (2021). A journey around decision-making: Searching for the "big picture" across disciplines. *European Management Journal*, *39*(1), 9–21.

Adkins, L. (2010). *Coaching agile teams*. Upper Saddle River, NJ: Addison-Wesley.

Adler, N. J. (1991). *International dimensions of organizational behavior* (2nd ed.). Boston, MA: PWS-Kent.

Adler, P. S., & Borys, B. (1996). Two types of bureaucracy: Enabling and coercive. *Administrative Science Quarterly*, *41*, 61–89.

Aertsen, T., & Gelders, D. (2011). Differences between the public and private communication of rumors. A pilot survey in Belgium. *Public Relations Review*, *37*(3), 281–291.

AFSCME v. State of Washington, 578 F. supp. 846 (W.D. Wash. 1983).

Aguinis, H. (1993). Action research and scientific method: Presumed discrepancies and actual similarities. *Journal of Applied Behavioral Science*, *29*(4), 416–431.

Aguinis, H., Nesler, M. S., Hosoda, M., & Tedeschi, J. T. (1994). The use of influence tactics in persuasion. *The Journal of Social Psychology*, *134*(4), 429–438.

Aguinis, H., Ramani, R. S., Campbell, P. K., Bernal-Turnes, P., Drewry, J. M., & Edgerton, B. T. (2017). Most frequently cited sources, articles, and authors in industrial-organizational psychology textbooks: Implications for the science–practice divide, scholarly impact, and the future of the field. *Industrial and Organizational Psychology*, *10*(4), 507–557.

Aguinis, H., Villamor, I., Lazzarini, S. G., Vassolo, R. S., Amorós, J. E., & Allen, D. G. (2020). Conducting management research in Latin America: why and what's in it for you? *Journal of Management*, *46*(5), 615–636.

Ahmed, F., Zhao, F., & Faraz, N. A. (2020). How and when does inclusive leadership curb psychological distress during a crisis? Evidence from the COVID-19 outbreak. *Frontiers in Psychology*, *11*, 1898–1918.

Aisenbrey, S., & Brückner, H. (2014). Gender inequality by choice? The effects of aspirations on gender inequality in wages. In I. Schoon & J. S. Eccles (Eds.), *Gender differences in aspirations and attainment: A life course perspective* (pp. 456–474). New York: Cambridge University Press.

Akkermans, J., Brenninkmeijer, V., Blonk, R., & Schaufeli, W. (2014, April). CareerSKILLS: Effectiveness of a career development intervention for young employees. Proceedings of the 11th European Academy of Occupational Health Psychology, Looking at the past, planning for the future: capitalizing on OHP multidisciplinarity, London, UK.

Albemarle Paper v. Moody, 74–389, 422 US 405 (Supreme Court of the United States 1975).

Alcivar, I., & Abad, A. G. (2016). Design and evaluation of a gamified system for ERP training. *Computers in Human Behavior*, *58*, 109–118.

Alderfer, C. P. (1972). *Existence, relatedness, and growth: Human needs in organizational settings*. New York: Free Press.

Alge, B. J. (2001). Effects of computer surveillance on perceptions of privacy and procedural justice. *Journal of Applied Psychology*, *86*(4), 797–804.

Alimo-Metcalfe, B., & Alban-Metcalfe, R. J. (2001). The development of a new transformational leadership questionnaire. *Journal of Occupational and Organizational Psychology*, *74*(1), 1–27.

Allen, D. G., Weeks, K. P., & Moffitt, K. R. (2005). Turnover intentions and voluntary turnover: The moderating roles of self-monitoring, locus of control, proactive personality, and risk aversion. *Journal of Applied Psychology*, *90*(5), 980–990.

Allen, R. W., & Porter, L. W. (Eds.). (1983). *Organizational influence processes*. Glenview, IL: Scott, Foresman.

Allen, T. D., Finkelstein, L. M., & Poteet, M. L. (2009). *Designing workplace mentoring programs: An evidence-based approach.* New York: Wiley-Blackwell.

Allen, T. D., French, K. A., Dumani, S., & Shockley, K. M. (2020). A cross-national meta-analytic examination of predictors and outcomes associated with work–family conflict. *Journal of Applied Psychology, 105*(6), 539–576.

Allen, T. D., & Rush, M. C. (1998). The effects of organizational citizenship behavior on performance judgments: A field study and a laboratory experiment. *Journal of Applied Psychology, 83*(2), 247–260.

Al-Mashaan, O. S. (2003). Comparison between Kuwaiti and Egyptian teachers in Type A behavior and job satisfaction: A cross-cultural study. *Social Behavior and Personality, 31*(5), 523–534.

Alper, S., Tjosvold, D., & Law, K. S. (2000). Conflict management, efficacy, and performance in organizational teams. *Personnel Psychology, 53*(3), 625–642.

American Management Association. (2019). *The latest on workplace monitoring and surveillance.* Retrieved 6/15/2021 from www.amanet.org/articles/the-latest-on-workplace-monitoring-and-surveillance/

American Psychological Association. (2002). *Ethical principles of psychologists and code of conduct.* Retrieved from www.apa.org/ethics/code2002.html

Anakwe, U. P., & Greenhaus, J. H. (1999). Effective socialization of employees: Socialization content perspective. *Journal of Managerial Issues, 11*(3), 315–329.

Anderson, L., & Wilson, S. (1997). Critical incident technique. In D. L. Whetzel & G. R. Wheaton (Eds.), *Applied measurement methods in industrial psychology* (pp. 89–112). Palo Alto, CA: Davies-Black.

Andersson, L. M., & Pearson, C. M. (1999). Tit for tat? The spiraling effect of incivility in the workplace. *Academy of Management Review, 24*(3), 452–471.

Andreassen, C. S. (2013). Work addiction. In P. M. Miller (Ed.), *Comprehensive addictive behaviors and disorders, Vol. 1: Principles of addiction* (pp. 837–845). San Diego, CA: Elsevier.

Argyris, C. (1964). *Integrating the individual and the organization.* New York: Wiley.

Aron, A., Coups, E. J., & Aron, E. N. (2013). *Statistics for Psychology* (6th ed.). Boston: Pearson.

Arthur, J. B., & Huntley, C. L. (2005). Ramping up the organizational learning curve: Assessing the impact of deliberate learning on organizational performance under gainsharing. *Academy of Management Journal, 48*(6), 1159–1170.

Arvey, R. D., & Begalla, M. E. (1975). Analyzing the homemaker job using the Position Analysis Questionnaire (PAQ). *Journal of Applied Psychology, 60*, 513–518.

Arvey, R. D., Maxwell, S. E., & Salas, E. (1992). The relative power of training evaluation designs under difficult cost configurations. *Journal of Applied Psychology, 77*, 155–160.

Ashford, S. J., & Detert, J. (2015). Get the boss to buy in: Learn to sell your ideas up the chain of command. *Harvard Business Review, 93*(1–2), 72–79.

Ashkanasy, N. M., Ayoko, O. B., & Jehn, K. A. (2014). Understanding the physical environment of work and employee behavior: An affective events perspective. *Journal of Organizational Behavior, 35*(8), 1169–1184.

Askew, K., & Coovert, M. D. (2013). Online decision-making. In Y. Amichai-Hamburger (Ed.), *The social net: Understanding our online behavior* (2nd ed., pp. 99–119). New York: Oxford University Press.

Athanasopoulou, A., & Dopson, S. (2018). A systematic review of executive coaching outcomes: Is it the journey or the destination that matters the most? *The Leadership Quarterly, 29*(1), 70–88.

Atwater, L. E., Brett, J. F., & Waldman, D. (2003). Understanding the benefits and risks of multi-source feedback. In S. E. Murphy & R. E. Riggio (Eds.), *The future of leadership development* (pp. 89–106). Mahwah, NJ: Erlbaum.

Atwater, L. E., Carey, J. A., & Waldman, D. A. (2001). Gender and discipline in the workplace: Wait until your father gets home. *Journal of Management, 27*(5), 537–561.

Atwater, L. E., & Elkins, T. (2009). Diagnosing, understanding, and dealing with counterproductive work behavior. In J. W. Smither & M. London (Eds.), *Performance management: Putting research into action* (pp. 359–410). San Francisco, CA: Jossey-Bass.

Atwater, L. E., Waldman, D. A., Atwater, D., & Cartier, P. (2000). An upward feedback field experiment: Supervisors' cynicism, reactions, and commitment to subordinates. *Personnel Psychology, 53*(2), 275–297.

Avery, D. R., Dumas, T. L., George, E., Joshi, A., Loyd, D. L., van Knippenberg, D., Wang, M., & Xu, H. (2021). Racial biases in the publication process: Exploring expressions and solutions. *Journal of Management* (in press), 7–16.

Avery, D. R., & McKay, P. F. (2006). Target practice: An organizational impression management approach to attracting minority and female job applicants. *Personnel Psychology, 59*, 157–187.

Avery, D. R., Richeson, J. A., Hebl, M. R., & Ambady, N. (2009). It does not have to be uncomfortable: The role of behavioral scripts in Black–White interracial interactions. *Journal of Applied Psychology, 94*(6), 1382.

Avolio, B. J., Avey, J. B., & Quisenberry, D. (2010). Estimating return on leadership development investment. *The Leadership Quarterly, 21*(4), 633–644.

Avolio, B. J., Reichard R.J., Hannah, S. T., Walumbwa, F. O., & Chan, A. (2009). A meta-analytic review of leadership impact research: Experimental and quasi-experimental studies. *The Leadership Quarterly, 20*(5), 764–784.

Axtell, C. M., Holman, D. J., Unsworth, K. L., Wall, T. D., Waterson, P. E., & Harrington, E. (2000). Shopfloor innovation: Facilitating the suggestion and implementation of ideas. *Journal of Occupational and Organizational Psychology, 73*(3), 265–285.

Ayman, R., Chemers, M. M., & Fiedler, F. (1995). The contingency model of leadership effectiveness: Its levels of analysis. *Leadership Quarterly, 6*(2), 147–167.

Aziz, S., Wuensch, K. L., & Duffrin, C. (2015). Workaholism, exercise, and stress-related illness. *Journal of Workplace Behavioral Health, 30*(4), 393–406.

Bacharach, S. B., & Lawler, E. J. (1998). Political alignments in organizations: Contextualization, mobilization, and coordination. In R. M. Kramer & M. A. Neale (Eds.), *Power and influence in organizations* (pp. 67–88). Thousand Oaks, CA: Sage.

Bachman, J. G., Bowers, D. G., & Marcus, P. M. (1968). Bases of supervisory power: A comparative study in five organizational settings. In A. S. Tannenbaum (Ed.), *Control in organizations* (pp. 229–238). New York: McGraw-Hill.

Back, M. D., Stopfer, S. V., Gaddis, S., Schmukle, S. C., Egloff, B., & Gosling, S. D. (2010). Facebook profiles reflect actual personality, not self-idealization. *Psychological Science, 21*, 372–374. doi:10.1177/0956797609360756

Bader, A. K., Kemper, L. E., & Froese, F. J. (2019). Who promotes a value-in-diversity perspective? A fuzzy set analysis of executives' individual and organizational characteristics. *Human Resource Management, 58*(2), 203–217.

Badura, K. L., Grijalva, E., Newman, D. A., Yan, T. T., & Jeon, G. (2018). Gender and leadership emergence: A meta-analysis and explanatory model. *Personnel Psychology, 71*(3), 335–367.

Bailey, C., & Fletcher, C. (2002). The impact of multiple source feedback on management development: Findings from a longitudinal study. *Journal of Organizational Behavior, 23*(7), 853–867.

Bailey, S. F., & Ferguson, A. J. (2013). Not just intergroup: The role of status within groups in the Sandusky scandal. *Industrial and Organizational Psychology, 6*(2), 149–152.

Baird, J. E. (1977). *The dynamics of organizational communication.* New York: Harper & Row.

Baldassarre, L., & Finken, B. (2015). GE's real-time performance development. *Harvard Business Review*, August 12. https://hbr.org/2015/08/ges-real-time-performance-development

Balkin, D. B., & Gomez-Mejia, L. R. (Eds.). (1987). *New perspectives on compensation.* Englewood Cliffs, NJ: Prentice Hall.

Baltes, B. B., Briggs, T. E., Huff, J. W., Wright, J. A., & Neuman, G. A. (1999). Flexible and compressed workweek schedules: A meta-analysis of their effects on work-related criteria. *Journal of Applied Psychology, 84*(4), 496–513.

Baltes, B. B., Dickson, M. W., Sherman, M. P., Bauer, C. C., & LaGanke, J. S. (2002). Computer-mediated communication and group decision making: A meta-analysis. *Organizational Behavior and Human Decision Processes, 87*(1), 156–179.

Bambacas, M., & Patrickson, M. (2008). Interpersonal communication skills that enhance organisational commitment. *Journal of Communication Management, 12*(1), 51–72.

Bandura, A. (1997). *Self-efficacy: The exercise of control.* San Francisco, CA: W. H. Freeman.

Bandura, A., & Walters, R. H. (1977). *Social learning theory* (Vol. 1). Prentice Hall.

Barber, A. E., Wesson, M. J., Roberson, Q. M., & Taylor, M. S. (1999). A tale of two job markets: Organizational size and its effects on hiring practices and job search behavior. *Personnel Psychology, 52*, 841–867.

Bardach, L., Rushby, J. V., Kim, L. E., & Klassen, R. M. (2020). Using video-and text-based situational judgement tests for teacher selection: A quasi-experiment exploring the relations between test format, subgroup differences, and applicant reactions. *European Journal of Work and Organizational Psychology*, 1–14.

Bareil, C. (2013). Paradigms about resistance to change. *Organization Development Journal, 31*(3), 59–71.

Barken, R., Denton, M., Sayin, F. K., Brookman, C., Davies, S., & Zeytinoglu, I. U. (2018). The influence of autonomy on personal support workers' job satisfaction, capacity to care, and intention to stay. *Home Health Care Services Quarterly, 37*(4), 294–312.

Barling, J., Weber, T., & Kelloway, E. K. (1996). Effects of transformational leadership training on attitudinal and financial outcomes: A field experiment. *Journal of Applied Psychology, 81*(6), 827–832.

Barnett, R. B., & Bradley, L. (2007). The impact of organizational support for career development on career satisfaction. *Career Development International, 12*(7), 617–636.

Barney, C. E., & Elias, S. M. (2010). Flex-time as a moderator of the job stress-work motivation relationship: A three nation investigation. *Personnel Review, 39*(4), 487–502.

Bar-On, R. (1997). BarOn emotional quotient inventory. Multi-health systems.

Baron, R. A. (1986). *Behavior in organizations: Understanding and managing the human side of work* (2nd ed.). Boston, MA: Allyn & Bacon.

Baron, R. S. (2005). So right it's wrong: Groupthink and the ubiquitous nature of polarized group decision making. *Advances in Experimental Social Psychology, 37*, 219–253.

Barrett, G. V., Phillips, J. S., & Alexander, R. A. (1981). Concurrent and predictive validity designs: A critical reanalysis. *Journal of Applied Psychology, 66*, 1–6.

Barringer, M. W., & Milkovich, G. T. (1998). A theoretical exploration of the adoption and design of flexible benefit plans: A case of human resource innovation. *Academy of Management Review, 23*(2), 305–324.

Bartol, K. M., & Martin, D. C. (1988). Influences on managerial pay allocations: A dependency perspective. *Personnel Psychology, 41*(2), 361–378.

Bartol, K. M., & Martin, D. C. (1990). When politics pays: Factors influencing managerial compensation decisions. *Personnel Psychology, 43*(3), 599–614.

Bass, B. M. (1954). The leaderless group discussion. *Psychological Bulletin, 51*, 465–492.

Bass, B. M. (1981). *Stogdill's handbook of leadership* (rev. and enl. ed.). New York: Free Press.

Bass, B. M., & Avolio, B. J. (1997). *Manual for the multifactor leadership questionnaire*. Palo Alto, CA: Mindgarden.

Bass, B. M., & Bass, R. (2008). *The Bass handbook of leadership*. New York: Free Press.

Bass, B. M., & Riggio, R. E. (2006). *Transformational leadership* (2nd ed.). Mahwah, NJ: Erlbaum.

Bauer, T. N., & Erdogan, B. (2011). Organizational socialization: The effective onboarding of new employees. In S. Zedeck (Ed.), *APA handbook of industrial and organizational psychology, Vol. 3: Maintaining, expanding, and contracting the organization* (pp. 51–64). Washington, DC: American Psychological Association.

Bauer, T. N., & Erdogan, B. (Eds.). (2016). *The Oxford handbook of leader–member exchange*. New York: Oxford University Press.

Bauer, T. N., Erdogan, B., Caughlin, D., Ellis, A. M., & Kurkoski, J. (2020). Jump-starting the socialization experience: The longitudinal role of Day 1 newcomer resources on adjustment. *Journal of Management*, (in press).

Bauer, T. N., Perrot, S., Liden, R. C., & Erdogan, B. (2019). Understanding the consequences of newcomer proactive behaviors: The moderating contextual role of servant leadership. *Journal of Vocational Behavior, 112*, 356–368.

Bauer, T. N., Truxillo, D. M., Jones, M. P., & Brady, G. (2020). Privacy and cybersecurity challenges, opportunities, and recommendations: Personnel selection in an era of online application systems and big data. In S. E. Woo, L. Tay, & R. W. Proctor (Eds.), *Big data in psychological research* (pp. 393–409). Washington, DC: American Psychological Association.

Bayo-Moriones, A., & Larraza-Kintana, M. (2009). Profit-sharing plans and affective commitment: Does the context matter? *Human Resource Management, 48*(2), 207–226.

Bays, G. (2007). Let's talk: Preparing students for speaking and listening in the workplace. In C. L. Selfe (Ed.), *Resources in technical communication: Outcomes and approaches* (pp. 281–291). Amityville, NY: Baywood.

Bazerman, M. H., Giuliano, T., & Appleman, A. (1984). Escalation of commitment in individual and group decision making. *Organizational Behavior and Human Performance, 33*(2), 141–152.

Bear, J. B. (2019). The caregiving ambition framework. *Academy of Management Review, 44*(1), 99–125.

Beehr, T. A. (1985). Organizational stress and employee effectiveness: A job characteristics approach. In T. A. Beehr & R. S. Bhagat (Eds.), *Human stress and cognition in organizations: An integrated perspective* (pp. 57–81). New York: Wiley.

Belkin, L. Y., Becker, W. J., & Conroy, S. A. (2020). The invisible leash: The impact of organizational expectations for email monitoring after-hours on employee resources, well-being, and turnover intentions. *Group & Organization Management, 45*(5), 709–740.

Bell, M. P., Berry, D., Leopold, J., & Nkomo, S. (2021). Making Black Lives Matter in academia: A black feminist call for collective action against anti-blackness in the academy. *Gender, Work & Organization, 28*, 39–57.

Bell, S. T., Brown, S. G., Colaneri, A., & Outland, N. (2018). Team composition and the ABCs of teamwork. *American Psychologist, 73*(4), 349–362.

Bellotti, V., Ducheneaut, N., Howard, M., Smith, I., & Grinter, R. E. (2005). Quality versus quantity: E-mail centric task management and its relation with overload. *Human-Computer Interaction, 20*(1–2), 89–138.

Beltrán-Martín, I., & Roca-Puig, V. (2013). Promoting employee flexibility through HR practices. *Human Resource Management, 52*(5), 645–674.

Benne, K. D., & Sheats, P. (1948). Functional roles of group members. *Journal of Social Issues, 4*, 41–49.

Bennett, G. K. (1981) *Hand-tool dexterity test manual*, revised, The Psychological Corporation, Harcourt Brace Jovanovich.

Bennett, G. K. (2008). *Bennett mechanical comprehension test*. Pearson.

Bennett, R. J., & Robinson, S. L. (2000). Development of a measure of workplace deviance. *Journal of Applied Psychology, 85*(3), 349–360.

Benson, G. S., & Lawler, E. E. (2016). Employee involvement: Research foundations. In M. J. Grawitch & D. W. Ballard (Eds.), *The psychologically healthy workplace: Building a win-win environment for organizations and employees* (pp. 13–33). Washington, DC: American Psychological Association.

Bergman, M. E., & Jean, V. A. (2016). Where have all the "workers" gone? A critical analysis of the unrepresentativeness of our samples relative to the labor market in the industrial–organizational psychology literature. *Industrial and Organizational Psychology, 9*(1), 84–113.

Berkery, E., Morley, M. J., Tiernan, S., & Peretz, H. (2020). From start to finish: Flexi-time as a social exchange and its impact on organizational outcomes. *European Management Journal, 38*(4), 591–601.

Berkery, E., Morley, M. J., Tiernan, S., Purtill, H., & Parry, E. (2017). On the uptake of flexible working arrangements and the association with human resource and organizational performance outcomes. *European Management Review, 14*(2), 165–183.

Bernardin, H. J., Hagan, C. M., Kane, J. S., & Villanova, P. (1998). Effective performance management: A focus on precision, customers, and situational constraints. In J. W. Smither (Ed.), *Performance appraisal: State of the art in practice* (pp. 3–48). San Francisco, CA: Jossey-Bass.

Bernerth, J. B., & Walker, H. J. (2020). Altered states or much to do about nothing? A study of when cannabis is used in relation to the impact it has on performance. *Group & Organization Management, 45*(4), 459–478.

Bernthal, P. R., & Insko, C. A. (1993). Cohesiveness without group-think: The interactive effects of social and task cohesion. *Group and Organization Management, 18*(1), 66–87.

Berry, C. M., Lelchook, A. M., & Clark, M. A. (2012). A meta-analysis of the interrelationships between employee lateness, absenteeism, and turnover: Implications for models of withdrawal behavior. *Journal of Organizational Behavior, 33*(5), 678–699.

Berson, J. (2014). Why companies fail to engage today's workforce: The overwhelmed employee. *Forbes*, March 15. www.forbes.com/sites/joshbersin/2014/03/15/why-companies-fail-to-engage-todays-workforce-the-overwhelmed-employee/#65281ca44726

Bertua, C., Anderson, N., & Salgado, J. F. (2005). The predictive validity of cognitive ability tests: A UK meta-analysis. *Journal of Occupational and Organizational Psychology, 78*, 387–409.

Bezrukova, K., Spell, C. S., Perry, J. L., & Jehn, K. A. (2016). A meta-analytical integration of over 40 years of research on diversity training evaluation. *Psychological Bulletin, 142*(11), 1227–1274.

Bhagat, R. S. (1983). Effects of stressful life events on individual performance effectiveness and work adjustment processes within organizational settings: A research model. *Academy of Management Review, 8*, 660–671.

Bipp, T., & van Dam, K. (2014). Extending hierarchical achievement motivation models: The role of motivational needs for achievement goals and academic performance. *Personality and Individual Differences, 64*, 157–162.

Birdi, K. (2020). Insights on impact from the development, delivery, and evaluation of the CLEAR IDEAS innovation training model. *European Journal of Work and Organizational Psychology, 30*(3), 400–414.

Birnbaum, M. H., & Sotoodeh, Y. (1991). Measurement of stress: Scaling the magnitudes of life changes. *Psychological Science, 2*, 236–243.

Bisbey, T. M., Reyes, D. L., Traylor, A. M., & Salas, E. (2019). Teams of psychologists helping teams: The evolution of the science of team training. *American Psychologist, 74*(3), 278–289.

Bisbey, T. M., Traylor, A., & Salas, E. (2020). *Implications of the changing nature of work for training.* Cambridge University Press. https://doi.org/10.1017/9781108278034.017

Blacksmith, N., Willford, J. C., & Behrend, T. S. (2016). Technology in the employment interview: A meta-analysis and future research agenda. *Personnel Assessment and Decisions, 2*(1), 2–20.

Blake, R. R., Shepard, H. A., & Mouton, J. S. (1964). *Managing intergroup conflict in industry.* Houston, TX: Gulf.

Bligh, M. C., & Kohles, J. C. (2009). The enduring allure of charisma: How Barack Obama won the historic 2008 presidential election. *The Leadership Quarterly, 20*(3), 483–492.

Bligh, M. C., Kohles, J. C., & Meindl, J. R. (2004). Charisma under crisis: Presidential leadership, rhetoric, and media responses before and after the September 11th terrorist attacks. *The Leadership Quarterly, 15*(2), 211–239.

Block, P. (1987). *The empowered manager.* San Francisco, CA: Jossey-Bass.

Bloom, N. (2020, 6/1). *How working from home works out.* Retrieved 6/16/2021 from https://siepr.stanford.edu/research/publications/how-working-home-works-out

Boies, K., & Howell, J. M. (2006). Leader–member exchange in teams: An examination of the interaction between relationship differentiation and mean LMX in explaining team-level outcomes. *The Leadership Quarterly, 17*(3), 246–257.

Bolino, M. C., Hsiung, H., Harvey, J., & LePine, J. A. (2015). "Well, I'm tired of tryin'!" Organizational citizenship behavior and citizenship fatigue. *Journal of Applied Psychology, 100*(1), 56–74.

Bolino, M. C., Kelemen, T. K., & Matthews, S. H. (2021). Working 9-to-5? A review of research on nonstandard work schedules. *Journal of Organizational Behavior, 42*(2), 188–211.

Bolton, L. R., Becker, L. K., & Barber, L. K. (2010). Big Five trait predictors of differential counterproductive work behavior dimensions. *Personality and Individual Differences, 49*(5), 537–541.

Bonaccio, S., Connelly, C. E., Gellatly, I. R., Jetha, A., & Ginis, K. A. M. (2020). The participation of people with disabilities in the workplace across the employment cycle: employer concerns and research evidence. *Journal of Business and Psychology, 35*(2), 135–158.

Bonaccio, S., Dalal, R. S., Highhouse, S., Ilgen, D. R., Mohammed, S., & Slaughter, J. E. (2010). Taking workplace decisions seriously: This conversation has been fruitful! *Industrial and Organizational Psychology, 3*(4), 455–464.

Bonaccio, S., O'Reilly, J., O'Sullivan, S. L., & Chiocchio, F. (2016). Nonverbal behavior and communication in the workplace: A review and an agenda for research. *Journal of Management, 42*(5), 1044–1074.

Bono, J. E., Foldes, H. J., Vinson, G., & Muros, J. P. (2007). Workplace emotions: The role of supervision and leadership. *Journal of Applied Psychology, 92*(5), 1357–1367.

Bono, J. E., & Judge, T. A. (2003). Core self-evaluations: A review of the trait and its role in job satisfaction and job performance. *European Journal of Personality, 17*(1 suppl.), S5–S18.

Bono, J. E., & Judge, T. A. (2004). Personality and transformational and transactional leadership: A meta-analysis. *Journal of Applied Psychology, 89*(5), 901–910.

Bono, J. E., & Vey, M. A. (2005). Toward understanding emotional management at work: A quantitative review of emotional labor research. In C. E. J. Härtel, W. J. Zerbe, & N. M. Ashkanasy (Eds.), *Emotions in organizational behavior* (pp. 213–233). Mahwah, NJ: Erlbaum.

Booth, R. T. (1986). Machinery hazards. In J. Ridley (Ed.), *Safety at work* (2nd ed., pp. 549–571). London: Butterworth.

Booth-Kewley, S., & Friedman, H. S. (1987). Psychological predictors of heart disease: A quantitative review. *Psychological Bulletin, 101*(3), 343–362.

Booysen, L. (2014). The development of inclusive leadership practice and processes. In B. M. Ferdman & B. R. Deane (Eds.), *Diversity at work: The practice of inclusion* (pp. 296–329). Jossey-Bass.

Borman, W. C. (1986). Behavior-based rating scales. In R. A. Berk (Ed.), *Performance assessment: Methods and applications* (pp. 100–200). Baltimore, MD: Johns Hopkins University Press.

Born, D. H., & Mathieu, J. E. (1996). Differential effects of survey-guided feedback: The rich get richer and the poor get poorer. *Group & Organization Management, 21*(4), 388–403.

Boswell, W. R., & Boudreau, J. W. (2002). Separating the developmental and evaluative performance appraisal uses. *Journal of Business and Psychology, 16*(3), 391–412.

Boswell, W. R., & Olson-Buchanan, J. B. (2004). Experiencing mistreatment at work: The role of grievance filing, nature of mistreatment, and employee withdrawal. *Academy of Management Journal, 47*, 129–139.

Bowling, N. A., Alarcon, G. M., Bragg, C. B., & Hartman, M. J. (2015). A meta-analytic examination of the potential correlates and consequences of workload. *Work & Stress, 29*(2), 95–113.

Bowling, N. A., Wagner, S. H., & Beehr, T. A. (2018). The facet satisfaction scale: An effective affective measure of job satisfaction facets. *Journal of Business and Psychology, 33*(3), 383–403.

Bradley-Geist, J. C., Rivera, I., & Geringer, S. D. (2015). The collateral damage of ambient sexism: Observing sexism impacts bystander self-esteem and career aspirations. *Sex Roles, 73*(1), 29–42.

Bragger, J. D., Kutcher, E., Morgan, J., & Firth, P. (2002). The effects of the structured interview on reducing biases against pregnant job applicants. *Sex Roles, 46*(7), 215–226.

Brannick, M. T., Levine, E. L., & Morgeson, F. P. (2007). *Job and work analysis: Methods, research, and applications for human resource management* (2nd ed.). Thousand Oaks, CA: Sage.

Brannon, D., Streit, A., & Smyer, M. A. (1992). The psychosocial quality of nursing home work. *Journal of Aging and Health, 4*, 369–389.

Brass, D. J., & Burkhardt, M. E. (1993). Potential power and power use: An investigation of structure and behavior. *Academy of Management Journal, 36*(3), 441–470.

Braver, M. C. W., & Braver, S. L. (1988). Statistical treatment of the Solomon four-group design: A meta-analytic approach. *Psychological Bulletin, 104*, 150–154.

Bray, D. W., Campbell, R. J., & Grant, D. L. (1974). Formative years in business: A long-term AT&T study of managerial lives. Wiley-Interscience.

Breaugh, J. A. (2017). The contribution of job analysis to recruitment. In H. W. Goldstein & C. S. Elaine D. Pulakos, & Jonathan Passmore (Eds.), *The Wiley Blackwell handbook of the psychology of recruitment, selection and employee retention* (pp. 12–28). John Wiley.

Brecher, E., Bragger, J., & Kutcher, E. (2006). The structured interview: Reducing biases toward job applicants with physical disabilities. *Employee Responsibilities and Rights Journal, 18*(3), 155–170.

Brenan, M. (2020). COVID-19 and remote work: An update. Gallup. Retrieved from https://news.gallup.com/poll/321800/covid-remote-work-update.aspx

Brewer, M. B. (1991). The social self: On being the same and different at the same time. *Personality and Social Psychology Bulletin, 17*(5), 475–482.

Brito v. Zia Co., 478 F.2d 1200 (10th. Cir. 1973).

Britt, T. W., Adler, A. B., & Bartone, P. T. (2001). Deriving benefits from stressful events: The role of engagement in meaningful work and hardiness. *Journal of Occupational Health Psychology, 6*(1), 53–63.

Brodbeck, F. C., Zapf, D., Prumper, J., & Frese, M. (1993). Error handling in office work with computers: A field study. *Journal of Occupational and Organizational Psychology, 66*, 303–317.

Brotheridge, C. M., & Grandey, A. A. (2002). Emotional labor and burnout: Comparing two perspectives of "people work." *Journal of Vocational Behavior, 60*(1), 17–39.

Brough, P. (2018). *Advanced research methods for applied psychology: Design, analysis and reporting.* Abingdon, UK: Routledge.

Brown, J., Cooper, C., & Kirkcaldy, B. (1996). Occupational stress among senior police officers. *British Journal of Psychology, 87*(1), 31–41.

Brown, K. T., & Ostrove, J. M. (2013). What does it mean to be an ally? The perception of allies from the perspective of people of color. *Journal of Applied Social Psychology, 43*(11), 2211–2222.

Brown, S. G., & Stuhlmacher, A. F. (2020). Affect and workplace judgment and decision-making. In L. Q. Yang & R. Cropanzano (Eds.), *The Cambridge handbook of workplace affect* (pp. 174–184). Cambridge University Press.

Brown, V. R., & Paulus, P. B. (1996). A simple dynamic model of social factors in group brainstorming. *Small Group Research, 27*(1), 91–114.

Brown, V. R., & Vaughn, E. D. (2011). The writing on the (Facebook) wall: The use of social networking sites in hiring decisions. *Journal of Business Psychology, 26*, 219–225. doi: 10.1007/s10869-011-9221-x

Brummel, B., Newman, E., Arnold, B., & Slaughter, A. (2019). Sexual harassment and sexual assault training needs analysis for journalists. *Industrial and Organizational Psychology, 12*(1), 115–118.

Buch, K., & Spangler, R. (1990). The effects of quality circles on performance and promotions. *Human Relations, 43*(6), 573–582.

Buchko, A. A. (1992). Employee ownership, attitudes, and turn over: An empirical assessment. *Human Relations, 45*(7), 711–733.

Buckett, A., Becker, J. R., Melchers, K. G., & Roodt, G. (2020). How different indicator-dimension ratios in assessment center ratings affect evidence for dimension factors. *Frontiers in Psychology, 11*, 459–506.

Buckly, R. (1993). *Job analysis and examination specifications study.* Sacramento, CA: Department of Real Estate.

Burgess, R. (1968). Communication networks: An experimental reevaluation. *Journal of Experimental Social Psychology, 4*(3), 324–337.

Burke, R. J. (1993). Organizational-level interventions to reduce occupational stressors. *Work & Stress, 7*(1), 77–87.

Burke, R. J. (2000). Workaholism in organizations: psychological and physical well-being consequences. *Stress Medicine, 16*(1), 11–16.

Burke, W. W. (1987). *Organization development: A normative view.* Reading, MA: Addison-Wesley.

Burns, J. M. (1978). *Leadership.* New York: Harper & Row.

Butterfield, L. D., Borgen, W. A., Amundson, N. E., & Asa-Sophia, T. M. (2005). Fifty years of the critical incident technique: 1954–2004 and beyond. *Qualitative Research, 5*, 475–497.

Byrne, B. M. (1993). The Maslach Burnout Inventory: Testing for factorial validity and invariance across elementary, intermediate, and secondary teachers. *Journal of Occupational and Organizational Psychology, 66*(3), 197–212.

Byrne, D. G., & Reinhart, M. I. (1989). Work characteristics, occupational achievement, and the Type A behaviour pattern. *Journal of Occupational Psychology, 62*(3), 123–134.

Cable, D. M., & Parsons, C. K. (2001). Socialization tactics and person-organization fit. *Personnel Psychology, 54*(1), 1–23.

Caligiuri, P., Tarique, I., & Jacobs, R. (2009). Selection for international assignments. *Human Resource Management Review, 19*, 251–262.

Callinan, M., & Robertson, I. T. (2000). Work sample testing. *International Journal of Selection and Assessment, 8*, 248–260.

Campbell, D. J., Campbell, K. M., & Chia, H. (1998). Merit pay, performance appraisal, and individual motivation: An analysis and alternative. *Human Resource Management, 37*(2), 131–146.

Campbell, D. J., & Furrer, D. M. (1995). Goal setting and competition as determinants of task performance. *Journal of Organizational Behavior, 16*(4), 377–389.

Campbell, D. J., & Lee, C. (1988). Self-appraisal in performance evaluation: Development versus evaluation. *Academy of Management Review, 13*, 302–314.

Campbell, D. T., & Stanley, J. C. (1963). *Experimental and quasi-experimental designs for research.* Chicago, IL: Rand McNally.

Campion, M. A., Cheraskin, L., & Stevens, M. J. (1994). Career-related antecedents and outcomes of job rotation. *Academy of Management Journal, 37*(6), 1518–1542.

Campion, M. A., & McClelland, C. L. (1991). Interdisciplinary examination of the costs and benefits of enlarged jobs: A job design quasi-experiment. *Journal of Applied Psychology, 76*(2), 186–198.

Campion, M. A., Palmer, D. K., & Campion, J. E. (1998). Structuring employment interviews to improve reliability, validity, and users' reactions. *American Psychological Society, 7*(3), 77–82.

Campion, M. C., Campion, E. D., & Campion, M. A. (2015). Improvements in performance management through the use of 360 feedback. *Industrial and Organizational Psychology: Perspectives on Science and Practice*, 8(1), 85–93.

Campion, M. C., Campion, E. D., & Campion, M. A. (2019). Using practice employment tests to improve recruitment and personnel selection outcomes for organizations and job seekers. *Journal of Applied Psychology*, 104(9), 1089.

Cannon-Bowers, J. A., Rhodenizer, L., Salas, E., & Bowers, C. A. (1998). A framework for understanding pre-practice conditions and their impact on learning. *Personnel Psychology*, 51(2), 291–320.

Cannon-Bowers, J. A., & Salas, E. (1997). A framework for developing team performance measures in training. In M. T. Brannick, E. Salas, & C. Prince (Eds.), *Team performance assessment and measurement: Theory, methods, and applications* (pp. 45–62). Hillsdale, NJ: Erlbaum.

Cannon-Bowers, J. A., Salas, E., & Converse, S. (1990). Cognitive psychology and team training: Training shared mental models and complex systems. *Human Factors Society Bulletin*, 33(12), 1–4.

Caplan, R. D., & Jones, K. W. (1975). Effects of workload, role ambiguity, and Type A personality on anxiety, depression, and heart rate. *Journal of Applied Psychology*, 60(6), 713–719.

Carayon, P. (1994). Stressful jobs and non-stressful jobs: A cluster analysis of office jobs. *Ergonomics*, 37(2), 311–323.

Carayon, P., & Zijlstra, F. (1999). Relationship between job control, work pressure and strain: Studies in the USA and The Netherlands. *Work & Stress*, 13(1), 32–48.

Carey, J. M., & Kacmar, C. J. (1997). The impact of communication mode and task complexity on small group performance and member satisfaction. *Computers in Human Behavior*, 13(1), 23–49.

Carless, S. A., & De Paola, C. (2000). The measurement of cohesion in work teams. *Small Group Research*, 31(1), 71–88.

Carlson, B. C., & Thompson, J. A. (1995). Job burnout and job leaving in public school teachers: Implications for stress management. *International Journal of Stress Management*, 2(2), 15–29.

Carpenter, C. S. (2007). Workplace drug testing and worker drug use. *Health Services Research*, 42(2), 795–810.

Carroll, S. J., Paine, F. T., & Ivancevich, J. J. (1972). The relative effectiveness of training methods: Expert opinion and research. *Personnel Psychology*, 25, 495–510.

Carson, P. P., Carson, K. D., & Roe, C. W. (1993). Social power bases: A meta-analytic examination of interrelationships and outcomes. *Journal of Applied Social Psychology*, 23(14), 1150–1169.

Carter, D. R., DeChurch, L. A., Braun, M. T., & Contractor, N. S. (2015). Social network approaches to leadership: An integrative conceptual review. *Journal of Applied Psychology*, 100(3), 597–622.

Cartwright, D. (1968). The nature of group cohesiveness. In D. Cartwright & A. Zander (Eds.), *Group dynamics: Research and theory* (3rd ed., pp. 91–109). New York: Harper & Row.

Cascio, W. F. (1987). *Applied psychology in personnel management* (3rd ed.). Englewood Cliffs, NJ: Prentice Hall.

Cascio, W. F. (2003). *Managing human resources: Productivity, quality of work life, profits* (6th ed.). Burr Ridge, IL: Irwin/McGraw-Hill.

Cascio, W. F., Alexander, R. A., & Barrett, G. V. (1988). Setting cutoff scores: Legal, psychometric, and professional issues and guidelines. *Personnel Psychology*, 41(1), 1–24.

Catanzaro, D., Moore, H., & Marshall, T. R. (2010). The impact of organizational culture on attraction and recruitment of job applicants. *Journal of Business and Psychology*, 25(4), 649–662.

Cathy, L., & Farah, L. (2020). *The COVID-19 pandemic has changed education forever. This is how*. Retrieved 7/9/2021 from www.weforum.org/agenda/2020/04/coronavirus-education-global-covid19-online-digital-learning/

Cattell, R. B., Eber, H. W., & Tatsuoka, M. M. (1970). *Handbook for the sixteen personality factor questionnaire (16PF)*. Institute for Personality & Ability Testing.

Cecil, J. (2001). Computer-aided fixture design: A review and future trends. *International Journal of Advanced Manufacturing Technology*, 18(11), 790–793.

Chang, C., Rosen, C. C., & Levy, P. E. (2009). The relationship between perceptions of organizational politics and employee attitudes, strain, and behavior: A meta-analytic examination. *Academy of Management Journal*, 52(4), 779–801.

Chang, E. H., & Milkman, K. L. (2020). Improving decisions that affect gender equality in the workplace. *Organizational Dynamics*, 49(1), 100709–100713.

Chao, G. T., Walz, P. M., & Gardner, P. D. (1992). Formal and informal mentorships: A comparison on mentoring functions and contrast with nonmentored counterparts. *Personnel Psychology*, 45(3), 619–636.

Chapman, J. (2006). Anxiety and defective decision making: An elaboration of the groupthink model. *Management Decision*, 44(10), 1391–1404.

Chatman, J. A., & Jehn, K. A. (1994). Assessing the relationship between industry characteristics and organizational culture: How different can you be? *Academy of Management Journal*, 37(3), 522–553.

Chawla, N., Gabriel, A. S., da Motta Veiga, S. P., & Slaughter, J. E. (2019). Does feedback matter for job search self-regulation? It depends on feedback quality. *Personnel Psychology*, 72(4), 513–541.

Chen, P. Y., & Spector, P. E. (1991). Negative affectivity as the underlying cause of correlations between stressors and strains. *Journal of Applied Psychology, 76*(3), 398–407.

Chen, X., Hui, C., & Sego, D. J. (1998). The role of organizational citizenship behavior in turnover: Conceptualization and preliminary tests of key hypotheses. *Journal of Applied Psychology, 83*(6), 922–931.

Chen, Y., & Fulmer, I. S. (2018). Fine-tuning what we know about employees' experience with flexible work arrangements and their job attitudes. *Human Resource Management, 57*(1), 381–395.

Chernyak-Hai, L., & Rabenu, E. (2018). The new era workplace relationships: Is social exchange theory still relevant? *Industrial and Organizational Psychology, 11*(3), 456–481.

Chesney, M. A., & Rosenman, R. H. (1980). Type A behaviour in the work setting. In C. L. Cooper & R. Payne (Eds.), *Current concerns in occupational stress* (pp. 187–212). Chichester, UK: Wiley.

Cheung, H. K., Lindsey, A., King, E., & Hebl, M. R. (2016). Beyond sex: Exploring the effects of femininity and masculinity on women's use of influence tactics. *Gender in Management: An International Journal, 31*(1), 43–60.

Cheung, J. H., Burns, D. K., Sinclair, R. R., & Sliter, M. (2017). Amazon Mechanical Turk in organizational psychology: An evaluation and practical recommendations. *Journal of Business and Psychology, 32*(4), 347–361.

Chiaburu, D. S., Oh, I., Berry, C. M., Li, N., & Gardner, R. G. (2011). The five-factor model of personality traits and organizational citizenship behaviors: A meta-analysis. *Journal of Applied Psychology, 96*(6), 1140–1166.

Chiu, S., & Tsai, W. (2007). The linkage between profit sharing and organizational citizenship behavior. *International Journal of Human Resource Management, 18*(6), 1098–1115.

Cho, I., & Payne, S. C. (2016). Other important questions: When, how, and why do cultural values influence performance management. *Industrial and Organizational Psychology, 9*(2), 343–350.

Choi, Y. J., Chan, L., & Jacobs, R. L. (2015). The hierarchical linear relationship among structured on-the-job training activities, trainee characteristics, trainer characteristics, training environment characteristics, and organizational characteristics of workers in small and medium-sized companies. *Human Resource Development International, 18*(5), 499–520.

Christensen, J. F. (2020). Weird ways of normalizing: Queering diversity research through norm critique. In A. Risberg, F. Villesèche, & S. N. Just (Eds.), *The Routledge companion to organizational diversity research methods* (pp. 59–72). New York: Routledge.

Christensen, J. F., Mahler, R., & Teilmann-Lock, S. (2020). GenderLAB: Norm-critical design thinking for gender equality and diversity. *Organization*, 1350508420961528

Chua, P. K., & Mazmanian, M. (2020). Are you one of us? Current hiring practices suggest the potential for class biases in large tech companies. *Proceedings of the ACM on Human-Computer Interaction, 4*(CSCW2), 1–20.

Chung, B. G., Ehrhart, K. H., Shore, L. M., Randel, A. E., Dean, M. A., & Kedharnath, U. (2020). Work group inclusion: Test of a scale and model. *Group & Organization Management, 45*(1), 75–102.

Church, A. H., & Waclawski, J. (2001). Hold the line: An examination of line vs. staff differences. *Human Resource Management, 40*(1), 21–34.

Church, A. H., Walker, A. G., & Brockner, J. (2002). Multisource feedback for organization development and change. In J. Waclawski & A. H. Church (Eds.), *Organization development: A data-driven approach to organizational change* (pp. 27–54). San Francisco, CA: Jossey-Bass.

Cialdini, R. B. (2008). *Influence: Science and practice* (5th ed.). Boston, MA: Pearson.

Cislak, A., Formanowicz, M., & Saguy, T. (2018). Bias against research on gender bias. *Scientometrics, 115*(1), 189–200.

Clark, M. A., Smith, R. W., & Haynes, N. J. (2020). The multidimensional workaholism scale: Linking the conceptualization and measurement of workaholism. *Journal of Applied Psychology, 105*(11), 1281–1307.

Clark, M. C. (2005, July). *The cost of job stress*. Retrieved from www.mediate.com/articles/clarkM1.cfm

Claypoole, V. L., & Szalma, J. L. (2019). Electronic performance monitoring and sustained attention: Social facilitation for modern applications. *Computers in Human Behavior, 94*, 25–34.

Clay-Warner, J., Reynolds, J., & Roman, P. (2005). Organizational justice and job satisfaction: A test of three competing models. *Social Justice Research, 18*(4), 391–409.

Cleveland, J. N., Murphy, K. R., & Williams, R. E. (1989). Multiple uses of performance appraisal: Prevalence and correlates. *Journal of Applied Psychology, 74*(1), 130–135.

Cobb, A. T. (1984). An episodic model of power: Toward an integration of theory and research. *Academy of Management Review, 9*(3), 482–493.

Cohen, S. (1980). Aftereffects of stress on human behavior and social behavior: A review of research and theory. *Psychological Bulletin, 88*, 82–108.

Cohen, S. G., Ledford, G. E., Jr., & Spreitzer, G. M. (1996). A predictive model of self-managing work team effectiveness. *Human Relations, 49*(5), 643–676.

Cohen-Charash, Y., & Spector, P. E. (2001). The role of justice in organizations: A meta-analysis. *Organizational Behavior and Human Decision Processes, 86*(2), 278–321.

Cole, N. D., & Flint, D. H. (2004). Perceptions of distributive and procedural justice in employee benefits: Flexible versus traditional benefit plans. *Journal of Managerial Psychology, 19*(1), 19–40.

Colella, A., Hebl, M., & King, E. (2017). One hundred years of discrimination research in the *Journal of Applied Psychology*: A sobering synopsis. *Journal of Applied Psychology, 102*(3), 500–513.

Collins, C. J., Hanges, P. J., & Locke, E. A. (2004). The relationship of achievement motivation to entrepreneurial behavior: A meta-analysis. *Human Performance, 17*(1), 95–117.

Collins, C. J., & Smith, K. G. (2006). Knowledge exchange and combination: The role of human resource practices in the performance of high-technology firms. *Academy of Management Journal, 49*(3), 544–560.

Collins, D. (1995). Death of a gainsharing plan: Power politics and participatory management. *Organizational Dynamics, 24*(1), 23–38.

Conger, J. A. (1993). The brave new world of leadership training. *Organizational Dynamics, 21*(3), 46–58.

Conger, J. A., & Kanungo, R. N. (1987). Toward a behavioral theory of charismatic leadership in organizational settings. *Academy of Management Review, 12*(4), 637–647.

Conger, J. A., & Kanungo, R. N. (1988). The empowerment process: Integrating theory and practice. *Academy of Management Review, 13*(3), 471–482.

Conlon, D. E., & Ross, W. H. (1993). The effects of partisan third parties on negotiator behavior and outcome perception. *Journal of Applied Psychology, 78*(2), 280–290.

Conroy, S. A. (2019). Setting base pay rates: integrating compensation practice with human capital value creation and value capture. In *Handbook of research on strategic human capital resources*. Edward Elgar Publishing.

Converse, S., Cannon-Bowers, J., & Salas, E. (1993). Shared mental models in expert team decision making. *Individual and Group Decision Making: Current Issues, 221*, 221–246.

Conway, J. M., Jako, R. A., & Goodman, D. F. (1995). A meta-analysis of interrater and internal consistency reliability of selection interviews. *Journal of Applied Psychology, 80*(5), 565–579.

Cooke, N. J., Kiekel, P. A., Salas, E., Stout, R., Bowers, C., & Cannon-Bowers, J. (2003). Measuring team knowledge: A window to the cognitive underpinnings of team performance. *Group Dynamics: Theory, Research, and Practice, 7*(3), 179–199.

Cooley, E. (1994). Training an interdisciplinary team in communication and decision-making skills. *Small Group Research, 25*(1), 5–25.

Cooper, C. L., Dewe, P. J., & O'Driscoll, M. P. (2002). *Organizational stress: A review and critique of theory, research, and applications*. Thousand Oaks, CA: Sage.

Cooper, C. L., Dyck, B., & Frohlich, N. (1992). Improving the effectiveness of gainsharing: The role of fairness and participation. *Administrative Science Quarterly, 37*(3), 471–490.

Cooper, C. L., Sloan, S. G., & Williams, S. (1988). *The occupational stress indicator: Management guide*. Oxford: NFER-Nelson.

Cooper-Thomas, H. (2009). The role of newcomer–insider relationships during organizational socialization. In R. L. Morrison & S. L. Wright (Eds.), *Friends and enemies in organizations* (pp. 32–56). Springer.

Cordes, C. L., & Dougherty, T. W. (1993). A review and an integration of research on job burnout. *Academy of Management Review, 18*, 621–656.

Cortina, J. M., Goldstein, N. B., Payne, S. C., Davison, H. K., & Gilliland, S. W. (2000). The incremental validity of interview scores over and above cognitive ability and conscientiousness scores. *Personnel Psychology, 53*(2), 325–351.

Cortina, L. M. (2008). Unseen injustice: Incivility as modern discrimination in organizations. *Academy of Management Review, 33*(1), 55–75.

Costa, P. T., & McCrae, R. R. (1992). Neo personality inventory-revised (NEO PI-R). Odessa, FL: Psychological Assessment Resources.

Coyle-Shapiro, J. A.-M. (2000). TQM and organizational change: A longitudinal study of the impact of a TQM intervention on work attitudes. *Research in Organizational Change and Development, 12*, 129–169.

Crawford, J. (1981). *Crawford small parts dexterity test*. San Antonio, TX: The Psychological Corporation.

Crenshaw, K. W. (2017). *On intersectionality: essential writings*. New Press.

Cropanzano, R., & Grandey, A. A. (1998). If politics is a game, then what are the rules? Three suggestions for ethical management. In M. Schminke (Ed.), *Managerial ethics: Moral management of people and processes* (pp. 133–152). Mahwah, NJ: Erlbaum.

Cropanzano, R., Howes, J. C., Grandey, A. A., & Toth, P. (1997). The relationship of organizational politics and support to work behaviors, attitudes, and stress. *Journal of Organizational Behavior, 18*, 159–180.

Cruz-Cunha, M. M. (2012). *Handbook of research on serious games as educational, business and research tools*. IGI Global.

Cuadrado, D., Salgado, J. F., & Moscoso, S. (2021). Personality, intelligence, and counterproductive academic behaviors: A meta-analysis. *Journal of Personality and Social Psychology, 120*(2), 504–537.

Culbertson, S. S., Weyhrauch, W. S., & Huffcutt, A. I. (2017). A tale of two formats: Direct comparison of matching situational and behavior description interview questions. *Human Resource Management Review, 27*(1), 167–177.

Cummings, N. A., & Follette, W. T. (1976). Brief psychotherapy and medical utilization: An eight-year follow-up. In H. Dorken (Ed.), *The professional psychologist today: New developments in law, health, insurance, and health practice* (pp. 176–197). San Francisco, CA: Jossey-Bass.

Curado, C., Henriques, P. L., & Ribeiro, S. (2015). Voluntary or mandatory enrollment in training and the motivation to transfer training. *International Journal of Training and Development, 19*(2), 98–109.

Curtis, M. B., Robertson, J. C., Cockrell, R. C., & Fayard, L. D. (2020). Peer ostracism as a sanction against wrongdoers and whistleblowers. *Journal of Business Ethics, 1*, 1–22.

Dada, S., Ashworth, H. C., Bewa, M. J., & Dhatt, R. (2021). Words matter: political and gender analysis of speeches made by heads of government during the COVID-19 pandemic. *BMJ Global Health, 6*(1), e003910

Dahl, M. S. (2011). Organizational change and employee stress. *Management Science, 57*(2), 240–256.

Dahling, J. J., Taylor, S. R., Chau, S. L., & Dwight, S. (2016). Why does coaching matter? A multilevel model linking managerial coaching effectiveness and frequency to sales goal attainment. *Personnel Psychology, 69*, 863–894.

Dalal, R. S., Bonaccio, S., Highhouse, S., Ilgen, D., Mohammed, S., & Slaughter, J. (2010). What if industrial–organizational psychology decided to take workplace decisions seriously? *Industrial and Organizational Psychology, 3*(4), 386–405.

da Motta Veiga, S. P., & Gabriel, A. S. (2016). The role of self-determined motivation in job search: A dynamic approach. *Journal of Applied Psychology, 101*(3), 350.

Danna, K., & Griffin, R. W. (1999). Health and well-being in the workplace: A review and synthesis of the literature. *Journal of Management, 25*(3), 357–384.

Darioly, A., & Mast, M. S. (2014). The role of nonverbal behavior in leadership. In R. E. Riggio & S. J. Tan (Eds.). *Leader interpersonal and influence skills: The soft skills of leadership* (pp. 73–100). New York: Routledge.

Davis, K. (1968). Success of chain-of-command oral communication in a manufacturing management group. *Academy of Management Journal, 11*(4), 379–387.

Davis, M. F., & Green, J. (2020, 04/23/2020). Three hours longer, the Pandemic workday has obliterated work-life balance. *Bloomberg.* Retrieved from www.bloomberg.com/news/articles/2020-04-23/working-from-home-in-covid-era-means-three-more-hours-on-the-job

Davis-Blake, A., & Broschak, J. P. (2009). Outsourcing and the changing nature of work. *Annual Review of Sociology, 35*, 321–340.

Davison, H. K., Antonik, C., Kaszycki, A., DuVernet, A., & Oppler, S. (2020). SIOP Income and Employment Survey. *The Industrial-Organizational Psychologist, 58*(1), 1–2.

Day, D. V. (2013). Training and developing leaders: Theory and research. In M. G. Rumsey, (Ed.), *The Oxford handbook of leadership* (pp. 76–93). New York: Oxford University Press.

Dean Jr., J. W., Yoon, S. J., & Susman, G. I. (1992). Advanced manufacturing technology and organization structure: Empowerment or subordination? *Organization Science, 3*(2), 203–229.

DeChurch, L. A., & Mesmer-Magnus, J. R. (2010). Measuring shared team mental models: A meta-analysis. *Group Dynamics: Theory, Research, and Practice, 14*(1), 1–14.

Deci, E. L., Connell, J. P., & Ryan, R. M. (1989). Self-determination in a work organization. *Journal of Applied Psychology, 74*(4), 580–590.

Decker, P. J., & Nathan, B. R. (1985). *Behavior modeling training: Principles and applications.* New York: Praeger.

De Dreu, C. K. W. (2008). The virtue and vice of workplace conflict: Food for (pessimistic) thought. *Journal of Organizational Behavior, 29*(1), 5–18.

De Dreu, C. K. W., & Weingart, L. R. (2003). Task versus relationship conflict, team performance, and team member satisfaction: A meta-analysis. *Journal of Applied Psychology, 88*(4), 741–749.

De Dreu, C. K. W., & West, M. A. (2001). Minority dissent and team innovation: The importance of participation in decision making. *Journal of Applied Psychology, 86*(6), 1191–1201.

de Lara, P. Z. M. (2006). Research note: Fear in organizations: Does intimidation by formal punishment mediate the relationship between interactional justice and workplace Internet deviance? *Journal of Managerial Psychology, 21*(6), 580–592.

Delaney, M. L., & Royal, M. A. (2017). Breaking engagement apart: The role of intrinsic and extrinsic motivation in engagement strategies. *Industrial and Organizational Psychology, 10*(1), 127–140.

DeMatteo, J. S., Eby, L. T., & Sundstrom, E. (1998). Team-based rewards: Current empirical evidence and directions for future research. In B. M. Staw & L. L. Cummings (Eds.), *Research in organizational behavior* (Vol. 20, pp. 141–148). Greenwich, CT: Jai Press.

Demerouti, E., Bakker, A. B., Nachreiner, F., & Schaufeli, W. B. (2001). The job demands–resources model of burnout. *Journal of Applied Psychology*, *86*(3), 499–512.

Demerouti, E., Bakker, A. B., Xanthopoulou, D., Taris, T., Peeters, M., & De Witte, H. (2019). Job demands–resources theory and the role of individual cognitive and behavioral strategies. In T. Taris, M. Peeters, & H. De Witten (Eds.), *The fun and frustration of modern working life: Contributions from an occupational health psychology perspective* (pp. 94–104). Pelckmans Pro.

DeNisi, A. S., & Murphy, K. R. (2017). Performance appraisal and performance management: 100 years of progress? *Journal of Applied Psychology*, *102*(3), 421–433.

Denison, D. R. (1996). What is the difference between organizational culture and organizational climate? A native's point of view on a decade of paradigm wars. *Academy of Management Review*, *21*(3), 619–654.

Derous, E. (2017). Ethnic minorities' impression management in the interview: helping or hindering? *Frontiers in Psychology*, *8*, 86–97.

Derous, E., Buijsrogge, A., Roulin, N., & Duyck, W. (2016). Why your stigma isn't hired: A dual-process framework of interview bias. *Human Resource Management Review*, *26*(2), 90–111.

Derous, E., Nguyen, H.-H. D., & Ryan, A. M. (2020). Reducing ethnic discrimination in resume-screening: a test of two training interventions. *European Journal of Work and Organizational Psychology*, *30*(2), 1–15.

Devine, D. J., Clayton, L. D., Philips, J. L., Dunford, B. B., & Melner, S. B. (1999). Teams in organizations: Prevalence, characteristics, and effectiveness. *Small Group Research*, *30*(6), 678–711.

Devine, D. J., Habig, J. K., Martin, K. E., Bott, J. P., & Grayson, A. L. (2004). Tinsel town: A top management simulation involving distributed expertise. *Simulation & Gaming*, *35*(1), 94–134.

de Vries, R. E., Bakker-Pieper, A., & Oostenveld, W. (2010). Leadership = communication? The relations of leaders' communication styles with leadership styles, knowledge sharing and leadership outcomes. *Journal of Business and Psychology*, *25*(3), 367–380.

Dewettinck, K., & van Ameijde, M. (2011). Linking leadership empowerment behaviour to employee attitudes and behavioural intentions: Testing the mediating role of psychological empowerment. *Personnel Review*, *40*(3), 284–305.

Dierdorff, E. C. (2012). Using secondary sources of work information to improve work analysis. In M. A. Wilson, W. Bennett, G. G. Shanan, & G. M. Alliger (Eds.), *The handbook of work analysis methods, systems, applications, and science of work measurement in organizations* (pp. 81–92). New York: Taylor & Francis.

Dierdorff, E. C., & Surface, E. A. (2008). If you pay for skills, will they learn? Skill change and maintenance under a skill-based pay system. *Journal of Management*, *34*(4), 721–743.

Dietz-Uhler, B., Bishop-Clark, C., & Howard, E. (2005). Formation of and adherence to a self-disclosure norm in an on-line chat. *CyberPsychology & Behavior*, *8*(2), 114–120.

DiFonzo, N., Bordia, P., & Rosnow, R. L. (1994). Reining in rumors. *Organizational Dynamics*, *23*(1), 47–62.

DiMatteo, M. R., Shugars, D. A., & Hays, R. D. (1993). Occupational stress, life stress, and mental health among dentists. *Journal of Occupational and Organizational Psychology*, *66*(2), 153–162.

Dinh, J. E., Lord, R. G., Gardner, W. L., Meuser, J. D., Liden, R. C., & Hu, J. (2014). Leadership theory and research in the new millennium: Current theoretical trends and changing perspectives. *The Leadership Quarterly*, *25*(1), 36–62.

Dipboye, R. L. (1994). Structured and unstructured selection interviews: Beyond the job-fit model. *Research in Personnel and Human Resources Management*, *12*, 79–123.

Dixon, M. L., & Hart, L. K. (2010). The impact of path–goal leadership styles on work group effectiveness and turnover intention. *Journal of Managerial Issues*, *22*(1), 52–69.

Dominick, P. G. (2009). Forced rankings: Pros, cons, and practices. In J. W. Smither & M. London (Eds.), *Performance management: Putting research into action* (pp. 411–443). San Francisco: Jossey-Bass.

Donaldson, T., Earl, J. K., & Muratore, A. M. (2010). Extending the integrated model of retirement adjustment: Incorporating mastery and retirement planning. *Journal of Vocational Behavior*, *77*(22), 279–289.

Dormann, C., & Zapf, D. (2001). Job satisfaction: A meta-analysis of stabilities. *Journal of Organizational Behavior*, *22*(5), 483–504.

Dornburg, C. C., Stevens, S. M., Hendrickson, S. M. L., & Davidson, G. S. (2009). Improving extreme-scale problem solving: Assessing electronic brainstorming effectiveness in an industrial setting. *Human Factors*, *51*(4), 519–527.

Dorsey, D., & Mueller-Hanson, R. (2017). Performance management that makes a difference: An evidence-based approach. SHRM Science to Practice Series.

Dotlich, D. L., & Noel, J. L. (1998). *Action learning*. San Francisco, CA: Jossey-Bass.

Drape, J. (2012, 06/22/2012). Sandusky guilty of sexual abuse of 10 young boys. *The New York Times*. Retrieved from www.nytimes.com/2012/06/23/sports/ncaafootball/jerry-sandusky-convicted-of-sexually-abusing-boys.html

Dray, K. K., Smith, V. R., Kostecki, T. P., Sabat, I. E., & Thomson, C. R. (2020). Moving beyond the gender binary: Examining workplace perceptions of nonbinary and transgender employees. *Gender, Work & Organization*, *27*(6), 1181–1191.

Driskell, J. E., Willis, R. P., & Copper, C. (1992). Effect of overlearning on retention. *Journal of Applied Psychology, 77*(5), 615–622.

Drucker, P. F. (1954). *The practice of management.* New York: Harper & Row.

Duane, M., Reimal, E., & Lynch, M. (2017). *Criminal background checks and access to jobs.* Urban Institute.

Dumdum, U. R., Lowe, K. B., & Avolio, B. J. (2002). A meta-analysis of transformational and transactional leadership correlates of effectiveness and satisfaction: An update and extension. In B. J. Avolio & F. J. Yammarino (Eds.), *Transformational and charismatic leadership: The road ahead* (pp. 39–70). Oxford, UK: JAI/Elsevier.

Dunnette, M. D., Campbell, J. P., & Hakel, M. D. (1967). Factors contributing to job satisfaction and dissatisfaction in six occupational groups. *Organizational Behavior and Human Performance, 2*(2), 143–174.

Dutton, J. E., & Ashford, S. J. (1993). Selling issues to top management. *Academy of Management Review, 18*(3), 397–428.

Dutton, J. E., Ashford, S. J., O'Neill, R. M., Hayes, E., & Wierba, E. E. (1997). Reading the wind: How middle managers assess the context for selling issues to top managers. *Strategic Management Journal, 18*(5), 407–423.

Dutton, J. E., Ashford, S. J., O'Neill, R. M., & Lawrence, K. A. (2001). Moves that matter: Issue selling and organizational change. *Academy of Management Journal, 44*(4), 716–736.

Dwyer, D. J., & Ganster, D. C. (1991). The effects of job demands and control on employee attendance and satisfaction. *Journal of Organizational Behavior, 12*(7), 595–608.

Eagly, A. H., Johannesen-Schmidt, M. C., & Van Engen, M. L. (2003). Transformational, transactional, and laissez-faire leadership styles: A meta-analysis comparing women and men. *Psychological Bulletin, 129*(4), 569–591.

Eagly, A. H., & Johnson, B. T. (1990). Gender and leadership style: A meta-analysis. *Psychological Bulletin, 108*(2), 233–256.

Eagly, A. H., & Karau, S. J. (2002). Role congruity theory of prejudice toward female leaders. *Psychological Review, 109*(3), 573–598.

Eagly, A. H., Nater, C., Miller, D. I., Kaufmann, M., & Sczesny, S. (2020). Gender stereotypes have changed: A cross-temporal meta-analysis of US public opinion polls from 1946 to 2018. *American Psychologist, 75*(3), 301–316.

Eatough, E. M., Meier, L. L., Igic, I., Elfering, A., Spector, P. E., & Semmer, N. K. (2016). You want me to do what? Two daily diary studies of illegitimate tasks and employee well-being. *Journal of Organizational Behavior, 37*(1), 108–127.

Eberly, M. B., Holtom, B. C., Lee, T. W., & Mitchell, T. R. (2009). Control voluntary turnover by understanding its causes. In E. A. Locke (Ed.), *Handbook of principles of organizational behavior* (Vol. 123). John Wiley.

Eby, L. T. (2007). Understanding relational problems in mentoring. In T. D. Allen & L. T. Eby (Eds.), *The Blackwell handbook of mentoring: A multiple perspectives approach* (pp. 323–344). Blackwell.

Eby, L. T., Shockley, K. M., Bauer, T. N., Edwards, B., Homan, A. C., Johnson, R., Lang, J. W., Morris, S. B., & Oswald, F. L. (2020). Methodological checklists for improving research quality and reporting consistency. *Industrial and Organizational Psychology, 13*(1), 76–83.

Eden, D. (1990). *Pygmalion in management.* Lexington, MA: Lexington Books.

Eden, D., & Shani, A. B. (1982). Pygmalion goes to boot camp: Expectancy, leadership, and trainee performance. *Journal of Applied Psychology, 67*(2), 194–199.

Efraty, D., & Sirgy, M. J. (1990). The effects of quality of working life (QWL) on employee behavioral responses. *Social Indicators Research, 22*(1), 31–47.

Eisenbach, R., Watson, K., & Pillai, R. (1999). Transformational leadership in the context of organizational change. *Journal of Organizational Change Management, 12*(2), 80–88.

Eisenberg, E. M., & Witten, M. G. (1987). Reconsidering openness in organizational communication. *Academy of Management Review, 12*(3), 418–426.

Eisenberger, R., Armeli, S., Rexwinkel, B., Lynch, P. D., & Rhoades, L. (2001). Reciprocation of perceived organizational support. *Journal of Applied Psychology, 86*(1), 42–51.

Elenkov, S. E. (1998). Can American management concepts work in Russia? A cross-cultural comparative study. *California Management Review, 40*(4), 133–156.

Ellis, A. P. J. (2006). System breakdown: The role of mental models and transactive memory in the relationship between acute stress and team performance. *Academy of Management Journal, 49*, 576–589.

Ely, R. J., & Thomas, D. A. (2001). Cultural diversity at work: The effects of diversity perspectives on work group processes and outcomes. *Administrative Science Quarterly, 46*(2), 229–273.

Ensher, E. A., & Murphy, S. E. (2005). *Power mentoring: How successful mentors and proteges get the most out of their relationships.* San Francisco, CA: Jossey-Bass.

Ensher, E. A., Thomas, C., & Murphy, S. E. (2001). Comparison of traditional, step-ahead, and peer mentoring on protégés' support, satisfaction, and perceptions of career success: A social exchange perspective. *Journal of Business and Psychology, 15*(3), 419–438.

Erdogan, B., & Bauer, T. N. (2014). Leader-member exchange (LMX) theory: The relational approach to leadership. In D. V. Day (Ed.), *The Oxford handbook of leadership and organizations* (pp. 407–433). Oxford University Press.

Erdogan, B., Karaeminogullari, A., Bauer, T. N., & Ellis, A. M. (2020). Perceived overqualification at work: Implications for extra-role behaviors and advice network centrality. *Journal of Management, 46*(4), 583–606.

Erfurt, J. C., Foote, A., & Heirich, M. A. (1992). The cost-effectiveness of worksite wellness programs for hypertension, weight loss, smoking cessation, and exercise. *Personnel Psychology, 45*(1), 5–27.

Erickson, R. J., Nichols, L., & Ritter, C. (2000). Family influences on absenteeism: Testing an expanded process model. *Journal of Vocational Behavior, 57*(2), 246–272.

Eschleman, K. J., Bowling, N. A., & Alarcon, G. M. (2010). A meta-analytic examination of hardiness. *International Journal of Stress Management, 17*(4), 277–307.

Esser, J. K. (1998). Alive and well after 25 years: A review of group-think research. *Organizational Behavior and Human Decision Processes, 73*(2–3), 116–141.

Etzion, D. (2003). Annual vacation: Duration of relief from job stressors and burnout. *Anxiety, Stress, and Coping, 16*(2), 213–226.

Evans, G. W., & Johnson, D. (2000). Stress and open-office noise. *Journal of Applied Psychology, 85*(5), 779–783.

Evers, W. J., Brouwers, A., & Tomic, W. (2006). A quasi-experimental study on management coaching effectiveness. *Consulting Psychology Journal: Practice and Research, 58*, 174–182.

Evertz, L., Kollitz, R., & Süß, S. (2019). Electronic word-of-mouth via employer review sites—the effects on organizational attraction. *International Journal of Human Resource Management, 32*, 1–30.

Ezerins, M. E., & Ludwig, T. D. (2021). A behavioral analysis of incivility in the virtual workplace. *Journal of Organizational Behavior Management* (in press), 1–24.

Fagenson, E. A. (1989). The mentor advantage: Perceived career/job experiences of protégés vs. non-protégés. *Journal of Organizational Behavior, 10*(4), 309–320.

Fagenson, E. A., & Burke, W. W. (1990). The activities of organization development practitioners at the turn of the decade of the 1990s: A study of their predictions. *Group and Organization Studies, 15*(4), 366–380.

Fantuzzo, J. W., Riggio, R. E., Connelly, S., & Dimeff, L. A. (1989). Effects of reciprocal peer tutoring on academic achievement and psychological adjustment: A component analysis. *Journal of Educational Psychology, 81*(2), 173–177.

Farh, C. I., & Chen, G. (2018). Leadership and member voice in action teams: Test of a dynamic phase model. *Journal of Applied Psychology, 103*(1), 97–110.

Farh, J. L., & Dobbins, G. H. (1989). Effects of comparative performance information on the accuracy of self-ratings and agreement between self- and supervisor ratings. *Journal of Applied Psychology, 74*(4), 606–610.

Farrell, D., & Petersen, J. C. (1982). Patterns of political behavior in organizations. *Academy of Management Review, 7*(3), 403–412.

Feher, A., & Vernon, P. A. (2021). Looking beyond the Big Five: A selective review of alternatives to the Big Five model of personality. *Personality and Individual Differences, 169*, 110002.

Feldman, D. C. (1976). A contingency theory of socialization. *Administrative Science Quarterly, 21*, 433–454.

Feldman, D. C. (1984). The development and enforcement of group norms. *Academy of Management Review, 9*(1), 47–53.

Ferdman, B. M. (2010). Teaching inclusion by example and experience: Creating an inclusive learning environment. In B. B. McFeeters, K. M. Hannum, & L. Booysen (Eds.), *Leading across differences: Cases and perspectives—Facilitator's guide* (pp. 37–50). Pfeiffer.

Ferdman, B. M., Prime, J., & Riggio, R. E. (2020). *Inclusive leadership: Transforming diverse lives, workplaces, and societies.* Routledge.

Ferrara, M., Romano, V., Steel, D. H., Gupta, R., Iovino, C., van Dijk, E. H., & Romano, M. R. (2020). Reshaping ophthalmology training after COVID-19 pandemic. *Eye, 34*(11), 2089–2097.

Ferreira, R. R., da Silva Abbad, G., & Mourao, L. (2015). Training needs analysis at work. In K. Kraiger, J. Passmore, N. R. dos Santos, & S. Malvezzi (Eds.), *The Wiley Blackwell handbook of the psychology of training, development, and performance improvement* (pp. 32–49). Chichester, UK: Wiley-Blackwell.

Ferris, G. R., Frink, D. D., Galang, M. C., Zhou, J., Kacmar, K. M., & Howard, J. L. (1996). Perceptions of organizational politics: Prediction, stress-related implications, and outcomes. *Human Relations, 49*(2), 233–266.

Ferris, G. R., Frink, D. D., Gilmore, D. C., & Kacmar, K. M. (1994). Understanding as an antidote for the dysfunctional consequences of organizational politics as a stressor. *Journal of Applied Social Psychology, 24*(13), 1204–1220.

Ferris, G. R., & Hochwater, W. A. (2011). Organizational politics. In S. Zedeck (Ed.), *APA handbook of industrial and organizational psychology* (Vol. 3, pp. 435–459). Washington, DC: American Psychological Association.

Ferris, G. R., Perrewé, P. L., Anthony, W. P., & Gilmore, D. C. (2000). Political skill at work. *Organizational Dynamics, 28*, 25–37.

Ferris, G. R., & Treadway, D. C. (Eds.). (2012). *Politics in organizations: Theory and research considerations*. New York: Routledge/ Taylor & Francis.

Festinger, L. (1957). *A theory of cognitive dissonance*. Evanston, IL: Row, Peterson.

Fiedler, F. E. (1967). *A theory of leadership effectiveness*. New York: McGraw-Hill.

Fine, S. A., & Cronshaw, S. F. (1999). *Functional job analysis: A foundation for human resources management*. Mahwah, NJ: Erlbaum.

Finegan, J. E. (2000). The impact of person and organizational values on organizational commitment. *Journal of Occupational and Organizational Psychology, 73*(2), 149–169.

Fisher, C. B. (2016). *Decoding the ethics code: A practical guide for psychologists* (2nd ed.). Thousand Oaks, CA: Sage.

Fisher, C. D. (2000). Mood and emotions while working: missing pieces of job satisfaction? *Journal of Organizational Behavior, 21*(2), 185–202.

Fisher, G. G., Truxillo, D. M., Finkelstein, L. M., & Wallace, L. E. (2017). Age discrimination: Potential for adverse impact and differential prediction related to age. *Human Resource Management Review, 27*(2), 316–327.

Flanagan, J. C. (1954). The critical incidents technique. *Psychological Bulletin, 51*, 327–358.

Fletcher, C. (2015). 360-degree feedback as a developmental tool. In K. Kraiger, J. Passmore, N. R. dos Santos, & S. Malvezzi (Eds.). *The Wiley handbook of the psychology of training, development and performance improvement* (pp. 486–502). Chichester, UK: John Wiley.

Fletcher, C., & Perry, E. L. (2001). Performance appraisal and feedback: A consideration of national culture and a review of contemporary research and future trends. In N. Anderson, D. S. Ones, H. K. Sinangil, & C. Viswesvaran (Eds.), *Personnel Psychology* (Vol. 1, pp. 127–144). Sage.

Fodor, E. M. (1976). Group stress, authoritarian style of control, and use of power. *Journal of Applied Psychology, 61*(3), 313–318.

Follmer, K. B., & Jones, K. S. (2018). Mental illness in the workplace: An interdisciplinary review and organizational research agenda. *Journal of Management, 44*(1), 325–351.

Fonner, K. L., & Roloff, M. E. (2010). Why teleworkers are more satisfied with their jobs than are office-based workers: When less contact is beneficial. *Journal of Applied Communication Research, 38*(4), 336–361.

Ford, J. K., Baldwin, T. T., & Prasad, J. (2018). Transfer of training: The known and the unknown. *Annual Review of Organizational Psychology and Organizational Behavior, 5*, 201–225.

Ford, J. K., & Noe, R. A. (1987). Self-assessed training needs: The effects of attitudes toward training, managerial level, and function. *Personnel Psychology, 40*(1), 39–53.

Ford, R. C., & Randolph, W. A. (1992). Cross-functional structures: A review and integration of matrix organizations and project management. *Journal of Management, 18*(2), 267–294.

Forsyth, D. R. (2006). *Group dynamics* (4th ed.). Pacific Grove, CA: Brooks/Cole.

Fox, S., & Spector, P. E. (Eds.). (2005). *Counterproductive work behavior: Investigations of actors and targets*. Washington, DC: American Psychological Association.

Franke, R. H., & Kaul, J. D. (1978). The Hawthorne experiments: First statistical interpretation. *American Sociological Review, 43*, 623–643.

Frederiksen, N. (1962). Factors in in-basket performance. *Psychological Monographs, 76* (Entire issue no. 541).

French, J. L., & Rosenstein, J. (1984). Employee ownership, work attitudes, and power relationships. *Academy of Management Journal, 27*(4), 861–869.

French, J. R. P., & Caplan, R. D. (1972). Organizational stress and individual strain. In A. J. Marrow (Ed.), *The failure of success* (pp. 30–66). New York: AMACOM.

French, J. R. P., Caplan, R. D., & Harrison, R. V. (1982). *The mechanisms of job stress and strain*. Chichester, UK: Wiley.

French, J. R. P., & Raven, B. H. (1959). The bases of social power. In D. Cartwright (Ed.), *Studies in social power* (pp. 150–167). Ann Arbor, MI: University of Michigan Press.

Frese, M., & Zapf, D. (1988). Methodological issues in the study of work stress: Objective vs. subjective measurement of work stress and the question of longitudinal studies. In C. L. Cooper & R. Payne (Eds.), *Courses, coping and consequences of stress at work* (pp. 375–411). New York: Wiley.

Frieder, R. E., Van Iddekinge, C. H., & Raymark, P. H. (2016). How quickly do interviewers reach decisions: An examination of interviewers' decision-making time across applicants. *Journal of Occupational and Organizational Psychology, 89*(2), 223–248.

Friedman, H. S., Hall, J. A., & Harris, M. J. (1985). Type A behavior, nonverbal expressive style, and health. *Journal of Personality and Social Psychology, 48*(5), 1299–1315.

Fritz, C., Ellis, A. M., Demsky, C. A., Lin, B. C., & Guros, F. (2013). Embracing work breaks: Recovering from work stress. *Organizational Dynamics*, *42*(4), 274–280.

Frone, M. R. (2008). Are work stressors related to employee substance use? The importance of temporal context assessments of alcohol and illicit drug use. *Journal of Applied Psychology*, *93*(1), 199–206.

Frone, M. R. (2011). Alcohol and illicit drug use in the workforce and workplace. In J. C. Quick & L. E. Tetrick (Eds.), *Handbook of occupational health psychology* (2nd ed., pp. 277–296). Washington, DC: American Psychological Association.

Fry, W., & Slocum, J. W. (1984). Technology, structure, and work-group effectiveness: A test of a contingency model. *Academy of Management Journal*, *27*, 221–246.

Fu, P. P., & Yukl, G. (2000). Perceived effectiveness of influence tactics in the United States and China. *Leadership Quarterly*, *11*(2), 251–266.

Fuller, J. A., Stanton, J. M., Fisher, G. G., Spitzmüller, C., Russell, S. S., & Smith, P. C. (2003). A lengthy look at the daily grind: Time series analysis of events, mood, stress, and satisfaction. *Journal of Applied Psychology*, *88*(6), 1019–1033.

Gaffney, S. (2005). Career development as a retention and succession planning tool. *Journal for Quality and Participation*, *28*(3), 7–10.

Gagné, M., & Deci, E. L. (2005). Self-determination theory and work motivation. *Journal of Organizational Behavior*, *26*(4), 331–362.

Gagné, M., & Deci, E. L. (2014). *The history of self-determination theory in psychology and management*. Oxford University Press.

Gaines, J. H. (1980). Upward communication in industry: An experiment. *Human Relations*, *33*(12), 929–942.

Gaither, S. E., Apfelbaum, E. P., Birnbaum, H. J., Babbitt, L. G., & Sommers, S. R. (2018). Mere membership in racially diverse groups reduces conformity. *Social Psychological and Personality Science*, *9*(4), 402–410. https://doi.org/10.1177/1948550617708013

Galaif, E. R., Newcomb, M. D., & Carmona, J. V. (2001). Prospective relationships between drug problems and work adjustment in a community sample of adults. *Journal of Applied Psychology*, *86*(2), 337–350.

Galbraith, J. R. (2008). Organization design. In T. G. Cummings (Ed.), *Handbook of organization development* (pp. 325–352). Sage.

Gallos, J. V. (Ed.). (2006). *Organization development*. San Francisco, CA: Jossey-Bass.

Ganster, D. C., Fusilier, M. R., & Mayes, B. T. (1986). Role of social support in the experience of stress at work. *Journal of Applied Psychology*, *71*(1), 102–110.

Ganster, D. C., & Rosen, C. C. (2013). Work stress and employee health: A multidisciplinary review. *Journal of Management*, *39*(5), 1085–1122.

Garavan, T., McCarthy, A., Sheehan, M., Lai, Y., Saunders, M. N., Clarke, N., Carbery, R., & Shanahan, V. (2019). Measuring the organizational impact of training: The need for greater methodological rigor. *Human Resource Development Quarterly*, *30*(3), 291–309.

Garbers, Y., & Konradt, U. (2014). The effect of financial incentives on performance: A quantitative review of individual and team-based financial incentives. *Journal of Occupational and Organizational Psychology*, *87*(1), 102–137.

García-Morales, V. J., Matias-Reche, F., & Verdú-Jover, A. J. (2011). Influence of internal communication on technological proactivity, organizational learning, and organizational innovation in the pharmaceutical sector. *Journal of Communication*, *61*(1), 150–177.

Gardner, B., Rose, J., Mason, O., Tyler, P., & Cushway, D. (2005). Cognitive therapy and behavioural coping in the management of work-related stress: An intervention study. *Work & Stress*, *19*(2), 137–152.

Gardner, D. M., & Alanis, J. M. (2020). Together we stand: Ally training for discrimination and harassment reduction. *Industrial and Organizational Psychology*, *13*(2), 196–199.

Gavin, D. (2013). Starbucks exceptionalism: An institutional ethnographic exploration of coffee culture in America. *Journal of Psychological Issues in Organizational Culture*, *4*(3), 44–58.

Gavin, J. F. (1984). Survey feedback: The perspectives of science and practice. *Group and Organization Studies*, *9*(1), 29–70.

Gegenfurtner, A., Zitt, A., & Ebner, C. (2020). Evaluating webinar-based training: A mixed methods study of trainee reactions toward digital web conferencing. *International Journal of Training and Development*, *24*(1), 5–21.

Geiger, M., Olderbak, S., Sauter, R., & Wilhelm, O. (2018). The "g" in faking: Doublethink the validity of personality self-report measures for applicant selection. *Frontiers in Psychology*, *9*, 2153–2161.

Gelfand, M. J., Aycan, Z., Erez, M., & Leung, K. (2017). Cross-cultural industrial organizational psychology and organizational behavior: A hundred-year journey. *Journal of Applied Psychology*, *102*(3), 514–529.

George, J. M. (1989). Mood and absence. *Journal of Applied Psychology*, *74*(2), 317–324.

George, J. M. (1991). State or trait: Effects of positive mood on prosocial behaviors at work. *Journal of Applied Psychology*, *76*(2), 299–307.

George, J. M., & Jones, G. R. (1996). The experience of work and turnover intentions: Interactive effects of value attainment, job satisfaction, and positive mood. *Journal of Applied Psychology*, *81*(3), 318–325.

Georgesen, J. C., & Harris, M. J. (1998). Why's my boss always holding me down? A meta-analysis of power effects on performance evaluations. *Personality and Social Psychology Review*, *2*(3), 183–195.

Georgiou, K., Gouras, A., & Nikolaou, I. (2019). Gamification in employee selection: The development of a gamified assessment. *International Journal of Selection and Assessment*, *27*(2), 91–103.

Ghielen, S. T. S., De Cooman, R., & Sels, L. (2021). The interacting content and process of the employer brand: Person–organization fit and employer brand clarity. *European Journal of Work and Organizational Psychology*, *30*(2), 292–304.

Ghislieri, C., Molino, M., & Cortese, C. G. (2018). Work and organizational psychology looks at the fourth industrial revolution: How to support workers and organizations? *Frontiers in Psychology*, *9*, 2365.

Ghodse, H. (Ed.). (2005). *Tackling drug use and misuse in the workplace*. Aldershot, UK: Gower.

Ghorpade, J. V. (1988). *Job analysis: A handbook for the human resource director*. Englewood Cliffs, NJ: Prentice Hall.

Gibb, J. R. (1961). Defensive communication. *Journal of Communication*, *11*(3), 81–84.

Gibson, J. L., Payne, S. C., Morgan, W. B., & Allen, J. A. (2018). The Society for Industrial and Organizational Psychology's guidelines for education and training: An executive summary of the 2016/2017 revision. *American Psychologist*, *73*(5), 678–682. https://doi.org/10.1037/amp0000266

Gibson, L. K., Finnie, B., & Stuart, J. L. (2015). A mathematical model for exploring the evolution of organizational structure. *International Journal of Organizational Analysis*, *23*, 21–40.

Gilbert, J. A., & Ivancevich, J. M. (2000). A re-examination of organizational commitment. *Journal of Social Behavior and Personality*, *14*, 385–396.

Gilbreth, F. B. (1916). Motion study in surgery. *Canadian Journal of Medicine and Surgery*, *1*, 1–10.

Gilin Oore, D., Leiter, M. P., & LeBlanc, D. E. (2015). Individual and organizational factors promoting successful responses to workplace conflict. *Canadian Psychology*, *56*(3), 301–310.

Gioaba, I., & Krings, F. (2017). Impression management in the job interview: An effective way of mitigating discrimination against older applicants? *Frontiers in Psychology*, *8*, 770–779.

Gist, M. E. (1987). Self-efficacy: Implications for organizational behavior and human resource management. *Academy of Management Review*, *12*(3), 472–485.

Gist, M. E., Schwoerer, C., & Rosen, B. (1989). Effects of alternative training methods on self-efficacy and performance in computer software training. *Journal of Applied Psychology*, *74*(6), 884–891.

Giumetti, G. W., Schroeder, A. N., & Switzer, F. S. (2015). Forced distribution rating systems: When does "rank and yank" lead to adverse impact? *Journal of Applied Psychology*, *100*(1), 180–193.

Goffin, R. D., & Gellatly, I. R. (2001). A multi-rater assessment of organizational commitment: Are self-report measures biased? *Journal of Organizational Behavior*, *22*(4), 437–451.

Goldberg, C. B., & Waldman, D. A. (2000). Modeling employee absenteeism: Testing alternative measures and mediated effects based on job satisfaction. *Journal of Organizational Behavior*, *21*(6), 665–676.

Goldman, R. B. (1976). *A work experiment: Six Americans in a Swedish plant*. New York: Ford Foundation.

Goldstein, I. L., & Ford, J. K. (2002). Training in organisations: Needs assessment, development, and evaluation. In S. Wheelan (Ed.), *The Handbook of group research and practice* (4 ed., pp. 539–546). Wadsworth/Thomson Learning.

Gonzalez, M. F., Capman, J. F., Martin, N. R., Johnson, T. M., Theys, E. R., & Boyce, A. S. (2019). Personality and the ADA: Ameliorating fairness concerns and maintaining utility. *Industrial and Organizational Psychology*, *12*(2), 151–156.

Gonzalez-Mulé, E., DeGeest, D. S., McCormick, B. W., Seong, J. Y., & Brown, K. G. (2014). Can we get some cooperation around here? The mediating role of group norms on the relationship between team personality and individual helping behaviors. *Journal of Applied Psychology*, *99*(5), 988–999.

Goodwin, V. L., Bowler, W. M., & Whittington, J. L. (2009). A social network perspective on LMX relationships: Accounting for the instrumental value of leader and follower networks. *Journal of Management*, *35*(4), 954–980.

Gorman, J. C., Grimm, D. A., Stevens, R. H., Galloway, T., Willemsen-Dunlap, A. M., & Halpin, D. J. (2020). Measuring real-time team cognition during team training. *Human Factors*, *62*(5), 825–860.

Gottsacker, J. (2020). Waging war against prior pay: The pay structure that reenforces the systemic gender discrimination in the workplace. *Saint Louis University Law Journal*, *64*, 113–146.

Gough, H. G. (1984). A managerial potential scale for the California Psychological Inventory. *Journal of Applied Psychology*, *69*, 233–240.

Gough, H. G. (1987). California psychological inventory: Administrator's guide. Consulting Psychologists Press.

Gouldner, A. W. (1960). The norm of reciprocity: A preliminary statement. *American Sociological Review*, *25*, 161–178.

Grady, C. (2020, Feb 24). Some say the Me Too movement has gone too far. The Harvey Weinstein verdict proves that's false. *Vox*. Retrieved from www.vox.com/culture/2020/2/24/21150966/harvey-weinstein-rape-conviction-sexual-predatory-assault-me-too-too-far

Grandey, A. A. (2001). Family friendly policies: Organizational justice perceptions of need-based allocations. In R. Cropanzano (Ed.), *Justice in the workplace: From theory to practice* (pp. 145–173). Mahwah, NJ: Erlbaum.

Grandey, A. A., Houston III, L., & Avery, D. R. (2019). Fake it to make it? Emotional labor reduces the racial disparity in service performance judgments. *Journal of Management*, *45*(5), 2163–2192.

Granrose, C. S. (1997). Cross-cultural socialization of Asian employees in U.S. organizations. In C. S. Granrose & S. Oskamp (Eds.), *Cross-cultural work groups* (pp. 186–211). Thousand Oaks, CA: Sage.

Graves, L. M., & Karren, R. J. (1996). The employee selection interview: A fresh look at an old problem. *Human Resource Management*, *35*(2), 163–180.

Gray, B., & Ariss, S. S. (1985). Politics and strategic change across organizational life cycles. *Academy of Management Review*, *10*(4), 707–723.

Greenberg, J., & Baron, R. A. (1997). *Behavior in organizations* (6th ed.). Upper Saddle River, NJ: Prentice Hall.

Greenberg, J., & Ornstein, S. (1983). High status job title as compensation for underpayment: A test of equity theory. *Journal of Applied Psychology*, *68*(2), 285–297.

Greenberger, D. B., & Strasser, S. (1986). Development and application of a model of personal control in organizations. *Academy of Management Review*, *11*(1), 164–177.

Greer, L. L., Caruso, H. M., & Jehn, K. A. (2011). The bigger they are, the harder they fall: Linking team power, team conflict, and performance. *Organizational Behavior and Human Decision Processes*, *116*(1), 116–128.

Greer, L. L., & Dannals, J. E. (2017). Conflict in teams. In E. Salas, R. P. Rico, & J. Passmore (Eds.), *The Wiley Blackwell handbook of team dynamics, teamwork, and collaborative working* (pp. 317–344). John Wiley.

Greer, L. L., de Jong, B. A., Schouten, M. E., & Dannals, J. E. (2018). Why and when hierarchy impacts team effectiveness: A meta-analytic integration. *Journal of Applied Psychology*, *103*(6), 591–613.

Greer, L. L., Van Bunderen, L., & Yu, S. (2017). The dysfunctions of power in teams: A review and emergent conflict perspective. *Research in Organizational Behavior*, *37*, 103–124.

Greer, L. L., & van Kleef, G. A. (2010). Equality versus differentiation: The effects of power dispersion on group interaction. *Journal of Applied Psychology*, *95*(6), 1032–1044.

Griffeth, R. W., Hom, P. W., & Gaertner, S. (2000). A meta-analysis of antecedents and correlates of employee turnover: Update, moderator tests, and research implications for the new millennium. *Journal of Management*, *26*(3), 463–488.

Griffin, B. (2015). Collective norms of engagement link to individual engagement. *Journal of Managerial Psychology*, *30*(7), 847–860.

Griggs v. Duke Power Co. (1971). 401 U.S. 424, 3EPD p8137, 3 FEP Cases 175.

Grossman, R., & Burke-Smalley, L. A. (2018). Context-dependent accountability strategies to improve the transfer of training: A proposed theoretical model and research propositions. *Human Resource Management Review*, *28*(2), 234–247.

Grossman, R., Heyne, K., & Salas, E. (2015). Game- and simulation-based approaches to training. In K. Kraiger, J. Passmore, N. R. dos Santos, & S. Malvezzi (Eds.), *The Wiley Blackwell handbook of the psychology of training, development, and performance improvement* (pp. 205–223). Chichester, UK: Wiley-Blackwell.

Grossman, R., & Salas, E. (2011). The transfer of training: what really matters. *International Journal of Training and Development*, *15*(2), 103–120.

Gubler, T., & Pierce, L. (2014). Healthy, wealthy, and wise: Retirement planning predicts employee health improvements. *Psychological Science*, *25*(9), 1822–1830.

Guion, R. M. (1965). *Personnel testing*. New York: McGraw-Hill.

Gully, S. M., Devine, D. J., & Whitney, D. J. (1995). A meta-analysis of cohesion and performance: Effects of level of analysis and task interdependence. *Small Group Research*, *26*(4), 497–520.

Gupta, N., & Beehr, T. A. (1979). Job stress and employee behaviors. *Organizational Behavior and Human Performance*, *23*, 373–387.

Gurtner, J. (2015). Effective virtual learning environments. In K. Kraiger, J. Passmore, N. R. dos Santos, & S. Malvezzi (Eds.), *The Wiley Blackwell handbook of the psychology of training, development, and performance improvement* (pp. 188–204). Chichester, UK: Wiley-Blackwell.

Guzzo, R. A., Jette, R. D., & Katzell, R. A. (1985). The effects of psychologically based intervention programs on worker productivity: A meta-analysis. *Personnel Psychology*, *38*(2), 275–292.

Gyllenhammer, P. (1977). *People at work*. Reading, MA: Addison-Wesley.

Hack-Polay, D. (2018). Putting across tangibility: Effectiveness of case-study-based teaching of organisational behaviour. In D. Hack-Polay (Ed.), *Teaching human resources and organizational behavior at the college level* (pp. 211–225). IGI.

Hackett, R. D., & Bycio, P. (1996). An evaluation of employee absenteeism as a coping mechanism among hospital nurses. *Journal of Occupational and Organizational Psychology, 69*(4), 327–328.

Hackman, J. R. (1990). *Groups that work (and those that don't)*. San Francisco, CA: Jossey-Bass.

Hackman, J. R. (1998). Why teams don't work. In R. S. Tindale (Ed.), *Theory and research on small groups* (pp. 245–267). New York: Plenum Press.

Hackman, J. R., Hackman, R. J., & Oldham, G. R. (1980). *Work redesign*. Addison-Wesley.

Hackman, J. R., & Oldham, G. R. (1975). Development of the job diagnostic survey. *Journal of Applied Psychology, 60*(2), 159–170.

Hackman, J. R., & Oldham, G. R. (1976). Motivation through the design of work: Test of a theory. *Organizational Behavior and Human Performance, 16*(2), 250–279.

Hackney, K. J., & Perrewé, P. L. (2018). A review of abusive behaviors at work: The development of a process model for studying abuse. *Organizational Psychology Review, 8*(1), 70–92.

Hakstian, R. A., & Cattell, R. B. (1975–1982). *Manual for the Comprehensive Ability Battery (CAB)*. Institute for Personality and Ability Testing.

Hall, R. J., Workman, J. W., & Marchioro, C. A. (1998). Sex, task, and behavioral flexibility effects on leadership perceptions. *Organizational Behavior and Human Decision Processes, 74*(1), 1–32.

Halpern, D. F., & Murphy, S. E. (Eds.). (2005). *From work–family balance to work–family interaction: Changing the metaphor*. Mahwah, NJ: Lawrence Erlbaum.

Halpin, A. W., & Winer, B. J. (1957). A factorial study of the leader behavior descriptions. In R. M. Stogdill & A. E. Coons (Eds.), *Leader behavior: Its description and measurement*. Columbus, OH: Ohio State University Bureau of Business Research.

Hamdani, M. R., Valcea, S., & Buckley, M. R. (2014). The relentless pursuit of construct validity in the design of employment interviews. *Human Resource Management Review, 24*(2), 160–176.

Hamilton, K., Shih, S., Tesler, R., & Mohammed, S. (2014). Team mental models and intragroup conflict. In O. B. Ayokko, N. M. Ashkanasy, & K. A. Jehn (Eds.), *Handbook of conflict management research* (pp. 239–253). Northampton, MA: Edward Elgar.

Hammer, T. H., & Landau, J. C. (1981). Methodological issues in the use of absence data. *Journal of Applied Psychology, 66*(5), 574–581.

Han, J. H., Bartol, K. M., & Kim, S. (2015). Tightening up the performance–pay linkage: Roles of contingent reward leadership and profit-sharing in the cross-level influence of individual pay-for-performance. *Journal of Applied Psychology, 100*(2), 417–430.

Hanlon, S. C., Meyer, D. G., & Taylor, R. R. (1994). Consequences of gainsharing: A field experiment revisited. *Group & Organization Management, 19*(1), 87–111.

Hannum, K. M., Martineau, J. W., & Reinelt, C. (Eds.). (2007). *The handbook of leadership development evaluation*. Hoboken, NJ: John Wiley.

Hansen, B., & McNichols, D. (2020). Information and the persistence of the gender wage gap: Early evidence from California's salary history ban (0898–2937). National Bureau of Economic Research.

Harman, R. P., Ellington, J. K., Surface, E. A., & Thompson, L. F. (2015). Exploring qualitative training reactions: Individual and contextual influences on trainee commenting. *Journal of Applied Psychology, 100*(3), 894–893.

Harris, L., Cooper-Thomas, H., Smith, P., & Smollan, R. (2020). Reclaiming the social in socialization: A practice-based understanding of newcomer adjustment. *Human Resource Development Quarterly, 31*(2), 193–211.

Harris, R., Simons, M., Willis, P., & Carden, P. (2003). Exploring complementarity in on- and off-job training for apprenticeships. *International Journal of Training and Development, 7*(2), 82–92.

Harris, T. E. (1993). *Applied organizational communication: Perspectives, principles, and pragmatics*. Hillsdale, NJ: Erlbaum.

Harrison, J. K. (1992). Individual and combined effects of behavior modeling and the cultural assimilator in crosscultural management training. *Journal of Applied Psychology, 77*(6), 952–962.

Harrison, M. S., & Thomas, K. M. (2009). The hidden prejudice in selection: A research investigation on skin color bias. *Journal of Applied Social Psychology, 39*(1), 134–168.

Harrison, T. M. (1985). Communication and participative decision making: An exploratory study. *Personnel Psychology, 38*(1), 93–116.

Hart, R. K. (2001). Constituting relationships in communication: An interdisciplinary approach to understanding peer relationships in geographically dispersed teams. In M. M. Beyerlein, D. A. Johnson, & S. T. Beyerlein (Eds.), *Virtual teams* (pp. 85–106). New York: Elsevier/JAI Press.

Härtel, C. E. J. (1998). Recent advances in diversity research: When diversity has positive outcomes for organizations and when it does not. *The Industrial-Organizational Psychologist*, *36*, 57–60.

Harvey, S., Blouin, C., & Stout, D. (2006). Proactive personality as a moderator of outcomes for young workers experiencing conflict at work. *Personality and Individual Differences*, *40*(5), 1063–1074.

Hathaway, S. R. & McKinley, J. C. (1970). *Minnesota Multiphasic Personality Inventory*. Psychological Corp.

Hatmaker, D. M., & Park, H. H. (2014). Who are all these people? Longitudinal changes in new employee social networks within a state agency. *The American Review of Public Administration*, *44*(6), 718–739.

Hauenstein, N. M. A. (1998). Training raters to increase the accuracy of appraisals and the usefulness of feedback. In J. W. Smither (Ed.), *Performance appraisal: State of the art in practice* (pp. 404–442). San Francisco, CA: Jossey-Bass.

Haug, C. (2015). What is consensus and how is it achieved in meetings? Four types of consensus decision making. In J. A. Allen, N. Lehman-Willenbrock, & S. G. Rogelberg (Eds.), *The Cambridge handbook of meeting science* (pp. 556–584). New York: Cambridge University Press.

Hayes, T. L., Kaylor, L. E., & Oltman, K. A. (2020). Coffee and controversy: How applied psychology can revitalize sexual harassment and racial discrimination training. *Industrial and Organizational Psychology*, *13*(2), 117–136.

Haynes, S. G., Feinleib, M., Levine, S., Scotch, N. A., & Kannel, W. B. (1978). The relationship of psychosocial factors to coronary heart disease in the Framingham study: II. Prevalence of coronary heart disease. *American Journal of Epidemiology*, *107*, 384–402.

Hazle, M. C., Hill, K. P., & Westreich, L. M. (2020). Workplace cannabis policies: A moving target. *Cannabis and Cannabinoid Research* (in press).

He, H., Baruch, Y., & Lin, C.-P. (2014). Modeling team knowledge sharing and team flexibility: The role of within-team competition. *Human Relations*, *67*(8), 947–978.

He, Y., Donnellan, M. B., & Mendoza, A. M. (2019). Five-factor personality domains and job performance: A second order meta-analysis. *Journal of Research in Personality*, *82*, 103848.

He, Y., Wang, Y., & Payne, S. C. (2019). How is safety climate formed? A meta-analysis of the antecedents of safety climate. *Organizational Psychology Review*, *9*(2–3), 124–156.

Heaney, C. A., Price, R. H., & Rafferty, J. (1995). Increasing coping resources at work: A field experiment to increase social support, improve work team functioning, and enhance employee mental health. *Journal of Organizational Behavior*, *16*(4), 335–353.

Heavey, A. L., Holwerda, J. A., & Hausknecht, J. P. (2013). Causes and consequences of collective turnover: A meta-analytic review. *Journal of Applied Psychology*, *98*(3), 412–453.

Hekman, D. R., Johnson, S. K., Foo, M.-D., & Yang, W. (2017). Does diversity-valuing behavior result in diminished performance ratings for non-white and female leaders? *Academy of Management Journal*, *60*(2), 771–797.

Hemingway, M. A., & Smith, C. S. (1999). Organizational climate and occupational stressors as predictors of withdrawal behaviours and injuries in nurses. *Journal of Occupational and Organizational Psychology*, *72*(3), 285–299.

Hempel, J. (2005). Why the boss really had to say goodbye. *Business Week*, July 4, 10.

Herd, A. M., Cumberland, D. M., Lovely, W. A., & Bird, A. (2018). The use of assessment center methodology to develop students' global leadership competencies: A conceptual framework and applied example. In *Advances in global leadership* (Vol. 11, pp. 175–196). Emerald.

Herd, J. A. (1988). Physiological indices of job stress. In J. J. Hurrell, L. R. Murphy, S. L., Sauter, & C. L. Cooper (Eds.), *Occupational stress issues and developments in research* (pp. 124–154). Philadelphia, PA: Taylor & Francis.

Hernandez, M., Avery, D. R., Volpone, S. D., & Kaiser, C. R. (2019). Bargaining while Black: The role of race in salary negotiations. *Journal of Applied Psychology*, *104*(4), 581–592.

Hernandez, T. R., Bergman, M. E., & Liu, S.-N. C. (2020). Why is training the only answer? *Industrial and Organizational Psychology*, *13*(2), 147–153.

Herpertz, S., Nizielski, S., Hock, M., & Schütz, A. (2016). The relevance of emotional intelligence in personnel selection for high emotional labor jobs. *PLoS One*, *11*(4), e0154432.

Hershcovis, M. S., & Bhatnagar, N. (2017). When fellow customers behave badly: Witness reactions to employee mistreatment by customers. *Journal of Applied Psychology*, *102*(11), 1528.

Hertel, G., Konradt, U., & Orlikowski, B. (2004). Managing distance by interdependence: Goal setting, task interdependence, and team-based rewards in virtual teams. *European Journal of Work and Organizational Psychology*, *13*(1), 1–28.

Herzberg, F. (1966). *Work and the nature of man*. Cleveland, OH: World.

Hickman, L., Bosch, N., Ng, V., Saef, R., Tay, L., & Woo, S. E. (2021). Automated video interview personality assessments: Reliability, validity, and generalizability investigations. *Journal of Applied Psychology* (in press).

Hideg, I., & Krstic, A. (2020). The quest for workplace gender equality in the 21st century: Where do we stand and how can we continue to make strides? *Canadian Journal of Behavioural Science*, *53*(2), 106–113.

Hill, G. W. (1982). Group versus individual performance: Are N+1 heads better than one? *Psychological Bulletin, 91*(3), 517–539.

Hillebrandt, A., & Barclay, L. J. (2017). Comparing integral and incidental emotions: Testing insights from emotions as social information theory and attribution theory. *Journal of Applied Psychology, 102*(5), 732.

Hinds, P. J., Patterson, M., & Pfeffer, J. (2001). Bothered by abstraction: The effect of expertise on knowledge transfer and subsequent novice performance. *Journal of Applied Psychology, 86*(6), 1232–1243.

Hinkin, T. R., & Schriesheim, C. A. (1989). Development and application of new scales to measure French and Raven (1959) bases of social power. *Journal of Applied Psychology, 74*, 561–567.

Hinkin, T. R., & Schriesheim, C. A. (1994). An examination of subordinate-perceived relationships between leader reward and punishment behavior and leader bases of power. *Human Relations, 47*(7), 779–800.

Ho, M. (2016). Investment in learning increases for fourth straight year. *Talent and Development.* Retrieved from www.td.org/magazines/td-magazine/investment-in-learning-increases-for-fourth-straight-year

Hobson, C. J., & Delunas, L. (2001). National norms and life-event frequencies for the revised social readjustment rating scale. *International Journal of Stress Management, 8*, 299–314.

Hochschild, A. R. (1983). *The managed heart: Commercialization of human feeling.* Berkeley, CA: University of California Press.

Hocker, J. L., & Wilmot, W. W. (1985). *Interpersonal conflict* (2nd ed.). Dubuque, IA: Brown.

Hoffman, B. J., & Woehr, D. J. (2009). Disentangling the meaning of multisource performance rating source and dimension factors. *Personnel Psychology, 62*(4), 735–765.

Hoffman, C. C., Nathan, B. R., & Holden, L. M. (1991). A comparison of validation criteria: Objective versus subjective performance measures and self- versus supervisor ratings. *Personnel Psychology, 44*, 601–619.

Hofstede, G. (1980). *Culture's consequences: International differences in work-related values.* Beverly Hills, CA: Sage.

Hofstede, G. (1997). *Cultures and organizations: Software of the mind.* New York: McGraw-Hill.

Hofstede, G., Neuijen, B., Ohayv, D., & Sanders, G. (1990). Measuring organizational cultures: A qualitative and quantitative study across twenty cases. *Administrative Science Quarterly, 35*, 286–316.

Hogan, R. (1985). Hogan personnel selection series. Minneapolis, MN: National Computer Systems.

Hogh, A., Mikkelsen, E. G., & Hansen, A. M. (2012). Impact of bullying on workers. In N. Tehrani (Ed.), *Workplace bullying: Symptoms and solutions* (pp. 21–34). New York: Routledge/Taylor & Francis.

Hollander, E. P. (1978). *Leadership dynamics: A practical guide to effective relationships.* New York: Free Press.

Hollander, E. P. (1985). Leadership and power. In G. Lindzey & E. Aronson (Eds.), *The handbook of social psychology* (3rd ed., pp. 485–538). New York: Random House.

Holmes IV, O., Jiang, K., Avery, D. R., McKay, P. F., Oh, I.-S., & Tillman, C. J. (2021). A meta-analysis integrating 25 years of diversity climate research. *Journal of Management, 47*(6), 1357–1382.

Holmes IV, O., Whitman, M. V., Campbell, K. S., & Johnson, D. E. (2016). Exploring the social identity threat response framework. *Equality, Diversity and Inclusion: An International Journal, 35*(3), 205–220.

Holmes, T. H., & Rahe, R. H. (1967). The social readjustment rating scale. *Journal of Psychosomatic Research, 11*, 213–218.

Holten, A.-L., Hancock, G. R., & Bøllingtoft, A. (2019). Studying the importance of change leadership and change management in layoffs, mergers, and closures. *Management Decision, 58*(3), 393–409.

Honeywell-Johnson, J. A., & Dickinson, A. M. (1999). Small group incentives: A review of the literature. *Journal of Organizational Behavior Management, 19*(2), 89–120.

Hong, L., & Page, S. E. (2004). Groups of diverse problem solvers can outperform groups of high-ability problem solvers. *Proceedings of the National Academy of Sciences of the United States of America, 101*(46), 16385–16389. https://doi.org/10.1073/pnas.0403723101

Hoon, H., & Tan, T. M. L. (2008). Organizational citizenship behavior and social loafing: The role of personality, motives, and contextual factors. *The Journal of Psychology, 142*(1), 89–108.

Hosking, D. M. (2007). Not leaders, not followers: A post-modern discourse of leadership processes. In B. Shamir, R. Pillai, M. Bligh, & M. Uhl-Bien (Eds.), *Follower-centred perspectives on leadership: A tribute to the memory of James R. Meindl, Information Age, Charlotte, NC* (pp. 243–263). Information Age.

Hough, L. M., & Connelly, B. S. (2013). Personality measurement and use in industrial and organizational psychology. In K. F. Geisinger (Ed.), *APA handbook of testing and assessment in psychology, Vol. 1: Test theory and testing and assessment in industrial and organizational psychology* (pp. 501–531). Washington, DC: American Psychological Association.

Hough, L. M., & Oswald, F. L. (2005). They're right, well . . . mostly right: Research evidence and an agenda to rescue personality testing from 1960s insights. *Human Performance, 18*(4), 373–387.

House, R. J. (1971). A path–goal theory of leader effectiveness. *Administrative Science Quarterly, 1*, 321–339.

House, R. J. (1977). A 1976 theory of charismatic leadership. In J. G. Hunt & L. L. Larsen (Eds.), *Leadership: The cutting edge* (pp. 189–207). Carbondale, IL: Southern Illinois University Press.

House, R. J., Hanges, P. J., Javidan, M., Dorfman, P. W., & Gupta, V. (Eds.). (2004). *Culture, leadership, and organizations: The GLOBE study of 62 societies*. Thousand Oaks, CA: Sage.

Houston, L., & Grandey, A. A. (2013). What we don't know can hurt us: A call for stereotype-congruent impression management tactics. *Industrial and Organizational Psychology, 6*(4), 433–437.

Howard, G. S., & Dailey, P. R. (1979). Response-shift bias: A source of contamination of self-report measures. *Journal of Applied Psychology, 64*(2), 144–150.

Howell, J. M., & Avolio, B. J. (1993). Transformational leadership, transactional leadership, locus of control, and support for innovation: Key predictors of consolidated business unit performance. *Journal of Applied Psychology, 78*(6), 891–902.

Howell, J. M., & Hall-Merenda, K. E. (1999). The ties that bind: The impact of leader–member exchange, transformational and transactional leadership, and distance on predicting follower performance. *Journal of Applied Psychology, 84*(5), 680–694.

Howell, T. M., Harrison, D. A., Burris, E. R., & Detert, J. R. (2015). Who gets credit for input? Demographic and structural status cues in voice recognition. *Journal of Applied Psychology, 100*(6), 1765.

Hu, X., Kaplan, S., & Dalal, R. S. (2010). An examination of blue- versus white-collar workers' conceptualizations of job satisfaction facets. *Journal of Vocational Behavior, 76*(2), 317–325.

Huffcutt, A. I., Roth, P. L., & McDaniel, M. A. (1996). A meta-analytic investigation of cognitive ability in employment interview evaluations: Moderating characteristics and implications for incremental validity. *Journal of Applied Psychology, 81*(5), 459–473.

Hughes, A. M., Gregory, M. E., Joseph, D. L., Sonesh, S. C., Marlow, S. L., Lacerenza, C. N., Benishek, L. E., King, H. B., & Salas, E. (2016). Saving lives: A meta-analysis of team training in healthcare. *Journal of Applied Psychology, 101*(9), 1266–1304.

Hughes, A. M., Zajac, S., Woods, A. L., & Salas, E. (2020). The role of work environment in training sustainment: A meta-analysis. *Human Factors, 62*(1), 166–183.

Hughes, R. L., Ginnett, R. C., & Curphy, G. J. (1996). *Leadership: Enhancing the lessons of experience* (2nd ed.). Chicago, IL: Irwin.

Hulsheger, U. R., Lang, J. W. B., & Maier, G. W. (2010). Emotional labor, strain, and performance: Testing reciprocal relationships in a longitudinal panel study. *Journal of Occupational Health Psychology, 15*(4), 505–521.

Hunt, G. T. (1980). *Communication skills in the organization*. Englewood Cliffs, NJ: Prentice Hall.

Hunter, E. M., & Wu, C. (2016). Give me a better break: Choosing workday break activities to maximize resource recovery. *Journal of Applied Psychology, 101*(2), 302.

Hunter, J. E., & Schmidt, F. L. (1982). Fitting people to jobs: The impact of personnel selection on national productivity. *Human Performance and Productivity, 1*, 233–284.

Hurrell, J. J., Murphy, L. R., Sauter, S. L., & Cooper, C. L. (Eds.). (1988). *Occupational stress issues and developments in research*. Philadelphia, PA: Taylor & Francis.

Hyland, A. M., & Muchinsky, P. M. (1991). Assessment of the structural validity of Holland's model with job analysis (PAQ) information. *Journal of Applied Psychology, 76*, 75–80.

Ilgen, D. R., & Höllenback, J. H. (1977). The role of job satisfaction in absence behavior. *Organizational Behavior and Human Performance, 19*, 148–161.

Ingold, P. V., Dönni, M., & Lievens, F. (2018). A dual-process theory perspective to better understand judgments in assessment centers: The role of initial impressions for dimension ratings and validity. *Journal of Applied Psychology, 103*(12), 1367–1378.

Ironson, G. H., Smith, P. C., Brannick, M. T., Gibson, W. M., & Paul, K. B. (1989). Construction of a job in general scale: A comparison of global, composite, and specific measures. *Journal of Applied Psychology, 74*(2), 193–200.

Isaac, R. G., Zerbe, W. J., & Pitt, D. C. (2001). Leadership and motivation: The effective application of expectancy theory. *Journal of Managerial Issues, 13*(2), 212–226.

Isenberg, D. J. (1986). Group polarization: A critical review. *Journal of Personality and Social Psychology, 50*(6), 1141–1151.

Islam, S., Lyew, A., & Moran, B. (2021). A 30,000-foot view of human capital consulting firm Twitter use. *Journal of Organizational Psychology, 21*(2), 57–69.

Ivancevich, J. M., & Matteson, M. T. (1980). *A managerial perspective: Stress and work*. Glenview, IL: Scott Foresman.

Jackson, D. J., Michaelides, G., Dewberry, C., & Kim, Y.-J. (2016). Everything that you have ever been told about assessment center ratings is confounded. *Journal of Applied Psychology, 101*(7), 976–994.

Jackson, P. B., & Finney, M. (2002). Negative life events and psychological distress among young adults. *Social Psychology Quarterly, 65*, 186–201.

Jackson, S. E., Brett, J. F., Sessa, V. I., Cooper, D. M., Julin, J. A., & Peyronnin, K. (1991). Some differences make a difference: Individual dissimilarity and group heterogeneity as correlates of recruitment, promotions, and tenure. *Journal of Applied Psychology, 76*(5), 675–689.

Jackson, S. E., & Joshi, A. (2011). Work team diversity. In S. Zedeck (Ed.), *APA handbook of industrial and organizational psychology* (Vol. 1, pp. 651–686). Washington, DC: American Psychological Association.

Jackson, S. E., Schwab, R. L., & Schuler, R. S. (1986). Toward an understanding of the burnout phenomenon. *Journal of Applied Psychology, 71*(4), 630–640.

Jacobs, R. R. (1986). Numerical rating scales. In R. A. Berk (Ed.), *Performance assessment: Methods and applications* (pp. 82–99). Baltimore, MD: Johns Hopkins University Press.

Jamal, M. (1999). Job stress, Type-A behavior, and well-being: A cross-cultural examination. *International Journal of Stress Management, 6*(1), 57–67.

Jamieson, D. W., Barnett, R. C., & Buono, A. F. (Eds.). (2016). *Consultation for organizational change revisited.* Charlotte, NC: Information Age.

Janis, I. L. (1972). *Victims of groupthink: A psychological study of foreign policy decisions and fiascoes.* Boston, MA: Houghton Mifflin.

Javed, B., Naqvi, S. M. M. R., Khan, A. K., Arjoon, S., & Tayyeb, H. H. (2019). Impact of inclusive leadership on innovative work behavior: The role of psychological safety. *Journal of Management & Organization, 25*(1), 117–136.

Jayasingam, S., & Yong, J. R. (2013). Affective commitment among knowledge workers: The role of pay satisfaction and organization career management. *The International Journal of Human Resource Management, 24*(20), 3903–3920.

Jenkins, C. D., Zyzanski, S. J., & Rosenman, R. H. (1979). *Manual for the Jenkins activity survey.* New York: Psychological Corporation.

Jensen, J. M., Opland, R. A., & Ryan, A. M. (2010). Psychological contracts and counterproductive work behaviors: Employee responses to transactional and relational breach. *Journal of Business and Psychology, 25*(4), 555–568.

Jette, M. (1984). Stress coping through physical activity. In A. S. Sethi & R. S. Schuler (Eds.), *Handbook of organizational stress coping strategies* (pp. 215–231). Cambridge, MA: Ballinger.

Jex, S. M., Bliese, P. D., Buzzell, S., & Primeau, J. (2001). The impact of self-efficacy on stressor–strain relations: Coping style as an explanatory mechanism. Journal of applied psychology, 86(3), 401.

Jiang, L., & Lavaysse, L. M. (2018). Cognitive and affective job insecurity: A meta-analysis and a primary study. *Journal of Management, 44*(6), 2307–2342.

Jimmieson, N. L. (2000). Employee reactions to behavioural control under conditions of stress: The moderating role of self-efficacy. *Work & Stress, 14*(3), 262–280.

Jimmieson, N. L., & Terry, D. J. (1993). The effects of prediction, understanding, and control: A test of the stress antidote model. *Anxiety, Stress, and Coping, 6*(3), 179–199.

Jimmieson, N. L., & Terry, D. J. (1999). The moderating role of task characteristics in determining responses to a stressful work simulation. *Journal of Organizational Behavior, 20*(5), 709–736.

Johnson, J. J. (2000). Differences in supervisor and non-supervisor perceptions of quality culture and organizational climate. *Public Personnel Management, 29*(1), 119–128.

Johnson, J. R., Bernhagen, M. J., Miller, V., & Allen, M. (1996). The role of communication in managing reductions in work force. *Journal of Applied Communication Research, 24*, 139–164.

Johnson, R. A. (2003). *Whistleblowing: When it works—and why.* Boulder, CO: Lynne Rienner.

Johnson, S. K. (2008). I second that emotion: Effects of emotional contagion and affect at work on leader and follower outcomes. *The Leadership Quarterly, 19*(1), 1–19.

Johnson, S. K. (2009). Do you feel what I feel? Mood contagion and leadership outcomes. *The Leadership Quarterly, 20*(5), 814–827.

Johnson, S. K. (2019). *Diversity at SIOP. Technical report for the Society for Industrial/Organizational Psychology.* SIOP.

Johnson, S. K. (2020). *Inclusify: The power of uniqueness and belonging to build innovative teams.* Harper Collins Business.

Johnson, S. K., & Dipboye, R. L. (2008). Effects of charismatic content and delivery on follower task performance: The moderating role of task charisma conduciveness. *Group & Organization Management, 33*(1), 77–106.

Johnson, S. K., Garrison, L. L., Hernez-Broome, G., Fleenor, J. W., & Steed, J. L. (2012). Go for the goal(s): Relationship between goal setting and transfer of training following leadership development. *Academy of Management Learning & Education, 11*(4), 555–569.

Johnson, S. K., & Lambert, B. K. (2020). Why diversity needs inclusion and how leaders make it happen. In *Inclusive Leadership* (pp. 60–69). Routledge.

Johnson, S. K., Murphy, S. E., Zewdie, S., & Reichard, R. J. (2008). The strong, sensitive type: Effects of gender stereotypes and leadership prototypes on the evaluation of male and female leaders. *Organizational Behavior and Human Decision Processes, 106*(1), 39–60.

Johnson, S. K., Sitzmann, T., & Nguyen, A. T. (2014). Don't hate me because I'm beautiful: Acknowledging appearance mitigates the "beauty is beastly" effect. *Organizational Behavior and Human Decision Processes, 125*(2), 184–192.

Johnston, J. H., Driskell, J. E., & Salas, E. (1997). Vigilant and hypervigilant decision making. *Journal of Applied Psychology, 82,* 614–622.

Jones, K. P., Arena, D. F., Nittrouer, C. L., Alonso, N. M., & Lindsey, A. P. (2017). Subtle discrimination in the workplace: A vicious cycle. *Industrial and Organizational Psychology, 10*(1), 51–76.

Jones, K. P., Peddie, C. I., Gilrane, V. L., King, E. B., & Gray, A. L. (2016). Not so subtle: A meta-analytic investigation of the correlates of subtle and overt discrimination. *Journal of Management, 42*(6), 1588–1613.

Jones, K. S., & Carpenter, N. C. (2014). Toward a sociocultural psychological approach to examining stereotype threat in the workplace. *Industrial and Organizational Psychology, 7*(3), 429–433.

Jones, K. S., Newman, D. A., Su, R., & Rounds, J. (2020). Black–White differences in vocational interests: Meta-analysis and boundary conditions. *Journal of Business and Psychology, 36,* 1–19.

Josefy, M., Kuban, S., Ireland, R. D., & Hitt, M. A. (2015). All things great and small: Organizational size, boundaries of the firm, and a changing environment. *Academy of Management Annals, 9*(1), 715–802.

Jubb, P. B. (1999). Whistleblowing: A restrictive definition and interpretation. *Journal of Business Ethics, 21*(1), 77–94.

Judge, T. A., & Higgins, C. A. (1998). Affective disposition and the letter of reference. *Organizational Behavior and Human Decision Processes, 75,* 207–221.

Judge, T. A., Parker, S., Colbert, A. E., Heller, D., & Ilies, R. (2001). Job satisfaction: A cross-cultural review. In N. Anderson, D. S. Ones, H. K. Sinangil, & C. Viswesvaran (Eds.), *Handbook of industrial, work and organizational psychology* (Vol. 2, pp. 25–52). London: Sage.

Judge, T. A., Piccolo, R. F., & Ilies, R. (2004). The forgotten ones? The validity of consideration and initiating structure in leadership research. *Journal of Applied Psychology, 89*(1), 36–51.

Judge, T. A., Thoresen, C. J., Bono, J. E., & Patton, G. K. (2001). The job satisfaction–job performance relationship: A qualitative and quantitative review. *Psychological Bulletin, 127*(3), 376–407.

Judge, T. A., Weiss, H. M., Kammeyer-Mueller, J. D., & Hulin, C. L. (2017). Job attitudes, job satisfaction, and job affect: A century of continuity and of change. *Journal of Applied Psychology, 102*(3), 356–374.

Jung, E. J., & Lee, S. (2015). The combined effects of relationship conflict and the relational self on creativity. *Organizational Behavior and Human Decision Processes, 130,* 44–57.

Kacmar, K. M., Andrews, M. C., Van Rooy, D. L., Chris Steilberg, R., & Cerrone, S. (2006). Sure everyone can be replaced . . . but at what cost? Turnover as a predictor of unit-level performance. *Academy of Management Journal, 49*(1), 133–144.

Kacmar, K. M., & Baron, R. A. (1999). Organizational politics: The state of the field, links to related processes, and an agenda for future research. *Research in Personnel and Human Resources Management, 7,* 1–39.

Kacmar, K. M., Witt, L. A., Zivnuska, S., & Gully, S. M. (2003). The interactive effect of leader–member exchange and communication frequency on performance ratings. *Journal of Applied Psychology, 88*(4), 764–772.

Kahn, R. L., & Katz, D. (1960). Leadership practices in relation to productivity and morale. In D. Cartwright & A. Zander (Eds.), *Group dynamics: Research and theory* (2nd ed., pp. 554–571). Elmsford, NY: Row, Peterson.

Kalinoski, Z. T., Steele-Johnson, D., Peyton, E. J., Leas, K. A., Steinke, J., & Bowling, N. A. (2013). A meta-analytic evaluation of diversity training outcomes. *Journal of Organizational Behavior, 34*(8), 1076–1104.

Kammeyer-Mueller, J., Wanberg, C., Rubenstein, A., & Song, Z. (2013). Support, undermining, and newcomer socialization: Fitting in during the first 90 days. *Academy of Management Journal, 56*(4), 1104–1124.

Kampkötter, P., & Marggraf, K. (2015). Do employees reciprocate to intra-firm trainings? An analysis of absenteeism and turnover. *International Journal of Human Resource Management, 26*(22), 2888–2907.

Kanfer, R., & Ackerman, P. L. (1989). Motivation and cognitive abilities: An integrative/aptitude-treatment approach to skill acquisition. *Journal of Applied Psychology, 74*(4), 657–690.

Kanfer, R., & Chen, G. (2016). Motivation in organizational behavior: History, advances and prospects. *Organizational Behavior and Human Decision Processes, 136,* 6–19.

Kanfer, R., Frese, M., & Johnson, R. E. (2017). Motivation related to work: A century of progress. *Journal of Applied Psychology, 102*(3), 338–355.

Kantrowitz, T. M., Dawson, C. R., & Fetzer, M. S. (2011). Computer adaptive testing (CAT): A faster, smarter, and more secure approach to pre-employment testing. *Journal of Business Psychology, 26,* 227–232.

Kaplan, A. (1964). *The conduct of inquiry.* New York: Harper & Row.

Kaptein, M. (2011a). From inaction to external whistleblowing: The influence of the ethical culture of organizations on employee responses to observed wrongdoing. *Journal of Business Ethics, 98*(3), 513–530.

Kaptein, M. (2011b). Understanding unethical behavior by unraveling ethical culture. *Human Relations, 64*(6), 843–869.

Karau, S. J., & Williams, K. D. (1993). Social loafing: A meta-analytic review and theoretical integration. *Journal of Personality and Social Psychology, 65*(4), 681–706.

Karkoulian, S., Assaker, G., & Hallak, R. (2016). An empirical study of 360-degree feedback, organizational justice, and firm sustainability. *Journal of Business Research*, *69*(5), 1862–1867.

Kath, L. M., Salter, N. P., Bachiochi, P., Brown, K. G., & Hebl, M. (2020). Teaching IO psychology to undergraduate students: Do we practice what we preach? *Industrial and Organizational Psychology*, *13*(4), 443–460.

Katz, D., & Kahn, R. L. (1966). *The social psychology of organizations*. New York: Wiley.

Katzell, R. A., & Austin, J. T. (1992). From then to now: The development of industrial-organizational psychology in the United States. *Journal of Applied Psychology*, *77*, 803–835.

Kausel, E. E., Culbertson, S. S., & Madrid, H. P. (2016). Overconfidence in personnel selection: When and why unstructured interview information can hurt hiring decisions. *Organizational Behavior and Human Decision Processes*, *137*, 27–44.

Keeler, K. R., Kong, W., Dalal, R. S., & Cortina, J. M. (2019). Situational strength interactions: Are variance patterns consistent with the theory? *Journal of Applied Psychology*, *104*(12), 1487–1513.

Keeter, S., Kennedy, C., & Deane, C. (2020). *Understanding how 2020 election polls performed and what it might mean for other kinds of survey work*. Pew Research. Retrieved 4/14/2021 from www.pewresearch.org/fact-tank/2020/11/13/understanding-how-2020s-election-polls-performed-and-what-it-might-mean-for-other-kinds-of-survey-work/

Keller, A. C., & Semmer, N. K. (2013). Changes in situational and dispositional factors as predictors of job satisfaction. *Journal of Vocational Behavior*, *83*(1), 88–98.

Keller, L. M., Bouchard, T. J., Arvey, R. D., Segal, N. L., & Dawis, R. V. (1992). Work values: Genetic and environmental issues. *Journal of Applied Psychology*, *77*(4), 79–88.

Kellermanns, F. W., Floyd, S. W., Pearson, A. W., & Spencer, B. (2008). The contingent effect of constructive confrontation on the relationship between shared mental models and decision quality. *Journal of Organizational Behavior*, *29*(1), 119–137.

Kenny, D. A., & Zaccaro, S. J. (1983). An estimate of variance due to traits in leadership. *Journal of Applied Psychology*, *68*, 678–685.

Kenyon, R. (2005). The business benefits of apprenticeships: The English employers' perspective. *Education & Training*, *47*(4), 366–373.

Keys, B., & Wolfe, J. (1990). The role of management games and simulations in education and research. *Journal of Management*, *16*(2), 307–336.

Kierein, N. M., & Gold, M. A. (2000). Pygmalion in work organizations: A meta-analysis. *Journal of Organizational Behavior*, *21*(8), 913–928.

Kiesler, S., & Sproull, L. (1992). Group decision making and communication technology. *Organizational Behavior and Human Decision Processes*, *52*(1), 96–123.

Kilman, R. H., Saxton, M. J., & Serpa, R. (Eds.). (1985). *Gaining control of the corporate culture*. San Francisco, CA: Jossey-Bass.

Kim, J. E., & Moen, P. (2001). Moving into retirement: Preparation and transitions in late midlife. In M. E. Lachman (Ed.), *Handbook of midlife development* (pp. 487–527). Hoboken, NJ: Wiley.

Kim, J.-Y., Hsu, N., Newman, D. A., Harms, P., & Wood, D. (2020). Leadership perceptions, gender, and dominant personality: The role of normality evaluations. *Journal of Research in Personality*, *87*, 103984.

Kim, K. Y., Atwater, L., Patel, P. C., & Smither, J. W. (2016). Multisource feedback, human capital, and the financial performance of organizations. *Journal of Applied Psychology*, *101*(11), 1569–1584.

Kim, M., Beehr, T. A., & Prewett, M. S. (2018). Employee responses to empowering leadership: A meta-analysis. *Journal of Leadership & Organizational Studies*, *25*(3), 257–276.

King, E. B., Avery, D. R., Hebl, M. R., & Cortina, J. M. (2018). *Systematic subjectivity: How subtle biases infect the scholarship review process*. Sage.

Kipnis, D. (1976). *The powerholders*. Chicago, IL: University of Chicago Press.

Kipnis, D., Schmidt, S. M., & Wilkinson, I. (1980). Intraorganizational influence tactics: Explorations in getting one's way. *Journal of Applied Psychology*, *65*, 440–452.

Kirby, E. G., Kirby, S. L., & Lewis, M. A. (2002). A study of the effectiveness of training proactive thinking. *Journal of Applied Social Psychology*, *32*, 1538–1549.

Kirk, A. K., & Brown, D. F. (2003). Employee assistance programs: A review of the management of stress and well-being through workplace counseling and consulting. *Australian Psychologist*, *38*(2), 138–143.

Kirkcaldy, B. D., & Cooper, C. L. (1993). The relationship between work stress and leisure style: British and German managers. *Human Relations*, *46*(5), 669–675.

Kirkpatrick, D. L. (1959). Techniques for evaluating training programs. *Journal of the American Society of Training Directors*, *13*, 3–32.

Kirkpatrick, D. L. (1978). Evaluating in-house training programs. *Training and Development Journal, 32,* 6–9.

Kirkpatrick, S. A., & Locke, E. A. (1996). Direct and indirect effects of three core charismatic leadership components on performance and attitudes. *Journal of Applied Psychology, 81*(1), 36–51.

Kirmeyer, S. L., & Dougherty, T. W. (1988). Work load, tension, and coping: Moderating effects of supervisor support. *Personnel Psychology, 41*(1), 125–139.

Kirnan, J. P., Alfieri, J. A., Bragger, J. D., & Harris, R. S. (2009). An investigation of stereotype threat in employment tests 1. *Journal of Applied Social Psychology, 39*(2), 359–388.

Klein, F. B., Hill, A. D., Hammond, R., & Stice-Lusvardi, R. (2021). The gender equity gap: A multistudy investigation of within-job inequality in equity-based awards. *Journal of Applied Psychology, 106*(5), 734–753.

Klein, H. J., & Mulvey, P. W. (1995). Two investigations of the relationships among group goals, goal commitment, cohesion, and performance. *Organizational Behavior and Human Decision Processes, 61*(1), 44–53.

Klein, K. J. (1987). Employee stock ownership and employee attitudes: A test of three models. *Journal of Applied Psychology, 72*(2), 319–332.

Klein, K. J., & House, R. J. (1995). On fire: Charismatic leadership and levels of analysis. *Leadership Quarterly, 6*(2), 183–198.

Kleine, A. K., Rudolph, C. W., & Zacher, H. (2019). Thriving at work: A meta-analysis. *Journal of Organizational Behavior, 40*(9–10), 973–999.

Knight, C., Patterson, M., & Dawson, J. (2017). Building work engagement: A systematic review and meta-analysis investigating the effectiveness of work engagement interventions. *Journal of Organizational Behavior, 38*(6), 792–812.

Knight, C., Patterson, M., & Dawson, J. (2019). Work engagement interventions can be effective: A systematic review. *European Journal of Work and Organizational Psychology, 28*(3), 348–372.

Kobasa, S. C. (1982). The hardy personality: Toward a social psychology of stress and health. In G. S. Sanders & J. Suls (Eds.), *The social psychology of health and illness* (pp. 3–32). Hillsdale, NJ: Erlbaum.

Kobasa, S. C., & Puccetti, M. C. (1983). Personality and social resources in stress resistance. *Journal of Personality & Social Psychology, 45*(4), 839–850.

Koch, A. J., D'Mello, S. D., & Sackett, P. R. (2015). A meta-analysis of gender stereotypes and bias in experimental simulations of employment decision making. *Journal of Applied Psychology, 100*(1), 128–161.

Koehler, J. W., Anatol, K. W. E., & Applbaum, R. L. (1981). *Organizational communication: Behavioral perspectives* (2nd ed.). New York: Holt, Rinehart & Winston.

Koenig, A. M., Eagly, A. H., Mitchell, A. A., & Ristikari, T. (2011). Are leader stereotypes masculine? A meta-analysis of three research paradigms. *Psychological Bulletin, 137*(4), 616–642.

Komaki, J. L. (1986). Toward effective supervision: An operant analysis and comparison of managers at work. *Journal of Applied Psychology, 71*(2), 270–279.

Komaki, J. L., Coombs, T., & Schepman, S. (1991). Motivational implications of reinforcement theory. In R. M. Steers & L. W. Porter (Eds.), *Motivation and work behavior* (5th ed., pp. 87–107). New York: McGraw-Hill.

Komaki, J. L., Desselles, M. L., & Bowman, E. D. (1989). Definitely not a breeze: Extending an operant model of effective supervision to teams. *Journal of Applied Psychology, 74*(3), 522–529.

Kondrasuk, J. N. (1981). Studies in MBO effectiveness. *Academy of Management Review, 6*(3), 419–430.

Korczynski, M. (2003). Communities of coping: Collective emotional labour in service work. *Organization, 10*(1), 55–79.

Kossek, E., Baltes, B., & Matthews, R. (2011). Focal article. How work–family research can finally have an impact in the workplace. *Industrial and Organizational Psychology: Perspectives on Science and Practice, 4,* 352–369.

Kossek, E. E., & Lambert, S. J. (Eds.). (2005). *Work and life integration: Organizational, cultural, and individual perspectives.* Mahwah, NJ: Erlbaum.

Kossek, E. E., & Nichol, V. (1992). The effects of on-site child care on employee attitudes and performance. *Personnel Psychology, 45*(3), 485–509.

Kossek, E. E., & Zonia, S. C. (1993). Assessing diversity climate: A field study of reactions to employer efforts to promote diversity. *Journal of Organizational Behavior, 14*(1), 61–81.

Koster, F., de Grip, A., & Fouarge, D. (2011). Does perceived support in employee development affect personnel turnover? *International Journal of Human Resource Management, 22*(11), 2403–2418.

Kottke, J. L., & Shultz, K. S. (1997). Using an assessment center as a developmental tool for graduate students: A demonstration. In R. E. Riggio & B. T. Mayes (Eds.), *Assessment centers: Research and applications* (pp. 289–302). Corte Madera, CA: Select Press.

Koval, C. Z., & Rosette, A. S. (2020). The natural hair bias in job recruitment. *Social Psychological and Personality Science, 12,* 741–750.

Kozan, M. K., Ergin, C., & Varoglu, K. (2014). Bases of power and conflict intervention strategy: A study of Turkish managers. *International Journal of Conflict Management, 25,* 38–60.

Kozlowski, S. W. J., & Ilgen, D. R. (2006). Enhancing the effectiveness of work groups and teams. *Psychological Science in the Public Interest, 7*(3), 77–124.

Krackhardt, D. (1990). Assessing the political landscape: Structure, cognition, and power in organizations. *Administrative Science Quarterly, 35*(2), 342–369.

Krackhardt, D., & Porter, L. W. (1986). The snowball effect: Turnover embedded in communication networks. *Journal of Applied Psychology, 71*(1), 50–55.

Kraiger, K., & Ford, J. K. (2021). The science of workplace instruction: Learning and development applied to work. *Annual Review of Organizational Psychology and Organizational Behavior, 8,* 45–72.

Kraiger, K., Ford, J. K., & Salas, E. (1993). Application of cognitive, skill-based and affective theories of learning outcomes to new methods of training evaluation. *Journal of Applied Psychology, 78*(2), 311–328.

Kraiger, K., Passmore, J., dos Santos, N. R., & Malvezzi, S. (2015). *The Wiley Blackwell handbook of the psychology of training, development, and performance improvement.* John Wiley.

Kravitz, D. A., & Balzer, W. K. (1992). Context effects in performance appraisal: A methodological critique and empirical study. *Journal of Applied Psychology, 77*(1), 24–31.

Kristof-Brown, A. L., Zimmerman, R. D., & Johnson, E. C. (2005). Consequences of individuals' fit at work: A meta-analysis of person–job, person–organization, person–group, and person–supervisor fit. *Personnel Psychology, 58*(2), 281–342.

Kuhn, W. (2010). Proclaiming the everlasting gospel to all people: Toward a creative adventist mission response. *Kerygma, 6*(2), 42–52.

Kumara, U. A., & Koichi, F. (1989). Employee satisfaction and job climate: An empirical study of Japanese manufacturing employees. *Journal of Business and Psychology, 3,* 315–329.

Kume, T. (1985). Managerial attitudes toward decision-making: North America and Japan. In W. B. Gudykunst, L. P. Stewart, & S. Ting-Toomey (Eds.), *Communication, culture, and organizational processes* (pp. 231–251). Beverly Hills, CA: Sage.

Kwon, B., & Farndale, E. (2020). Employee voice viewed through a cross-cultural lens. *Human Resource Management Review, 30*(1), 1–11.

Lacerenza, C. N., Marlow, S. L., Tannenbaum, S. I., & Salas, E. (2018). Team development interventions: Evidence-based approaches for improving teamwork. *American Psychologist, 73*(4), 517–531.

Lacerenza, C. N., Reyes, D. L., Marlow, S. L., Joseph, D. L., & Salas, E. (2017). Leadership training design, delivery, and implementation: A meta-analysis. *Journal of Applied Psychology, 102*(12), 1686–1718.

Lalonde, C., & Adler, C. (2015). Information asymmetry in process consultation: An empirical research on leader-client/consultant relationship in healthcare organizations. *Leadership & Organization Development Journal, 36,* 177–211.

Lam, S. S. K., Hui, C., & Law, K. S. (1999). Organizational citizenship behavior: Comparing perspectives of supervisors and subordinates across four international samples. *Journal of Applied Psychology, 84*(4), 594–601.

Lam, W., Huang, X., & Snape, E. (2007). Feedback-seeking behavior and leader-member exchange: Do supervisor attributed motives matter? *Academy of Management Journal, 50*(2), 348–363.

Lambert, L. S., Tepper, B. J., Carr, J. C., Holt, D. T., & Barelka, A. J. (2012). Forgotten but not gone: An examination of fit between leader consideration and initiating structure needed and received. *Journal of Applied Psychology, 97*(5), 913–930.

Landy, F. J. (1989). *Psychology of work behavior* (4th ed.). Pacific Grove, CA: Brooks/Cole.

Landy, F. J., Farr, J. F., & Farr, J. L. (1983). *The measurement of work performance: Methods, theory, and applications.* Academic Press.

Langan-Fox, J. (2001). Communication in organizations: Speed, diversity, networks and influence on organizational effectiveness, human health, and relationships. In N. Anderson, D. S. Ones, H. K. Sinangil, & C. Viswesvaran (Eds.), *Handbook of industrial, work, & organizational psychology* (pp. 188–205). London: Sage.

Lange, T. (2009). Attitudes, attributes, and institutions determining job satisfaction in Central and Eastern Europe. *Human Relations, 31*(1), 81–97.

Langfred, C. W. (1998). Is group cohesiveness a double-edged sword? An investigation of the effects of cohesiveness on performance. *Small Group Research, 29*(1), 124–143.

Larson, E. W., & Gobeli, D. H. (1987). Matrix management: Contradictions and insights. *California Management Review, 29*(4), 126–138.

Larwood, L., Wright, T. A., Desrochers, S., & Dahir, V. (1998). Extending latent role and psychological contract theories to predict intent to turnover and politics in business organizations. *Group & Organization Management, 23*(2), 100–123.

Latack, J. C., & Foster, L. W. (1985). Implementation of compressed work schedules: Participation and job redesign as critical factors for employee acceptance. *Personnel Psychology, 38*(1), 75–92.

Latané, B., Williams, K., & Harkins, S. (1979). Many hands make light the work: The causes and consequences of social loafing. *Journal of Personality and Social Psychology, 37*(6), 822–832.

Latham, G. P. (1988). Human resource training and development. *Annual Review of Psychology, 39*(1), 545–582.

Latham, G. P. (2001). The reciprocal transfer of learning from journals to practice. *Applied Psychology: An International Review, 50,* 201–211.

Lau, V. C. S., Au, W. T., & Ho, J. M. C. (2003). A qualitative and quantitative review of antecedents of counterproductive behavior in organizations. *Journal of Business and Psychology, 18*(1), 73–99.

Law, R., Dollard, M. F., Tuckey, M. R., & Dormann, C. (2011). Psychosocial safety climate as a lead indicator of workplace bullying and harassment, job resources, psychological health and employee engagement. *Accident Analysis and Prevention, 43*(5), 1782–1793.

Lawler, E. E. (1971). *Pay and organizational effectiveness.* New York: McGraw-Hill.

Lawler, E. E. (1987). Paying for performance: Future directions. In D. B. Balkin & L. R. Gomez-Mejia (Eds.), *New perspectives on compensation* (pp. 162–168). Englewood Cliffs, NJ: Prentice Hall.

Lawler III, E. E., Mohrman, S. A., & Ledford, G. E. (1992). *Employee involvement and total quality management: Practices and results in Fortune 1000 companies.* San Francisco, CA: Jossey-Bass.

Lawong, D., Ferris, G. R., Hochwarter, W., & Maher, L. (2019). *Recruiter political skill and organization reputation effects on job applicant attraction in the recruitment process: A multi-study investigation.* Career Development International.

Lazarus, R. S. (1991). Psychological stress in the workplace. *Journal of Social Behavior and Personality, 6,* 1–13.

Leana, C. R. (1985). A partial test of Janis' groupthink model: Effects of group cohesiveness and leader behavior on defective decision making. *Journal of Management, 11*(1), 5–18.

Le Blanc, P. M., & González-Romá, V. (2012). A team level investigation of the relationship between Leader–Member Exchange (LMX) differentiation, and commitment and performance. *The Leadership Quarterly, 23*(3), 534–544.

Ledford, G. E., Lawler, E. E., & Mohrman, S. A. (1988). The quality circle and its variations. In J. P. Campbell & R. J. Campbell (Eds.), *Productivity in organizations* (pp. 255–294). San Francisco, CA: Jossey-Bass.

Lee, C., Earley, P. C., & Hanson, L. A. (1988). Are Type As better performers? *Journal of Organizational Behavior, 9*(3), 263–269.

Lee, C-c., Lin, Y-h., Huan, H.-c., Huang, W.-w., & Teng, H.-h. (2015). The effects of task interdependence, team cooperation, and team conflict on job performance. *Social Behavior and Personality, 43*(4), 529–536.

Lee, F. (1993). Being polite and keeping MUM: How bad news is communicated in organizational hierarchies. *Journal of Applied Social Psychology, 23*(14), 1124–1149.

Lee, S. Y., Hanson, M. D., & Cheung, H. K. (2019). Incorporating bystander intervention into sexual harassment training. *Industrial and Organizational Psychology, 12*(1), 52–57.

Lee, T. W., & Mitchell, T. R. (1994). An alternative approach: The unfolding model of voluntary employee turnover. *Academy of Management Review, 19*(1), 51–89.

Lee, T. W., Mitchell, T. R., Sablynski, C. J., Burton, J. P., & Holtom, B. C. (2004). The effects of job embeddedness on organizational citizenship, job performance, volitional absences, and voluntary turnover. *Academy of Management Journal, 47*(5), 711–722.

Lee, Y., Berry, C. M., & Gonzalez-Mulé, E. (2019). The importance of being humble: A meta-analysis and incremental validity analysis of the relationship between honesty-humility and job performance. *Journal of Applied Psychology, 104*(12), 1535–1546.

Lefkowitz, J. (2016). The maturation of a profession: A work psychology for the new millennium. In I. McWha-Hermann, D. C. Maynard, & M. O'Neill (Eds.), *Humanitarian work psychology and the global development agenda: Case studies and interventions* (pp. 200–204). New York: Routledge/Taylor & Francis.

Lefkowitz, J. (2017). *Ethics and values in industrial-organizational psychology.* Taylor & Francis.

Leibowitz, Z. B., Kaye, B. L., & Farren, C. (1986). *Designing career development systems.* Pfeiffer.

Leisenring, M. (2020). Women still have to work three months longer to equal what men earned in a year. www.census.gov/library/stories/2020/03/equal-pay-day-is-march-31-earliest-since-1996.html

LePine, J. A., Hanson, M. A., Borman, W. C., & Motowidlo, S. J. (2000). Contextual performance and teamwork: Implications for staffing. In *Research in Personnel and Human Resources Management, 19,* 53–90.

LePine, J. A., Podsakoff, N. A., & LePine, M. A. (2005). A meta-analytic test of the challenge stressor–hindrance stressor framework: An explanation for inconsistent relationships among stressors and performance. *Academy of Management Journal, 48,* 764–775.

Lepold, A., Tanzer, N., Bregenzer, A., & Jiménez, P. (2018). The efficient measurement of job satisfaction: Facet-items versus facet scales. *International Journal of Environmental Research and Public Health, 15*(7), 1362–1381.

Leslie, L. M., & Manchester, C. F. (2011). Work–family conflict is a social issue not a women's issue. *Industrial and Organizational Psychology, 4*(3), 414–417.

Levashina, J., Hartwell, C. J., Morgeson, F. P., & Campion, M. A. (2014). The structured employment interview: Narrative and quantitative review of the research literature. *Personnel Psychology, 67*(1), 241–293.

Levi, L., Frankenhaeuser, M., & Gardell, B. (1986). The characteristics of the workplace and the nature of its social demands. In S. G. Wolf & A. J. Finestone (Eds.), *Occupational stress: Health and performance at work* (pp. 54–67). Littleton, MA: PSG.

Lewis, D. (2002). Whistleblowing procedures at work: What are the implications for human resource practitioners? *Business Ethics: A European Review, 11*(3), 202–209.

Li, W. D., Zhang, Z, Song, Z., & Arvey, R. D. (2016). It is also in our nature: Genetic influences on work characteristic and in explaining their relationship with well-being. *Journal of Organizational Behavior, 37*(6), 868–888.

Liden, R. C., Wayne, S. J., Jaworski, R. A., & Bennett, N. (2004). Social loafing: A field investigation. *Journal of Management, 30*(2), 285–304.

Liden, R. C., Wayne, S. J., & Stilwell, D. (1993). A longitudinal study on the early development of leader–member exchanges. *Journal of Applied Psychology, 78*(4), 662–674.

Liebowitz, S. J., & de Meuse, K. P. (1982). The application of team building. *Human Relations, 35*(1), 1–18.

Lieke, L., Johns, G., Lyons, B. J., & ter Hoeven, C. L. (2016). Why and when do employees imitate the absenteeism of co-workers? *Organizational Behavior and Human Decision Processes, 134*, 16–30.

Likert, R. (1967). *The human organization.* New York: McGraw-Hill.

Lim, S., & Cortina, L. M. (2005). Interpersonal mistreatment in the workplace: The interface and impact of general incivility and sexual harassment. *Journal of Applied Psychology, 90*(3), 483–496.

Lim, V. K. G. (1996). Job insecurity and its outcomes: Moderating effects of work-based and nonwork-based social support. *Human Relations, 49*(2), 171–194.

Lin, S.-H. J., Ma, J., & Johnson, R. E. (2016). When ethical leader behavior breaks bad: How ethical leader behavior can turn abusive via ego depletion and moral licensing. *Journal of Applied Psychology, 101*(6), 815.

Linos, E., & Riesch, N. (2020). Thick red tape and the thin blue line: A field study on reducing administrative burden in police recruitment. *Public Administration Review, 80*(1), 92–103.

Lipman-Blumen, J. (2005). *The allure of toxic leadership.* New York: Oxford University Press.

Liu, J., Kwan, H. K., Fu, P. P., & Mao, Y. (2013). Ethical leadership and job performance in China: The roles of workplace friendships. *Journal of Occupational and Organizational Psychology, 86*(4), 564–584.

Liu, S., Liu, P., Wang, M., & Zhang, B. (2021). Effectiveness of stereotype threat interventions: A meta-analytic review. *Journal of Applied Psychology, 106*(6), 921–949.

Liu, Y., Ferris, G. R., Xu, J., Weitz, B. A., & Perrewé, P. L. (2014). When ingratiation backfires: The role of political skill in the ingratiation-internship performance relationship. *Academy of Management Learning & Education, 13*(4), 569–586.

Livingston, R. W., Rosette, A. S., & Washington, E. F. (2012). Can an agentic Black woman get ahead? The impact of race and interpersonal dominance on perceptions of female leaders. *Psychological Science, 23*(4), 354–358.

Lloyd, K. J., Boer, D., & Voelpel, S. C. (2017). From listening to leading: Toward an understanding of supervisor listening within the framework of leader–member exchange theory. *International Journal of Business Communication, 54*(4), 431–451.

Locke, E. A. (1968). Toward a theory of task motivation and incentives. *Organizational Behavior and Human Performance, 3*(2), 157–189.

Locke, E. A., Latham, G. P., & Erez, M. (1988). The determinants of goal commitment. *Academy of Management Review, 13*(1), 23–39.

Loden, M., & Rosener, J. B. (1991). *Workforce America! Managing employee diversity as a vital resource.* Homewood, IL: Business One Irwin.

London, M., & Beatty, R. W. (1993). 360-degree feedback as a competitive advantage. *Human Resource Management, 32*(2–3), 353–372.

Loo, R. (1994). The evaluation of stress management services by Canadian organizations. *Journal of Business and Psychology, 9*(2), 129–136.

Lopez, F. J., Hou, N., & Fan, J. (2019). Reducing faking on personality tests: Testing a new faking-mitigation procedure in a US job applicant sample. *International Journal of Selection and Assessment, 27*(4), 371–380.

Louis, M. R., Posner, B. Z., & Powell, G. N. (1983). The availability and helpfulness of socialization practices. *Personnel Psychology, 36*(4), 857–866.

Lounsbury, J. W., & Hoopes, L. L. (1986). A vacation from work: Changes in work and nonwork outcomes. *Journal of Applied Psychology, 71*(3), 392–401.

Lowe, K. B., Kroeck, K. G., & Sivasubramaniam, N. (1996). Effectiveness correlates of transformational and transactional leadership: A meta-analytic review of the MLQ literature. *Leadership Quarterly, 7*(3), 385–425.

Lowry, S. M., Maynard, H. B., & Stegemerten, G. J. (Eds.). (1940). *Time and motion study and formulas for wage incentives* (3rd ed.). New York: McGraw-Hill.

Luan, S., Reb, J., & Gigerenzer, G. (2019). Ecological rationality: Fast-and-frugal heuristics for managerial decision making under uncertainty. *Academy of Management Journal, 62*(6), 1735–1759.

Lucas, J. L., & Heady, R. B. (2002). Flextime commuters and their driver stress, feelings of time urgency, and commute satisfaction. *Journal of Business and Psychology, 16*(4), 565–572.

Ludwig, T. D., & Geller, E. S. (1997). Assigned versus participative goal setting and response generalization: Managing injury control among professional pizza deliverers. *Journal of Applied Psychology, 82*, 253–261.

Lukacik, E.-R., Bourdage, J. S., & Roulin, N. (2020). Into the void: A conceptual model and research agenda for the design and use of asynchronous video interviews. *Human Resource Management Review* (in press), 100789.

Lundberg, C., Gudmundson, A., & Andersson, T. D. (2009). Herzberg's Two-Factor Theory of work motivation tested empirically on seasonal workers in hospitality and tourism. *Tourism Management, 30*(6), 890–899.

Macan, T. H., & Dipboye, R. L. (1994). The effects of the application on processing of information from the employment interview. *Journal of Applied Social Psychology, 24*, 1291–1314.

Macey, W. H., & Schneider, B. (2008). Engaged in engagement: We are delighted we did it. *Industrial and Organizational Psychology, 1*(1), 76–83.

Machlowitz, M. M. (1976). Working the 100-hour week—and loving it. *The New York Times*, October 3, p. 45.

Mackay, M. M., Allen, J. A., & Landis, R. S. (2017). Investigating the incremental validity of employee engagement in the prediction of employee effectiveness: A meta-analytic path analysis. *Human Resource Management Review, 27*(1), 108–120.

Mackenzie, M. L. (2010). Manager communication and workplace trust: Understanding manager and employee perceptions in the e-world. *International Journal of Information Management, 30*(6), 529–541.

Maddi, S. R., Harvey, R. H., Khoshaba, D. M., Fazel, M., & Resurreccion, N. (2009). Hardiness training facilitates performance in college. *The Journal of Positive Psychology, 4*(6), 566–577.

Madera, J. M., & Hebl, M. R. (2012). Discrimination against facially stigmatized applicants in interviews: an eye-tracking and face-to-face investigation. Journal of Applied Psychology, 97(2), 317.

Madera, J. M., Hebl, M. R., & Martin, R. C. (2009). Gender and letters of recommendation for academia: Agentic and communal differences. *Journal of Applied Psychology, 94*(6), 1591–1599.

Madera, J. M., King, E. B., & Hebl, M. R. (2013). Enhancing the effects of sexual orientation diversity training: The effects of setting goals and training mentors on attitudes and behaviors. *Journal of Business and Psychology, 28*(1), 79–91.

Madjar, N., Greenberg, E., & Chen, Z. (2011). Factors for radical creativity, incremental creativity, and routine, noncreative performance. *Journal of Applied Psychology, 96*(4), 730–743.

Majumdar, B., & Ray, A. (2011). Transformational leadership and innovative work behaviour. *Journal of the Indian Academy of Applied Psychology, 37*(1), 140–148.

Mann, R. B., & Decker, P. J. (1984). The effect of key behavior distinctiveness on generalization and recall in behavior modeling training. *Academy of Management Journal, 27*(4), 900–909.

Manz, C. C., Fugate, M., Hom, P. W., & Millikin, J. P. (2015). When having to leave is a "good thing": A case for positive involuntary turnover. *Organizational Dynamics, 44*, 57–64.

Marks, M. A., Sabella, M. J., Burke, C. S., & Zaccaro, S. J. (2002). The impact of cross-training on team effectiveness. *Journal of Applied Psychology, 87*(1), 3–13.

Marks, M. L., & Mirvis, P. H. (2010). *Joining forces*. San Francisco, CA: Jossey-Bass.

Markus, M. L. (1994). Electronic mail as the medium of managerial choice. *Organization Science, 5*, 502–527.

Marlow, S. L., Lacerenza, C. N., Paoletti, J., Burke, C. S., & Salas, E. (2018). Does team communication represent a one-size-fits-all approach? A meta-analysis of team communication and performance. *Organizational Behavior and Human Decision Processes, 144*, 145–170.

Marlow, S. L., Lacerenza, C. N., Reyes, D., & Salas, E. (2017). The science and practice of simulation-based training in organizations. In K. G. Brown (Ed.), *The Cambridge handbook of workplace training and employee development* (pp. 256–277). Cambridge University Press.

Marshall, J., & Rossett, A. (2014). Perception of barriers to the evaluation of workplace learning programs. *Performance Improvement Quarterly, 27*, 7–26.

Martineau, J. W., & Preskill, H. (2002). Evaluating the impact of organization development interventions. In J. Waclawski & A. H. Church (Eds.), *Organization development: A data-driven approach to organizational change* (pp. 286–301). San Francisco, CA: Jossey-Bass.

Martinez, L. R., White, C. D., Shapiro, J. R., & Hebl, M. R. (2016). Selection BIAS: Stereotypes and discrimination related to having a history of cancer. *Journal of Applied Psychology, 101*(1), 122–128. https://doi.org/10.1037/apl0000036

Martins, L. L. (2011). Organizational change and development. In S. Zedeck (Ed.), *APA handbook of industrial and organizational psychology* (Vol. 3, pp. 691–728). Washington, DC: American Psychological Association.

Martocchio, J. J., & Webster, J. (1992). Effects of feedback and cognitive playfulness on performance in microcomputer software training. *Personnel Psychology, 45*(3), 553–578.

Marx, R. D. (1982). Relapse prevention for managerial training: A model for maintenance of behavior change. *Academy of Management Review, 7*(3), 433–441.

Maslach, C. (2005). Understanding burnout: Work and family issues. In D. F. Halpern & S. E. Murphy (Eds.), *From work–family balance to work–family interaction: Changing the metaphor* (pp. 99–114). Mahwah, NJ: Erlbaum.

Maslach, C., & Jackson, S. E. (1986). *MBI: Maslach Burnout Inventory*. Palo Alto, CA: Consulting Psychologists Press.

Maslow, A. H. (1965). *Eupsychian management*. Homewood, IL: Irwin.

Maslow, A. H. (1970). *Motivation and personality* (2nd ed.). New York: Harper & Row.

Mathieu, J. E., Hofmann, D. A., & Farr, J. L. (1993). Job perception–job satisfaction relations: An empirical comparison of three competing theories. *Organizational Behavior and Human Decision Processes, 56*(3), 370–387.

Mathieu, J. E., Martineau, J. W., & Tannenbaum, S. I. (1993). Individual and situational influences on the development of self-efficacy: Implications for training effectiveness. *Personnel Psychology, 46*(1), 125–147.

Matteson, M. T., & Ivancevich, J. M. (1987). *Controlling work stress: Effective human resource and management strategies*. San Francisco, CA: Jossey-Bass.

Mattingly, V., & Kraiger, K. (2019). Can emotional intelligence be trained? A meta-analytical investigation. *Human Resource Management Review, 29*(2), 140–155.

Maurer, T. J., & Chapman, E. F. (2013). Career success in relation to individual and situational variables from the employee development literature. *Journal of Vocational Behavior, 83*(3), 450–465.

Mayer, J. D. (2002). MSCEIT: Mayer-Salovey-Caruso emotional intelligence test. Toronto, Canada: Multi-Health Systems.

Mayer, J. D., Caruso, D. R., & Salovey, P. (2016). The ability model of emotional intelligence: Principles and updates. *Emotion Review, 8*(4), 290–300.

Mayes, B. T. (1995). *Power and organizational politics*. Unpublished manuscript.

Mayes, B. T., & Allen, R. W. (1977). Toward a definition of organizational politics. *Academy of Management Review, 2*(4), 672–678.

Mayo, E. (1933). *The human problems of an industrial civilization*. Cambridge: Harvard University Press.

McCarthy, J. M., Bauer, T. N., Truxillo, D. M., Anderson, N. R., Costa, A. C., & Ahmed, S. M. (2017). Applicant perspectives during selection: A review addressing "So what?," "What's new?," and "Where to next?" *Journal of Management, 43*(6), 1693–1725.

McClelland, D. C. (1961). *The achieving society*. New York: Van Nostrand.

McClelland, D. C. (1970). The two faces of power. *Journal of International Affairs, 24*, 29–47.

McClelland, D. C. (1975). *Power: The inner experience*. New York: Irvington Press.

McClelland, D. C. (1980). Motive dispositions: The merits of operant and respondent measures. In L. Wheeler (Ed.), *Review of personality and social psychology* (Vol. 1, pp. 10–41). Beverly Hills, CA: Sage.

McClelland, D. C., & Boyatzis, R. E. (1982). Leadership motive pattern and long-term success in management. *Journal of Applied Psychology, 67*(6), 737–743.

McClelland, D. C., & Franz, C. E. (1992). Motivational and other sources of work accomplishments at mid-life: A longitudinal study. *Journal of Personality, 60*(4), 679–707.

McConkie, M. L. (1979). A clarification of the goal setting and appraisal processes in MBO. *Academy of Management Review, 4*(1), 29–40.

McCord, M. A., Joseph, D. L., Dhanani, L. Y., & Beus, J. M. (2018). A meta-analysis of sex and race differences in perceived workplace mistreatment. *Journal of Applied Psychology, 103*(2), 137.

McCormick, E. J. (1979). *Job analysis: Methods and applications*. New York: AMACOM.

McCormick, E. J., & Cooper, C. L. (1988). Executive stress: Extending the international comparison. *Human Relations, 41*(1), 65–72.

McCormick, E. J., Jeanneret, P. R., & Mecham, R. C. (1969). *Position analysis questionnaire*. West Lafayette, IN: Occupational Research Center, Purdue University.

McCredie, M. N., & Morey, L. C. (2019). Convergence between Thematic Apperception Test (TAT) and self-report: Another look at some old questions. *Journal of Clinical Psychology*, *75*(10), 1838–1849.

McFarland, L. A., & Ployhart, R. E. (2015). Social media: A contextual framework to guide research and practice. *Journal of Applied Psychology*, *100*(6), 1653–1677.

McFarland, L. A., Reeves, S., Porr, W. B., & Ployhart, R. E. (2020). Impact of the COVID-19 pandemic on job search behavior: An event transition perspective. *Journal of Applied Psychology*, *105*, 1207–1217.

McFillen, J. M., O'Neil, D. A., Balzer, W. K., & Vareny, G. H. (2013). Organizational diagnosis: An evidence-based approach. *Journal of Change Management*, *13*(2), 223–246.

McKay, P. F., & Avery, D. R. (2006). What has race got to do with it? Unraveling the role of racioethnicity in job seekers' reactions to site visits. *Personnel Psychology*, *59*, 395–429.

McKay, P. F., Avery, D. R., & Morris, M. A. (2008). Mean racial-ethnic differences in employee sales performance: The moderating role of diversity climate. *Personnel Psychology*, *61*(2), 349–374.

McKay, P. F., Avery, D. R., Tonidandel, S., Morris, M. A., Hernandez, M., & Hebl, M. R. (2007). Racial differences in employee retention: Are diversity climate perceptions the key? *Personnel Psychology*, *60*(1), 35–62.

McLaughlin, M., & Cox, E. (2015). *Leadership coaching: Developing braver leaders*. New York: Routledge/Taylor & Francis.

McMurry, R. N. (1947). The problem of resistance to change in industry. *Journal of Applied Psychology*, *31*(6), 589–593.

McTernan, W. P., Dollard, M. F., & LaMontagne, A. D. (2013). Depression in the workplace: An economic cost analysis of depression-related productivity loss attributable to job strain and bullying. *Work & Stress*, *27*(4), 321–338.

Meade, A. W., Michels, L. C., & Lautenschlager, G. J. (2007). Are Internet and paper-and-pencil personality tests truly comparable? An experimental design measurement invariance study. *Organizational Research Methods*, *10*(2), 322–345.

Meehl, P. (1954). *Clinical vs. statistical prediction: A theoretical analysis and review of the evidence*. Minneapolis, MN: University of Minnesota Press.

Mehrabian, A. (1981). *Silent messages* (2nd ed.). Belmont, CA: Wadsworth.

Meinecke, A. L., Klonek, F. E., & Kauffeld, S. (2017). Appraisal participation and perceived voice in annual appraisal interviews: Uncovering contextual factors. *Journal of Leadership & Organizational Studies*, *24*(2), 230–245.

Melson-Silimon, A., Harris, A. M., Shoenfelt, E. L., Miller, J. D., & Carter, N. T. (2019). Personality testing and the Americans with Disabilities Act: Cause for concern as normal and abnormal personality models are integrated. *Industrial and Organizational Psychology*, *12*(2), 119–132.

Melson-Silimon, A., Salter, N. P., & Carter, N. T. (2021). A historical review of industrial-organizational psychology's role in the study of LGBTQ employees' workplace experiences. In L. L. Koppes, J. C. Bryan, & K. Murphy (Eds.), *Historical perspectives in industrial and organizational psychology* (Vol. 2, pp. 161–183). Routledge.

Mesmer-Magnus, J. R., & Viswesvaran, C. (2007). Expatriate management: A review and directions for research in expatriate selection, training, and repatriation. In M. M. Harris (Ed.), *Handbook of research in international human resource management* (pp. 183–206). Mahwah, NJ: Lawrence Erlbaum.

Meyer, J. P., & Allen, N. J. (1997). *Commitment in the workplace: Theory, research, and application*. Thousand Oaks, CA: Sage.

Meyer, J. P., Allen, N. J., & Smith, C. A. (1993). Commitment to organizations and occupations: Extension and test of a three-component conceptualization. *Journal of Applied Psychology*, *78*(4), 538–551.

Mhatre, K. H., & Riggio, R. E. (2014). Charismatic and transformational leadership: Past, present, and future. In D. V. Day (Ed.), *Oxford handbook of leadership and organizations* (pp. 221–240). New York: Oxford University Press.

Miceli, M. P. (1993). Justice and pay system satisfaction. In R. Cropanzano (Ed.), *Justice in the workplace: Approaching fairness in HRM* (pp. 257–283). Hillsdale, NJ: Erlbaum.

Michaelsen, L. K., Watson, W. E., & Black, R. H. (1989). A realistic test of individual versus group consensus decision making. *Journal of Applied Psychology*, *74*(5), 834–839.

Migliano, S. (2020, 11/18/2020). *Employee surveillance software demand up 51% since start of pandemic*. Retrieved 6/16/2021 from www.top10vpn.com/research/covid-employee-surveillance/

Mills, M. J., & Culbertson, S. S. (2017). The elephant in the family room: Work–family considerations as central to evolving HR and IO. *Industrial and Organizational Psychology*, *10*(1), 26–31.

Mills, P. R., Kessler, R. C., Cooper, J., & Sullivan, S. (2007). Impact of a health promotion program on employee health risks and work productivity. *American Journal of Health Promotion*, *22*(1), 45–53.

Millsap, R. E., & Kwok, O. (2004). Evaluating the impact of partial factorial invariance on selection in two populations. *Psychological Methods*, *9*(1), 93–115.

Miner, J. B. (1983). The unpaved road from theory: Over the mountains to application. In R. H. Kilmann, K. W. Thomas, D. P. Slevin, R. Nath, & S. L. Jerrel (Eds.), *Producing useful knowledge for organizations* (pp. 37–68). New York: Praeger.

Mintzberg, H. (1973). *The nature of managerial work*. New York: Harper & Row.

Mintzberg, H. (1984). Power and organization life cycles. *Academy of Management Review, 9*(2), 207–224.

Mio, J. S., & Goishi, C. K. (1988). The employee assistance program: Raising productivity by lifting constraints. In P. Whitney & R. B. Ochman (Eds.), *Psychology and productivity* (pp. 105–125). New York: Plenum Press.

Miraglia, M., & Johns, G. (2021). The social and relational dynamics of absenteeism from work: A multilevel review and integration. *Academy of Management Annals, 15*(1), 37–67.

Miron, D., & McClelland, D. C. (1979). The impact of achievement motivation training on small businesses. *California Management Review, 21*(4), 13–28.

Mishra, J. (1990). Managing the grapevine. *Public Personnel Management, 19*(2), 213–228.

Mitchell, T. R., Hopper, H., Daniels, D., Falvy, J. G., & Ferris, G. R. (1998). Power, accountability, and inappropriate actions. *Applied Psychology: An International Review, 47*, 497–517.

Mitchell, T. R., & Kalb, L. S. (1982). Effects of job experience on supervisor attributions for a subordinate's poor performance. *Journal of Applied Psychology, 67*(2), 181–188.

Mitra, A., Gupta, N., & Jenkins, G. D. (1997). A drop in the bucket: When is a pay raise a pay raise? *Journal of Organizational Behavior, 18*(2), 117–137.

Mitra, A., Gupta, N., & Shaw, J. D. (2011). A comparative examination of traditional and skill-based pay plans. *Journal of Managerial Psychology, 26*(4), 278–296.

Mitz, A., & Wayne, C. (2014). Group decision making in conflict: From groupthink to polythink in the war in Iraq. In P. T. Coleman, M. Deutsch, & E. C. Marcus (Eds.), *The handbook of conflict resolution: Theory and practice* (3rd ed., pp. 331–352). San Francisco: Jossey-Bass.

Mohammed, S., Ferzandi, L., & Hamilton, K. (2010). Metaphor no more: A 15-year review of the team mental model construct. *Journal of Management, 36*(4), 876–910.

Molinsky, A., & Margolis, J. (2006). The emotional tightrope of downsizing: Hidden challenges for leaders and their organizations. *Organizational Dynamics, 35*, 145–159.

Mone, M. A., McKinley, W., & Barker, V. L. (1998). Organizational decline and innovation: A contingency framework. *Academy of Management Review, 23*(1), 115–132.

Moore, S., Grunberg, L., & Greenberg, E. (2006). Surviving repeated waves of organizational downsizing: The recency, duration, and order effects associated with different forms of layoff contact. *Anxiety, Stress & Coping: An International Journal, 19*(3), 309–329.

Mor Barak, M. E. (2011). *Managing diversity: Toward a globally inclusive workplace* (2nd ed.). Sage.

Mor Barak, M. E., Cherin, D. A., & Berkman, S. (1998). Organizational and personal dimensions in diversity climate: Ethnic and gender differences in employee perceptions. *The Journal of Applied Behavioral Science, 34*(1), 82–104.

Morgeson, F. P., Brannick, M. T., & Levine, E. L. (2019). *Job and work analysis: Methods, research, and applications for human resource management*. Sage.

Morse, N. C., & Reimer, E. (1956). The experimental change of a major organizational variable. *Journal of Abnormal and Social Psychology, 52*(1), 120–129.

Motowidlo, S. J., Packard, J. S., & Manning, M. R. (1986). Occupational stress: Its causes and consequences for job performance. *Journal of Applied Psychology, 71*, 618–629.

Mousa, S. (2020). Building social cohesion between Christians and Muslims through soccer in post-ISIS Iraq. *Science, 369*(6505), 866–870.

Mowbray, P. K., Wilkinson, A., & Tse, H. H. (2015). An integrative review of employee voice: Identifying a common conceptualization and research agenda. *International Journal of Management Reviews, 17*(3), 382–400.

Mowday, R. T., Steers, R., & Porter, L. W. (1979). The measurement of organizational commitment. *Journal of Vocational Behavior, 14*, 224–247.

Mu, J. (2015). Marketing capability, organizational adaptation and new product development performance. *Industrial Marketing Management, 49*, 151–166.

Muchinsky, P. M. (1977). Organizational communication: Relationships to organizational climate and job satisfaction. *Academy of Management Journal, 20*(4), 592–607.

Muchinsky, P. M. (1993). Validation of intelligence and mechanical aptitude tests in selecting employees for manufacturing jobs. *Journal of Business and Psychology, 7*, 373–382.

Mueser, K. T., Rosenberg, S. D., & Rosenberg, H. J. (2009). *Treatment of posttraumatic stress disorder in special populations: A cognitive restructuring program*. Washington, DC: American Psychological Association.

Mullen, J. E., & Kelloway, E. K. (2009). Safety leadership: A longitudinal study of the effects of transformational leadership on safety outcomes. *Journal of Occupational and Organizational Psychology, 82*(2), 253–272.

Munnoch, K., & Bridger, R. (2008). The relationship between a mechanical comprehension test and weapons-training task. *Military Psychology*, *20*(2), 95–101.

Munsterberg, H. (1913). *On the witness stand; essays on psychology and crime*. Doubleday, Page.

Munyon, T. P., Summers, J. K., Thompson, K. M., & Ferris, G. R. (2015). Political skill and work outcomes: A theoretical extension, meta-analytic investigation, and agenda for the future. *Personnel Psychology*, *68*(1), 143–184.

Munz, D. C., & Kohler, J. M. (1997). Do worksite stress management programs attract the employees who need them and are they effective? *International Journal of Stress Management*, *4*(1), 1–11.

Murphy, S. A., Beaton, R. D., Pike, K. C., & Johnson, L. C. (1999). Occupational stressors, stress responses, and alcohol consumption among professional firefighters: A prospective, longitudinal analysis. *International Journal of Stress Management*, *6*(3), 179–196.

Murphy, S. E. (2002). Leader self-regulation: The role of self-efficacy and multiple intelligences. In R. E. Riggio, S. E. Murphy, & P. J. Pirozzolo (Eds.), *Multiple intelligences and leadership* (pp. 165–186). Mahwah, NJ: Erlbaum.

Muse, L. A., Harris, S. G., & Field, H. S. (2003). Has the inverted-U theory of stress and job performance had a fair test? *Human Performance*, *16*, 349–364.

Myers, D. G., & Lamm, H. (1976). The group polarization phenomenon. *Psychological Bulletin*, *83*(4), 602–627.

Nahrgang, J. D., Morgeson, F. P., & Hofmann, D. A. (2011). Safety at work: A meta-analytic investigation of the link between job demands, job resources, burnout, engagement, and safety outcomes. *Journal of Applied Psychology*, *96*, 71–94. doi:10.1037/a0021484

Naranjo-Valencia, J. C., Jimenez-Jimenez, D., & Sanz-Valle, R. (2011). Innovation or imitation? The role of organizational culture. *Management Decision*, *49*(1), 55–72.

Narayanan, L., Menon, S., & Spector, P. (1999). A cross-cultural comparison of job stressors and reactions among employees holding comparable jobs in two countries. *International Journal of Stress Management*, *6*(3), 197–212.

Nathan, P. E. (1983). Failures in prevention: Why we can't prevent the devastating effect of alcoholism and drug abuse. *American Psychologist*, *38*(4), 459–467.

Near, J. P., Dworkin, T. M., & Miceli, M. P. (1993). Explaining the whistle-blowing process: Suggestions from power theory and justice theory. *Organization Science*, *4*(3), 393–411.

Nesnidol, S., & Highhouse, S. (2020). Personality and intelligence in employee selection. In B. J. Caducci & C. S. Nave (Eds.), *The Wiley encyclopedia of personality and individual differences: Clinical, applied, and cross-cultural research* (pp. 511–515). John Wiley.

Neuman, G. A., Edwards, J. E., & Raju, N. S. (1989). Organizational development interventions: A meta-analysis of their effects on satisfaction and other attitudes. *Personnel Psychology*, *42*(3), 461–489.

Newman, D. A., & Lyon, J. S. (2009). Recruitment efforts to reduce adverse impact: Targeted recruiting for personality, cognitive ability, and diversity. *Journal of Applied Psychology*, *94*(2), 298–317.

Newman, S. A., & Ford, R. C. (2021). Five steps to leading your team in the virtual COVID-19 workplace. *Organizational Dynamics*, *50*(1), 1–11.

Ng, T. W. H., Butts, M. M., Vandenberg, R. J., DeJoy, D. M., & Wilson, M. G. (2006). Effects of management communication, opportunity for learning, and work schedule flexibility on organizational commitment. *Journal of Vocational Behavior*, *68*(3), 474–489.

Nguyen, H.-H. D., & Ryan, A. M. (2008). Does stereotype threat affect test performance of minorities and women? A meta-analysis of experimental evidence. *Journal of Applied Psychology*, *93*(6), 1314–1334.

Nicklin, J. M., & Roch, S. G. (2009). Letters of recommendation: Controversy and consensus from expert perspectives. *International Journal of Selection and Assessment*, *17*(1), 76–91.

Nie, Y., Chua, B. L., Yeung, A. S., Ryan, R. M., & Chan, W. Y. (2015). The importance of autonomy support and the mediating role of work motivation for well-being: Testing self-determination theory in a Chinese work organisation. *International Journal of Psychology*, *50*(4), 245–255.

Niederman, F., & Volkema, R. J. (1999). The effects of facilitator characteristics on meeting preparation, set up, and implementation. *Small Group Research*, *30*(3), 330–360.

Nishii, L. H. (2013). The benefits of climate for inclusion for gender-diverse groups. *Academy of Management Journal*, *56*(6), 1754–1774.

Nishii, L. H., & Rich, R. E. (2014). Creating inclusive climates in diverse organizations. In B. M. Ferdman & B. R. Deane (Eds.), *Diversity at work: The practice of inclusion* (pp. 330–363). Jossey-Bass.

Nisula, A., & Kianto, A. (2016). The role of knowledge management practices in supporting employee capacity for improvisation. *The International Journal of Human Resource Management*, *27*, 1920–1937.

Noe, R. A. (1986). Trainees' attributes and attitudes: Neglected influences on training effectiveness. *Academy of Management Review, 11*(4), 736–749.

Nossiter, V. (1979). A new approach toward resolving the line and staff dilemma. *Academy of Management Review, 4*(1), 103–106.

O'Bannon, D. P., & Pearce, C. L. (1999). An exploratory examination of gainsharing in service organizations: Implications for organizational citizenship behavior and pay satisfaction. *Journal of Managerial Issues, 11*(3), 363–378.

O'Boyle, E. H., Forsyth, D. R., & O'Boyle, A. S. (2011). Bad apples or bad barrels: An examination of group- and organizational-level effects in the study of counterproductive work behavior. *Group and Organization Management, 36*(1), 39–69.

O'Connell, B. (2020, 6/13/2020). *Performance management evolves: Annual appraisals are falling out of favor as companies open lines of communication and provide regular feedback and coaching to workers.* Society for Human Resource Management (SHRM). Retrieved 6/16/2021 from www.shrm.org/hr-today/news/all-things-work/pages/performance-management-evolves.aspx

O'Connor, J. (1977). *O'Connor finger dexterity test.* Lafayette, IN: Lafayette Instrument.

O'Donovan, R., & McAuliffe, E. (2020). A systematic review exploring the content and outcomes of interventions to improve psychological safety, speaking up and voice behaviour. *BMC Health Services Research, 20*(1), 1–11.

O'Driscoll, M. P., & Eubanks, J. L. (1993). Behavioral competencies, goal-setting, and OD practitioner effectiveness. *Group & Organization Management, 18*(3), 308–327.

Offermann, L. R., Basford, T. E., Graebner, R., Jaffer, S., De Graaf, S. B., & Kaminsky, S. E. (2014). See no evil: Color blindness and perceptions of subtle racial discrimination in the workplace. *Cultural Diversity and Ethnic Minority Psychology, 20*(4), 499.

Offermann, L. R., Matos, K., & DeGraaf, S. B. (2014). Estan hablando de mi? Challenges for multilingual organizations. *Journal of Managerial Psychology, 29*(6), 644–660.

O'Leonard, K. (2014). *The corporate learning factbook: Benchmarks, trends and analysis of the U.S. training market.* Bersin.

Olian, J. D., Carroll, S. J., & Giannantonio, C. M. (1993). Mentor reactions to protégés: An experiment with managers. *Journal of Vocational Behavior, 43*(2), 266–278.

Oliver, N. (1990). Work rewards, work values, and organizational commitment in an employee-owned firm: Evidence from the U.K. *Human Relations, 43*(6), 513–526.

O'Malley, A. L., & Gregory, J. B. (2011). Don't be such a downer: Using positive psychology to enhance the value of negative feedback. *The Psychologist-Manager Journal, 14*(4), 247–264.

O'Neil, J., & Marsick, V. J. (2014). Action learning coaching. *Advances in Developing Human Resources, 16*(2), 202–221.

Ones, D. S. (2005). Personality at work: Raising awareness and correcting misconceptions. *Human Performance, 18*(4), 389–404.

Ones, D. S., & Viswesvaran, C. (1998). The effects of social desirability and faking on personality and integrity assessment for personnel selection. *Human Performance, 11*, 245–269.

Ones, D. S., & Viswesvaran, C. (2007). A research note on the incremental validity of job knowledge and integrity tests for predicting maximal performance. *Human Performance, 20*(3), 293–303.

Ones, D. S., Viswesvaran, C., & Schmidt, F. L. (2017). Realizing the full potential of psychometric meta-analysis for a cumulative science and practice of human resource management. *Human Resource Management Review, 27*(1), 201–215.

Onyeador, I. N., Wittlin, N. M., Burke, S. E., Dovidio, J. F., Perry, S. P., Hardeman, R. R., Dyrbye, L. N., Herrin, J., Phelan, S. M., & van Ryn, M. (2020). The value of interracial contact for reducing anti-Black bias among non-Black physicians: A cognitive habits and growth evaluation (CHANGE) study report. *Psychological Science, 31*(1), 18–30.

Oostrom, J. K., Lehmann-Willenbrock, N., & Klehe, U.-C. (2019). A new scoring procedure in assessment centers: Insights from interaction analysis. *Personnel Assessment and Decisions, 5*(1), 5–14.

Orbach, M., Demko, M., Doyle, J., Waber, B. N., & Pentland, A. (2015). Sensing informal networks in organizations. *American Behavioral Scientist, 59*(4), 508–524.

O'Reilly, C. A. (1978). The intentional distortion of information in organizational communication: A laboratory and field approach. *Human Relations, 31*(2), 173–193.

O'Reilly, C. A. (1989). Corporations, culture, and commitment: Motivation and social control in organizations. *California Management Review, 31*(4), 9–25.

O'Reilly, C. A., & Chatman, J. A. (1996). Culture as social control: Corporations, cults, and commitment. *Research in Organizational Behavior, 18*, 157–200.

O'Reilly, C. A., Chatman, J. A., & Caldwell, D. (1991). People and organizational culture: A Q-sort approach to assessing person-organization fit. *Academy of Management Journal, 34*(3), 487–516.

O'Reilly, C. A., & Roberts, K. H. (1976). Relationships among components of credibility and communication behaviors in work units. *Journal of Applied Psychology, 61*(1), 99–102.

O'Reilly, C. A. and Tushman, M. L. (2004). The ambidextrous organization. *Harvard Business Review, 82*(4), 74–83.

Organ, D. W. (1988). *Organizational citizenship behavior: The good soldier syndrome.* Lexington, MA: Lexington.

Organ, D. W. (1990). The motivational basis of organizational citizenship behavior. In B. M. Staw & L. L. Cummings (Eds.), *Research in organizational behavior* (Vol. 14, pp. 43–72). Greenwich, CT: JAI Press.

Organ, D. W. (2018). Organizational citizenship behavior: Recent trends and developments. *Annual Review of Organizational Psychology and Organizational Behavior, 80,* 295–306.

Organ, D. W., & Ryan, K. (1995). A meta-analytic review of attitudinal and dispositional predictors of organizational citizenship behavior. *Personnel Psychology, 48,* 775–802.

Ortega, J. (2001). Job rotation as a learning mechanism. *Management Science, 47*(10), 1361–1370.

Osborn, A. F. (1957). *Applied imagination.* New York: Charles Scribner's.

Ostroff, C. (1993). The effects of climate and personal influences on individual behavior and attitudes in organizations. *Organizational Behavior and Human Decision Processes, 56*(1), 56–90.

Ostroff, C., & Ford, J. K. (1989). Assessing training needs: Critical levels of analysis. In I. L. Goldstein (Ed.), *Training and development in organizations* (pp. 25–62). San Francisco, CA: Jossey-Bass.

Ostroff, C., & Kozlowski, S. W. J. (1992). Organizational socialization as a learning process: The role of information acquisition. *Personnel Psychology, 45*(4), 849–874.

Ostroff, C., & Kozlowski, S. W. J. (1993). The role of mentoring in the information gathering processes of newcomers during early organizational socialization. *Journal of Vocational Behavior, 42*(2), 170–183.

Ostrove, J. M., & Brown, K. T. (2018). Are allies who we think they are? A comparative analysis. *Journal of Applied Social Psychology, 48*(4), 195–204.

Ostrove, J. M., Kornfeld, M., & Ibrahim, M. (2019). Actors against ableism? Qualities of nondisabled allies from the perspective of people with physical disabilities. *Journal of Social Issues, 75*(3), 924–942.

O'Sullivan, M. (2005). Emotional intelligence and deception detection: Why most people can't "read" others, but a few can. In R. E. Riggio & R. S. Feldman (Eds.), *Applications of nonverbal communication* (pp. 215–253). Mahwah, NJ: Erlbaum.

Oswald, F. L., Behrend, T. S., Putka, D. J., & Sinar, E. (2020). Big data in industrial-organizational psychology and human resource management: Forward progress for organizational research and practice. *Annual Review of Organizational Psychology and Organizational Behavior, 7,* 505–533.

Otis, A. S. (1929). *Self-administering test of mental ability.* Tarrytown-on-Hudson, NY: World.

Owen, H. F., & Arnold, J. N. (1942). Purdue Blueprint Reading Test. Purdue University, University book store.

Palmer, A. (2020, 6/16/2020). *Amazon is rolling out cameras that can detect if warehouse workers are following social distancing rules.* Retrieved 6/16/2021 from www.cnbc.com/2020/06/16/amazon-using-cameras-to-enforce-social-distancing-rules-at-warehouses.html

Paludi, M. A. (Ed.).(2015). *Bullies in the workplace: Seeing and stopping adults who abuse their co-workers and employees.* Santa Barbara, CA: Praeger/ABC-CLIO.

Pande, P. S., Neuman, R. P., & Cavanagh, R. R. (2000). *The Six Sigma way: How GE, Motorola, and other top companies are honing their performance.* New York: McGraw-Hill.

Parasuraman, S., & Alutto, J. A. (1984). Sources and outcomes of stress in organizational settings: Toward the development of a structural model. *Academy of Management Journal, 27*(2), 330–350.

Parker, C. P., Dipboye, R. L., & Jackson, S. L. (1995). Perceptions of organizational politics: An investigation of antecedents and consequences. *Journal of Management, 21*(5), 891–912.

Parker, D. W., Holesgrove, M., & Pathak, R. (2015). Improving productivity with self-organised teams and agile leadership. *International Journal of Productivity and Performance Management, 64*(1), 112–128.

Parker, K., Minkin, R., & Bennett, J. (2020). Economic fallout from COVID-19 continues to hit lower-income Americans the hardest. *Pew Research Center,* 21.

Parker, S. K. (2014). Beyond motivation: Job and work design for development, health, ambidexterity, and more. *Annual Review of Psychology, 65,* 661–691.

Parr, A. D., Lanza, S. T., & Bernthal, P. (2016). Personality profiles of effective leadership performance in assessment centers. *Human Performance, 29*(2), 143–157.

Parsons, H. M. (1974). What happened at Hawthorne? *Science, 183,* 922–932.

Patall, E. A., Cooper, H., & Robinson, J. C. (2008). The effects of choice on intrinsic motivation and related outcomes: A meta-analysis of research findings. *Psychological Bulletin, 134*(2), 270–300.

Paul, J., & Jefferson, F. (2019). A comparative analysis of student performance in an online vs. face-to-face environmental science course from 2009 to 2016. *Frontiers in Computer Science, 1,* 1–9.

Paulus, P. B., & Dzindolet, M. T. (1993). Social influence processes in group brainstorming. *Journal of Personality and Social Psychology, 64*(4), 575–586.

Paustian-Underdahl, S. C., Walker, L. S., & Woehr, D. J. (2014). Gender and perceptions of leadership effectiveness: A meta-analysis of contextual moderators. *Journal of Applied Psychology, 99*(6), 1129–1141.

Pearce, C. L., & Conger, J. A. (Eds.). (2003). *Shared leadership: Reframing the hows and whys of leadership.* Thousand Oaks, CA: Sage.

Pearce, J. L., Stevenson, W. B., & Perry, J. L. (1985). Managerial compensation based on organizational performance: A time series analysis of the effects of merit pay. *Academy of Management Journal, 28*(2), 261–278.

Peck, J. A., & Levashina, J. (2017). Impression management and interview and job performance ratings: A meta-analysis of research design with tactics in mind. *Frontiers in Psychology, 8*, 201–211.

Pelled, L. H., & Xin, K. R. (1999). Down and out: An investigation of the relationship between mood and employee withdrawal behavior. *Journal of Management, 25*(6), 875–895.

Peluchette, J. V. E., & Karl, K. (2018). "She's got the look": Examining feminine and provocative dress in the workplace. In A. M. Broadbridge & S. L. Fielden (Eds.), *Research handbook of diversity and careers* (pp. 116–128). Edward Elgar.

Peretz, H., & Fried, Y. (2012). National cultures, performance appraisal practices, and organizational absenteeism and turnover: A study across 21 countries. *Journal of Applied Psychology, 97*(2), 448–459.

Perrewé, P. L., Zellars, K. L., Rossi, A. M., Ferris, G. R., Kacmar, C. J., Liu, Y., Zinko, R., & Hochwater, W. A. (2005). Political skill: An antidote in the role overload-strain relationship. *Journal of Occupational Health Psychology, 10*(3), 239–250.

Perrow, C. (1970). *Organizational analysis: A sociological perspective.* Belmont, CA: Wadsworth.

Perry, N. (1998). Indecent exposures: Theorizing whistleblowing. *Organization Studies, 19*(2), 235–257.

Peters, D., Calvo, R. A., & Ryan, R. M. (2018). Designing for motivation, engagement and wellbeing in digital experience. *Frontiers in Psychology, 9*, 797–810.

Phetmisy, C. N., & King, D. D. (2021). The ubiquitous effects of financial stress during pandemics and beyond: Opportunities for industrial and organizational psychology. *Industrial and Organizational Psychology, 14*(1–2), 90–93.

Phillips, K. W., Liljenquist, K. A., & Neale, M. A. (2009). Is the pain worth the gain? The advantages and liabilities of agreeing with socially distinct newcomers. *Personality and Social Psychology Bulletin, 35*(3), 336–350. https://doi.org/10.1177/0146167208328062

Phillips, K. W., Northcraft, G. B., & Neale, M. A. (2006). Surface-level diversity and decision-making in goups: When does deep-level similarity help? *Group Processes & Intergroup Relations, 9*(4), 467–482. https://doi.org/10.1177/1368430206067557

Pingitore, R., Dugoni, B. L., Tindale, R. S., & Spring, B. (1994). Bias against overweight job applicants in a simulated employment interview. *Journal of Applied Psychology, 79*(6), 909–917.

Pinkley, R. L., Brittain, J., Neale, M. A., & Northcraft, G. B. (1995). Managerial third-party dispute intervention: An inductive analysis of intervenor strategy selection. *Journal of Applied Psychology, 80*(3), 386–402.

Pinzler, I. K., & Ellis, D. (1989). Wage discrimination and comparable worth: A legal perspective. *Journal of Social Issues, 45*, 51–65.

Pirola-Merlo, A. (2010). Agile innovation: The role of team climate in rapid research and development. *Journal of Occupational and Organizational Psychology, 83*(4), 1075–1084.

Piszczek, M. M., & Pimputkar, A. S. (2020). Flexible schedules across working lives: Age-specific effects on well-being and work. *Journal of Applied Psychology* (forthcoming). https://doi.org/ 10.1037/apl0000844

Plachy, R. (1998). *More results-oriented job descriptions: 226 models to use or adapt with guidelines for creating your own.* ACACOM.

Ployhart, R. E., Schmitt, N., & Tippins, N. T. (2017). Solving the supreme problem: 100 years of selection and recruitment at the *Journal of Applied Psychology. Journal of Applied Psychology, 102*(3), 291–304.

Podsakoff, P. M., & MacKenzie, S. B. (1997). Impact of organizational citizenship behavior on organizational performance: A review and suggestions for future research. *Human Performance, 10*, 133–151.

Podsakoff, P. M., MacKenzie, S. B., Paine, J. B., & Bachrach, D. G. (2000). Organizational citizenship behaviors: A critical review of the theoretical and empirical literature and suggestions for future research. *Journal of Management, 26*(3), 513–563.

Podsakoff, P. M., & Schriesheim, C. A. (1985). Field studies of French and Raven's bases of power: Critique, reanalysis, and suggestions for future research. *Psychological Bulletin, 97*(3), 387–411.

Pogrebtsova, E., Luta, D., & Hausdorf, P. A. (2020). Selection of gender-incongruent applicants: No gender bias with structured interviews. *International Journal of Selection and Assessment, 28*(1), 117–121.

Poon, J. M. L. (2003). Situational antecedents and outcomes of organizational politics perceptions. *Journal of Managerial Psychology, 18*, 138–155.

Porter, C. M., & Rigby, J. R. (2021). The turnover contagion process: An integrative review of theoretical and empirical research. *Journal of Organizational Behavior, 42*(2), 212–228.

Porter, L. W., Allen, R. W., & Angle, H. L. (1981). The politics of upward influence in organizations. In B. Staw (Ed.), *Research in organizational behavior* (pp. 109–149). Greenwich, CT: JAI Press.

Porter, L. W., & Lawler, E. E. (1968). *Managerial attitudes and performance.* Homewood, IL: Irwin.

Porter, L. W., & Roberts, K. H. (1976). Communication in organizations. In M. D. Dunnette (Ed.), *Handbook of industrial and organizational psychology* (pp. 1553–1589). Skokie, IL: Rand McNally.

Porter, L. W., Steers, R. M., Mowday, R. T., & Boulian, P. V. (1974). Organizational commitment, job satisfaction, and turnover among psychiatric technicians. *Journal of Applied Psychology, 59*(5), 603–609.

Post, J. M., & Panis, L. K. (2011). Crimes of obedience: "Groupthink" at Abu Ghraib. *International Journal of Group Psychotherapy, 61*(1), 49–66.

Postmes, T., Spears, R., & Cihangir, S. (2001). Quality of decision making and group norms. *Journal of Personality and Social Psychology, 80*(6), 918–930.

Powers, K. (2019). History of industrial organizational psychology. In B. Mosher & R. Cox IV (Eds.), *Workplace psychology.* Chemeketa Press.

Primoff, E. (1975). *How to prepare and conduct job element examinations.* Personnel Research and Development Center, Washington, DC: U.S. Government Printing Office.

Pritchard, R. D., Hollenback, J., & DeLeo, P. J. (1980). The effects of continuous and partial schedules of reinforcement on effort, performance, and satisfaction. *Organizational Behavior and Human Performance, 25*(3), 336–353.

Probst, T. M. (2003). Exploring employee outcomes of organizational restructuring: A Solomon four-group study. *Group & Organization Management, 28*(3), 416–439.

Pulakos, E. D., Arad, S., Donovan, M. A., & Plamondon, K. E. (2000). Adaptability in the workplace: Development of a taxonomy of adaptive performance. *Journal of Applied Psychology, 85*, 612–624.

Pulakos, E. D., Hanson, R. M., Arad, S., & Moye, N. (2015). Performance management can be fixed: An on-the-job experiential learning approach for complex behavior change. *Industrial and Organizational Psychology, 8*(1), 51–76.

Putka, D. J., & Hoffman, B. J. (2013). Clarifying the contribution of assessee-, dimension-, exercise-, and assessor-related effects to reliable and unreliable variance in assessment center ratings. *Journal of Applied Psychology, 98*(1), 114–133.

Qiadan, E., Tziner, A., & Waismel-Manor, R. (2012). Differences in the perceived effectiveness of influence tactics among Jews and Arabs: The mediating role of cultural values 1. *Journal of Applied Social Psychology, 42*(4), 874–889.

Quiñones, M. A. (1997). Contextual influences on training effectiveness. In M. A. Quiñones & A. Ehrenstein (Eds.), *Training for a rapidly changing workplace: Applications of psychological research* (pp. 177–199). Washington, DC: American Psychological Association.

Rabelo, V. C., Robotham, K. J., & McCluney, C. L. (2020). "Against a sharp white background": How Black women experience the white gaze at work. *Gender, Work & Organization, 28*, 1840–1858.

Rademacher, R., Simpson, D., & Marcdante, K. (2010). Critical incidents as a method for teaching professionalism. *Medical Teacher, 32*, 244–249.

Rafaeli, A., & Pratt, M. G. (Eds.). (2006). *Artifacts and organizations: Beyond mere symbolism.* Mahwah, NJ: Erlbaum.

Rafferty, A. E., & Griffin, M. A. (2006). Perceptions of organizational change: A stress and coping perspective. *Journal of Applied Psychology, 91*(5), 1154–1162.

Ragins, B. R., & Cotton, J. L. (1993). Gender and willingness to mentor in organizations. *Journal of Management, 19*(1), 97–116.

Ragins, B. R., & Cotton, J. L. (1999). Mentor functions and outcomes: A comparison of men and women in formal and informal mentoring relationships. *Journal of Applied Psychology, 84*(4), 529–550.

Ragins, B. R., Cotton, J. L., & Miller, J. S. (2000). Marginal mentoring: The effects of type of mentor, quality of relationship, and program design on work and career attitudes. *Academy of Management Journal, 43*(6), 1177–1194.

Ragins, B. R., & Ehrhardt, K. (2021). Gaining perspective: The impact of close cross-race friendships on diversity training and education. *Journal of Applied Psychology, 106*(6), 856–881.

Ragins, B. R., Lyness, K. S., Williams, L. J., & Winkel, D. (2014). Life spillovers: The spillover of fear of home foreclosure to the workplace. *Personnel Psychology, 67*(4), 763–800.

Ragins, B. R., & Scandura, T. A. (1993, April). *Expected costs and benefits of being a mentor.* Paper presented at 8th Annual Conference of the Society for Industrial/Organizational Psychology, San Francisco, CA.

Ramawickrama, J., Opatha, H., & Puspakumari, M. (2017). A synthesis towards the construct of job performance. *International Business Research, 10*(10), 1–16.

Randel, A. E., Galvin, B. M., Shore, L. M., Ehrhart, K. H., Chung, B. G., Dean, M. A., & Kedharnath, U. (2018). Inclusive leadership: Realizing positive outcomes through belongingness and being valued for uniqueness. *Human Resource Management Review, 28*(2), 190–203.

Rantanen, M., Mauno, S., Kinnunen, U., & Rantanen, J. (2011). Do individual coping strategies help or harm in the work-family conflict situation? Examining coping as a moderator between work-family conflict and well-being. *International Journal of Stress Management, 18*(1), 24–48.

Rao, V. S. (1995). Effects of teleconferencing technologies: An exploration of comprehension, feedback, satisfaction and role-related differences. *Group Decision and Negotiation, 4*(3), 251–272.

Rasskazova, E., Ivanova, T., & Sheldon, K. (2016). Comparing the effects of low-level and high-level worker need-satisfaction: A synthesis of the self-determination and Maslow need theories. *Motivation and Emotion, 40*(4), 541–555.

Rattan, A., & Dweck, C. S. (2018). What happens after prejudice is confronted in the workplace? How mindsets affect minorities' and women's outlook on future social relations. *Journal of Applied Psychology, 103*(6), 676.

Raven, B. H. (1992). A power/interaction model of interpersonal influence: French & Raven thirty years later. *Journal of Social Behavior and Personality, 7*, 217–244.

Raven, B. H., Schwarzwald, J., & Koslowsky, M. (1998). Conceptualizing and measuring a power/interaction model of interpersonal influence. *Journal of Applied Social Psychology, 28*(4), 307–322.

Raven, J., & Raven, J. (2003). Raven Progressive Matrices. In R. S. McCallum (Ed.), Handbook of nonverbal assessment (pp. 223–237). Kluwer Academic/Plenum Publishers.

Raver, J. L., & Nishii, L. H. (2010). Once, twice, or three times as harmful? Ethnic harassment, gender harassment, and generalized workplace harassment. *Journal of Applied Psychology, 95*(2), 236–254.

Reiley, P. J., & Jacobs, R. R. (2016). Ethics matter: Moderating leaders' power use and followers' citizenship behavior. *Journal of Business Ethics, 134*(1), 69–81.

Reilly, R. R., & McGourty, J. (1998). Performance appraisal in team settings. In J. W. Smither (Ed.), *Performance appraisal: State of the art in practice* (pp. 244–277). San Francisco, CA: Jossey-Bass.

Reinsch Jr, N. L., & Beswick, R. W. (1995). Preferences for sending word-processed versus handwritten messages: An exploratory study. *Journal of Business and Technical Communication, 9*(1), 45–62.

Rennesund, A. B., & Saksvik, P. O. (2010). Work performance norms and organizational efficacy as cross-level effects on the relationship between individual perceptions of self-efficacy, overcommitment, and work-related stress. *European Journal of Work and Organizational Psychology, 19*(6), 629–653.

Rentsch, J. R., & Steel, R. P. (1998). Testing the durability of job characteristics as predictors of absenteeism over a six-year period. *Personnel Psychology, 51*(1), 165–190.

Rest, J. R. (1986). *Moral development: Advances in research and theory*. Praeger.

Rice, B. (1982). The Hawthorne defect: Persistence of a flawed theory. *Psychology Today, 16*(2), 70–74.

Rice, R. W. (1978). Construct validity of the least preferred coworker (LPC) score. *Psychological Bulletin, 85*(6), 1199–1237.

Riggio, R. E. (1987). *The charisma quotient*. New York: Dodd-Mead.

Riggio, R. E. (2001). Interpersonal sensitivity research and organizational psychology: Theoretical and methodological applications. In J. A. Hall & F. Bernieri (Eds.), *Measurement of interpersonal sensitivity* (pp. 305–317). Mahwah, NJ: Erlbaum.

Riggio, R. E. (2005). Business applications of nonverbal communication. In R. E. Riggio & R. S. Feldman (Eds.), *Applications of nonverbal communication* (pp. 119–138). Mahwah, NJ: Erlbaum.

Riggio, R. E., Chaleff, I., & Lipman-Blumen, J. (Eds.). (2008). *The art of followership*. San Francisco: Jossey-Bass.

Riggio, R. E., & Cole, E. J. (1992). Agreement between subordinate and superior ratings of supervisory performance and effects on self- and subordinate job satisfaction. *Journal of Occupational and Organizational Psychology, 65*(2), 151–158.

Riggio, R. E., & Cole, E. J. (1995, August). *Stress and coping processes in on-duty firefighters*. Paper presented at meeting of the American Psychological Association, Toronto, Canada.

Riggio, R. E., Mayes, B. T., & Schleicher, D. J. (2003). Using assessment center methods for outcome assessment. *Journal of Management Inquiry, 12*, 68–78.

Riggio, R. E., Murphy, S. E., & Pirozzolo, F. J. (Eds.). (2002). *Multiple intelligences and leadership*. Mahwah, NJ: Erlbaum.

Riggio, R. E., & Reichard, R. J. (2008). The emotional and social intelligences of effective leadership: An emotional and social skill approach. *Journal of Managerial Psychology, 23*(2), 169–185.

Riggio, R. E., & Throckmorton, B. (1988). The relative effects of verbal and nonverbal behavior, appearance, and social skills on evaluations made in hiring interviews. *Journal of Applied Social Psychology, 18*(4), 331–348.

Riordan, C. A. (1989). Images of corporate success. In R. A. Giacalone & P. Rosenfeld (Eds.), *Impression management in the organization* (pp. 87–103). Hillsdale, NJ: Erlbaum.

Rios, K., & Mackey, C. D. (2020). *Group cohesion*. https://doi.org/10.1093/acrefore/9780190236557.013.742

Rioux, S. M., & Penner, L. A. (2001). The causes of organizational citizenship behavior: A motivational analysis. *Journal of Applied Psychology*, *86*(6), 1306–1314.

Ritchie, R. J., & Moses, J. L. (1983). Assessment center correlates of women's advancement into middle management: A 7-year longitudinal analysis. *Journal of Applied Psychology*, *68*, 227–231.

Robbins, S. P. (1979). *Organizational behavior: Concepts and controversies*. Englewood Cliffs, NJ: Prentice Hall.

Robbins, T. L. (1995). Social loafing on cognitive tasks: An examination of the "sucker effect". *Journal of Business and Psychology*, *9*(3), 337–342.

Roberson, L., & Kim, R. (2014). Stereotype threat research hits the sweet spot for organizational psychology. *Industrial and Organizational Psychology*, *7*(3), 450–452.

Roberson, L., & Kulik, C. T. (2007). Stereotype threat at work. *Academy of Management Perspectives*, *21*(2), 24–40.

Roberson, Q., King, E., & Hebl, M. (2020). Designing more effective practices for reducing workplace inequality. *Behavioral Science & Policy*, *6*(1), 39–49.

Robinson, A. N., Arena, D. F., Lindsey, A. P., & Ruggs, E. N. (2020). Expanding how we think about diversity training. *Industrial and Organizational Psychology*, *13*(2), 236–241.

Roche, G. R. (1979). Much ado about mentors. *Harvard Business Review*, *57*, 14–19.

Rodgers, R., & Hunter, J. E. (1991). Impact of management by objectives on organizational productivity. *Journal of Applied Psychology*, *76*(2), 322–336.

Rodríguez-Bailón, R., Moya, M., & Yzerbyt, V. (2000). Why do superiors attend to negative stereotypic information about their subordinates? Effects of power legitimacy on social perception. *European Journal of Social Psychology*, *30*(5), 651–671.

Roethlisberger, F. J., & Dickson, W. J. (1939). *Management and the worker*. Cambridge, MA: Harvard University Press.

Rogelberg, S. G., & Rumery, S. M. (1996). Gender diversity, team decision quality, time on task, and interpersonal cohesion. *Small Group Research*, *27*(1), 79–90.

Rose, R. M. (1987). Neuroendocrine effects of work stress. In J. C. Quick, R. S. Bhagat, J. E. Dalton, & J. D. Quick (Eds.), *Work stress: Health care systems in the workplace* (pp. 130–147). New York: Praeger.

Rosen, C. C., Klein, K. J., & Young, K. M. (1986). *Employee ownership in America: The equity solution*. Lexington, MA: Lexington Books.

Rosen, C. C., Levy, P. E., & Hall, R. J. (2006). Placing perceptions of politics in the context of the feedback environment, employee attitudes, and job performance. *Journal of Applied Psychology*, *91*(1), 211–220.

Rosenman, R. H. (1978). The interview method of assessment of the coronary-prone behavior pattern. In T. M. Dembroski, S. M. Weiss, J. L. Shields, S. G. Haynes, & M. Feinlib (Eds.), *Coronary-prone behavior* (pp. 55–69). New York: Springer-Verlag.

Rosenman, R. H., Friedman, M., Strauss, R., Warm, M., Kositchek, R., Hahn, W., & Werthessen, N. T. (1964). A predictive study of coronary heart disease: The Western Collaborative Group Study. *Journal of the American Medical Association*, *189*, 15–22.

Rosenthal, R. (1991). *Meta-analytic procedures for the social sciences* (2nd ed.). Newbury Park, CA: Sage.

Rosenthal, R. (1994). Interpersonal expectancy effects: A 30-year perspective. *Current Directions in Psychological Science*, *3*(6), 176–179.

Rosette, A. S., de Leon, R. P., Koval, C. Z., & Harrison, D. A. (2018). Intersectionality: Connecting experiences of gender with race at work. *Research in Organizational Behavior*, *38*, 1–22.

Rosette, A. S., Koval, C. Z., Ma, A., & Livingston, R. (2016). Race matters for women leaders: Intersectional effects on agentic deficiencies and penalties. *The Leadership Quarterly*, *27*(3), 429–445.

Rosette, A. S., & Tost, L. P. (2010). Agentic women and communal leadership: How role prescriptions confer advantage to top women leaders. *Journal of Applied Psychology*, *95*(2), 221–235.

Rospenda, K. M., Richman, J. A., Ehmke, J. L. Z., & Zlatoper, K. W. (2005). Is workplace harassment hazardous to your health? *Journal of Business and Psychology*, *20*(1), 95–110.

Rost-Roth, M. (2010). Intercultural training. In D. Matsumoto (Ed.), *APA handbook of intercultural communication* (pp. 293–315). Washington, DC: American Psychological Association.

Roth, P. L., Bobko, P., & McFarland, L. A. (2005). A meta-analysis of work sample test validity: Updating and integrating some classic literature. *Personnel Psychology*, *58*, 1009–1037.

Roth, P. L., & Campion, J. E. (1992). An analysis of the predictive power of the panel interview and pre-employment tests. *Journal of Occupational and Organizational Psychology*, *65*(1), 51–60.

Roth, P. L., Van Iddekinge, C. H., DeOrtentiis, P. S., Hackney, K. J., Zhang, L., & Buster, M. A. (2017). Hispanic and Asian performance on selection procedures: A narrative and meta-analytic review of 12 common predictors. *Journal of Applied Psychology*, *102*(8), 1178.

Rothausen, T. J., Gonzalez, J. A., & Griffin, A. E. C. (2009). Are all the parts there everywhere? Facet job satisfaction in the United States and the Philippines. *Asia Pacific Journal of Management*, *26*(4), 681–700.

Rothausen, T. J., & Henderson, K. E. (2019). Meaning-based job-related well-being: Exploring a meaningful work conceptualization of job satisfaction. *Journal of Business and Psychology, 34*(3), 357–376.

Rousseau, V., & Aubé, C. (2018). When leaders stifle innovation in work teams: The role of abusive supervision. *Journal of Business Ethics, 151*(3), 651–664.

Roznowski, M. (1989). Examination of the measurement properties of the Job Descriptive Index with experimental items. *Journal of Applied Psychology, 74*(5), 805–814.

Rudert, S. C., Ruf, S., & Greifeneder, R. (2020). Whom to punish? How observers sanction norm-violating behavior in ostracism situations. *European Journal of Social Psychology, 50*(2), 376–391.

Rudolph, C. W., Allan, B., Clark, M., Hertel, G., Hirschi, A., Kunze, F., Shockley, K., Shoss, M., Sonnentag, S., & Zacher, H. (2021). Pandemics: Implications for research and practice in industrial and organizational psychology. *Industrial and Organizational Psychology, 14*(1–2), 1–35.

Ruggs, E., & Hebl, M. (2012). Diversity, inclusion, and cultural awareness for classroom and outreach education. In B. Bogue & E. Cady (Eds.), *Apply research to practice (ARP) resources* (pp. 1–16). AWE Online.

Ruggs, E. N., & Avery, D. R. (2020). Organizations cannot afford to stay silent on racial injustice. *MIT Sloan Management Review, 61*(4), 1–3.

Ruggs, E. N., Hebl, M. R., Rabelo, V. C., Weaver, K. B., Kovacs, J., & Kemp, A. S. (2016). Baltimore is burning: Can IO psychologists help extinguish the flames? *Industrial and Organizational Psychology, 9*(3), 525–547.

Ruggs, E. N., Law, C., Cox, C. B., Roehling, M. V., Wiener, R. L., Hebl, M. R., & Barron, L. (2013). Gone fishing: I–O psychologists' missed opportunities to understand marginalized employees' experiences with discrimination. *Industrial and Organizational Psychology, 6*(1), 39–60.

Ruggs, E. N., Martinez, L. R., & Hebl, M. R. (2011). How individuals and organizations can reduce interpersonal discrimination. *Social and Personality Psychology Compass, 5*(1), 29–42.

Rupp, D. E., Song, Q. C., & Strah, N. (2020). Addressing the so-called validity–diversity trade-off: Exploring the practicalities and legal defensibility of Pareto-optimization for reducing adverse impact within personnel selection. *Industrial and Organizational Psychology, 13*(2), 246–271.

Russell, J. S. (1984). A review of fair employment cases in the field of training. *Personnel Psychology, 37*, 261–276.

Ryan, A. M., & Derous, E. (2019). The unrealized potential of technology in selection assessment. *Journal of Work and Organizational Psychology, 35*(2), 85–92.

Ryan, A. M., & Ployhart, R. E. (2014). A century of selection. *Annual Review of Psychology, 65*, 693–717.

Ryan, R. M., & Deci, E. L. (2000). Self-determination theory and the facilitation of intrinsic motivation, social development, and well-being. *American Psychologist, 55*(1), 68–78.

Rynes, S. L. (1988). *The employment interview as a recruitment device* (Publication Number 1988-05-29) Cornell University.

Rynes, S. L. (1993). When recruitment fails to attract: Individual expectations meet organizational realities in recruitment. In H. Schuler, J. L. Farr, & M. Smith (Eds.), *Personnel selection and assessment: Individual and organizational perspectives* (pp. 27–40). Hillsdale, NJ: Erlbaum.

Sachdev, A. R., Grossman, R., & Burke-Smalley, L. A. (2019). Beyond "checking the box": Using accountability to promote the effectiveness of sexual misconduct training. *Industrial and Organizational Psychology, 12*(1), 100–105.

Sackett, P. R., & Mullen, E. J. (1993). Beyond formal experimental design: Towards an expanding view of the training evaluation process. *Personnel Psychology, 46*, 613–627.

Sadowski-Rasters, G., Duysters, G., & Sadowski, B. M. (2006). *Communication and cooperation in the virtual workplace: Teamwork in computer-mediated-communication.* Northampton, MA: Edward Elgar.

Sajjadiani, S., Sojourner, A. J., Kammeyer-Mueller, J. D., & Mykerezi, E. (2019). Using machine learning to translate applicant work history into predictors of performance and turnover. *Journal of Applied Psychology, 104*(10), 1207–1225.

Saks, A. M. (2006). Antecedents and consequences of employee engagement. *Journal of Managerial Psychology, 21*(7), 600–619.

Salancik, G. R., & Pfeffer, J. (1977). Who gets power and how they hold on to it: A strategic-contingency model of power. *Organizational Dynamics, 5*(3), 3–21.

Salas, E., & Cannon-Bowers, J. A. (2001). The science of training: A decade of progress. *Annual Review of Psychology, 52*(1), 471–499.

Salas, E., DiazGranados, D., Klein, C., Burke, C. S., Stagl, K. C., Goodwin, G. F., & Halpin, S. M. (2008). Does team training improve team performance? A meta-analysis. *Human Factors, 50*(6), 903–933.

Salas, E., Kozlowski, S. W., & Chen, G. (2017). A century of progress in industrial and organizational psychology: Discoveries and the next century. *Journal of Applied Psychology, 102*(3), 589–598.

Salas, E., Rozell, D., Mullen, B., & Driskell, J. E. (1999). The effect of team building on performance: An integration. *Small Group Research, 30*(3), 309–329.

Salas, E., Salazar, M. R., Feitosa, J., & Kramer, W. S. (2014). Collaboration and conflict in teams. In B. Schneider & K. M. Barbera (Eds.), *Oxford handbook of organizational climate and culture* (pp. 382–399). New York: Oxford University Press.

Salgado, J. F., Anderson, N., Moscoso, S., Bertua, C., & de Fruyt, F. (2003). International validity generalization of GMA and cognitive abilities: A European community meta-analysis. *Personnel Psychology, 56*, 573–605.

Salimäki, A., & Jämsén, S. (2010). Perceptions of politics and fairness in merit pay. *Journal of Managerial Psychology, 25*(3), 229–251.

Sallis, J. F., Johnson, C. C., Trevorrow, T. R., Hovell, M. F., & Kaplan, R. M. (1985, August). *Worksite stress management: Anything goes?* Paper presented at the meeting of the American Psychological Association, Los Angeles, CA.

Sanchez-Hucles, J. V., & Davis, D. D. (2010). Women and women of color in leadership: Complexity, identity, and intersectionality. *American Psychologist, 65*(3), 171–181.

Santos, C. M., Uitdewilligen, S., & Passos, A. M. (2015). Why is your team more creative than mine? The influence of shared mental models on intra-group conflict, team creativity and effectiveness. *Creativity and Innovation Management, 24*(4), 645–658.

Sarkar-Barney, S. (2004). The role of national culture in enhancing training effectiveness: A framework. In *Cultural ergonomics*. Emerald.

Sawang, S., O'Connor, P. J., Kivits, R. A., & Jones, P. (2020). Business owner-managers' job autonomy and job satisfaction: Up, down or no change? *Frontiers in Psychology, 11*, 1508–1522.

Sawyer, J. E., Latham, W. R., Pritchard, R. D., & Bennett, W. R., Jr. (1999). Analysis of work group productivity in an applied setting: Application of a time series panel design. *Personnel Psychology, 52*(4), 927–947.

Scandura, T. A., & Graen, G. B. (1984). Moderating effects of initial leader-member exchange status on the effects of a leadership intervention. *Journal of Applied Psychology, 69*(3), 428–436.

Scandura, T. A., & Williams, E. A. (2001). An investigation of the moderating effects of gender on the relationships between mentorship initiation and protégé perceptions of mentoring functions. *Journal of Vocational Behavior, 59*(3), 342–363.

Scarpello, V., & Campbell, J. P. (1983). Job satisfaction: Are all the parts there? *Personnel Psychology, 36*(3), 577–600.

Scarpello, V., & Vandenberg, R. J. (1992). Generalizing the importance of occupational and career views to job satisfaction attitudes. *Journal of Organizational Behavior, 13*(2), 125–140.

Schalken, N., & Rietbergen, C. (2017). The reporting quality of systematic reviews and meta-analyses in industrial and organizational psychology: A systematic review. *Frontiers in Psychology, 8*, 1395.

Schaufeli, W. B., Shimazu, A., Hakanen, J., Salanova, M., & De Witte, H. (2019). An ultra-short measure for work engagement: The UWES-3 validation across five countries. *European Journal of Psychological Assessment, 35*(4), 577–591.

Schaumberg, R. L., & Flynn, F. J. (2017). Clarifying the link between job satisfaction and absenteeism: The role of guilt proneness. *Journal of Applied Psychology, 102*(6), 982.

Schein, E. H. (1969). *Process consultation: Its role in organization development*. Reading, MA: Addison-Wesley.

Schein, E. H. (1992). *Organizational culture and leadership* (2nd ed.). San Francisco, CA: Jossey-Bass.

Schleicher, D. J., Baumann, H. M., Sullivan, D. W., & Yim, J. (2019). Evaluating the effectiveness of performance management: A 30-year integrative conceptual review. *Journal of Applied Psychology, 104*(7), 851–887.

Schleicher, D. J., Bull, R. A., & Green, S. G. (2009). Rater reactions to forced distribution rating systems. *Journal of Management, 35*(4), 899–927.

Schleicher, D. J., Day, D. V., Mayes, B. T., & Riggio, R. E. (2002). A new frame for frame of reference training: Enhancing the construct validity of assessment centers. *Journal of Applied Psychology, 87*, 735–746.

Schmidt, F. L., Hunter, J. E., Mc Kenzie, R. C., & Muldrow, T. W. (1979). Impact of valid selection procedures on work-force productivity. *Journal of Applied Psychology, 64*, 609–626.

Schmidt, R. A., & Bjork, R. A. (1992). New conceptualizations of practice: Common principles in these paradigms suggest new concepts for training. *Psychological Science, 3*(4), 207–217.

Schminke, M., Ambrose, M. L., & Cropanzano, R. S. (2000). The effect of organizational structure on perceptions of procedural fairness. *Journal of Applied Psychology, 85*(2), 294–304.

Schneider, B., Brief, A. P., & Guzzo, R. A. (1996). Creating a climate and culture for sustainable organizational change. *Organizational Dynamics, 24*(4), 7–19.

Schneider, B., Erhart, M. G., & Macey, W. H. (2011). Perspectives on organizational climate and culture. In S. Zedeck (Ed.), *APA handbook of industrial and organizational psychology* (Vol. 1, pp. 373–414). Washington, DC: American Psychological Association.

Schneider, B., Ehrhart, M. G., & Macey, W. H. (2013). Organizational climate and culture. *Annual Review of Psychology, 64*, 361–388.

Schneider, J., & Locke, E. A. (1971). A critique of Herzberg's incident classification system and a suggested revision. *Organizational Behavior and Human Performance, 6*(4), 441–457.

Schriesheim, C. A., Hinkin, T. R., & Podsakoff, P. M. (1991). Can ipsative and single-item measures produce erroneous results in field studies of French and Raven's (1959) five bases of power? An empirical investigation. *Journal of Applied Psychology, 76*(1), 106–114.

Schwatka, N. V., Goldenhar, L. M., Johnson, S. K., Beldon, M. A., Tessler, J., Dennerlein, J. T., Fullen, M., & Trieu, H. (2019). A training intervention to improve frontline construction leaders' safety leadership practices and overall jobsite safety climate. *Journal of Safety Research, 70*, 253–262.

Schweiger, D. M., Sandberg, W. R., & Ragan, J. W. (1986). Group approaches for improving strategic decision making: A comparative analysis of dialectical inquiry, devil's advocacy, and consensus. *Academy of Management Journal, 29*(1), 51–71.

Scott, G., Leritz, L. E., & Mumford, M. D. (2004). The effectiveness of creativity training: A quantitative review. *Creativity Research Journal, 16*, 361–388.

Scott, K. D., & Taylor, G. S. (1985). An examination of conflicting findings on the relationship between job satisfaction and absenteeism: A meta-analysis. *Academy of Management Journal, 28*, 599–612.

Scott, W. D. (1908). *The psychology of advertising.* New York: Arno Press.

Selye, H. (1976). *The stress of life* (rev. ed.). New York: McGraw-Hill.

Sergent, K., & Stajkovic, A. D. (2020). Women's leadership is associated with fewer deaths during the COVID-19 crisis: Quantitative and qualitative analyses of United States governors. *Journal of Applied Psychology, 105*(8), 771–789.

Sethi, A. S. (1984). Meditation for coping with organizational stress. In A. S. Sethi & R. S. Schuler (Eds.), *Handbook of organizational stress coping strategies* (pp. 145–165). Cambridge, MA: Ballinger.

Sethi, A. S., & Schuler, R. S. (Eds.). (1984). *Handbook of organizational stress coping strategies.* Cambridge, MA: Ballinger.

Seyranian, V., & Bligh, M. C. (2008). Presidential charismatic leadership: Exploring the rhetoric of social change. *The Leadership Quarterly, 19*(1), 54–76.

Shachaf, P. (2008). Cultural diversity and information and communication technology impacts on global virtual teams: An exploratory study. *Information & Management, 45*(2), 131–142.

Shahani, C., Weiner, R., & Streit, M. K. (1993). An investigation of the dispositional nature of the time management construct. *Anxiety, Stress, and Coping, 6*(3), 231–243.

Shaiken, H. (1984). *Work transformed: Automation and labor in the computer age.* New York: Holt, Rinehart & Winston.

Shaw, J. D., Gupta, N., Mitra, A., & Ledford, G. E. (2005). Success and survival of skill-based pay. *Journal of Management, 31*(1), 28–49.

Shaw, M. E. (1964). Communication networks. *Advances in Experimental Social Psychology, 1*, 111–147.

Shaw, M. E. (1978). Communication networks fourteen years later. In L. Berkowitz (Ed.), *Group processes* (pp. 351–362). New York: Academic Press.

Shaw, M. E. (1981). *Group dynamics: The psychology of small group behavior* (3rd ed.). New York: McGraw-Hill.

Sherif, M., Harvey, O. J., White, B. J., Hood, W. R., & Sherif, C. W. (1961). *Intergroup conflict and cooperation: The robbers cave experiment.* Norman, OK: Institute of Group Relations.

Shibly, S. A. (2019). Mapping the holistic impact of realistic job preview-pre-recruitment phase, post-recruitment phase and marketing spillover effect. *Journal of Organizational Psychology, 19*(1), 70–78.

Shin, S. J. (2015). Leadership and creativity: The mechanism perspective. In C. E. Shalley, M. A. Hitt, & J. Zhou (Eds.), *The Oxford handbook of creativity, innovation, and entrepreneurship* (pp. 17–30). New York: Oxford University Press.

Shockley, K. M., Clark, M. A., Dodd, H., & King, E. B. (2020). Work–family strategies during COVID-19: Examining gender dynamics among dual-earner couples with young children. *Journal of Applied Psychology, 106*, 15–28.

Shore, L. M., Cleveland, J. N., & Sanchez, D. (2018). Inclusive workplaces: A review and model. *Human Resource Management Review, 28*(2), 176–189.

Shore, L. M., Randel, A. E., Chung, B. G., Dean, M. A., Holcombe Ehrhart, K., & Singh, G. (2011). Inclusion and diversity in work groups: A review and model for future research. *Journal of Management, 37*(4), 1262–1289.

Shore, L. M., & Wayne, S. J. (1993). Commitment and employee behavior: Comparison of affective commitment and continuance commitment with perceived organizational support. *Journal of Applied Psychology, 78*(5), 774–780.

Shoss, M. K., Jundt, D. K., Kobler, A., & Reynolds, C. (2016). Doing bad to feel better? An investigation of within- and between-person perceptions of counterproductive work behavior as a coping tactic. *Journal of Business Ethics, 137*(3), 571–587.

Shouksmith, G., & Burrough, S. (1988). Job stress factors for New Zealand and Canadian air traffic controllers. *Applied Psychology: An International Review, 37*(3), 263–270.

SHRM. (2012). *The use of criminal background checks in hiring decisions.* Alexandria: Society for Human Resource Management.

Sia, C.-L., Tan, B. C. Y., & Wei, K.-K. (2002). Group polarization and computer-mediated communication: Effects of communication cues, social presence, and anonymity. *Information Systems Research, 13*(1), 70–90.

Sias, P. M., & Jablin, F. M. (1995). Differential superior-subordinate relations, perceptions of fairness, and coworker communication. *Human Communication Research, 22*(1), 5–38.

Silva, S. A., & Fugas, C. S. (2016). Influence of peer norms. In S. Clarke, T. M. Probst, F. Guldenmund, & J. Passmore (Eds.), *The Wiley Blackwell handbook of the psychology of occupational safety and workplace health* (pp. 61–82). New York: Wiley/Blackwell.

SimanTov-Nachlieli, I., & Bamberger, P. (2021). Pay communication, justice, and affect: The asymmetric effects of process and outcome pay transparency on counterproductive workplace behavior. *Journal of Applied Psychology, 106*(2), 230.

Simmons, P. O. (1993). The Judd test for Lotus 1–2–3. *HR Magazine, 38*, 33–36.

Simon, S. J., & Werner, J. M. (1996). Computer training through behavior modeling, self-paced, and instructional approaches: A field experiment. *Journal of Applied Psychology, 81*(6), 648–659.

Sims, R. L., & Keenan, J. P. (1998). Predictors of external whistle-blowing: Organizational and intrapersonal variables. *Journal of Business Ethics, 17*(4), 411–421.

Singletary, S. L., & Hebl, M. R. (2009). Compensatory strategies for reducing interpersonal discrimination: The effectiveness of acknowledgments, increased positivity, and individuating information. *Journal of Applied Psychology, 94*(3), 797.

Sitzmann, T., & Johnson, S. K. (2012). The best laid plans: Examining the conditions under which a planning intervention improves learning and reduces attrition. *Journal of Applied Psychology, 97*(5), 967–981.

Sitzmann, T., & Weinhardt, J. M. (2019). Approaching evaluation from a multilevel perspective: A comprehensive analysis of the indicators of training effectiveness. *Human Resource Management Review, 29*(2), 253–269.

Slemp, G. R., Kern, M. L., Patrick, K. J., & Ryan, R. M. (2018). Leader autonomy support in the workplace: A meta-analytic review. *Motivation and Emotion, 42*(5), 706–724.

Smart Richman, L., & Leary, M. R. (2009). Reactions to discrimination, stigmatization, ostracism, and other forms of interpersonal rejection: a multimotive model. *Psychological Review, 116*(2), 365–383.

Smith, A. N., Watkins, M. B., Burke, M. J., Christian, M. S., Smith, C. E., Hall, A., & Simms, S. (2013). Gendered influence: A gender role perspective on the use and effectiveness of influence tactics. *Journal of Management, 39*(5), 1156–1183.

Smith, C. A., Organ, D. W., & Near, J. P. (1983). Organizational citizenship behavior: Its nature and antecedents. *Journal of Applied Psychology, 68*(4), 653–663.

Smith, D. B., & Shields, J. (2013). Factors related to social service workers' job satisfaction: Revisiting Herzberg's motivation to work. *Administration in Social Work, 37*(2), 189–198.

Smith, E., & Smith, V. (2005). *Apprenticeships: their role in economies and societies across the globe* (Vol. 47). Emerald.

Smith, L., & Folkard, S. (1993). The impact of shiftwork on personnel at a nuclear power plant: An exploratory survey study. *Work & Stress, 7*(4), 341–350.

Smith, P., Balzer, W., Brannick, M., Chia, W., Eggleston, S., Gibson, W., Johnson, B., Josephson, H., Paul, K., & Reilly, C. (1987). The revised JDI: A facelift for an old friend. *The Industrial-Organizational Psychologist, 24*(4), 31–33.

Smith, P. C., Kendall, L. M., & Hulin, C. L. (1969). *The measurement of satisfaction in work and retirement.* Chicago, IL: Rand McNally.

Smith, P. C., Kendall, L. M., & Hulin, C. L. (1985). Job descriptive index. In *The measurement of satisfaction in work and retirement.* Bowling Green, OH: Bowling Green State University.

Smither, J. W., Wohlers, A. J., & London, M. (1995). A field study of reactions to normative versus individualized upward feedback. *Group & Organization Management, 20*(1), 61–89.

Smith-Jentsch, K. A., Jentsch, F. G., Payne, S. C., & Salas, E. (1996). Can pretraining experiences explain individual differences in learning? *Journal of Applied Psychology, 81*(1), 110–116.

Snyder, R. A., & Morris, J. H. (1984). Organizational communication and performance. *Journal of Applied Psychology, 69*(3), 461–465.

Society for Industrial and Organizational Psychology (SIOP). (2018). Principles for the validation and use of personnel selection procedures. *Industrial and Organizational Psychology: Perspectives on Science and Practice, 11(Supl 1)*, 2–97. https://doi.org/10.1017/iop.2018.195

Society for Industrial and Organizational Psychology (SIOP). (2016). *Guidelines for education and training in industrial-organizational psychology.* Retrieved from www.siop.org/Events-Education/Graduate-Training-Program/Guidelines-for-Education-and-Training

Soderlund, J. (2015). Project-based organizations: What are they? In F. Chiocchio, E. K. Kelloway, & B. Hobbs (Eds.), *The psychology and management of project teams* (pp. 74–100). New York: Oxford University Press.

Solomon, R. L. (1949). An extension of control group design. *Psychological Bulletin, 46*, 137–150.

Somech, A., Desivilya, H. S., & Lidogoster, H. (2009). Team conflict management and team effectiveness: The effects of task interdependence and team identification. *Journal of Organizational Behavior, 30*(3), 359–378.

Song, Z., Li, W., & Arvey, R. D. (2011). Associations between dopamine and serotonin genes and job satisfaction: Preliminary evidence from the Add Health Study. *Journal of Applied Psychology, 96*(6), 1223–1233.

Sonnentag, S., Brodbeck, F. C., Heinbokel, T., & Stolte, W. (1994). Stressor–burnout relationship in software development teams. *Journal of Occupational and Organizational Psychology, 67*(4), 327–341.

Sonnentag, S., & Zijlstra, F. R. H. (2006). Job characteristics and off-job activities as predictors of need for recovery, well-being, and fatigue. *Journal of Applied Psychology, 91*(2), 330–350.

Soroko, E. (2012). The presentation of self in letters of application: A mixed-method approach. *Journal of Employment Counseling, 49*, 4–17.

Sparks, K., & Cooper, C. L. (1999). Occupational differences in the work-strain relationship: Towards the use of situation-specific models. *Journal of Occupational and Organizational Psychology, 72*(2), 219–229.

Spector, P. E. (1987). Interactive effects of perceived control and job stressors on affective reactions and health outcomes for clerical workers. *Work and Stress, 1*(2), 155–162.

Spector, P. E. (1992). A consideration of the validity and meaning of self-report measures of job conditions. In C. L. Cooper & I. T. Richardson (Eds.), *International review of industrial and organizational psychology* (Vol. 7, pp. 123–151). New York: Wiley.

Spector, P. E. (1997). *Job satisfaction: Application, assessment, causes, and consequences.* Thousand Oaks, CA: Sage.

Spence, J. T., & Robbins, A. S. (1992). Workaholism: Definition, measurement, and preliminary results. *Journal of Personality Assessment, 58*(1), 160–178.

Spielberger, C. D., & Reheiser, E. C. (1994). The job stress survey: Measuring gender differences in occupational stress. *Journal of Social Behavior and Personality, 9*(2), 199–218.

Spieler, I., Scheibe, S., Stamov-Roßnagel, C., & Kappas, A. (2017). Help or hindrance? Day-level relationships between flextime use, work–nonwork boundaries, and affective well-being. *Journal of Applied Psychology, 102*(1), 67–87.

Spreitzer, G. M. (1996). Social structural characteristics of psychological empowerment. *Academy of Management Journal, 39*(2), 483–504.

Spreitzer, G. M., Cohen, S. G., & Ledford, G. E., Jr. (1999). Developing effective self-managing work teams in service organizations. *Group & Organization Management, 24*(3), 340–366.

Stahelski, A. J., Frost, D. E., & Patch, M. E. (1989). Use of socially dependent bases of power: French and Raven's theory applied to workgroup leadership. *Journal of Applied Social Psychology, 19*(4), 283–297.

Stan, S., Arnold, T. J., McAmis, G., & Evans, K. R. (2021). Salesperson socialization to the consumption of organizationally provided support services: Differences between high-and low-performing salespeople. *Journal of Marketing Theory and Practice, 29*(3), 271–288.

Standage, M., & Ryan, R. M. (2020). Self-determination theory in sport and exercise. *Handbook of Sport Psychology, 1*, 37–56.

Staw, B. M., & Ross, J. (1985). Stability in the midst of change: A dispositional approach to job attitudes. *Journal of Applied Psychology, 70*(3), 469–480.

Stearns, J., & White, C. (2018). Can paid sick leave mandates reduce leave-taking? *Labour Economics, 51*, 227–246.

Steele, C. M., & Aronson, J. (1998). Stereotype threat and the test performance of academically successful African Americans. *Journal of Personality and Social Psychology, 69*, 797–811.

Steele, C. M., Spencer, S. J., & Aronson, J. (2002). Contending with group image: The psychology of stereotype and social identity threat. *Advances in Experimental Social Psychology, 34*, 379–440.

Steelman, L. A., & Wolfeld, L. (2018). The manager as coach: The role of feedback orientation. *Journal of Business and Psychology, 33*(1), 41–53.

Steers, R. M., & Porter, L. W. (Eds.). (1991). *Motivation and work behavior* (5th ed.). New York: McGraw-Hill.

Stein, F. (2001). Occupational stress, relaxation therapies, exercise and biofeedback. *Work: Journal of Prevention, Assessment & Rehabilitation, 17*(3), 235–246.

Steinberg, B. A., Klatt, M., & Duchemin, A.-M. (2017). Feasibility of a mindfulness-based intervention for surgical intensive care unit personnel. *American Journal of Critical Care, 26*(1), 10–18.

Steinmann, B., Ötting, S. K., & Maier, G. W. (2016). Need for affiliation as a motivational add-on for leadership behaviors and managerial success. *Frontiers in Psychology, 7*, 1972–1985.

Sternberg, R. J. (2002). Successful intelligence: A new approach to leadership. In R. E. Riggio, S. E. Murphy, & F. J. Pirozzolo (Eds.), *Multiple intelligences and leadership* (pp. 9–28). Mahwah, NJ: Erlbaum.

Stevens, C. K. (1998). Antecedents of interview interactions, interviewers' ratings, and applicants' reactions. *Personnel Psychology, 51*(1), 55–85.

Stevens, M. J., & Campion, M. A. (1994). The knowledge, skill, and ability requirements for teamwork: Implications for human resource management. *Journal of Management, 20,* 503–530.

Stogdill, R. M. (1948). Personal factors associated with leadership: A survey of the literature. *Journal of Psychology, 25*(1), 35–71.

St-Onge, S. (2000). Variables influencing the perceived relationship between performance and pay in a merit pay environment. *Journal of Business and Psychology, 14*(3), 459–479.

Stork, D., & Richards, W. D. (1992). Nonrespondents in communication network studies. *Group and Organization Management, 17*(2), 193–209.

Sturman, M. C., Hannon, J. M., & Milkovich, G. T. (1996). Computerized decision aids for flexible benefits decisions: The effects of an expert system and decision support system on employee intentions and satisfaction with benefits. *Personnel Psychology, 49*(4), 883–908.

Suh, J. Y. (2021). Age discrimination in the workplace hurts us all. *Nature Aging, 1*(2), 147–147.

Suleiman, J., & Watson, R. T. (2008). Social loafing in technology-supported teams. *Computer Supported Cooperative Work, 17*(4), 291–301.

Sutherland, V. J., & Cooper, C. L. (1988). Sources of work stress. In J. J. Hurrell, L. R. Murphy, S. L., Sauter, & C. L. Cooper (Eds.), *Occupational stress issues and developments in research* (pp. 3–40). Philadelphia, PA: Taylor & Francis.

Svyantek, D. J., Goodman, S. A., Benz, L. L., & Gard, J. A. (1999). The relationship between organizational characteristics and team building success. *Journal of Business and Psychology, 14*(2), 265–283.

Szkudlarek, B., Osland, J. S., Nardon, L., & Zander, L. (2020). Communication and culture in international business: Moving the field forward. *Journal of World Business, 55*(6), 1–9.

Takalkar, P., & Coovert, M. D. (1994). International replication note: The dimensionality of job satisfaction in India. *Applied Psychology: An International Review, 43*(3), 415–426.

Tang, T. L., Tollison, P. S., & Whiteside, H. D. (1996). The case of active and inactive quality circles. *The Journal of Social Psychology, 136*(1), 57–67.

Taormina, R. J. (2009). Organizational socialization: The missing link between employee needs and organizational culture. *Journal of Managerial Psychology, 24*(7), 650–676.

Tarakci, M., Greer, L. L., & Groenen, P. J. F. (2016). When does power disparity help or hurt group performance? *Journal of Applied Psychology, 101*(3), 415–429.

Tarigan, V., & Ariani, D. W. (2015). Empirical study relations job satisfaction, organizational commitment, and turnover intention. *Advances in Management and Applied Economics, 5*(2), 21–42.

Taris, T. W., Kalimo, R., & Schaufeli, W. B. (2002). Inequity at work: Its measurement and association with worker health. *Work & Stress, 16*(4), 287–301.

Tay, L., Ng, V., Malik, A., Zhang, J., Chae, J., Ebert, D. S., Ding, Y., Zhao, J., & Kern, M. (2018). Big data visualizations in organizational science. *Organizational Research Methods, 21*(3), 660–688.

Taylor, F. W. (1911). *The principles of scientific management.* New York: Harper.

Tehrani, N., & Piper, N. (2011). Traumatic stress in the police service. In N. Tehrani (Ed.), *Managing trauma in the workplace: Supporting workers and organizations* (pp. 17–32). New York: Routledge.

Tenhiälä, A., & Salvador, F. (2014). Looking inside glitch mitigation capability: The effect of intraorganizational communication channels. *Decision Sciences, 45*(3), 437–466.

Tepper, B. J., Duffy, M. K., & Shaw, J. D. (2001). Personality moderators of the relationship between abusive supervision and subordinates' resistance. *Journal of Applied Psychology, 86*(5), 974–983.

Thacker, R. A., & Wayne, S. (1995). An examination of the relationship between upward influence tactics and assessments of promotability. *Journal of Management, 21*(4), 739–756.

Tharenou, P. (2001). The relationship of training motivation to participation in training and development. *Journal of Occupational and Organizational Psychology, 74*(5), 599–621.

Thomas, K. W. (1976). Conflict and conflict management. In M. Dunnette (Ed.), *Handbook of industrial and organizational psychology* (pp. 889–936). Chicago, IL: Rand McNally.

Thomas, K. W. (1992). Conflict and negotiation processes in organizations. In M. D. Dunnette & L. M. Hough (Eds.), *Handbook of industrial and organizational psychology* (Vol. 3, 2nd ed., pp. 651–717). Palo Alto, CA: Consulting Psychologists Press.

Thomason, S. J., Weeks, M., Bernardin, H. J., & Kane, J. (2011). The differential focus of supervisors and peers in evaluations of managerial potential. *International Journal of Selection and Assessment, 19*(1), 82–97.

Thoroughgood, C. N., & Padilla, A. (2013). Destructive leadership and the Penn State scandal: A toxic triangle perspective. *Industrial and Organizational Psychology, 6*(2), 144–149.

Thornton III, G. C., & Kedharnath, U. (2013). Work sample tests. In K. F. Geisinger (Ed.), *APA handbook of testing and assessment in psychology, Vol. 1: Test theory and testing and assessment in industrial and organizational psychology* (pp. 533–550). Washington, DC: American Psychological Association.

Tiffin, J. (1968). *Purdue pegboard.* West Lafayette, IN: Science Research Associates.

Tippins, N. T. (2015). Technology and assessment in selection. *Annual Review of Organizational Psychology and Organizational Behavior, 2*(1), 551–582.

Tjosvold, D. (1984). Effects of crisis orientation on managers' approach to controversy in decision making. *Academy of Management Journal, 27*(1), 130–138.

Tjosvold, D. (1998). Cooperative and competitive goal approach to conflict: Accomplishments and challenges. *Applied Psychology: An International Review, 47*(3), 285–342.

Tjosvold, D., Morishima, M., & Belsheim, J. A. (1999). Complaint handling on the shop floor: Cooperative relationships and open-minded strategies. *The International Journal of Conflict Management, 10*(1), 45–68.

Tjosvold, D., XueHuang, Y., Johnson, D. W., & Johnson, R. T. (2008). Social interdependence and orientation toward life and work. *Journal of Applied Social Psychology, 38*(2), 409–435.

Törnroos, M., Jokela, M., & Hakulinen, C. (2019). The relationship between personality and job satisfaction across occupations. *Personality and Individual Differences, 145*, 82–88.

Tosi, H., & Tosi, L. (1987). What managers need to know about knowledge-based pay. In D. B. Balkin & L. R. Gomez-Mejia (Eds.), *New perspectives on compensation* (pp. 43–48). Englewood Cliffs, NJ: Prentice Hall.

Towler, A. J., & Dipboye, R. L. (2001). Effects of trainer expressiveness, organization, and trainee goal orientation on training outcomes. *Journal of Applied Psychology, 86*(4), 664–673.

Trahan, W. A., & McAllister, H. A. (2002). Master's level training in industrial/organizational psychology: Does it meet the SIOP guidelines? *Journal of Business and Psychology, 16*, 457–465.

Trevor, C. O., Gerhart, B., & Boudreau, J. W. (1997). Voluntary turnover and job performance: Curvilinearity and the moderating influences of salary growth and promotions. *Journal of Applied Psychology, 82*(1), 44–61.

Trippe, B., & Baumoel, D. (2015). Beyond the Thomas–Kilmann model: Into extreme conflict. *Negotiation Journal, 31*(2), 89–103.

Truxillo, D. M., Donahue, L. M., & Sulzer, J. L. (1996). Setting cutoff scores for personnel selection tests: Issues, illustrations, and recommendations. *Human Performance, 9*(3), 275–295.

Tschan, F. (1995). Communication enhances small group performance if it conforms to task requirements: The concept of ideal communication cycles. *Basic and Applied Social Psychology, 17*(3), 371–393.

Tucker, F. D. (1985). A study of the training needs of older workers: Implications for human resources development planning. *Public Personnel Management, 14*(1), 85–95.

Tuckey, M. R., & Neall, A. M. (2014). Workplace bullying erodes job and personal resources: Between- and within-person perspectives. *Journal of Occupational Health Psychology, 19*(4), 413–424.

Tung, R. L. (1997). International and intranational diversity. In C. S. Granrose & S. Oskamp (Eds.), *Cross-cultural work groups* (pp. 163–185). Thousand Oaks, CA: Sage.

Tziner, A. (1982). Differential effects of group cohesiveness types: A clarifying overview. *Social Behavior and Personality, 10*, 227–239.

Uhl-Bien, M. (2004). Relationship development as a key ingredient for leadership development. In S. E. Murphy & R. E. Riggio (Eds.), *The future of leadership development* (pp. 129–147). Mahwah, NJ: Lawrence Erlbaum.

Uhl-Bien, M. (2011). Relational leadership and gender: From hierarchy to relationality. In W. P. & M. Painter-Morland (Eds.), *Leadership, Gender, and Organization: Issues in Business Ethics* (Vol. 27, pp. 65–74). Dordrecht: Springer.

Uhl-Bien, M., Graen, G., & T. Scandura. (2000). Implications of leader–member exchange (LMX) for strategic human resource management systems: Relationships as social capital for competitive advantage. In G. R. Ferris (Ed.), *Research in personnel and human resource management* (Vol. 18, pp. 137–185). JAI Press.

Uhl-Bien, M., Riggio, R. E., Lowe, K. B., & Carsten, M. K. (2014). Followership theory: A review and research agenda. *The Leadership Quarterly, 25*(1), 83–104.

United States v. City of Chicago, 77–1171 (7th Cir. 1978).

Ury, W., Brett, J., & Goldberg, S. (1988). *Getting disputes resolved: Designing systems to cut the costs of conflict.* San Francisco, CA: Jossey-Bass.

U.S. Department of Labor. (1991). *Dictionary of occupational titles* (4th ed.). Washington, DC: U.S. Government Printing Office.

U.S. Department of Labor. (2016). *Employer compensation and benefit statistics.* Retrieved from www.bls.gov/home.htm

U.S. Department of Labor Office of Federal Contract Compliance Program. (2020). *Global Conciliation Agreement Between the U.S. Department of Labor Office of Federal Contract Compliance Programs and WELLS FARGO BANK, N.A.* Retrieved from www.dol.gov/sites/dolgov/files/ofccp/foia/files/2020-08-11WellsFargoCA_Redacted3.pdf

Vale, C.D., & Prestwood, J.S. (1987). *Manual for the MCAB: Minnesota Clerical Assessment Battery*. St. Paul, MN: Assessment Systems Corp.

van Beek, I., Taris, T. W., & Schaufeli, W. B. (2011). Workaholic and work engaged employees: Dead ringers or world's apart? *Journal of Occupational and Health Psychology*, *16*(4), 468–482.

Van Coller-Peter, S., & Burger, Z. (2019). A guiding framework for multi-stakeholder contracting in executive coaching. *SA Journal of Human Resource Management*, *17*(1), 1–11.

van de Vliert, E., Euwema, M. C., & Huismans, S. E. (1995). Managing conflict with a subordinate or a superior: Effectiveness of conglomerated behavior. *Journal of Applied Psychology*, *80*(2), 271–281.

Van den Broeck, A., Carpini, J., & Diefendorff, J. (2019). How much effort will I put into my work? It depends on your type of motivation. In R. Ryan (Ed.), *The Oxford handbook of human motivation* (2nd ed., pp. 354–372). John Wiley. https://doi.org/10.1093/oxfordhb/9780190666453.013.27

van Dorssen-Boog, P., de Jong, J., Veld, M., & Van Vuuren, T. (2020). Self-leadership among healthcare workers: A mediator for the effects of job autonomy on work engagement and health. *Frontiers in Psychology*, *11*, 1420–1432.

Van Dun, D. H., Hicks, J. N., & Wilderom, C. P. M. (2017). Values and behaviors of effective lean managers: Mixed-methods exploratory research. *European Management Journal*, *35*(2), 174–186.

Van Dyne, L., Graham, J. W., & Dienesch, R. M. (1994). Organizational citizenship behavior: Construct redefinition, measurement, and validation. *Academy of Management Journal*, *37*(4), 765–802.

Van Eerde, W., & Azar, S. (2020). Too late? What do you mean? Cultural norms regarding lateness for meetings and appointments. *Cross-Cultural Research*, *54*(2–3), 111–129.

Van Eerde, W., & Thierry, H. (1996). Vroom's expectancy models and work-related criteria: A meta-analysis. *Journal of Applied Psychology*, *81*(5), 575–586.

Van Wingerden, J., Bakker, A. B., & Derks, D. (2016). A test of a job demands–resources intervention. *Journal of Managerial Psychology*, *31*, 686–701. https://doi.org/10.1108/JMP-03-2014-0086

Vanhove, A. J., Herian, M. N., Perez, A. L., Harms, P. D., & Lester, P. B. (2016). Can resilience be developed at work? A meta-analytic review of resilience-building programme effectiveness. *Journal of Occupational and Organizational Psychology*, *89*(2), 278–307.

Vaziri, H., Casper, W. J., Wayne, J. H., & Matthews, R. A. (2020). Changes to the work–family interface during the COVID-19 pandemic: Examining predictors and implications using latent transition analysis. *Journal of Applied Psychology*, *105*(10), 1073–1087.

Verbeke, W. (2000). A revision of Hofstede's (1990) organizational practices scale. *Journal of Organizational Behavior*, *21*(5), 587–602.

Verquer, M. L., Beehr, T. A., & Wagner, S. H. (2003). A meta-analysis of relations between person–organization fit and work attitudes. *Journal of Vocational Behavior*, *63*(3), 473–489.

Vigoda, E. (2001). Reactions to organizational politics: A cross-cultural examination in Israel and Britain. *Human Relations*, *54*(11), 1483–1518.

Vigoda-Gadot, E., & Angert, L. (2007). Goal setting theory, job feedback and OCB: Lessons from a longitudinal study. *Basic and Applied Social Psychology*, *29*(2), 119–128.

Vinchur, A. J., & Koppes, L. L. (2011). A historical survey of research and practice in industrial and organizational psychology. In S. Zedeck (Ed.), *APA handbook of industrial and organizational psychology* (Vol. 1, pp. 3–36). Washington, DC: American Psychological Association.

Viswesvaran, C., & Ones, D. S. (2018). Non-test methods and techniques used in employee selection. In D. S. Ones, N. Anderson, C. Viswesvaran, & H. K. Sinangil (Eds.), *The SAGE handbook of industrial, work & organizational psychology: Personnel psychology and employee performance* (pp. 451–473). Washington, DC: American Psychological Association.

Viswesvaran, C., Sanchez, J. I., & Fisher, J. (1999). The role of social support in the process of work stress: A meta-analysis. *Journal of Vocational Behavior*, *54*(2), 314–334.

Vodanovich, S. J. (2003). Psychometric measures of boredom: A review of the literature. *Journal of Psychology: Interdisciplinary and Applied*, *137*(6), 569–595.

Volmer, J., Niessen, C., Spurk, D., Linz, A., & Abele, A. E. (2011). Reciprocal relationships between leader–member exchange (LMX) and job satisfaction: A cross-lagged analysis. *Applied Psychology*, *60*(4), 522–545.

Volpone, S. D., Tonidandel, S., Avery, D. R., & Castel, S. (2015). Exploring the use of credit scores in selection processes: Beware of adverse impact. *Journal of Business and Psychology*, *30*(2), 357–372.

Volz-Peacock, M., Carson, B., & Marquardt, M. (2016). Action learning and leadership development. *Advances in Developing Human Resources*, *18*(3), 318–333.

Vongas, J. G., & Al Hajj, R. (2015). The evolution of empathy and women's precarious leadership appointments. *Frontiers in Psychology, 6*, 1751–1769.

Voskuijl, O. F., & van Sliedregt, T. (2002). Determinants of interrater reliability of job analysis: A meta-analysis. *European Journal of Psychological Assessment, 18*, 52–62.

Voyles, E. C., & Nadler, J. T. (2020). Intersectionality and future research directions. In J. T. Nadler & E. C. Voyles (Eds.), *Stereotypes: The incidence and impacts of bias* (pp. 185–220). Praeger.

Vroom, V. H. (1964). *Work and motivation.* New York: Wiley.

Vroom, V. H., & Jago, A. G. (1978). On the validity of the Vroom–Yetton model. *Journal of Applied Psychology, 63*(2), 151–162.

Vroom, V. H., & Jago, A. G. (1988). *The new leadership: Managing participation in organizations.* Englewood Cliffs, NJ: Prentice Hall.

Vroom, V. H., & Jago, A. G. (1995). Situation effects and levels of analysis in the study of leader participation. *Leadership Quarterly, 6*(2), 169–181.

Vroom, V. H., & Yetton, P. W. (1973). *Leadership and decision-making.* Pittsburgh, PA: University of Pittsburgh Press.

Waclawski, J., & Church, A. H. (Eds.). (2002). *Organization development: A data-driven approach to organizational change.* San Francisco, CA: Jossey-Bass.

Wageman, R., & Baker, G. (1997). Incentives and cooperation: The joint effects of task and reward interdependence on group performance. *Journal of Organizational Behavior, 18*(2), 139–158.

Wageman, R., Gardner, H., & Mortensen, M. (2012). Teams have changed: Catching up to the future. *Industrial and Organizational Psychology, 5*(1), 48–52.

Wagstaff, M. F., del Carmen Triana, M., Kim, S., & Al-Riyami, S. (2015). Responses to discrimination: Relationships between social support seeking, core self-evaluations, and withdrawal behaviors. *Human Resource Management, 54*(4), 673–687.

Waldman, D. A., Atwater, L. E., & Antonioni, D. (1998). Has 360-degree feedback gone amok? *Academy of Management Executive, 12*(2), 86–94.

Waldman, D. A., & Korbar, T. (2004). Student assessment center performance in prediction of early career success. *Academy of Management Learning & Education, 3*(2), 151–167.

Wallace, L. E., Stelman, S. A., & Chaffee, D. S. (2016). Ratee reactions drive performance appraisal success (and failure). *Industrial and Organizational Psychology, 9*(2), 310–314.

Wallach, M. A., Kogan, N., & Bem, D. J. (1962). Group influence on individual risk taking. *Journal of Abnormal and Social Psychology, 65*(2), 75–86.

Walton, R. E., & Dutton, J. M. (1969). The management of interdepartmental conflict: A model and review. *Administrative Science Quarterly, 14*, 73–84.

Walz, S. M., & Niehoff, B. P. (1996). Organizational citizenship behaviors and their effect on organizational effectiveness in limited-menu restaurants. In J. B. Keys & L. N. Dosier (Eds.), *Academy of management best paper proceedings* (pp. 307–311). Briarcliff Manor, NY: Academy of Management.

Wanberg, C. R., & Banas, J. T. (2000). Predictors and outcomes of openness to changes in a reorganizing workplace. *Journal of Applied Psychology, 85*(1), 132–142.

Wanberg, C. R., Gavin, M. B., & Bunce, L. W. (1999). Perceived fairness of layoffs among individuals who have been laid off: A longitudinal study. *Personnel Psychology, 52*(1), 59–84.

Wang, D., Waldman, D. A., & Zhang, Z. (2014). A meta-analysis of shared leadership and team effectiveness. *Journal of Applied Psychology, 99*(2), 181–198.

Wanous, J. P., Reichers, A. E., & Hudy, M. J. (1997). Overall job satisfaction: How good are single-item measures? *Journal of Applied Psychology, 82*(2), 247–252.

Wanous, J. P., Reichers, A. E., & Malik, S. D. (1984). Organizational socialization and group development: Toward an integrative perspective. *Academy of Management Review, 9*(4), 670–683.

Wasik, B. (1984). *Teaching parents effective problem solving: A handbook for professionals.* Chapel Hill: University of North Carolina Press.

Watson v. Fort Worth Bank and Trust, 798 F.2d 791 (5th Cir. 1986) rev. 487 U.S. 977 (1988).

Waung, M., McAuslan, P., DiMambro, J. M., & Miegoć, N. (2017). Impression management use in resumes and cover letters. *Journal of Business and Psychology, 32*(6), 727–746.

Wax, A., Coletti, K. K., & Ogaz, J. W. (2018). The benefit of full disclosure: A meta-analysis of the implications of coming out at work. *Organizational Psychology Review, 8*(1), 3–30.

Wayne, S. J., Liden, R. C., Graf, I. K., & Ferris, G. R. (1997). The role of upward influence tactics in human resource decisions. *Personnel Psychology, 50*(4), 979–1006.

Weber, M. (1947). *The theory of social and economic organizations* (A. M. Henderson & T. Parsons, Trans.). New York: Free Press.

Wech, B. A., Mossholder, K. W., Steel, R. P., & Bennett, N. (1998). Does work group cohesiveness affect individuals' performance and organizational commitment? A cross-level examination. *Small Group Research, 29*(4), 472–494.

Wechsler, D. (1981). *WAIS-R manual: Wechsler adult intelligence scale – revised*. New York: Harcourt-Brace-Jovanovich.

Weenig, M. W. H. (1999). Communication networks in the diffusion of an innovation in an organization. *Journal of Applied Social Psychology, 29*(5), 1072–1092.

Weinberg, A. (2016). When the work is not enough: The sinister stress of boredom. In G. Fink (Ed.). *Handbook of stress, Vol. 1: Stress: Concepts, cognition, emotion, and behavior* (pp. 195–201). San Diego, CA: Elsevier Academic Press.

Weisband, S. P., Schneider, S. K., & Connolly, T. (1995). Computer-mediated communication and social information: Status salience and status differences. *Academy of Management Journal, 38*(4), 1124–1151.

Weiss, D. J., Dawis, R. V., England, G. W., & Lofquist, L. H. (1967). Manual for the Minnesota Satisfaction Questionnaire. In *Minnesota studies on vocational rehabilitation* (Vol. 22). Minneapolis, MN: University of Minnesota Industrial Relations Center.

Welbourne, T. M., & Ferrante, C. J. (2008). To monitor or not to monitor: A study of individual outcomes from monitoring one's peers under gainsharing and merit pay. *Group & Organization Management, 33*(2), 139–162.

Wells, K. (2011). More research with a purpose: Advancing work–family program utilization. *Industrial and Organizational Psychology, 4*(3), 402–405.

Wertheim, E. H., & Donnoli, M. (2012). Do offender and victim typical conflict styles affect forgiveness? *International Journal of Conflict Management, 23*(1), 57–76.

Westman, M., & Eden, D. (1997). Effects of a respite from work on burnout: Vacation relief and fade-out. *Journal of Applied Psychology, 82*(4), 516–527.

Wexley, K. N., & Baldwin, T. T. (1986). Post-training strategies for facilitating positive transfer: An empirical exploration. *Academy of Management Journal, 29*(3), 503–520.

Wexley, K. N., & Latham, G. P. (2001). *Developing and training human resources in organizations* (3rd ed.). Englewood Cliffs, NJ: Prentice-Hall.

Whalen, T., & Wright, D. (2000). *The business case for web-based training*. Boston, MA: Artech House.

Wheaton, G. R., & Whetzel, D. L. (1997). Contexts for developing applied measurement instruments. In D. L. Whetzel & G. R. Wheaton (Eds.), *Applied measurement methods in industrial psychology* (pp. 1–10). Palo Alto, CA: Davies-Black.

Wheeler, D. D., & Janis, I. L. (1980). *A practical guide for making decisions*. New York: Free Press.

White, R. P., & Shullman, S. L. (2012). Thirty years of global leadership training: A cross-cultural odyssey. *Consulting Psychology Journal, 64*(4), 268–278.

Wichman, A. (1994). Occupational differences in involvement with ownership in an airline employee ownership program. *Human Relations, 47*(7), 829–846.

Wiesenfeld, B. M., Raghuram, S., & Garud, R. (2001). Organizational identification among virtual workers: The role of need for affiliation and perceived work-based social support. *Journal of Management, 27*(2), 213–229.

Wildman, J. L., Bedwell, W. L., Salas, E., & Smith-Jentsch, K. A. (2011). Performance measurement at work: A multilevel perspective. In S. Zedeck (Ed.), *APA handbook of industrial and organizational psychology, Vol. 1: Building and developing the organization* (pp. 303–341). Washington, DC: American Psychological Association.

Wilhelmy, A., Kleinmann, M., König, C. J., Melchers, K. G., & Truxillo, D. M. (2016). How and why do interviewers try to make impressions on applicants? A qualitative study. *Journal of Applied Psychology, 101*(3), 313–332.

Wilkie, D. (2015). Is the annual performance review dead? GE is latest company to reject time-consuming paperwork and yearly appraisals. *SHRM Better Workplaces Better World*. Retrieved 6/29/2021, from www.shrm.org/ResourcesAndTools/hr-topics/employee-relations/Pages/performance-reviews-are-dead.aspx

Williams, J. R., & Levy, P. E. (1992). The effects of perceived system knowledge on the agreement between self-ratings and supervisor ratings. *Personnel Psychology, 45*(4), 835–847.

Williams, J. S., & Lowman, R. L. (2018). The efficacy of executive coaching: An empirical investigation of two approaches using random assignment and a switching-replications design. *Consulting Psychology Journal: Practice and Research, 70*(3), 227–249.

Williams, K. Y., & O'Reilly III, C. A. (1998). Demography and diversity in organizations: A review of 40 years of research. *Research in Organizational Behavior, 20*, 77–140.

Williams, M. (2016). Being trusted: How team generational age diversity promotes and undermines trust in cross-boundary relationships. *Journal of Organizational Behavior, 37*(3), 346–373.

Williams, M. T. (2020). Psychology cannot afford to ignore the many harms caused by microaggressions. *Perspectives on Psychological Science, 15*(1), 38–43.

Williams, T. C., & Rains, J. (2007). Linking strategy to structure: The power of systematic organization design. *Organization Development Journal*, 25(2), 163–170.

Williamson, L. G., Campion, J. E., Malos, S. B., Roehling, M. V., & Campion, M. A. (1997). Employment interview on trial: Linking interview structure with litigation outcomes. *Journal of Applied Psychology*, 82, 900–912.

Wilson, K. Y. (2010). An analysis of bias in supervisor narrative comments in performance appraisal. *Human Relations*, 63(12), 1903–1933.

Winter, D. G. (1973). *The power motive*. New York: Free Press.

Wise, S. (2014). Can a team have too much cohesion? The dark side to network density. *European Management Journal*, 32, 703–711.

Witt, L. A. (1998). Enhancing organizational goal congruence: A solution to organizational politics. *Journal of Applied Psychology*, 83, 666–674.

Witt, L. A., & Nye, L. G. (1992). Gender and the relationship between perceived fairness of pay or promotion and job satisfaction. *Journal of Applied Psychology*, 77(6), 910–917.

Wittig, M. A., & Berman, S. L. (1992). Wage structure analysis: An empirical approach to pay equity in segregated jobs. *Social Justice Research*, 5, 291–317.

Wolf, F. M. (1986). *Meta-analysis: Quantitative methods for research synthesis*. Beverly Hills, CA: Sage.

Wonderlic, E. F. (1983). *Wonderlic Personnel Test*. Northfield, IL: Wonderlic.

Woodley, H. J., Bourdage, J. S., Ogunfowora, B., & Nguyen, B. (2016). Examining equity sensitivity: An investigation using the Big Five and HEXACO models of personality. *Frontiers in Psychology*, 6, 2000–2015.

Woodward, J. (1965). *Industrial organization: Theory and practice*. London: Oxford University Press.

World Economic Forum. (2019). *Global Gender Gap Report 2020*. Retrieved from www3.weforum.org/docs/WEF_GGGR_2020.pdf

Wright, R. R., Mohr, C. D., Sinclair, R. R., & Yang, L. (2015). Sometimes less is more: Directed coping with interpersonal stressors at work. *Journal of Organizational Behavior*, 36(6), 786–805.

Wright, T. A., & Cropanzano, R. (1998). Emotional exhaustion as a predictor of job performance and voluntary turnover. *Journal of Applied Psychology*, 83(3), 486–493.

Xin, K. R., & Tsui, A. S. (1996). Different strokes for different folks? Influence tactics by Asian-American and Caucasian-American managers. *Leadership Quarterly*, 7(1), 109–132.

Xu, E., Huang, X., Ouyang, K., Liu, W., & Hu, S. (2020). Tactics of speaking up: The roles of issue importance, perceived managerial openness, and managers' positive mood. *Human Resource Management*, 59(3), 255–269.

Yaffe, T., & Kark, R. (2011). Leading by example: The case of leader OCB. *Journal of Applied Psychology*, 96(4), 806–826.

Yalabik, Z. Y. (2013). Mergers and acquisitions: Does organizational socialization matter? *Human Resource Development International*, 16(5), 519–537.

Yang, L. Q., Che, H., & Spector, P. E. (2008). Job stress and well-being: An examination from the view of person-environment fit. *Journal of Occupational and Organizational Psychology*, 81(3), 567–587.

Yang, J., & Mossholder, K. W. (2004). Decoupling task and relationship conflict: The role of intragroup emotional processing. *Journal of Organizational Behavior*, 25(5), 589–605.

Yates, J., & Orlikowski, W. J. (1992). Genres of organizational communication: A structurational approach to studying communication and the media. *Academy of Management Review*, 17(2), 299–326.

Yen, H. R., & Niehoff, B. P. (2004). Organizational citizenship behaviors and organizational effectiveness: Examining relationships in Taiwanese banks. *Journal of Applied Social Psychology*, 34(8), 1617–1637.

Yoon, M. H., & Suh, J. (2003). Organizational citizenship behaviors and service quality as external effectiveness of contact employees. *Journal of Business Research*, 56(8), 597–611.

Yorks, L. (1979). *Job enrichment revisited*. New York: AMACOM.

Yost, A. B., Behrend, T. S., Howardson, G., Darrow, J. B., & Jensen, J. M. (2019). Reactance to electronic surveillance: A test of antecedents and outcomes. *Journal of Business and Psychology*, 34(1), 71–86.

Young, A. M., & Perrewé, P. L. (2000). What did you expect? An examination of career-related support and social support among mentors and protégés. *Journal of Management*, 26(4), 611–632.

Yukl, G. A. (1998). *Leadership in organizations* (4th ed.). Englewood Cliffs, NJ: Prentice Hall.

Yukl, G. A., & Falbe, C. M. (1991). Importance of different power sources in downward and lateral relations. *Journal of Applied Psychology*, 76(3), 416–423.

Yun, G. J., Donahue, L. M., Dudley, N. M., & McFarland, L. A. (2005). Rater personality, rating format, and social context: Implications for performance appraisals. *International Journal of Selection and Assessment*, 13(2), 97–107.

Zaccaro, S. J., & Banks, D. (2004). Leader visioning and adaptability: Bridging the gap between research and practice on developing the ability to manage change. *Human Resource Management, 43*(4), 367–380.

Zahn, G. L. (1991). Face-to-face communication in an office setting. *Communication Research, 18*(6), 737–754.

Zaniboni, S., Kmicinska, M., Truxillo, D. M., Kahn, K., Paladino, M. P., & Fraccaroli, F. (2019). Will you still hire me when I am over 50? The effects of implicit and explicit age stereotyping on resume evaluations. *European Journal of Work and Organizational Psychology, 28*(4), 453–467.

Zanin, A. C., Bisel, R. S., & Adame, E. A. (2016). Supervisor moral talk contagion and trust-in-supervisor: Mitigating the workplace moral mum effect. *Management Communication Quarterly, 30*(2), 147–163.

Zhang, L. (2020). An institutional approach to gender diversity and firm performance. *Organization Science, 31*(2), 439–457.

Zhao, H. H., Li, N., Harris, T. B., Rosen, C. C., & Zhang, X. (2020). Informational advantages in social networks: The core-periphery divide in peer performance ratings. *Journal of Applied Psychology, 106*, 1093–1102.

Zhou, J., & George, J. M. (2001). When job dissatisfaction leads to creativity: Encouraging the expression of voice. *Academy of Management Journal, 44*(4), 682–696.

Zhu, D. H. (2014). Group polarization in board decisions about CEO compensation. *Organization Science, 25*(2), 552–571.

Zhu, J., Xu, S., & Zhang, B. (2020). The paradoxical effect of inclusive leadership on subordinates' creativity. *Frontiers in Psychology, 10*, 2960–2969.

Zivnuska, S. L., Carlson, D. S., Carlson, J. R., Harris, K. J., Harris, R. B., & Valle, M. (2020). Information and communication technology incivility aggression in the workplace: Implications for work and family. *Information Processing & Management, 57*(3), 1–9.

INDEX

Note: The Index uses US spelling. Page numbers in *italic* refer to Figures; page numbers in **bold** refer to Tables